# HISTORICAL DICTIONARY

The historical dictionaries present essential information on a broad range of subjects, including American and world history, art, business, cities, countries, cultures, customs, film, global conflicts, international relations, literature, music, philosophy, religion, sports, and theater. Written by experts, all contain highly informative introductory essays on the topic and detailed chronologies that, in some cases, cover vast historical time periods but still manage to heavily feature more recent events.
Brief A–Z entries describe the main people, events, politics, social issues, institutions, and policies that make the topic unique, and entries are cross-referenced for ease of browsing. Extensive bibliographies are divided into several general subject areas, providing excellent access points for students, researchers, and anyone wanting to know more. Additionally, maps, photographs, and appendixes of supplemental information aid high school and college students doing term papers or introductory research projects. In short, the historical dictionaries are the perfect starting point for anyone looking to research in these fields.

# Historical Dictionaries of U.S. Politics and Political Eras

Jon Woronoff, Series Editor

*From the Great War to the Great Depression*, by Neil A. Wynn, 2003.
*Revolutionary America*, by Terry M. Mays, 2005.
*Early American Republic*, by Richard Buel Jr., 2006.
*Jacksonian Era and Manifest Destiny*, by Terry Corps, 2006.
*Reagan–Bush Era*, by Richard S. Conley, 2007.
*Kennedy–Johnson Era*, by Richard Dean Burns and Joseph M. Siracusa, 2008.
*Nixon–Ford Era*, by Mitchell K. Hall, 2008.
*Roosevelt–Truman Era*, by Neil A. Wynn, 2008.
*Eisenhower Era*, by Burton I. Kaufman and Diane Kaufman, 2009.
*Progressive Era*, by Catherine Cocks, Peter C. Holloran, and Alan Lessoff, 2009.
*Gilded Age*, by T. Adams Upchurch, 2009.
*Political Parties*, by Harold F. Bass Jr., 2010.
*George W. Bush Era*, by Richard S. Conley, 2010.
*United States Congress*, by Scot Schraufnagel, 2011.
*Colonial America*, by William Pencak, 2011.
*Civil War and Reconstruction, Second Edition*, by William L. Richter, 2012.
*Clinton Era*, by Richard S. Conley, 2012.
*Old South, Second Edition*, by William L. Richter, 2013.
*Carter Era*, by Diane Kaufman and Scott Kaufman, 2013.
*From the Great War to the Great Depression, Second Edition*, by Neil A. Wynn, 2014.
*Barack Obama Administration*, by Michael J. Pomante II and Scot Schraufnagel, 2014.
*Kennedy–Johnson Era, Second Edition*, by Richard Dean Burns and Joseph M. Siracusa, 2015.
*U.S. Supreme Court*, by Artemus Ward, Christopher Brough, and Robert Arnold, 2015.
*American Frontier*, by Jay H. Buckley and Brenden W. Rensink, 2015.
*U.S. Presidency*, by Richard S. Conley, 2016.
*U.S. Constitution*, by Richard S. Conley, 2016.

# Historical Dictionary of the U.S. Constitution

Richard S. Conley

ROWMAN & LITTLEFIELD
Lanham • Boulder • New York • London

Published by Rowman & Littlefield
A wholly owned subsidiary of The Rowman & Littlefield Publishing Group, Inc.
4501 Forbes Boulevard, Suite 200, Lanham, Maryland 20706
www.rowman.com

Unit A, Whitacre Mews, 26-34 Stannary Street, London SE11 4AB



British Library Cataloguing in Publication Information Available

**Library of Congress Cataloging-in-Publication Data**

Names: Conley, Richard Steven
Title: Historical dictionary of U.S. Constitution / Richard S. Conley.
Description: Lanham : Rowman & Littlefield, [2016] | Series: Historical dictionaries of U.S. politics and political eras | Includes bibliographical references.
Identifiers: LCCN 2016011954 (print) | LCCN 2016012460 (ebook) | ISBN 9781442271883 (hardcover : alk. paper) | ISBN 9781442271876 (electronic)
Subjects: LCSH: Constitutional history—United States—Dictionaries. | Constitutional law—United States—Dictionaries. | United States—Politics and government—Dictionaries. | Constitutional history—United States—Dictionaries—Sources. | United States. Constitution—Dictionaries.
Classification: LCC KF4548.5 .C66 2016 (print) | LCC KF4548.5 (ebook) | DDC 342.73003—dc23
LC record available at http://lccn.loc.gov/2016011954

∞ The paper used in this publication meets the minimum requirements of American National Standard for Information Sciences Permanence of Paper for Printed Library Materials, ANSI/NISO Z39.48-1992.

Printed in the United States of America.

To my treasured son, a father's blessing, Arthur Patrick Conley

"The Constitution only gives people the right to pursue happiness. You have to catch it yourself." —Benjamin Franklin

# Contents

# Editor's Foreword

As constitutions go, that of the United States is regarded as one of the best. It is written in one succinct charter, while some others are not written, even in part, or consist of a maze of sometimes contradictory documents and statements made at different times. It is fairly easy to understand by an ordinary person, while even lawyers cannot make sense of some others. It has been around for a long time and is likely to remain, whereas in some places each new strong leader adopts a new one. Above all, it is flexible and can be adapted to changing times and circumstances, as shown by its longevity and relatively few amendments. For these and other reasons, most foreigners envy the U.S. Constitution, and most Americans like it too. Admittedly, there is some criticism now, which is all right and even positive as long as it is informed and constructive. And there's the rub, as too much criticism of it is partisan and leaves little room for compromise. More serious, there are signs that many citizens and students no longer know much about the Constitution . . . or even care.

So, if anyone is not familiar or wishes to fill in the background or details, this *Historical Dictionary of the United States Constitution* is an excellent starting point. The chronology is quite extensive and traces key events from the framing to the present. The list of acronyms can come in handy while reading. The introduction provides considerable insight into the framing and functioning of the Constitution. The most important, and largest, section is the dictionary, with entries on the Framers and notable Supreme Court justices, the various articles and all the amendments, crucial cases, and some essential terminology. There are also many helpful appendixes that provide useful background. And those wanting to know more are well served by the extensive bibliography.

This volume was written by Richard S. Conley, who is ideally suited to the task. He is an associate professor at the University of Florida, where he has been teaching since 1998. He focuses on comparative politics, which gives him a broad view, and specializes on the U.S. presidency and executive–legislative relations, very close to the topics at hand. He has written extensively, including numerous articles, and has edited or authored several books, the most recent dealing with the Ronald Reagan and George W. Bush administrations. Of particular note, Dr. Conley is also the author of the historical dictionaries on the Reagan–Bush, George

W. Bush, and Clinton eras. No wonder he covers the subject so thoroughly and almost instinctively knows what will interest potential readers. For all of this we can be thankful at a time when a reliable guide to the Constitution is so badly needed.

Jon Wornoff
Series Editor

# Preface

The United States Constitution is the cornerstone of the American experiment in self-governance. The Framers who gathered at Independence Hall in Philadelphia in the summer of 1787 set out to "form a more perfect union"—one that could remedy the dysfunctions of the Articles of Confederation. The document they produced, haltingly and as a result of ample compromise, has endured 229 years regardless of its imperfections. The text remains unchanged notwithstanding the 27 amendments adopted between 1791 and 1992. But interpretations of the scope of fundamental civil liberties, civil rights, and governmental power within a separated institutional structure have varied considerably over time as the nation has confronted challenges ranging from civil war, world wars, and the War on Terrorism to economic calamity and technological change. Its simplicity and malleability are potentially the Constitution's greatest attributes and its Achilles' heel, the locus of continuing debates more than two centuries after its adoption.

The objective of this volume is to provide students, scholars, and citizens with an accessible and thorough reference tool on the contours of constitutional history. The endeavor proved cathartic in the sense that the myriad subjects, personalities, and Supreme Court cases covered in the book represent so much of what I *wish* I had time to detail in the introductory American government course I routinely teach at the University of Florida but cannot in a 16-week survey class. As such, I trust that the volume will contribute to greater civic knowledge about our foundational charter and the paramount importance of its enduring legacy for rallying the political engagement, debate, and deliberation central to the ethos of a healthy democracy.

In order to facilitate the rapid and efficient location of information and to make this book as useful a reference tool as possible, extensive cross-references have been provided in the dictionary section. Within individual entries, terms that have their own entries are in **boldface type** the first time they appear. Related terms that do not appear in the text are indicated in the *See also*. *See* refers to other entries that deal this topic.

The entries provide an in-depth explanation of Articles I through VII, the Bill of Rights, and the subsequent 17 amendments. Brief biographies of key Framers, including those opposed to ratification, alongside the bibliography furnish a starting point to research further key historical figures whose philosophical understandings buttressed the Founding and what they expected. Moreover, the appendixes provide information on some of the pivotal debates between Federalists and Anti-Federalists, which perhaps more than the Convention debates themselves offer significant insight into normative concerns about the shape of the experiment in self-governance. Much of the volume centers on key Supreme Court cases that trace the ebb and flow of interpretation of constitutional rights. Every effort has been made to situate those cases objectively within historical contexts, and once again, the bibliography provides valuable historical and contemporary resources for further research. In sum, these features of the volume furnish a constructive basis from which to juxtapose the Framers' intentions with historical and contemporary developments that have had far-reaching implications for our understanding of what constitutional governance is and *should be*.

That question sparked many lively dinner table conversations among me, my wife, and our six-year-old son as I undertook this endeavor. I am indebted to my perceptive and loving spouse, Cindy, for patiently supporting and encouraging my sometimes lonely work on the computer early in the mornings and late at night and helping me flesh out points of detail. I also thank the many colleagues at various conferences in the past several years who have challenged the precepts of my thinking on the Constitution, as well as the Department of Political Science at the University of Florida for support of this work. In particular, I thank Irwin Morris and the Liberty Fund for the exciting conference on the Constitution that I attended in 2007 in Tampa, which was in many ways a precursor to this work. The series editor, Jon Woronoff, has provided essential feedback and a sharp eye for this and the several other manuscripts I have been privileged to write for this series, and I am grateful for his confidence in me. Finally, it is my son, Patrick, to whom I dedicate this oeuvre. He and his generation will inherit the spirited American constitutional legacy that for over two centuries the men and women of this nation have sought to preserve, protect, and defend. As James Madison reflected, "The happy Union of these States is a wonder; their Constitution a miracle; their example the hope of Liberty throughout the world." I hope readers will share my excitement in reviving vigorous and dynamic conversations, from the kitchen to the public square, about constitutional debates old and new.

Richard S. Conley

# Acronyms and Abbreviations

| | |
|---|---|
| ACLU | American Civil Liberties Union |
| BCRA | Bipartisan Campaign Reform Act |
| CDA | Communications Decency Act |
| CFPB | Consumer Financial Protection Bureau |
| CIA | Central Intelligence Agency |
| CLEO | chief law enforcement officer |
| CRS | Congressional Research Service |
| CSA | Controlled Substances Act |
| DEA | Drug Enforcement Agency |
| DOMA | Defense of Marriage Act |
| ERA | Equal Rights Amendment |
| FBI | Federal Bureau of Investigation |
| FEC | Federal Elections Commission |
| FECA | Federal Elections Campaign Act |
| FISA | Foreign Intelligence Surveillance Act |
| INS | Immigration and Naturalization Service |
| IRS | Internal Revenue Service |
| IQ | intelligence quotient |
| NAACP | National Association for the Advancement of Colored Persons |
| NAEP | National Assessment of Progress |
| NARAL | National Abortion and Reproductive Rights Action League |
| NIRA | National Industrial Recovery Act |
| NLRB | National Labor Relations Board |
| NOW | National Organization for Women |
| NRA | National Rifle Association |
| NSA | National Security Agency |
| RFRA | Religious Freedom Restoration Act |

| | |
|---|---|
| UCMJ | Uniform Code of Military Justice |
| VMI | Virginia Military Institute |

# Chronology

**1776 4 July:** Drafted by Thomas Jefferson, the Declaration of Independence is adopted.

**1781 2 February:** Articles of Confederation ratified by all 13 states.

**1783 3 September:** Treaty of Paris formally ends war between the United States and Great Britain.

**1785 25 March:** Delegates from Maryland and Virginia meet at the home of George Washington in Mount Vernon to discuss navigation rights, resulting in the Mount Vernon Compact between the states.

**1786 August:** Shays's Rebellion commences. **11 September:** Heeding calls from James Madison and the Virginia General Assembly, delegates from Delaware, New Jersey, New York, Pennsylvania, and Virginia meet in Annapolis, Maryland, to discuss interstate commerce issues. **14 September:** Annapolis Convention adjourns and sends report to state legislatures and Congress calling for a convention to amend the Articles of Confederation.

**1787 21 February:** Congress formally calls for a constitutional convention "for the sole and express purpose of revising the Articles of Confederation and reporting to Congress and the several legislatures such alterations and provisions therein and when agreed to in Congress and confirmed by the States render the Federal Constitution adequate to the exigencies of Government and the preservation of the Union." **25 May:** Delegates convene in Philadelphia, Pennsylvania; George Washington is elected presiding office of the Convention. **29 May:** The Virginia Plan favoring large states is presented by Edmund Randolph. **15 June:** William Paterson presents the New Jersey Plan, which favors small states. **16 July:** The Committee of Eleven report presents the Great or Connecticut Compromise, which proposes proportional representation based on population for the House of Representatives and equal representation of the states in the Senate. **24 July:** Committee of Detail begins drafting the Constitution. **6 August:** Committee of Detail presents draft Constitution. **1–8 September:** Committee of Eleven (Postponed Matters) reports recommendations. **12 September:** Committee of Style presents final draft of the Constitution. **15 September:** State delegations unanimously approve draft of the Constitution. **17 September:** Convention adjourns after 39 delegates sign the Constitution. **20 September:** Constitution received by Congress. **27 September:** First Anti-Federalist letter published against ratification of the Constitution. **27 October:** First Federalist Paper penned under the pseudonym Publius is published. **7 December:** Delaware ratifies the Constitution. **12 December:** Pennsylvania ratifies the Constitution. **18 December:** New Jersey ratifies the Constitution.

**1788 2 January:** Georgia ratifies the Constitution. **9 January:** Connecticut ratifies the Constitution. **6 February:** Massachusetts ratifies the Constitution. **24 March:** Rhode Island rejects the Constitution in a popular referendum. **28 April:** Maryland ratifies the Constitution. **23 May:** South Carolina ratifies the Constitution. **21 June:** New Hampshire ratifies the Constitution; Constitution is officially established as nine of 13 states ratified. **25 June:** Virginia ratifies the Constitution. **26 July:** New York ratifies the Constitution. **13 September:** Congress certifies ratification of the Constitution and establishes meeting date of new government and date for the presidential election. **15 December–10 January 1789:** First presidential election.

**1789 4 February:** Electoral College convenes for the first time; George Washington elected. **4 March:** The First Congress of the United States convenes at Federal Hall in New York City. **6 April:** Congress certifies George Washington as president, John Adams as vice president. **30 April:** George Washington inaugurated first president of the United States. **25 September:** Congress approves 12 amendments to the Constitution. **21 November:** North Carolina ratifies the Constitution.

**1790 2 February:** Supreme Court commences its first term with John Jay as chief justice. **29 May:** Rhode Island ratifies the Constitution.

**1791 10 January:** Vermont ratifies the Constitution and applies for statehood in the Union. **15 December:** First 10 amendments to the Constitution, the Bill of Rights, ratified.

**1795 7 February:** Ratification of the Eleventh Amendment, overturning the Supreme Court decision in *Chisholm v. Georgia* (1793).

**1802 24 February:** The Supreme Court, under Chief Justice John Marshall, decides *Marbury v. Madison*, extending judicial review to include actions of other branches of the government.

**1804 15 June:** Ratification of the Twelfth Amendment altering Electoral College procedure for choosing the president and vice president.

**1810 25 March:** Supreme Court decides *Fletcher v. Peck*, first case in which a state law is invalidated as unconstitutional.

**1819 6 March:** Supreme Court decides *McCulloch v. Maryland*, striking down Maryland's attempt to tax the Bank of the United States.

**1824 2 March:** Supreme Court decides *Gibbons v. Ogden* regarding interstate commerce.

**1833 16 February:** Supreme Court decides *Barron v. Baltimore*, ruling that the Bill of Rights does not apply to the states.

**1857 6 March:** Supreme Court decides *Dred Scott v. Sanford*, ruling that slaves are not citizens.

**1861 4 February:** Southern states that seceded from the Union form the Confederate States of America. **12 April:** Civil War commences with the Battle of Fort Sumter, South Carolina.

**1865 9 April:** Civil War ends with General Robert E. Lee's surrender to Ulysses S. Grant in Appomattox, Virginia. **14 April:** President Abraham Lincoln assassinated. **6 December:** Ratification of the Thirteenth Amendment abolishing slavery.

**1868 9 July:** Ratification of the Fourteenth Amendment, clarifying citizenship rights and guaranteeing that no state may abridge the privileges and immunities of its citizens, due process of the law, or equal protection of the law.

**1870 3 February:** Ratification of the Fifteenth Amendment, providing to citizens the right to vote regardless of color or race.

**1873 14 April:** Supreme Court decides the *Slaughterhouse Cases*, narrowing interpretation of the Fourteenth Amendment's privileges and immunities clause.

**1875 29 March:** Supreme Court decides *Minor v. Happersett*, contending that the Fourteenth Amendment does not provide women a right to vote.

**1876 27 March:** Supreme Court decides *U.S. v. Reese*, asserting that the Fifteenth Amendment does not guarantee blacks right to vote.

**1883 15 October:** Supreme Court decides the *Civil Rights Cases*, concluding that neither the Thirteenth nor the Fourteenth Amendment enables Congress to protect blacks from individual actions or discrimination.

**1896 18 May:** Supreme Court decides *Plessy v. Ferguson*, affirming "separate but equal" facilities for blacks and whites.

**1913 3 February:** Sixteenth Amendment ratified, establishing income tax. **8 April:** Ratification of the Seventeenth Amendment, providing for direct election of senators.

**1919 16 January:** Ratification of Eighteenth Amendment, prohibiting production, sale, and transport of alcohol. **3 March:** In *Schenck v. United States*, Supreme Court articulates "clear and present danger test" regarding First Amendment free speech rights.

**1920 16 January:** Prohibition (Eighteenth Amendment) takes effect. **18 August:** Ratification of the Nineteenth Amendment providing women the right to vote.

**1925 8 June:** Supreme Court incorporates First Amendment free speech rights in *Gitlow v. New York*.

**1933 23 January:** Ratification of the Twentieth Amendment, providing for the term of the president to commence on 20 January instead of in March. **5 December:** Ratification of Twenty-First Amendment, repealing the Eighteenth Amendment and Prohibition.

**1935 2 May:** Supreme Court decides *Schechter Poultry Co. v. U.S.*, strikes down major elements of President Franklin Roosevelt's New Deal as unconstitutional.

**1944 11 October:** Supreme Court decides *Korematsu v. United States*, affirming constitutionality of executive action limiting civil liberties of Japanese Americans.

**1947 21 March:** Ratification of the Twenty-Second Amendment, limiting the president to two terms in office.

**1954 17 May:** Supreme Court decides *Brown v. Board of Education*, invalidating "separate but equal" facilities for blacks and whites as unconstitutional; decision spurs desegregation efforts around the nation.

**1961 29 March:** Ratification of the Twenty-Third Amendment, providing Electoral College vote to the District of Columbia. **19 June:** Supreme Court decides *Mapp v. Ohio*, articulating "exclusionary rule" for evidence gathered by police not in accordance with Fourth Amendment protections.

**1962 25 June:** Supreme Court decides *Engel v. Vitale*, striking down official prayer in public schools.

**1963 18 March:** Supreme Court decides *Gideon v. Wainwright*, taking an expansive view of the Sixth Amendment right to assistance of counsel in criminal matters.

**1964 23 January:** Ratification of the Twenty-Fourth Amendment to abolish the poll tax.

**1965 7 June:** Supreme Court decides *Griswold v. Connecticut*, affirming right to birth control information from medical providers.

**1966 13 June:** Supreme Court decides *Miranda v. Arizona*, establishing that criminal confessions are not voluntary under the Fifth Amendment unless the defendant is made aware of his or her rights.

**1967 10 February:** Ratification of the Twenty-Fifth Amendment, outlining procedure for presidential disability and succession.

**1971 1 July:** Ratification of the Twenty-Sixth Amendment, extending the vote to 18-year-olds.

**1972 9 June:** Supreme Court decision in *Furman v. Georgia* holds that inconsistent application of the death penalty amounts to cruel and unusual punishment under the Eighth Amendment; ruling commences a four-year moratorium on the death penalty.

**1973 22 June:** Supreme Court decides *Roe v. Wade*, confirming a woman's right to abortion.

**1976 30 January:** Supreme Court decides *Buckley v. Valeo*, invalidating campaign spending limits. **2 July:** Supreme Court decision in *Gregg v. Georgia* reestablishes death penalty.

**1982 30 June:** Equal Rights Amendment to the Constitution fails despite extended ratification deadline.

**1983 23 June:** Supreme Court decision in *INS v. Chadha* strikes down one-house legislative veto as unconstitutional.

**1989 1 June:** Supreme Court decision in *Texas v. Johnson* invalidates a Texas law banning flag burning on grounds of First Amendment protections and symbolic speech.

**1992 7 May:** Ratification of the Twenty-Seventh Amendment, prohibiting congressional pay raises from taking effect until the following term of office.

**1993 28 June:** Supreme Court decision in *Shaw v. Reno* imposes standard of strict scrutiny on congressional districts that are racially gerrymandered.

**1997 26 June:** In *Reno v. ACLU,* Supreme Court strikes down the Communications Decency Act for violating free speech provisions under the First Amendment.

**2000 12 December:** Supreme Court decides *Bush v. Gore,* ending local recounts and allowing Florida's certification of electoral votes for George W. Bush, who subsequently wins the Electoral College.

**2003 26 June:** Supreme Court decides *Lawrence v. Texas,* affirming the constitutionality of homosexual relations.

**2004 28 June:** Supreme Court decides *Rasul v. Bush* and *Hamdan v. Rumsfeld,* affirming the constitutionality of detention of suspected terrorists, but foreign nationals have due process rights to challenge their detention.

**2008 26 June:** Supreme Court decision in *D.C. v. Heller* affirms Second Amendment right to gun ownership for lawful self-protection and invalidates local gun restrictions.

**2015 26 June:** Supreme Court decides *Obergefell v. Hodges,* invalidating state bans on homosexual marriage under the Fourteenth Amendment.

# Introduction

## THE CONTEXT OF THE FOUNDING OF THE AMERICAN REPUBLIC, 1783–1789

The United States Constitution, the nation's foundational charter, arose from the difficulties precipitated by the anachronistic governing structure the Articles of Confederation left in place following independence from Great Britain. That latter document was no more than a "league of friendship" that provided a minimalist framework for the states to wage the Revolutionary War collectively.[1] George Washington's many frustrations with the Continental Congress are well documented.[2] But it was after victory at Yorktown, the departure of the British, and in the immediate years after ratification of the Treaty of Paris in 1784 that the articles' deficits became increasingly apparent at the dawn of an era as full of peril as it was promise. The covenant had not created a central or national government of any variety. States—which regarded themselves essentially as sovereign nations—willfully gave little power to the Continental Congress during the conflict, and even more so thereafter. Further, the articles were structurally flawed insofar as there was no executive to enforce the laws passed by Congress, nor was there a judiciary capable of arbitrating disputes. The result was a growing and dangerous paralysis. The outlook for the survival of civil society, let alone the birth of a unified republic, seemed bleak as storm clouds loomed on the horizon. The inchoate nation fell under the burden of heavy foreign debts incurred during the Revolutionary War, and the Continental currency collapsed by 1782. Colonial powers—including the British to the north and the Spanish to the south—potentially threatened domestic security alongside sporadic attacks by natives. States engaged in tariff wars with one another, disrupting internal commerce and barring the development of a national economy. Veterans of the Revolutionary War, who had been promised pay for their military service but never received any, ultimately took up arms to protest the foreclosure of their farms and shops as Congress remained immobilized and state governments largely refused to intervene.

Indeed, the chaos that ensued during Shays's Rebellion in Fall 1786—perhaps more than the Annapolis Convention called for by James Madison to discuss protectionist trade barriers erected by the states—catalyzed calls for a national conference to sort out debt, trade, and governance issues.[3] The delegates from the states who ultimately met at Independence Hall in Philadelphia beginning in May 1787 were, according to Charles Beard, most interested in protecting their own property.[4] Shays's Rebellion, in this view, demonstrated the potential for the destruction of the landowning elite's economic interests by an unruly, populist mob. A more benign and perhaps more widely held perspective is that the Framers of the Constitution were enlightened statesmen who gave primacy to civil liberties and limited government above their own welfare and for whom protection of wealth and property was less preponderant than a commitment to the principles of democratic governance.

In either case, the Framers confronted a dearth of clear, real-world examples of democratic structures in the late 18th century upon which they could draw as they contemplated the only acceptable political configuration to the generation that had thrown off the yoke of King George III: a republic. It is vital to recall that the French Revolution had not yet occurred, the *Déclaration des Droits de l'Homme et du Citoyen* had not been drafted, and most European nation-states were led by monarchs whose divine right to govern derived from the blessings of the church. Federalism was an intriguing theory without much empirical foundation. Although alliances at the heart of the Swiss confederation dated to the 13th century, the founding of the federal state (*Confederatio Helvetica*) was still six decades away.

Trained primarily in philosophy and law, many of the Framers were, to be sure, familiar with seminal Greek and Roman works on politics and normative democracy, including those by Plato, Aristotle, and Cicero. Similarly, the writings of Hobbes, Locke, Montesquieu, and Rousseau indubitably influenced their understanding of social contract theory and models of potential institutional structures. But as Robert Dahl posits, their prospects for successful "constitutional engineering" were circumscribed:

> The knowledge of the Framers—some of them, certainly—may well have been the best available in 1787. But reliable knowledge about constitutions appropriate to a large representative republic was, at best, meager. History had produced no truly relevant models of representative government on the scale the United States had already attained, not to mention the scale it would reach in the years to come. As much as many of the delegates admired the British constitution, it was far from a suitable model. Nor could the Roman Republic provide much of a guide. The famous Venetian Republic, illustrious though it had been, was governed by a hereditary aristocracy of fewer than two thousand men and was already tottering: a decade after the Convention an upstart Corsican would knock it over in a featherweight military attack. Whatever knowledge the delegates could gain from historical experience was, then, only marginally relevant at best.[5]

As Ben Franklin responded when queried about the type of government Americans would have, "a republic—if you can keep it." The document that ultimately emerged from the Constitutional Convention on 17 September 1787 reflected not only significant compromise but considerable "leaps of faith" in a grand experiment in self-governance. And it was a "hard sell" at times during the Convention and during the ratification debate. James Madison's initial design for a new constitution became the starting point for the debate. Far from fashioning a governing structure that favored *direct* democracy, Madison carefully devised what would become known as the Virginia Plan.[6] The proposal accentuated *representative democracy* and was painstakingly crafted on the federal principle to arrive at an acceptable equilibrium between national and state power. Those fearful of an overbearing central government, known as the Anti-Federalists, would reject any other scheme out of hand. And many later did so despite Madison's best efforts to address their qualms.

The task of striking the appropriate balance not only in federal–state authority but also in the institutional structure of the central government itself was first assigned to the Committee on Detail, chaired by John Routledge of South Carolina, and later to the Committee on Postponed Matters, which was composed of 11 members including Madison, Rufus King of Massachusetts, Roger Sherman of Connecticut, Gouverneur Morris of Pennsylvania, and Pierce Butler of South Carolina.[7] The issue of representation in Congress waxed between the Virginia Plan, which favored the large states, and the New Jersey Plan, which favored the less populous states. The Connecticut (or Great) Compromise, proposed by Roger Sherman, carried the day by calling for equal representation for the states in the Senate (with senators appointed by state legislatures) and representation in the House based on population. There was ample support for the Three-Fifths Compromise, proposed by Sherman and James Wilson, which counted slaves as three-fifths of a person for purposes of enumeration and thereby all but ensured the continuation of the institution of bondage for blacks in southern states for the foreseeable future. All but a few Framers, including Wilson and Alexander Hamilton, were generally wary of a strong executive and were far more comfortable lodging power in the legislature. Not only were the Framers split on whether the office of the presidency should be unitary or plural, but they also disagreed on how the executive should be chosen. Edmund Randolph's presentation of the Virginia Plan provided Congress with the authority to appoint a "national executive." William Paterson, author of the New Jersey Plan, proposed a "federal executive" chosen by Congress and devoid of a veto power. Elbridge Gerry recommended that the president be chosen by state governors. Alexander Hamilton, by contrast, supported a "supreme executive," and James Wilson pressed for a single "magistrate" with "energy, dispatch and responsibility." Ultimately, the threat of internecine power struggles within a multiple-executive structure convinced the Framers of the soundness of a unitary office. The Electoral College, a territorially based formula for electing the executive, was yet another example of compromise as well as the Framers' preference for *indirect* democracy. Slates of electors based on congressional representation would ultimately choose the president via an Electoral College. Notwithstanding a majority, the decision would fall back upon the House of Representatives, where Madison believed it would return "nineteen times out of twenty"—and much to the delight of proponents of legislative government. Beyond George Washington, the presiding officer at the Convention, few imagined other candidates who could match his character and veneration to carry the Electoral College in the future.

The final draft of the Constitution sought not only to remedy the weaknesses of the Articles of Confederation but also to include safeguards for the new democratic structure based on a separation of powers between the branches. The munificent enumerated powers of Congress in Article I, including the regulation of interstate commerce, the establishment of post offices, and borrowing money, were complemented by the "necessary and proper" or "elastic" clause, which gave the legislature the power to enforce laws—a clause that had been painfully absent in the Articles of Confederation. Article VI elucidated that the Constitution was the supreme law of the land and takes precedence over state laws. The president was to share the war power with Congress, with the former able to take swift actions to "repel sudden attacks" while the latter would have the authority to declare war formally. Moreover, presidential appointments to executive departments and the judiciary would be subjected to majority Senate approval and treaties to a supermajority. Presidents could veto bills but not absolutely: Congress was given the last word with a two-thirds vote in both the House and the Senate. Further, presidents, like judges, could be removed by impeachment in Congress with a two-thirds majority in the Senate for "high crimes and misdemeanours," a phrase the Committee on Postponed Matters failed to define more fully. Finally, Congress itself also faced restrictions, including a prohibition on bills of attainder, ex post facto laws, granting of titles of nobility, and the suspension of habeas corpus outside situations of rebellion or for purposes of public safety.

Anti-Federalists remained unconvinced that the charter was adequate to preclude tyranny. Elbridge Gerry, George Mason, and Edmund Randolph rose to the forefront in opposition to the document the Committee on Style produced for signature. While variably successful in altering the final draft to include an additional method for amending the Constitution and language on impeachment, the faction's biggest objection was the absence of a bill of rights that set in stone civil liberties. They drew upon recent history as they had witnessed it. Between the Revolutionary War and the Constitutional Convention, the 13 states had drawn up 17 constitutions between them, all of which had some preamble, preface, or detailed outline of individual rights the government could not abrogate. Madison supported the idea of a bill of rights in the federal constitution,[8] but Mason and Gerry were overruled in their quest for such an appendix by the rest of the members of the Committee on Style, who were anxious to adjourn. Gerry, Mason, and Randolph ultimately refused to sign the document, and a dozen other delegates left before the proceedings terminated. Rhode Island had never sent delegates, and New York's left early. Such was the context in which the remaining delegates put their signatures to the document and prepared to send it to the states for ratification.

Article VII of the Constitution required that nine of 13 states ratify the document for its approval. The fate of the charter would be tied to the heated debate between Federalists who supported it and Anti-Federalists who opposed it, as each side framed its arguments in newspaper editorials of the day. The collection of 85 essays penned by James Madison, Alexander Hamilton, and John Jay, known as the Federalist Papers, was a coordinated effort to convince a sometimes skeptical public and circumspect state legislatures to approve the Constitution.[9] The compendium provides the most authoritative insight into the Framers' essential understanding of how the new republic was to operate and buttress the nation's pursuit of democratic rule. As was the custom of the era, Madison, Hamilton, and Jay used a pseudonym—Publius—to identify their writings.

Federalists confronted a less organized yet resolute opposition by Anti-Federalists, including George Clinton, Robert Yates, Samuel Bryan, Arthur Lee, and Benjamin Workman, who outlined their opposition to the Constitution in essays published under the pseudonyms Cato, Brutus, Centinel, Cincinnatus, and Philadelphiensis, respectively, as well as "The Federal Farmer" (whose identity is not clear but likely Richard Henry Lee, Melancton Smith, or Mercy Otis Smith).[10] In their pleas Anti-Federalists cited the presidency as a "military king," viewed the Senate as an institution that would descend into the foibles of aristocracy, and chastised the delegates at the Convention for exceeding their authority in supplanting the Articles of Confederation (a charge that Congress dismissed on 20 September 1787). Nonetheless, as vital to the Anti-Federalists' case as the written essays were the speeches given by Patrick Henry. Henry did not partake in the Constitutional Convention but argued eloquently at Virginia's ratification convention against the project, contending that it provided a framework for the federal government to usurp the power of the states. Of the Framers he asked rhetorically, "what right had they to say 'we the people' instead We the States?" and contended that the absence of a bill of rights was "the most fatal plan that could possibly be conceived to enslave a free people."[11]

The Anti-Federalists lost their larger case to Madison's compelling arguments based on pluralist political theory, most notably articulated in Federalist nos. 10 and 51, and Hamilton's and Jay's defense of the executive and judiciary, respectively. Ten months after the Constitution—which had been drafted in secret—was sent to the states, Delaware's legislature ratified it unanimously. Pennsylvania, New Jersey, Georgia, Connecticut, Massachusetts, Maryland, South Carolina, and New Hampshire followed suit; by 21 June 1788 the requisite nine states had approved it. Ratifying states' calls for amendments regarding a bill of rights helped push success in Virginia and New York the same year. North Carolina ratified the Constitution in September 1789. Rhode Island, which rejected ratification overwhelmingly by popular referendum in 1788, became the final state to ratify the Constitution in May 1790. On 25 September 1789 the First Congress adopted 12 proposed constitutional amendments. The 10 that were ratified on 15 December 1791 enshrined the Bill of Rights, the most important if sometimes disregarded contribution of the Anti-Federalists, and which guaranteed precious individual liberties ranging from freedom of speech, assembly, conscience, and press and redress of grievances in the First Amendment to the reserved powers in the Tenth Amendment.

Ratification of the Constitution enshrined an American form of "exceptionalism" that would demarcate the nation's character for future generations. Its principles, as defined here, included the Revolutionary ideals of republicanism and representative democracy, limited government, and personal liberty. These principles are outlined in a *written* framework that set forth the relationship between the separated branches of government and that government and its citizens, including a charter of *negative* freedoms that protected the individual from government intrusion. Few countries in the 18th century had written constitutions, and Great Britain still does not have one. Still, critics of the Constitution point to its many alleged omissions and the Framers' narrow and putatively elitist construction of the notion of "democracy." Although the preamble eloquently cites *natural rights* to which men are entitled from God, the men who wrote the document did not consider the rights of women, ethnic minorities, or natives, and they institutionalized slavery. Moreover, the democratic process in the early republic was limited to the few who met eligibility for voting, were white, and owned substantial property. All told "democracy" extended to very few citizens.[12]

When the First Congress took up office alongside President George Washington in 1789, setting up the federal court system with passage of the Judiciary Act and filling seats on the Supreme Court were among the top priorities. Perhaps few Framers, including Alexander Hamilton, who contended that the Supreme Court was the "least dangerous branch," foresaw the future role that the judiciary would play in interpreting the Constitution, fleshing out the meaning of many of its provisions, and addressing rights deemed implicit. Neither could the Framers have anticipated a cataclysmic civil war just 71 years after the Founding, waves of immigrants in the 19th century that would test the mettle of the application of individual rights, nor two world wars and a massive depression in the 20th century that would transform not only the role of the presidency within the delicate institutional balance but also the fundamental role of the federal government in larger political, social, and economic systems. In retrospect, contemporary theories of "path dependency" in political science and history seemingly would have provided little guidance or prediction of how the fledgling nation and its ideals printed on parchment would develop from 1789 onward. Questions abounded: How far would protections in the Bill of Rights extend? Did implied powers exist in the Constitution, and if so, what were the parameters? How was the "peculiar institution" of slavery, as Alexis de Tocqueville asserted in *Democracy in America*, compatible in the long term with personal liberty, democratic development, and territorial expansion? Were the constitutional framework and separation of powers to be interpreted so narrowly that they were a "straightjacket" or "suicide pact" that limited the federal government to the point of potential paralysis in times of crisis? Or would the founding charter be adaptable to evolving governing contexts and social change, and hinder or promote the expansion of democracy, equality, and essential freedoms? Such questions, for better or for worse, would place the Supreme Court front and center in controversies that would from time to time shake the nation to its core.

## CONSTITUTIONAL INTERPRETATION, THE SUPREME COURT, AND THE NATION'S FIRST CENTURY

If, as Supreme Court Justice Charles Evans Hughes opined, "The Constitution is what judges say it is," any academic foray into the evolution of interpretations of its scope and meaning necessitates a sharp focus on judicial constructs in pivotal Supreme Court decisions over time. Readers are cautioned, however, that the entries in the dictionary that follows do *not* make up a comprehensive compendium of Supreme Court cases, a history of the high court, or an anthology of justices' biographies. Nor is that the objective of the present volume. Students interested in the dynamics of the Supreme Court, its procedures, and its membership are urged to consult the *Historical Dictionary of the U.S. Supreme Court* (2015) authored by Artemus Ward, Christopher Brough, and Robert Arnold in this series for Scarecrow Press. Rather, the Supreme Court cases, and to a lesser degree basic procedural issues, covered in *this* dictionary are those judged by the author to represent the most critical historical and contemporary decisions regarding interpretations of Articles I to VII, the Bill of Rights, and the Civil War Amendments (Thirteenth, Fourteenth, and Fifteenth Amendments), in particular. Every effort has been made to situate the context of the dispute and the constitutional provision at issue in such cases. Moreover, the outcome of the case includes the vote split among justices as well as excerpts of majority and dissenting opinions, where appropriate, that lend insight into the court's decision-making rationale and minority perspectives.

Just as the nation's first president, George Washington, founded critical precedents for the office of the presidency by establishing a cabinet, cementing the commander-in-chief role in domestic affairs during the Whiskey Rebellion, and buttressing presidential primacy in the realm of foreign relations with the Neutrality Proclamation, Chief Justice John Marshall played a decisive role in securing the Supreme Court's constitutional position as a coequal branch of government vis-à-vis Congress and the president in the early Republic.[13] Article III of the Constitution elucidated that the Supreme Court was a court of original jurisdiction, where cases are first heard, as well as an appellate court. Its original jurisdiction extends to cases affecting foreign ministers and ambassadors, maritime law, any case to which the United States government is a party, disputes between the states and between a state and citizens of another state, and disputes between a state or citizens of a state and foreign nations. The Constitution was silent, however, on the larger notion of *judicial review* by the Supreme Court of the actions of other branches of the federal government.

The case of *Marbury v. Madison* in 1803 settled the issue of judicial review definitively. Arising from the "midnight appointments" of outgoing Federalist president John Adams in 1801, the case centered on the refusal of Democratic-Republican President Thomas Jefferson's secretary of state, James Madison, to provide appointed justice William Marbury a writ of mandamus to take up his judgeship. While the dispute, per se, is intriguing for its political implications, the mere fact that the Marshall Court exerted its authority and claimed the right to pass judgment on actions of other branches of the federal government, in this case the executive, affected the balance of national institutions considerably. Aware of detractors' allegations that the high court was usurping authority, Marshall wrote eloquently in the unanimous majority opinion:

> The judicial power of the United States is extended to all cases arising under the constitution. Could it be the intention of those who gave this power, to say that, in using it, the constitution should not be looked into? That a case arising under the constitution should be decided without examining the instrument under which it arises? This is too extravagant to be maintained. In some cases then, the constitution must be looked into by the judges. And if they can open it at all, what part of it are they forbidden to read, or to obey?

As Congress and the states fine-tuned presidential elections with ratification of the Twelfth Amendment in 1804, the Marshall Court played a critical role in clarifying the parameters of federal and state power, as well as in expounding understandings of the inapplicability of the federal

Bill of Rights to the states in the early 19th century. In *Fletcher v. Peck* (1810) the Supreme Court invalidated a state law for the first time and accentuated the sanctity of contracts. In *McCulloch v. Maryland* (1819) the court found that the State of Maryland had exceeded its authority when it taxed the Bank of the United States (as Marshall bristled, "the power to tax is the power to destroy"). In *Gibbons v. Ogden* (1824) Congress's power to regulate interstate commerce was found to extend to navigation of waterways. And in *Barron v. Baltimore* (1833) the Bill of Rights was interpreted *not* to apply to state actions but only to the federal government. The case would have far-reaching implications beyond the Nullification Crisis of 1832, in which the Force Bill, Andrew Jackson's saber-rattling, and a compromise over the "Tariff of Abominations" put to rest, at least temporarily, John C. Calhoun's notion that states could annul federal laws with which they disagreed.[14]

Marshall's successor as chief justice, Roger Taney, oversaw one of the most momentous Supreme Court cases that foreshadowed the opening salvos of the American Civil War.[15] If the Framers had missed a critical opportunity to eradicate slavery at the Constitutional Convention, the Taney Court affirmed the constitutionality of indentured servitude at a critical juncture in time as Kansas bled and the presidency of James Buchanan floundered. In the decision in *Dred Scott v. Sanford* (1857) free and enslaved blacks were found *not* to be citizens of the United States and therefore had no basis from which to sue at the federal level. Moreover, in the 7–2 decision the justices asserted the Missouri Compromise of 1820 was unconstitutional (although it had been superseded by the Kansas–Nebraska Act of 1854), as Congress had no authority to regulate the institution of slavery in territories acquired after the founding of the United States in 1789. The decision further exacerbated the tensions between abolitionists and proponents of slavery as the nation edged toward nearly a half decade of civil conflict that would commence with the presidential election of 1860, the secession of the southern states, and the shots fired at Fort Sumter, South Carolina.

Taney was at the center of another constitutional controversy just a few years later as he reviewed the question of President Abraham Lincoln's wartime suspension of the writ of habeas corpus. The case underscored the critical axiom of the court's lack of enforcement authority. In *Ex Parte Merryman* (1861) Taney ruled that only Congress could suspend habeas corpus and the president's actions were unconstitutional. Lincoln, in turn, defied Taney's ruling and refused to turn over a Maryland militiaman, John Merryman, to the courts. Five years later, in *Ex Parte Milligan* (1866) the court, under Chief Justice Salmon P. Chase, held only that Lincoln's unilateral establishment of military tribunals was unconstitutional because civilian courts were still in operation.

As Lincoln's successor, Andrew Johnson, would battle the Radical Republicans in Congress over Reconstruction policy and ultimately face impeachment, Congress passed and the states ultimately ratified the Thirteenth, Fourteenth, and Fifteenth Amendments to the Constitution in 1865, 1869, and 1870, respectively. The Civil War Amendments, or Reconstruction Amendments as they were known, explicitly abolished slavery; made the Bill of Rights apply to the states by guaranteeing due process, privileges and immunities, and equal protection under the law; and granted citizenship rights to newly freed blacks.[16] In other words, the amendments sought to overturn the prior court rulings in *Barron* and *Dred Scott*, in particular, and rendered moot the Three-Fifths Compromise. Southern states assented to the amendments as a condition of reestablishing congressional representation and a return to the full privileges of statehood, which would come only after the departure of federal troops following the Hayes–Tilden Compromise in the disputed presidential election of 1876.

The Civil War Amendments had been on the books for only a few short years when the decision in the *Slaughterhouse Cases* (1873) elucidated that the Supreme Court intended to construe the Fourteenth Amendment in narrow terms and invert the intent of its framers by asserting it did not apply to the states. In *U.S. v. Reese* (1876) it became clear that the Fifteenth Amendment, too, was to be interpreted in such a way as to abrogate the voting rights of blacks. Finally, the *Civil Rights Cases* (1883) further elaborated that Congress, according to the court, had no authority under the Fourteenth Amendment to enforce the Civil Rights Act of 1875 and its provisions against racial discrimination. History wrote a particularly dark chapter for freedmen as states and local governments effected "black codes" aimed at paying African Americans low wages and keeping them in debt, passed so-called Jim Crow laws to segregate the races, and implemented poll taxes, literacy tests, and grandfather clauses to disenfranchise blacks.[17] Under Chief Justice Melville Fuller, the Supreme Court confirmed the constitutionality of "separate but equal" facilities for blacks in the landmark case of *Plessy v. Ferguson*, which remained the formal law of the land for 58 years. Perhaps never in American history had the spirit or the letter of the Constitution, as amended, been so subverted and the concept of natural rights for those granted citizenship and freed from the bondage of slavery been so thoroughly sabotaged.

## FROM THE PROGRESSIVE ERA AND SELECTIVE INCORPORATION TO THE WARREN COURT IN THE 20TH CENTURY

The early 20th century was significant for the Progressive movement heralded by the election of Presidents Theodore Roosevelt and Woodrow Wilson that led to the adoption of the Sixteenth, Seventeenth, and Nineteenth Amendments. The period was similarly notable for conservatism in the form of Prohibition and the ratification of the Eighteenth Amendment and President William Howard Taft's one-term reversion to a "strict constructionist" view of national institutions that defied the ethos of the Progressive Era, if not an illiberalism that was later tolerated with respect to civil liberties in the aftermath of World War I and the First Red Scare.

In response to the decision in *Pollock v. Farmers' Loan & Trust Co.* (1895), Congress and the states overrode the Supreme Court and in 1913 adopted the Sixteenth Amendment, which established an income tax without apportioning it among the states or per the Census. Proponents cited the alleged consolidation of wealth by industrialists and other affluent individuals as justification for passage of an amendment that detractors of the Internal Revenue Service continue to rue every 15 April. The direct election of senators provided by the adoption of the Seventeenth Amendment in 1913 enhanced the ideal of popular democracy but arguably eroded an important ideal of the federal principle of state influence so cherished by many Anti-Federalists. But the amendment may also be to blame for the frequent condition of "divided government" or split-party control of the presidency and Congress, and in particular the phenomenon of haphazard midterm loss for the president's party in the upper chamber (which sometimes reverses party control, as in 1946, 1954, 1994, 2006, and 2010), beginning in the 20th century. Finally, the Nineteenth Amendment, ratified in 1919, represented the culmination of decades of efforts of suffragettes to secure the women's vote at the national level. In 1875, the Supreme Court had held in *Minor v. Happersett* that the Fourteenth Amendment's "privileges and immunities" clause did not provide for a right to vote. Although new states such as Utah and Wyoming in the West had granted the women's vote, Susan B. Anthony, Elizabeth Cady Stanton, and Carrie Chapman Catt realized a hard-fought dream when President Warren Harding called Congress into special session to approve the measure and it was quickly ratified by the states.

The temperance movement celebrated its own victory in 1919 with ratification of the Eighteenth Amendment, which banned the production, transport, and sale of intoxicating liquors without defining them.[18] Drinking such beverages privately or possessing alcohol was *not* illegal. The Volstead Act, adopted over President Woodrow Wilson's veto, sought to provide a framework for enforcement of the nation's first attempt to regulate social policy by a constitutional amendment. From 1920, when the amendment went into effect, until its repeal in 1933 with ratification of the Twenty-First Amendment, Prohibition provided fodder for brutal criminal gangs, who took over the illegal transport of alcohol, alongside moonshiners who produced it. The Roaring '20s were remembered as much for the widespread "speakeasy" underground drinking establishments and the viciousness of gangsters such as Al Capone as for economic prosperity and jazz music.

The First Red Scare, the scores of anarchy laws passed by the states, and the federal Espionage Act of 1919, rather ironically, furnished the context in which the Supreme Court began selectively *incorporating* the Bill of Rights—extending civil liberties protections to apply to state governments through the Fourteenth Amendment.[19] In 1833, the high court had decided in *Barron v. Baltimore* that the first 10 amendments to the U.S. Constitution had no bearing on state actions. *Au fur et à mesure* the Supreme Court veered from that 19th-century precedent and slowly overturned the narrow interpretation of the Civil War Amendments during Reconstruction and through the early 20th century. One of the first cases, *Gitlow v. New York* (1925), regarded freedom of speech and explicitly invalidated the finding in *U.S. v. Cruikshank* (1876) that the First Amendment did not apply to state governments. Although socialist Benjamin Gitlow's conviction under a state anarchy law was upheld, the Taft Court held that the Fourteenth Amendment protections of due process, equal protection, and privileges and immunities preclude states from infringing on freedom of speech and freedom of the press. As with the ruling in *U.S. v. Schenck* six years earlier, in which Justice Oliver Wendell Holmes articulated the "clear and present danger" test, First Amendment guarantees of free speech are qualified.

The following decade, under Chief Justice Charles Evans Hughes, the Supreme Court incorporated other First Amendment freedoms. In *Near v. Minnesota* (1933) the majority established an extraordinarily high bar for the notion of "prior restraint," or governmental efforts to stop print media publication of materials. Moreover, the freedom of assembly was incorporated in *DeJonge v. Oregon* (1937) and the free exercise clause incorporated in *Cantwell v. Connecticut* (1940).

It was the Supreme Court under Chief Justice Earl Warren—one of two appointments that President Dwight Eisenhower alluded to as "mistakes"—that not only were other significant guarantees in the Bill of Rights incorporated but also segregation was found to violate the Fourteenth Amendment.[20] Indeed, in the watershed case of *Brown v. Board of Education* (1954), the court elucidated that separate facilities for white and black students were "inherently unequal" and ordered the desegregation of school districts around the nation "with all deliberate speed." Overturning the *Plessy* decision of 58 years earlier marked the beginning of the advancement of rights for blacks, who were aided considerably in the 1960s by President Lyndon Johnson's Great Society and War on Poverty agendas, as well as by significant legislation such as the Voting Rights Act of 1965.

The "rights revolution" during the Warren Court was most pronounced with respect to criminal rights.[21] The majority elaborated in *Mapp v. Ohio* (1961) that Fourth Amendment protections extend to state and local police actions, and illegally gathered evidence must be excluded from trials. In *Gideon v. Wainwright* (1963) the court took an expansive view of the

Sixth Amendment's provision for the right of "assistance of counsel" and asserted that due process required states to provide indigent defendants counsel at no charge. The Warren Court further expanded the reach of the Sixth Amendment in the decision in *Miranda v. Arizona* (1966), asserting that a defendant's confession may not be deemed voluntary unless the defendant understands his or her rights to remain silent and have counsel present during questioning. Finally, the Warren Court incorporated the Eighth Amendment protections against cruel and unusual punishment to the state level in *Robinson v. California* (1962) and the First Amendment right to petition government for redress of grievances in *Edwards v. South Carolina* (1963).

From the Great Depression through the late 1960s, Americans also added six more amendments to the founding charter. The Twentieth Amendment, ratified in 1933, coincided with the election of Franklin D. Roosevelt a year earlier and the birth of the modern presidency. Moving the date on which presidents take office from March to 20 January following the November election solved at least partially the lengthy lame-duck status of outgoing chief executives and the disadvantage of a four-month lead time for a new president to assume office and implement his agenda. It was nearly two decades after ratification of the Twenty-First Amendment in 1933, which ended Prohibition, that Congress and the states ratified another change to the presidency. The Twenty-Second Amendment, adopted in 1951, limited a president to two four-year terms. The amendment was at least in part a response to the unprecedented four elections won by Franklin D. Roosevelt from 1932 to 1944 and his subsequent health issues and sudden death just three months into his fourth term. A decade later, ratification of the Twenty-Third Amendment extended voting rights to citizens of the District of Columbia, who gained representation in the Electoral College for the first time. The Twenty-Fourth Amendment did away with the poll tax in 1964, a year notable for passage of the Civil Rights Act and the election of President Lyndon Baines Johnson, whose commitment to equality for African Americans took shape amid the controversial War on Poverty and Great Society agendas. Finally, the Twenty-Fifth Amendment, ratified in 1967, fine-tuned the parameters of presidential disability and succession. Impetus for such clarification grew not only from past historical experience (such as Woodrow Wilson's infirmity in his second term) but also from the assassination of President John F. Kennedy in 1963.

## FROM THE BURGER COURT TO THE NEW MILLENNIUM: THE DECLINE OF CONSTITUTIONAL CONSENSUS?

As the continuing tumult of the Vietnam War, the assassinations of Robert F. Kennedy and Martin Luther King in 1968, and the departure of

President Lyndon B. Johnson from politics gave way to the 1970s and the presidency of Richard Milhous Nixon, the nation wrestled not only with political issues but also social questions probably never contemplated by the Framers. Warren Burger became chief justice of the Supreme Court in 1969, the same year the high court affirmed in *Tinker v. Des Moines* students' rights under the First Amendment to protest the war in Southeast Asia by wearing armbands, despite schools' objections. Regardless, from abortion and a host of First Amendment interpretations to allegations of corruption in the White House, pressing civil rights issues, and questions regarding Eighth Amendment protections, the Burger Court walked amid a potential minefield.[22]

As President Nixon endeavored to end the conflict in Vietnam and achieve "peace with honor," the administration launched a frontal assault on the freedom of the press by attempting to enjoin the *New York Times* and the *Washington Post* from printing the so-called Pentagon Papers. The classified government report documented the Johnson administration's alleged "disinformation campaign" regarding the war, and Nixon judged that publication might jeopardize negotiating with the North Vietnamese. In 1971 in *New York Times Co. v. U.S.* , the Supreme Court held that the government had not met the "heavy burden" required for prior restraint and confirmed the newspapers' right to publish the material.

But if the Vietnam War was continuing to tear at the fabric of American society, the issue of abortion would add to the nation's melancholy. In 1973 the high court reviewed the hodgepodge state regulations regarding abortion and concluded in a 7–2 decision a woman's right to terminate a pregnancy was constitutionally protected by an implicit "right to privacy" under the Fourteenth Amendment. The justices noted, however, that the right had to be balanced with the legitimate state interest in protecting women's health and human life. In the immediate aftermath of the decision, and across the four decades that followed, not only would that balance prove elusive but the political debate would morph into one of the most intense and divisive in the post–World War II era.

Pivotal First Amendment issues centered on the establishment clause, obscenity, the parameters of freedom of the press, and campaign finance. In *Lemon v. Kurtzman* (1971) the high court weighed in on the question of religion and public education, holding that any laws regarding religion must "avoid excessive entanglement" between the state and religion, must be secular in nature, and must neither advance nor retard religion. In *Miller v. California* (1973) the court established a three-part test to determine what material may be considered obscene. In doing so, the justices erected a nearly insurmountable threshold by concluding that such material must lack "serious literary, artistic, political, or scientific value." In *Miami Herald v. Tornillo* (1974) the court struck down a Florida law mandating "equal time" be given to political candidates in print newspapers, buttressing the differences in the way that the First Amendment applies to print versus broadcast media. Finally, in *Buckley v. Valeo* (1976) the court held that spending in political campaigns is equivalent to free speech, struck down a central element of the Federal Campaign Election Act of 1974, and established an important precedent for future debates over the regulation of money in political campaigns.

The Supreme Court also passed judgment on the reach of executive privilege in the presidency and dealt the deathblow to President Richard Nixon's attempt to conceal his involvement in the Watergate scandal. Nixon claimed that conversations he taped with advisors were confidential and beyond the reach of the special prosecutor investigating the burglary at the Democratic Party headquarters at the Watergate Hotel in Washington, DC, and the subsequent cover-up. When Nixon refused to comply with a subpoena to turn over recorded material, the justices—in a unanimous decision—ordered the president to hand over the tapes. Within months the final chapter of the scandal was written with Nixon's resignation in August 1974.

Additionally, the Burger Court grappled with the question of cruel and unusual punishment prohibited by the Eighth Amendment. In 1972 the majority's ruling in *Furman v. Georgia* resulted in a moratorium on the death penalty due to a lack of consistency in states' application of capital punishment. Four years later in *Gregg v. Georgia* the court held that the death penalty was *not* fundamentally a violation of the Eighth Amendment and reaffirmed criteria—including crimes eligible for capital punishment, jury review, and appeals processes—that states must meet to avoid unconstitutional practices.

The Burger Court walked a very fine line with regard to affirmative action. The case of *Regents of the University of California v. Bakke* (1978) was the first litigation of its kind with regard to formal policies aimed at promoting racial diversity in higher education. Opponents to such policies decried alleged "reverse discrimination" against whites. Proponents contended that institutional programs were vital in redressing past discrimination against various minority groups. The high court held that race could be one factor—but not the overriding factor—in university admissions decisions. Both sides of the debate could view the ruling as the glass half empty or half full.

Finally, in 1983 the Burger Court weighed in on a paramount issue regarding the separation of powers. At issue in *INS v. Chadha* was the constitutionality of the "legislative veto," whereby Congress can retroactively reject presidential actions. The court held that a single-chamber legislative veto violated the presentment clause of the Constitution and the principle of bicameralism and invalidated the practice—though the legislative and executive branches continue to utilize it for the sake of convenience and in defiance of the ruling.

By most scholarly and journalistic accounts, the Supreme Court under Chief Justice William Rehnquist took a turn toward a more conservative approach to constitutional interpretation in the mid-1980s, though not universally. The justices would revisit the battle lines on the most contentious contemporary debates, many of which contributed to the increasing polarization between liberals and conservatives and Democrats and Republicans during the presidencies of Ronald Reagan, George H. W. Bush, William Clinton, and the first term of George W. Bush. The issues ranged from abortion and affirmative action to the War on Terror.[23]

The court was particularly critical of governmental affirmative action programs and legislative reapportionment schemes intended to enhance minority representation in Congress. The first blow to champions of affirmative action came in 1987 in the case of *Richmond v. Croson*. The justices held that local government "set-asides" of contracts for minority-owned businesses were unconstitutional where the intent was to counter societal discrimination. A similar ruling on federal set-aside programs was elaborated in *Adarand v. Peña* in 1995. With regard to public education, in *Grutter v. Bollinger* (2003) the justices concluded that the affirmative action program at the University of Michigan Law School was tailored narrowly enough in favoring underrepresented minority groups to pass constitutional muster. However, in *Gratz v. Bollinger* (2003) the court ruled that the admissions system at the University of Michigan that automatically awarded "points" to minority students violated equal protection under the Fourteenth Amendment. Regarding gender discrimination, the Rehnquist Court struck down the Virginia Military Institute's ban on admitting women from the state-subsidized postsecondary school in *U.S. v. Virginia* (1996). In the cases of alleged "racial gerrymandering" in *Shaw v. Reno* (1993) and *Miller v. Johnson* (1995), the court affirmed that race could be one criterion—but not the overriding criterion—in legislative redistricting and struck down oddly shaped majority-minority districts drawn by state legislatures as a violation of Fourteenth Amendment protections.

First Amendment protections also came into sharp focus. In *Texas v. Johnson* (1989) the Rehnquist Court struck down a Texas law that banned burning the American flag as a violation of symbolic speech. A year later in *U.S. v. Eichman* the justices invalidated a federal prohibition on flag desecration. In *Reno v. ACLU* (1997) the court determined that the vagaries of congressional legislation aimed at protecting minors from obscene electronic communications was a free speech violation. With respect to the establishment clause, in *Lee v. Weisman* (1992), the high court invalidated prayers at public school graduation ceremonies and in *Santa Fe Independent School District v. Doe* (2000) held that prayers before high school football games were similarly unconstitutional. In *Zelman v. Simmons-Harris* (2002) the court found that narrowly tailored school voucher programs with secular purposes did *not* violate the establishment clause.

Finally, regarding free association, the court held in *Boy Scouts of America v. Dale* (2000) that a private organization could exclude homosexuals.

Abortion and capital punishment issues also occupied the court's agenda. In *Webster v. Reproductive Health Services* (1989) the justices found that states could legislate regarding abortion. In *Planned Parenthood v. Casey* (1992) a plurality reinforced that finding, so long as regulations did not impose an "undue burden" on women. In *McCleskey v. Kemp* (1987) the court rejected arguments that African Americans were more likely to receive the death penalty than whites and rebuffed statistics that purportedly suggested racism in the application of capital punishment.

The Rehnquist Court also struggled with the question of individual rights in several domains. First, in *Lawrence v. Texas* (2004) the justices overturned state sodomy laws that prohibited consensual homosexual acts. The decision reversed the ruling in *Bowers v. Hardwick* (1986) of two decades earlier and was a major victory for gay rights advocates. The terrorist attacks of 11 September 2001 and the subsequent War on Terror prosecuted by President George W. Bush spawned several cases about the constitutional rights of detained enemy combatants. In *Rasul v. Bush* (2004) the court determined that civilian courts in the U.S. had jurisdiction to hear habeas corpus cases stemming from the imprisonment of detainees at Guantanamo Bay, Cuba. In *Hamdi v. Rumsfeld* (2004) it confirmed the due process rights of detainees.

The Rehnquist Court also reviewed the parameters of congressional and presidential power and played a pivotal role in the 2000 presidential election outcome. In *U.S. v. Lopez* (1995) the court's decision was the first to limit congressional power under the commerce clause in a case that involved gun rights. In *Gonzales v. Raich* (2005), however, the justices upheld the right of Congress to criminalize marijuana under the commerce clause, even if states allowed for the medical use of cannabis. In *Clinton v. City of New York* (1998) the court found that the "enhanced rescission authority," or "line-item veto," the Republican 104th Congress begrudgingly gave to President William Clinton as part of the Contract with America agenda of House Speaker Newt Gingrich violated the separation of powers. Congress cannot give away legislative powers, which are its exclusive domain per Article I.

In 2000 a divided court was thrown in the midst of the most divisive presidential election outcome since 1876.[24] The certification of Electoral College votes in Florida, where ballot and voting problems had occurred, would determine whether Democrat Albert Gore Jr. or Republican George W. Bush became president. For 36 days the nation collectively held its breath as county-level recounts were undertaken and the two partisan camps challenged the process in the state courts, and ultimately in the Supreme Court. By a 5–4 decision, the high court essentially put an end to the recounts by asserting that the disparate processes for reassessing ballots violated the Fourteenth Amendment right to equal protection.

The decision in *Bush v. Gore* (2000) paved the way for the Florida secretary of state, Katherine Harris, to certify that Bush—whose brother Jeb was governor of the Sunshine State—had carried the state by 537 votes. Republicans breathed a sigh of relief while many Democrats remained convinced that the election had been hijacked by the federal judiciary.

The year 2005 marked the passing of the torch to Chief Justice John Roberts. In the last decade the Supreme Court has never seemed so divided or the interpersonal acrimony between the justices more palpable on constitutional issues ranging from abortion, affirmative action, and civil rights to campaign finance and Second Amendment issues.[25] Early cases during the presidency of George W. Bush included the lingering question of enemy combatant detainees held in Guantanamo Bay, Cuba, and their legal rights. In *Hamdan v. Rumsfeld* (2006) the justices struck down the military commissions established by the president to try the suspects captured in the War on Terror for violating the Uniform Code of Military Justice (UCMJ) and the Geneva Conventions. In *Boumediene v. Bush* (2008) the majority declared that the Military Commissions Act passed by Congress in 2006 was unconstitutional and that enemy combatants had a right to habeas corpus to challenge their detentions in civilian courts.

Controversial social issues also dominated the Roberts Court's constitutional interpretations. In *Gonzales v. Carhart* (2006) a narrow majority on the high court affirmed a congressional prohibition on late-term abortions, igniting the fury of pro-choice advocates. With Associate Justice Anthony Kennedy assuming the pivotal swing vote, the court struck down portions of the federal Defense of Marriage Act (DOMA) that defined marriage as the union of one man and one woman in *U.S. v. Windsor* (2013). Two years later—in the *Obergefell v. Hodges* decision that was cheered by gay rights advocates and held in contempt by conservatives—Kennedy provided the opinion that same-sex marriage was a constitutional right under the Fourteenth Amendment and struck down bans against the practice enacted in 29 states.

Apart from emotional battles surrounding the redefinition of marriage, perhaps no other issue proved as divisive as local attempts to impose strict gun controls in two of the nation's urban centers with unacceptably high crime and murder rates. In *District of Columbia v. Heller* (2008) the court narrowly upheld the Second Amendment right to keep a firearm in the federal district for self-defense. In *McDonald v. City of Chicago* (2010) a slim majority used the same principles to incorporate the Second Amendment right to bear arms through the Fourteenth Amendment and apply it to the states.

Major civil rights cases regarding affirmative action in secondary and postsecondary education also left the court divided. In *Parents Involved in Community Schools v. Seattle School District* (2007) the justices split 4–4–1 while invalidating a voluntary desegregation plan that assigned students to schools on the basis of racial classifications that were not sufficiently narrowly tailored to a compelling government interest. In *Fisher v. University of Texas* (2013) the justices stopped short of ending affirmative action in higher education, remanding a case to a federal appeals court in which the plaintiff had sued over the university's race-conscious admissions policy. The justices determined that the appeals court had erred by failing to apply strict scrutiny to the university's admission policy while affirming the precedent in *Grutter v. Bollinger* (2003).

Finally, the Supreme Court's ruling in *Citizens United v. Federal Elections Commission* (2009) on the issue of campaign finance drew an uncharacteristic rebuke from President Obama in his State of the Union address to Congress and the nation in January 2010. The surreal setting, which featured the president's verbal browbeating of the justices who ruled that the First Amendment prohibited governmental prohibitions on political expenditures by independent groups, included several justices on the majority shaking their heads in disapprobation with scowls on their faces. The scene seemed to encapsulate the hyperpartisanship that now characterizes the American Republic, and the chasm between the political left and right with respect to constitutional interpretation in the 21st century. The sudden passing of Associate Justice Antonin Scalia, a Reagan appointee, in February 2016 almost certainly presages one of the most spectacular nomination battles in recent memory that will dominate the presidential election and may leave the court as divided as ever—and without a crucial fifth vote for months if not years to come.

The question that naturally arises in this contemporary era of partisan and ideological polarization in the electorate, extraordinary tension among the justices in the highest court in the land, and the seeming aggrandizement of federal power quite often at the expense of the states is how and whether the Constitution can remain the reference point for debate about present dilemmas in governance and social policy when there is ostensibly less consensus about its relevance, usefulness, or authority and the legitimacy of the Supreme Court to resolve issues. Proponents of "strict constructionism" yearn for a return to the "original intent" of the Framers and denounce deviations from the orthodoxy of the precepts of the foundational charter dating to the Convention debates and the campaign for ratification. Progressives dismiss elements of the Constitution as a "charter of negative freedoms" and champion the alleged malleability of the document to advocate for a greater role of the federal government in social, economic, and regulatory affairs.

The structure of national political institutions, of course, looks much different today than in 1789. To the probable disappointment of the Framers of the Republic, over the course of the last two and a quarter centuries momentum has swung decidedly away from the preponderance of legislative government to presidential dominance. But the investment of greater power in the executive scarcely yielded a panacea with the advent of the modern presidency beginning in 1932. The "shadow" of successful heroic, rhetorical, and policy leadership exercised by Franklin Roosevelt, conditioned by economic crisis and the last declared war by Congress, has become as increasingly elusive as it is long.[26] Indeed, the nation's last two chief executives—George W. Bush and Barack H. Obama—have proven the most polarizing in a generation, and their questionable unilateral actions are at the core of much consternation on either side of the political divide. It is doubtful that the "great man" theory of executive leadership can dispel the nation's woes, from terrorism to the astronomical debt, by a constitutionally dubious stroke of a pen. Moreover, faith in those elected to Congress is at an all-time low since polls have been taken. Careerism on Capitol Hill has replaced notions of a "citizen legislature," and gridlock within Congress and between the presidency and Congress is now the standard in an era of divided party control. Further, esteem for the Supreme Court has dropped to disturbing levels as ideological differences and rancor between the justices have been more fully exposed. The frequent 5–4 decisions on matters ranging from gun rights to campaign spending mirror the chasm in the electorate. Finally, trust in the media, which is supposed to act as a guardian for the people's interests and keep public officials accountable, has all but evaporated in an era when one's partisanship likely determines from which cable news station or Internet websites one derives political information.

Regardless, this is *not* the first time in American history that constitutional dissensus and political consternation have caused confusion and chaos, if not social upheaval. Examples are bountiful: the nullification crisis of 1832 that pitted states' rights against the federal government; the election of 1860 and the subsequent Civil War; the narrow interpretations of the Fourteenth and Fifteenth Amendments and their wholesale forsaking by the Supreme Court during Reconstruction with respect to the protection of the rights of African Americans; First Amendment challenges during the First Red Scare after World War I and the Espionage Act; the McCarthy Era in the 1950s; and the elections of 1896 and 1932 with respect to economic and social regulation. Each of these examples placed into clear conflict constitutional interpretations of civil liberties and civil rights or conceptualizations of the role of the national government. The Republic survived. Crises were averted or resolved, and at least some semblance of broad harmony and agreement followed, often evidenced by electoral realignments that legitimized national policies, if even haltingly. Will the nation today return to such equilibrium?

Addressing the nation's current state of malaise requires a return to a spirited discussion about what the Constitution means to generations old and new without losing sight of the Framers' republican principles. It also mandates a civic debate that can include honest, intellectual disagreements about interpretation. Such a debate must take place in a public space in which political parties, pundits, and ordinary citizens talk *to* one another rather than *past* one another. Keeping and fine-tuning the

Republic's constitutional order ultimately depends on an informed citizenry that reveres the rule of law in the spirit of those who gathered in Philadelphia in 1787 and will hold those who govern the nation to account. Before policy considerations, elected officials' performance must be scored on adherence to and respect for the Constitution. Representative democracy is as much about process and fidelity to the rule of laws as it is about outcome.

Perhaps our real constitutional crisis is an alarming dearth of civic knowledge. A recent survey revealed that 70 percent of Americans did not know that the Constitution is the supreme law of the land. An Annenburg Public Policy Center survey found that only 38 percent of Americans could name all three branches of the U.S. government, and a third were unable to correctly name a single branch. And a National Assessment of Educational Progress (NAEP) survey of high school seniors showed that three-quarters could not name a single power granted to Congress by the Constitution.[27] As Judge Learned Hand wrote, "Liberty lies in the hearts of men and women: when it dies there, no constitution, no law, no court can even do much to help it." Such is a recipe for an unaccountable government that can inexorably sow the seeds of the tyranny that so troubled the Anti-Federalists. Whether their writings will once again find their way into the lexicon of contemporary political discourse, in the 2016 election and beyond, is unclear. But as the voters and students look to history for guidance about the future, perhaps this volume makes a small contribution in providing a basis from which to weigh our leaders' commitment to preserving, protecting, and defending our cherished, if sometimes neglected, foundational charter.

## NOTES

1. Lutz, Donald S. "The Articles of Confederation as the Background to the Federal Republic." *Publius: The Journal of Federalism* (1990): 55–70.
2. Moten, Matthew. *Presidents and Their Generals: An American History of Command in War*. Cambridge, MA: Belknap Press, 2014, Chapter 1.
3. Feer, Robert A. "Shays's Rebellion and the Constitution: A Study in Causation." *New England Quarterly* (1969): 388–410.
4. Beard, Charles A. *An Economic Interpretation of the Constitution of the United States*. New York: Simon and Schuster, 2012.
5. Dahl, Robert. *How Democratic Is the American Constitution?* New Haven, CT: Yale University Press, 2001, pp. 8–9.
6. Banning, Lance. *The Sacred Fire of Liberty: James Madison and the Founding of the Federal Republic*. Ithaca, NY: Cornell University Press, 1998, see Chapter 4.

7. For a full record of the Convention proceedings, see Farrand, Max (ed.). *The Records of the Federal Convention of 1787*. New Haven, CT: Yale University Press, 1911.
8. Labunski, Richard. *James Madison and the Struggle for the Bill of Rights*. New York: Oxford University Press, 2006.
9. Genovese, Michael A. (ed.). *The Federalist Papers*. New York: Palgrave-Macmillan, 2010.
10. Ketcham, Ralph (ed.). *The Anti-federalist Papers and the Constitutional Convention Debates*. New York: Penguin, 2003.
11. Patrick Henry, Virginia Ratifying Convention, 4 June 1788. http://press-pubs.uchicago.edu/founders/documents/preambles14.html; Virginia Ratifying Convention, 9 June 1788. http://www.constitution.org/rc/rat_va_07.htm.
12. Steinfeld, Robert J. "Property and Suffrage in the Early American Republic." *Stanford Law Review* (1989): 335–376.
13. Hobson, Charles F. *The Great Chief Justice: John Marshall and the Rule of Law*. Lawrence: University Press of Kansas, 1996.
14. See Maier, Pauline. "The Road Not Taken: Nullification, John C. Calhoun, and the Revolutionary Tradition in South Carolina." *The South Carolina Historical Magazine* (1981): 1–19.
15. On Taney's life and legacy, see Smith, Charles William. *Roger B. Taney: Jacksonian Jurist*. Chapel Hill: The University of North Carolina Press, 1936.
16. Maltz, Earl M. *Civil Rights, the Constitution, and Congress, 1863–1869*. Lawrence: University Press of Kansas, 1990.
17. See Woodward, C. Vann. *The Strange Career of Jim Crow*. New York: Oxford University Press, 2001.
18. Hamm, Richard F. *Shaping the Eighteenth Amendment: Temperance Reform, Legal Culture, and the Polity, 1880–1920*. Chapel Hill: University of North Carolina Press, 1995.
19. Curtis, Michael Kent. *No State Shall Abridge: The Fourteenth Amendment and the Bill of Rights*. Durham, NC: Duke University Press, 1990.
20. Belknap, Michal R., and Earl Warren. *The Supreme Court Under Earl Warren, 1953–1969*. Columbia: University of South Carolina Press, 2005.
21. Kamisar, Yale. "The Warren Court and Criminal Justice: A Quarter-Century Retrospective." *Tulsa Law Journal* 31 (1995): 1–56.
22. See Blasi, Vincent (ed.). *The Burger Court: The Counter-Revolution that Wasn't*. New Haven, CT: Yale University Press, 1983.
23. See Tushnet, Mark. *A Court Divided: The Rehnquist Court and the Future of Constitutional law*. New York: W. W. Norton & Company, 2005.
24. Posner, Richard A. *Breaking the Deadlock: The 2000 Election, the Constitution, and the Courts*. Princeton, NJ: Princeton University Press, 2001.
25. Coyle, Marsha. *The Roberts Court: The Struggle for the Constitution*. New York: Simon & Schuster, 2014.

26. Leuchtenburg, William Edward. *In the Shadow of FDR: From Harry Truman to George W. Bush*. Cornell University Press, 2001.

27. See Dwyer, Devin. "United States of Ignorants? Americans Don't Know Constitution, Surveys Find." 24 March 2011, ABC News Online. http://abcnews.go.com/Politics/tea-party-enthusiasm-surveys-find-ignorance-us-constitution/story?id=13206667; Annenburg Public Policy Center. "New Annenberg Survey Asks: 'How Well Do Americans Understand the Constitution?'" http://www.annenbergpublicpolicycenter.org/new-annenberg-survey-asks-how-well-do-americans-understand-the-constitution/; Henthoff, Nate. "Our Constitution: How Many of Us Know It?" CATO Institute, 19 May 2011. http://www.cato.org/publications/commentary/our-constitution-how-many-us-know-it.

# A

## ABORTION

Defined as the medically induced termination of a pregnancy, abortion was legalized nationwide by the **Supreme Court** in the landmark ***Roe v. Wade*** decision of 1973. The justices who wrote the majority opinion contended that a woman's right to choose whether to terminate a pregnancy was protected by an inherent "right to privacy" in the Constitution under the **due process clause** of the **Fourteenth Amendment**. Prior to *Roe*, states had legislated varying degrees of access to abortion services, and some banned abortion procedures altogether. One precedent for this right to privacy came a decade earlier in the case of ***Griswold v. Connecticut*** (1965), which established the rights of individuals to obtain and use birth control.

Since *Roe*, conflicts have centered on state restrictions on access to abortions and abortion procedures. In ***Webster v. Reproductive Health Services*** (1989) the Supreme Court found a Missouri law that precluded the use of state funds and facilities for abortions constitutional. ***Planned Parenthood v. Casey*** (1992) established that restrictions on access to abortions must not place an "undue burden" on women. In *Stenberg v. Carhart* a Nebraska law banning "partial-birth" (late-term) abortions was found to violate the due process clause of the Fourteenth Amendment. In ***Gonzales v. Carhart*** (2007), however, the Supreme Court upheld the Partial-Birth Abortion Act passed by Congress in 2003 and found that restrictions on the procedure did not constitute an "undue burden" as enunciated in *Planned Parenthood v. Casey*. *See also* GENDER, GENDER DISCRIMINATION.

## ADAMS, JOHN (1735–1826)

The first vice president and second president of the United States was born in Quincy, Massachusetts. He graduated from Harvard College with an A.B. degree in 1755 and a law degree in 1758. Adams's opposition to British imperial rule in the American colonies commenced with his disapprobation of the Stamp Act of 1765. The "instructions" he drafted for the residents of Braintree (essentially a letter-writing campaign) to the Massachusetts legislature were replicated by the citizens of other towns in opposition to the tax. He published several articles in the *Boston Gazette* in which he outlined the colonists' belief that the tax violated their rights. He publicly denounced the act before the royal governor, contending that Massachusetts had not assented to the law because the colony had no representation in the English Parliament.

Adams was elected to the Massachusetts colonial legislature in 1770. A passionate proponent of the right to counsel, he defended that same year the British soldiers accused of the Boston Massacre, in which five civilians were killed. Six of the eight soldiers were acquitted. Two years later Adams became embroiled in the dispute over the British Parliament's authority over the colonies, ultimately publishing *Novanglus; or, A History of the Dispute with America, from Its Origin, in 1754, to the Present Time*. Contending that colonial legislatures were autonomous over their own affairs, Adams posited that the colonists' only allegiance was to the king alone in light of Britain's *unwritten* constitutional traditions.

Adams was a Massachusetts delegate at the first Continental Congress in 1774 and again at the second Congress from 1775 to 1777. It is during this time that he became firmly committed to independence from Britain. Drawing on **republican** principles elaborated by **Locke** and **Montesquieu**, Adams's treatise *Thoughts on Government* (1776) proved an influential, authoritative point of reference as the colonies drew up written constitutions following the **Declaration of Independence**. Adams had been asked to draft that document but deferred to **Thomas Jefferson**. Adams nevertheless played a central role in defending the declaration on the merits of republicanism and **natural rights**.

During the Revolutionary War, Adams oversaw the military effort as head of the Board of War and Ordnance. He negotiated peace with the British, helped the Massachusetts legislature design its constitution, and later won Dutch recognition of an independent America. In 1785 he was appointed minister to the Court of St. James, in effect becoming the first American ambassador to Britain.

Adams was elected vice president in 1789 and again in 1792, securing the second-highest number of electoral votes behind **George Washington** (the **Twelfth Amendment** was not adopted until 1804). Though Washington had significant confidence in Adams given his revolutionary credentials, the president did not consult with Adams on policy issues. Adams played an active role as president of the Senate and broke the most tie votes in U.S. history—29—but lamented the vice presidency as an otherwise "insignificant office."

Adams contested the 1796 presidential election as a **Federalist**, though enthusiasm for his candidacy in Federalist circles was less than solid among those who preferred **Alexander Hamilton**. Although South Carolina Governor **Charles Pinckney** also ran as a Federalist, Adams's primary opponent was Democratic-Republican candidate Thomas Jefferson, who had served as secretary of state under Washington. The campaign, which marked the opening salvo of the First Party System, was bitter and degenerated into vicious attacks on the character of both candidates by supporters and detractors, though Adams and Jefferson failed to campaign actively themselves as the traditions of the day mandated. Adams carried the northern states, while Jefferson won the southern states; Adams prevailed in the Electoral College by three votes over Jefferson, who became vice president.

Intense political conflict between Federalists and the Democratic-Republican opposition resulted in the passage of the **Alien and Sedition Acts**, signed by Adams in 1798. The bills were a product of continuing hostilities between Democratic-Republican sympathizers of the French Revolution and the Federalists, who were convinced that the country was nearing an outbreak of civil war. The four laws passed by Congress enabled the president to deport dangerous individuals, changed residency requirements for citizenship, and made it a crime punishable by a fine and incarceration to level malicious and false allegations against the government. The bills, which were aimed at tempering criticism of the government, were only selectively enforced. Nevertheless, the prosecutions of several newspaper editors and a Democratic-Republican member of Congress gained widespread public attention, and the bills become a major point of contention in the presidential election of 1800.

Adams's reelection effort was marred by political infighting within the Federalist camp—to wit, Hamilton's support of Charles Pinckney's candidacy, Aaron Burr's ability to secure a Jefferson victory in New York, and Jefferson's popularity in the more populous southern states due to the counting of slaves via the Three-Fifths Compromise. Jefferson prevailed in the Electoral College by eight votes, 73 to 65.

Adams's influence nevertheless remained great with respect to the Federalists' legacy in the judiciary. The president won confirmation of **John Marshall**, who became the longest-serving **chief justice** of the **Supreme Court**. Marshall's tenure from 1801 to 1835 proved decisive in solidifying the Supreme Court as a coequal branch of government vis-à-vis the presidency and Congress and in interpreting constitutional questions ranging from judicial review (***Marbury v. Madison***, 1803) to interstate commerce (***Gibbons v. Ogden***, 1824) and the balance between state and federal authority (***McCulloch v. Maryland***, 1819). Less successful were other of Adams's "midnight appointments" to the judiciary. Passage of the Judiciary Act of 1801 by the lame-duck Federalist Congress enabled Adams to make 16 new appointments to the federal circuit courts prior to leaving office. Congress repealed those posts in 1802.

Adams returned to Quincy, Massachusetts, in 1801 to undertake his autobiography. He spent much of his time in retirement writing and attempting to defend his legacy and political views, most notably against the previous attacks on his character by Alexander Hamilton. In perhaps one of the nation's most uncanny twists of fate, both Adams and Jefferson died on the same date, 4 July 1826, within hours of each other. Adams is buried at the United First Parish Church in Quincy, Massachusetts. The Adams National Historical Park at 1250 Hancock Street in Quincy comprises three historic houses, the John Adams Birthplace, the John Quincy Adams Birthplace, the Old House at Peace field as well as the 1870 Stone Library, the 1873 Adams Carriage House, and 12 acres of historic grounds, including a formal garden and orchard.

**ADAMS, SAMUEL (1722–1803)**

A native of Boston, Massachusetts, Adams became a key leader in the American Revolution. He opposed the Stamp Act of 1765 and organized the Boston Tea Party of 1773, which resulted in the Coercive Acts a year later. He served as a legislator in Massachusetts from 1765 to 1774 and was a delegate to the Continental Congress. A signer of the **Declaration of Independence**, Adams gravitated to the Democratic-Republican Party headed by **Thomas Jefferson** in the 1790s. From 1794 to 1797, he served as governor of Massachusetts. He died on 2 October 1803 and is interred at the Granary Burying Ground in Boston. He was a second cousin to **John Adams**, the second president of the United States.

***ADARAND V. PEÑA* (1995)**

This **Supreme Court civil rights** case focused on federal "**set-asides**" or contracts for disadvantaged businesses. At issue was a U.S. Department of Transportation contractor's decision to award a subcontract to a minority-owned (disadvantaged) business. Adarand Constructors Inc. had submitted a proposal to complete guardrail work on an interstate highway but lost the contract to Gonzales Construction, a business classified as disadvantaged. The bid by Gonzales Construction was higher than that of Adarand.

In a 5–4 ruling, the high court found that racial classifications are subject to **strict scrutiny**, that they must be tailored narrowly to further compelling governmental interests, and that the federal government must uphold **due process** under the **Fifth Amendment** just as states must under the **Fourteenth Amendment** to avoid discriminatory practices. The ruling, which targeted the presumption of disadvantage based solely on race, essentially overturned *Metro Broadcasting Inc. v. FCC* (1990) and was a serious blow to federal **affirmative action** programs of this type. *See also RICHMOND V. CROSON* (1989).

**ADVICE AND CONSENT**

Article II, Section 2, of the Constitution necessitates Senate approval of presidential **appointments** and treaties. Presidential appointments to the courts, cabinet, and ambassadorships require a simple majority vote of the upper chamber. Treaties require a two-thirds threshold of the Senate for approval.

The Founders were deeply split over executive and judicial appointments. The advice and consent clause was the result of an uneasy compromise at the Constitutional Convention among advocates of a strong presidency, including **Alexander Hamilton**; proponents of a strong legislature, such as **James Madison**; and **Anti-Federalists** concerned more generally with the possibility of executive tyranny. Hamilton had envisaged no congressional role in presidential appointments in **Federalist Paper** no. 66. Madison had proposed a Senate majority "veto" of appointments.

**AFFIRMATIVE ACTION**

Affirmative action programs constitute a category of constitutional **civil rights** and may be defined as programs at the federal, state, and local levels designed to remedy or redress past injustices, discrimination, or otherwise aid disadvantaged minority groups in employment and education. Much of the contemporary debate over affirmative action centers on whether such programs should be temporary or institutionalized, whether "quotas" in education and employment are constitutional, and whether race- or ethnicity-based criteria for such programs should be replaced by economic means testing. The constitutional issue with which federal courts have grappled is whether affirmative action programs violate the **Fifth Amendment** (federal government) and **Fourteenth Amendment** (states) in terms of **due process** and **equal protection**.

In the realm of employment, governmental affirmative action plans targeted to minority businesses have been narrowed in recent decades. At issue has been "**set-asides**" of governmental contracts for minority-owned businesses. In ***Richmond v. Croson*** (1989) the **Supreme Court** found that the city government's preference in awarding contracts to minority businesses violated the equal protection clause of the Fourteenth Amendment. The landmark federal case involving the U.S. Department of Transportation known as ***Adarand v. Peña*** (1995) established that set-asides for minority businesses must be viewed through the lens of **strict scrutiny** and racial classifications must have a compelling governmental interest that are narrowly tailored.

Specific employment practices and the implementation of affirmative action programs have frequently involved not only questions of race but also **gender**. Many cases have been brought about with reference to the statutory language in Title VII of the Civil Rights Act of 1964. Others have focused on broad constitutional questions. In *Wygant v. Jackson Board of Education* (1986), the court found employers may not use race to protect less senior minority employees from layoffs and all candidates, regardless of gender and race, can compete for employment on the basis of their qualifications. In ***Johnson v. Transportation Agency, Santa Clara County*** (1987) the Supreme Court decided that a voluntary affirmative action plan, for which gender was one consideration for promotion, was constitutional.

Over the last five decades, there has been significant litigation over affirmative action programs in higher education. With respect to college admissions, the case of ***Regents of the University of California v. Bakke*** (1978) established that universities' attempts to set aside a quota of seats violated the 1964 Civil Rights Act, but that race could be one of several factors used in admission decisions. In *Grove City v. Bell* (1984) federal affirmative action programs were deemed to apply to the entire institution of education rather than just the program receiving federal money; Congress overrode the Supreme Court's decision in the 1988 Civil Rights Restoration Act. In ***Gratz v. Bollinger*** (2003) the high court struck down a University of Michigan program that awarded additional "points" to minorities for admissions consideration, but affirmed that university's law school admissions policy that considered race as one of several factors in ***Grutter v. Bollinger*** (2003). In *Fisher v. University of Texas* (2013) the Supreme Court reaffirmed the standard of strict scrutiny in using race as a criterion for college admissions and required that such policies be narrowly tailored. In ***Schuette v. Coalition to Defend Affirmative Action*** (2014) a Michigan constitutional amendment banning affirmative action in college admissions was upheld. In 2007 the court found that the use of race as a "tiebreaker" for high school admissions violated the Fourteenth Amendment and was neither narrowly tailored nor reflected a compelling government interest (***Parents Involved in Community Schools v. Seattle School District***).

**ALIEN AND SEDITION ACTS**

One of the first challenges to free speech guarantees in the **First Amendment**, the Alien and Sedition Acts consisted of four laws (the Naturalization Act, the Alien Act, the Alien Enemies Act, and the Sedition Act) passed by the **Federalist** Congress and signed into law by President **John Adams** in 1798. Fear of anarchy and an impending war with France following the French Revolution, as well as Federalists' political considerations given relentless Democratic-Republican criticism of Adams's administration, undergirded the statutes. The Naturalization Act mandated 14 years' residency for citizenship (an increase of nine years), reflecting Federalists' suspicion that European-born sympathizers of France might undermine the government. To halt propagandists, the Alien Act enabled the president to jail or deport foreign nationals (aliens) considered "dangerous to the peace and safety of the United States."

**Thomas Jefferson** and his Democratic-Republican Party, the Federalists' chief political rivals, were widely considered Francophiles and received the backing of French and Irish immigrants, in particular. Adams and the Federalists, fearing insurrection, hoped to further silence Democratic-Republican criticism with the Sedition Act, which made it a punishable offense of a fine and imprisonment to "write, print or utter . . . false, scandalous, and malicious writing or writings against the government of the United States with the intent to defame" the President or Congress. The acts were a central feature of the 1800 presidential campaign, in which Jefferson prevailed. The new Seventh Congress repealed the Naturalization Act in 1802, while the Alien Act expired in 1800 and the Sedition Act elapsed in 1801.

**AMENDMENTS (FORMULA)**

*See* ARTICLE V (CONSTITUTION).

**AMERICAN CIVIL LIBERTIES UNION (ACLU)**

Founded in 1920 amid the Red Scare following World War I, the ACLU purports to champion **civil liberties** of individuals and is a not-for-profit group. Along with individual representation before federal, state, and local courts, the ACLU also files **amicus curiae** briefs in court cases. The organization has a long history of defending plaintiffs with regard to protections in the **Bill of Rights**. Examples include ***Everson v. Board of Education*** (1947) regarding the establishment clause and the separation of church and state, ***Engle v. Vitale*** (1962) regarding school prayer, ***Miranda v. Arizona*** (1966) involving the **Fifth Amendment** and self-incrimination, symbolic speech during the Vietnam War as in ***U.S. v. O'Brien*** (1967), ***New York Times Co. v. United States*** (1971) entailing **prior restraint** and **First Amendment** guarantees of freedom of the press, **gay rights** and the right to privacy as in the case of ***Bowers v. Hardwick*** (1986), state bans on interracial marriage as in ***Loving v. Virginia*** (1967), and First Amendment rights in electronic communications in ***Reno v. ACLU*** (1997). In 2014 the organization had expenditures totaling just more than $133 million.

**AMICUS CURIAE**

Latin for "friend of the court," amicus curiae are unsolicited legal briefs sent to the courts by organizations, advocacy groups, law firms, and government agencies that are not party to a pending case. The briefs contain legal arguments and opinions aimed at influencing the outcome of a case as judges deliberate on the merits.

**ANNAPOLIS CONVENTION**

A precursor to the Constitutional Convention in Philadelphia in July 1787, the Annapolis Convention was a meeting of the states called by **James Madison** to discuss trade and other difficulties arising from the failings of the **Articles of Confederation** in the post-Revolutionary period. Only five states attended: Delaware, New Jersey, New York, Pennsylvania, and Virginia. However, the report of the conferees detailed the protectionist trade barriers erected by the states that inhibited economic exchange and Congress's inability to regulate interstate commerce under the articles. The findings of the Annapolis Convention, along with the civil chaos unleashed during **Shays's Rebellion**, are thought to have been instrumental in convincing states to send delegates to the 1787 Constitutional Convention to address the shortcomings of the Articles of Confederation and create a national government.

**ANTI-FEDERALIST, ANTI-FEDERALISM**

The term *Anti-Federalist* connotes those who opposed replacing the **Articles of Confederation** during the debate concerning the ratification of the Constitution from 1787 to 1788. Anti-Federalists favored greater state authority and autonomy and were particularly concerned about **civil liberties** and the structure of the executive. Anti-Federalists worried that the proposed office of the presidency would evolve into a monarchy and degenerate into the type of tyranny under King George III that the colonists had eschewed.

Authors under various pseudonyms, such as "Brutus," "**Cato**," and "Philadelphiensis," penned articles and expositions against ratification of the Constitution ("The Anti-Federalist Papers"), which were published in newspapers in response to the arguments of **James Madison** ("Publius"), **John Jay**, and **Alexander Hamilton** in the collection of essays widely known now as the **Federalist Papers**. **Patrick Henry** and **George Clinton** were among the most vocal Anti-Federalists.

The structure of the proposed government was a bitter point of contention for Anti-Federalists. Rebuffing the arguments of Alexander Hamilton in Federalist Papers nos. 67–77, Anti-Federalists viewed the presidential office as a precursor to monarchy, martial law, and repression. They viewed Congress's ability to regulate interstate **commerce** as a sham to protect the interests of the wealthy. And they not only disagreed fundamentally about the causes of the failure of the Articles of Confederation but also viewed a strong central government as a usurpation of **states' rights**.

The Anti-Federalists were able to influence neither the initial characteristics of the Constitution nor approval of it. Their persistence, however, convinced ratifying conventions in at least four states to adopt language that the Constitution be amended to include a bill of rights. When the new Constitution entered into effect in 1789, Congress passed a total of 12 amendments that were sent to the states. Ten of these amendments—known universally as the **Bill of Rights**—were ratified by the states in 1791 and enshrine guarantees against government interference with basic individual liberties. Following the ratification of the Constitution and the adoption of the Bill of Rights, the Anti-Federalists' raison d'être ceased. The vestiges of the movement were largely subsumed in **Thomas Jefferson**'s Democratic-Republican Party, the primary opposition to **John Adams** and Alexander Hamilton.

## APPOINTMENT POWER

**Article II**, Section 2, of the Constitution states that the president "shall nominate, and by and with the advice and consent of the Senate, shall appoint ambassadors, other public ministers and consuls, judges of the **Supreme Court**, and all other officers of the United States, whose appointments are not herein otherwise provided for, and which shall be established by law." The appointment power is a prime example of a "shared power" between the president and the Senate. Unlike treaties, which require the approval of two-thirds of the Senate, only a majority of senators is necessary to confirm a nominee.

Historically, comity between the president and Senate has been greatest for cabinet appointments. The Senate usually defers to the president's nominations. One great exception was during the presidency of Andrew Johnson during **Reconstruction**. Congress passed the **Tenure of Office**

**Act** requiring Senate approval before the president could remove a member of his cabinet. Although the act was repealed and deemed unconstitutional in 1926, congressional Republicans used Johnson's sacking of Secretary of War Edwin M. Stanton as a pretext for impeaching the president.

Presidential appointments to the federal and appellate courts, as well as to the Supreme Court, are generally successful—but can occasionally stir partisan and ideological battles between the branches. Presidents have generally followed the norm of senatorial courtesy, whereby they secure the approval of the two senators hailing from a nominee's state before proceeding with the formal nomination. Still, since the 1980s, anywhere from one to more than three dozen federal and appellate court nominees have been blocked as partisanship heightened under divided government.

Interbranch battles have been more spectacular for controversial Supreme Court nominees. Presidents **George Washington**, **James Madison**, John Tyler, James Polk, Ulysses Grant, Grover Cleveland, Herbert Hoover, Richard M. Nixon, and Ronald W. Reagan had one or more of their high court nominees rejected by a majority of the Senate.

Article II, Section 2, of the Constitution also provides for "recess appointments," which are temporary. The proviso states that the "President shall have power to fill up all vacancies that may happen during the recess of the Senate, by granting commissions which shall expire at the end of their next session." Such appointments must be confirmed by a majority vote by the end of the Senate's next session (usually within a year period since the end of World War II) or the position becomes vacant.

Recess appointments have occasionally engendered conflict between the president and the Senate—particularly when the president's party does not control a majority in the upper chamber. Presidents can use recess appointments strategically by appointing individuals who might not be expected to be confirmed under normal circumstances. While the Constitution is clear that the president can make *intersession* appointments (when the Senate adjourns *sine die*), the greatest controversy in recent decades is whether presidents can make *intrasession* recess appointments. The Senate (and House of Representatives) typically work on a nine-to-12-month calendar, but often take breaks during that time for federal holidays and summer vacation typically in August.

The Constitution is silent on how many days the Senate must be adjourned to enable a recess appointment. President George W. Bush made a number of intrasession recess appointments that drew the ire of Senate majority leader Harry Reid (D-NV) after Republicans lost control of the upper chamber in the 2006 midterm elections. Reid was able to halt recess appointments by keeping the Senate in session continually by holding pro forma meetings during which no business was conducted. Reid and fellow Democrats were concerned that Bush was attempting a "court-packing" scheme akin to what Presidents **John Adams** and Franklin D. Roosevelt had attempted to ensure ideological dominance in the judiciary beyond their elective mandates. In 2014 the Supreme Court issued a rebuke to President Barack H. Obama for recess appointments he made to the National Labor Relations Board (NLRB). In ***NLRB v. Canning*** (2014), the high court determined unanimously that a Senate adjournment of less than 10 days is "presumptively too short" for a recess appointment. *See also MARBURY V. MADISON* (1803); TWENTY-FIFTH AMENDMENT.

**ARTICLE I (CONSTITUTION)**

The first article of the U.S. Constitution outlines the electoral and other rules, in addition to the enumerated powers, of Congress and also provides for limits to congressional power in the realm of **civil liberties** and states' powers. It is the longest and most detailed article in the foundational document.

Section 1 vests all legislative powers in Congress. While the **Supreme Court** has found that while Congress may assign regulatory power to executive departments and agencies, specific *legislative* powers may not be delegated to other branches.

Section 2 addresses elections, qualifications, apportionment, vacancies, and the basic leadership structure for the House of Representatives. Elections for the House are to occur every two years by popular vote. Eligible voters include those qualified to vote for the state legislature's most numerous chamber. The **Civil War Amendments**, the **Nineteenth Amendment**, the **Twenty-Fourth Amendment**, and the **Twenty-Sixth Amendment** to the Constitution largely preclude state restrictions on voter eligibility beyond the original wording of Section 2. Candidates for House elections must be at least 25 years old, a citizen of the United States for no less than seven years, and a resident of the state from which he or she is elected. Section 2 further elaborates that representatives (and taxes) will be apportioned based on population; the Three-Fifths Compromise language is included so that slaves counted as three-fifths of a person for representational purposes (the **Thirteenth Amendment** made this provision moot). The first "enumeration" or census to determine apportionment was to be completed within three years after the first meeting of Congress in 1789, and to take place subsequently on a decennial basis. The balance of Clause 3 discusses the exact representation of the 13 states in the House upon the entry into effect of the Constitution. Clause 4 clarifies that when a vacancy occurs in the House, it is the responsibility of the state governor to issue a writ for a special election; governors may not, therefore, appoint members to the House. Finally, the fifth clause provides that the House shall choose a speaker and other officers (without identifying the process) and grants to the lower chamber the sole power of impeachment, which is tantamount to bringing criminal charges against elected or appointed officials.

Section 3 details the modalities of the Senate. Clause 1 mandates that there are two senators per state who serve six-year terms and are chosen by state legislatures (direct election did not occur until passage of the **Seventeenth Amendment** in 1913). Clause 2 provides the basis for staggered representation in the Senate (one-third of the body is elected every two years), as members were initially divided into three "classes." The first class served only two years beginning in 1789, the second class served four years, and the third class served six years. Initially, vacancies in the Senate were to be filled by the state legislature; the Seventeenth Amendment, however, enables governors of states to fill vacancies, unlike for the House of Representatives. Clause 3 requires that to be eligible to serve in the upper chamber, senators must have attained the age of 30, be a resident of the U.S. for nine years, and reside in the state from which they are appointed (now popularly elected). Clause 4 makes the vice president the *president* of the Senate, but restricts his or her voting to tiebreaks only. Clause 5 calls for the Senate to choose its own officers without outlining the procedures, and enables the president pro tempore to preside over the upper chamber in the absence of the vice president. Finally, Clause 6 empowers the Senate to try cases of impeachment, over which the **chief justice** of the Supreme Court presides, and requires a two-thirds vote for conviction. Clause 7 explicates that the penalty for convictions stemming from impeachment is confined to removal from office and disqualification from holding future office. Nonetheless, officials who are impeached are also liable for criminal charges according to statute.

Section 4 specifies the rules for the timing of elections and mandates that Congress meet at a minimum once per year. Clause 1 leaves it to states to decide the times of elections, including primaries, while enabling Congress to establish national rules (such as making the general election the first Tuesday in November). Clause 2 requires that Congress meet on the first Monday of December, unless the legislature establishes a different date (today Congress generally meets the first week of January).

Section 5 outlines congressional procedures relative to the qualification of members, quorums, rules, the congressional journal, and adjournment. Clause 1 states that a majority of members present shall constitute a quorum, and that each chamber of Congress can define the qualifications of members and compel their attendance. Clause 2 empowers each chamber to adopt its own rules and expel members with a two-thirds vote. Clause 3 mandates that each chamber keep a journal of its proceedings to be published from time to time, and to record votes at the request of one-fifth of members. Clause 4 prohibits either chamber from adjourning for more than three days without the consent of the other chamber, or to relocate without the consent of the other chamber.

Section 6 takes up the parameters of congressional pay and privileges, and prohibits legislators from holding concurrent offices. Clause 1 specifies that members shall receive compensation while also receiving certain legal protections, including immunity from arrest while giving speeches or in debates notwithstanding charges of treason, felony, or breach of peace. Clause 2 prohibits members from holding any position in the executive branch while in Congress to ensure independence between the branches.

Section 7 details tax bills, the presentment clause, and the presidential veto. Clause 1 mandates that bills of revenue (taxation) must commence in the House of Representatives, though the Senate may propose and concur with amendments. Clause 2 (the presentment clause) elaborates that upon passage by the House and the Senate, all bills must be presented to the president. If the president signs the bill it becomes law; if he does not, he must return the bill, with his objections, to the chamber in which the bill originated. By a two-thirds margin in both chambers Congress may override a president's objections (veto). Clause 2 also outlines the "pocket veto"; if Congress sends the president a bill, goes out of session within 10 days, and the president does not sign the bill, the legislation is not considered passed. Clause 3 reiterates the president's veto prerogative, subject to a two-thirds override by Congress.

Section 8 describes the many enumerated powers of Congress. They include the following: (1) taxation and payment of debts; (2) borrowing money; (3) regulating foreign and interstate commerce, and commerce with Native American tribes; (4) establishing rules regarding naturalization and bankruptcy; (5) coining money and fixing standards of weights and measures; (6) punishing counterfeiters; (7) establishing post offices and roads; (8) awarding patents; (9) establishing lower courts; (10) defining and punishing piracy and felonies on the high seas; (11) declaring war, granting letters of marque and reprisal, and rules concerning captures on land and water; (12) raising and supporting armies; (13) providing and maintaining a navy; (14) rulemaking for the regulation of land and naval forces; (15) calling up the military to suppress insurrection and repel invasions; (16) organizing, arming, and disciplining the military; (17) exercising exclusive legislative power regarding the District of Columbia; and (18) making all laws "necessary and proper" for carrying out these powers.

The details of Section 8 were in large measure aimed not only at ensuring *legislative government* generally but rectifying the shortcomings of the **Articles of Confederation**. As one example, the "elastic clause" or "necessary and proper clause" clarifies that Congress shall have the authority to enforce the laws it passes. The legislature had no such power in the Articles. Further, Congress may set up lower federal courts (other than the Supreme Court), which it did in the Judiciary Act of 1789 and the structure of which has remained largely intact since. Controversies over Congress's enumerated powers have centered historically on federal–state conflicts, including taxation and interstate commerce, and the war power. The case of ***McCulloch v. Maryland*** (1819), involving a national bank chartered by Congress, clarified that states could not tax federal entities. The case of ***Gibbons v. Ogden*** (1824) extended the reach of congressional regulation of interstate navigation to navigation. Both of the aforementioned cases were overseen by chief justice **John Marshall**. In ***Schechter Poultry Corp. v. United States*** (1935), however, the high court invalidated part of Franklin Roosevelt's New Deal by finding unconstitutional congressional delegation of regulatory authority to the president in local matters. With respect to the war power, the age-old debate centers on unilateral presidential action and congressional declaration authority. Congress has not formally declared war against any nation since World War II. At dispute is the **War Powers Resolution** of 1973, passed in the Vietnam War era over President Richard Nixon's veto, which mandates that the president notify Congress and seek authorization for the use of troops abroad within 60 or 90 days; neither branch has pursued a definitive answer as to the constitutionality of the legislation with the Supreme Court for fear of eroding its authority.

Section 9 places limitations on congressional power. Congress was precluded from halting the importation of slaves before 1808 or imposing a tax on such import exceeding 10 dollars. There are three important civil liberties protections in Section 9. Congress cannot pass bills of attainder (calling for the capital punishment of an individual) or ex post facto laws (laws that are retroactively effective), nor can the writ of **habeas corpus** (the right to go before a judge and have charges heard following arrest) be suspended notwithstanding cases of rebellion or invasion. Other provisions prohibit taxes not based on the census, taxes imposed on exports from one state to another, preference of ports, or duties required from vessels from one state docking from another. These provisions were also a product of commerce issues that arose under the Articles of Confederation. Section 9 prohibits spending money from the Treasury without appropriations (which has caused government "shutdowns" when Congress and the president have been unable to agree on a budget in recent decades). Finally, Congress is prohibited from granting "titles of nobility," nor can any person accept foreign titles without congressional consent.

The tenth and final section places prohibitions on the states and thereby reinforces select enumerated powers of Congress, placing the same prohibitions on the states as the national legislature. Clause 1 precludes states from entering into treaties, granting letters of marque and reprisal, coining money, passing bills of attainder or ex post facto laws, impairing the obligation of contracts, or granting titles of nobility. Clause 2 bars states from imposing tariffs or duties on imported goods. And finally, Clause 3 excludes states from entering into treaties or engaging in war unless invaded or in a time of imminent danger. *See also CITY OF NEW YORK V. CLINTON* (1998); *INS (IMMIGRATION AND NATURALIZATION SERVICE) V. CHADHA* (1983); LINE-ITEM VETO.

**ARTICLE II (CONSTITUTION)**

The second article of the U.S. Constitution enumerates the powers of the president and, inter alia, specifies the process for the election of the president and sets out specific competencies of the office. Compared to Article I, which defines the powers of Congress in great detail, Article II is relatively vague and many provisions are open to interpretation. Scholars contend that the imprecisions and shared powers with the Senate, in particular, reflect the Founders' general fear of executive power in light of the colonial experience under King George III and a greater general trust in legislative government.

Article II was a product of ample and dogged compromise at the Constitutional Convention in Philadelphia in 1787. While many delegates may have been convinced that an executive—which had been absent from the **Articles of Confederation**—was necessary, they disagreed on a plural or unitary office, how to choose the president (Congress, the states, or the people), and which powers the office should hold.

Article II, Section 1 states that "The executive power shall be vested in a President of the United States" and that, along with vice president, he shall have a term of four years. The parameters of "executive power" are not defined but are generally understood in the context of the administration of laws. As one example, the president's ability to issue directives to cabinet departments and agencies using **executive orders** falls under executive power. Contemporary debates on the boundaries of **executive power** under this section include questions of the extent to which presidents can claim **executive privilege** to preclude public and congressional scrutiny of executive advice, as well as **signing statements** in which presidents have interpreted legislative intent, the constitutionality of statutes, or posited that they will refuse to enforce provisions of laws passed by Congress.

Section 1 details the method for selecting the president through an **Electoral College**. State legislatures appoint a total number of electors reflecting their state's representation in Congress: the number of representatives in the House plus two for the Senate. Until 1804 the candidate with the second-highest number of electoral votes became vice president. The **Twelfth Amendment** "encouraged" presidential and vice presidential candidates to run on the same ticket, as electors were mandated to cast ballots for both offices. Today all states save Maine and Nebraska apportion their electoral votes according to the unit rule, whereby the candidate who wins the most votes statewide receives the entirety of that state's electoral votes. Section I specifies that if no candidate wins a majority in the Electoral College, the election devolves to the House of Representatives, wherein each state delegation has a single vote for the presidency. Twice in U.S. history presidential elections have been thrown to the House: the contest between **Thomas Jefferson** and **John Adams** in 1800, and the match between Andrew Jackson and John Quincy Adams in 1824. The latter outcome was particularly controversial and bitter, as "Old Hickory" won a plurality of the vote, but the House—with Henry Clay's maneuvering—nevertheless chose Adams in what supporters of Jackson titled a "corrupt bargain."

Section 1 also delineates that the president must be a **natural-born citizen**, of at least age 35, and a resident of the United States for at least 14 years when the Constitution entered into force. The "natural-born citizen" provision reflected the Founders' concern that the fledgling republic might be susceptible to foreign subversion. From the Founders' historical reference point in the 18th century, empires were frequently forged through the marriages of monarchs. Today many voters and scholars suggest the provision is anachronistic and has precluded popularly elected, foreign-born officials such as former California Governor Arnold Schwarzenegger and former Michigan Governor Jennifer Granholm from pursuing the nation's highest office. The last attempt to amend the Constitution to alter the provision was in 2003. The proposal, sponsored by Senator Orrin Hatch of Utah, received no legislative action.

Finally, Section 1 sets forth the **succession** of power to the vice president in the case of disability and enables Congress to legislate the devolution of power in the case the death of both the president and vice president, provides for the compensation of the president, and mandates the oath of office each president must take. Congress has adopted legislation on presidential succession thrice, in 1792, 1886, and 1947 (current statute). As of 2015, the president's current annual salary is $400,000, with a yearly expense account totaling $50,000. The president's salary was increased by congressional statute from $200,000 to $400,000 effective in 2001.

Section 2 enumerates the president's most important powers and responsibilities. The president is **commander-in-chief** of the armed forces, has the power to commission officers, can grant reprieves and **pardons** (notwithstanding **impeachments**), and can ask his cabinet secretaries for their opinion. Section 2 also specifies presidential powers shared with the Senate, with the upper chamber's **advice and consent**. The president can make treaties with foreign countries but must secure the approval of two-thirds of the Senate. The president can nominate judges, ambassadors, and officials to head executive departments but must obtain a majority of senators' support for those nominations. The president can also make recess **appointments** to these latter posts when the Senate is not in session; such appointments expire at the end of the congressional term.

Section 3 advises that the president shall "from time to time" give the state of the union to Congress. There is no specific time frame (e.g., annually) mandated by the Constitution. **George Washington** gave the first state of the union before Congress in 1790. **Thomas Jefferson** ended the practice of delivering the state of the union in person, and presidents sent a written copy to Congress with little fanfare until 1913, when Woodrow Wilson reestablished the tradition of appearing before members in the Capitol.

The president may also recommend to Congress for their consideration "such measures as he shall judge necessary and expedient." There is no mandate, however, for Congress to act on presidential legislative requests. Moreover, the president cannot "dissolve" Congress as modern prime ministers can in one way or another in parliamentary systems. Section 3 authorizes the president to adjourn Congress only when the House and Senate cannot agree on a date. The president can, however, convene both houses of Congress into special session "on extraordinary occasions." From 1789 to 1932, presidents convened special sessions of both chambers of Congress a total of 27 times. Since 1933 presidents have only done so four times. The most recent and dramatic was Harry S. Truman's use of this tool in 1948 to call the Republican-led 80th Congress back into special session, a witty reelection tactic.

Section 3 grants the president an extremely important power in foreign affairs insofar as he "shall receive ambassadors and other public ministers." In essence, this provision entitles the president to "recognize" foreign governments by establishing diplomatic relations. In the last century presidents' decisions to recognize some countries, such as the Soviet Union in 1933 by Franklin D. Roosevelt, Israel in 1948 by Harry Truman, and Richard M. Nixon's pursuit of a normalization of relations with the People's Republic of China in the 1970s, have stirred controversy.

Finally, Section 3 obliges the president to "take care that the laws be faithfully executed." In practicality this provision gives the president ample latitude in deciding when and how to enforce laws. The **Supreme Court**, however, clarified in ***Marbury v. Madison*** (1803) that presidents cannot preclude officials in the executive branch from carrying out congressional legislation. Further, per ***Youngstown Sheet and Tube v. Sawyer*** (1952) the president cannot take a unilateral action outside the bounds of constitutional or statutory authority.

The fourth and last section of Article II provides that "The President, Vice President and all civil officers of the United States, shall be removed from office on impeachment for, and conviction of, treason, bribery, or other high crimes and misdemeanors." Treason and bribery are much easier to define than "high crimes and misdemeanors," which the provision leaves open to interpretation. It is on this basis that scholars generally concur that the Founders viewed impeachment as a largely *political* process. The House of Representatives adopts articles of impeachment, the Senate tries the impeachment, and a two-thirds vote is required to overturn an election and remove the president for malfeasance as defined by House allegations. Two presidents have been formally impeached: Andrew Johnson (1868) and William J. (Bill) Clinton (1998). Both were acquitted. The Judiciary Committee of the Democratic-led House of Representatives approved articles of impeachment against Richard M. Nixon in 1974, but the president resigned rather than face a trial in the Senate.

Scholars disagree whether the enumerated powers delineated in Article II, or the *informal* perquisites and prestige of the office, form the bases of presidential power. Article II underscores the many formal tasks of the president: chief legislator, chief military officer, chief judicial officer, chief diplomat, and chief administrator. Some scholars contend, however, that the office is fundamentally weak and the reservoir of presidential power is contingent upon successfully sharing power with Congress and persuading not only members on Capitol Hill but also key lobbying groups and grassroots supporters. *See also* VETO (POWER).

**ARTICLE III (CONSTITUTION)**

Consisting of three sections, Article III outlines the structure of the judicial branch of the federal government. Section 1 establishes a single **Supreme Court** but does not specify the number of justices, leaving the decision to Congress. Similarly, Section 1 grants Congress the power to establish "inferior" federal courts, which the legislature did in the Judiciary Act of 1789. Section 1 further elaborates that federal judges serve during "good behavior"—a life term—and that their salaries may not be diminished during their time of service; both provisions were aimed at ensuring the independence of judges.

Section 2 elucidates that the Supreme Court is both a court of original jurisdiction, where select types of cases are heard, and an appellate court. As a court of original jurisdiction, the Supreme Court hears (1) cases relating to ambassadors and "other public Ministers and Consuls" and all cases of admiralty and under maritime jurisdiction; (2) disputes involving the federal government; (3) disputes between the states; and (4) disputes involving foreign states. As an appellate court, notwithstanding claims of **habeas corpus** that often involve the **death penalty**, the Supreme Court only takes cases that are "ripe," or for which a real and adverse controversy exists, the state or federal appeals process has been exhausted, and the parties have standing. For the Supreme Court to hear a case, a **writ of certiorari** is required, whereby four of nine justices agree to hear the case. Finally, section 2 mandates that other than **impeachment**, jury trials are required in the jurisdiction in which a crime is committed and, when not committed in a state, shall be tried according to congressional direction (statute).

Section 3 defines treason and the parameters of punishment. Treason consists of "levying war" against the United States and requires either the testimony of two witnesses or confession in open court. Section 3 further assigns to Congress the punishment of treason but proscribes punishment for anyone else (such as family members) of any individual convicted of treason.

Article III does *not* explicitly mention **judicial review** of state actions or those of other branches of the federal government. Rather, judicial review was established in the case of ***Marbury v. Madison*** (1803), enunciated under **Chief Justice John Marshall**.

**ARTICLE IV (CONSTITUTION)**

Comprising four sections, Article IV of the Constitution addresses **full faith and credit**, state obligations regarding privileges and immunities and extradition, the admission of new states, and states' rights to republican government and protection from invasion and domestic insurrection.

Section 1 details that states must acknowledge the official acts, records, and court proceedings of other states. The Supreme Court ruled in *Mills v. Duryee* (1813) that this provision extends to the merits of legal cases from other states. However, the more contemporary controversy regarding full faith and credit centered on gay marriage and civil unions between same-sex couples. The **Defense of Marriage Act** (DOMA), passed in 1996, defined marriage as the union between a man and a woman for federal purposes and enabled states to decline to recognize same-sex marriages performed in other states. In 2013 the **Supreme Court** struck down portions of DOMA in the case titled ***U.S. v. Windsor***. In ***Obergefell v. Hodges*** (2015) the high court ruled that same-sex marriage was a constitutional right under the **Fourteenth Amendment**, that states are required to issue marriage licenses to same-sex couples, and that same-sex marriages in one state must be recognized in all other states.

**ARTICLE V (CONSTITUTION)**

The fifth article of the Constitution outlines the amending process. There are two possible routes by which the Constitution may be altered. The first consists of a proposal that receives the assent of two-thirds of both chambers of Congress, and which is ratified by three-quarters of the states. The second route, which has never been utilized as of 2015, is for two-thirds of states to call for a constitutional convention; amendments may then by ratified by three-quarters of legislatures or state ratifying conventions.

There have been 27 amendments to the Constitution. The **Bill of Rights**, the first 10 amendments, was proposed and adopted from 1789 to 1791. The **Eleventh Amendment** dealt with states' sovereign immunity. The **Twelfth Amendment** "encouraged" presidents and vice presidents to run on the same ticket and mandated that electors cast separate votes for each office. The **Civil War Amendments** (**Thirteenth**, **Fourteenth**, and **Fifteenth Amendments**) nationalized the Bill of Rights through selective **incorporation**. The **Seventeenth Amendment** provided for the direct election of senators. The **Eighteenth**, **Nineteenth**, and **Twentieth Amendments** provided for the prohibition of the sale of alcohol, gave the right to vote to women, and moved the beginning of the president's term from March to 20 January, respectively. The **Twenty-First Amendment** repealed prohibition and was the only amendment for which Congress mandated the type of ratification process (state convention). The **Twenty-Second Amendment** set the total number of terms a president can serve to two. The **Twenty-Third Amendment** extended **Electoral College** representation to the District of Columbia. The **Twenty-Fourth Amendment** abolished the **poll tax**. The **Twenty-Fifth Amendment** defined the role for selecting a vice president when that office becomes vacant, as well as presidential disabilities. The **Twenty-Sixth Amendment** established the right to vote for all citizens who obtain the age of 18. The **Twenty-Seventh Amendment** mandated that when Congress adopts pay raises for its members, such raises cannot go into effect until the following session.

There have been six proposed amendments to the Constitution approved by Congress but not ratified by the states. The first involved congressional apportionment in 1789. In 1810 Congress approved an amendment stripping anyone who accepted a title of nobility of citizenship. The Corwin Amendment in 1861, named for Senator Thomas Corwin of Ohio, was an effort to draw secessionist states of the South back into the Union on the promise of shielding them from constitutional amendments or congressional statutes regarding slavery. In 1924 a child labor amendment bill was approved by Congress, but by 1937 only 28 of 48 states had ratified the measure. Unlike these previous proposals, when Congress passed the **Equal Rights Amendment** (ERA) in March 1972, legislators set a deadline for ratification of the measure, which would have enshrined equality between men and women, of March 1979. The proposal was initially ratified by 35 states, but five later rescinded ratification; nine states rejected the proposal. Finally, in 1978 Congress approved an amendment to provide residents of Washington, DC, with full voting rights and gave states seven years to ratify the measure. The proposal failed, as only 16 states ratified the measure prior to the deadline.

**ARTICLE VI (CONSTITUTION)**

The sixth article of the Constitution addresses three points: debts, the supremacy of the document, and the prohibition of religious tests for public office. The first paragraph of Article VI clarifies that all debts and contracts that existed under the **Articles of Confederation** were to be just as valid under the new Constitution. **James Madison** addressed this point in **Federalist Paper** no. 10, contending that **federalism** would serve as a check against the excess of factions that might demand a wholesale elimination of financial obligations incurred under the old regime. He suggested that "A rage for paper money, for an abolition of debts, for an equal division of property, or for any other improper or wicked project, will be less apt to pervade the whole body of the Union than a particular member of it; in the same proportion as such a malady is more likely to taint a particular county or district, than an entire State."

The second paragraph contains the "supremacy clause." The Constitution and the laws and treaties adopted under it form the supreme law of the land. Several **Supreme Court** cases in the early Republic confirmed this parameter in state and federal power disputes, including ***McCulloch v. Maryland*** (1819) and ***Gibbons v. Ogden*** (1824). The third and final paragraph outlines that public servants at the federal and state levels must take an oath of office in which they affirm that they will uphold the Constitution. The paragraph also precludes any religious test for eligibility to serve in the "public Trust."

**ARTICLE VII (CONSTITUTION)**

The seventh article of the Constitution sets forth the terms of ratification of the Constitution adopted at the convention in Philadelphia in 1787. The assent of nine of 13 state legislatures (three-quarters) was necessary for the Constitution to enter into effect. Delaware was the first to ratify the Constitution on 7 December 1787; New Hampshire was the ninth state to do so on 21 June 1788. New York and Virginia ratified the Constitution before the new governmental structure officially commenced on 4 March 1789. North Carolina and Rhode Island ratified the Constitution in 1789 and 1790, respectively, as the **Bill of Rights** was sent to states for their consideration.

**ARTICLES OF CONFEDERATION**

The first formal, written constitution of the United States was known as the Articles of Confederation and Perpetual Union. The articles were drafted in 1777 and formally ratified by all 13 states in 1781. The primary objective of the articles was to enable the states to fight the Revolutionary War collectively. The articles were supplanted by the U.S. Constitution, which went into effect on 4 March 1789.

The Articles of Confederation did *not* create a national government, and the weaknesses of the structure agreed upon in 1776 became evident following the Revolutionary War. States had begrudgingly ceded power to Congress under the articles, and there was no executive, no judiciary, nor any means for Congress to enforce state compliance with laws it passed. In the period immediately following the Revolutionary War, severe problems of interstate commerce, debt to war veterans and foreign nations, potential military aggression from the British and Spanish, and possible civil anarchy exemplified by **Shays's Rebellion** in Massachusetts dogged the fledgling Republic. In September 1786 **James Madison** invited state representatives to the **Annapolis Convention** (the Meeting of Commissioners to Remedy Defects of the Federal Government) to discuss potential reforms. Although only five states heeded Madison's call, the meeting provided impetus for a wider constitutional convention ultimately held in Philadelphia in 1787. Following the convention, **Federalists** who favored the adoption of the constitutional structure, including

Madison, **Alexander Hamilton**, and **John Jay**, penned a host of articles in local newspapers known as the **Federalist Papers** to convince states to ratify the document. They were met with opposition by **Anti-Federalists**, who opposed strong central government, feared executive tyranny, and saw the lack of a **bill of rights** in the proposed constitution as anathema to a state-centered vision of post-Revolutionary America.

# B

**BAIL**

*See* EIGHTH AMENDMENT.

***BAKER V. CARR* (1962)**

This landmark **Supreme Court** case addressed the issue of legislative redistricting. The Tennessee case centered on a state constitutional mandate that districts for the legislative assembly be redrawn every 10 years according to the federal census. Charles Baker, whose state legislative district included Memphis, filed suit because the boundaries had not been updated since 1901. In a 6–2 decision the justices found his complaint to be "justiciable" and court intervention warranted in redistricting cases, reversing a longstanding doctrine whereby the high court refused to adjudicate "political questions." *See also MILLER V. JOHNSON* (1995); *REYNOLDS V. SIMS* (1964); *SHAW V. RENO* (1993); *WESBERRY V. SANDERS* (1964).

***BARRON V. BALTIMORE* (1833)**

This pivotal **Supreme Court** case was precedential in determining that the **Bill of Rights** did *not* apply to the states in the 19th century. The case arose when John Barron, who owned a wharf in Baltimore, sued when the city's public works program and construction all but destroyed his business. He won damages in a trial court, but an appeals court reversed the decision. In a unanimous decision penned by **Chief Justice John Marshall**, the justices on the Supreme Court found that Barron's complaint with reference to the "takings" clause in the **Fifth Amendment** was invalid. Marshall wrote that the first 10 amendments to the Constitution "contain no expression indicating an intention to apply them to the State governments. This court cannot so apply them."

The doctrine outlined in *Barron* was formally reversed after the Civil War with passage of the **Fourteenth Amendment** in 1866, which specifies that states cannot violate **due process** and **equal protection** of the law. Nonetheless, throughout **Reconstruction** states passed statutes such as **Jim Crow laws** that violated the rights of African Americans, and the ***Slaughterhouse Cases*** (1873) confirmed the high court's narrow interpretation of the scope of the Fourteenth Amendment, despite Chief Justice **Salmon Chase**'s dissent. It was not until the 1920s that the Supreme Court, through the **incorporation doctrine**, began to apply selectively the federal Bill of Rights to state actions.

***BENTON V. MARYLAND* (1969)**

The question of the **Fifth Amendment** prohibition against double jeopardy, and the **incorporation** of the prohibition to state trials via the **Fourteenth Amendment**, informed this landmark **Supreme Court** case. John Benton had been convicted of burglary but acquitted of larceny charges by a Maryland court. The Maryland Court of Appeals subsequently ruled that a state constitutional provision mandating that jurors swear an oath that they believed in God was illegal. Benton demanded and was accorded a new trial based on the Court of Appeals ruling. In his second trial, he was convicted of burglary and larceny. He asserted that the conviction for larceny in the second trial violated double jeopardy.

Writing for the majority, Associate Justice Thurgood Marshall posited that "It is clear that petitioner's larceny conviction cannot stand once federal double jeopardy standards are applied. Petitioner was acquitted of larceny in his first trial. Because he decided to appeal his burglary conviction, he is forced to suffer retrial on the larceny count as well. . . . He has . . . a valid double jeopardy plea which he cannot be forced to waive. Yet Maryland wants the earlier acquittal set aside, over petitioner's objections, because of a defect in the indictment. This it cannot do. Petitioner's larceny conviction cannot stand."

By incorporating the Fifth Amendment protection against double jeopardy, the court's ruling effectively overturned ***Palko v. Connecticut*** (1937).

**BILL OF ATTAINDER**

*See* ARTICLE I (CONSTITUTION).

**BILL OF RIGHTS**

The first 10 amendments to the Constitution, adopted between 1789 and 1791 at the behest of **Anti-Federalists**, constitute the Bill of Rights. The federal Constitution's protections of essential **civil liberties** mirror provisions adopted by the several states' constitutions during the Revolutionary period. The Bill of Rights may be viewed as a set of "negative freedoms" or freedom *from* governmental intrusion.

The **First Amendment** prohibits Congress from making any law establishing religion, impeding the free exercise of religion, or abridging freedom of the press, assembly, or the right to petition the government for grievances. The **Second Amendment** guarantees the right to keep and bear arms. The **Third Amendment** precludes the quartering of troops in civilian homes in times of peace. The **Fourth Amendment** bars unreasonable search and seizure, and mandates that warrants signed by a judge specify the place and things to be searched upon probable cause. The **Fifth Amendment** protects individuals from self-incrimination, prevents the government from trying an individual for the same crime more than once (double jeopardy), and mandates compensation for government takings of private property (eminent domain). The **Sixth Amendment** guarantees the right to a jury trial, to a speedy trial, to confront accusers, and to counsel in criminal proceedings. The **Seventh Amendment** confirms the right to a jury trial in civil proceedings. The **Eighth Amendment** guarantees that individuals may not be subjected to unreasonable bail or fines or cruel and unusual punishment. The **Ninth Amendment** clarifies that the enumeration of rights in the Constitution shall not be "construed to deny or disparage others retained by the people." The **Tenth Amendment** elucidates that powers not delegated to the federal government (i.e., "enumerated") in the Constitution are reserved to the states or the people, buttressing the principle of **federalism**.

**BLACK CODES**

Alongside **Jim Crow laws**, black codes were state and local laws and regulations adopted after the Civil War and during **Reconstruction** in the South that were aimed at disenfranchising and segregating freed slaves and denying them fundamental rights, including **Fourteenth Amendment** rights to **equal protection** and **due process** of law. Black codes survived until the early 20th century, when the **Supreme Court** began the slow process of selective **incorporation** of the **Bill of Rights** to the states. *See also* GRANDFATHER CLAUSE; *PLESSY V. FERGUSON* (1896); POLL TAX; *SLAUGHTERHOUSE CASES* (1873).

***BOLLING V. SHARPE* (1954)**

*See* REVERSE INCORPORATION.

***BOUMEDIENE V. BUSH* (2008)**

This **Supreme Court** case concerned the rights of suspected terrorists to challenge their indefinite detention at Guantanamo Bay, Cuba, and their prospective trial by military courts. The plaintiff, Lakhdar Boumediene, a Bosnian national born in Algeria, was arrested by U.S. troops in Bosnia for alleged ties to the terrorist organization al-Qaeda after the Bosnian courts found no grounds to hold him. He was subsequently transferred to and detained at the military facility in Cuba as an enemy combatant.

Boumediene's petition was a writ of **habeas corpus**, or the right to appear before a judge in a civilian court. By a 5–4 decision, Boumediene's petition was granted. Prior to this case, the Supreme Court held in ***Rasul v. Bush*** (2004) that U.S. courts did have the authority to determine whether detainees were unlawfully imprisoned and dismissed the argument that the facility in Cuba was beyond the reach of U.S. law. In ***Hamdan v. Rumsfeld*** (2006), the court had also decided a habeas corpus petition by a detainee, concluding that the military tribunals set up by the President George W. Bush by **executive order** were unconstitutional and could only be founded by an act of Congress. As a result, Congress passed the Military Commissions Act (2006) establishing military tribunals. The ruling in *Boumediene* found that the Military Commissions Act, as well, violated detainees' rights to habeas corpus. *See also* WAR ON TERROR, WAR ON TERRORISM.

***BOWERS V. HARDWICK* (1986)**

This case concerned **gay rights** and state sodomy laws that criminalized certain sexual activity as immoral or "against nature." While applying equally to heterosexual and homosexual couples, the latter were generally targeted under state laws. The Georgia case involved Michael Hardwick, who was sought by local police on an arrest warrant for public drunkenness. Upon entering Hardwick's residence to take him into custody, the officials found him engaged in sexual activity with another man. He was subsequently charged with violating a state sodomy law. He appealed the matter to the **Supreme Court** as a test case for gay rights with the assistance of the **American Civil Liberties Union** (ACLU). While the case ostensibly involved a right to privacy that had been elucidated in ***Griswold v. Connecticut*** (1965) and ***Roe V. Wade*** (1973), the justices ruled in a 5–4 decision that the Constitution did not confer any particular right to homosexual sodomy. The **concurring opinions** of the majority cited the "ancient roots" of moral teachings to buttress its verdict. The decision was overturned by the Supreme Court in 2004 in ***Lawrence v. Texas***.

***BOY SCOUTS OF THE UNITED STATES V. DALE* (2000)**

This **Supreme Court** case involved the question of **gay rights**. The Boy Scouts revoked the membership of James Dale in the organization when leaders learned he was homosexual and a gay rights activist. The Boy Scouts asserted that his sexual orientation conflicted with the organization's values.

Dale contended that his dismissal violated a New Jersey public accommodation law. In a 5–4 decision, the justices on the high court reversed a state supreme court ruling that Dale's reinstatement under the New Jersey law did not violate the Boy Scouts **First Amendment** rights to expressive association, since his reinstatement conveyed no particular message. Writing for the majority, **Chief Justice William Rehnquist** wrote that Dale's reinstatement "would, at the very least, force the organization to send a message, both to the young members and the world, that the Boy Scouts accepts homosexual conduct as a legitimate form of behavior." The decision was considered a major setback for gay rights advocates.

***BRANDENBURG V. OHIO* (1969)**

This **First Amendment** free speech case centered on an Ohio criminal syndicalism law that prohibited the advocacy of violence. Charles Brandenburg, a Ku Klux Klan member, was fined and sentenced to prison after leading a rally against racial and religious minorities under a statute adopted in 1919 during the First Red Scare following World War I. In a per curiam decision, the **Supreme Court** invalidated the Ohio law and established an "imminent lawless action" test. Government cannot prohibit or punish speech that is violent in abstract terms. Rather, the speech in question must have violent intent, constitute an imminent threat, and have the likelihood of inciting lawless action. As the Court held, "Ohio's

Criminal Syndicalism Act cannot be sustained. The Act punishes persons who 'advocate or teach the duty, necessity, or propriety' of violence 'as a means of accomplishing industrial or political reform'; or who publish or circulate or display any book or paper containing such advocacy; or who 'justify' the commission of violent acts 'with intent to exemplify, spread or advocate the propriety of the doctrines of criminal syndicalism'; or who 'voluntarily assemble' with a group formed 'to teach or advocate the doctrines of criminal syndicalism.' Neither the indictment nor the trial judge's instructions to the jury in any way refined the statute's bald definition of the crime in terms of mere advocacy not distinguished from incitement to imminent lawless action."

The case overturned the precedent set in ***Whitney v. California*** (1927), in which the conviction of a woman advocating syndicalism was upheld by the high court. *See also CHAPLINSKY V. NEW HAMPSHIRE* (1942); ESPIONAGE ACT (1917); FIGHTING WORDS; *SCHENCK V. UNITED STATES* (1919).

***BROWN V. BOARD OF EDUCATION OF TOPEKA* (1954)**

One of the most pivotal **civil rights** cases decided by the **Supreme Court** in U.S. history, *Brown* reversed the "separate but equal" doctrine enunciated in ***Plessy v. Ferguson*** (1896). The unanimous decision of the high court, led by **Chief Justice Earl Warren**, was that segregation in education was a violation of the **equal protection clause** of the **Fourteenth Amendment**.

In the class action lawsuit, National Association for the Advancement of Colored Persons (NAACP) lawyer Thurgood Marshall argued against de jure segregation on behalf of black families who had unsuccessfully attempted to enroll their children in all-white schools that were closer to their homes than the all-black schools that were farther away and substandard. The justices contended that separate educational facilities were "inherently" unequal. A year later, in *Brown II*, the court ordered school districts around the nation to desegregate with "all deliberate speed."

Resistance to the mandate was palpable in the South and reached a turning point in 1957 when President Dwight Eisenhower sent troops to Little Rock to preclude Arkansas Governor Orval Faubus from blocking integration of the public schools. Following the decision in *Brown*, school districts around the nation turned to inter- and intradistrict busing of students to achieve racial balance. The Supreme Court affirmed the constitutionality of the policy in ***Swann v. Charlotte-Mecklenburg*** (1970) but narrowed the scope of busing in ***Milliken v. Bradley*** (1974). *See also COOPER V. AARON* (1958).

**BRUTUS**

*See* ANTI-FEDERALIST, ANTI-FEDERALISM.

***BUCKLEY V. VALEO* (1976)**

This **Supreme Court** case addressed **First Amendment** issues regarding campaign finance. In a per curiam decision, the justices ruled that limits on candidates' campaign expenditures or independent groups, as mandated by the Federal Election Campaign Act Amendments of 1974, violated free speech protections. The court held that "A restriction on the amount of money a person or group can spend on political communication during a campaign necessarily reduces the quantity of expression by restricting the number of issues discussed, the depth of their exploration, and the size of the audience reached." The court did uphold, however, regulation of individual contributions to political candidates. *See also CITIZENS UNITED V. FEDERAL ELECTIONS COMMISSION (FEC)* (2010).

**BURGER, WARREN (1907–1995)**

A native of St. Paul, Minnesota, Burger earned a law degree from the University of Minnesota in 1931. He taught law at his alma mater until 1946 and worked in private practice until 1953, when President Dwight Eisenhower appointed him to the Department of Justice. Eisenhower then appointed him to the U.S. Court of Appeals for the District of Columbia in 1969. President Richard Nixon nominated him as **chief justice** of the **Supreme Court** in 1969. Burger served on the high court until 1986. Among the most pivotal cases Burger oversaw during his tenure were ***Swann v. Charlotte-Mecklenburg*** (1970), ***Lemon v. Kurtzman*** (1971), ***New York Times Co. v. United States*** (1971), ***Furman v. Georgia*** (1972), ***Miller v. California*** (1973), ***Miami Herald v. Tornillo*** (1974), ***Milliken v. Bradley*** (1974), ***U.S. v. Nixon*** (1974); ***Buckley v. Valeo*** (1976), ***Craig v. Boren*** (1976), ***Gregg v. Georgia*** (1976), ***INS v. Chadha*** (1983), and ***Bowers v. Hardwick*** (1986). Burger headed the Commission on the Bicentennial of the United States Constitution from 1982 to 1992. He died on 25 June 1995.

***BUSH V. GORE* (2000)**

This **Supreme Court** case ultimately decided the winner of the 2000 presidential election contest between Republican George W. Bush and Democrat Albert A. (Al) Gore. The outcome of the election depended on Florida's 25 **Electoral College** votes. Controversy first erupted over the use of the so-called butterfly ballot in Palm Beach County, which many voters—particularly the elderly—found confusing and caused them to vote for the wrong candidate. Early results from Florida's 67 counties on 8 November showed that Bush had defeated Gore by a margin of less than a half percent, which triggered an automatic machine recount of ballots under state law. By 10 November 2000, the statewide machine recount showed that Bush's lead had fallen to just over 300 votes. Using the discretion afforded him under Florida law, Gore petitioned four counties to conduct manual recounts: Broward, Miami-Dade, Palm Beach, and Volusia. Local election boards subsequently engaged in a painstaking recount of ballots, during which they attempted to determine voters' intentions when ballots were not completely punched through, leaving so-called chads.

Florida law required that counties submit their completed returns to the secretary of state no later than seven days following the election. Three of the four counties believed they could not meet that deadline. A state court ruled that the counties could later amend their returns, and the secretary of state had the discretion to amend the final results. Florida Secretary of State Katherine Harris noted on 14 November that she was in receipt of the results from all 67 counties, but since recounts in Broward, Miami-Dade, and Palm Beach continued, she would not certify the results until 26 November.

On 26 November, Harris certified that Bush had won Florida by 537 votes. The certification of Florida's 25 Electoral College votes put Bush over the necessary threshold of 270 to win the election. In a highly controversial move, Harris determined that there was no basis to amend the results of the disputed counties. Litigation ensued, and on 8 December the Florida Supreme Court, in a 4–3 decision, ordered a statewide manual recount of all votes. On 9 December, the U.S. Supreme Court halted the recount on a 5–4 decision and scheduled oral arguments. On 12 December, the court made an expedited decision and, in a 7–2 vote, contended that the lack of uniform standards in the county-level recounts violated the **equal protection clause** (**Fourteenth Amendment**) of the Constitution, thereby halting the recount and effectively enabling Bush to secure enough electoral votes to prevail in the election.

***BUSH V. VERA* (1996)**

This **Supreme Court voting rights** case focused on the question of **reapportionment** and racial **gerrymandering**. At issue were three districts drawn by the Texas legislature to enhance Hispanic and African American representation in Congress from the Lone Star State. Using the standard of **strict scrutiny** elaborated in the pivotal case of ***Shaw v. Reno*** (1993) and followed in ***Miller v. Johnson*** (1995), the high court struck down the district boundaries and asserted that the state had not narrowly tailored the redistricting plans to further a compelling government interest.

Associate Justice Sandra Day O'Connor authored the plurality opinion. She contended that "the State substantially neglected traditional districting criteria such as compactness, that it was committed from the outset to creating majority minority districts, and that it manipulated district lines to exploit unprecedentedly detailed racial data—[which] together weigh in favor of the application of strict scrutiny." She added, "Not only are the shapes of the districts bizarre; they also exhibit utter disregard of city limits, local election precincts, and voter tabulation district lines," and, citing the principle of **stare decisis**, asserted that "our precedents, which acknowledge voters as more than mere racial statistics, play an important role in defining the political identity of the American voter."

**BUTLER, PIERCE (1744–1822)**

Born in County Carlow, Ireland, Butler came to America in 1758 and resided in South Carolina. He attained the rank of brigadier general during the Revolutionary War. He represented the Palmetto State at the Constitutional Convention in 1787 in Philadelphia. He was the architect of the Fugitive Slave Clause in **Article IV** of the Constitution, which formally protected the institution, and advocated counting the entire slave population in states for the purposes of congressional representation, which resulted in the Three-Fifths Compromise in **Article I**. He became an ardent supporter of the ratification of the Constitution but did not attend his state's ratifying convention.

Butler served in the U.S. Senate for South Carolina from 1793 to 1796, and again from 1802 to 1804. He commenced his political career as a **Federalist**, gravitated to the Democratic-Republicans of Thomas Jefferson in 1795, and left the upper chamber an independent. He died on 15 February 1822 and is interred in Christ Churchyard in Philadelphia, Pennsylvania.

# C

## CAMPAIGN FINANCE

Since passage of the Federal Election Campaign Act (FECA) in 1971, the **Supreme Court** has struck down successive attempts to regulate spending as a violation of **First Amendment** guarantees of free speech. Limitations on campaign contributions by individuals and groups are regulated by the Federal Elections Commission (FEC), which was created in 1974 from amendments to the 1971 statute. These amendments placed restrictions on so-called hard-money contributions made by individuals and political action committees.

In the 1974 case of ***Buckley v. Valeo*** the high court invalidated *candidate* expenditure limits on the basis that they were at odds with "political expression at the core of our electoral process and of First Amendment Freedoms." The court affirmed expenditure limits on publicly funded campaigns, including presidential campaigns, in *Republican National Committee v. FEC* (1980) since presidential candidates are at liberty to decline public funding—and most have done so in the last several decades. Congress passed the 1974 amendments with an eye to "leveling the playing field" in presidential campaigns through public funding in light of the unprecedented amounts of unregulated money that flowed to Richard M. Nixon's reelection campaign in 1972.

The Bipartisan Campaign Reform Act (BCRA) passed by Congress in 2002 sought to eliminate soft money contributions to the Democratic and Republican National Committees and curb "electioneering communications" by nonparty organizations that garnered contributions from corporations or labor unions. The bill survived a 2003 challenge by the National Rifle Association (NRA) in the Supreme Court case *McConnell v. FEC*. However, the ban on so-called issue ads preceding primary and general elections was found unconstitutional in ***FEC v. Wisconsin Right to Life*** (2007). Further, the restrictions on independent expenditures by nonparty organizations were struck down by the high court in ***Citizens United v. FEC*** (2010) on First Amendment grounds. In 2014, the case of ***McCutcheon v. FEC*** invalidated limits on total individual contributions, such as contributions to national party committees, but maintained as constitutional the cap on contributions to individual candidates' campaigns.

## *CANTWELL V. CONNECTICUT* (1940)

This crucial **Supreme Court** case regarded the **incorporation doctrine** and was the first to apply the free exercise clause of the **First Amendment** to the states via the **Fourteenth Amendment**. At issue was a Connecticut law that required anyone soliciting for religious or charitable purposes to obtain a license from the state. Jesse Cantwell, a Jehovah's Witness, and his sons were arrested and convicted for violating the law, and for breach of peace, when they entered a largely Catholic neighborhood in New Haven, Connecticut, and passed out materials and played a phonograph that angered several men whom they stopped on the street. In a unanimous decision, the Supreme Court overturned Cantwell's conviction and invalidated the Connecticut solicitation law as a violation of the First Amendment. The state's permit process set out to determine whether the purpose of the individual or organization was "a religious one or is a bona fide object of charity or philanthropy" and whether it "conforms to reasonable standards of efficiency and integrity." The justices contended that local officials' efforts to determine what is and is not religious countermanded both "the freedom to believe and the freedom to act" enshrined in the First Amendment.

**CATO**

This pseudonym, or pen name, is usually attributed to **George Clinton**, an **Anti-Federalist** who wrote expositions against the ratification of the Constitution following the Philadelphia convention in 1787. *See also* FEDERALIST, FEDERALIST PARTY; FEDERALIST PAPERS.

***CHAPLINSKY V. NEW HAMPSHIRE* (1942)**

This **Supreme Court** case addressed limitations to the **First Amendment** guarantee of free speech insofar as "**fighting words**" are concerned. The case centered on a Jehovah's Witness, Walter Chaplinsky, who was using a public sidewalk to give pamphlets against organized religion to passersby. When the police attempted to remove Chaplinsky for blocking access to the roadway, he verbally assaulted the town marshal by using profanity. Convicted of violating a New Hampshire law barring offensive speech in public venues, Chaplinsky appealed his case to the highest court. The justices unanimously upheld his conviction and articulated the doctrine that "the lewd and obscene, the profane, the slanderous" and "fighting words" that seek to provoke others are not constitutionally protected speech. *See also SCHENCK V. UNITED STATES* (1919).

**CHASE, SALMON PORTLAND (1808–1873)**

Born in Cornish, New Hampshire, Chase spent his childhood in Ohio. He returned to his native Granite State and graduated from Dartmouth College in 1826. His pursuit of law took him to Washington, DC, where he read under Attorney General William Wirt. Admitted to the bar in 1829, he moved to Cincinnati and established a private law practice. An ardent opponent of slavery, Chase joined the Free Soil Party and became a U.S. Senator from the Buckeye State. In 1855 he won the governorship of Ohio, and he returned to the Senate in 1860. He quickly resigned his seat when President Abraham Lincoln appointed him secretary of the treasury. Lincoln nominated him as **chief justice** of the **Supreme Court** in December 1864. He served on the high court for eight years until his death on 7 May 1873. He is interred at Spring Grove Cemetery in Cincinnati, Ohio. As chief justice, Chase won acclaim for his balanced oversight of the impeachment trial of President Andrew Johnson in 1868. In two cases central to the **Reconstruction** Era, Chase ruled in *Mississippi v. Johnson* (1867) that the president could enforce Reconstruction measures and in ***Texas v. White*** (1869) that secession was unconstitutional and the Union indissoluble.

***CHICAGO, BURLINGTON & QUINCY RAILROAD CO. V. CITY OF CHICAGO*** **(1897)**

**CHICAGO, BURLINGTON & QUINCY RAILROAD CO. V. CHICAGO**

This **Supreme Court** case focused on **eminent domain** and the takings clause of the **Fifth Amendment**, and was the first such case to **incorporate** these rights through the **Fourteenth Amendment**. At issue were the City of Chicago's plans to widen a street that crossed through a railroad's property. Under an Illinois statute, a jury was to determine the amount of compensation when private land was taken for public use. A jury awarded one dollar to the railroad, which was unhappy with the amount and sued after the court rejected its petition for a new trial.

In a 7–1 decision, the Supreme Court sided with the state of Illinois. The majority specifically considered the question of Fifth Amendment **due process** of law, as applied through the Fourteenth Amendment, in determining fair compensation for the railroad. Writing for the majority, Associate Justice John Marshall Harlan asserted that "a judgment of a state court, even if it be authorized by statute, whereby private property is taken for the state or under its direction for public use, without compensation made or secured to the owner, is, upon principle and authority, wanting in the due process of law required by the fourteenth amendment of the Constitution of the United States, and the affirmance of such judgment by the highest court of the state is a denial by that state of a right secured to the owner by that instrument." The case solidified that takings of private property—whether by federal or state governments—require just compensation to the owner. *See also KELO V. CITY OF NEW LONDON* (2005).

**CHIEF JUSTICE**

The position of chief justice of the **Supreme Court** is appointed by the president, and, like all judicial and cabinet nominees, confirmation requires a majority vote of the Senate. The only formal, constitutional mandate for the chief justice is to preside over **impeachment** trials in the Senate. Informally, the chief justice has historically sworn in the president at the inaugural ceremony. The chief justice may be considered the "chief administrative officer" for the Supreme Court's work, including organizing the business of the highest court in the United States.

The relative influence of chief justices over associate justices on the Supreme Court regarding constitutional questions is questionable since the deliberations of the justices are closed to the public. Regardless, the chief justice often takes the lead in writing concurring or dissenting opinions for the Supreme Court. Such opinions may lend significant insight into chief justices' jurisprudential perspectives and approaches to constitutional controversies.

***CHISHOLM V. GEORGIA* (1793)**

*See* ELEVENTH AMENDMENT.

***CITIZENS UNITED V. FEDERAL ELECTIONS COMMISSION (FEC)* (2010)**

This landmark **Supreme Court** case centered on **First Amendment** guarantees of free speech as such guarantees relate to **campaign finance**. At issue was whether the nonprofit group Citizens United could air advertising and a film that criticized former first lady, New York senator, and 2008 presidential candidate Hillary Rodham Clinton. The Bipartisan Campaign Finance Reform Act (BCRA) passed by Congress in 2002 forbade "electioneering communications" by independent groups. By a 5–4 vote, the Supreme Court struck down the BCRA restrictions, contending that it was unconstitutional to limit independent communications by non- or for-profit organizations, including corporations and labor unions, on free speech grounds. *See also MCCUTCHEON V. FEC (FEDERAL ELECTIONS COMMISSION)* (2014).

***CITY OF BOERNE V. FLORES* (1997)**

This **Supreme Court** case focused on the constitutionality of the Religious Freedom Restoration Act (RFRA), passed by Congress in 1993. The statute represented a congressional response to a 1990 case in Oregon (*Employment Division v. Smith*, 1990) in which the high court validated a state law criminalizing the use of peyote, a custom in traditional Native American ceremonies. Critics charged that the decision set a precedent for greater state regulation of religious practices despite **First Amendment** protections. The RFRA mandated that the standard of **strict scrutiny**, which requires the government to show a compelling interest, apply to regulations concerning freedom of conscience.

The case centered on the application by the archbishop of San Antonio, Texas, Patrick Flores, to enlarge a Catholic Church in the city of Boerne, Texas. The church was located in a historic district, and the city government denied the archbishop a permit to expand the church on that basis. Flores contended that the denial contravened the RFRA, placing a burden on the parish without a compelling, justifiable government interest.

In a 6–3 decision, the majority on the Supreme Court found the RFRA unconstitutional. Writing the majority opinion, Associate Justice Anthony Kennedy noted that Congress had relied on the precepts of the **Fourteenth Amendment**, which forbid states from depriving individuals of life, liberty, or property, when drafting the statute. However, Kennedy contended that Congress had exceeded its authority: "RFRA is not a proper exercise of Congress' §5 enforcement power because it contradicts vital principles necessary to maintain separation of powers and the federal-state balance. . . . RFRA's most serious shortcoming . . . lies in the fact that it is so out of proportion to a supposed remedial or preventive object that it cannot be understood as responsive to, or designed to prevent, unconstitutional behavior. It appears, instead, to attempt a substantive change in constitutional protections, proscribing state conduct that the Fourteenth Amendment itself does not prohibit. Its sweeping coverage ensures its intrusion at every level of government, displacing laws and prohibiting official actions of almost every description and regardless of subject matter. . . . All told, RFRA is a considerable congressional intrusion into the States' traditional prerogatives and general authority to regulate for the health and welfare of their citizens, and is not designed to identify and counteract state laws likely to be unconstitutional because of their treatment of religion."

***CITY OF NEW YORK V. CLINTON* (1998)**

This case centered on the **line-item veto** legislation passed by Congress in 1996 that gave the president "enhanced rescission authority." The president could eliminate individual items in the budget passed by Congress, and the latter could restore the provisions with a simple majority vote. In a 6–3 decision the **Supreme Court** ruled that the Line Item Veto Act of 1996 violated the **presentment clause** in the Constitution. Specifically, all legislative powers belong to Congress per Article I. Presidents must either sign an entire bill or return it to Congress (**veto**) without their signature. There is no condition under which a president can strike down or repeal only part of a bill. A line-item veto power for the president would necessitate a constitutional amendment, as Congress cannot delegate its legislative powers.

**CIVIL LIBERTIES**

The term *civil liberties* may be defined as fundamental freedoms and individual rights, enshrined in law, from governmental interference. In the United States civil liberties are closely associated with the **Bill of Rights**—the first 10 amendments to the Constitution. Civil liberties also comprise limitations on congressional power, including the suspension of **habeas corpus** and passage of bills of attainder and ex post facto laws, outlined in **Article I**, Section 9, of the Constitution. Such provisions in the United States Constitution are a reflection of the Founders' emphasis on **natural rights**, elaborated in the **Declaration of Independence**, which also influenced *La déclaration des droits de l'homme et du citoyen* (Declaration of the Rights of Man and Citizen) during the French Revolution in August 1789.

The **First Amendment** to the Constitution precludes Congress from making any law respecting "an establishment of religion, or prohibiting the free exercise thereof; or abridging the freedom of speech, or of the press; or the right of the people peaceably to assemble, and to petition the Government for a redress of grievances."

The **Second Amendment**, which protects gun rights, elucidates that "A well regulated militia being necessary to the security of a free State, the right of the People to keep and bear arms shall not be infringed."

The **Third Amendment** states that "No soldier shall, in time of peace be quartered in any house, without the consent of the owner, nor in time of war, but in a manner to be prescribed by law."

The **Fourth Amendment** protects individuals from unlawful searches by the authorities: "The right of the people to be secure in their persons, houses, papers, and effects, against unreasonable searches and seizures, shall not be violated, and no Warrants shall issue, but upon probable cause, supported by Oath or affirmation, and particularly describing the place to be searched, and the persons or things to be seized."

The **Fifth Amendment** addresses legal rights, "double jeopardy," and "takings" by elaborating that "No person shall be held to answer for a capital, or otherwise infamous crime, unless on a presentment or indictment of a Grand Jury, except in cases arising in the land or naval forces, or in the Militia, when in actual service in time of War or public danger; nor shall any person be subject for the same offence to be twice put in jeopardy of life or limb; nor shall be compelled in any criminal case to be a witness against himself, nor be deprived of life, liberty, or property, without **due process** of law; nor shall private property be taken for public use, without just compensation."

The **Sixth Amendment** elaborates processual rights in the legal realm by stating that "In all criminal prosecutions, the accused shall enjoy the right to a speedy and public trial, by an impartial jury of the State and district wherein the crime shall have been committed, which district shall have been previously ascertained by law, and to be informed of the nature and cause of the accusation; to be confronted with the witnesses against him; to have compulsory process for obtaining witnesses in his favor, and to have the Assistance of Counsel for his defence."

The **Seventh Amendment** addresses civil law suits and mandates that "In Suits at common law, where the value in controversy shall exceed twenty dollars, the right of trial by jury shall be preserved, and no fact tried by a jury, shall be otherwise re-examined in any Court of the United States, than according to the rules of the common law."

The **Eighth Amendment** directs that "Excessive bail shall not be required, nor excessive fines imposed, nor cruel and unusual punishments inflicted."

The **Ninth Amendment** clarifies that "The enumeration in the Constitution, of certain rights, shall not be construed to deny or disparage others retained by the people."

And the **Tenth Amendment** states that "The powers not delegated to the United States by the Constitution, nor prohibited by it to the States, are reserved to the States respectively, or to the people." *See also* INCORPORATION DOCTRINE.

**CIVIL RIGHTS**

The term *civil rights* refers to citizens' demands for the government to take some action on their behalf, such as the enforcement of constitutional or statutory rights. **Affirmative action**, defined as governmental programs targeted to minority groups and designed to redress past discriminatory practices, falls under the rubric of civil rights in the post-1950s era. Early federal efforts to address civil rights focused on the plight of African Americans. Blacks suffered from discrimination in voting, employment, housing, and other forms of legal (de jure) segregation during and after **Reconstruction**, as evidenced by the **Supreme Court** decision in the ***Slaughterhouse Cases*** (1873), the passage of **Jim Crow laws**, and the high court's ruling in ***Plessy v. Ferguson*** in 1898, which entrenched the "separate but equal" doctrine. The expanded focus of efforts at integration of blacks in terms of education, as well as affirmative action programs for other minority groups, including Hispanics, Asian Americans, gays and lesbians, and women, has stirred ample controversy. Moreover, the Supreme Court has rendered important decisions on voting rights, employment discrimination, sexual harassment and **gender** equality, and religious freedom that fall within the category of civil rights.

In the realm of education, the landmark decision in ***Brown v. Board of Education*** (1954) overturned the "separate but equal" doctrine enunciated in *Plessy* 58 years earlier. In *Brown II* the Supreme Court mandated that public school districts around the country desegregate "with all deliberate speed." *Brown* had been preceded by two cases, ***Sweatt v. Painter*** (1950) and ***McLaurin v. Oklahoma State Regents*** (1950), in which justices struck down separate but equal classroom facilities at the college level. The high court, however, had no power to carry out its ruling in *Brown*, which met resistance in the South, in particular. President Dwight D. Eisenhower was forced to send the military—the 101st Airborne—to Little Rock, Arkansas, in 1957 to enforce desegregation over the objections of the state's governor, Orval Faubus, who had employed the state national guard to preclude black children from entering Little Rock High School. In ***Cooper v. Aaron*** (1958) the Supreme Court ruled unconstitutional the efforts of the Arkansas legislature to undermine desegregation of schools.

Still, the courts struggled to find ways to implement desegregation in education and tailor programs consistent with the **equal protection** of the law in the **Fourteenth Amendment**. In ***Swann v. Charlotte-Mecklenburg***

***Board of Education*** (1971) the Supreme Court ruled that busing across district lines as a means of achieving integration was constitutional. In ***Milliken v. Bradley*** (1974) busing was scaled back to districts in which past discrimination was evident, and interdistrict transfers were not to be used as a tool for a larger societal objective of achieving integration.

Voting rights fall under the rubric of civil rights. In 1962 the Supreme Court established federal oversight of redistricting cases involving congressional districts in the case of ***Baker v. Carr***. In 1964 the decisions in ***Reynolds v. Sims*** and ***Wesberry v. Sanders*** addressed issues of unequal population apportionment of congressional districts and mandated "one person, one vote" to ensure that districts were drawn fairly so as not to advantage more or less populated districts over one another. The **Twenty-Fifth Amendment** to the Constitution, adopted in 1964, abolished the **poll tax**. Passage of the Voting Rights Act of 1965 secured **voting rights** for African Americans with federal assistance, and within a decade erased disparities in the percentage of white and black registered voters. The case of ***Shaw v. Reno*** (1993) addressed "racial **gerrymandering**," or the drawing of congressional districts to favor election of minorities. The Supreme Court held that while states must take into account the mandates of the 1965 Voting Rights Act, drawing of districts along racial lines is subject to **strict scrutiny** under the equal protection clause of the Fourteenth Amendment. The high court reaffirmed this view in ***Miller v. Johnson*** (1995) when it struck down an oddly shaped Georgia congressional district with an African American majority. In ***Shelby County v. Holder*** (2013) the court invalidated a provision of the 1965 Voting Rights Act requiring states to gain "preclearance" from the Department of Justice before redrawing congressional districts. The majority contended that the formula to determine past discrimination by states is outdated.

Women's rights and gender discrimination constitute another subcomponent of civil rights. In the 19th and early 20th centuries, the focus was on voting rights. In ***Minor v. Happersett*** (1875) the Supreme Court ruled that the Constitution did *not* provide women with a right to vote. The suffrage movement ultimately prevailed in securing women's right to vote with passage of the **Nineteenth Amendment** to the Constitution in 1920. More recent cases have involved other questions of **gender discrimination**. In ***Reed v. Reed*** (1971) an Idaho law that gave preferential treatment to men as administrators of estates was struck down. In ***Craig v. Boren*** (1976) the Supreme Court enunciated the view that gender classifications were subject to **intermediate scrutiny**, whereby such classifications must reflect an important government objective. In ***Rostker v. Goldberg*** (1981) confining the military draft to men only was found constitutional. However, the court struck down discrimination based on gender for admissions to state-sponsored institutions of higher education in ***U.S. v. Virginia Military Institute*** (1996). In ***Johnson v. Transportation Agency*** (1986) the high court affirmed that, ceteris paribus, gender could be one factor in workplace promotions regarding affirmative action and did not violate equal protection of the laws.

Civil rights regarding homosexuals have also become a focus of intense controversy in the last three decades. In ***Bowers v. Hardwick*** (1986) the Supreme Court refused to confirm a constitutional right to homosexual activity based on sexual privacy and upheld a state ban on sodomy. Eighteen years later, in ***Lawrence v. Texas*** (2003), the court reversed its opinion and struck down state sodomy laws as a violation of **due process** of law. In ***Romer v. Evans*** (1996) the justices invalidated a Colorado state constitutional amendment that prohibited the consideration of homosexuals as a "protected class." In 2000, however, the Supreme Court found that private organizations could preclude the participation of homosexuals (***Boy Scouts of the United States v. Dale***, 2000). In ***U.S. v. Windsor*** (2013) the court invalidated parts of the Defense of Marriage Act (1996) that defined marriage as only between a man and a woman, finding the statute violated due process. In 2015 in the case ***Obergefell v. Hodges*** the Supreme Court declared gay marriage a constitutional right under the due process and equal protection clauses of the **Fourteenth Amendment** and struck down all state statutes and constitutional amendments banning the practice.

***CIVIL RIGHTS CASES* (1883)**

*See* FOURTEENTH AMENDMENT.

**CIVIL WAR AMENDMENTS**

The **Thirteenth**, **Fourteenth**, and **Fifteenth Amendments** together constitute the Civil War Amendments. These amendments were aimed at providing citizenship for newly freed slaves and ensuring that the federal Constitution was applied to state actions, including **due process** of law, **equal protection** of the laws, and citizenship. *See also* INCORPORATION DOCTRINE.

**CLINTON, GEORGE (1739–1812)**

Born in Little Britain, New York, Clinton enlisted in the British Army at age 18 and rose to the position of lieutenant during the French and Indian War. In 1759 he was elected Clerk of Ulster County, New York—a position he held for 52 years—and from 1768 to 1776 he served as a member of the New York Provincial Assembly.

He joined the Revolutionary War as a brigadier general in 1777 and was elected governor of New York the same year. He was reelected governor five times and remains New York's longest-serving executive, though he stayed in the Continental Army until 1783. He served with **George Washington** during the war and in 1783 negotiated the withdrawal of British troops following the Revolution.

A Founding Father and **Anti-Federalist** to whom some historians attribute the pen name **Cato** during the debates over the Constitution, Clinton remained opposed to the new **republican** framework until the **Bill of Rights** was ratified. In 1792 he was a candidate for vice president largely due to Jeffersonians' increasing distaste for **John Adams**, not out of opposition to Washington, who was running for a second term. Clinton received 50 **Electoral College** votes.

In 1804 **Thomas Jefferson** selected Clinton as his vice presidential candidate to replace Aaron Burr. In 1808, **James Madison** kept Clinton as his running mate. He is the only vice president other than John C. Calhoun to have served as vice president under two different presidents. He is also the first vice president to have died in office. He passed away from a heart attack on 20 April 1812 and was reinterred at Kingston, New York, in 1908. *See also* FEDERALIST PAPERS.

## COMMANDER-IN-CHIEF

**Article II**, Section 2, of the Constitution states that the "President shall be commander in chief of the Army and Navy of the United States, and of the militia of the several states, when called into the actual service of the United States." This provision ensures *civilian* control of the military. Contemporary chain of command was established for the Army, Navy, Air Force, and Marines in the 1947 National Security Act and the Goldwater-Nichols Act in 1986.

The president has no constitutional power to declare war. That provision belongs solely to Congress. However, presidents' unilateral decisions to engage U.S. troops abroad with or without congressional approval—particularly in the post–World War II period—has resulted in heated debates about the Founders' intentions, the separation of powers, and the need to reign in alleged presidential adventurism in the wake of the Korean War and the Vietnam War, in particular. The latter prompted Congress to pass the **War Powers Resolution**, over the objections of President Richard M. Nixon, in 1973. President George W. Bush's decision to invade Iraq in 2003, albeit with congressional support, renewed this crucial debate.

Congress has not formally declared war against any country since Imperial Japan and Nazi Germany in World War II. The Congressional Research Service (CRS) reported that between 1975 and 2003, presidents submitted 111 reports on troop deployments pursuant to the requirements of the War Powers Resolution.

## COMMERCE CLAUSE

The commerce clause is found in **Article I**, Section 8, Clause 3, of the Constitution and states that Congress shall have the power "to regulate commerce with foreign nations, and among the several states, and with the Indian tribes." The clause was aimed at rectifying one of the major shortcomings of the **Articles of Confederation** following the American Revolution, during which time states engaged in "trade wars" with one another. The impediments to building a national economy amid the postwar chaos prompted **James Madison** to call for states to attend the **Annapolis Convention** in 1786 as a means to begin to sort out economic challenges.

It is important to note that the commerce clause provides Congress the ability to regulate interstate and foreign commerce but leaves it to the states to regulate *intrastate* commerce. Historical **Supreme Court** cases regarding the commerce clause have centered largely on federal–state conflicts, such as navigation (***Gibbons v. Ogden***, 1824), what constitutes a "foreign state" or Indian tribe (*Cherokee Nation v. Georgia*, 1831), congressional delegation of regulatory power over local affairs to the executive (***Schechter Poultry Corp. v. United States***, 1935), and limitations on congressional regulation of national versus local commerce (***Gonzales v. Raich***, 2005; ***U.S. v. Lopez***, 1995).

**CONCURRING OPINION**

When the **Supreme Court** issues a decision on a constitutional matter, either the **chief justice** or the most senior associate justice (generally if the chief justice disagrees) writes the **majority opinion** on the case. A concurring opinion is an opinion authored by other justices on the high court in which they elaborate their particular reasons for supporting the majority. Often, concurring opinions expound different legal precedents or understandings of the case from the majority opinion, and thereby frequently provide important insights into how individual justices arrive at their decisions. *See also* DISSENTING OPINION.

**CONGRESS**

*See* ARTICLE I (CONSTITUTION).

***COOPER V. AARON*** **(1958)**

This **civil rights** era **Supreme Court** case pivoted on whether states were obligated to follow and enforce the high court's decisions. Following the decision in ***Brown v. Board of Education*** (1954), the Arkansas legislature battled desegregation by amending the state constitution and passing a statute that freed children from having to attend racially integrated schools. The Little Rock School Board, although it had proposed a desegregation plan consistent with *Brown*, asked the federal courts to suspend desegregation efforts for several years in light of Governor Orval Faubus's and the state legislature's opposition, which had precipitated President Eisenhower's decision to send troops to Central High School in 1957. In a unanimous decision, the Supreme Court denied the Little Rock School Board's request, citing **equal protection** of the law for black students. Moreover, the justices affirmed that the *Brown* decision was the law of the land per the supremacy clause of the Constitution and the doctrine of **judicial review** elaborated in ***Marbury v. Madison*** (1803).

***CRAIG V. BOREN*** **(1976)**

This **Supreme Court** case considered the constitutionality of **gender**-based classifications. The conflict centered on an Oklahoma law that barred the sale of 3.2 percent beer to men less than 21 years of age but allowed women over the age of 18 to purchase the beverage. The statute was challenged under the **Fourteenth Amendment equal protection clause** as discriminatory toward men. In a 7–2 decision, the justices on the high court invalidated the Oklahoma statute on the basis that the facts on which the state legislature relied (higher driving-while-intoxicated rates for males) did not correlate with the intended benefits of prohibiting beer sales to males. As such, the ruling established the standard of **intermediate scrutiny** in gender-based classifications, whereby the state must demonstrate specific objectives and how the statute achieves such objectives. *See also U.S. V. VIRGINIA* (1996).

**CRUEL AND UNUSUAL PUNISHMENT**

*See* DEATH PENALTY; EIGHTH AMENDMENT.

# D

## DEATH PENALTY

The constitutionality of capital punishment has been challenged as a violation of the **Eighth Amendment** prohibition on cruel and unusual punishment. The **Supreme Court** has upheld the constitutionality of the death penalty, but has also narrowed its applicability over time. As of late 2015, a total of 31 states and the federal government provide for executions of convicted criminals.

The Supreme Court first confirmed the constitutionality of the death penalty in 1879 in states and territories in *Wilkerson v. Utah*. In *Powell v. Alabama* (1932), three decades prior to the ruling in ***Gideon v. Wainwright*** (1963), indigent defendants who were not competent to represent themselves were to have counsel appointed by judges. In 1972 the high court struck down the death penalty in ***Furman v. Georgia***, essentially imposing a four-year moratorium on capital punishment in light of inconsistent or arbitrary application of death sentences for various crimes. In ***Gregg v. Georgia*** (1976) the Supreme Court reaffirmed that the death penalty was not, per se, a violation of the Eighth Amendment so long as explicit factors and procedures were established and/or a mandatory sentence for a particular crime was specified.

Since the decision in *Gregg*, the Supreme Court has narrowed the parameters of criminal cases eligible for the death penalty in a number of ways. In *Woodson v. North Carolina* (1976) the justices determined that mandatory death sentences for first-degree murder violated not only the Eighth but also the **Fourteenth Amendment**. According to *Lockett v. Ohio* (1978), sentencing authorities must be allowed to consider all potentially mitigating factors, and according to *Beck v. Alabama* (1980) juries must have the choice of lesser convictions, not simply a choice between a death sentence and acquittal. In *Ford v. Wainwright* (1986) the execution of insane individuals was found to be unconstitutional, as was the imposition of the death penalty on individuals aged 15 in *Thompson v. Oklahoma* (1988). In *Roper v. Simmons* (2005) the high court determined that the death penalty was unconstitutional for defendants who had committed their crimes at age 18 or less. The execution of mentally retarded defendants was found unconstitutional in *Atkins v. Virginia* (2002). In *Tennard v. Dretke* (2004) the Supreme Court ruled at *all* mitigating factors must be considered in both the trial and sentence phase in death penalty cases. In *Hill v. McDonough* (2006) defendants in death penalty cases were allowed to appeal their sentences on civil rights grounds, even if they had already done so via **habeas corpus**. In *Kennedy v. Louisiana* (2008) the death penalty was ruled unconstitutional if the victim's life was not taken. Per *House v. Bell* (2006), postconviction appeals may introduce DNA evidence.

Nonetheless, the Supreme Court has upheld not only execution procedures but also eligibility criteria for the application of the death penalty. In *Glass v. Louisiana* (1985) electrocution was found constitutional. Similarly, in *Baze v. Rees* (2008) lethal injection was found constitutional, as was use of a sedative for lethal injection in *Glossip v. Gross* (2015). In *Tyson v. Arizona* (1987) defendants who participated in a felony were found to be subject to the death penalty if they showed extreme indifference to human life. In ***McCleskey v. Kemp*** (1988) the court rejected arguments about general racial bias in death penalty cases as a violation of **due process**; defendants must instead show intentional discrimination. In *Kansas v. Marsh* (2008) the high court determined that the death penalty could be applied in cases in which the aggravating and mitigating factors were of equal weight. Finally, in *Hall v. Florida* (2014) intelligent quotient (IQ) tests alone were found insufficient to determine a defendant's eligibility for the death penalty based on intellectual disability. *See also ROBINSON V. CALIFORNIA* (1962).

**DECLARATION OF INDEPENDENCE**

This document, penned by **Thomas Jefferson** and adopted by the Continental Congress in Philadelphia on 4 July 1776, declared independence from the British Crown, detailed the rationale for the former colonies' revolt that had begun a year earlier, and affirmed **natural rights** that would form the philosophical basis for many of the **civil liberties** protections ultimately adopted in the Constitution and the **Bill of Rights**.

The preamble of the declaration is often cited as a straightforward and elegant elaboration of natural rights, as Jefferson writes that "We hold these truths to be self-evident, that all men are created equal, that they are endowed by their Creator with certain unalienable Rights, that among these are Life, Liberty and the pursuit of Happiness." By emphasizing individual rights that may not be compromised because they are God-given, the sentence accentuates a central Revolutionary ideal that challenges monarchs' claims to rule by divine right. Moreover, the document elucidates another core Revolutionary concept in terms of social contract theory: that a legitimate government must secure the *consent* of the governed and the people have a right to cast off the shackles of despotism when consent is lacking.

The balance of the declaration contains a litany of complaints against King George III—and not against the British people per se. Indictments include but are not limited to his failure to assent to colonial laws, corruption in the judiciary, imposition of taxes without consent, quartering of troops, and crimes on the high seas.

Fifty-six members of the Continental Congress signed the Declaration. John Hancock, the president of the Congress, was the first to affix his signature. The signatories were, in effect, signing their own death warrants as traitors to the Crown. Only five, however, were ultimately captured and died in the course of the Revolutionary War: George Walton, Thomas Heyward Jr., Arthur Middleton, Edward Rutledge, and Richard Stockton.

The theoretical origins of the declaration remain a wellspring of scholarly controversy and disagreement. Some credit British political theorist **John Locke**, who authored the *Second Treatise on Civil Government*, as influencing Jefferson. Others suggest continental influences. Regardless, Jefferson is known to have referenced his preamble to the Constitution of the State of Virginia as well as **George Mason**'s draft of the Virginia Declaration of Rights.

The original declaration is maintained for display at the Rotunda of the National Archives Building in Washington, DC, alongside copies of the Constitution and the Bill of Rights. As an example of **republican** political theory, the declaration is credited with enduring historical influence abroad, including the French Revolution and other independence movements in the 19th and 20th centuries, from Europe to Africa and Asia.

**DEFENSE OF MARRIAGE ACT (DOMA)**

Passed by a Republican-led Congress and signed into law by Democratic President William Clinton in 1996, this statute defined marriage as the union of one man and one woman and enabled states to refuse to recognize same-sex marriages performed in other states. Congressional action was prompted by a Hawaii case, *Baehr v. Miike* (1993), in which the state supreme court found that the government must demonstrate a compelling interest in denying same-sex couples the right to marry. Some legislators feared that other states would be forced to recognize same-sex marriages performed in Hawaii if that state legalized the right. Under the **full faith and credit clause** of **Article IV** of the Constitution, states must respect the "public acts, records, and judicial proceedings of every other state."

Passage of the law drew the ire of **gay rights** advocates, who had supported Clinton's presidential bid in 1992. Constitutional questions about the statute abounded, including whether congressional legislation could circumvent a constitutional provision. In 2011 President Barack Obama announced that his administration would no longer defend the statute in the legal arena. In a 5–4 decision in ***U.S. v. Windsor*** (2013) the **Supreme Court** struck down Section 3 of the statute, which defined marriage as the union of one man and one woman. The majority contended that the definition violated **Fifth Amendment** rights and constituted a "deprivation of liberty." In 2015 in the case of ***Obergefell v. Hodges*** the Supreme Court, in another 5–4 decision, invalidated Section 2 of DOMA by mandating that all states recognize same-sex marriages under the **due process clause** of the **Fourteenth Amendment**.

*DEJONGE V. OREGON* **(1937)**

This **Supreme Court** decision concerned the **incorporation doctrine** and the application of the **First Amendment** right to freedom of assembly to the states via the **Fourteenth Amendment**. At issue was an Oregon law that forbade the assembly of persons for any doctrine that "advocates crime, physical violence, sabotage, or any unlawful acts or methods as a means of accomplishing or effecting industrial or political change or revolution." Dirk DeJonge, a member of the Communist Party, made a speech in a public forum in the midst of a maritime strike in Portland. He was arrested and convicted of violating the Oregon criminal syndicalism statute. In a unanimous decision, the Supreme Court invalidated DeJonge's conviction. Writing for the majority, **Chief Justice Charles Evans Hughes** asserted that the right to freedom of assembly "cannot be denied without violating those fundamental principles of liberty and justice which lie at the base of all civil and political institutions."

*DENNIS V. UNITED STATES* **(1951)**

This **Supreme Court** ruling held that individuals do not have **First Amendment** rights to free speech, publication, or assembly if the intent is to overthrow the government. The case centered on 11 members of the Communist Party who were convicted of violating the 1940 Smith Act, which established it as a crime to call for the overthrow of the government. In a 7–2 decision the majority upheld the convictions. In his opinion, **Chief Justice Fred Vinson** invoked the "clear and present danger" test, asking "whether the gravity of the 'evil,' discounted by its improbability, justifies such invasion of free speech as necessary to avoid the danger." *See also BRANDENBURG V. OHIO* (1969); *GITLOW V. NEW YORK* (1925); *WHITNEY V. CALIFORNIA* (1927).

*DICKERSON V. UNITED STATES* **(2000)**

This **Supreme Court** case confirmed the requirement that suspected criminals must be read their constitutional rights consistent with the ruling in ***Miranda v. Arizona*** (1966). The case pivoted on a suspect's voluntary confession, after which he was informed of his right to remain silent or have counsel present during questioning. Prosecutors asserted that 18 U.S. Code § 3501, passed by Congress in 1968 following *Miranda*, provided that "a confession shall be admissible in evidence if it is voluntarily given." Writing for the majority in the 7–2 decision, **Chief Justice William Rehnquist** wrote that "Miranda announced a constitutional rule that Congress may not supersede legislatively."

**DISSENTING OPINION**

When the **Supreme Court** issues a decision on a constitutional matter, either the **chief justice** or the most senior associate justice (if the chief justice disagrees) writes the **majority opinion** on the case. A dissenting opinion is an opinion authored by other justices on the high court in which they elaborate their particular reasons for opposing the majority. Dissenting opinions generally elaborate the constitutional bases and provide legal precedents that buttress the justice's belief that the majority erred in its ruling.

***DISTRICT OF COLUMBIA V. HELLER* (2008)**

This **Supreme Court** case was the first in seven decades that took up the question of **Second Amendment** rights. The litigation resulted from legislation passed by the District of Columbia that banned the registration of handguns, required licenses for all pistols, and obliged gun owners to keep all firearms unloaded and either disassembled or trigger locked. A federal district court held that restrictions were constitutional and that Second Amendment protections extended only to "militias." A federal appeals court disagreed, prompting the high court to review the question.

In a 5–4 decision, the majority of justices on the Supreme Court invalidated the city's ban, asserting that Second Amendment rights did not just extend to individuals connected to militias such as the National Guard but also to individuals who wish to possess firearms for legitimate purposes such as self-protection. Writing for the majority, Associate Justice Antonin Scalia provided a detailed analysis of **original intent** as well as state constitutional amendments for gun ownership after the ratification of the Constitution. He posited that "the inherent right of self-defense has been central to the Second Amendment right. The handgun ban amounts to a prohibition of an entire class of 'arms' that is overwhelmingly chosen by American society for that lawful purpose. The prohibition extends, moreover, to the home, where the need for defense of self, family, and property is most acute. Under any of the standards of scrutiny that we have applied to enumerated constitutional rights, banning from the home 'the most preferred firearm in the nation to "keep" and use for protection of one's home and family' . . . would fail constitutional muster." *See also MCDONALD V. CITY OF CHICAGO* (2010).

***DRED SCOTT V. SANFORD* (1857)**

This landmark pre–Civil War **Supreme Court** decision, over which **Chief Justice Roger Taney** presided, found that blacks were not citizens of the United States. The case was brought by Dred Scott, a slave whose forced labor had been repeatedly leased out by his owner in free states. When Scott was unable to secure his freedom from the Missouri courts or buy his freedom from his owner's widow, he sued in federal court. In a 7–2 decision, the Supreme Court ruled that blacks—slave or free—were not citizens and therefore had no standing to sue under the provisions of **Article III** of the Constitution. Moreover, the high court overturned the Missouri Compromise of 1820 by asserting that Congress had no authority to legislate slavery in territories acquired *after* the Constitution entered into effect (i.e., the Louisiana Territory). Finally, the majority of justices agreed that simply because Scott had relocated to Wisconsin Territory (now Minnesota), a free territory, he was not a free man. Rather, Scott remained the property of his owner under Missouri law.

Far from resolving the slavery issue, as Taney had hoped, the decision galvanized abolitionists, stirred the resolve of slaveholders, and moved the nation closer toward civil war during the presidency of James Buchanan. The **Civil War Amendments** overturned the decision in *Dred Scott*. The **Thirteenth Amendment** abolished slavery, the **Fourteenth Amendment** gave citizenship rights to blacks, and the **Fifteenth Amendment** barred states from denying blacks the right to vote. In the **Reconstruction** era, however, those amendments were interpreted so narrowly by the Supreme Court as to abrogate the rights of blacks. *See also PLESSY V. FERGUSON* (1896); *SLAUGHTERHOUSE CASES* (1873); *U.S. V. REESE* (1876).

**DUE PROCESS (CLAUSE)**

This concept is a fundamental **civil liberty**. Due process may be understood as a protection against the government's ability to deprive an individual of life, liberty, and property. Legal proceedings are to be fair and impartial, and individuals have a right to be heard in a court of law and receive notice of such proceedings in advance. Moreover, laws are to be neither capricious nor arbitrary. The **Fifth Amendment** of the Constitution guarantees due process in the **Bill of Rights**. The right has been **incorporated** selectively across time to apply to states through the **Fourteenth Amendment** in successive **Supreme Court** cases beginning in the 20th century. *See also* EQUAL PROTECTION (CLAUSE).

# E

***EDWARDS V. SOUTH CAROLINA* (1963)**

This **Supreme Court** case regarded the **First Amendment** right of freedom of assembly and the freedom to petition the government for redress of grievances, and the **incorporation** of these rights to state actions through the **Fourteenth Amendment**. A crowd of more than 180 African American teachers and students marched peacefully on the state house in Columbia, South Carolina, in 1961 to petition for **civil rights**. When the police arrived to disperse the crowd, the protestors refused, sang patriotic songs, were arrested, and were later convicted for breaking the peace. Writing for the 8–1 majority that struck down the protestors' convictions, Supreme Court Associate Justice Potter Stewart called the protestors' exercise of their First Amendment rights an example of "their most pristine and classic form" and condemned efforts to "make criminal the peaceful expression of unpopular views." *See also DEJONGE V. OREGON* (1937).

**EIGHTEENTH AMENDMENT**

Ratified on 16 January 1919, this amendment went into effect exactly one year later and prohibited the "manufacture, sale, or transportation of intoxicating liquors within, the importation thereof into, or the exportation thereof from the United States and all territory subject to the jurisdiction thereof for beverage purposes." The amendment was a result of the temperance movement and was closely associated with the Progressive Era focus on corruption and criminality, which supporters of prohibition believed was aggravated by alcohol consumption. The Volstead Act of 1919 set forth the implementing language for the Eighteenth Amendment by defining the contours of "intoxicating liquor" and specifying a prohibition against the manufacture, sale, and so on of alcohol while not outlawing its use. The result was a decade of the illegal, underground sale of alcohol in "speakeasy" bars and rampant criminality by gangs, including Chicago's Al Capone, which took over the now-illegal industry. Thirteen years later, in 1933, the Eighteenth Amendment was repealed in entirety with ratification of the **Twenty-First Amendment**.

**EIGHTH AMENDMENT**

This amendment to the Constitution was ratified on 15 December 1791 and is part of the **Bill of Rights**. The **civil liberties** protections of the Eighth Amendment address excessive bail and fines and prohibit cruel and unusual punishment. The text reads: "Excessive bail shall not be required, nor excessive fines imposed, nor cruel and unusual punishments inflicted."

The amendment leaves a number of matters for interpretation. The **Supreme Court** held in *Stack v. Boyle* (1951) that bail for a defendant is excessive if a judge decides on a "figure higher than is reasonably calculated" to guarantee that the accused will appear at the trial. Bail is, however, *not mandated* by the Eighth Amendment. The high court asserted in *U.S. v. Salerno* (1987) that "the government's proposed conditions of release or detention not be 'excessive' in light of the perceived evil." Thus, judges have discretion, given the magnitude of the alleged crime, to withhold bail.

With respect to excessive fines, the pivotal court case was *Waters-Pierce Oil Co. v. Texas* (1909). The Supreme Court elucidated that excessive fines that violate the Eighth Amendment are those that are "so grossly excessive as to amount to a deprivation of property without **due process** of law." In *U.S. v. Bajakajian* (1998) the court struck down a $357,000 fine levied on an individual who violated the reporting requirements for taking more than $10,000 cash out of the country. The justices determined that the fine was "grossly disproportional" to the point that it was tantamount to cruel and unusual punishment.

The constitutionality of the **death penalty** has historically been front and center in debates about cruel and unusual punishment. In *Wilkerson v. Utah* (1879) the Supreme Court determined that capital punishment by firing squad did not violate the Eighth Amendment but that burning alive, drawing and quartering, and disembowelment were unconstitutional. The Eighth Amendment was incorporated to apply to the states through the **Fourteenth Amendment** in the case of ***Robinson v. California*** (1962). Two critical cases took place in the 1970s. In ***Furman v. Georgia*** (1972) the Supreme Court struck down the death penalty due to its lack of consistent application in several states. Four years later, however, in ***Gregg v. Georgia*** (1976) the majority of justices concluded that the death penalty was *not* inherently unconstitutional. Rather, its application was subject to objective criteria to limit its use and sentencing courts (and juries) must be able to take into account the character of the individual. The Supreme Court further elaborated in *Atkins v. Virginia* (2002) that the death penalty was unconstitutional for mentally handicapped individuals. In ***McCleskey v. Kemp*** (1987), however, the high court rejected arguments that blacks were statistically more likely to receive the death penalty than whites as a basis for overturning capital punishment.

**ELECTORAL COLLEGE**

The Electoral College process for selecting the president of the United States is outlined in **Article II**, Section 1, of the Constitution. Instead of voting directly for the president, voters cast ballots for a slate of electors in each state. The number of each state's electors equals the number of representatives in the House plus two for the Senate. The **Twenty-Third**

**Amendment**, adopted in 1961, provided a minimum of three electors for the District of Columbia. Currently, there are 538 electoral votes; 270 electoral votes are needed to win election. If there is no Electoral College majority, then the election is thrown to the House of Representatives, where each state has a single vote. Article II provides no guidelines on how that single vote is to be determined among members of the state delegation.

Several controversial elections have, indeed, been decided by the House. In 1800 **Thomas Jefferson** and Aaron Burr tied the electoral vote. Jefferson was chosen by the House, and the **Twelfth Amendment** was adopted in 1804 to "encourage" presidential and vice presidential candidates to run on the same ticket. In 1824 the race between Andrew Jackson, John Quincy Adams, and Henry Clay yielded no Electoral College majority. Jackson won a plurality of the popular vote, but the House chose Adams in what Jackson supporters called a "corrupt bargain." In 1876 Democrat Samuel Tilden prevailed over Republican Rutherford B. Hayes in the popular vote, but disputed returns in Florida, Louisiana, Oregon, and South Carolina threw the Electoral College vote into chaos. Rather than the House deciding the outcome, Florida, Louisiana, and South Carolina ultimately certified Hayes as the victor in exchange for ending military occupation during Reconstruction.

As the 1800, 1824, and 1876 elections underscore, the national popular vote is irrelevant in determining the winner of the presidential election. In 1888 Grover Cleveland outpolled Benjamin Harrison by approximately 90,000 votes nationally, but Harrison won the Electoral College by a comfortable margin. In 2000 Albert A. (Al) Gore won a half million more votes nationally than George W. Bush, but following the Florida recount ended by the **Supreme Court** case ***Bush v. Gore*** (2000), Bush prevailed in the Electoral College. Critics suggest that these empirical realities—and the theoretical likelihood that in a future election a candidate who wins the popular vote may lose the Electoral College again—is antithetical to democracy.

The possibility of a popular vote victory and an Electoral College defeat is exacerbated by the "unit rule," which 48 states employ. The unit rule, or "winner take all" provision, mandates that the entirety of a state's electoral votes go to whichever candidate obtains a plurality of the *statewide* vote. The result is that candidates who do exceedingly well in the popular vote beyond the necessary threshold to capture the state's electoral vote obtain a surplus number of ballots that have no effect in the Electoral College distribution. Gore's particularly strong showing in California in 2000 is a case in point: he won the state by nearly 1.3 million votes but derived no more than the maximum electoral votes in the Golden State (54). Only Maine and Nebraska currently employ an electoral vote distribution plan based on congressional districts and the state's at-large winner.

Other detractors of the Electoral College system point to the "faithless elector" possibility. This occurs when an elector pledged to a particular candidate casts his or her ballot for a different candidate. In response to some "faithless electors" who have exercised this prerogative in the past, largely as a protest to the system, more than half the states have passed laws binding electors to cast ballots for their pledge.

Abolition of the Electoral College or change to the selection process require a constitutional amendment. The most concerted effort was spearheaded by Democratic Senator Birch Bay and Democratic Representative Emmanuel Celler, who advocated a plurality rule for the Electoral College. The proposal died in the Senate in 1971, though President James E. (Jimmy) Carter suggested support for the institution's abolition during his term. Some scholars support a direct presidential vote as in France, while others have suggested adopting the Maine and Nebraska model, a congressional district plan, or some hybrid. Historical analysis suggests that a number of election outcomes would have been different under alternative proposals, but whether those outcomes would have been more "democratic" remains a point of intense controversy.

The Electoral College is best viewed as a system that reflected the Founders' 18th-century understanding of the political world. Fearful of direct democracy, they established a system consistent with the tenets of representative democracy. Key to this worldview was **federalism**, or the division of power between levels of government. States choose the delegates to the Electoral College (note that the unit rule is a contemporary development and not constitutionally mandated), and the localization of elections is consistent with the logic **James Madison** elaborated in **Federalist Papers** no. 10: that a "conflagration" (in this case, electoral fraud) in one part of the country was unlikely to foment in all parts. Indeed, in discussing possible electoral "mischief," **Alexander Hamilton** wrote in Federalist no. 68 that "The choice of SEVERAL, to form an intermediate body of electors, will be much less apt to convulse the community with any extraordinary or violent movements, than the choice of ONE who was himself to be the final object of the public wishes. And as the electors, chosen in each State, are to assemble and vote in the State in which they are chosen, this detached and divided situation will expose them much less to heats and ferments, which might be communicated from them to the people, than if they were all to be convened at one time, in one place." Whether the present-day system built on the foundations of the Founders' philosophical legacy serves the nation more than 200 years later is a hotly contested debate.

**ELEVENTH AMENDMENT**

Ratified on 7 February 1795, this amendment was a direct result of the **Supreme Court** decision in *Chisholm v. Georgia* (1793) and addressed the question of the sovereign immunity of the states. The text reads: "The Judicial power of the United States shall not be construed to extend to any suit in law or equity, commenced or prosecuted against one of the United States by Citizens of another State, or by Citizens or Subjects of any Foreign State." The amendment overturned the decision in *Chisholm*, in which the high court had ruled that federal courts had jurisdiction over claims by citizens against states and that states were *not* immune from lawsuits filed by citizens of another state. In effect, the Eleventh Amendment narrowed the interpretation of **Article III**, Section 2, of the Constitution, which specifies that federal judicial power extends to "Controversies between two or more States" and "between a State and Citizens of another State" and "between Citizens of different States."

**ELLSWORTH, OLIVER (1745–1807)**

A native of Windsor, Connecticut, Ellsworth graduated from Princeton University (the College of New Jersey) in 1766. Admitted to the bar in 1779 after reading law for four years, he served as a member of the Connecticut General Assembly from 1773 to 1776 and as a delegate to the Continental Congress from 1777 to 1784. He earned a judgeship in Connecticut in 1785 and was a delegate to the Constitutional Convention in Philadelphia in 1787. Ellsworth, along with **Roger Sherman**, helped broker the Connecticut or **Great Compromise**, which structured representation in Congress and resolved the conflict between small and large states at the Convention. He served as a senator in the First Congress beginning in 1789 and chaired the committee responsible for drafting the Judiciary Act of 1789.

In March 1796 President **George Washington** nominated him as **chief justice** of the **Supreme Court**. He resigned his position in September 1800. One of the most important cases over which he presided was *Hollingsworth v. Virginia* (1798), in which the high court contended that the president has no formal role in constitutional amendments and, further, that the **Eleventh Amendment** applied to cases pending before the judiciary prior to ratification. Ellsworth died on 26 November 1807. He is interred at the Old Cemetery in Somerville, Massachusetts.

**EMINENT DOMAIN**

This concept refers to private property that the government may take for some public use or purpose. The **Fifth Amendment** "takings" clause in the Constitution mandates that when governments take private property for public benefit, the property owner must be compensated. *See also CHICAGO, BURLINGTON & QUINCY RAILROAD CO. V. CITY OF CHICAGO* (1897); *KELO V. CITY OF NEW LONDON* (2005).

***ENGLE V. VITALE* (1962)**

This historic **Supreme Court** case addressed the constitutionality of school prayer. At issue was whether a nondenominational prayer, recited at a New York public school, violated the establishment clause of the **First Amendment**. The text of the voluntary prayer, as composed by state officials, was as follows: "Almighty God, we acknowledge our dependence upon Thee, and we beg Thy blessings upon us, our parents, our teachers and our country. Amen." A New York State court of appeals upheld the prayer, which was supported in the Supreme Court litigation by 22 states. The plaintiffs, three members of the Jewish faith and two others who did not belong to organized religions, were supported by several groups in urging a ban on the prayer. By a 6–1 margin, the Supreme Court ruled that the prayer, by its very nature, was a promotion of religion by the state that violated the establishment clause, regardless of the absence of coercion.

Writing the **majority opinion**, Associate Justice Hugo Black explained: "It is true that New York's establishment of its Regents' prayer as an officially approved religious doctrine of that State does not amount to a total establishment of one particular religious sect to the exclusion of all others—that, indeed, the governmental endorsement of that prayer seems relatively insignificant when compared to the governmental encroachments upon religion which were commonplace 200 years ago. To those who may subscribe to the view that, because the Regents' official prayer is so brief and general there can be no danger to religious freedom in its governmental establishment, however, it may be appropriate to say in the words of James Madison, the author of the First Amendment: '[I]t is proper to take alarm at the first experiment on our liberties. . . . Who does not see that the same authority which can establish Christianity, in exclusion of all other Religions, may establish with the same ease any particular sect of Christians, in exclusion of all other Sects? That the same authority which can force a citizen to contribute three pence only of his property for the support of any one establishment may force him to conform to any other establishment in all cases whatsoever?'" *See also LEE V. WEISMAN* (1992); *SANTA FE INDEPENDENT SCHOOL DISTRICT V. DOE* (2000).

**ENUMERATED POWERS**

Those powers specified in **Article I**, **Article II**, and **Article III** of the Constitution and delegated to Congress, the presidency, and the Supreme Court, respectively, are considered "enumerated" powers. The **Tenth Amendment** places restrictions on the power of the central government: "The powers not delegated to the United States by the Constitution, nor prohibited by it to the States, are reserved to the States respectively, or to the people."

**EQUAL PROTECTION (CLAUSE)**

Section 1 of the **Fourteenth Amendment** to the Constitution, adopted in 1868, states that "All persons born or naturalized in the United States, and subject to the jurisdiction thereof, are citizens of the United States and of the State wherein they reside. No State shall make or enforce any law which shall abridge the privileges or immunities of citizens of the United States; nor shall any State deprive any person of life, liberty, or property, without **due process** of law; *nor deny to any person within its jurisdiction the equal protection of the laws*" (emphasis added).

The objective of the Fourteenth Amendment was to guarantee citizenship rights, and to prohibit states from curtailing those of African Americans, in particular, by making the **Bill of Rights** apply to the states through the doctrine of **incorporation**. Beginning with the ***Slaughterhouse Cases*** (1873) during **Reconstruction** and extending through the "separate but equal" doctrine enunciated by the **Supreme Court** in ***Plessy v. Ferguson*** (1896), however, narrow interpretations of "equal protection of the laws" as inapplicable to the states enabled them to maintain segregation of the races through **black codes** and **Jim Crow laws**. Moreover, African Americans were disenfranchised through mechanisms such as the **poll tax**, literacy tests, and **grandfather clauses**.

Equal protection of the law was gradually applied to the state and federal governments beginning in the 20th century. The watershed case of ***Brown v. Board of Education*** (1954) heralded a revolution in **civil rights** and marked the beginning of the end of segregation. In *Brown* the Supreme Court held that separate-but-equal facilities in education were inherently *unequal*. That same year the high court elaborated the notion of **reverse incorporation** in *Bolling v. Sharpe*, asserting that Fourteenth Amendment equal protection applied to *federal* jurisdictions through the **Fifth Amendment**.

The equal protection clause is often at the center of litigation concerning **affirmative action** programs, **voting rights**, **gender discrimination**, and **gay rights**.

**EQUAL RIGHTS AMENDMENT (ERA)**

This proposed amendment to the Constitution, which addressed **gender** discrimination, was first introduced in Congress in 1923 following adoption of the **Nineteenth Amendment**. It did not reach the two-thirds vote threshold in both chambers of Congress until 1972. Section 1 of the amendment read: "Equality of rights under the law shall not be denied or abridged by the United States or by any State on account of sex." Congress provided a seven-year window for the states to ratify the amendment. The deadline was later extended for another three years, but by 1982 three-quarters of the states had not ratified the amendment, five states had rescinded their prior approval, and the ERA failed.

The ratification debate focused sharply on differing perspectives regarding gender roles in society. Moreover, many women who declared themselves "feminists" disagreed on how the purported protections afforded in the amendment would affect working women and homemakers. The ratification debate pitted the National Organization for Women (NOW) against conservative activist Phyllis Schlafly. Although the amendment has been reintroduced in every session of Congress since 1982, legislative action has not been forthcoming.

***ESCOBEDO V. ILLINOIS* (1964)**

*See MIRANDA V. ARIZONA* (1966).

**ESPIONAGE ACT (1917)**

This statute was passed by Congress shortly after the United States entered into World War I. Amid fears of anarchy during the First Red Scare, the legislation barred individuals from interfering with military operations or the recruitment of soldiers, took aim at insubordination in the military, and sought to preclude support of foreign enemies during the war. An amendment to the Espionage Act, commonly referred to as the Sedition Act of 1918, clearly challenged free speech rights under the **First Amendment** by banning "any disloyal, profane, scurrilous, or abusive language about the form of government of the United States . . . or the flag of the United States, or the uniform of the Army or Navy."

The Supreme Court upheld the constitutionality of the Espionage Act, its limits on free speech, and World War I–era convictions (including that of Socialist Party leader Eugene Debs) in the landmark case ***Schenck v. United States*** (1919). The essence of the statute has remained on the books despite revisions that include the McCarran Security Act of 1950 (passed over the veto of President Harry S. Truman) and legal challenges. Many cold war spies, including the Rosenbergs, Jonathan Pollard, and Aldrich Ames, were convicted under the act. In the post-9/11 era, the most spectacular conviction under the act was of Bradley (now Chelsea) Manning, who channeled hundreds of thousands of classified documents about military operations in Afghanistan and Iraq to WikiLeaks (an Internet site that discloses secret government information). *See also BRANDENBURG V. OHIO* (1969); *DENNIS V. UNITED STATES* (1951); *GITLOW V. NEW YORK* (1925); WAR ON TERROR, WAR ON TERRORISM; *WHITNEY V. CALIFORNIA* (1927).

**ESTABLISHMENT CLAUSE**

*See* FIRST AMENDMENT.

***EVERSON V. BOARD OF EDUCATION* (1947)**

This **Supreme Court** case pivoted on the question of whether a school district's reimbursement of transportation costs to New Jersey parents whose children attended public and private parochial schools violated the establishment clause of the **First Amendment**. In a 5–4 decision a majority on the court found that the reimbursement was, per se, constitutional because all students were eligible for reimbursements and funds were paid to parents, not to any religious institutions. Nevertheless, the majority decision penned by associate justice Hugo Black had a much broader scope that embraced **incorporation** of the **Bill of Rights** to state actions.

In effect, the majority applied the establishment clause to the states through the **Fourteenth Amendment**, arguing that "The 'establishment of religion' clause of the First Amendment means at least this: Neither a state nor the Federal Government can set up a church. Neither can pass laws which aid one religion, aid all religions or prefer one religion over another. Neither can force nor influence a person to go to or to remain away from church against his will or force him to profess a belief or disbelief in any religion. . . . No tax in any amount, large or small, can be levied to support any religious activities or institutions, whatever they may be called, or whatever form they may adopt to teach or practice religion. Neither a state nor the Federal Government can, openly or secretly, participate in the affairs of any religious organizations or groups and vice versa. In the words of Jefferson, the clause against establishment of religion by law was intended to erect 'a wall of separation between Church and State.'" *See also LEMON V. KURTZMAN* (1971); *ZELMAN V. SIMMONS-HARRIS* (2002).

***EX PARTE MERRYMAN* (1861)**

This controversial court case was a major test of constitutional law regarding presidential, congressional, and judicial power during the Civil War. On 27 April 1861 President Abraham Lincoln suspended **habeas corpus** and instituted martial law in the state of Maryland, where federal troops were being harassed and antiwar activists planned to disrupt railroads vital to the Union effort. Lieutenant John Merryman was arrested the following month for attempts to destroy key bridges on the rail line and charged with treason.

The military personnel at Fort McHenry, Maryland, denied an initial writ of habeas corpus from a Maryland federal district judge. Merryman's attorneys then sought the assistance of the **chief justice** of the **Supreme Court**, **Roger Taney**. Taney issued a writ for Merryman, which General George Cadwalader refused on the authority of President Lincoln. Taney subsequently penned a decision that reproved President Lincoln for an alleged abuse of power.

The chief justice believed that the president had arrogated and abused a congressional power to which he was not constitutionally entitled: "The clause in the Constitution which authorizes the suspension of the privilege of the writ of habeas corpus is in the ninth section of the first article. This article is devoted to the Legislative Department of the United States, and has not the slightest reference to the Executive Department." Taney continued several paragraphs later, noting: "It is the second article of the Constitution that provides for the organization of the Executive Department, and enumerates the powers conferred on it, and prescribes its duties. And if the high power over the liberty of the citizens now claimed was intended to be conferred on the President, it would undoubtedly be found in plain words in this article. But there is not a word in it that can furnish the slightest ground to justify the exercise of the power."

When Congress reconvened July 1861, the legislature refused to pass legislation authorizing Lincoln's suspension of habeas corpus. Two months later the president defied Taney a second time by ordering the imprisonment of members of the Maryland state legislature. Five months later Lincoln allowed the release of most prisoners. In December 1862 Congress ultimately passed legislation indemnifying the president, and

Lincoln again suspended habeas corpus in 1863, and the policy remained in effect until his successor, Andrew Johnson, reinstated it in 1865.

Lincoln's unilateral suspension of this core component of **civil liberties** protection in the Constitution remains one of the most contentious points of his presidency. Scholars continue to debate Taney's motives as well since the chief justice was a Democrat and political opponent of Lincoln. The Supreme Court ruled in ***Ex Parte Milligan*** (1866) that the use of military tribunals in lieu of civilian courts still in operation was unconstitutional. *See also BOUMEDIENE V. BUSH* (2008); *EX PARTE QUIRIN* (1942); *HAMDAN V. RUMSFELD* (2006).

***EX PARTE MILLIGAN* (1866)**

This post–Civil War **Supreme Court** case took up the question of military tribunals. Lambdin Milligan, along with four others, were tried and convicted by a military commission in Indiana in 1864 for plans to liberate Confederate soldiers and a host of other charges of disloyalty to the Union and sentenced to be hanged the following year. One of the lawyers who argued on Milligan's behalf was James Garfield, who would be elected president in 1880. In a unanimous decision, the high court ruled that while President Lincoln's suspension of **habeas corpus** was constitutional, it was *unconstitutional* to subject citizens to military trials when civilian courts were still in operation. The justices clarified that the suspension only entitled the government to hold the accused, not to try and execute them. *See also BOUMEDIENE V. BUSH* (2008); *EX PARTE MERRYMAN* (1861); *EX PARTE QUIRIN* (1942); *HAMDAN V. RUMSFELD* (2006).

***EX PARTE QUIRIN* (1942)**

This **Supreme Court** decision weighed the constitutionality of convictions of unlawful combatants by military tribunals during World War II. The case hinged on eight Germans—two of whom were born in the United States—who were captured after journeying via U-Boat to the East Coast with instructions to sabotage the U.S. war effort. All eventually disposed of their official military uniforms that identified them as members of the Nazi forces. After their capture, President Franklin D. Roosevelt issued an **executive order** establishing a military tribunal to prosecute them. All eight men were convicted, and six were executed. Attorney Kenneth Royall contended that the Nazi soldiers, having cast off their identifying uniforms, should not be prosecuted by a military tribunal because civil courts were still in operation and cited ***Ex Party Milligan*** (1866). Francis Biddle, the attorney general, argued that the Germans were unlawful combatants who had no recourse to civilian courts because the plans they sought to undertake were the same whether in or out of uniform.

In a unanimous decision, the justices on the high court sided with Biddle. Author of the opinion, **Chief Justice Harlan Fiske Stone**, wrote that "Lawful combatants are subject to capture and detention as prisoners of war by opposing military forces. Unlawful combatants are likewise subject to capture and detention, but in addition they are subject to trial and punishment by military tribunals for acts which render their belligerency unlawful." Stone further contended that such belligerents are "generally deemed not to be entitled to the status of prisoners of war, but to be offenders against the law of war subject to trial and punishment by military tribunals." The case was used unsuccessfully as a justification for military tribunals established by President George W. Bush via **executive order**, and later legislatively by Congress, to try unlawful enemy combatants captured in the **War on Terror**. *See also BOUMEDIENE V. BUSH* (2008); *EX PARTE MERRYMAN* (1861); *HAMDAN V. RUMSFELD* (2006).

**EX POST FACTO LAW**

*See* ARTICLE I (CONSTITUTION).

**EXCLUSIONARY RULE**

*See* FOURTH AMENDMENT; *MAPP V. OHIO* (1961); *U.S. V. LEON* (1984).

**EXECUTIVE ORDER**

An executive order is a presidential directive that interprets and implements congressional legislation, a treaty, or a constitutional provision. Executive orders fall squarely within the president's **executive power** and the constitutional provision in **Article II** that he "take care that the laws be faithfully executed." Executive orders directed to departments and agencies to take specific actions have the force of law and must be issued under statutory authority from Congress. Because congressional legislation is often broadly written, and the details of implementation are routinely left to the president's discretion, executive orders have become an increasingly important tool of presidential policymaking and administration.

In the early Republic, presidents used executive orders on relatively routine matters pertaining to the administration of federal agencies. Bold usage arguably commenced with President Theodore Roosevelt, who used executive orders to set aside federal lands for conservation. In the post–World War II period, there has been a significant increase in the usage of executive orders, which has had profound societal impacts, some of which have been highly contentious. Presidents John F. Kennedy and Lyndon B. Johnson used executive orders to prohibit discrimination in housing. At the height of economic chaos with high inflation and high unemployment, President Richard M. Nixon issued an executive order mandating "wage and price controls" to thwart more drastic congressional action, though he had previously rejected such an approach. President Barack H. Obama used executive orders to expand the reach of the Environmental Protection Agency to regulate greenhouse gases emitted from coal plants as a means to combat climate change.

Among the most controversial executive orders are those in the military realm. President Franklin D. Roosevelt issued a highly controversial executive order to intern Japanese Americans during World War II. President Harry Truman issued an executive order to seize the steel mills during the Korean War. President James E. (Jimmy) Carter pardoned draft evaders of the Vietnam War. President William J. Clinton sent troops to Bosnia. And President George W. Bush attempted to establish military tribunals to try enemy combatants in the **War on Terror**. *See also HIRABAYASHI V. UNITED STATES* (1943); *KOREMATSU V. UNITED STATES* (1944); *RASUL V. BUSH* (2004); *YOUNGSTOWN SHEET AND TUBE V. SAWYER* (1952).

**EXECUTIVE POWER**

**Article II**, Section 1, of the U.S. Constitution states, "The executive power shall be vested in a President of the United States of America." The Framers of the Constitution did not, however, define with exactitude the parameters of executive power, leaving the boundaries open to some interpretation. Article II of the Constitution lays out specific responsibilities and prerogatives of the president, including his role as **commander-in-chief**; his nomination power to the courts, to the **Supreme Court**, and to cabinet with the **advice and consent** of the Senate; his power to make treaties, also with the advice and consent of the Senate; his authority to grant **pardons** and reprieves; his power to receive ambassadors; and his power to convene Congress into special session. Article I, Section 7, of the Constitution also specifies that the president has the **veto power**—though Congress can override his decision with a two-thirds vote of both chambers. Finally, the president also has administrative power through **executive orders**, which he can use to implement laws passed by Congress.

One controversial issue surrounding executive power relates to "emergency powers" of the president. The Constitution does not *expressly* grant the president the war power—which Congress retains—or any additional prerogatives. Indeed, a close reading of the debate records of the Constitutional Convention shows that **James Madison** and **Elbridge Gerry** advocated the right of Congress to "declare" war and left the commander-in-chief function to the president in order to "repel sudden attacks"—as a defensive or protective mechanism in light of the collective-action problems of Congress they recognized and the 18th-century context of colonialism in which they lived. In general terms, presidential "emergency" powers require a grant of such authority by Congress. Nevertheless, President Abraham Lincoln's suspension of the writ of **habeas corpus** during the Civil War in 1861 was implemented without congressional approval and in spite of a Federal Court ruling in Maryland (***Ex Parte Merryman***) that found the action unconstitutional. Other actions Lincoln took, including the naval blockade of Fort Sumter, he took with the belief that Congress (which was not in session) would approve.

On the other hand, when President Franklin D. Roosevelt invoked "emergency powers" by issuing Executive Order 9066 mandating the internment of Japanese Americans during World War II, the **Supreme Court** held in ***Korematsu v. United States*** (1944) that his action was constitutional because Congress had declared war against imperial Japan and the president was responding to the urgency of war.

The Supreme Court, however, rejected the arguments of President Harry S. Truman when he seized privately owned steel mills in 1952 with the claim that he required the materials to carry out the Korean War effectively. In ***Youngstown Sheet and Tube v. Sawyer*** (1952) the high court contended that the president had no right to seize private property in the absence of congressional legislation authorizing such action. *See also* EXECUTIVE PRIVILEGE.

**EXECUTIVE PRIVILEGE**

This doctrine refers to the confidentiality of private communications and policy advice between the president and officials in the executive branch, including the cabinet and advisers in the White House, if the public disclosure of those communications would interrupt or impede executive decision making. While executive privilege is not explicitly mentioned in **Article II** of the Constitution, the precedent dates to the early Republic but is not an absolute. **George Washington** refused to disclose information to Congress on the Jay Treaty. **Thomas Jefferson** invoked executive privilege to preclude handing over documents subpoenaed by Aaron Burr in his treason trial, but **Chief Justice John Marshall** ruled in Burr's favor on a **Sixth Amendment** rationale and the president complied with the ruling. The most spectacular case in the 20th century was decided in ***U.S. v. Nixon*** (1974) when the high court rejected President Richard Nixon's refusal to disclose recorded tapes to a special prosecutor amid the Watergate scandal.

# F

**FAIRNESS DOCTRINE**
*See RED LION BROADCASTING CO. V. FCC (FEDERAL COMMUNICATIONS COMMISSION)* (1969).

**FAST-TRACK TRADE AUTHORITY**

This procedure, by which presidents are empowered by Congress to negotiate international trade agreements subject only to an "up or down vote" without amendment by the legislature, constitutes a form of "legislative veto" that was formally struck down by the **Supreme Court** in ***INS v. Chadha*** (1983), but it continues to operate between the branches despite the ruling. *See also* WAR POWERS RESOLUTION.

***FEC (FEDERAL ELECTIONS COMMISSION) V. WISCONSIN RIGHT TO LIFE* (2007)**

This **Supreme Court** case involved **campaign finance** legislation and **First Amendment** guarantees of free speech. The Bipartisan Campaign Finance Reform Act (BCRA), passed by Congress in 2002, placed restrictions on organizations' ability to fund "electioneering advertisements" or "issue ads" in which candidates were discussed but no specific endorsement or call for the defeat of a particular candidate was made. In a 5–4 decision, the court determined that such ads 30 days prior to a primary election or 60 days in advance of a general election were not subject to regulation unless there was "express advocacy" for a particular candidate. *See also CITIZENS UNITED V. FEDERAL ELECTIONS COMMISSION (FEC)* (2010); *MCCUTCHEON V. FEC (FEDERAL ELECTIONS COMMISSION)* (2014).

**FEDERALISM**

This term refers to the division of powers between levels of government on a territorial basis. Examples of countries with forms of federalism include Australia, Canada, Germany, Switzerland, and the United States. In each case the central government has certain **enumerated powers** while subnational units (states, provinces, *Länder*, cantons) have specific powers delegated or reserved to them. Systems with weaker central governments and strong subnational units are generally considered *confederations* (e.g., Canada, Switzerland).

In the United States, the Constitution provides states with a range of competences, largely through the **Tenth Amendment**, which reserves to the states (or the people) powers not specifically granted to the federal level. In some realms, such as taxation and regulation, the federal government and the states have *concurrent* powers. Federalism is expressed territorially through the division of powers between federal, state, local, and special district governments.

**FEDERALIST, FEDERALIST PARTY**

The term *Federalist* generally referred to supporters of the Constitution. They espoused the replacement of the **Articles of Confederation** with a new structure comprising a strong central government and championed financial policies to construct a national economy. Over the course of the Federalist presidencies of **George Washington** and **John Adams**, disputes about centralization of authority and implied powers of the federal government, fiscal policies, and the intractable and overarching question of whether the fledgling republic should support Great Britain or France in those countries' ongoing conflict, symbolized by the Jay Treaty and the Quasi-War with France, led to the emergence of the First Party System. The philosophical quarrel between the Federalists and Democratic-Republicans came to be embodied by the rivalry between **Alexander Hamilton** and **Thomas Jefferson**, respectively. By the election of 1800, Federalists maintained a hold on parts of New England, whereas the Democratic-Republican Party dominated the South and prevailed with Jefferson's election to the presidency and control of Congress.

Critics of the Federalists' support for monarchical Great Britain charged that they were not committed to the **republican** cause. Federalists, however, suggested that the degeneration of the French Revolution into the Terror and then to a military dictatorship under Napoléon Bonaparte represented a potential, if not inevitable, path for republican government absent moderation of the excesses of popular democracy. Ultimately, the Federalists' attempts to undermine their opposition led to the party's disappearance as a political force at the conclusion of the War of 1812, which Federalists ardently opposed. However, President John Adams's "midnight appointments" to the federal judiciary, and particularly **Chief Justice John Marshall**'s influence on the **Supreme Court** from 1801 to 1835, guaranteed Federalists' sway over the development of interpretations of the federal–state balance of power and enumerated powers of the central government, as well as the establishment of **judicial review** of federal and state laws. *See also MARBURY V. MADISON* (1803).

**FEDERALIST PAPERS**

Authored by **Alexander Hamilton**, **John Jay**, and **James Madison** under the pseudonym **Publius**, the Federalist Papers constitute 85 short essays published from 1787 to 1788 in support of ratification of the Constitution to replace the **Articles of Confederation**. Widely read, the Federalist Papers appeared in local newspapers. They were countered by **Anti-Federalist** essays written under various pseudonyms, including Brutus (Robert Yates) and **Cato** (**George Clinton**), in opposition to the proposed constitution, largely due to concerns about **civil liberties** and the power of the central government relative to the states.

The Federalist Papers are ordered by subject. All told, the essays cover issues of foreign influence and danger, the potential for disputes between the states, the failures of the articles, defense, economy, the structure of the three branches of the central government, and the rules governing election of members of the House and Senate and the president. The Framers of the Constitution were particularly influenced by the writings of philosophers **John Locke** and the Baron de **Montesquieu**, who advocated a separation of powers as a check on tyranny.

**FIFTEENTH AMENDMENT**

The final of three amendments passed after the Civil War during the era of **Reconstruction**, the Fifteenth addressed **voting rights**. It was ratified on 30 March 1870. The amendment reads: "The right of citizens of the United States to vote shall not be denied or abridged by the United States or by any State on account of race, color, or previous condition of servitude."

The objective of the amendment was to ensure voting rights for newly freed slaves. However, African Americans were routinely disenfranchised in southern states through **poll taxes**, **grandfather clauses**, and all-white primary elections. In 1876 the **Supreme Court** ruled in ***U.S. v. Reese*** that the Fifteenth Amendment did *not* provide a fundamental right to suffrage. It was not until the early 20th century that the Supreme Court began enforcing the spirit and letter of the amendment. In ***Guinn v. United States*** (1915) the majority struck down grandfather clauses. Over the course of the next four decades, the court dismantled the all-white primary system predominant in some states. Finally, the ratification of the **Twenty-Fourth Amendment**, which prohibited the poll tax, and passage of the Voting Rights Act of 1965 removed significant barriers to blacks' full participation in the electoral process as envisioned by the Fifteenth Amendment. *See also* CIVIL RIGHTS.

**FIFTH AMENDMENT**

This amendment, part of the **Bill of Rights**, was ratified on 15 December 1791. Its **civil liberties** protections include prohibitions against trials for capital crimes or felonies notwithstanding a grand jury indictment, self-incrimination, being tried for the same crime twice, and violation of **due process** of law. Further, the Fifth Amendment mandates that "takings" of private property by the government must be duly compensated. The text reads as follows: "No person shall be held to answer for a capital, or otherwise infamous crime, unless on a presentment or indictment of a Grand Jury, except in cases arising in the land or naval forces, or in the Militia, when in actual service in time of War or public danger; nor shall any person be subject for the same offence to be twice put in jeopardy of life or limb; nor shall be compelled in any criminal case to be a witness against himself, nor be deprived of life, liberty, or property, without due process of law; nor shall private property be taken for public use, without just compensation."

As with the other amendments that constitute the Bill of Rights, the Fifth has been selectively **incorporated** through the **Fourteenth Amendment** and made to apply to the states, not just the federal government. In ***Barron v. Baltimore*** (1833) the **Supreme Court** contended that compensation for takings of private property applied only to actions of the federal government—and held for the first time that the Bill of Rights did *not* apply to state-level actions in **eminent domain** cases. Sixty-four years later, in the eminent domain case of ***Chicago, Burlington & Quincy Railroad Co. v. City of Chicago*** (1897), the high court reversed course. In ***Kelo v. City of New London*** (2005) the Supreme Court broadened the scope of governmental power to take private property to combat urban blight.

With respect to self-incrimination, the landmark Supreme Court decision in ***Miranda v. Arizona*** (1966) remains the standard by which confessions are deemed voluntary and constitutional. Defendants held by authorities must be informed of their right to remain silent *prior* to any interrogation. Further, they must be made aware of their **Sixth Amendment** right to counsel during an interrogation (*see* GIDEON V. WAINWRIGHT (1963)). The typical statement police routinely provide defendants, known as the Miranda Warning, states, "You have the right to remain silent. Anything you say can and will be used in a court of law. You have the right to an attorney. If you cannot afford an attorney, one will be appointed for you. Do you understand these rights?" The decision in *Miranda,* which incorporated the right against self-incrimination, built on several earlier cases, including *Chambers v. Florida* (1940) and *Ashcraft v. Tennessee* (1944), in which the court found that prolonged interrogations were coerced and therefore unconstitutional.

With respect to double jeopardy—being tried for the same crime twice—the Supreme Court incorporated this protection via the Fourteenth Amendment in the 20th century. In ***Palko v. Connecticut*** (1937), a **death penalty** case, a majority on the court held that a defendant's conviction of a lesser crime, and a retrial in which he was convicted and received capital punishment, did *not* violate due process of law. The court reversed itself in ***Benton v. Maryland*** (1969), in which a majority of justices held that a defendant's conviction upon a second trial, after he had been acquitted of one of the charges in the first trial, violated due process.

The eventual incorporation of the Fifth Amendment right to due process through the Fourteenth Amendment has proven among the most controversial with respect to **civil rights** litigation. In ***Hirabayashi v. United States*** (1943) and ***Korematsu v. United States*** (1944) the Supreme Court ruled that presidential exclusion orders targeting Japanese Americans were constitutional during wartime and did not violate due process of law. A decade later, however, in *Bolling v. Sharpe* (1954), a segregation case, the court applied the doctrine of **reverse incorporation**, which held that the **equal protection clause** of the Fourteenth Amendment applies to the federal government through the Fifth Amendment right to due process. Opponents to **affirmative action** have frequently litigated such programs on this basis. Proponents of same-sex marriage, however, effectively overturned a federal ban on homosexual unions in ***U.S. v. Windsor*** (2013) on grounds of a "deprivation of liberty," paving the way for the landmark ruling in ***Obergefell v. Hodges*** (2015) that legalized same-sex marriage nationwide. One significant, contemporary controversy relating to the **War on Terror**, on which the Supreme Court has not ruled, is the constitutionality of targeting American citizens who are suspected terrorists by the U.S. military in foreign nations. Opponents charge that targeting alleged combatants for assassination violates not only due process but also **habeas corpus**.

**FIGHTING WORDS**

Fighting words constitute a class of speech that is *not* protected under the **First Amendment**. The constitutional right to free speech does not extend to language that is aimed at provoking others to violence. The controlling **Supreme Court** case on the question of fighting words was ***Chaplinsky v. New Hampshire*** (1942). *See also BRANDENBURG V. OHIO* (1969); *GITLOW V. NEW YORK* (1925); *SCHENCK V. UNITED STATES* (1919); *WHITNEY V. CALIFORNIA* (1927).

**FIRST AMENDMENT**

Adopted on 15 December 1791, the First Amendment is the cornerstone of the **Bill of Rights** in the Constitution. Its core **civil liberties** protections preclude Congress from making any law respecting an establishment of religion, impeding the free exercise of religion, abridging the freedom of speech, infringing on the freedom of the press, interfering with the right to peaceably assemble, or prohibiting the petitioning for a governmental redress of grievances. The First Amendment, like the following nine amendments in the Bill of Rights, was adopted at the behest of states with large numbers of **Anti-Federalists**, who opposed ratification of the Constitution due to a concern that adequate civil liberties protections were absent in the document. **James Madison**, principal architect of the Constitution, proposed a total of 20 amendments for which 12 were sent to the states and 10 were ultimately ratified.

The **Supreme Court** has set numerous boundaries in its historical interpretations of the establishment clause and the free exercise clause. As with other components of the Bill of Rights, the First Amendment has been made to apply to state actions by the **incorporation doctrine** and the **Fourteenth Amendment**. One of the earliest cases was ***Cantwell v. Connecticut*** (1940), in which the court struck down a state law requiring a license to pass out religious materials. In ***Everson v. Board of Education*** (1947) a narrow majority of justices gave its assent to a program to reimburse parents for transportation costs to private and parochial schools. In the case of ***Zorach v. Clauson*** (1952) the court similarly found that allowing children to leave public schools voluntarily for part of the day for religious instruction did not constitute a violation of the establishment clause. In ***Lemon v. Kurtzman*** (1971), however, the court invalidated laws that enabled states to pay the salaries of teachers in parochial schools. Most importantly, in *Lemon* the high court established a tripartite test for determining whether laws violate the establishment clause. In ***City of Boerne v. Flores*** (1997) the court quashed a congressional statute, the Religious Freedom Restoration Act of 1993, on the basis that the law was "not designed to identify and counteract state laws likely to be unconstitutional because of their treatment of religion." Finally, in ***Zelman v. Simmons-Harris*** (2002) the Supreme Court upheld **school vouchers** subject to a five-part test that drew from the precepts of *Lemon*.

School prayer is another controversial question in relation to the establishment clause. One of the earliest cases in the 20th century involved a New York law that mandated the recitation of a nondenominational prayer in public schools. The court invalidated the practice in ***Engle v. Vitale*** (1962). In a similar vein the Supreme Court ruled unconstitutional prayers at graduation ceremonies in public schools in ***Lee v. Weisman*** (1992). Finally, in ***Santa Fe Independent School District v. Doe*** (2000) the court struck down prayers at high school football games.

Free speech is one of the most complex elements of the First Amendment. One of the earliest challenges to freedom of expression came with passage of the **Alien and Sedition Acts** in 1798. In the 20th century, however, the Supreme Court drew distinctions between different *types* of speech, including symbolic speech and speech that is not protected by the Constitution. Speech that represents a "clear and present danger," as the court articulated in ***Schenck v. United States*** (1919), is not protected. Neither are **fighting words** aimed at inciting someone to anger, as the court elucidated in ***Chaplinsky v. New Hampshire*** (1942). In ***Gitlow v. New York*** (1925) the court determined that speech that would not be considered dangerous in peacetime could be considered dangerous and punishable in a time of war or national emergency. Many such cases like *Gitlow* arose during the First Red Scare after World War I. In ***Whitney v. California*** (1927) the court upheld convictions for communist organizers who violated a state statute barring the advocacy of the violent overthrow of the government. Similarly, in ***Dennis v. United States*** (1951) the court confirmed the constitutionality of the convictions of members of the Communist Party accused of advocating the overthrow of the government. It was not until 1969, in the case of ***Brandenburg v. Ohio***, that the court established an "imminent lawless action" test in judging the constitutionality of criminal syndicalism and "anarchy" laws adopted decades earlier.

Limits on **symbolic speech** are few. One of the few exceptions came in ***U.S. v. O'Brien*** (1968) when the Supreme Court refused to strike down a law banning the burning of draft cards during the Vietnam War but emphasized the noncummunicative impact of such conduct in frustrating government interest. The major precedential case, however, came in 1931 in ***Stromberg v. California*** when the court invalidated a California law that barred the public display of red flags, symbolic of communists. In ***Tinker v. Des Moines*** (1969) the court found that students' wearing of black armbands to protest the Vietnam War was constitutional. And in ***Texas v. Johnson*** (1989) and ***U.S. v. Eichman*** (1990) the court ruled that burning the American flag in protest constituted a protected speech right.

Freedom of the press is nearly limitless in terms of the print media. **Prior restraint**, or the government's attempt to preclude publication of material, is a nearly insurmountable obstacle. The controlling Supreme Court cases are ***Near v. Minnesota*** (1931) and ***New York Times Co. v. United States*** (1971). In the former the high court invalidated a Minnesota public nuisance law that was aimed at halting a newspaper publisher's tirades against minorities and local governmental officials. In the latter case, also known as the "Pentagon Papers," the court did not find that a national security rationale—in this case, the Nixon administration's plea that the publication of a secret government report could damage the peace process to end the Vietnam War—was justification for an injunction against the *New York Times* and *Washington Post*.

**Libel**—false statements against someone that are written, printed, or proclaimed in broadcast media—is not protected speech. However, the threshold for proving libel is high. In ***New York Times Co. v. Sullivan*** (1964) the Supreme Court asserted that newspapers were exempt from lawsuits if false statements were not made with reckless disregard for the truth. In ***Hustler Magazine Inc. v. Falwell*** (1988) the court invalidated an award to a television evangelist for emotional distress connected to libel, contending that no one could reasonably conclude a magazine's parody of him was factual.

One of the more controversial elements of free speech regards the question of a "right to reply" when someone is criticized, is attacked, or has his or her opinion condemned in the media. As with the regulation of public airwaves, the court has made a fundamental distinction between print and broadcast media. In ***Miami Herald v. Tornillo*** (1974) the Supreme Court struck down a Florida law that mandated that newspapers must give political candidates a right to reply in newspapers. In ***Red Lion Broadcasting Co. v. FCC*** (1969), however, the high court found that the fairness doctrine, which requires television broadcasters to air opposing views on controversial topics, was constitutional. As a public good, broadcast media are subject to greater regulation than private print media.

Another contentious free speech issue involves the definition of obscene material. The landmark case is ***Miller v. California*** (1973). In a narrow decision the Supreme Court ruled that obscene material is *not* protected under the First Amendment. However, the majority elaborated a three-part test to determine obscenity, and the threshold is quite high, including the conclusion that the material in question is void of serious literary, artistic, political, or scientific value. In ***Reno v. ACLU*** (1997) the court invalidated a congressional statute aimed at protecting minors from receiving allegedly obscene communications. The statute, according to the majority, was too vague and too restrictive.

Finally, **campaign finance** and regulation has been tied to the question of free speech. In the landmark case of ***Buckley v. Valeo*** (1976) the Supreme Court held that federal limits on candidates' campaign expenditures conflicted with First Amendment protections. In other words, campaign spending is tantamount to free speech. In ***FEC v. Wisconsin Right to Life*** (2007) the justices found that restrictions on "issue ads" in which independent groups oppose a candidate for office but do not advocate for another were unconstitutional. In ***Citizens United v. FEC*** (2010) a narrow majority on the court struck down provisions of the 2002 Bipartisan Campaign Finance Reform Act (BCRA) that precluded independent groups from airing "electioneering communications." In ***McCutcheon v. FEC*** (2014) the court invalidated BCRA's aggregate limits on individuals' campaign contributions (although limits on how much a particular candidate could *receive* were ruled constitutional).

With respect to peaceable assembly, there have only been a handful of Supreme Court cases. The earliest dates to 1876 in ***U.S. v. Cruikshank***, in which the majority refused to incorporate the right to prohibit states from abridging this civil liberty through the **Fourteenth Amendment**. In ***DeJonge v. Oregon*** (1937) the court overturned the conviction of an Oregon communist who was convicted of violating a state law barring the assembly of persons that "advocates crime, physical violence, sabotage, or any unlawful acts" aimed at political change or revolution. In ***Edwards v. South Carolina*** (1963) the high court struck down the conviction of **civil rights** protestors at the South Carolina state capitol was an unconstitutional violation of the right to assembly and to petition the government for redress of grievances. *See also BOY SCOUTS OF THE UNITED STATES V. DALE* (2000).

***FLETCHER V. PECK* (1810)**

This case was the first in the history of the republic in which the **Supreme Court** overturned a state law under **judicial review**. At issue were property rights and the contracts clause in **Article I**, Section 10, of the Constitution. The contract clause states that "No State shall . . . pass any Bill of Attainder, ex post facto Law, or Law impairing the Obligation of Contracts, or grant any Title of Nobility."

As a result of widespread bribery of its members, the Georgia legislature permitted the sale of 30 million acres of land at less than two cents per acre in 1795. The acreage, known as the Yazoo lands, would later become the states of Alabama and Mississippi. A year later the electorate repudiated the incumbent legislators and replaced them, and the new state legislature voided the transfer of lands. Most property owners refused to accept repayment by the legislature and in turn sold their lands to other private interests.

Robert Fletcher had purchased a tract of acreage from John Peck while the statute nullifying the transfer of lands was still in effect. The contract between the buyer and the seller stated that the title to the 15,000 acres was not affected by the decisions of the Georgia state legislature. The question was whether Peck had clear title to the land when he sold it to Fletcher. If the 1796 act by the state legislature was unconstitutional, both Fletcher *and* Peck were able to secure their lands.

In a 4–1 ruling, the Supreme Court found that Georgia had abrogated the contract clause of the Constitution by repealing the grants of land in 1796. Writing for the majority, **Chief Justice John Marshall** posited that "When a law is in its nature a contract, when absolute rights have vested under that contract, a repeal of the law cannot divest those rights." In effect, the court found that Peck had entered into two valid contracts—one with the legislature, another with Fletcher—and he was an innocent third party. The 1795 grants, despite the evidence of corruption in the legislature, were valid. The repeal was an unconstitutional ex post facto law insofar as it sought to strip land buyers of their purchase for wrongs committed by the sellers.

**FOREIGN INTELLIGENCE SURVEILLANCE COURT (FISA COURT)**

Established by congressional statute in 1978, the FISA Court authorizes requests for warrants for wiretaps and electronic surveillance and other searches of suspected spies and terrorists by U.S. domestic law enforcement, such as the Federal Bureau of Investigation (FBI) and the Department of Justice, and intelligence agencies, such as the National Security Agency (NSA). The FISA Court was created to enable intelligence agencies to carry out their missions while still complying with **Fourth Amendment** guarantees against unreasonable searches and seizures.

The FISA Court was thrust into the midst of controversy in 2013 when a former Central Intelligence Agency employee, Edward Snowden, revealed that the court had issued a top secret order that mandated that the cell phone carrier Verizon furnish phone records of its customers to the NSA as part of the ongoing **War on Terror**. Critics charge that the FISA Court is unaccountable and a potential threat to **civil liberties** because all of its proceedings occur ex parte, or with information provided to judges only by government agencies without the defendant's knowledge and without counsel, and there is inadequate oversight by Congress or the public of the court's activities.

**FOURTEENTH AMENDMENT**

Ratified on 9 July 1868, this was the second post–Civil War amendment adopted during the **Reconstruction** Era. The first section clarified that all persons born or naturalized in the United States are citizens of the United States and the states in which they reside. Moreover, Section 1 prohibits any state from making or enforcing "any law which shall abridge the privileges or immunities of citizens of the United States; nor shall any State deprive any person of life, liberty, or property without **due process** of law; nor deny to any person within its jurisdiction the **equal protection** of the laws."

Section 2 effectively eliminated the Three-Fifths Compromise originally set forth in **Article I** of the Constitution by mandating that "representatives shall be apportioned among the several States according to their respective numbers, counting the whole number of persons in each State, excluding Indians not taxed." Section 3 prohibits anyone who had taken an oath of office and engaged in rebellion against the United States from public service, notwithstanding a two-thirds vote by Congress. Section 4 lifts any obligation on the federal or state governments from paying any debt or obligation "incurred in aid of insurrection or rebellion against the United States, or any claim for the loss of emancipation of any slave." Finally, Section 5 enables Congress to enforce the amendment by appropriate legislation.

While Sections 2–4 of the Fourteenth Amendment may be anachronistic, Section 1 provisions prohibiting states from breaching "privileges or immunities," "due process of law," and "equal protection of the laws" have been among the most vehemently contested constitutional issues in the last century and a half. Section 1 first represented an effort by Republicans in Congress to take aim at the **black codes** passed in the South that infringed on African Americans' newly found freedoms after doubts that **civil rights** legislation could be effectively enforced. But even passage of the amendment scarcely guaranteed the enforcement of its provisions. In the ***Slaughterhouse Cases*** (1873) the **Supreme Court** took a narrow view of equal protection of the laws and ruled that the Fourteenth Amendment did *not* apply to state actions. In the *Civil Rights Cases* (1883), a consolidation of five cases, the high court struck down the 1875 Civil Rights Act, which set out to prohibit segregation, as unconstitutional. In 1896 the Supreme Court affirmed "separate but equal" facilities for the races in the ***Plessy v. Ferguson*** decision. That doctrine remained in place for 58 years until the Supreme Court overturned it in the landmark case of ***Brown v. Board of Education*** (1954).

It was not until the early 20th century that the Supreme Court selectively **incorporated** the **Bill of Rights** to state actions through the Fourteenth Amendment's provisions for privileges and immunities, due process, and equal protection of the laws. **First Amendment** rights relative to free speech were incorporated in ***Gitlow v. New York*** (1925) and for **symbolic speech** in ***Stromberg v. California*** (1931); concerning the establishment clause in ***Cantwell v. Connecticut*** (1940) and ***Everson v. Board of Education*** (1947); with respect to assembly in ***DeJonge v. Oregon*** (1937); and regarding petition for the redress of grievances in ***Edwards v. South Carolina*** (1963). **Second Amendment** rights were confirmed in

***McDonald v. City of Chicago*** (2010); **Fourth Amendment** rights in ***Mapp v. Ohio*** (1961); **Fifth Amendment** rights to not self-incriminate in ***Miranda v. Arizona*** (1966) and double jeopardy in ***Palko v. Connecticut*** (1937); **Sixth Amendment** rights in ***Gideon v. Wainwright*** (1963); and **Eighth Amendment** rights regarding cruel and unusual punishment in ***Robinson v. California*** (1962).

The Fourteenth Amendment remains at the center of controversy with respect to contemporary civil rights and **affirmative action**, **voting rights**, **gender discrimination**, and **gay rights** issues that have come before the Supreme Court. In ***Roe v. Wade*** (1973) the high court elucidated an implied right to privacy in the Bill of Rights that struck down state restrictions on **abortion**. Other critical cases include ***Adarand v. Peña*** (1995) and ***Regents of the University of California v. Bakke*** (1978) on affirmative action; ***Shaw v. Reno*** (1993) and ***Miller v. Johnson*** (1995) on racial **gerrymandering**; ***Craig v. Boren*** (1976), ***Johnson v. Transportation Agency, Santa Clara County*** (1987), and ***U.S. v. Virginia*** (1996) regarding gender; and ***U.S. v. Windsor*** (2013) and ***Obergefell v. Hodges*** (2015) with respect to same-sex marriage. *See also* INTERMEDIATE SCRUTINY; ORDINARY SCRUTINY; STRICT SCRUTINY.

**FOURTH AMENDMENT**

This fundamental set of **civil liberties** protections was adopted as an amendment to the Constitution on 15 December 1791. The text of the amendment reads: "The right of the people to be secure in their persons, houses, papers, and effects, against unreasonable searches and seizures, shall not be violated, and no Warrants shall issue, but upon probable cause, supported by Oath or affirmation, and particularly describing the place to be searched, and the persons or things to be seized."

In barring authorities from unreasonable search and seizures, the Fourth Amendment mandates that warrants for searches authorized by the courts must be limited in scope and meet two tests. The first is that the requester must demonstrate and affirm probable cause, or a rational foundation for the belief that criminality or contraband will be discovered. The second is that the specific place and items to be seized, including the arrest of an individual, must be delineated in the writ or warrant issued by a judge. Probable cause, as the **Supreme Court** enunciated in *Carroll v. United States* (1925), is subject to a "common sense" standard, such as the search of an automobile when it is not feasible to secure a warrant and criminality is suspected. The Supreme Court set forth a standard of reasonableness in *Chandler v. Miller* (1997): "To be reasonable under the Fourth Amendment, a search ordinarily must be based on individualized suspicion of wrongdoing. But particularized exceptions to the main rule are sometimes warranted based on 'special needs, beyond the normal need for law enforcement.' . . . When such 'special needs' are alleged, courts must undertake a context-specific inquiry, examining closely the competing private and public interests advanced by the parties."

Evidence from unconstitutional searches is inadmissible in trial courts, per the high court's landmark ruling in ***Mapp v. Ohio*** (1961), which effectively **incorporated** Fourth Amendment protections to state actions. The "exclusionary rule" was first adopted in 1914 at the federal level in *Weeks v. United States*. In 1939 the Supreme Court held that all secondary evidence from illegal searches and seizure was inadmissible in court as "fruit of the poisonous tree," as Justice Felix Frankfurter asserted in *Nardone v. United States*. In ***U.S. v. Leon*** (1984), however, the Supreme Court elaborated an exception to the strict standard in *Mapp* by validating illegal searches by authorities that were conducted "in good faith."

One of the most controversial issues regarding Fourth Amendment protections in the contemporary era has been the question of warrantless wiretaps and the **War on Terror**. In *Katz v. United States* (1967) the Supreme Court ruled that electronic listening devices constituted a violation of the right to privacy under Fourth Amendment protections and that wiretapping is a form of search. In 1978 Congress passed the **Foreign Intelligence Surveillance Act** (FISA), which established a special court to review governmental requests for wiretaps. Following the terrorist attacks on 11 September 2001, the FISA provisions for court approval were relaxed and broad authority was granted to the president under the USA PATRIOT Act. In the administration of George W. Bush the president claimed to have the authority to wiretap individuals without a specific warrant, including U.S. citizens, who were in communication with suspected al-Qaeda terrorists. In 2007 the **American Civil Liberties Union** (ACLU) unsuccessfully sued for federal review of the matter and a circuit court refused to rule on the program's constitutionality after dismissing the case for the petitioner's lack of standing. During the presidency of Barack H. Obama, the National Security Agency's (NSA) electronic eavesdropping program was continued. Although a federal circuit court judge in one instance ruled that evidence obtained against one suspected terrorist was illegally obtained, an appeals court overturned the decision. Moreover, the Obama administration supported congressional legislation that was aimed at indemnifying telephone companies cooperating in providing "metadata" on phone activity to the government. In 2013 a former NSA contract employee, Edward Snowden, released tens of thousands of pages of classified material to the press that documented government oversight in the domestic realm, stirring ample debate and forcing him to flee prosecution in the United States.

**FRANKLIN, BENJAMIN (1706–1790)**

A central figure in the founding of the American Republic, Franklin was born in Boston, Massachusetts. His scientific contributions include inventions such as the lightening rod and bifocal glasses. He championed colonial unity during the Revolutionary War and represented colonial interests in Britain, including efforts to repeal the Stamp Act. He was the first ambassador to France, serving from 1778 to 1785. From 1785 to 1788, he served as governor of Pennsylvania. He was the publisher of the *Pennsylvania Chronicle* newspaper and the *Pennsylvania Gazette*, as well as author of *Poor Richard's Almanack*. Franklin was a delegate to the Constitutional Convention in 1787 and is the only individual to have signed the **Declaration of Independence**, the Constitution, the Treaty of Alliance with France, and the Treaty of Paris that ended the war with Britain. In his later years he became a champion for the abolition of slavery. He died on 17 April 1790 and is interred at Christ Church Burial Ground in Philadelphia, Pennsylvania.

**FREE SPEECH**

*See* FIRST AMENDMENT.

**FULL FAITH AND CREDIT CLAUSE**

Detailed in **Article IV**, Section 1, of the Constitution, the full faith and credit clause mandates that states must recognize "public acts, records, and judicial proceedings of every other state." As one example, a driver's license in one state must be recognized as valid in any of the other 49 states.

In the 1990s a major controversy erupted with respect to full faith and credit regarding same-sex marriage. Anticipating that the Hawaii state supreme court would legalize same-sex marriage, Congress passed the **Defense of Marriage Act**, which enabled states to disregard same-sex marriages in other states. The penultimate question was whether Congress could allow states to circumvent a constitutional provision by statute rather than by amendment. In a 5–4 decision in ***U.S. v. Windsor*** (2013) the **Supreme Court** struck down Section 3 of the statute, which defined marriage as the union of one man and one woman. The majority contended that the definition violated **Fifth Amendment** rights and constituted a "deprivation of liberty." In 2015 in the case of ***Obergefell v. Hodges*** the Supreme Court, in another 5–4 decision, invalidated Section 2 of DOMA by mandating that all states recognize same-sex marriages under the **due process clause** of the **Fourteenth Amendment**.

**FULLER, MELVILLE WESTON (1833–1910)**

A native of Augusta, Maine, Fuller graduated from Bowdoin College in 1853 and read law in Bangor, Maine, following a brief course of legal studies at Harvard. After serving as August city solicitor, he relocated to Chicago in 1856. In 1863 he was elected to the Illinois House of Representatives. President Grover Cleveland nominated Fuller to the position of **chief justice** of the **Supreme Court** in 1888. During his tenure on the high court, he also served on the Venezuela–British Guiana Border Commission and on the Court of Permanent Arbitration in The Hague, Netherlands. He died on 4 July 1910 and is interred at Graceland Cemetery in Chicago.

***FURMAN V. GEORGIA* (1972).**

This **Supreme Court** decision centered on the **death penalty**, and the criteria utilized by states for capital punishment in criminal cases. The Georgia case concerned a man involved in a robbery who claimed to have accidentally tripped on a firearm while fleeing, killing his victim. Because the victim died during the commission of a felony, the accused, William Henry Furman, was found guilty of murder and sentenced to death. The case was combined with several others, including rape cases in Georgia and Texas for which the death penalty was applied.

By a 5-4 margin, the High Court's per curiam decision read, in part: "The Court holds that the imposition and carrying out of the death penalty in these cases constitute **cruel and unusual punishment** in violation of the **Eighth** and **Fourteenth Amendments**." Although a plurality opinion, the majority took issue with the arbitrary nature of the application of the death penalty. As a result, the decision placed a de facto moratorium on capital punishment. In subsequent years, state governments and Congress passed a host of laws aimed at surmounting indiscriminate application of capital punishment. In ***Gregg v. Georgia*** (1976), the Supreme Court ruled that the death penalty was not, per se, cruel and unusual punishment, effectively reinstating the constitutionality of its use. *See also* DUE PROCESS (CLAUSE); HABEAS CORPUS; *MCCLESKEY V. KEMP* (1988); *ROBINSON V. CALIFORNIA* (1962)

# G

**GAY RIGHTS**

The contemporary debate about constitutional protections for homosexuals has centered largely on state sodomy laws, overt discrimination, and same-sex marriage. The **Supreme Court** refused to invalidate a Georgia law that forbade homosexual acts in ***Bowers v. Hardwick*** (1986). The high court reversed its position two decades later when it struck down a Texas sodomy law in ***Lawrence v. Texas*** (2004), thereby essentially nullifying such laws nationally.

With respect to discrimination against homosexuals, the Supreme Court has made a distinction between public laws and private organizations. In ***Romer v. Evans*** (1996) the justices invalidated a Colorado state constitutional amendment that prohibited the consideration of homosexuals as a "protected class." In 2000, however, the Supreme Court found that private organizations could preclude the participation of homosexuals (***Boy Scouts of the United States v. Dale***).

The other major constitutional controversy has involved same-sex marriage. In response to a potential legalization of same-sex marriage in Hawaii, Congress passed the **Defense of Marriage Act** (DOMA), which defined marriage as the union of one man and one woman. The statute enabled states to circumvent the **full faith and credit clause** of **Article IV** and not recognize same-sex marriages performed in other states. In ***U.S. v. Windsor*** (2013) the Supreme Court struck down the definition of marriage in DOMA on **Fifth Amendment** grounds. Two years later in ***Obergefell v. Hodges*** (2015) the high court struck down another portion of DOMA on **Fourteenth Amendment due process** grounds and legalized same-sex marriage in all 50 states, invalidating bans on the practice adopted in 29 states. *See also* HOLLINGSWORTH V. PERRY (2013).

**GENDER, GENDER DISCRIMINATION**

Women's rights and gender discrimination constitute a subcomponent of **civil rights**. Women's struggle for equal rights historically has focused on **voting rights**, educational and workplace discrimination, and the associated issues of **affirmative action**. With respect to voting, the **Supreme Court** rejected an inherent, constitutional right to vote for women in the landmark case ***Minor v. Happersett*** (1875). Forty-five years later the issue was settled when the suffragette and progressive movements were successful in ratifying the **Twentieth Amendment**. Supporters of the **Equal Rights Amendment** failed to secure ratification of the proposal in 1982.

Questions of educational and workplace discrimination with respect to gender are guided by **due process** of law and **equal protection** in the **Fourteenth Amendment**. In ***Reed v. Reed*** (1971) an Idaho law that gave preferential treatment to men as administrators of estates was struck down. In ***Craig v. Boren*** (1976) the Supreme Court enunciated the view that gender classifications were subject to **intermediate scrutiny**, whereby such classifications must reflect an important government objective. The court struck down discrimination based on gender for admissions to state-sponsored institutions of higher education in ***U.S. v. Virginia*** (1996). In ***Johnson v. Transportation Agency, Santa Clara County*** (1986) the high court affirmed that, ceteris paribus, gender could be one factor in workplace promotions regarding affirmative action and did not violate equal protection of the laws. In ***Rostker v. Goldberg*** (1981), however, the high court ruled that confining the military draft to men only was constitutional. The latter issue remains unsettled as of 2015, when the military lifted the ban from women's participation in all combat roles.

In 1973 the Supreme Court ruled that women were entitled to seek **abortions** under the Constitution in ***Roe v. Wade***. The high court has since confirmed the legality of some state restrictions on the procedure in the cases of ***Webster v. Reproductive Health Services*** (1989), ***Planned Parenthood v. Casey*** (1992), and ***Gonzales v. Carhart*** (2007) regarding late-term abortions.

**GERRY, ELBRIDGE THOMAS (1744–1814)**

Born in Marblehead, Massachusetts, Gerry played an instrumental role in organizing the Revolutionary War. A signer of both the **Declaration of Independence** and the **Articles of Confederation**, he was a delegate to the Constitutional Convention in Philadelphia in 1787 but refused to sign the Constitution in the absence of a bill of rights. He was elected to the First Congress in 1788 and championed the adoption of the **Bill of Rights**, or the first 10 amendments to the Constitution, alongside states' rights. He is immortalized in the lexicon of American politics for the **gerrymander**, or legislative districts drawn for partisan advantage, given his oddly shaped district in Massachusetts. Chosen as President **James Madison**'s vice presidential candidate in 1812, Gerry died a year and a half into his term on 23 November 1814. He is buried in the Congressional Cemetery in Washington, DC, and is the only signer of the Declaration buried in the nation's capital. *See also* ANTI-FEDERALIST, ANTI-FEDERALISM.

**GERRYMANDERING**

Named for **Elbridge Gerry**, whose odd-shaped congressional district in Massachusetts in the 1790s resembled a salamander and was called a "gerrymander" by a local newspaper, this term connotes the intentional drawing of legislative districts for political (partisan) advantage. **Article**

I, Section 2, and the **Fourteenth Amendment** of the Constitution require that each state have at least one representative and that representation must be equal on the basis of population. Since state legislatures are responsible for redrawing congressional districts following the decennial census, the partisan composition of state legislatures has a significant bearing on the practice, and whether Democrats or Republicans may solidify an advantage. State legislatures' redistricting practices are now frequently the subject of litigation by public interest groups and the Department of Justice.

Since passage of the Voting Rights Act of 1965, "racial gerrymandering"—the drawing of districts to advantage the potential for minority representation in Congress—has drawn judicial scrutiny. "Majority-minority" districts were challenged in two major **Supreme Court** cases. In ***Shaw v. Reno*** (1993) the high court ruled that the drawing of districts on the basis of race was subject to the standard of **strict scrutiny**. In ***Miller v. Johnson*** (1995) the court struck down an oddly shaped district in Georgia allegedly drawn on the basis of racial considerations as a violation of the **equal protection clause** of the Fourteenth Amendment. *See also REYNOLDS V. SIMS* (1964); *WESBERRY V. SANDERS* (1964).

***GIBBONS V. OGDEN* (1824)**

This landmark **Supreme Court** case considered Congress's right to regulate interstate **commerce** in **Article I** of the Constitution. The conflict emerged when the New York state legislature granted a monopoly to steamboat operators Robert Fulton and Robert Livingston to operate exclusively in the state's waters. The monopoly began requiring licensing fees for out-of-state operators. Thomas Gibbons, who operated a business between New Jersey and New York under a federal coastal license, challenged the monopoly on the basis that only Congress had the power to regulate commerce between the states. In a unanimous decision, the Supreme Court overturned the New York licensing requirement for out-of-state operators, arguing that the federal licensing legislation passed by Congress superseded the state law per the **supremacy clause** of the Constitution. **Chief Justice John Marshall**'s opinion clarified the interpretation of commerce, which Congress has the sole right to regulate, "among the several states" to include navigation.

***GIDEON V. WAINWRIGHT* (1963)**

This **Supreme Court** case extended the **Sixth Amendment** right to counsel to trials at the state level through the **incorporation** doctrine of the **Fourteenth Amendment**. Prior to *Gideon*, the high court had ruled in *Powell v. Alabama* (1932) that state courts had to appoint counsel to defendants in capital cases who otherwise could not mount their own defense due to illiteracy. In *Johnson v. Zerbst* (1938) the Supreme Court extended the appointment of counsel to all defendants in federal cases who could not afford an attorney. In *Betts v. Brady* (1942), however, the Supreme Court refused to mandate that state courts appoint counsel to defendants charged with other serious crimes, notwithstanding a demonstration of "special circumstances." In 1961, in the case of *Hamilton v. Alabama*, the Supreme Court expanded the right to counsel to capital cases in state courts even if there was no evidence of "ignorance, feeble mindedness, illiteracy, or the like."

Earl Gideon faced charges of burglary in the state of Florida. Too poor to hire an attorney on his own, he requested and was denied counsel by the state. He contended that his Sixth Amendment right to counsel, via the Fourteenth Amendment application to the states, had been violated. In a unanimous decision, the Supreme Court held that state courts must appoint attorneys for any indigent defendant charged with a felony, generally defined as a crime punishable by imprisonment of greater than one year.

Associate Justice Hugo Black authored the **majority opinion**. He posited that "The right to be heard would be, in many cases, of little avail if it did not comprehend the right to be heard by counsel. Even the intelligent and educated layman has small and sometimes no skill in the science of law. If charged with crime, he is incapable, generally, of determining for himself whether the indictment is good or bad. He is unfamiliar with the rules of evidence. Left without the aid of counsel, he may be put on trial without a proper charge, and convicted upon incompetent evidence, or evidence irrelevant to the issue or otherwise inadmissible. He lacks both the skill and knowledge adequately to prepare his defense, even though he have a perfect one. He requires the guiding hand of counsel at every step in the proceedings against him. Without it, though he be not guilty, he faces the danger of conviction because he does not know how to establish his innocence." *See also MIRANDA V. ARIZONA* (1966); WARREN, EARL (1891–1974).

***GITLOW V. NEW YORK* (1925)**

This paramount **First Amendment** case about the right to free speech took place against the backdrop of the First Red Scare following World War I. Benjamin Gitlow, a socialist who distributed copies of his "Left Wing Manifesto" in opposition to the U.S. government, was convicted of violating a New York state criminal anarchy law and was sentenced to five to 10 years in prison.

With the assistance of the **American Civil Liberties Union** (ACLU), Gitlow appealed his conviction on the basis that the state of New York had violated his right to free speech through the **incorporation doctrine** of the **Fourteenth Amendment**. The **Supreme Court**, in a 7–2 decision that may appear contradictory, upheld Gitlow's conviction and ruled that his speech in question was not protected under the First Amendment. However, the majority of justices also found that state governments are *not* permitted to deny their citizens the fundamental right of freedom of expression outlined in the **Bill of Rights**. As such, *Gitlow* was one of the first cases to delineate the parameters of free speech and place standards on the criminalization of unprotected speech. *See also BRANDENBURG V. OHIO* (1969); *CHAPLINSKY V. NEW HAMPSHIRE* (1942); *DENNIS V. UNITED STATES* (1951); ESPIONAGE ACT (1917); FIGHTING WORDS; *SCHENCK V. UNITED STATES* (1919); *WHITNEY V. CALIFORNIA* (1927).

### *GOMILLION V. LIGHTFOOT* (1960)

This **voting rights** case decided by the **Supreme Court** addressed efforts by the state of Alabama to alter the boundaries of the city of Tuskegee as a means of excluding African American voters and creating an all-white constituency. The case arose following passage of the 1957 Civil Rights Act and black activists' growing success in registering voters within the city's confines, threatening the white majority's numbers. The state **gerrymander** created a 28-sided boundary around the city that froze out blacks from the constituency.

In a unanimous decision authored by Associate Justice Felix Frankfurter, the Supreme Court invalidated the Tuskegee gerrymander on the basis of the **Fifteenth Amendment** guarantee that states could not bar individuals from voting on the basis of race, color, or condition of previous servitude. In his majority opinion Frankfurter asserted that "A statute which is alleged to have worked unconstitutional deprivations of petitioners' rights is not immune to attack simply because the mechanism employed by the legislature is a redefinition of municipal boundaries. According to the allegations here made, the Alabama Legislature has not merely redrawn the Tuskegee city limits with incidental inconvenience to the petitioners; it is more accurate to say that it has deprived the petitioners of the municipal franchise and consequent rights and to that end it has incidentally changed the city's boundaries. While in form this is merely an act redefining metes and bounds, if the allegations are established, the inescapable human effect of this essay in geometry and geography is to despoil colored citizens, and only colored citizens, of their theretofore enjoyed voting rights. . . . When a State exercises power wholly within the domain of state interest, it is insulated from federal judicial review. But such insulation is not carried over when state power is used as an instrument for circumventing a federally protected right."

The case was critical as a precedent to the court's future review of voting rights and gerrymandering, particularly in the case of ***Baker v. Carr*** (1962).

### *GONZALES V. CARHART* (2007)

This **Supreme Court** case centered on the Partial-Birth Abortion Ban Act of 2003 that prohibited late-term (third-trimester) **abortions**. The legislation, signed by President George W. Bush, made no exception for the life of the mother. Two federal courts found the legislation unconstitutional. In a 5–4 decision the high court ruled that the law did not impose an "undue burden" on women. Abortion rights groups, including Planned Parenthood, which argued the case in front of the Supreme

Court, contended that the ruling was a major setback for women's reproductive rights. *See also* GENDER, GENDER DISCRIMINATION; *PLANNED PARENTHOOD V. CASEY* (1992); *ROE V. WADE* (1973); *WEBSTER V. REPRODUCTIVE HEALTH SERVICES* (1989).

***GONZALES V. RAICH* (2005)**

This **Supreme Court** case focused on the power of Congress, through the **commerce clause**, to criminalize through federal law individuals who grew medicinal marijuana in states that had adopted exemptions for marijuana use for medical reasons. The case arose after California voters approved an initiative legalizing medical marijuana. The initiative conflicted with federal law, as the Controlled Substances Act (CSA) did not provide any exemption for medical marijuana. The Drug Enforcement Agency (DEA), which was tasked with seizing and destroying the plants grown by individuals, asserted that federal law trumped state law. Moreover, proponents of the CSA posited that individuals' use of marijuana affected interstate commerce, enabling Congress to regulate or prohibit the cultivation, use, or distribution of the drug under its enumerated powers in **Article I** of the Constitution.

Two California residents sued, contending that Congress had exceeded its authority under the commerce clause. In addition, Angel Raich argued that her life was at risk without the use of medical marijuana. The Ninth Circuit Court of Appeals concurred with Raich and coplaintiff Diane Monson and enjoined the federal government from enforcing the CSA. By a 6–3 decision, the Supreme Court reversed the Ninth Circuit Court's ruling and upheld Congress's ability to criminalize personal marijuana use. In his **majority opinion**, Associate Justice John Paul Stevens rejected claims that the personal use of cannabis for medical purposes was a distinguishing factor. Citing a New Deal–era case, *Wickard v. Fillburn* (1942), regarding wheat regulation, Stevens contended that "Congress can regulate purely intrastate activity that is not itself 'commercial,' in that it is not produced for sale, if it concludes that failure to regulate that class of activity would undercut the regulation of the interstate market in that commodity . . . the case for the exemption comes down to the claim that a locally cultivated product that is used domestically rather than sold on the open market is not subject to federal regulation. Given the findings in the CSA and the undisputed magnitude of the commercial market for marijuana, our decisions in *Wickard* v. *Filburn* and the later cases endorsing its reasoning foreclose that claim."

**GRANDFATHER CLAUSE**

The "grandfather clause" was a mechanism used by southern states during and after **Reconstruction** to disenfranchise African American voters despite passage of the **Fifteenth Amendment**. In effect, statutory provisos or state constitutional amendments conditioned voting eligibility on whether an individual's grandfather was eligible to vote as of approximately the end of the Civil War in the 1860s. Since African Americans were not considered citizens of the United States until the Emancipation Proclamation and passage of the Fifteenth Amendment, grandfather clauses, along with the **poll tax** and literacy tests, precluded blacks from voting. *See also* CIVIL RIGHTS; *GUINN V. UNITED STATES* (1915); JIM CROW LAWS; TWENTY-FOURTH AMENDMENT; VOTING RIGHTS.

***GRATZ V. BOLLINGER* (2003)**

This **civil rights** case focused on an **affirmative action** program in higher education. At issue was a "point system" utilized by the University of Michigan that gave a "bonus" to minority applicants. Two white students, Jennifer Gratz and Patrick Hamacher, were denied admission to the university in 1995 and 1997, respectively. They subsequently sued the university, contending that the award of bonus points to underrepresented groups violated their **Fourteenth Amendment** rights. In a 6–3 decision, the **Supreme Court** held that because the university's "freshman admissions policy is not narrowly tailored to achieve respondents' asserted interest in diversity, the policy violates the **equal protection clause**." Citing the prior case of ***Regents of the University of California v. Bakke*** (1978), the majority asserted that nothing in that rule "signaled that a university may employ whatever means it desires to achieve diversity without regard to the limits imposed by **strict scrutiny**." *See also* *GRUTTER V. BOLLINGER* (2003).

**GREAT COMPROMISE**

Also known as the Connecticut Compromise, the Great Compromise reconciled competing plans for legislative representation in the new national government at the Constitutional Convention in Philadelphia in 1787. At the core of the debate was the representation of large- and small-population states. The **New Jersey Plan**, articulated by William Paterson, advocated a unicameral legislature for Congress in which states each had a single vote, as under the **Articles of Confederation**. The **Virginia Plan**, also known as the Randolph Plan (for Edmund Randolph), proposed a bicameral legislature in which representation would be weighted by population.

Fashioned by **Oliver Ellsworth** and **Roger Sherman**, the Great Compromise melded the two proposals to settle the difficulties of securing small-population and large-population states. The lower chamber of the legislature, the House of Representatives, would be elected on the basis of state population. (The Three-Fifths Compromise would further detail that slaves would count as three-fifths of a person for representation in the House; the **Fourteenth Amendment** repealed this provision in 1868.) Seats in the upper chamber of the legislature, the Senate, would be apportioned equally and members chosen by state legislatures (until the **Seventeenth Amendment**, adopted in 1913).

***GREGG V. GEORGIA* (1976)**

This landmark **Supreme Court** decision reversed the moratorium on the imposition of the **death penalty** in *Furman v. Georgia* four years earlier. In *Furman* the high court asserted that state laws regarding capital punishment suffered from arbitrariness and a lack of consistent standards in the application of the death penalty. As such, the majority found under *Furman* that the lack of standards violated the **Eighth Amendment** regarding cruel and unusual punishment, though a majority could not agree on a controlling opinion on what those standards should be.

The *Gregg* case represented the consolidation of five different death penalty cases. The petitioners had been convicted of murder and had their sentences upheld at the state level. The states in question—Georgia, Florida, Louisiana, North Carolina, and Texas—had all changed their death penalty statutes in the aftermath of *Furman*.

In a 7–2 decision, the Supreme Court held that imposition of the death penalty does *not* automatically constitute a violation of Eighth Amendment rights. Instead, the majority articulated a two-pronged approach to constitutional review. First, a jury must apply objective standards that limit its discretion, and its decision must be subject to meaningful appellate review. Second, whether a judge or jury pronounces such a sentence, a defendant's character and record must be considered; mandatory sentencing is therefore unconstitutional. The high court held that the Georgia, Florida, and Texas guidelines passed muster. The justices rejected the Louisiana and North Carolina guidelines on the basis that they included mandatory imposition of the death penalty or were too rigid, respectively. *See also* BURGER, WARREN (1907–1995).

***GRISWOLD V. CONNECTICUT* (1965)**

This historic **Supreme Court** case concerned a Connecticut law that prohibited the use of contraceptives. Estelle Griswold and a colleague, Dr. Buxton of the Yale Medical School, set up a Planned Parenthood clinic in New Haven, Connecticut, and were convicted and fined for discussing contraception with patients. On appeal to the high court, the justices decided by a 7–2 margin that a "right to privacy" that protected marital relations existed implicitly in the Constitution.

The author of the **majority opinion**, Associate Justice William O. Douglas, contended that "The present case, then, concerns a relationship lying within the zone of privacy created by several fundamental constitutional guarantees. And it concerns a law which, in forbidding the use of contraceptives, rather than regulating their manufacture or sale, seeks to achieve its goals by means having a maximum destructive impact upon that relationship. Such a law cannot stand in light of the familiar principle, so often applied by this Court, that a governmental purpose to control or prevent activities constitutionally subject to state regulation may not be achieved by means which sweep unnecessarily broadly and thereby invade the area of protected freedoms." The **concurring opinions** in the ruling cited both the **Ninth Amendment** (reservation clause) as well the **Fifth Amendment** right not to self-incriminate and the **Fourteenth Amendment** right to **due process** and protection from governmental interference to buttress the conclusion. The watershed ruling provided part of the rationale in the case of ***Roe v. Wade*** (1973), which legalized **abortion** nationwide.

*GRUTTER V. BOLLINGER* **(2003)**

This **Supreme Court** case pivoted on the question of **affirmative action** in higher education. At issue was the admissions policy of the University of Michigan Law School, which used race as a factor and contended that the institution's policy served a "compelling interest in achieving diversity among its student body." Barbara Grutter, a white student with impressive academic credentials, was denied admission and argued that the Law School utilized race as a predominant factor in admissions decisions that advantaged minority students, thereby violating **equal protection** under the **Fourteenth Amendment**.

In a 5–4 decision, the majority of justices ruled that the admissions policy did not violate the Constitution and was consistent with the prior decision in ***Regents of the University of California v. Bakke*** (1978) insofar as the school had not erected a system that was tantamount to the imposition of quotas. While the admissions policy favored "underrepresented minority groups," it passed muster under **strict scrutiny** by considering individual factors other than race. *See also* CIVIL RIGHTS; *GRATZ V. BOLLINGER* (2003).

*GUINN V. UNITED STATES* **(1915)**

This **Supreme Court** case involved **voting rights** and the constitutionality of **grandfather clauses** and literacy tests that were adopted by states to disenfranchise African Americans. The case turned on an amendment to the Oklahoma state constitution that mandated a literacy test unless a voter was able to prove that his grandfather had been eligible to vote prior to the end of the Civil War, or had been a citizen of a foreign nation. As a result of the wording, illiterate whites were able to vote, but blacks were not.

By an 8–0 decision, the court held that the Oklahoma amendment violated the **Fifteenth Amendment**. In writing the **majority opinion**, **Chief Justice Edward White** averred that "The establishment of a literacy test for exercising the suffrage is an exercise by the State of a lawful power vested in it not subject to the supervision of the Federal courts. Whether a provision in a suffrage statute may be valid under the Federal Constitution if it is so connected with other provisions that are invalid as to make the whole statute unconstitutional is a question of state law, but, in the absence of any decision by the state court, this court may, in a case coming from the Federal courts, determine it for itself. The suffrage and literacy tests in the amendment of 1910 to the constitution of Oklahoma are so connected with each other that the unconstitutionality of the former renders the whole amendment invalid."

Although the court's ruling formally nullified grandfather clauses in a host of southern states, the practice, alongside the **poll tax**, continued until the latter was abolished with the **Twenty-Fourth Amendment** in 1964 and the federal government increased involvement in voter registration and elections oversight following passage of the Voting Rights Act of 1965. *See also* JIM CROW LAWS.

**GUN RIGHTS**

*See* SECOND AMENDMENT.

# H

**HABEAS CORPUS**

Generally translated from the longer Latin phrase "habeas corpus ad subiiciendum et recipiendum" as "keep the body to put it in hand (of law) and retake it," this fundamental **civil liberties** protection in the Constitution is found in **Article I**, Section 9, and constitutes a writ that requires that a prisoner appear before a court to have the legality of his or her detention reviewed. Many death penalty cases are appealed on an emergency basis via habeas corpus to the **Supreme Court**, prior to authorities' carrying out the sentence, to challenge the legality of the court-imposed sentence, the controlling court's jurisdiction, or the expiration of the sentence.

The Constitution elucidates that "The privilege of the writ of habeas corpus shall not be suspended, unless when in cases of rebellion or invasion the public safety may require it." President Abraham Lincoln suspended the writ several times during the Civil War. He defied **Chief Justice Roger Taney** in the case ***Ex Parte Merryman*** (1861) by refusing to release arrested prisoners to the court. In ***Ex Parte Milligan*** (1866) the Supreme Court ruled that Lincoln's detention of prisoners had been constitutional, but the use of military tribunals while civil courts were in operation was not legal.

In the contemporary era, habeas corpus petitions have centered again on the question of military tribunals. In ***Ex Parte Quirin*** (1942) the Supreme Court upheld the convictions of Germans captured out of uniform in the United States. The **War on Terror** spawned a number of challenges to the detention of "unlawful enemy combatants." In ***Boumediene v. Bush*** (2008), a suspected terrorist detainee held at Guantanamo Bay, Cuba, successfully challenged his indefinite detention without court review. In ***Rasul v. Bush*** (2004) the Supreme Court held that detainees had such a right and that the military base in Cuba was *not* beyond the reach of the Constitution. Similarly, in ***Hamdi v. Rumsfeld*** (2004) the high court found that citizens could challenge their detention while contending that the president had the authority to detain unlawful enemy combatants. In ***Hamdan v. Rumsfeld*** (2006) the Supreme Court invalidated the establishment of military commissions to try suspected terrorists that President George W. Bush had set up via **executive order**. *See also* EIGHTH AMENDMENT.

***HAMDAN V. RUMSFELD* (2006)**

This **Supreme Court** case concerned military tribunals that the administration of George W. Bush set up to try suspected enemy combatants in the **War on Terror**. Salim Ahmed Hamdan, a Yemeni national captured in Afghanistan who was al-Qaeda terrorist Osama bin Laden's driver, was detained as an "enemy combatant" at the naval base at Guantanamo Bay, Cuba. He filed a **habeas corpus** petition to the high court, contending that his detention violated protections afforded by the Geneva Conventions and challenging the constitutionality of the military tribunals.

In a 5–3 decision, the Supreme Court held that the president did not have the authority to set up military commissions unilaterally and that such commissions required congressional legislation. Further, the justices held that the military commissions violated the Geneva Conventions, as well as the Uniform Code of Military Justice (UCMJ). **Chief Justice John Roberts** recused himself from the case.

Associate Justice John Paul Stevens delivered the **majority opinion**, in which he asserted that the government's argument that "military discipline and, therefore, the Armed Forces' efficient operation, are best served if the military justice system acts without regular interference from civilian courts . . . is inapt because Hamdan is not a service member. Second, the view that federal courts should respect the balance Congress struck when it created 'an integrated system of military courts and review procedures' is inapposite, since the tribunal convened to try Hamdan is not part of that integrated system. . . . [T]he most relevant precedent is ***Ex parte Quirin***, where the Court, far from abstaining pending the conclusion of ongoing military proceedings, expedited its review because of (1) the public importance of the questions raised, (2) the Court's duty, in both peace and war, to preserve the constitutional safeguards of civil liberty, and (3) the public interest in a decision on those questions without delay. . . . The Government has identified no countervailing interest that would permit federal courts to depart from their general duty to exercise the jurisdiction Congress has conferred on them." *See also* *BOUMEDIENE V. BUSH* (2008); *HAMDI V. RUMSFELD* (2004); *RASUL V. BUSH* (2004).

***HAMDI V. RUMSFELD* (2004)**

This **Supreme Court** case involved a **habeas corpus** petition by Yaser Esam Hamdi, who was captured in Afghanistan and suspected of being a Taliban fighter in the **War on Terror**. Hamdi was detained at Guantanamo Bay, Cuba, as an "enemy combatant" when the military learned that he had dual citizenship in the United States and Saudi Arabia.

A federal court in the Fourth Circuit overturned a district court ruling and posited that Hamdi did not have the right to challenge his indefinite detention. The federal court contended that his detention was constitutional under **Article II** of the Constitution, which gives the president broad latitude in times of war. Hamdi subsequently petitioned the high court for relief. A majority of justices contended that President George W.

Bush had the authority to detain unlawful enemy combatants, but that citizens have the fundamental right to challenge their detention. As Associate Justice Sandra Day O'Connor wrote in the **majority opinion** joined by **Chief Justice John Roberts**, "a citizen-detainee seeking to challenge his classification as an enemy combatant must receive notice of the factual basis for his classification, and a fair opportunity to rebut the Government's factual assertions before a neutral decisionmaker. . . . At the same time, the exigencies of the circumstances may demand that, aside from these core elements, enemy combatant proceedings may be tailored to alleviate their uncommon potential to burden the Executive at a time of ongoing military conflict." *See also BOUMEDIENE V. BUSH* (2008); *HAMDAN V. RUMSFELD* (2006); *RASUL V. BUSH* (2004).

**HAMILTON, ALEXANDER (1755–1804)**

Born in the West Indies as an illegitimate child to a father who abandoned him, Hamilton was orphaned at age 13 when his mother died. He made his way to New Jersey and ultimately studied at King's College (modern-day Columbia University), where he took up the Revolutionary cause. During the Revolutionary War, Hamilton served as aide-de-camp to General **George Washington**. He later practiced law and became a pivotal figure in crafting the institutional framework of the new Republic. He attended not only the Annapolis Conference called for by **James Madison** in 1786 to discuss the weaknesses of the **Articles of Confederation** but also the convention in Philadelphia a year later that shaped the Constitution, and he was a signatory to the foundational document. Hamilton wrote many of the **Federalist Papers** in support of the new Constitution alongside **James Madison** and **John Jay**. His essays include the most consequential and robustly passionate defenses of the powers and functions of the presidency in Federalist nos. 67–77, from the **veto power** to rebuffing critics who warned of an inevitable tyranny. In Federalist no. 70 he posited that "energy in the executive is a leading character in the definition of good government."

In 1789, when the new Constitution entered into effect, President Washington appointed Hamilton the first secretary of the treasury. An anglophile, Hamilton often butted heads with Secretary of State **Thomas Jefferson** over policy toward Great Britain and France. Hamilton's financial policies also placed him at odds with others, including James Madison, which heralded future conflicts that would become exacerbated in the administration of **John Adams** and helped ground the First Party Era. Hamilton resigned as treasury secretary in 1795 in the midst of a scandal involving an extramarital affair. He returned to law practice but remained a close advisor to President Washington. He helped draft the president's Farewell Address delivered in 1797.

Hamilton's poor relationship with John Adams, their mutual enmity, and his maneuvering in the 1800 election ultimately proved his undoing. He first tried to undermine Adams by convincing Federalist electors to cast their votes for **Charles C. Pinckney** in lieu of Adams. When Adams was defeated, Hamilton then turned to manipulate votes to ensure that Thomas Jefferson prevailed over Aaron Burr, whom Hamilton despised. Hamilton was shot and killed in a duel with Burr on 11 July 1804. He is buried at Trinity Church Cemetery in Manhattan, New York.

**HATE SPEECH**

*See* FIRST AMENDMENT.

**HENRY, PATRICK (1736–1799)**

An influential Founder of the American Republic, Henry was born in Hanover County, Virginia. He became an attorney in 1760 after reading law and soon became enmeshed in the Revolutionary cause against King George III. He is best known for his refrain "Give me liberty, or give me death" in a speech in the House of Burgesses in Virginia in 1775, which served as a rallying cry to mobilize forces for independence against Great Britain. Following the Revolution, Henry became an **Anti-Federalist** opposed to ratification of the Constitution. He feared a centralized government at the expense of the states and viewed **civil liberties** protections in the proposed constitution inadequate. He became a champion for the adoption of the **Bill of Rights** from 1789 to 1791. He later broke with the emerging Republican Party of **Thomas Jefferson**, supporting **Federalist John Adams** in the late 1790s as the country debated the aftermath of the French Revolution. Henry died on 6 June 1799 and is buried at Red Hill Patrick Henry National Memorial near Brookneal, Virginia.

**HIGH CRIMES AND MISDEMEANORS**

*See* IMPEACHMENT.

***HIRABAYASHI V. UNITED STATES* (1943)**

This **Supreme Court** case reviewed the constitutionality of **Executive Order** 9066, issued by President Franklin D. Roosevelt following the Japanese attack on Pearl Harbor, Hawaii. That attack heralded the United States' entry into World War II. The executive order empowered the armed forces to impose a curfew and other restrictions on Japanese Americans before they were remanded to internment camps. A University of Washington student, Gordon Hirabayashi, violated the curfew order, was arrested, and was convicted. The constitutional question centered on whether the executive order violated the **Fifth Amendment** right to **due process** by targeting a minority group for exclusion.

The Supreme Court rebuffed Hirabayashi's arguments and upheld his conviction and the executive order. Writing for a unanimous court, **Chief Justice Harlan Fiske Stone** posited that "the aim of Congress and the Executive was the protection against sabotage of war materials and utilities in areas thought to be in danger of Japanese invasion and air attack. We have stated in detail facts and circumstances with respect to the American citizens of Japanese ancestry residing on the Pacific Coast which support the judgment of the war-waging branches of the Government that some restrictive measure was urgent. We cannot say that these facts and circumstances, considered in the particular war setting, could afford no ground for differentiating citizens of Japanese ancestry from other groups in the United States. The fact alone that attack on our shores was threatened by Japan, rather than another enemy power, set these citizens apart from others who have no particular associations with Japan." *See also KOREMATSU V. UNITED STATES* (1944).

***HOLLINGSWORTH V. PERRY* (2013)**

This **Supreme Court** case regarded **gay rights** and the issue of a ban on same-sex marriage adopted via a ballot initiative in California. The case commenced as *Perry v. Schwarzenegger* at the federal district level in California when a circuit court judge ruled that Proposition 8, which was passed by voters in November 2008 and prohibited same-sex marriages, violated **equal protection** under the **Fourteenth Amendment**. Two successive governors of the state—Arnold Schwarzenegger, a Republican, and Jerry Brown, a Democrat—refused to challenge the ruling and support Proposition 8. In a 5–4 ruling, the majority of justices on the Supreme Court asserted that the proponents of the ballot measure lacked standing under **Article III** of the Constitution to challenge the federal court's determination if the state government refused to contest the ruling. The ruling effectively legalized same-sex marriage in California. *See also OBERGEFELL V. HODGES* (2015); *U.S. V. WINDSOR* (2013).

**HUGHES, CHARLES EVANS (1862–1948)**

Born in Glens Falls, New York, Hughes graduated from Madison (now Colgate) University and earned a law degree from Columbia Law School (1882). He worked in private practice and taught law thereafter and was counsel to a special committee in the New York legislature investigating utility company corruption. In 1906 he defeated William Randolph Hearst, the newspaper mogul, for the governorship of New York and was the only Republican to win a statewide office in that election. He cultivated ties with leading GOP Progressives, including Theodore Roosevelt and William Howard Taft, and the latter appointed him to the **Supreme Court** in 1910.

Six years later Hughes resigned from the Supreme Court to challenge incumbent Democratic President Woodrow Wilson for the Oval Office. Although Hughes's record as New York Governor was impressive, the Progressive Party supported Wilson, which distracted from Hughes's progressive policies and focused attention on his more conservative stances on taxation and economics. The very close outcome hinged on California, where Wilson narrowly prevailed to win reelection on the refrain that he had kept the country out of World War I.

In 1921 Hughes returned to public service when President Warren Harding appointed him secretary of state. In 1930 President Herbert Hoover appointed him **chief justice** of the Supreme Court, and he would serve on the high court until 1941, during which time he variably supported and challenged important elements of President Franklin D.

Roosevelt's New Deal and quietly sought to undermine his court-packing plan. Hughes died on 27 August 1948 in Osterville, Massachusetts, and is buried at Woodlawn Cemetery in Bronx, New York.

***HUSTLER MAGAZINE INC. V. FALWELL* (1988)**

This **Supreme Court** case focused on the question of **libel** and free speech under the **First Amendment**. Jerry Fallwell, a prominent evangelical Baptist minister and conservative political activist, sued *Hustler Magazine* and its owner, Larry Flynt, for its parody of him. The satirical story line included charges of incest between Falwell and his mother and a replica of advertising from an Italian aperitif for which celebrities had been spoofed about their first sexual experience. Falwell had been awarded $150,000 by a federal circuit court on the basis of emotional distress from the article, not on libel. That court decided that a reasonable person would not have concluded that the parody of Falwell constituted "facts," but that the emotional distress was intentional.

The Supreme Court ruled in an 8–0 decision that the lower court had erred in awarding Falwell a judgment. Public figures are not eligible to receive compensation for emotional distress under the First Amendment. The lawsuit was cast as a 1996 movie entitled *The People vs. Larry Flynt* produced by Oliver Stone.

# I

**IMPEACHMENT**

**Article II**, Section 4, of the Constitution provides that the "President, Vice President, and all civil officers" of the United States are subject to removal. The House of Representatives has the sole power of impeachment, and the Senate the sole power to try the impeachment. A two-thirds vote of the Senate is required for removal. The chief justice of the **Supreme Court** is the presiding judge at a Senate trial.

Article II, Section 4, states that "treason, bribery, or other high crimes and misdemeanors" are the only basis for impeachment and removal. Since 1797 only 16 federal officials, including two presidents, have been impeached. Of the total of seven convictions in the Senate, all have been judges.

While treason and bribery are offenses rooted in legal precedent in English common law, the Founders furnished no interpretation as to what constitutes a "high crime or misdemeanor." They realized that impeachment was likely to be a politicized affair, and the bicameral process and supermajority vote required for removal was a safeguard against abuse. As **Alexander Hamilton** wrote in **Federalist** no. 65, "A well-constituted court for the trial of impeachments is an object not more to be desired than difficult to be obtained in a government wholly elective. The subjects of its jurisdiction are those offenses which proceed from the misconduct of public men, or, in other words, from the abuse or violation of some public trust. They are of a nature which may with peculiar propriety be denominated POLITICAL, as they relate chiefly to injuries done immediately to the society itself. The prosecution of them, for this reason, will seldom fail to agitate the passions of the whole community, and to divide it into parties more or less friendly or inimical to the accused. In many cases it will connect itself with the pre-existing factions, and will enlist all their animosities, partialities, influence, and interest on one side or on the other; and in such cases there will always be the greatest danger that the decision will be regulated more by the comparative strength of parties, than by the real demonstrations of innocence or guilt."

Indeed, the two formal impeachments of presidents in the history of the Republic demonstrate strong political overtones by the executives' detractors. Andrew Johnson offended many radical Republicans in Congress by engaging in a speechmaking tour in which he castigated members for **Reconstruction** policies in the South. Congress responded by passing the **Tenure of Office Act**, which prohibited the president from firing members of his cabinet without legislative approval. Although the act was repealed and later declared unconstitutional by the Supreme Court in *Myers v. United States* (1926), Johnson's firing of his secretary of war, Edward M. Stanton, was used as a pretext for impeachment by the House in 1868. At Johnson's Senate trial, the dynamics of which John F. Kennedy documented in his prize-winning book *Profiles in Courage*, the vote for removal was just one shy of the two-thirds requirement.

William J. (Bill) Clinton was impeached by the House of Representatives in December 1998 on the charges of obstruction of justice and perjury. The charges stemmed from his involvement in, and alleged attempts to cover up, a sexual relationship he had with a White House intern, Monica Lewinsky, during an independent counsel investigation conducted by Kenneth Starr. A separate charge of perjury and another for abuse of power failed a House vote. The successful votes for impeachment were adopted largely along party lines, save a handful of members of Congress who crossed the aisle. When Senators voted on whether to remove Clinton, conviction on the perjury charge failed 45–55, and failed 50–50 on obstruction of justice.

However, it is a near certitude that Richard M. Nixon would have been convicted by the Senate and removed from office in 1974 had he not resigned the presidency. Following revelations of taped recordings Nixon made with White House staff and operatives surrounding the Watergate break-in at the Democratic Party headquarters in Washington, DC, and the Supreme Court case ***U.S. v. Nixon*** (1974) in which the president was ordered to turn over the tapes to prosecutors despite his claim of **executive privilege**, the Judiciary Committee of the House of Representatives had voted overwhelmingly for three articles of impeachment—obstruction of justice, abuse of power, and failure to comply with subpoenas. Nixon resigned the presidency on 9 August 1974 after a group of Republican Senators informed him of the likelihood of removal by the upper chamber if the articles of impeachment moved forward. Gerald R. Ford issued a full **pardon** to Nixon less than a month later.

The only member of a president's cabinet to have been impeached was William Belknap, the secretary of war to President Ulysses S. Grant, who was accused of abusing his power to set up "traderships" on military bases for western settlers. Belknap resigned the day the articles of impeachment were approved by the House.

**IMPLIED POWERS**

While **enumerated powers** in the Constitution are those specifically granted to national institutions in **Articles I**, **II**, and **III**, implied powers are those that are not explicitly stated but considered to derive from enumerated powers. The most common reference for Congress is the "necessary and proper clause" (or "elastic clause") outlined in Article I, Section 8, which provides that the legislature shall have the power to "make all Laws which shall be necessary and proper for carrying into Execution the foregoing Powers, and all other Powers vested by this Constitution in the Government of the United States, or in any Department or Officer thereof." Many court challenges have sprung forth from the implied powers of Congress, but the **Supreme Court** has interpreted congressional power broadly. The paramount case was ***McCulloch v. Maryland*** (1819). Although the Constitution is silent on a national bank, **Chief Justice John Marshall**, writing for the majority, struck down Maryland's attempts to tax the bank and reaffirmed congressional power and asserted that "the sound construction of the Constitution must allow to the national legislature that discretion with respect to the means by which the powers it confers are to be carried into execution which will enable that body to perform the high duties assigned to it in the manner most beneficial to the people."

The Supreme Court's power of **judicial review** is another example of an implied power. Nowhere in Article III or in the balance of the Constitution is the purview of the Supreme Court to pass judgment on state actions, or actions of the legislature and the executive at the national level, stated explicitly. Yet Chief Justice Marshall elucidated that such an implied power existed when the Supreme Court agreed to decide the case of ***Marbury v. Madison*** (1803), which focused on Secretary of State **James Madison**'s refusal to issue a writ of mandamus to William Marbury, a "midnight" judicial appointment under outgoing President **John Adams** in 1801.

The scope of implied constitutional powers for the presidency has proven far more controversial, in large measure due to the vagaries of Article II. For example, while Section 1 solidifies that the president has the "executive power," the boundaries of such are undefined. Presidential claims of **executive privilege**, or the right to withhold information from Congress, the public, and others, have proven highly controversial. In recent decades presidents have been criticized for issuing **signing statements** in which they challenge the constitutionality of bills, or suggest they will not enforce provisions, when they sign statutes into law. As another example, Section 3 states that the president "shall take Care that the Laws be faithfully executed" but provides no guidance on implementation or enforcement. **Executive orders**, which require a statutory framework, are an implied power deriving from Section 3. Most contentious, however, are presidential claims to "emergency powers," on which the Constitution is silent.

Scholars disagree whether presidents can legitimately claim extraordinary authority in times of national emergency or war. President Lincoln believed so, suspending the writ of **habeas corpus** unilaterally during the Civil War and defying Chief Justice **Roger Taney** in ***Ex Parte Merryman*** (1861). Congress later approved of Lincoln's actions in ***Ex Parte Milligan*** (1866). In the contemporary era, presidential claims to emergency powers have typically been connected to war and international conflict, with powers allegedly deriving from their commander-in-chief role. The Supreme Court's record on this account has been mixed. President Franklin Roosevelt's internment of Japanese Americans during World War II was affirmed in ***Korematsu v. United States*** (1944), while his establishment of military tribunals to try captured German enemy combatants was sanctioned in ***Ex Parte Quirin*** (1942). In ***U.S. v. Curtiss-Wright Export Corp.*** (1936) the high court suggested that in the realm of foreign policy, the president's implied powers were almost limitless. Nonetheless, President Harry Truman's seizure of steel mills during the Korean War was struck down in ***Youngstown Sheet and Tube v. Sawyer*** (1952). Further, President George W. Bush's indefinite detention of unlawful enemy combatants and the establishment of military commissions in the **War on Terror** were challenged in the cases of ***Boumediene v. Bush*** (2008), ***Hamdan v. Rumsfeld*** (2006), ***Hamdi v. Rumsfeld*** (2004), and ***Rasul v. Bush*** (2004).

**INCORPORATION DOCTRINE**

The incorporation doctrine refers to the process by which the federal **Bill of Rights**, the first 10 amendments to the Constitution, has been made to apply to the states, particularly through the **due process clause** of the **Fourteenth Amendment**. Across time the application has been gradual (i.e., selective incorporation) through successive **Supreme Court** cases following the Civil War and **Reconstruction**.

The case of ***Barron v. Baltimore*** (1833) was precedential insofar as the Supreme Court held that state governmental actions were *not* within the purview of the Bill of Rights, and that the latter regarded only the federal government. Following the Civil War, Congress passed the **Thirteenth**, Fourteenth, and **Fifteenth Amendments**, which explicitly made provisions for due process of law, immunities and privileges, and **equal protection** of the laws found in the **Fifth Amendment** to state governments' actions, in addition to citizenship rights for newly freed blacks. The **Civil War Amendments**, as they are often called, were essentially rebuffed by the high court in the ***Slaughterhouse Cases*** (1873), in which the narrow interpretation of privileges and immunities essentially exempted state governments from the reach of the **Fourteenth Amendment**. Moreover, in ***U.S. v. Cruikshank*** (1876) the court elaborated that **First Amendment** protections did not extend to state governments.

Beginning in the 1920s, the Supreme Court began to reverse course. In ***Gitlow v. New York*** (1925) the court found that the First Amendment could apply to state laws. Freedom of the press and **prior restraint** at the state level were addressed in ***Near v. Minnesota*** (1933). With respect to freedom of assembly, the court incorporated the First Amendment to state actions in ***DeJonge v. Oregon*** (1937). Petitioning for the redress of grievances at the state level was incorporated with ***Edwards v. South Carolina*** (1963). The establishment clause and the free exercise clause were applied to the states in ***Everson v. Board of Education*** (1947) and ***Cantwell v. Connecticut*** (1940).

Incorporation of the **Second Amendment** was affirmed in ***McDonald v. City of Chicago*** (2010). The **Fourth Amendment** provision against unreasonable search and seizure was incorporated via ***Mapp v. Ohio*** (1961) and the articulation of the exclusionary rule. The contours of the Fifth Amendment provision against self-incrimination were extended to the states in ***Miranda v. Arizona*** (1966); the takings provision was incorporated in ***Chicago, Burlington & Quincy Railroad Co. v. City of Chicago*** (1897) (*see also* KELO V. CITY OF NEW LONDON (2005)). Among the most important provisions of the **Sixth Amendment** was the incorporation of the right to counsel in ***Gideon v. Wainwright*** (1963). The **Eighth Amendment** ban on cruel and unusual punishment was incorporation in ***Robinson v. California*** (1962). *See also* REVERSE INCORPORATION.

***INS (IMMIGRATION AND NATURALIZATION SERVICE) V. CHADHA* (1983)**

**INS V. CHADHA (1983)**

This **Supreme Court** case pivoted on the constitutionality of the "legislative veto" and the separation of powers between the legislative and executive branches. At issue was a section of the Immigration and Nationality Act that empowered either the House or the Senate to veto the decision of the attorney general, to whom Congress delegated authority, to allow a deportable immigrant alien to remain in the country. When the House of Representatives overrode the attorney general's decision not to deport Jagdish Chadha, whose citizenship was recognized neither by India nor Kenya (leaving him without citizenship anywhere), Chadha sued to halt his deportation from the United States based on the congressional resolution.

In a 7–2 decision, the Supreme Court found that the act's provision for a one-chamber legislative veto violated the **presentment clause** in **Article I**. While Congress may delegate authority to the executive branch, the legislature must accept the consequences of the executive's decisions and cannot take actions that alter the rights or responsibilities of those outside the legislative branch, including officials in the executive branch. The justices found the House resolution ordering Chadha's deportation invalid and unenforceable.

The court's decision in *Chadha* did not end use of the legislative veto, however. Indeed, the **War Powers Resolution**, which mandates that presidents inform Congress of military actions abroad and secure legislative support after the deployment of troops, remains in place, and neither Congress nor the executive has chosen to litigate the statute's constitutionality. Similarly, **fast-track trade authority**, a process by which Congress delegates to the president the authority to negotiation international trade agreements subject to an "up-or-down" vote without amendments, is another form of the legislative veto.

**INTERMEDIATE SCRUTINY**

This term refers to the standards applied in **judicial review** of the constitutionality of policies that are challenged on the basis of **equal protection** (**Fourteenth Amendment**). **Gender**-based classifications fall into this category. To pass the intermediate scrutiny test, a law that appears to discriminate must further an important government interest by ways that are substantially related to that interest. Intermediate scrutiny is a more scrupulous standard than rational basis review, but not as rigorous as **strict scrutiny**, which demands that challenged statutes be narrowly tailored and serve a compelling government interest. *See also CRAIG V. BOREN* (1976); *JOHNSON V. TRANSPORTATION AGENCY, SANTA CLARA COUNTY* (1987); *REED V. REED* (1971); *ROSTKER V. GOLDBERG* (1981).

# J

**JAY, JOHN (1745–1829)**

A native of Rye, New York, Jay was the first **chief justice** of the **Supreme Court**. He graduated from King's College (present-day Columbia University) in 1764. After reading law, he was admitted to the bar in 1768. A delegate to both the First and Second Continental Congresses, he was elected president of the Continental Congress in 1778 and served in the New York militia during the Revolutionary War. Along with **John Adams**, **Benjamin Franklin**, **Thomas Jefferson**, and Henry Laurens, he negotiated the Treaty of Paris in 1783, which ended the conflict with Britain. A **Federalist**, Jay coauthored the **Federalist Papers** (nos. 2, 3, 4, 5, and 64) in the quest to ratify the Constitution to replace the **Articles of Confederation**. President **George Washington** nominated him as the first chief justice of the United States in September 1789, and he remained in that position until 1795. A year earlier, in 1794, he negotiated the Jay Treaty with Britain, which improved trade relations with that country and angered Democratic-Republicans such as Jefferson, who favored maintaining closer relations with France. Jay resigned as chief justice in 1795 to become governor of New York. He eschewed a second appointment as chief justice by President John Adams, who in turn nominated **John Marshall** for the position. Jay died on 17 May 1829 and is buried on his son's farm in Rye, New York.

**JEFFERSON, THOMAS (1743–1826)**

The nation's third president was born in Albemarle County, Virginia, and graduated from the College of William and Mary in 1762. Considered one of the most erudite men to have held the office of the president, Jefferson served as governor of Virginia during the Revolutionary War and authored the **Declaration of Independence** in 1776. From 1784 to 1789, he served as ambassador to France. President **George Washington** appointed Jefferson the first secretary of state in 1789. He soon found himself at odds with Secretary of the Treasury **Alexander Hamilton**'s economic policies and differed with the latter over support of Great Britain in that country's war with France, as well as the Jay Treaty. A Francophile, Jefferson resigned as secretary of state when French ambassador Edmund Genêt was recalled.

Jefferson emerged as the Democratic-Republican candidate for the presidency in 1796. **John Adams** won the electoral contest, but with the second-highest number of electoral votes Jefferson became vice president under the rules prior to adoption of the **Twelfth Amendment**. He opposed the Quasi-War with France as well as the **Alien and Sedition Acts**, which he worked to undermine at the state level with the Kentucky Resolutions.

In the 1800 presidential election, neither Jefferson nor Aaron Burr culled a majority of votes in the **Electoral College**. The election was thrown to the **Federalist**-controlled House of Representatives, which ultimately chose Jefferson after 36 ballots. Over the course of his two terms, Jefferson reigned in governmental spending and debt. He supported the establishment of the U.S. Military Academy in West Point, New York, and was a proponent of Indian removal. Foreign affairs, however, dominated much of his time in office from 1801 to 1809. The Barbary Wars marked the first armed conflict abroad, though Congress never formally declared war per its constitutional authority. When North African pirates threatened U.S. shipping on the high seas, Jefferson sent the navy to protect American vessels, bombarded Tripoli, and ultimately signed a peace agreement ending the conflict. In 1802 Jefferson sought to purchase New Orleans from the French, and Napoléon Bonaparte offered to sell all French possessions, resulting in the Louisiana Purchase, which doubled the nation's size and removed French colonial interests as an impediment from westward expansion—but also raised the constitutionality of the purchase by opponents. Still, the president faced the difficult task of keeping the United States neutral in the conflicts between Britain and France. The British stepped up harassment of U.S. merchant ships and impressed captured sailors into naval service. Jefferson responded with the Embargo Act of 1807, which halted trade with Britain and had a significantly negative impact on the U.S. economy. He signed a repeal of the measure, which Federalists steadfastly opposed, shortly before leaving office in 1809.

Jefferson left office in 1809 and returned to his Virginia home, Monticello, and 10 years later established the University of Virginia. He died on 4 July 1826, just hours after the passing of John Adams. He is interred at Monticello.

**JIM CROW LAWS**

Adopted by states and local governments in the South following **Reconstruction**, Jim Crow laws mandated racial segregation of whites and blacks in public facilities, including transportation and education. De jure segregation, although clearly a violation of the **Civil War Amendments** aimed at enforcing blacks' **civil rights**, commenced in 1877 and endured formally until 1954. In the ***Slaughterhouse Cases*** (1873) the **Supreme Court** decided that the privileges and immunities clause in the **Fourteenth Amendment** did not apply to states, and thereby emboldened legislatures to enact laws that buttressed racial discrimination. In 1890 Louisiana passed a "separate but equal" law for rail transportation, mandating similar yet segregated facilities for blacks and whites (which were scarcely equal in reality). In ***Plessy v. Ferguson*** (1896) the Supreme Court affirmed the constitutionality of the policy, which was not overturned until the 1954 case of ***Brown v. Board of Education***.

Jim Crow laws had far-reaching and lasting impacts on African Americans in the political and social realms. Combined with the so-called **black codes**, Jim Crow laws kept African Americans economically disadvantaged and prohibited them from voting via **poll taxes**, literacy tests, and **grandfather clauses** that prohibited them from voting unless their grandparents had been citizens (and none were prior to Reconstruction). In the social realm sexual relations and marriages between the races were prohibited, and blacks were refused service in public and private facilities or forced to use separately designated areas (drinking fountains, restrooms, lunch counters) and compelled to attend separate educational institutions. Lynchings and murders abounded, causing an untold number of deaths for which all-white juries in the South generally acquitted alleged perpetrators.

De jure segregation has, in the eyes of many analysts, been replaced with de facto segregation in the last 40 or 50 years due to residential mobility patterns in which minorities constitute majority populations in urban areas as many whites moved to the suburbs. Battles to redress a long history of segregation include busing children as a means to overcome past discrimination and enforce integration; the Supreme Court approved busing in ***Swann v. Charlotte-Mecklenburg Board of Education*** (1971) and then narrowed the scope of such programs in ***Milliken v. Bradley*** (1974). The **Twenty-Fourth Amendment**, adopted in 1964, abolished the poll tax. Beginning with President Richard Nixon's Philadelphia Plan in the 1970s, the federal government has created numerous **affirmative action** programs to combat discrimination, precipitating constitutional conflicts ranging from government **set-asides** of contracts to allegations of "reverse discrimination" against whites that putatively violates Fourteenth Amendment protections. *See also ADARAND V. PEÑA* (1995); *LOVING V. VIRGINIA* (1967); *RICHMOND V. CROSON* (1989).

## *JOHNSON V. TRANSPORTATION AGENCY, SANTA CLARA COUNTY* (1987)

## JOHNSON V. TRANSPORTATION AGENCY, SANTA CLARA COUNTY

This **Supreme Court** case centered on the question of **gender discrimination**. At issue was the decision of a local transportation authority to promote a female employee over a male employee, both of whom were equally qualified, as part of an **affirmative action** program. The plaintiff, Paul Johnson, argued that preferential treatment based on gender violated **equal protection** under the **Fourteenth Amendment**. The case was subject to the test of **intermediate scrutiny** by the high court, which ruled 6–3 that gender could be used as one factor in promotion decisions. Further, the majority contended that the agency's policy did not establish a quota system based on gender and did not create an absolute barrier to the advancement of male employees. *See also CRAIG V. BOREN* (1976).

**JUDICIAL ACTIVISM**

This term refers to debates about the **Supreme Court**'s constitutional interpretations. Critics regard rulings allegedly based on political considerations, that privilege individual justices' political opinions, or that appear to substitute judge's policy preferences in deciding cases to constitute judicial activism (often referred to as "legislating from the bench"). Conservatives often criticize the court for purportedly failing to follow the original intent of the Founders. Liberals often decry decisions that putatively take a restrictive view of governmental power.

**JUDICIAL REVIEW**

Judicial review is the principle that the **Supreme Court** has the **implied power** not only to pass judgment on state laws but also on the actions of the other two branches of the federal government, the presidency and Congress. Although many scholars assert that **Article III** provides an implied power of judicial review to the high court, the term *judicial review* is not found in the Constitution. Rather, the principle was established in the precedential case of ***Marbury v. Madison*** (1803) under **Chief Justice John Marshall.**

# K

***KELO V. CITY OF NEW LONDON* (2005)**

This **Supreme Court** case hinged on the constitutional interpretation of the "takings" clause in the **Fifth Amendment** and the definition of "public use" relative to **eminent domain**. The case arose when the City of New London, Connecticut, proposed a comprehensive development plan that sought to condemn buildings in a neighborhood and ultimately transfer the property to a private development corporation. Susette Kelo and other plaintiffs contended that the city's actions were unconstitutional and an abuse of government power. In a 5–4 decision the Supreme Court asserted that the city's policy was legal and for public use, and set forth a set of criteria on which to assess economic development takings on the basis of legitimate government purpose. These included planning, the expenditure of public funds, the state of blight in the community, and the process by which a nongovernmental developer was chosen. *See also CHICAGO, BURLINGTON & QUINCY RAILROAD CO. V. CITY OF CHICAGO* (1897).

**KING, RUFUS (1755–1827)**

Born in Scarborough, Maine (then part of Massachusetts), King graduated from Harvard (1777) and was admitted to the Massachusetts bar three years later. He was a Massachusetts delegate during the Constitutional Convention in 1787 and signer of the Constitution. After serving briefly in the New York legislature, he was appointed to the U.S. Senate in 1789. A **Federalist**, King supported the Jay Treaty and was appointed minister to Great Britain in 1796 by President **George Washington**. He was **Charles Cotesworth Pinckney**'s running mate for the vice presidency in the latter's unsuccessful challenges to **Thomas Jefferson** and **James Madison** in the elections of 1804 and 1808, respectively. He was elected to the Senate once again in 1813, reelected in 1819, and served until 1825. His Senate career was notable for his opposition to slavery.

In 1816 King was the last Federalist to stand for a presidential election. The election took place as the Federalist Party imploded, discredited for opposition to the War of 1812 and the controversy over the party's secessionist overtones in New England during the Hartford Convention of 1814–1815. He lost decisively, carrying only three of 19 states against James Monroe. King died on 29 April 1827 and is interred at Grace Church Cemetery in Jamaica, Queens, New York.

***KOREMATSU V. UNITED STATES* (1944)**

This landmark **Supreme Court** case pivoted on President Franklin D. Roosevelt's issuance of **Executive Order** 9066, which mandated that Japanese Americans, regardless of their citizenship, be placed in internment camps during World War II. Fred Korematsu knowingly violated a Civilian Restrictive Order that precluded the presence of Japanese Americans from military areas on the West Coast of the United States and evaded internment. Korematsu was convicted and appealed his case to the Supreme Court on **Fifth Amendment, due process** grounds. In a 6–3 decision the justices upheld Korematsu's conviction, asserting that during wartime the protection of the nation outweighed individual rights. In November 1983 the controversial conviction was vacated *coram nobis* by a U.S. district court in Northern California on the basis that the government had utilized false information against Korematsu in the Supreme Court case. *See also HIRABAYASHI V. UNITED STATES* (1943).

# L

***LAWRENCE V. TEXAS* (2003)**

This **Supreme Court** case focused on **gay rights** and the issue of state sodomy laws that criminalized sexual activity between homosexuals. In 1986 in the case of ***Bowers v. Hardwick*** the high court refused to invalidate state sodomy laws on the basis of an **implied** right to privacy in the Constitution as the justices had done for **abortion** in ***Roe v. Wade*** (1973).

The case centered on the arrest of John Lawrence in Harris County, Texas, after police were called to his home and officers allegedly found him engaged in oral sex with another man. Lawrence, who was combative, was charged with "deviate sex" under a Texas homosexual conduct statute. Lawrence and his partner, Tyrone Garner, ultimately pled no contest to charges and were fined $125 and court costs, setting up a set of appeals. One Texas court found the state statute unconstitutional, while the Texas Court of Criminal Appeals found it legal.

In a 6–3 decision, five of the justices on the Supreme Court contended that the law violated **due process** rights under the **Fourteenth Amendment**, while Associate Justice Sandra Day O'Connor cited a violation of **equal protection** of the laws. In effect, the ruling overturned *Bowers* and solidified constitutional protections for gays relative to consensual, private relations. The decision elucidated that community or moral objections were insufficient to justify criminalization of homosexual activity and thereby invalidated sodomy laws around the country.

***LEE V. WEISMAN* (1992)**

This **Supreme Court** case focused on the establishment clause of the **First Amendment** of the Constitution regarding voluntary school prayer. The litigation pivoted on the decision of the principle of a Rhode Island public middle school to invite a Jewish rabbi to deliver a benediction at graduation ceremonies. The family of one student, Deborah Weisman, sued. In a 5–4 decision the high court found that even though the prayer was voluntary and the student did not have to stand during its recitation, the establishment clause precluded both nonsectarian *and* traditional prayers specific to a particular faith. *See also ENGLE V. VITALE* (1962); *SANTA FE INDEPENDENT SCHOOL DISTRICT V. DOE* (2000).

**LEGISLATIVE VETO**

*See* FAST-TRACK TRADE AUTHORITY; *INS (IMMIGRATION AND NATURALIZATION SERVICE) V. CHADHA* (1983).

***LEMON V. KURTZMAN* (1971)**

This landmark **Supreme Court** case focused on the question of legislation pertaining to religion and the establishment clause of the **First Amendment**. The particulars of the case involved Pennsylvania and Rhode Island education statutes that enabled the state to pay the salaries of teachers in parochial schools if they used public school materials (Pennsylvania) or to supplement private school teachers' salaries (Rhode Island).

In a unanimous decision, the Supreme Court invalidated the states' practices. The more important legacy of the case, however, was that the high court articulated a three-part test that set a precedent for determining whether legislation violates the establishment clause. First, any legislation regarding religion must avoid "excessive government entanglement" in religious affairs. Second, the effect of the law must be neither to advance nor retard religious practice. And finally, the law must have a secular purpose. *See also SANTA FE INDEPENDENT SCHOOL DISTRICT V. DOE* (2000).

**LIBEL**

Also known as defamation of character, the definition of *libel* is to print, broadcast, or represent in images known falsities about an individual that harm his or her reputation. Constitutional questions have focused on public officials and **First Amendment** guarantees of free speech and freedom of the press. In ***New York Times Co. v. Sullivan*** (1964) the **Supreme Court** ruled that public officials could only prevail in libel suits when the news media published material with the knowledge that it was false or "with reckless disregard" about its falsity. In ***Hustler Magazine Inc. v. Falwell*** (1988) the Supreme Court reversed a damages award to Jerry Falwell, a reverend and conservative activist, after a magazine had published a parody of him that alleged, inter alia, incest. The justices held that no reasonable person would have interpreted the parody as factual. In effect, the court has established a relatively high threshold for public officials to prevail in libel cases vis-à-vis the print or broadcast media.

**LINE-ITEM VETO**

The line-item veto is an instrument by which the executive can annul specific items (or lines) in appropriations legislation. Forty-four states have a provision for gubernatorial line-item vetoes, though provisos for a legislative override of those vetoes vary considerably.

Presidents dating to Gerald R. Ford argued that a line-item veto power at the national level would enable the executive to halt wasteful spending and reduce government expenditures and deficits allegedly caused by congressional "pork-barrel" programs and special interests. Congressional Republicans passed the Line-Item Veto Act of 1996 as part of the House majority's policy platform known as the Contract with America. The act gave President William J. (Bill) Clinton "enhanced rescission authority." Any item vetoes could be overridden by a simple majority in Congress.

Clinton used the authority 82 times from the time of the bill's passage until early 1998. However, a group of senators led by Robert Byrd of West Virginia sued in federal court to declare the line-item veto unconstitutional. In February 1998, a New York federal court agreed and struck the law down. The **Supreme Court** weighed in on the issue following an appeal, and in ***Clinton v. City of New York*** (1998) the justices decided by a 6–3 decision that the law violated the **presentment clause** in Article I, Section 7, of the Constitution. The high court determined that the law contravened the provision that the president either sign an entire bill or return it to Congress, and that there was no condition under which the president could strike down only part of a bill.

### *LOCHNER V. NEW YORK* (1905)

This landmark **Supreme Court** case under **Chief Justice Melville Fuller** set a critical precedent from the Progressive Era through the Great Depression with respect to the federal government's efforts to regulate the economy. At issue was a New York State law (the Bakeshop Act) that precluded bakers from working any more than 10 hours a day or a total of 60 hours per week. In a 5–4 decision written by Associate Justice Rufus Peckham, the majority held that the law violated the **due process clause** of the **Fourteenth Amendment**. Peckham contended that the law was "not a legitimate exercise of the police power of the State, but an unreasonable, unnecessary and arbitrary interference with the right and *liberty of the individual to contract* in relation to labor, and, as such, it is in conflict with, and void under, the Federal Constitution" (emphasis added).

Peckham continued, arguing that "It is manifest to us that the limitation of the hours of labor as provided for in this section of the statute under which the indictment was found, and the plaintiff in error convicted, has no such direct relation to, and no such substantial effect upon, the health of the employee as to justify us in regarding the section as really a health law. It seems to us that the real object and purpose were simply to regulate the hours of labor between the master and his employees (all being men *sui juris*) in a private business, not dangerous in any degree to morals or in any real and substantial degree to the health of the employees. Under such circumstances, the freedom of master and employee to contract with each other in relation to their employment, and in defining the same, cannot be prohibited or interfered with without violating the Federal Constitution."

The decision in *Lochner* created a significant barrier to Progressives, in particular, who championed greater labor and economic regulation. Indeed, in the 1930s the high court struck down a number of New Deal policies proposed by President Franklin D. Roosevelt and passed by Congress, prompting the former to launch an unsuccessful "packing scheme" aimed at increasing the number of justices on the Supreme Court. The Lochner "era" terminated in 1937 with the decision in the case of *West*

*Coast Hotel Co. v. Parrish,* in which the majority upheld minimum-wage legislation in the state of Washington, reversing a 1923 precedent.

**LOCKE, JOHN (1632–1704)**

One of the great British Enlightenment philosophers, Locke studied at Oxford and is best known for the influence his *Two Treatises on Government* had on the American Founding. The work focused on despotism and the monarchy, social contract theory, and the centrality of consent of the governed for political legitimacy. Such critical ideas, including the concept of **natural rights**, are best expressed in the **Declaration of Independence** penned by **Thomas Jefferson**. Locke's writings also influenced continental thinkers including **Montesquieu**, whose *Esprit des Lois* also motivated the Founders' thinking about the separation of powers in government.

***LOVING V. VIRGINIA*** **(1967)**

This landmark **civil rights** case regarded the issue of interracial marriage. The lawsuit was brought before the **Supreme Court** after Richard and Mildred Loving were sentenced to a year in prison for violating a Virginia "anti-miscegenation" statute that forbade whites from marrying "colored" individuals. Richard Loving was Caucasian; Mildred Loving was African American. Sixteen other states had similar prohibitions on interracial marriage when the Supreme Court took up the issue.

In a unanimous decision written by **Chief Justice Earl Warren**, the high court struck down the Virginia law as a violation of the **due process** and **equal protection clauses** of the **Fourteenth Amendment**. The justices found that marriage is a fundamental civil right, and the Virginia law was aimed primarily at perpetuating white supremacy because intermarriage between whites and others was the only targeted classification in the statute. *See also OBERGEFELL V. HODGES* (2015).

# M

## MADISON, JAMES (1751–1836)

Coauthor of the **Federalist Papers**, principal architect of the Constitution, and the fourth president, Madison was born near Port Conway, Virginia. A graduate of Princeton University (1771), he served in the state legislature of Virginia from 1776 to 1779. He served in Congress from 1780 to 1783 and then again in the state legislature from 1784 to 1786. He called for the Annapolis Convention in 1786 for the states to discuss dysfunctions of the **Articles of Confederation** in the post-Revolutionary period. During the Constitutional Convention of 1787 in Philadelphia, Madison was a leading author of the nation's foundational document, a signatory to it, and a defender of its contents in the debates prior to ratification. In 1789 he was elected to the First Congress and championed the adoption of the **Bill of Rights**, the first 10 amendments to the Constitution.

Like his friend **Thomas Jefferson**, Madison came to oppose Secretary of the Treasury **Alexander Hamilton**'s economic policies during the presidency of **George Washington**, including the chartering of the First Bank of the U.S. Moreover, he favored continued alliance with France and disagreed with President Washington's Neutrality Proclamation and opposed the Jay Treaty, solidifying the growing rift between **Federalists** and Jefferson's Democratic-Republicans. During the presidency of **John Adams**, he disagreed with the Quasi-War with France and was abhorred by the **Alien and Sedition Acts**, drafting the Virginia Resolutions in protest.

President Thomas Jefferson appointed Madison secretary of state in 1801. He supported the Louisiana Purchase as well as the trade embargo against Great Britain in 1807. Jefferson stood down for reelection in 1808, and Madison received the Democratic-Republican Party nomination for the presidency over James Monroe. In the general election he faced Federalist **Charles Cotesworth Pinckney**, whose party had all but collapsed outside the states of New England. Madison and vice presidential candidate **George Clinton** won nearly two-thirds of the popular vote and carried 12 of 17 states in the **Electoral College**.

Madison's presidency was dominated largely by foreign affairs. On the domestic front, he opposed rechartering the Bank of the U.S. Internationally, the Napoleonic Wars in Europe spilled over into the United States insofar as British trade policy was concerned. Great Britain forbade neutral countries from trading with France, and its impressment of

American sailors and rallying of natives against settlers helped precipitate the War of 1812. He was assisted by "War Hawks" in Congress, including Henry Clay. Antiwar opponents supported DeWitt Clinton in 1812, but Madison was reelected with the support of 11 of 18 states.

Opinion of Madison was as topsy-turvy as the course of the war itself. The British burned the White House in August 1814. But William Henry Harrison's victories and Andrew Jackson's triumph at the Battle of New Orleans gave way to the "Era of Good Feelings" and renewed patriotism and optimism, even if neither the United States nor the British achieved any territorial gain. After vetoing the rechartering of the bank in 1814, Madison came to accept it in 1816 to steer the nation on a sound economic path. The Treaty of Ghent with the British provided the framework for significantly improved future relations. The Federalist opposition all but disappeared.

Madison retired to his tobacco plantation in Montpelier, Virginia, in 1817. James Monroe succeeded him as president. Saddled with debt, Madison became the president of the University of Virginia in 1826. In poor physical and questionable mental health in his postpresidential years, he died on 28 June 1836. He is buried in the family cemetery on the Montpelier estate.

**MAJORITY OPINION**

In **Supreme Court** decisions, a majority opinion is the written conclusion of more than half the justices. Typically, the **chief justice** pens the majority opinion. If the chief justice is not in the majority, the most senior associate justice on the court generally writes the opinion. Majority opinions, like **dissenting opinions**, provide a legal rationale for the justices' views of the case, including the precedents and constitutional interpretations they employed to arrive at their decision. *See also* CONCURRING OPINION.

***MAPP V. OHIO* (1961)**

This landmark **Supreme Court** case involved the **incorporation** of the **Fourth Amendment** prohibitions against unreasonable search and seizure to the states. The court elaborated the principle of the "exclusionary rule" in criminal proceedings, whereby an unconstitutional seizure of evidence by the police must be excluded at all levels of government. The case pivoted on a search of Dolree Mapp's apartment in Cleveland, where police alleged she was harboring a fugitive. The authorities ultimately entered her apartment, presenting a piece of paper claiming to be a warrant, which they confiscated from her, and then seized pornographic material from Mapp's apartment. A valid warrant was never produced. She was convicted and sentenced to seven years for violating an Ohio statute regarding obscene materials.

In a 6–3 decision the Supreme Court overturned Mapp's conviction. In the **majority opinion** Associate Justice Tom C. Clark argued that "If letters and private documents can thus be seized and held and used in evidence against a citizen accused of an offense, the protection of the Fourth Amendment declaring his right to be secure against such searches and seizures is of no value, and, so far as those thus placed are concerned, might as well be stricken from the Constitution. The efforts of the courts and their officials to bring the guilty to punishment, praiseworthy as they are, are not to be aided by the sacrifice of those great principles established by years of endeavor and suffering which have resulted in their embodiment in the fundamental law of the land." The decision clarified that "all evidence obtained by searches and seizures in violation of the Constitution is, by [the Fourth Amendment], inadmissible in a state court." The case was one of the most important for the court's review of criminal rights under **Chief Justice Earl Warren** in the 1960s. *See also GIDEON V. WAINWRIGHT* (1963); *MIRANDA V. ARIZONA* (1966).

***MARBURY V. MADISON* (1803)**

This **Supreme Court** case, over which **Chief Justice John Marshall** presided, set forth the doctrine of **judicial review**. The case revolved around a "midnight appointment" by outgoing **Federalist** President **John Adams** in 1801. William Marbury was appointed justice of the peace for the District of Columbia. When **Thomas Jefferson** took office in 1801, his secretary of state, **James Madison**, refused to deliver Marbury's commission. Marbury subsequently petitioned the Supreme Court for remedy.

The high court found that Madison's failure to give Marbury his commission was unconstitutional. However, the Supreme Court refused to compel Madison to do so by writ of mandamus. Indeed, writing for the unanimous opinion, Chief Justice Marshall contended that the provision in the Judiciary Act of 1789 that enabled Marbury to seek a writ of mandamus from the Supreme Court was itself unconstitutional because that provision conflicted with **Article III** of the Constitution.

The longer-term significance of this landmark case is that by taking the matter, per se, the Supreme Court established the right of judicial review—to pass judgments on the constitutionality of actions of the other two coequal branches of government, Congress and the executive. As such, the case was critical in setting the relative boundaries between the three branches of government and in this case subjected executive branch decisions to judicial scrutiny. *See also* EXECUTIVE PRIVILEGE; *EX PARTE MERRYMAN* (1861); *EX PARTE QUIRIN* (1942); *HAMDAN V. RUMSFELD* (2006); *KOREMATSU V. UNITED STATES* (1944); *NEW YORK TIMES CO. V. UNITED STATES* (1971); *U.S. V. NIXON* (1974); *YOUNGSTOWN SHEET AND TUBE V. SAWYER* (1952).

**MARRIAGE EQUALITY**

*See* GAY RIGHTS.

**MARSHALL, JOHN (1755–1835)**

Born in Fauquier County, Virginia, Marshall was a Revolutionary War veteran. He was elected to the Virginia legislature in 1782 after studying law and was a member of the state's ratifying convention for the Constitution in 1788. In 1796 President **John Adams** commissioned Marshall, along with **Elbridge Gerry** and **Charles Cotesworth Pinckney**, to go to Paris to end hostilities between France and the United States. Marshall wrote the dispatches that led to the exposure of the XYZ Affair and subsequently precipitated the Quasi-War with France. Adams appointed him secretary of state in 1800 after Marshall had been elected to Congress. As Adams's presidency came to a close, in 1801 the president appointed Marshall **chief justice** of the **Supreme Court** after **John Jay** refused the position.

Marshall was perhaps the most influential chief justice in American history. His sway was extensive in championing an expansive view of enumerated powers in the Constitution and centralizing power in the federal government, insuring the **Federalists**' influence well after the party had disappeared by 1816 as a political force with **Rufus King**'s abortive quest for the presidency. In 1803 Marshall's ruling in the case of ***Marbury v. Madison*** established the doctrine of judicial review and buttressed the high court's coequal constitutional status with the presidency and Congress. Marshall oversaw the conspiracy trial of Aaron Burr. His narrow construction of the grounds for treason, and Burr's acquittal, placed the chief justice at growing odds with President **Thomas Jefferson**, who had called for Burr's conviction. Marshall's rulings in a host of other cases, including ***Fletcher v. Peck*** (1810), ***McCulloch v. Maryland*** (1819), ***Gibbons v. Ogden*** (1824), and ***Barron v. Baltimore*** (1833), had profound impacts on the federal–state balance of power and established significant precedents.

Marshall served as chief justice for 34 years. He died on 6 July 1835 at the age of 79. He is buried at Shockoe Cemetery in Richmond, Virginia.

**MASON, GEORGE, IV (1725–1792)**

Born in Virginia, Mason served in the Virginia colonial legislature (House of Burgesses), organized the militia in Virginia at the beginning of the American Revolutionary War, and was the principle architect of the Virginia Declaration of Rights, which emphasized the concept of **natural rights** and preceded the **Declaration of Independence** penned by **Thomas Jefferson**. He served as a delegate to the Constitutional Convention in 1787 but did not sign the document. An **Anti-Federalist**, Mason feared the absence of individual rights in the Constitution and was a **states' rights** advocate. He pressed for the inclusion of a **Bill of Rights** to secure individual **civil liberties**, which was eventually ratified through the first 10 amendments after the Constitution was adopted. Mason died on 7 October 1792 and is interred at his home, Gunston Hall, in Mason Neck, Virginia.

***MCCLESKEY V. KEMP* (1988)**

This **death penalty** case in the **Supreme Court** pivoted on the question of racism in capital punishment cases. The case turned on the conviction of Warren McCleskey, an African American who murdered a white police officer in Atlanta, Georgia. A jury found aggravating circumstances, as the murder was committed during an armed robbery, and recommended a sentence of death—which the trial court followed.

McCleskey appealed the sentence by alleging that racial discrimination played a role in the jury's decision and thereby violated his **Fourteenth Amendment** rights to **equal protection**. He cited a study headed by David Baldus, who found that blacks who killed whites in Georgia were more than four times more likely to receive the death penalty. In a 5–4 decision the Supreme Court rejected Baldus's statistical study and rejected the argument that the death penalty was, per se, cruel and unusual. Writing for the majority, Associate Justice Lewis Powell held that "There is no evidence that the legislature either enacted the statute to further a racially discriminatory purpose or maintained the statute because of the racially disproportionate impact suggested by the Baldus study." Citing ***Gregg v. Georgia*** (1976), the majority opinion further contended that Georgia's capital punishment system was neither arbitrary nor capricious and therefore did not violate the **Eighth Amendment** prohibition on cruel and unusual punishment.

### *MCCONNELL V. FEC* (2003)

*See* CAMPAIGN FINANCE.

### *MCCULLOCH V. MARYLAND* (1819)

This early landmark **Supreme Court** case was critical in delineating congressional power and the contours of **federalism**. At issue was a tax that the state of Maryland imposed on the Second Bank of the United States, created by an act of Congress. The Maryland legislature passed a statute that imposed fines for transactions at banks not specifically chartered by the state legislature. James McCulloch, president of the federal bank in Baltimore, refused to pay the fines.

The Supreme Court case revolved around the question of the **implied powers** of Congress. The state of Maryland contended that the Constitution was silent on the question of banks and that no enumerated power to create them was accorded to Congress. Maryland contended that "necessary and proper" should be narrowly interpreted as those laws passed for the execution of enumerated powers only.

In a unanimous decision authored by **Chief Justice John Marshall**, the justices invalidated the Maryland statute. Marshall made reference to the First Bank of the United States, chartered by Congress in 1791 and championed by **Alexander Hamilton**, cited the supremacy of the Constitution and states' ratification of the document, and provided an expansive view of the necessary and proper clause in **Article I**. While the Constitution did not specifically enumerate the power for Congress to establish a bank, Marshall asserted that "the power to tax involves the power to destroy," and elaborated that the states "have no power, by taxation or otherwise, to retard, impede, burden or in any manner control the operations of the constitutional laws enacted by Congress." In effect, Marshall argued that the necessary and proper clause, as a power and not a prohibition on Congress, enables the legislature to *implement* established powers in Article I. As Marshall concluded, "the sound construction of the constitution must allow to the national legislature that discretion, with respect to the means by which the powers it confers are to be carried into execution, which will enable that body to perform the high duties assigned to it, in the manner most beneficial to the people. Let the end be legitimate, let it be within the scope of the constitution, and all means which are appropriate, which are plainly adapted to that end, which are not prohibited, but consist with the letter and spirit of the constitution, are constitutional."

***MCCUTCHEON V. FEC (FEDERAL ELECTIONS COMMISSION)* (2014)**

This **Supreme Court** case concerned **campaign finance**. The central question was the constitutionality of ceilings placed on individual monetary contributions to candidates and national political parties. The Federal Election Campaign Act (FECA), passed by Congress in 1971, limited aggregate annual contributions to parties and candidates; the Bipartisan Campaign Reform Act (BCRA), passed in 2002, revised the limits on a biennial basis. Although the Supreme Court had ruled in ***Buckley v. Valeo*** (1976) that aggregate limits on contributions to campaigns were constitutional, businessman Shawn McCutcheon challenged the regulation when he approached the limits in the election cycle because he still wished to support other candidates' campaigns.

In a 5–4 decision the Supreme Court confirmed that a limit on how much money an individual *campaign* could receive was legal, but overturned aggregate limits in *individuals' spending* as a violation of the **First Amendment**. Writing for the majority, **Chief Justice John Roberts** contended that "The government may no more restrict how many candidates or causes a donor may support than it may tell a newspaper how many candidates it may endorse." *See also CITIZENS UNITED V. FEDERAL ELECTIONS COMMISSION (FEC)* (2010); *FEC (FEDERAL ELECTIONS COMMISSION) V. WISCONSIN RIGHT TO LIFE* (2007).

***MCDONALD V. CITY OF CHICAGO* (2010)**

This **Second Amendment Supreme Court** case focused on local ordinances that banned handguns and placed restrictions on the possession of other firearms. The constitutional question was, in light of the high court's prior decision in ***District of Columbia v. Heller*** (2008), whether Second Amendment rights were **incorporated** via the **Fourteenth Amendment** and must be applied to the states. In *Heller* the court found that the Second Amendment applied directly since Washington, DC, is under federal control.

In a 5–4 decision the majority of justices invalidated the restrictions on gun ownership at the state and local levels. Following its rationale in *Heller*, the court emphasized the traditional right to gun ownership as "deeply rooted." Associate Justice Samuel Alito accentuated **due process** in the decision, while Clarence Thomas reasoned that restrictions at the state level violated the privileges and immunities clause of the Fourteenth Amendment.

***MCLAURIN V. OKLAHOMA STATE REGENTS* (1950)**

This **civil rights** case regarding segregation in higher education was a precursor to the landmark decision by the **Supreme Court** in ***Brown v. Board of Education*** (1954). George McLaurin, an African American, contended that the "separate" facilities provided to him by the University of Oklahoma were scarcely equal, as they included a desk in the hallway and the cafeteria. In a unanimous decision, the justices on the Supreme Court ruled that it was a violation of the **equal protection clause** of the **Fourteenth Amendment** for public universities to treat students differently on the basis of race. The decision invalidated the restrictions on which the University of Oklahoma had made McLaurin's admission contingent. Decided by the court the same day as ***Sweatt v. Painter***, the case was instrumental in commencing the reversal of de jure segregation of the races and the doctrine of "separate but equal" enunciated in ***Plessy v. Ferguson*** (1896).

***MIAMI HERALD V. TORNILLO* (1974)**

This **Supreme Court** case pivoted on the question of **First Amendment** rights regarding freedom of the press. The constitutional issue was whether a Florida statute giving candidates for political office a "right to reply" in newspapers that editorialized on their candidacies violated the free press clause. Pat Tornillo, who had been critiqued by the *Miami Herald* in his bid for a seat in the Florida legislature, demanded that the newspaper publish his response. The newspaper demurred. The Florida Supreme Court held that the statute and Tornillo's right to respond were legal.

In a unanimous decision, the Supreme Court invalidated the Florida statute as a violation of the First Amendment. Writing for the Court, **Chief Justice Warren Burger** posited that "press responsibility is not mandated by the Constitution and . . . cannot be legislated." Further, Burger contended that the Florida law represented an "intrusion into the function of editors in choosing what material goes into a newspaper and in deciding on the size and content of the paper and the treatment of public issues and officials." *See also NEW YORK TIMES CO. V. SULLIVAN* (1964); *RED LION BROADCASTING CO. V. FCC (FEDERAL COMMUNICATIONS COMMISSION)* (1969).

**MILITARY TRIBUNALS**

This term refers to courts-martial, or noncivilian trials conducted by military authorities. Historically, the constitutionality of military tribunals has been questioned three times: during the Civil War, during World War II, and after the attacks of 11 September 2001 and in the ensuing **War on Terror**. Under contemporary standards, military tribunals operate under the Uniform Code of Military Justice (UCMJ).

Abraham Lincoln's suspension of the writ of **habeas corpus** in 1861, and again in 1863, during the Civil War resulted in the decision ***Ex Parte Merryman*** (1861). **Chief Justice Roger Taney** ordered the release of a prisoner arrested under the president's order, but Lincoln refused to comply. The court later affirmed Lincoln's actions in ***Ex Parte Milligan*** (1867) but invalidated the use of military tribunals when civil courts were still in operation.

During World War II, the court took up the question of the use of military tribunals to try Nazi saboteurs who were captured out of uniform. The high court affirmed President Franklin D. Roosevelt's **executive order** establishing military tribunals in the case of ***Ex Parte Quirin*** (1942).

Following the terrorist attacks on New York City and the Pentagon in Washington, DC, on 11 September 2001, President George W. Bush intended to try "unlawful enemy combatants" captured in Afghanistan in military tribunals. Detainees, held at military facilities in Guantanamo Bay, Cuba, challenged the constitutionality of military tribunals or commissions by filing habeas corpus petitions to have their cases heard before a civilian judge. In ***Rasul v. Bush*** (2004) the Supreme Court held that U.S. courts had the authority to determine whether detainees were unlawfully imprisoned. In ***Hamdan v. Rumsfeld*** (2006) justices struck down the military commissions created by Bush via executive order. In ***Boumediene v. Bush*** (2008) the high court invalidated military commissions established by Congress and ruled that the Military Commissions Act violated prisoners' rights to habeas corpus.

***MILLER V. CALIFORNIA* (1973)**

This landmark **First Amendment Supreme Court** case focused on obscenity. At issue was a California law that made it a misdemeanor crime for the possession, publishing, printing, or distribution of any obscene matter. Marvin Miller, a pornographic film and book distributor, was convicted for violating the statute after sending advertising material that depicted sexual acts. The constitutional issue was whether the state statute was inconsistent with the fundamental right of freedom of expression.

In a 5–4 decision, the Supreme Court ruled that obscene material is *not* protected under the First Amendment. However, the justices modified the test of what may qualify as obscene articulated in the cases of *Roth v. United States* (1957) and *Memoirs v. Massachusetts* (1966) and established a very high bar. A three-pronged test included (1) whether the average person, applying contemporary community standards, would find that the work, taken as a whole, appeals to the prurient interest; (2) whether the work depicts or describes, in a patently offensive way, sexual conduct specifically defined by the applicable state law; and (3) whether the work, taken as a whole, lacks serious literary, artistic, political, or scientific value. *See also RENO V. ACLU (AMERICAN CIVIL LIBERTIES UNION)* (1997).

***MILLER V. JOHNSON* (1995)**

This **civil rights** case concerned **voting rights** and the constitutionality of racial **gerrymandering**. The **Supreme Court** case focused on the redrawing of Georgia's Eleventh Congressional District following the 1990 Census. A group of white voters sued over redistricting by the state assembly that allegedly aimed to help elect an African American member of Congress by constructing a constituency that defied geographic logic, as it ran from Atlanta east to Augusta and south to Savannah. The Georgia legislature did so to satisfy "preclearance" demands by the Department of Justice with respect to the Voting Rights Act; under Justice guidelines, given Georgia's African American population, the state was entitled to an additional majority-black district. The constitutional question was whether the use of race to draw the district violated the **equal protection clause** of the **Fourteenth Amendment**.

In a 5–4 decision that applied the rule of **strict scrutiny** laid out in ***Shaw v. Reno*** (1993), Anthony Kennedy delivered the **majority opinion** that invalidated the district, the structure of which reflected no compelling government interest. He noted that "Appellants cannot refute the claim of racial gerrymandering by arguing the Legislature complied with traditional districting principles, since those factors were subordinated to racial objectives. Nor are there tangible communities of interest spanning the District's hundreds of miles that can be called upon to rescue the plan." *See also WESBERRY V. SANDERS* (1964).

***MILLIKEN V. BRADLEY* (1974)**

This **Supreme Court** case dealt with the issue of school desegregation following the landmark ruling in ***Brown v. Board of Education*** (1954). At issue was the question of bussing students across district lines to achieve racial balance. The Supreme Court had legitimized the use of bussing in the case of ***Swann v. Charlotte-Mecklenburg Board of Education*** in 1971.

In Swann, however, the High Court did not distinguish between de jure segregation in which school districts had adopted legal rules aimed at separating the races and de facto segregation stemming from residential mobility patterns (e.g., "white flight" from inner cities in the 1960s and 1970s) or the drawing of lines without overt racist intentions. Milliken involved schools in the city of Detroit, which were among the most segregated racially in the nation. The National Association for the Advancement of Colored Persons (NAACP) sued the Detroit school district for allegedly drawing school boundaries to enhance segregation. A district court agreed, fashioning a remedy to distribute more white students across the city's schools via bussing than the school district had planned.

In a 5-4 decision authored by **Chief Justice Warren Burger**, the Supreme Court disavowed the lower court's ruling as "wholly impermissible" and affirmed that the drawing of seemingly arbitrary district lines were not unconstitutional if the school district had no intent of exacerbating segregation. The decision was widely considered a significant loss for **civil rights** groups, and arguably contributed to the long term problem of resolving continuing segregation of school districts, whatever the cause.

### *MINOR V. HAPPERSETT* (1875)

This **voting rights** case concerned women's suffrage and **gender discrimination**. Virginia Minor was precluded from registering to vote in Missouri, where only men were allowed suffrage under the state constitution. Minor sued, contending that her citizenship rights and **due process** and privileges and immunities under the **Fourteenth Amendment** of the federal Constitution had been violated. The **Supreme Court** ruled unanimously against Minor, contending that the Fourteenth Amendment did not confer any inherent right to vote for women—or anyone. As **Chief Justice Morrison Waite** wrote on behalf of the majority, "Certainly, if the courts can consider any question settled, this is one. For nearly ninety years the people have acted upon the idea that the Constitution, when it conferred citizenship, did not necessarily confer the right of suffrage." Adoption of the **Nineteenth Amendment** to the Constitution in 1920 effectively invalidated the high court's ruling. *See also* EQUAL RIGHTS AMENDMENT (ERA).

### *MIRANDA V. ARIZONA* (1966)

The lead case, including three others that the **Supreme Court** reviewed simultaneously on the question of police interrogations, the **Fifth Amendment** right not to self-incriminate, and the **Sixth Amendment** right to counsel, the landmark decision in *Miranda* solidified the constitutional rights of the accused. The decision built on the ruling in *Escobedo v. Illinois* two years earlier when the court held that suspects had the right to counsel during police interrogations.

At issue was the confession of Ernesto Miranda, who signed a form after several hours of police interrogation, that he raped an 18-year-old woman. Miranda signed the form, which noted that he did so "voluntarily and of my own free will, with no threats, coercion, or promises of immunity, and with full knowledge of my legal rights, understanding any statement I make may be used against me." The statement was used at Miranda's trial, at which he was convicted of rape and kidnapping and sentenced to 20 or more years in prison for each count. At the trial and in his appeal of the convictions, Miranda's attorney argued that the confession was not voluntary and should not have been allowed into evidence.

**Chief Justice Earl Warren** penned the majority opinion that overturned Miranda's conviction on Fifth and Sixth Amendment grounds. The ruling elucidated that for a confession to be voluntary, a suspect had to be informed of his or her right not to self-incriminate, as well as the right to legal counsel, *before* any police interrogation commenced. Further, as Warren asserted, "If the individual indicates in any manner, at any time prior to or during questioning, that he wishes to remain silent, the interrogation must cease. . . . If the individual states that he wants an attorney, the interrogation must cease until an attorney is present. At that time, the individual must have an opportunity to confer with the attorney and to have him present during any subsequent questioning."

The ruling gave rise to the implementation of "Miranda warnings" issued by police to arrestees to ensure that criminal suspects are aware of their constitutional rights. Generally, the warning informs the defendant of his or right to remain silent, that anything said can be used against the defendant, the right to have counsel present for all questioning, and the right to have counsel appointed if the defendant cannot afford counsel.

Ernesto Miranda was retried following the Supreme Court decision and convicted on the basis of witness testimony. He was sentenced to 20 years in prison, paroled in 1972, and murdered in 1976. Ironically, the defendant charged in connection with his murder exercised his right to remain silent and was released.

The precedent set in *Miranda* survived an important congressional challenge in the case of ***Dickerson v. United States*** (2000). The Supreme Court invalidated a federal law that purported to overturn the necessity of Miranda warnings by instructing judges to admit voluntary statements regardless of whether the defendant had been informed of his or her constitutional rights. *See also GIDEON V. WAINWRIGHT* (1963).

**MONTESQUIEU, CHARLES-LOUIS DE SECONDAT, BARON DE LA BRÈDE ET DE (1689–1755)**

Born in the Aquitaine region of southwest France, Montesquieu was an Enlightenment thinker whose political work *L'Esprit des Lois* (Spirit of the Laws, 1748), which championed a political structure notable for the separation of powers between the executive, legislature, and judiciary, had a profound impact on the American Founding and the Constitution. **James Madison**, principle architect of the drafting of the Constitution, called him an "oracle," and **Alexander Hamilton** refereed to him as the "celebrated" Montesquieu for his political thought. Montesquieu's writings, like those of **John Locke**, played a central role in the Framers' understandings of constitution making and the structural foundations of a **republican** form of government that could best protect liberty and **natural rights**.

**MORRIS, GOUVERNEUR (1752–1816)**

Born in Westchester County, New York, Morris graduated from King's College (now Columbia University) in 1768. He served in the New York provincial congress during the American Revolution and served in the militia. With **John Jay** and Robert Livingston, he helped draft New York's first state constitution. He served in the state legislature and from 1778 to 1779 in the Continental Congress. He was one of the signers of the **Articles of Confederation**. Morris played a central role in the Constitutional Convention in Philadelphia in 1787. A nationalist with aristocratic sympathies, he served most notably on the committee on postponed matters and style, and is credited with penning large sections of the document, including the preamble, of which he was a signatory. In 1792 President **George Washington** appointed him minister to France to replace **Thomas Jefferson**. He remained in Europe until 1799, served in the Senate briefly, and was defeated as a **Federalist** in 1802 in a bid for reelection. An ardent foe of Jefferson's Democratic-Republican Party, Morris opposed the War of 1812 with Britain. From 1810 to 1813 he served as chair of the Erie Canal Commission. He died on 6 November 1816 and is interred at St. Ann's Episcopal Churchyard in the Bronx, New York City.

***MULLER V. OREGON* (1908)**

This pivotal **Supreme Court** decision reflected differential treatment of men and women in the early 20th century. Although in ***Lochner v. New York*** (1905) the court, under **Chief Justice Melville Fuller**, held that labor laws limiting the number of hours bakers could work was a violation of the "liberty of contract," in *Muller* the majority ruled that laws restricting the hours women could work were justified insofar as the state had a legitimate interest in protecting their health. In the unanimous opinion authored by Associate Justice David Brewer, he cited the importance of women's health with respect to their role as mothers. *See also* GENDER, GENDER DISCRIMINATION.

# N

## NATURAL RIGHTS

Understood as universal rights that cannot be abridged by government, the concept of natural rights was at the heart of the American Revolution and the Founding of the Republic. The theory is closely aligned with Enlightenment thinker **John Locke**, who discussed "life, liberty, and the pursuit of property" as fundamental rights in his *Second Treatise of Government*. **George Mason** articulated a version of the ideal in the Virginia Declaration of Rights in 1776, prior to the **Declaration of Independence**, when he wrote that "all men are born equally free" and hold "certain inherent natural rights, of which they cannot, by any compact, deprive or divest their posterity." **Thomas Jefferson** substituted "life, liberty, and the pursuit of happiness" (in lieu of "property") in the Declaration of Independence, emphasizing the *inalienable* nature of these rights, granted by God, before outlining King George III's oppressive policies toward the colonies. A government that violates the natural rights of its citizens is susceptible to legitimate rebellion, as the Continental Congress declared in 1776. The concept of natural rights was clearly at odds with 18th-century royalist thinking, as the sovereign derived his powers from God through the authority of the church. *See also* REPUBLICANISM, REPUBLICAN POLITICAL THEORY.

## NATURAL-BORN CITIZEN

**Article II**, Section 1, of the Constitution states that "No person except a natural born Citizen, or a Citizen of the United States, at the time of the Adoption of this Constitution, shall be eligible to the Office of President; neither shall any Person be eligible to that Office who shall not have attained to the Age of thirty-five Years, and been fourteen Years a Resident within the United States." Similarly, in reference to the vice president, the **Twelfth Amendment** states "No person constitutionally ineligible to the office of President shall be eligible to that of Vice-President of the United States."

The Constitution does not define "natural born citizen," and the **Supreme Court** has not dealt with it in any case. The general interpretation of "natural born" is that one must be born on U.S. soil or to a parent with U.S. citizenship to be eligible for the presidency. "Naturalized" citizens born in other countries are therefore ineligible.

The Founders' rationale for this constitutional provision stemmed from their 18th-century perspective on politics. For centuries in Europe, kingdoms were forged and lost by marriages between monarchs. In **Federalist** no. 68 **Alexander Hamilton** expressed concerns about potential attempts by foreign powers to gain influence within and undermine the inchoate Republic: "Nothing was more to be desired than that every practicable obstacle should be opposed to cabal, intrigue, and corruption. These most deadly adversaries of republican government might naturally have been expected to make their approaches from more than one quarter, but chiefly from the desire in foreign powers to gain an improper ascendant in our councils."

Critics of this provision of presidential eligibility suggest that it is anachronistic in the 21st century, as there is little concern that naturalized citizens would represent foreign powers in the presidency. Indeed, detractors of the provision argue that it has precluded worthy and popular candidates from seeking the office. For example, Democrat Jennifer Granholm, former governor of Michigan, and former Republican California Governor Arnold Schwarzenegger, were recently barred from running because they were born in Canada and Austria, respectively.

Controversies have erupted in the last several decades over presidential eligibility. Critics of Barack H. Obama contended that he was born in Kenya, where his father was a citizen, and demanded that he produce his birth certificate. When the State of Hawaii finally made the official record available, many "birthers" remained unconvinced. Questions also surrounded Republican presidential candidate John McCain's eligibility in 2008. McCain was born on a U.S. military base in Panama, where his father was stationed. Finally, Texas Senator Ted Cruz, who is (as of late 2015) running as a Republican candidate for president in the 2016 election, was born in Calgary, Alberta, Canada, to a Cuban father and an American mother. Some have suggested he is ineligible to seek the presidency.

The dogged questions surrounding eligibility prompted the Congressional Research Service to investigate the interpretation of "natural born." A report completed in 2011 concludes, "The weight of scholarly legal and historical opinion appears to support the notion that 'natural born Citizen' means one who is entitled under the Constitution or laws of the United States to U.S. citizenship 'at birth' or 'by birth,' including any child born 'in' the United States, the children of United States citizens born abroad, and those born abroad of one citizen parent who has met U.S. residency requirements."

### *NEAR V. MINNESOTA* (1931)

This **Supreme Court** case centered on the issue of **prior restraint**, or government efforts to preclude the publication of printed material. Jay Near began printing a newspaper entitled *The Saturday Press* in Minneapolis in which he expounded his bigoted views against a host of groups. Near had taken aim at local public officials in his paper for alleged corruption. A state trial court and the state supreme court enjoined Near from publishing his putatively offensive views about the officials under a Minnesota public nuisance law that precluded publishing, selling, or distributing a "malicious, scandalous and defamatory newspaper."

Near contended that the Minnesota law violated his **First Amendment** right to freedom of the press. By a 5–4 decision the majority of justices on the Supreme Court agreed and used the **incorporation doctrine** of the **Fourteenth Amendment** to apply First Amendment freedoms to state-level actions. According to the **majority opinion** written by **Chief Justice Charles Evans Hughes**, "we hold the statute, so far as it authorized the proceedings in this action . . . to be an infringement of the liberty of the press guaranteed by the Fourteenth Amendment. We should add that this decision rests upon the operation and effect of the statute, without regard to the question of the truth of the charges contained in the particular periodical. The fact that the public officers named in this case, and those associated with the charges of official dereliction, may be deemed to be impeccable cannot affect the conclusion that the statute imposes an unconstitutional restraint upon publication."

The precedent-setting case established an almost insurmountable threshold for government at any level in the United States to bar print publications, even with respect to classified material. *See also NEW YORK TIMES CO. V. UNITED STATES* (1971).

**NECESSARY AND PROPER CLAUSE**

*See* ARTICLE I (CONSTITUTION).

**NEW JERSEY PLAN**

Also known as the Paterson Plan (named for William Paterson), the New Jersey Plan was offered as a blueprint for the structure of national institutions at the Constitutional Convention in 1787 in Philadelphia. The plan favored small-population states by proposing a unicameral legislature based on equal representation (one vote) for each state, similar to the structure in the **Articles of Confederation**. The proposal was generated in response to the **Virginia Plan**, which called for a bicameral legislature based on population. The debate that ensued set the stage for the emergence of the **Great Compromise** (also known as the Connecticut Compromise), by which representation in the House of Representatives would be weighted by population and states would be equally represented in the Senate. *See also* SEVENTEENTH AMENDMENT.

***NEW YORK TIMES CO. V. SULLIVAN* (1964)**

This **First Amendment Supreme Court** case considered the question of freedom of the press and **libel**. The case centered on press coverage of the **civil rights** movement in the 1960s in southern states. L. B. Sullivan, the Montgomery, Alabama, public safety commissioner, sued when the *New York Times* published a full-page advertisement regarding police actions and contended, inter alia, that civil rights leader Martin Luther King had been arrested seven times when he had only been arrested four times. The advertisement also contained other inaccurate accountings of the situation in Montgomery. Sullivan contended that the allegations were defamatory. Sullivan's libel suit was one of dozens filed in southern states against the news media's reporting on the civil rights movement.

In a unanimous decision, the justices on the high court used the **incorporation doctrine** to hold that the First Amendment applied through the **Fourteenth Amendment** and indemnified newspapers from libel suits for false statements if such statements were not made without reckless disregard for the truth. Writing the **majority opinion** for the court, Associate Justice William Brennan asserted, "Injury to official reputation affords no more warrant for repressing speech that would otherwise be free than does factual error. . . . If neither factual error nor defamatory content suffices to remove the constitutional shield from criticism of official conduct, the combination of the two elements is no less inadequate. . . . The constitutional guarantees require, we think, a federal rule that prohibits a public official from recovering damages for a defamatory falsehood relating to his official conduct unless he proves that the statement was made with 'actual malice'—that is, with knowledge that it was false or with reckless disregard of whether it was false or not." In establishing an "actual malice" standard for libel suits by public officials, the court set an extremely high threshold to challenge newspaper reporting. *See also HUSTLER MAGAZINE INC. V. FALWELL* (1988).

***NEW YORK TIMES CO. V. UNITED STATES* (1971)**

Also known as the "Pentagon Papers," this **Supreme Court** case pivoted on efforts by the administration of Richard Nixon to preclude newspapers from publishing sensitive documents relating to the Vietnam War titled "History of U.S. Decision-Making Process on Viet Nam Policy." The *New York Times* had obtained the top-secret report commissioned by the then secretary of defense Robert S. McNamara during the presidency of Lyndon Johnson on U.S. strategy in Indochina. Daniel Ellsberg, a former military analyst, had copied the report and released it. Using elements of the **Espionage Act** of 1917, Nixon and his attorney general, John Mitchell, sought a restraining order to halt the *New York Times* and *Washington Post* from publishing articles on the report. Nixon feared exposure of the report, which documented the Johnson administration's public disinformation campaign on the conflict, would subvert ongoing negotiations to end the war in Vietnam. The government claimed **prior restraint**—in this case, precluding the publication of material written by the government itself—was imperative to protect national security.

In a 6–3 per curiam decision the majority on the Supreme Court agreed with two lower courts that the prohibition on the publication of the material violated the **First Amendment** right to freedom of the press. Citing ***Near v. Minnesota*** (1931), the **majority opinion** asserted that "Any system of prior restraints of expression comes to this Court bearing a heavy presumption against its constitutional validity" and further that the government "carries a heavy burden of showing justification for the imposition of such a restraint." According to the justices, the government "had not met that burden." In Associate Justice Thurgood Marshall's **concurring opinion**, he disagreed, saying that "the President's power to conduct foreign affairs and his position as Commander in Chief give him authority to impose censorship on the press to protect his ability to deal effectively with foreign nations and to conduct the military affairs of the country."

**NINETEENTH AMENDMENT**

Ratified on 18 August 1920, this Progressive Era amendment to the Constitution enshrined women's right to vote. The text reads: "The right of citizens of the United States to vote shall not be denied or abridged by the United States or by any State on account of sex." The amendment effectively overturned the **Supreme Court** decision in ***Minor v. Happersett*** (1875), in which the majority ruled that the Constitution did not provide a fundamental right to vote to women.

Several western states and territories, including Wyoming, Utah, and Washington, extended the right to vote to women from the late 1860s to the early 1880s, bolstering the efforts of the suffragette movement headed by Susan B. Anthony and Elizabeth Cady Stanton. The first introduction of the amendment in Congress came in 1878 and was made by California Senator Aaron Sargent. As it languished in the legislature for more than three decades, the suffragette movement's state-level victories combined with the rise of progressive politics, including the election of Democrat Woodrow Wilson in 1912, to reignite the movement. The Supreme Court dismissed a case challenging the constitutionality of the amendment, inter alia, on grounds that several state constitutions that denied women the right to vote conflicted with the amendment and that two others had not followed proper legislative procedure in their ratifications in *Lesser v. Garnett* (1922).

**NINTH AMENDMENT**

Ratified on 15 December 1791, the Ninth Amendment reads: "The enumeration in the Constitution, of certain rights, shall not be construed to deny or disparage others retained by the people." At issue were arguments *against* the inclusion of a **Bill of Rights** in the Constitution. **Federalists** contended that a listing of rights might lead to an inadvertent if not wholesale expansion of congressional power, in particular, under **Article I**, Section 8. The language of the amendment drew heavily from **James Madison**'s several drafts, which sought to quell concerns that "by enumerating exceptions to the grant of power, it would disparage those rights which were not placed in that enumeration." Madison emphasized that "the constitution is a bill of powers, the great residuum being the rights of the people." In sum, the courts have generally interpreted the Ninth Amendment as a hedge against the expansion of government power insofar as fundamental rights may not be breached simply because they were not specifically **enumerated** in the Constitution.

***NLRB (NATIONAL LABOR RELATIONS BOARD) V. CANNING* (2014)**

This **Supreme Court** case reviewed the president's recess **appointment power** under **Article II**, Section 2, of the Constitution. Litigation followed President Barack Obama's appointments to the National Labor Relations Board and the Consumer Financial Protection Bureau (CFPB) when the Senate was, in his view, out of session. The nominations sparked political controversy when Senate Republicans vowed to block the appointments. In the case of Richard Coudray's nomination to the CFPB, Republicans filibustered the nomination and Democrats were unable to invoke cloture (60 votes) to proceed to an up-or-down vote. Obama bypassed the Senate in January 2012 when he granted Coudray a recess appointment. Republicans contended that the Senate was *not* officially out of session. The petitioner in the case, Noel Canning, contended that his business had been adversely affected by the NLRB appointments. He asserted that three members had been chosen by the president via recess appointments that were allegedly unconstitutional.

The central question with which the court struggled was the length of time the Senate had to be out of session for a recess appointment to be constitutional. Writing for the majority, Associate Justice Stephen Breyer noted that "We hold that, for purposes of the Recess Appointments Clause, the Senate is in session when it says it is, provided that, under its own rules, it retains the capacity to transact Senate business." The majority opinion further elaborated that the Senate is not officially out of session unless the House of Representatives concurs in adjournment. Most importantly, the court found that pro forma sessions of the Senate do not count as recesses as the Senate is still able to transact business. Thus the unanimous opinion placed limits on the president's appointment power, as recesses must be of substantial length for the Article II clause to take effect.

# O

## OATH OF OFFICE

**Article II**, Section 1, of the United States Constitution elucidates that the president, before he enters on the execution of the office, take the following oath or affirmation: "I do solemnly swear (or affirm) that I will faithfully execute the Office of President of the United States, and will to the best of my Ability, preserve, protect and defend the Constitution of the United States." The Constitution does not specify who shall administer the oath of office, but in standard practice the **chief justice** of the **Supreme Court** does so. In the modern era presidents generally place their right hand on the Bible during the administration of the oath. The practice of using a Bible dates to **George Washington**, though some presidents, including **John Quincy Adams** and Theodore Roosevelt, did not use a Bible. Moreover, although presidents routinely end the oath with the phrase "so help me God," there is no constitutional requirement that they do so. After they complete the oath of office, presidents typically give their inaugural address, which in the modern era generally sketches the president's domestic and foreign policy vision for his term.

## *OBERGEFELL V. HODGES* (2015)

This **Supreme Court** case reviewed the question of **gay rights** with respect to state-level bans on homosexual marriage. The case represented the consolidation of six cases from lower federal courts and followed the decision in ***U.S. v. Windsor*** (2013), in which the court struck down provisions of the **Defense of Marriage Act** (DOMA).

In a 5–4 decision the majority on the high court posited that same-sex marriage was a fundamental right and that state bans violated the **equal protection** and **due process clauses** of the **Fourteenth Amendment**. The decision confirmed that states must issue marriage licenses to same-sex couples nationwide. Citing the decision in ***Loving v. Virginia*** (1967) that struck down laws barring individuals of different races from marrying, Associate Justice Anthony Kennedy's **majority opinion** described marriage as a fundamental liberty, a right of personal choice, a right to intimate association, and a safeguard to children and families not contingent on procreation, and contended that it was "demeaning to lock same-sex couples out of a central institution of the Nation's society."

**Dissenting opinions** on the majority's conclusions were particularly visceral, highlighting significant disagreement on the court reflected in the larger public debate. **Chief Justice John Roberts** chastised his colleagues for failing to allow the democratic process to play out in the states: "Many people will rejoice at this decision, and I begrudge none their celebration. But for those who believe in a government of laws, not of men, the majority's approach is deeply disheartening. . . . Five lawyers have closed the debate and enacted their own vision of marriage as a matter of constitutional law. Stealing this issue from the people will for many cast a cloud over same-sex marriage, making a dramatic social change that much more difficult to accept." Associate Justice Antonin Scalia was more pointed in his critique, writing, "If, even as the price to be paid for a fifth vote, I ever joined an opinion for the Court that began: 'The Constitution promises liberty to all within its reach, a liberty that includes certain specific rights that allow persons, within a lawful realm, to define and express their identity,' I would hide my head in a bag. The Supreme Court of the United States has descended from the disciplined legal reasoning of **John Marshall** and Joseph Story to the mystical aphorisms of the fortune cookie."

The majority and dissenting opinions highlight central debates surrounding **judicial activism** and **original intent**. *See also BOWERS V. HARDWICK* (1986); CIVIL RIGHTS; *HOLLINGSWORTH V. PERRY* (2013); *LAWRENCE V. TEXAS* (2003); *ROMER V. EVANS* (1996).

**OBSCENITY**

*See MILLER V. CALIFORNIA* (1973).

**ORDINARY SCRUTINY**

Ordinary scrutiny refers to **judicial review** and the "rational basis" approach of the **Supreme Court** in its interpretations of the constitutionality of statutes and government actions. Under standards of ordinary scrutiny, the government must show only a legitimate state interest. Regulatory affairs serve as one example. However, the court applies **intermediate scrutiny** in cases involving some questionable classifications, such as **gender**. In these cases, the classification must serve an important and substantially related state interest. The most stringent review falls under **strict scrutiny**. In cases regarding race and **civil rights**, religion, and **voting rights**, for example, "suspect classifications" must serve a compelling government interest. Thus it is incumbent upon the government to show how laws or actions do *not* discriminate and shifts the burden of proof to the government away from the plaintiff. *See also ADARAND V. PEÑA* (1995); AFFIRMATIVE ACTION; *CRAIG V. BOREN* (1976); *JOHNSON V. TRANSPORTATION AGENCY, SANTA CLARA COUNTY* (1987); *LOVING V. VIRGINIA* (1967); *MILLER V. JOHNSON* (1995); *REYNOLDS V. SIMS* (1964); *SHAW V. RENO* (1993); *U.S. V. VIRGINIA* (1996).

**ORIGINAL INTENT**

The normative doctrine of original intent suggests that in its interpretations of the Constitution and **judicial review** of federal and state actions and statutes, the **Supreme Court** should follow as closely as possible the rationale of the Founders. Emphasis is placed on understanding how constitutional provisions were interpreted at the time of their drafting and ratification. One starting point is the debates at the Constitutional Convention in Philadelphia in 1787. Another is to assess the arguments in the **Federalist Papers**.

The notion is closely aligned to conservative critiques of the court and allegations of **judicial activism**, particularly on social matters, in the contemporary era roughly beginning with the tenure of **Chief Justice Earl Warren** in the 1950s. Examples include **abortion** and the decision in ***Roe v. Wade*** (1973), in which the court found a "right to privacy" that enabled women to seek abortions legally in all 50 states, as well as the decision in ***Obergefell v. Hodges*** (2014), in which the court held that homosexuals had a right to marry under the **due process clause** of the **Fourteenth Amendment**. Since the Constitution does not specifically mention such rights, a strict construction approach suggests they do not exist. Moreover, from this perspective, reference to the Fourteenth Amendment should be taken in the context of post–Civil War debates on the ratification of the amendment and the intent regarding citizenship rights in which **gay rights** were not considered.

Critics of this approach posit that such interpretations make the Constitution a "straightjacket" or "suicide pact" that hamstrings social progress. The debate represents a classic disagreement between those who favor a narrow reading of the Constitution that limits government and those who view it as an evolving document that empowers the court to apply interpretations that reflect changes in society.

# P

## *PALKO V. CONNECTICUT* (1937)

This **Supreme Court** case considered the **incorporation** of the **Fifth Amendment** prohibition on double jeopardy to criminal trials in the states. Frank Palka (whose name was misspelled on the appeal paperwork) was originally convicted by a Connecticut court of second-degree murder. The prosecution appealed the decision based on errors of law and won a new trial at which Palka was convicted of first-degree murder and given the **death penalty**. Palka appealed the second trial, contending that his **due process** rights under the **Fourteenth Amendment** had been violated as double jeopardy had attached in the first trial.

By a margin of 8–1, the Supreme Court ruled against Palka. Writing the majority opinion, Associate Justice Benjamin Cardozo wrote that "The state is not attempting to wear the accused out by a multitude of cases with accumulated trials. It asks no more than this, that the case against him shall go on until there shall be a trial free from the corrosion of substantial legal error. . . . The conviction of appellant is not in derogation of any privileges or immunities that belong to him as a citizen of the United States." Palka was executed in the electric chair in April 1938. *See also BENTON V. MARYLAND* (1969).

## PARCHMENT BARRIERS

This often-cited phrase was first articulated by **James Madison** in **Federalist Paper** no. 48 during the debate over the ratification of the Constitution. Madison discusses the "encroaching nature" of government power vis-à-vis individual liberties and the separation of powers, and reflects: "Will it be sufficient to mark, with precision, the boundaries of these departments, in the constitution of the government, and to trust to these parchment barriers against the encroaching spirit of power? This is the security which appears to have been principally relied on by the compilers of the most of the American constitutions. But experience assures us, that the efficacy of the provision has been greatly overrated; and that some more adequate defense is indispensably necessary for the more feeble, against the more powerful, members of the government. The legislative department is everywhere extending the sphere of its activity, and drawing all power into its impetuous vortex."

In effect, Madison differed from many Founders insofar as he contended that the major threat to liberty was the legislative branch and *not* the executive, though he worried about the latter's "necessity to war."

His main argument was that the separation of powers, per se, on paper was an inadequate guarantee of the protection against the abuse of government power. As he wrote at the end of the letter, "The conclusion which I am warranted in drawing from these observations is, that a mere demarcation on parchment of the constitutional limits of the several departments, is not a sufficient guard against those encroachments which lead to a tyrannical concentration of all the powers of government in the same hands." Madison did not specify the particulars of a "sufficient guard." However, the **Anti-Federalists**' successful demands for a federal **Bill of Rights** took up many of most important safeguards for individual liberty that occupied Madison's concerns in Federalist no. 48.

**PARDON POWER**

**Article II**, Section 2, of the Constitution states that the president "shall have Power to Grant Reprieves and Pardons and Offenses against the United States, except in Cases of **Impeachment**." The Constitution is silent on the criteria the president should exercise in determining an individual's eligibility for a pardon. The president can grant a full pardon to a person convicted of a federal crime or issue conditional pardons that forgive the convicted person partially by reducing a penalty to a specified number of years, or alter a penalty with conditions. Franklin D. Roosevelt issued the most pardons, 3,687; William Henry Harrison and James Garfield issued none.

Pardons have often proven controversial in the history of the presidency. In 1795 **George Washington** issued pardons to two men convicted of treason who were involved in the Whiskey Rebellion in Pennsylvania a year earlier. Washington took the action to halt further civil chaos the tax on whiskey had generated. In 1858 President James Buchanan pardoned Mormon leader Brigham Young for his alleged involvement in the "Utah Massacre" of a westward-bound wagon train during a yearlong standoff with federal authorities. In 1886 President Grover Cleveland pardoned Fitz John Porter, a Union general who had been disgraced at the Second Battle of Bull Run during the Civil War and court-martialed. In 1921 President Warren Harding commuted socialist Eugene Debs's sentence for an espionage conviction to time served (two years) but stopped short of issuing a full pardon. In 1971 President Richard M. Nixon commuted labor and suspected Mafia leader Jimmy Hoffa's 13-year sentence to time served (four years). Nixon himself was pardoned in 1974 by President Gerald R. Ford, just a month after Nixon resigned in the face of certain removal from office for his involvement in the Watergate scandal. President James E. (Jimmy) Carter commuted the sentence of Patty Hearst, who had been involved in a bank robbery by a guerilla group, and in 2001 President William J. Clinton issued a full pardon as Hearst was thought to have been brainwashed by her captors.

In the last several decades, presidential pardons have received greater scrutiny when those pardoned were involved in allegedly unconstitutional or extraconstitutional operations, are relatives of the president, or the "process" set forth by the Department of Justice for the consideration of presidential pardons was not followed. In 1992, for example, President George H. W. Bush pardoned former Defense Secretary Caspar Weinberger and five others involved in the Iran-Contra scandal; Bush had served as vice president under President Ronald W. Reagan when the arms-for-hostages plan was hatched. On the last day of his term on 20 January 2001, President William J. Clinton pardoned a total of 140 persons, including his half brother, Roger Clinton, and Susan McDougal, who had been implicated in the Whitewater land deal in Arkansas in which Clinton had been implicated. In these and other pardons, such as those of former House Ways and Means Committee Chair Dan Rostenkowski and millionaire ex-patriot Marc Rich, Clinton had not consulted the Department of Justice guidelines and recommendations on pardons.

Of the more humorous grants of clemency, George W. Bush and Barack H. Obama both pardoned turkeys from the White House oven on Thanksgiving eve, a tradition that dates to the presidency of John F. Kennedy.

***PARENTS INVOLVED IN COMMUNITY SCHOOLS V. SEATTLE SCHOOL DISTRICT* (2007)**

**PARENTS V. SEATTLE SCHOOL DISTRICT**

This **Supreme Court civil rights** case involved the question of voluntary efforts by local school boards to promote racial diversity in Seattle, Washington, and Louisville, Kentucky. Unlike ***Brown v. Board of Education*** (1954), in which the court struck down de jure (state-sanctioned) segregation, this case centered on racial classifications used by the school districts to promote diversity and avoid racial isolation in light of de facto segregation as a result of residential mobility patterns. The case was decided on the standard of **strict scrutiny**.

The decision, in similar fashion to ***Regents of the University of California v. Bakke*** (1978), was divided. A majority of five justices found that the school districts' plans were not "narrowly tailored" in light of racial classifications and a "tiebreak" system of assigning children to schools by race. On the other hand, another majority of five justices (with Associate Justice Anthony Kennedy the determining vote) held that the school districts *did* have a compelling interest in promoting racial diversity. The court followed prior standards regarding the use of race in higher education in the cases of ***Grutter v. Bollinger*** (2003) and ***Gratz v. Bollinger*** (2003).

**PENTAGON PAPERS**

*See NEW YORK TIMES CO. V. UNITED STATES* (1971); PRIOR RESTRAINT.

***PIERCE V. SOCIETY OF SISTERS* (1925)**

This landmark **Supreme Court** case considered an Oregon law designed to eliminate private and parochial schools and mandate that children attend public schools. The case was *not* litigated on **First Amendment** grounds relative to freedom of conscience. Rather, a unanimous majority on the court took an expansive view of the **Fourteenth Amendment** right to **due process** under the law and applied it to state actions, striking down the Oregon statute. Associate Justice James McReynolds wrote the **majority opinion**, asserting that the law "unreasonably interferes with the liberty of parents and guardians to direct the upbringing and education of children under their control: as often heretofore pointed out, rights guaranteed by the Constitution may not be abridged by legislation which has no reasonable relation to some purpose within the competency of the State." The decision in *Pierce* heralded a dawning period in the 1920s and beyond in which the court embraced the **incorporation doctrine**, selectively, to make the **Bill of Rights** apply fully to the states.

**PINCKNEY, CHARLES COTESWORTH (1745–1825)**

Born in Charleston, South Carolina, and educated in England, Pinckney fought in the Revolutionary War and was captured and held as a prisoner of war by the British from 1780 to 1782. He represented South Carolina at the Constitutional Convention in 1787, was a signatory to the Constitution, and was influential in the state's ratification of the Constitution in 1788. President **George Washington** appointed Pinckney to replace James Monroe as ambassador to France in 1796, but the Revolutionary government (Directory) refused to receive him. President **John Adams** commissioned Pinckney, along with **John Marshall** and **Elbridge Gerry**, to Paris to end hostilities between the United States and France, but the terms proposed by the French resulted in the XYZ Affair.

A **Federalist**, Pinckney was John Adams's vice presidential running mate in 1800. He was the party's presidential candidate against **Thomas Jefferson** in 1804 and against **James Madison** in 1808, but carried only two and five states, respectively. In his postpolitical career, Pinckney helped found the University of South Carolina. He died on 16 August 1825 and is buried in St. Michael's Churchyard in Charleston, South Carolina.

***PLANNED PARENTHOOD V. CASEY* (1992)**

This milestone **Supreme Court** case involved a series of restrictions to **abortions** passed by the state of Pennsylvania. Antiabortion activists regarded the case as an opportunity to invalidate the tenets of ***Roe v. Wade*** (1973). The high court declined to do so. In effect, plurality decisions among the justices upheld a 24-hour waiting period for abortions, parental consent for abortions by minors, and informed consent provisions. The justices, however, struck down a spousal notification proviso, arguing that abused women, in particular, would cede too much power to their husbands and exacerbate their condition.

The main thrust of the case was to overturn the **strict scrutiny** standard in state restrictions on abortions. Following Justice Sandra Day O'Connor's earlier opinion in *Akron v. Akron Center for Reproductive*

*Health,* the court enunciated the benchmark of an "undue burden" in assessing restrictions. Moreover, a plurality of the justices set aside the trimester formula in *Roe,* contending that state interest in the life of the fetus may obtain prior to the end of the first semester, in light of medical advances, and restrictions on abortion may be imposed except in the case of the life or health of the mother. *See also GONZALES V. CARHART* (2007); *WEBSTER V. REPRODUCTIVE HEALTH SERVICES* (1989).

***PLESSY V. FERGUSON* (1896)**

In this landmark **civil rights** case, the **Supreme Court** affirmed the constitutionality of "separate but equal" facilities for the races mandated by state laws. Alongside **Jim Crow** laws, **black codes**, **grandfather clauses**, and **poll taxes**, the case represented the culmination of losses for the rights of African Americans in the late nineteenth century that **Reconstruction** era amendments to the Constitution (the **Thirteenth**, **Fourteenth**, and **Fifteenth Amendments**) were aimed at enshrining.

The case centered on a Louisiana man, Homer Plessy, who challenged a state law mandating separate facilities for blacks and whites on railroads. Plessy, who was one-eighth black, boarded a train car reserved for whites. He was asked to move to the car reserved for blacks and was arrested when he refused. A state court in Orleans Parish rejected his arguments that the state law violated his Thirteen and Fourteenth Amendment rights, upheld the state's ability to regulate policies for railways within its borders, and fined Plessy $25.

In a 7-1 opinion for which Associate Justice Henry B. Brown wrote the majority opinion, the High Court rejected arguments that the Louisiana statute violated equal protection of the laws or placed blacks in an inferior position in society. Citing the ***Civil Rights Cases***, the ***Slaughterhouse Cases***, and a Boston case regarding the segregation of educational facilities, Brown contended that Fourteenth Amendment protections were to be narrowly construed: "It is claimed by the plaintiff in error that, in any mixed community, the reputation of belonging to the dominant race, in this instance the white race, is property in the same sense that a right of action or inheritance is property. Conceding this to be so for the purposes of this case, we are unable to see how this statute deprives him of, or in any way affects his right to, such property. If he be a white man and assigned to a colored coach, he may have his action for damages against the company for being deprived of his so-called property. Upon the other hand, if he be a colored man and be so assigned, he has been deprived of no property, since he is not lawfully entitled to the reputation of being a white man."

Associate Justice John Marshall Harlan was the only member of the court to dissent from the opinion. in line with his prior objections to the Court's interpretation of Reconstruction era amendments, he wrote "While there may be in Louisiana persons of different races who are not citizens of the United States, the words in the act 'white and colored races' necessarily include all citizens of the United States of both races residing in that State. So that we have before us a state enactment that compels, under penalties, the separation of the two races in railroad passenger coaches, and makes it a crime for a citizen of either race to enter a coach that has been assigned to citizens of the other race . . . In respect of civil rights common to all citizens, the Constitution of the United States does not, I think, permit any public authority to know the race of those entitled to be protected in the enjoyment of such rights. Every true man has pride of race, and, under appropriate circumstances, when the rights of others, his equals before the law, are not to be affected, it is his privilege to express such pride and to take such action based upon it as to him seems proper. But I deny that any legislative body or judicial tribunal may have regard to the race of citizens when the civil rights of those citizens are involved. Indeed, such legislation as that here in question is inconsistent not only with that equality of rights which pertains to citizenship, National and State, but with the personal liberty enjoyed by everyone within the United States."

The doctrine of "separate but equal" remained in the formal law of the land for 58 years. In 1954, the Supreme Court, under **Chief Justice Earl Warren**, rejected the segregation of races in education as inherently unequal in ***Brown v. Board of Education***. The Court's reversal in *Brown* was complemented by constitutional amendments, including the abolition of the poll tax in 1964 with the ratification of the **Twenty-Fourth Amendment**, and congressional statutes such as the Civil Rights Act of 1964 and the Voting Rights Act of 1965 that were central to the Civil Rights Movement for African Americans in the 1950s and 1960s. *See also* AFFIRMATIVE ACTION; DUE PROCESS (CLAUSE); EQUAL PROTECTION (CLAUSE); INCORPORATION DOCTRINE.

**POCKET VETO**

This unique form of presidential disapproval of congressional legislation stems from the **presentment clause** in **Article I**, Section 7, of the Constitution. The president must either sign or **veto** legislation passed by both chambers of Congress within 10 days. However, if Congress adjourns, sine die, within that 10-day period, and the president does not sign the bill, the bill does not become law. The president need take no other action since Congress is no longer in session to receive a veto message. It is incumbent upon Congress to pass the bill anew and present it to the president in the next session. Presidents often pocket veto private bills and legislation rushed by Congress at the end of a session, generally without great fanfare or media scrutiny.

**POLL TAX**

A poll tax is an amount of money an individual must pay to the county in which he or she is registered for the right to vote. From **Reconstruction** until the adoption of the **Twenty-Fourth Amendment** in 1964, poll taxes were implemented by local authorities on a discriminatory basis in many southern states to discourage or preclude African Americans from exercising their **voting rights**. *See also* CIVIL RIGHTS; FIFTEENTH AMENDMENT; JIM CROW LAWS.

**PREROGATIVE POWER**

This term refers to the president's unilateral assertion of authority based on an interpretation of constitutional powers. Although **Article II** of the Constitution sets forth various concrete provisions—or express powers—for the exercise of presidential responsibilities (**commander-in-chief**, receive ambassadors, issue **pardons**, make treaties, and appoint judges and members of his cabinet with the **advice and consent** of the Senate), the boundaries of **executive power** are nonetheless subject to some ambiguity because the Founders did not specify them as they did for Congress in **Article I**. At one extreme is the "stewardship theory," articulated by President Theodore Roosevelt, that suggested that presidential action is legitimate as long as there is no constitutional prohibition on that action. At the other extreme, his rival William Howard Taft took a literalist approach to argue that presidential actions were illegitimate absent a specific constitutional grant of power.

Historically, the "prerogative presidency" has been most closely associated with President Abraham Lincoln's conduct during the Civil War. Lincoln took a number of extraordinary actions, such as the naval blockade of Charleston, South Carolina, and the suspension of the writ of **habeas corpus**, based on his understanding of the **oath of office** and with the assumption that Congress would ratify his decisions. As Lincoln wrote to A. G. Hodges in 1864, "I have never understood that the presidency conferred upon me an unrestricted right to act. . . . I did understand, however, that my oath to preserve the Constitution to the best of my ability imposed upon me the duty of preserving, by every indispensable means, that government—that nation, of which the Constitution was the organic law. . . . I felt that measures otherwise unconstitutional might become lawful by becoming indispensable to the preservation of the Constitution through the preservation of the nation."

In the post–World War II period, presidents' claims to prerogative powers have sometimes been successfully challenged. Harry S. Truman's seizure of steel mills during the Korean War was struck down by the **Supreme Court** in ***Youngstown Sheet and Tube v. Sawyer*** (1952). Richard Nixon's claim of **executive privilege** over recordings that implicated him in the Watergate scandal was denied by the high court in ***U.S. v. Nixon*** (1974). George W. Bush's effort to set up military tribunals for enemy combatants in the **War on Terror** was struck down in ***Hamdan v. Rumsfeld*** in 2006.

Still, presidents' interpretations of their authority, particularly as commander-in-chief and in the realm of foreign policy, have a long history of precedent that buttresses claims. **George Washington** was the first president to exercise prerogative power in this domain with the Neutrality

Proclamation. And prerogative power may also extend to matters that intersect the role as commander-in-chief and domestic affairs. Washington's handling of the Whiskey Rebellion and Dwight D. Eisenhower's decision to send the army to Little Rock, Arkansas, in 1957 to uphold the Supreme Court decision in ***Brown v. Board of Education*** (1954) are but two examples. Nevertheless, in military matters, Congress became more assertive in the 1970s with the passage of the **War Powers Resolution** over President Nixon's **veto**. Whether that legislative act has weakened presidential prerogative in foreign and military affairs remains a significant debate. *See also* SIGNING STATEMENT.

**PRESENTMENT CLAUSE**

**Article I**, Section 7, of the Constitution outlines the process by which a bill becomes law. The identical bill must be passed by a majority of the House of Representatives and the Senate. The bill is then sent to the president for his signature.

If the president does not object to the bill, and does not sign it within 10 days, the bill becomes law. The exception is a **pocket veto**, whereby Congress adjourns during the 10-day period—and without the president's signature, the law is invalid. Alternatively, the president may choose to **veto** the bill and return it to Congress with his objections. In that case, Congress retains the final word: a two-thirds vote of the House and Senate is required to override the president and enact the bill. *See also CITY OF NEW YORK V. CLINTON* (1998); *INS (IMMIGRATION AND NATURALIZATION SERVICE) V. CHADHA* (1983).

***PRINTZ V. UNITED STATES* (1997)**

Although this **Supreme Court** case superficially involved the question of handgun regulation and the **Second Amendment**, the larger implications concerned **federalism**. When Congress passed the Brady Handgun Violence Prevention Act in 1993, the bill mandated that a background-check system be established to preclude sales of firearms to individuals who were already barred from purchasing them. Interim rules mandated that the seller of the firearms fill out a form with the purchaser's information, verify the purchaser's identity, and forward all material to the local chief law enforcement officer (CLEO). The CLEO, in turn, had to research within five days whether the sale was legitimate using available state and federal resources.

Chief law enforcement officers from Montana and Arizona disputed the provision, contending that the federal government had no right to compel local governments to enforce federal law. In a 5–4 ruling, the majority on the court ruled the interim provisions unconstitutional. Writing the **majority opinion**, Justice Antonin Scalia expressed concern about "the effect that federal control of state officers would have upon the first element of the 'double security' alluded to by Madison: the division of power between State and Federal Governments. It would also have an effect upon the second element: the separation and equilibration of powers between the three branches of the Federal Government itself. The Constitution does not leave to speculation who is to administer the laws enacted by Congress; the President, it says, 'shall take Care that the Laws be faithfully executed' . . . personally and through officers whom he appoints." Following the decision, many localities chose to voluntarily comply with the Brady Bill's interim provisions.

**PRIOR RESTRAINT**

This term refers to governmental suppression of speech or publication of material that has yet to take place. The notion of prior restraint conflicts with the fundamental freedoms, including press and speech, in the **First Amendment**. Two landmark **Supreme Court** cases have guided **judicial review** of state laws and government action to preclude newspapers from publishing offensive, allegedly harmful, or otherwise sensitive government documents with national security implications. First, in ***Near v. Minnesota*** (1931) the court invalidated a Minnesota public nuisance law that sought to make a newspaper publisher's offensive comments and invectives about local officials a crime in an effort to shut down his enterprise. Second, in ***New York Times Co. v. United States*** (1971) the court halted efforts by the Nixon administration to enjoin the *New York Times* and the *Washington Post* from publishing a series of articles (the "Pentagon Papers"), including a detailed government report on military strategy, for fear of complicating a negotiated settlement to end the Vietnam War. All told, the two precedential cases established nearly insurmountable barriers to government censorship of print media.

**PUBLIUS**

This pseudonym or pen name was used by **Alexander Hamilton**, **John Jay**, and **James Madison** in their collection of 85 essays known as the **Federalist Papers** to support ratification of the Constitution. *See also* ANTI-FEDERALIST, ANTI-FEDERALISM; CATO.

# Q

**QUARTERING (TROOPS)**
*See* THIRD AMENDMENT.

# R

***RASUL V. BUSH* (2004)**

This **Supreme Court** case emanated from the **War on Terror** following the terrorist attacks on 11 September 2001. The constitutional issue was the right of **habeas corpus** for unlawful enemy combatants detained at the U.S. military facility in Guantanamo Bay, Cuba. Shafiq Rasul, a British national who was captured among Taliban operatives during the U.S.-led invasion of Afghanistan in 2001, filed a habeas corpus petition in U.S. civilian court. The administration of George W. Bush sought to try enemy combatants in military tribunals and used the precedent in ***Ex Parte Quirin*** (1942) as a justification. A federal circuit and appellate court both denied Rasul's petition. The Supreme Court, however, reversed the lower courts' decision and in a 6–3 decision ruled that enemy combatants did have recourse to civil courts. Although Rasul was released into British custody before the finding, the decision was considered a major setback for the Bush administration. *See also BOUMEDIENE V. BUSH* (2008); *HAMDI V. RUMSFELD* (2004).

**RATIFICATION**

*See* ARTICLE VII (CONSTITUTION).

**REAPPORTIONMENT**

This term refers to the process for determining representation in the House of Representatives. **Article I**, Section 2, of the Constitution details that "Representatives and direct Taxes shall be apportioned among the several States which may be included within this Union, according to their respective Numbers, which shall be determined by adding to the whole Number of free Persons, including those bound to Service for a Term of Years, and excluding Indians not taxed, three fifths of all other Persons." The Three-Fifths Compromise whereby slaves were counted as three-fifths of a person to determine states' representation in the House was superseded by the **Fourteenth Amendment** following the Civil War: "Representatives shall be apportioned among the several States according to their respective numbers, counting the whole number of persons in each State, excluding Indians not taxed. But when the right to vote at any election for the choice of electors for President and Vice-President of the United States, Representatives in Congress, the Executive and Judicial officers of a State, or the members of the Legislature thereof, is denied to any of the male inhabitants of such State, being twenty-one years of age, and citizens of the United States, or in any way abridged, except for participation in rebellion, or other crime, the basis of representation therein shall be reduced in the proportion which the number of such male citizens shall bear to the whole number of male citizens twenty-one years of age in such State." Every state must have at least one representative in the House, regardless of population.

Article I, Section 2, mandates that reapportionment must take place every 10 years following the Census. State legislatures determine district boundaries, and significant controversies have plagued reapportionment efforts across time. The **Supreme Court** was loath to take up "political questions" surrounding **voting rights** and reapportionment until the 20th century. In 1962 the high court reversed its position in the case of ***Baker v. Carr***. Federal redistricting cases have focused on skewed representation between rural and urban areas, as well as **gerrymandering**, or the drawing of districts by state legislatures for partisan gain or to enhance minority representation. Congress set the number of representatives in the House at a total of 435 in the Reapportionment Act of 1929. *See also MILLER V. JOHNSON* (1995); *REYNOLDS V. SIMS* (1964); *SHAW V. RENO* (1993); *SHELBY COUNTY V. HOLDER* (2013); *WESBERRY V. SANDERS* (1964).

**RECONSTRUCTION**

Following the American Civil War, the era of Reconstruction (1865–1877) was begun under President Andrew Johnson as a means of restoring the states of the former Confederacy to the Union. Passage of the **Thirteenth**, **Fourteenth**, and **Fifteenth Amendments** to the Constitution was aimed at ensuring citizenship rights for former slaves, eradicating discrimination against blacks, and, most importantly, making the **due process** and **equal protection clauses** apply to the states (**incorporation doctrine**). Little progress was made during the period, however, when the **Supreme Court** decision in the ***Slaughterhouse Cases*** (1873) elucidated an exceedingly narrow view of the reach of the Fourteenth Amendment, in particular. Moreover, the period witnessed the rise of **Jim Crow laws** aimed at keeping the franchise from blacks and solidifying segregation of the races. Reconstruction ended when the last federal troops stationed in the southern states left in 1877. The withdrawal of federal troops was a result of the compromise in the **Electoral College** following the disputed election between Republican Rutherford B. Hayes and Democrat Samuel J. Tilden in 1876.

***RED LION BROADCASTING CO. V. FCC (FEDERAL COMMUNICATIONS COMMISSION)* (1969)**

This significant **Supreme Court** ruling concerned the "fairness doctrine" requiring television and radio broadcasters to present opposing views on controversial issues. The fairness doctrine was implemented by the FCC in 1949, and the regulations were justified on the basis of the scarcity of the broadcast spectrum. The central question was whether the broadcaster in the case, Red Lion Broadcasting, could be compelled to air the views of an individual, Fred Cook, who had been personally attacked on air by a television evangelist. The broadcaster contended that the FCC had overstepped its regulatory authority and interfered with **First Amendment** guarantees to freedom of speech and freedom of the press.

In delivering the **majority opinion** for the court, Associate Justice Byron White underscored the centrality of First Amendment rights in the broadcasting realm but also held the FCC's regulation of a right to reply as constitutional. White wrote: "It is the right of the public to receive suitable access to social, political, esthetic, moral, and other ideas and experiences which is crucial here. That right may not constitutionally be abridged either by Congress or by the FCC. . . . Although broadcasting is clearly a medium affected by a First Amendment interest . . . differences in the characteristics of new media justify differences in the First Amendment standards applied to them."

The ruling accentuates fundamental differences in the regulation of print and broadcast media (in an earlier era vis-à-vis broadcast media). As a "public good," broadcast media are subject to greater governmental regulation. Print media, however, are exempt from "equal time" rules on controversial issues or "right to reply" regulation as the Supreme Court enunciated in ***Miami Herald Publishing Co. v. Tornillo*** (1974). The FCC stopped enforcing the fairness doctrine in 1987. With the proliferation of broadcast channels and cable television channels, the doctrine became largely unenforceable. *See also* PRIOR RESTRAINT.

**REDISTRICTING**

*See* GERRYMANDERING; REAPPORTIONMENT.

***REED V. REED* (1971)**

This **Supreme Court** case centered on the question of **gender discrimination**. At issue was an Idaho law that mandated that "males must be preferred to females" in the appointment of administrators of estates. Sally and Cecil Reed, who were separated, each applied in probate court to administer their minor son's estate following his death. The court appointed Cecil Reed, and Sally Reed challenged the ruling on the basis of the **equal protection clause** of the **Fourteenth Amendment**.

The Supreme Court unanimously struck down the Idaho law. Writing for the majority, **Chief Justice Warren Burger** asserted that "To give a mandatory preference to members of either sex over members of the other, merely to accomplish the elimination of hearings on the merits, is to make the very kind of arbitrary legislative choice forbidden by the Equal Protection Clause of the Fourteenth Amendment; and whatever may be said as to the positive values of avoiding intrafamily controversy, the choice in this context may not lawfully be mandated solely on the basis of sex." *See also* INTERMEDIATE SCRUTINY.

***REGENTS OF THE UNIVERSITY OF CALIFORNIA V. BAKKE* (1978)**

This landmark **Supreme Court civil rights** decision focused on **affirmative action** as implemented in college admission policies. The constitutional issue involved the use of race to justify a quota of students admitted to university programs. The litigation was brought about by Allan Bakke, who had applied twice to the University of California, Davis Medical School and was denied admission. Upon discovering that the university had "set aside" a quota of seats reserved for minority applicants, and that his test scores exceeded those of some of the minority students who had been admitted—and who received extra admission points based on race—Bakke contended the policy had violated his right to **equal protection** under the **Fourteenth Amendment**. The university had adopted the affirmative action program voluntarily, and posited that while integration was not the issue, the historical lack of minority doctors in the field of health practice justified the policy.

The case split the justices on the high court deeply, as reflected in the plurality opinion that Associate Justice Lewis Powell penned. Powell contended that "The State certainly has a legitimate and substantial interest in ameliorating, or eliminating where feasible, the disabling effects of identified discrimination." But he also argued that "It may be assumed that the reservation of a specified number of seats in each class for individuals from the preferred ethnic groups would contribute to the attainment of considerable ethnic diversity in the student body. But petitioner's argument that this is the only effective means of serving the interest of diversity is seriously flawed. In a most fundamental sense, the argument misconceives the nature of the state interest that would justify consideration of race or ethnic background. It is not an interest in simple ethnic diversity, in which a specified percentage of the student body is in effect guaranteed to be members of selected ethnic groups, with the remaining percentage an undifferentiated aggregation of students. The diversity that furthers a compelling state interest encompasses a far broader array of qualifications and characteristics, of which racial or ethnic origin is but a single, though important, element. Petitioner's special admissions program, focused solely on ethnic diversity, would hinder, rather than further, attainment of genuine diversity."

Since there was no controlling **majority opinion**, the decision did not provide concrete guidance for the future. Essentially, race could be considered as one of several factors in university admissions decisions—but could not constitute the sole criterion. The court ordered Bakke's admission and struck down the special program for minorities. Bakke entered the medical school in 1978. *See also GRATZ V. BOLLINGER* (2003); *GRUTTER V. BOLLINGER* (2003).

**REHNQUIST, WILLIAM HUBBS (1924–2005)**

A native of Milwaukee, Wisconsin, Rehnquist was a World War II veteran who later received degrees from Harvard University and a law degree from Stanford, where he graduated first in his class. He clerked for **Supreme Court** Justice Robert Jackson before taking up private practice in Arizona from 1953 to 1969. Rehnquist worked in President Richard

Nixon's Office of White House Counsel from 1969 to 1971. Nixon nominated him to associate justice of the Supreme Court to replace John Marshall Harlan in 1971.

Rehnquist evinced a conservative voting record as an associate justice, writing critical opinions on desegregation and opposing the ***Roe v. Wade*** (1973) decision that legalized abortion. When **Chief Justice** Warren Burger retired in 1986, President Ronald Reagan nominated Rehnquist to take his place. He was confirmed by a Senate vote of 65–25. Antonin Scalia was later tapped by Reagan to fill the associate justice position created by Rehnquist's vacancy. Rehnquist presided over the impeachment trial of President William Clinton in 1999. Rehnquist died of complications from thyroid cancer on 3 September 2005. His support for states' rights, particularly in reference to the wall separating church from state, is one of his most controversial legacies. President George W. Bush nominated John Roberts to succeed Rehnquist.

**RELIGIOUS FREEDOM RESTORATION ACT (RFRA) (1993)**

*See CITY OF BOERNE V. FLORES* (1997).

***RENO V. ACLU (AMERICAN CIVIL LIBERTIES UNION)* (1997)**

This **Supreme Court** case arose in connection with the Communications Decency Act (CDA) passed by Congress in 1996 and addressed **First Amendment** rights relative to the Internet. Provisions of the statute criminalized the knowing transmission of obscene material via the Internet to minors under the age of 18. The statute prohibited intentionally sending a communication to minors "that, in context, depicts or describes, in terms patently offensive as measured by contemporary community standards, sexual or excretory activities or organs."

Associate Justice John Paul Stevens wrote the **majority opinion** and was joined by six others on the high court invalidating the law. Stevens asserted that "We are persuaded that the CDA lacks the precision that the First Amendment requires when a statute regulates the content of speech. In order to deny minors access to potentially harmful speech, the CDA effectively suppresses a large amount of speech that adults have a constitutional right to receive and to address to one another. That burden on adult speech is unacceptable if less restrictive alternatives would be at least as effective in achieving the legitimate purpose that the statute was enacted to serve." Stevens concluded the opinion by noting that "governmental regulation of the content of speech is more likely to interfere with the free exchange of ideas than to encourage it." *See also* PRIOR RESTRAINT.

**REPUBLICANISM, REPUBLICAN POLITICAL THEORY**

Republicanism holds that the sovereignty of a nation is ultimately vested in the people and emphasizes individual rights, the rule of law, and civic virtue and participation. The concept of popular sovereignty rejects a monarchy in which a king or queen is sovereign and rules by divine right and bloodline, and was at the center of Revolutionary thought in the 18th century. The United States is a constitutional republic in which fundamental liberties are outlined in the foundational document. Republican theory is reflected in the Constitution's emphasis on **natural rights**, the enumeration of the powers of the central government, and provisions for frequent elections to the legislature and executive that seek to secure popular control of governing institutions. *See also* BILL OF RIGHTS; DECLARATION OF INDEPENDENCE; LOCKE, JOHN (1632–1704); MONTESQUIEU, CHARLES-LOUIS DE SECONDAT, BARON DE LA BRÈDE ET DE (1689–1755).

**RESERVED POWERS**

The **Tenth Amendment** to the Constitution addresses the question of those powers *not* **enumerated** in **Articles I to VII**. The amendment reads "The powers not delegated to the United States by the Constitution, nor prohibited by it to the States, are reserved to the States respectively, or to the people." Reserved powers are a fundamental principle of **federalism** and the division of powers between levels of government. Further, the concept is an important component of **republican political theory** that informed the Founders' thinking about the security of individual rights and the balancing of interests (or factions). As James Madison wrote in **Federalist Paper** no. 51, "happily for the *republican cause*, the practicable sphere may be carried to a very great extent, by a judicious modification and mixture of the *federal principle*." In contemporary debates proponents of limited government and **states' rights** rely on the Tenth Amendment to argue against overreach by the central government and the accumulation of power by the federal level vis-à-vis the states.

**REVERSE INCORPORATION**

This concept stems from the notion that the **equal protection clause** of the **Fourteenth Amendment**, aimed at the states, applies to the federal government through the **Fifth Amendment** right to **due process**. In other words, rights intended to protect individuals in the states apply to the federal level as a matter of due process. As one example, the **Supreme Court** ruled in *Bolling v. Sharpe* (1954), a companion case to ***Brown v. Board of Education*** (1954), that Washington, DC, schools had to desegregate even though the city is under federal control. Similarly, in the **affirmative action** case of ***Adarand v. Peña*** (1995) the court held a federal program to the **strict scrutiny** standard based on the equal protection clause of the Fourteenth Amendment, as applied through the Fifth Amendment.

***REYNOLDS V. SIMS* (1964)**

This **Supreme Court** case addressed **voting rights**. Specifically, the case took up the question of state legislative districts that were, in some cases, drawn with highly disproportionate populations. Voters in Birmingham, Alabama, brought suit as state senate districts had disparities as high as 41:1 in terms of the apportioning of population across the geography of the Cotton State. In Alabama as in other states, malapportionment was particularly egregious in terms of the overrepresentation of rural areas at the expense of urban regions.

The court had taken up the issue of voting rights initially in ***Baker v. Carr*** (1962), pulling back from the position that reapportionment constituted a "political question" in which the court did not wish to intervene. In an 8–1 decision the majority invalidated malapportionment and mandated that the voting districts of state legislatures have roughly equal populations. The decision was based on the **equal protection clause** of the **Fourteenth Amendment**. The majority stressed the centrality of "one person, one vote," as central to **republican** governance.

Writing the **majority opinion**, **Chief Justice Earl Warren** asserted: "Legislators represent people, not trees or acres. Legislators are elected by voters, not farms or cities or economic interests. As long as ours is a representative form of government, and our legislatures are those instruments of government elected directly by and directly representative of the people, the right to elect legislators in a free and unimpaired fashion is a bedrock of our political system. It could hardly be gainsaid that a constitutional claim had been asserted by an allegation that certain otherwise qualified voters had been entirely prohibited from voting for members of their state legislature. And, if a State should provide that the votes of citizens in one part of the State should be given two times, or five times, or 10 times the weight of votes of citizens in another part of the State, it could hardly be contended that the right to vote of those residing in the disfavored areas had not been effectively diluted. It would appear extraordinary to suggest that a State could be constitutionally permitted to enact a law providing that certain of the State's voters could vote two, five, or 10 times for their legislative representatives, while voters living elsewhere could vote only once. And it is inconceivable that a state law to the effect that, in counting votes for legislators, the votes of citizens in one part of the State would be multiplied by two, five, or 10, while the votes of persons in another area would be counted only at face value, could be constitutionally sustainable." *See also MILLER V. JOHNSON* (1995); *SHAW V. RENO* (1993); *WESBERRY V. SANDERS* (1964).

***RICHMOND V. CROSON* (1989)**

This **Supreme Court civil rights** case considered the question of "**set-asides**" in government-awarded contracts for minority-owned businesses as part of **affirmative action**. As Associate Justice Sandra Day O'Connor noted in writing the **majority opinion**, "In this case, we confront once again the tension between the **Fourteenth Amendment**'s guarantee of equal treatment to all citizens, and the use of race-based measures to ameliorate the effects of past discrimination on the opportunities enjoyed by members of minority groups in our society." The case focused on the city of Richmond, Virginia, where the local government set a target of awarding approximately one-third of municipal contracts to minority-owned business given African Americans' historical lack of access to such contracts.

Alluding to the decision in ***Regents of the University of California v. Bakke*** (1978), O'Connor wrote, "While there is no doubt that the sorry history of both private and public discrimination in this country has contributed to a lack of opportunities for black entrepreneurs, this observation, standing alone, cannot justify a rigid racial quota in the awarding of public contracts in Richmond, Virginia. Like the claim that discrimination in primary and secondary schooling justifies a rigid racial preference in medical school admissions, an amorphous claim that there has been past discrimination in a particular industry cannot justify the use of an unyielding racial quota." Applying **strict scrutiny** to the case, the majority struck down the city's practice as a violation of **equal protection** under the Fourteenth Amendment in a 7–2 decision. The outcome was a major setback for proponents of affirmative action and laid the groundwork for the case of ***Adarand v. Peña*** (1995), in which minority set-asides for federal contracts were similarly invalidated.

**RIGHT TO COUNSEL**

*See GIDEON V. WAINWRIGHT* (1963); SIXTH AMENDMENT.

**ROBERTS, JOHN GLOVER, JR. (1955–)**

Born in Buffalo, New York, Roberts grew up in Indiana. He earned both his undergraduate and law degree from Harvard University, where he was law review editor. He clerked for Second Circuit Court of Appeals Judge Henry Friendly and later for **Supreme Court** Justice **William Rehnquist**. From 1982 to 1986, he worked in the Office of White House Counsel in the Reagan administration. After several years in private law practice, he served in the administration of George H. W. Bush as deputy solicitor general from 1989 to 1992, arguing the government's position before the Supreme Court. He served briefly on the U.S. Court of Appeals for the District of Columbia in 1992 and ruled on the case of ***Hamdan v. Rumsfeld***, which was later appealed to the Supreme Court and decided in 2006. His judgeship was never confirmed by Congress, and he returned to private law practice and taught at Georgetown University following the elder Bush's unsuccessful reelection bid.

He was ultimately nominated by President George W. Bush to the U.S. Court of Appeals for the District of Columbia in 2003, and he served in that position until 2005. In July 2005, Bush nominated Roberts to replace retiring Supreme Court Justice Sandra Day O'Connor. However, when **Chief Justice** William Rehnquist died in September 2005, Bush rescinded the nomination for O'Connor's seat and nominated Roberts for chief justice. Roberts was confirmed by the Senate by a 78–22 margin in late September. A Catholic, Roberts is widely viewed as a moderate. He supported restrictions on **abortion** but has not supported overturning the landmark case of ***Roe v. Wade*** (1973). He came under intense condemnation by conservatives for his position supporting the Affordable Care Act, but he disagreed poignantly with the **majority opinion** in ***Obergefell v. Hodges*** (2015) that legalized same-marriage nationwide and represented a significant victory for **gay rights** advocates.

***ROBINSON V. CALIFORNIA* (1962)**

This **Supreme Court** case addressed the **Eighth Amendment** and "cruel and unusual punishment." The case focused on whether the Eighth Amendment prohibited only *forms of punishment* or whether the *criminalization of certain behavior* violated the Constitutional protection through the incorporation of the **Bill of Rights** via the **Fourteenth Amendment**. At issue was a California state statute that made "addiction to the use of narcotics" a misdemeanor crime, punishable by imprisonment. Further, an individual was eligible for prosecution "at any time before he reforms" and regardless of displaying antisocial behavior or possessing narcotics.

In a 6–2 ruling for which Associate Justice Potter Stewart penned the **majority opinion**, the justices held that addiction constituted a disease that cannot be constitutionally criminalized. Addiction, Stewart posited, "is apparently an illness which may be contracted innocently or involuntarily. We hold that a state law which imprisons a person thus afflicted as a criminal, even though he has never touched any narcotic drug within the State or been guilty of any irregular behavior there, inflicts a cruel and unusual punishment in violation of the Fourteenth Amendment. To be sure, imprisonment for ninety days is not, in the abstract, a punishment which is either cruel or unusual. But the question cannot be considered in the abstract. Even one day in prison would be a cruel and unusual punishment for the 'crime' of having a common cold."

***ROE V. WADE* (1973)**

This landmark **Supreme Court** ruling with regard to women's **abortion** rights has shaped a generation of sharp political debate. At issue was a Texas law restricting abortions. Norma McCorvey (alias Jane Roe) originally sought an abortion in Texas by falsely claiming she had been raped. Texas only allowed abortions in cases of rape or incest. Ultimately denied access to an abortion, Roe sued. A federal district court found in her favor based on the **Ninth Amendment** (reservation of rights to the people) but refused to enjoin the Texas law. Dallas district attorney Henry Wade represented the State of Texas.

In a 7–2 decision justices on the Supreme Court ruled against the Texas legal restrictions on abortion by referencing an implicit "right to privacy" under the **due process clause** of the **Fourteenth Amendment**. The roots of that implied right to privacy were enunciated in ***Griswold v. Connecticut*** (1965). The **concurring opinions** of the justices emphasized the question of the viability of the fetus outside the mother's womb, contending that abortion was constitutional during the first trimester. Beyond the first trimester, abortion was legal when the mother's life and health were at stake. State laws regarding abortion restrictions were subject to **strict scrutiny** and a compelling government interest, the highest threshold in **judicial review**.

Critics charge that the decision in *Roe* was poor constitutional law and that a right to privacy was "invented" to justify abortion. Further, since Norma McCorvey had given birth prior to the high court's ruling, she had neither standing to represent other women nor to argue the case on her own behalf under the doctrine of mootness. The justices posited an exception in which the situation was likely to be repeated but might "evade review." Women's rights groups, such as the National Organization for Woman (NOW) and the National Abortion Rights Action League (NARAL), hailed the decision and have sought to protect the decision from state efforts to restrict abortion procedures. *See also* GENDER, GENDER DISCRIMINATION; *GONZALES V. CARHART* (2007); *PLANNED PARENTHOOD V. CASEY* (1992); *WEBSTER V. REPRODUCTIVE HEALTH SERVICES* (1989).

***ROMER V. EVANS* (1996)**

This **Supreme Court** case dealt with the issue of **gay rights** in Colorado and had major implications nationally. At issue was Amendment 2 to the Colorado constitution, adopted by voters via the initiative process in 1992. The amendment forbade governments in Colorado from recognizing homosexuals as a protected class of any variety: "Neither the State of Colorado, through any of its branches or departments, nor any of its agencies, political subdivisions, municipalities or school districts, shall enact, adopt or enforce any statute, regulation, ordinance or policy whereby homosexual, lesbian or bisexual orientation, conduct, practices or relationships shall constitute or otherwise be the basis of or entitle any person or class of persons to have or claim any minority status, quota preferences, protected status or claim of discrimination." The amendment passed by a 53–47 percent margin. Proponents contended the initiative was aimed at curbing **affirmative action**, while opponents maintained it targeted homosexuals for overt discrimination.

Although a state trial court had ruled that the amendment violated **equal protection** and was subject to **strict scrutiny**, the decision by the Supreme Court emphasized that the amendment, while abrogating the **Fourteenth Amendment**, did not even pass the standard of **ordinary scrutiny** whereby the state must show a legitimate interest on a rational basis. In writing the majority opinion for the six justices who voted to invalidate the amendment, Associate Justice Anthony Kennedy argued that the amendment "deprives gays and lesbians even of the protection of general laws and policies that prohibit arbitrary discrimination in governmental and private settings and that "Its sheer breadth is so discontinuous with the reasons offered for it that the amendment seems inexplicable by anything but animus toward the class that it affects; it lacks a rational relationship to legitimate state interests." Kennedy terminated the opinion by opining that "We must conclude that Amendment 2 classifies homosexuals not to further a proper legislative end but to make them unequal to everyone else. This Colorado cannot do. A State cannot so deem a class of persons a stranger to its laws."

In his **dissenting opinion**, joined by **Chief Justice William Rehnquist** and Associate Justice Clarence Thomas, Associate Justice Antonin Scalia contended that "The Court has mistaken a Kulturkampf for a fit of spite. The constitutional amendment before us here is not the manifestation of a 'bare . . . desire to harm' homosexuals . . . but is rather a modest attempt by seemingly tolerant Coloradans to preserve traditional sexual mores against the efforts of a politically powerful minority to revise those mores through use of the laws."

The case was a major turning point in the evolution of gay rights since the court had demurred from invalidating state sodomy laws in ***Bowers v. Hardwick*** (1986). Eight years later the Supreme Court overturned *Bowers* in ***Lawrence v. Texas*** (2003), and the following decade extended marriage rights to same-sex couples in ***Obergefell v. Hodges*** (2015). In each of these cases Justice Kennedy authored the majority opinion.

***ROSTKER V. GOLDBERG* (1981)**

This **gender discrimination** case addressed the question of the draft, or Selective Service. The controversy centered on congressional legislation in 1980 reauthorizing the draft and mandating that young men register for the Selective Service. President Jimmy Carter had called for the reauthorization following the Soviet invasion of Afghanistan a year early. The president challenged Congress to alter the system to include women, but the legislation ultimately passed with the requisite funding levels to register men only. Many legislators concluded that because the branches of the armed forces prohibited women from engaging in combat, mandating that women sign up for the Selective Service was counterproductive.

The case arose when a longstanding opponent to the draft, Bernard Rostker, won a lower-court decision that the reinstitution of the draft for men only violated the **due process clause** of the **Fifth Amendment**. Rostker had litigated the draft since the early 1970s.

In a 6–3 decision, the **Supreme Court** reversed the lower court's decision. Writing the **majority opinion**, Associate Justice **William Rehnquist** maintained that "This case is quite different from several of the gender-based discrimination cases we have considered in that, despite appellees' assertions, Congress did not act 'unthinkingly' or 'reflexively and not for any considered reason.' The question of registering women for the draft not only received considerable national attention and was the subject of wide-ranging public debate, but also was extensively considered by Congress in hearings, floor debate, and in committee." He further elaborated that "Women as a group . . . unlike men as a group, are not eligible for combat. The restrictions on the participation of women in combat in the Navy and Air Force are statutory. . . . The reason women are exempt from registration is not because military needs can be met by drafting men. This is not a case of Congress arbitrarily choosing to burden one of two similarly situated groups, such as would be the case with an all-black or all-white, or an all-Catholic or all-Lutheran, or an all-Republican or all-Democratic registration. Men and women, because of the combat restrictions on women, are simply not similarly situated for purposes of a draft or registration for a draft. Congress' decision to authorize the registration of only men, therefore, does not violate the Due Process Clause."

**ROUTLEDGE, JOHN (1739–1800)**

A native of Charleston, South Carolina, in Colonial America, Routledge studied law at the Inns of Court in England and was admitted to the English bar in 1760. In 1761 Rutledge was elected to the South Carolina Commons House of Assembly. In 1764 he was appointed attorney general of South Carolina by the king's governor. He first took up the Revolutionary War cause by serving as the youngest delegate to the Stamp Act Congress of 1765, which petitioned King George III for repeal of the act.

Rutledge served on the South Carolina delegation to the Constitutional Convention in 1787 in Philadelphia and headed the Committee on Detail. He served at the South Carolina Ratification Convention the following year. In fall 1789 President **George Washington** nominated Rutledge one of the original associate justices of the **Supreme Court** of the United States. The Senate confirmed Routledge in September 1789, but Routledge resigned to become chief justice in South Carolina's highest court. In August 1795, Washington nominated Rutledge **chief justice** of the federal Supreme Court. He served as a recess **appointment** for only four months as his Senate confirmation failed by a vote of 10–14. He had publicly spoken against the Jay Treaty, supported by President Washington, and angered **Federalists**. He died on 21 June 1800 and is buried in St. Michael's Churchyard in Charleston, South Carolina.

# S

**SAME-SEX MARRIAGE**

*See* GAY RIGHTS; *HOLLINGSWORTH V. PERRY* (2013); *OBERGEFELL V. HODGES* (2015); *U.S. V. WINDSOR* (2013).

***SANTA FE INDEPENDENT SCHOOL DISTRICT V. DOE* (2000)**

This **Supreme Court** case took up anew the question of school prayer and the establishment clause of the **First Amendment**. A Texas public high school allowed prayer at high school football games following a school election in which a majority of students supported the policy. Per a prior lower-court ruling, prayers had to be nonsectarian and nonproselytizing. Several parents who objected to the policy commenced litigation and were identified as "Doe" to preclude harassment.

In a 6–3 decision, the Supreme Court invalidated the school's practice. Drawing on the precedent in ***Lee v. Weisman*** (1992), the majority concluded the prayers at football games violated the establishment clause and concurred with a federal district court ruling in favor of Doe. The author of the **majority opinion**, Associate Justice John Paul Stevens, concluded that "the Constitution also requires that the Court keep in mind the myriad, subtle ways in which Establishment Clause values can be eroded . . . and guard against other different, yet equally important, constitutional injuries. One is the mere passage by the District of a policy that has the purpose and perception of government establishment of religion. . . . [T]he policy's text and the circumstances surrounding its enactment reveal that it has such a purpose." He elaborated that "Another constitutional violation warranting the Court's attention is the District's implementation of an electoral process that subjects the issue of prayer to a majoritarian vote. Through its election scheme, the District has established a governmental mechanism that turns the school into a forum for religious debate and empowers the student body majority to subject students of minority views to constitutionally improper messages."

Three justices, including **Chief Justice William Rehnquist** and Associate Justices Antonin Scalia and Clarence Thomas, joined in penning a strong **dissenting opinion** in which they chastised the majority for applying the most rigid standard elaborated in ***Lemon v. Kurtzman*** (1971) in the Texas case. The minority contended that "The Court distorts existing precedent to conclude that the school district's student-message program is invalid on its face under the Establishment Clause. But even more disturbing than its holding is the tone of the Court's opinion; it bristles with hostility to all things religious in public life. Neither the holding nor the tone of the opinion is faithful to the meaning of the Establishment Clause, when it is recalled that George Washington himself, at the request of the very Congress which passed the **Bill of Rights**, proclaimed a day of 'public thanksgiving and prayer, to be observed by acknowledging with grateful hearts the many and signal favors of Almighty God.'"

### *SCHECHTER POULTRY CORP. V. UNITED STATES* (1935)

This **Supreme Court** case addressed the constitutionality of the National Industrial Recovery Act (NIRA) passed by Congress during the presidency of Franklin D. Roosevelt amid the Great Depression. The legislation empowered the executive to implement a series of regulations, including wage and price controls, union organizing, and the determination of "fair competition." The constitutional issue centered on whether Congress had overstepped its bounds in delegating such broad regulatory authority to the president.

In a unanimous decision, the Supreme Court struck down the NIRA, contending that Congress had violated the **separation of powers** in its delegation of authority to the president and had also exceeded its authority under the **commerce clause** in **Article I** of the Constitution. The author of the **majority opinion**, **Chief Justice Charles Evans Hughes**, outlined in great detail that "Extraordinary conditions, such as an economic crisis, may call for extraordinary remedies, but they cannot create or enlarge constitutional power," that "Congress is not permitted by the Constitution to abdicate, or to transfer to others, the essential legislative functions with which it is vested," that "Congress may leave to selected instrumentalities the making of subordinate rules within prescribed limits, and the determination of facts to which the policy, as declared by Congress, is to apply; but it must itself lay down the policies and establish standards," and that "The delegation of legislative power sought to be made to the President . . . is unconstitutional and the Act is also unconstitutional, as applied in this case, because it exceeds the power of Congress to regulate interstate commerce and invades the power reserved exclusively to the States." Finally, with respect to "codes of fair competition," the court asserted that "Congress cannot delegate legislative power to the President to exercise an unfettered discretion to make whatever laws he thinks may be needed or advisable for the rehabilitation and expansion of trade and industry."

The decision marked the opening salvo in a conflict between the court and President Roosevelt over New Deal policies that prompted him to engage in an unsuccessful "court-packing" plan aimed at expanding the court's membership from nine to 12 justices. Remarkably, over the course of Roosevelt's second term, the court reversed its position on a score of New Deal policies it had previously invalidated.

### *SCHENCK V. UNITED STATES* (1919)

This **Supreme Court** case elaborated the "clear and present danger test" for **First Amendment** free speech rights. The case stemmed from congressional passage of the 1917 **Espionage Act** during World War I and the First Red Scare, advocated by President Woodrow Wilson to combat opponents of the war effort. Inter alia, the statute made it a crime (1) to convey information with intent to interfere with the operation or success of the armed forces of the United States or to promote the success of its enemies (violations were punishable by death or imprisonment of up to 30 years); and (2) to convey false reports or false statements with intent to interfere with the operation or success of the military or naval forces of the United States or to promote the success of its enemies when the United States is at war, to cause or attempt to cause insubordination, disloyalty, mutiny, refusal of duty, in the military or naval forces of the United States, or to willfully obstruct the recruiting or enlistment service of the United States (violations were punishable by a maximum fine of $10,000 or by imprisonment for not more than 20 years or both).

Charles Schenck, a prominent socialist, had been convicted for violating the Espionage Act by handing out leaflets to men who had recently been drafted into the war. He appealed his conviction to the Supreme Court. His principle argument was the Espionage Act violated the First Amendment guarantee that Congress shall make no law abridging the freedom of speech.

In a unanimous **majority opinion** famously authored by Associate Justice Oliver Wendell Holmes, the court upheld Schenck's conviction under the Espionage Act and distinguished between types of speech and the *context* of protected speech. Key to the majority ruling was Schenck's intention to undermine the draft through the language in his flyers. Holmes expounded that "the character of every act depends upon the circumstances in which it is done. The most stringent protection of free speech would not protect a man in falsely shouting fire in a theatre and causing a panic." He elaborated that "The question in every case is whether the words used are used in such circumstances and are of such a nature as to create a clear and present danger that they will bring about the substantive evils that Congress has a right to prevent. It is a question of proximity and degree. When a nation is at war, many things that might be said in time of peace are such a hindrance to its effort that their utterance will not be endured so long as men fight, and that no Court could regard them as protected by any constitutional right."

Holmes's analogies to yelling "Fire!" in a crowded theater and his assertion that there are differences in protected and unprotected speech in peacetime and wartime, respectively, represented an important distinction in the interpretation of the First Amendment. The case set important precedents that would play a role in future questions about the limits of the First Amendment, including ***Gitlow v. New York*** (1925), ***Brandenburg v. Ohio*** (1969), and ***Chaplinsky v. New Hampshire*** (1942).

## SCHOOL PRAYER

*See ENGLE V. VITALE* (1962); FIRST AMENDMENT; *LEE V. WEISMAN* (1992); *SANTA FE INDEPENDENT SCHOOL DISTRICT V. DOE* (2000).

## SCHOOL VOUCHERS

This term refers to a government program in which parents can redeem tuition fees at a private or parochial school. The constitutional question pivots on whether such programs are inconsistent with the establishment clause of the **First Amendment**. *See also ZELMAN V. SIMMONS-HARRIS* (2002).

## *SCHUETTE V. COALITION TO DEFEND AFFIRMATIVE ACTION* (2014)

This landmark **Supreme Court** case focused on **affirmative action** in higher education and voters' ability to end such programs via referenda. The case stemmed from a 2006 amendment to the Michigan state constitution, adopted by voters as a ballot initiative that prohibited affirmative action, notwithstanding federal mandates. The critical part of the amendment read: "The state shall not discriminate against, or grant preferential treatment to, any individual or group on the basis of race, sex, color, ethnicity, or national origin in the operation of public employment, public education, or public contracting." The ballot initiative followed the high court's decisions in ***Gratz v. Bollinger*** (2003), in which a "point system" for university admissions was found unconstitutional, but in ***Grutter v. Bollinger*** (2003) a more narrowly tailored program for law school admissions was upheld. Opponents of the amendment contended that the amendment violated the **equal protection clause** of the **Fourteenth Amendment**.

Associate Justice Anthony Kennedy wrote the plurality opinion; he was joined by **Chief Justice John Roberts** and Associate Justice Samuel Alito, while Antonin Scalia and Stephen Breyer penned **concurring opinions**. In upholding the state constitutional ban, the justices cited different rationales. Citing the democratic process, Kennedy posited that "This case is not about how the debate about racial preferences should be resolved. It is about who may resolve it. There is no authority in the Constitution of the United States or in this Court's precedents for the Judiciary to set aside Michigan laws that commit this policy determination to the voters. . . . Deliberative debate on sensitive issues such as racial preferences all too often may shade into rancor. But that does not justify removing certain court-determined issues from the voters' reach. Democracy does not presume that some subjects are either too divisive or too profound for public debate." Scalia asserted that "we confront a frighteningly bizarre question: Does the Equal Protection Clause of the Fourteenth Amendment forbid what its text plainly requires? Needless to say (except that this case obliges us to say it), the question answers itself." Scalia further emphasized that "we have emphasized the near-limitless sovereignty of each State to design its governing structure as it sees fit."

Justice Sonia Sotomayor was joined by Ruth Bader Ginsburg in her dissent. She opined that "We are fortunate to live in a democratic society. But without checks, democratically approved legislation can oppress minority groups. For that reason, our Constitution places limits on what a majority of the people may do. This case implicates one such limit: the guarantee of equal protection of the laws. Although that guarantee is traditionally understood to prohibit intentional discrimination under existing laws, equal protection does not end there. Another fundamental strand of our equal protection jurisprudence focuses on process, securing to all citizens the right to participate meaningfully and equally in self-government. . . . A majority of the Michigan electorate changed the basic rules of the political process in that State in a manner that uniquely disadvantaged racial minorities." *See also BROWN V. BOARD OF EDUCATION OF TOPEKA* (1954); CIVIL RIGHTS; *PARENTS INVOLVED IN COMMUNITY SCHOOLS V. SEATTLE SCHOOL DISTRICT* (2007); *REGENTS OF THE UNIVERSITY OF CALIFORNIA V. BAKKE* (1978).

**SECOND AMENDMENT**

This **civil liberties** protection in the **Bill of Rights**, adopted on 15 December 1791, states that "A well regulated Militia, being necessary to the security of a free State, the right of the people to keep and bear Arms, shall not be infringed." Historical and contemporary debates have centered on the Founders' intent with particular reference to "militia." In *U.S. v. Miller* (1939) the **Supreme Court** found that a prohibition against the transportation of a sawed-off shotgun across state lines was *not* unconstitutional. The majority concluded that such weapons had no relation to the necessities of a "well regulated militia." The case was remanded to a lower federal court, but the death of one of the plaintiffs precluded a definitive conclusion to the litigation. Gun right advocates nonetheless have asserted that the court confirmed the right to keep and bear other types of arms, as the majority underscored that state laws historically contained "Clauses intended to insure the possession of arms and ammunition by all who were subject to military service [and] appear in all the important enactments concerning military affairs." Opponents of gun rights contend that the ruling confirmed that firearms ownership is connected only to the purpose of militias, such as the National Guard.

In ***District of Columbia v. Heller*** (2008) the Supreme Court held that the District of Columbia's ban on handguns was unconstitutional. The narrow majority found that Second Amendment rights extended not just to those in "militias" such as the National Guard, but also to those who wished to possess firearms for other legitimate purposes such as self-protection. Because the District of Columbia is under federal control, the ruling applied only to federal "enclaves." In ***McDonald v. City of Chicago*** (2010) the high court, in another narrow **majority opinion**, struck down a local ordinance that outlawed handguns and thereby **incorporated** Second Amendment rights, through the **Fourteenth Amendment**, to the states.

Several other contemporary cases have dealt with federal laws that have attempted to regulate gun ownership. In ***U.S. v. Lopez*** (1995) the court held that a "gun free school zone" statute passed by Congress exceeded the legislature's authority under the **commerce clause**. In ***Printz v. United States*** (1997) a majority on the court found that provisions of the Brady Handgun Violence Act of 1993, which mandated that local law enforcement determine whether local sales of firearms were legal, was unconstitutional as a violation of **federalism** and division of powers between levels of government.

**SELECTIVE INCORPORATION**

*See* INCORPORATION DOCTRINE.

**SELF-INCRIMINATION**

*See* FIFTH AMENDMENT.

**SEPARATION OF POWERS**

This term refers to the division of responsibilities, functions, and authority between branches of the federal level of government in the United States. The separation of powers is found in **Articles I**, **II**, and **III** of the Constitution, which detail **enumerated powers** granted to Congress, the president, and the **Supreme Court**, respectively. As the **Tenth Amendment** specifies, those powers not granted to the federal level are **reserved** to the states or the people. **Federalism**, or the division of powers *between* levels of government, is consistent with the general concept of the separation of powers.

The Founders of the American Republic were profoundly influenced by Enlightenment philosophers, including **John Locke** and the Baron de **Montesquieu**, who proposed that a concentration of power in any single branch threatened tyranny. **Alexander Hamilton**, **James Madison**, and **John Jay** elegantly elaborated arguments in favor of the separation of powers in the **Federalist Papers**, which informed the debate about the ratification of the Constitution following the Convention in Philadelphia in 1787. **Anti-Federalists** feared that despite such constitutional engineering, an overbearing central government menaced state sovereignty and **civil liberties** were inadequately protected absent the **Bill of Rights**. Madison even lamented in Federalist no. 48 that mere **parchment barriers** might not be sufficient to preclude one branch—in his view the legislature—from dominating the executive and judiciary.

In effect, as political scientist Richard Neustadt contended, the Constitution may well have created "separated institutions *sharing* powers" more than a wholesale separation. The document is replete with examples of the intermingling of powers between the branches, especially between the president and Congress, including **appointments**, treaty making, and the **veto**. Similarly, the federal level and the states enjoy concurrent powers, such as regulation and taxation.

Contemporary critics of the Constitution suggest that executive power, in particular, threatens the balance of power between the branches. The presidential war power, claims of **executive privilege**, the use of **executive orders** to bypass the legislature, presidents' assertions that statutes will not be enforced in **signing statements**, and Congress's putative loss of or failure to utilize the "power of the purse" portend ominous implications for the separation of powers from this perspective.

**SET-ASIDES**

In controversies surrounding **affirmative action**, this term refers to a quota of government contracts or seats in higher education admissions reserved for minorities. The **Supreme Court** has rejected the use of race alone in such policies and applied **strict scrutiny** to such matters. With respect to government contracts, in ***Richmond v. Croson*** (1989) the use of race to target minority-owned businesses disadvantaged by general discrimination in the past was invalidated. The high court similarly struck down a similar set-aside program at the federal level in ***Adarand v. Peña*** (1995).

In higher education the court has rejected quotas while asserting that race may be one of several factors in admissions decisions. The landmark case was ***Regents of the University of California v. Bakke*** (1978), in which the justices ruled that while the set-aside of a percentage of seats for minorities in the University of California, Davis Medical School was unconstitutional, race could be one of several criteria used in the admissions process. *See also* CIVIL RIGHTS; *GRATZ V. BOLLINGER* (2003); *GRUTTER V. BOLLINGER* (2003); *SCHUETTE V. COALITION TO DEFEND AFFIRMATIVE ACTION* (2014).

**SEVENTEENTH AMENDMENT**

Ratified on 31 May 1913, this amendment to the Constitution superseded the **Article I** provision that senators be elected from state legislatures. The Seventeenth Amendment codified popular election of senators and enabled state legislatures to empower governors to make temporary appointments in the case of vacancies until a special election can be called. The first nationwide popular election of Senators occurred in 1914, a midterm election in which the Democratic Party made most gains in the upper chamber during the presidency of Woodrow Wilson.

The amendment arose out the populist movement in the late 19th and early 20th centuries. Progressives, including newspaper magnate William Randolph Hearst, brought to light alleged corruption in Congress. Three-time Democratic Party nominee for the presidency William Jennings Bryan campaigned vigorously for the amendment and, as secretary of state in 1913, proclaimed its passage. Regardless, the popular election of senators had major implications for **federalism** and the **original intent** of the Framers, including **Anti-Federalists**, who regarded the appointment of senators by state legislatures as critical to maintain a balance between the national government and the interests of states.

**SEVENTH AMENDMENT**

Ratified on 15 December 1791, this straightforward amendment to the Constitution is part of the **Bill of Rights** and provides for a jury trial in civil cases. The text reads: "In Suits at common law, where the value in controversy shall exceed twenty dollars, the right of trial by jury shall be preserved, and no fact tried by a jury, shall be otherwise re-examined in any Court of the United States, than according to the rules of the common law." Although not formally **incorporated** by a **Supreme Court** ruling, states have generally provided for the same provision.

***SHAW V. RENO* (1993)**

This **Supreme Court voting rights** case centered on the question of racial **gerrymandering**. At issue was a North Carolina congressional district (12th) that was drawn by the state legislature, per the Voting Rights Act of 1965, to improve the representation of African Americans. The state legislature did so at the behest of the Department of Justice following **reapportionment** from the 1990 Census. The proposed district was approximately 160 miles long and was, in places, as narrow as the lane boundaries along Interstate 85. Critics charged that the geographic boundaries made no historical or other sense, apart from creating a majority of black voters in the district.

White voters sued, contending that the proposed district was tantamount to "reverse discrimination" that violated **equal protection** of the law under the **Fourteenth Amendment**. In a 5–4 decision, the majority on the Supreme Court invalidated the district and held that redistricting efforts that involved racial classification were subject to **strict scrutiny**. Writing the **majority opinion**, Associate Justice Sandra Day O'Connor noted that "redistricting legislation that is so bizarre on its face that it is 'unexplainable on grounds other than race' . . . demands the same close scrutiny that we give other state laws that classify citizens by race."

O'Connor, joined by four other justices, including **Chief Justice William Rehnquist**, further posited that "reapportionment is one area in which appearances do matter. A reapportionment plan that includes in one district individuals who belong to the same race, but who are otherwise widely separated by geographical and political boundaries, and who may have little in common with one another but the color of their skin, bears an uncomfortable resemblance to political apartheid. It reinforces the perception that members of the same racial group—regardless of their age, education, economic status, or the community in which the live—think alike, share the same political interests, and will prefer the same candidates at the polls. We have rejected such perceptions elsewhere as impermissible racial stereotypes." Finally, she submitted that "The message that such districting sends to elected representatives is equally pernicious. When a district obviously is created solely to effectuate the perceived common interests of one racial group, elected officials are more likely to believe that their primary obligation is to represent only the members of that group, rather than their constituency as a whole. This is altogether antithetical to our system of representative democracy."

The case was a bellwether for future constitutional litigation concerning minority-majority congressional districts. By establishing the standard for strict scrutiny when race appears to be the "overriding, predominant force" and when "a reapportionment plan may be so highly irregular and bizarre in shape that it rationally cannot be understood as anything other than an effort to segregate voters based on race," the court set the stage for the invalidation of Georgia's 11th congressional district in 1995 in ***Miller v. Johnson*** and several minority-majority districts in Texas in ***Bush v. Vera*** (1996).

**SHAYS'S REBELLION**

This uprising, spearheaded by Daniel Shays of Massachusetts, galvanized calls for a stronger central government following the Revolutionary War. Shays, like many veterans, faced significant obstacles in obtaining pay promised for his military service. Moreover, the lack of available credit made it impossible for many subsistence farmers to pay their debts, resulting in widespread property seizures sanctioned by state courts. In 1786 Shays and approximately 4,000 men protested against the Massachusetts state government's seeming obduracy on their plight. The rebellion was put down with a militia, and harsh penalties were levied upon those who had partaken. The Disqualification Act barred the rebels from holding elective office to pursue legislatively the objectives of the rebellion. Some rebels were convicted. However, most were pardoned or had their sentences commuted. And Governor Bowdoin, who had supported the Disqualification Act, lost reelection in 1787 to John Hancock. Some modest tax and other reforms were subsequently enacted.

Regardless, for many prominent leaders, including **George Washington** and **James Madison**, the rebellion accentuated the problems with the **Articles of Confederation** following the Revolution, particularly the lack of a central government that could govern effectively or promote economic expansion and secure property rights. Washington, in correspondence with Henry Knox, wrote, "Let us have a government by which our lives, liberties, and properties will be secured, or let us know the worst at once." The rebellion catalyzed Madison's call to states to attend the **Annapolis Convention** to discuss trade issues in September 1786. While only a few states attended, calls for reform continued to resound. **John Jay**, for example, cited how the "inefficiency of the Federal government" had become manifest.

The relative influence of Shays's Rebellion on the adoption of the Constitution in 1787 remains a point of disagreement among scholars. Historian Charles Beard argued that the rebellion mobilized the propertied classes in post-Revolutionary America to fashion an antidemocratic constitution that precluded radicalism and civil chaos that could destroy their fortunes. Beard contends that the Founders were less concerned with Enlightenment political theory than protecting their own economic interests. Others reject Beard's fundamental thesis, highlighting the Founders' focus on **natural rights** and the influence of **John Lock**, the Baron de **Montesquieu**, and others on the drafting of the Constitution and the adoption of the **Bill of Rights**.

***SHELBY COUNTY V. HOLDER* (2013)**

This pivotal **Supreme Court voting rights** case centered on several provisions of the Voting Rights Act of 1965, as reauthorized by Congress in 2006, the most important of which (Section 4b) obliged nine select southern states to secure "preclearance" from the Department of Justice (or the U.S. District Court) prior to making any changes to state voting laws. The other provision of the act that was challenged concerned the formula for determining which states were mandated to obtain preclearance based on past discrimination.

The locality of Shelby County, Alabama, sued in federal district court in an effort to overturn the provisions. The U.S. District Court for the District of Columbia, as well as the U.S. Court of Appeals for the District of Columbia, ruled the provisions constitutional and critical to protect the voting rights of minorities. By a 5–4 decision, however, the Supreme Court invalidated the preclearance requirement.

**Chief Justice John Roberts** penned the **majority opinion**. The majority concluded that Congress had exceeded its authority under the **Fourteenth** and **Fifteenth Amendments**, with important ramifications for **federalism** and state sovereignty. Roberts contended that "States must beseech the Federal Government for permission to implement laws that they would otherwise have the right to enact and execute on their own," and "despite the tradition of equal sovereignty, the Act applies to only nine States (and several additional counties). While one State waits months or years and expends funds to implement a validly enacted law, its neighbor can typically put the same law into effect immediately, through the normal legislative process. Even if a noncovered jurisdiction is sued, there are important differences between those proceedings and preclearance proceedings; the preclearance proceeding 'not only switches the burden of proof to the supplicant jurisdiction, but also applies substantive standards quite different from those governing the rest of the nation.'"

The majority also held that the formula for preclearance was based on "40-year-old facts having no logical relation to the present day." Roberts elaborated that "If Congress had started from scratch in 2006, it plainly could not have enacted the present coverage formula." Noting that the provisions for preclearance were originally to have expired five years after enactment in 1965, Roberts asserted that "Nearly 50 years later, things have changed dramatically . . . '[v]oter turnout and registration rates now approach parity. Blatantly discriminatory evasions of federal decrees are rare. And minority candidates hold office at unprecedented levels.' . . . The tests and devices that blocked access to the ballot have been forbidden nationwide for over 40 years."

The majority left the door open for Congress to revisit the issue, noting that "Congress may draft another formula based on current conditions. Such a formula is an initial prerequisite to a determination that exceptional conditions still exist justifying such an 'extraordinary departure from the traditional course of relations between the States and the Federal Government.'" The case prompted a host of states to adopt voter identification laws, which remain the subject of significant controversy and litigation as of 2015.

**SHERMAN, ROGER (1721–1793)**

Born in Newton, Massachusetts, Sherman was admitted to the bar in Connecticut in 1754 despite no formal legal training. He served in the Connecticut legislature from 1755 to 1758 and again from 1760 to 1761 before he was appointed to a judgeship in 1762. In 1766 he was elected to the Governor's Council of the Connecticut General Assembly, on which he served 19 years. He served on the state's superior court from 1766 to 1789, at which time he resigned to serve in the First Congress of the United States. He also served as mayor of New Haven, Connecticut, from 1784 until his death in 1793.

Sherman helped draft the **Declaration of Independence** and was one of the most influential members of the Constitutional Convention in Philadelphia in 1787, notwithstanding his terse speaking style. An ardent supporter of the **Virginia Plan**, he was the architect of the **Great Compromise** alongside **Oliver Ellsworth**. He is the only Founder to have signed the Association (or Continental Association) in 1774 that imposed a boycott on Great Britain, the **Articles of Confederation**, the Declaration of Independence, and the Constitution.

Sherman died from typhoid fever on 23 July 1793. Originally buried in New Haven Green, his remains were reinterred in the Grove Street Cemetery adjacent to the campus of Yale University.

**SIGNING STATEMENT**

This term refers to the presidents' comments and statements made when signing a bill into law. Presidents often make such statements during bill signing ceremonies at the White House. The practice dates to the presidency of **James Madison** and has been used with increased frequency since World War II.

Scholars have analyzed signing statements and have uncovered that presidents use them for a variety of purposes. Some statements are rhetorical and serve to congratulate or criticize Congress on the legislation or portions of it, or to take credit for bills themselves. Others instruct agencies on administrative details. The most controversial type of signing statements involves presidential challenges to the constitutionality of bills and interpretations of the enforceability of provisions.

Although there was an increase in challenge to bills under Presidents Gerald R. Ford, James E. (Jimmy) Carter, and Ronald W. Reagan, the most significant controversy over signing statements occurred during the presidency of George W. Bush. From 2001 to 2008, Bush utilized signing statements more expansively than any U.S. president to challenge parts of bills rather than veto them outright. Critics charged that the practice was tantamount to an unconstitutional **line-item veto** or otherwise violated the **presentment clause**. Bush used signing statements to object to more than 130 bills and more than 1,200 specific legislative provisions, drawing rebukes from the American Bar Association, sparking a lively debate among legal and presidency scholars, and prompting congressional hearings on proposals to curb the practice.

There is no constitutional provision or federal statute providing the president with a "signing statement power." Neither the federal courts nor the **Supreme Court** have validated or invalidated the legal force of signing statements. Efforts to pass a bill restricting their use to challenge laws failed in the Senate in 2006. President Barack H. Obama promised to curb use of signing statements during his presidential campaign in 2008 and during his first term issued only 21 signing statements. *See also* EXECUTIVE ORDER.

**SIXTEENTH AMENDMENT**

Ratified on 3 February 1913, this amendment to the Constitution enabled the federal government to impose a direct tax on income. The amendment reads: "The Congress shall have power to lay and collect taxes on incomes, from whatever source derived, without apportionment among the several States, and without regard to any census or enumeration." The principle source of federal revenues prior to the amendment derived from excise and customs taxes. The amendment was a response to the **Supreme Court** decision in *Pollock v. Farmers' Loan and Trust Co.* (1895), in which the majority ruled that property and other taxes provided for in the Wilson-Gormann Tariff Act of 1894 violated the provision for apportioned direct taxes according to the Census in **Article I**. The Sixteenth Amendment effectively overturned this decision. Today the Internal Revenue Service (IRS), part of the Department of the Treasury, collects personal, corporate, and other forms of income per congressional statutes on rates. Opponents of the income tax argue for the repeal of the Sixteenth Amendment and call for a "flat" or across-the-board consumption tax to replace the complexities of the current system and to eliminate "loopholes" in the tax code.

**SIXTH AMENDMENT**

Ratified on 15 December 1791, this amendment to the Constitution is part of the **Bill of Rights**. Its **civil liberties** protections address criminal trials and right to counsel. The text of the amendment reads: "In all criminal prosecutions, the accused shall enjoy the right to a speedy and public trial, by an impartial jury of the State and district wherein the crime shall have been committed, which district shall have been previously ascertained by law, and to be informed of the nature and cause of the accusation; to be confronted with the witnesses against him; to have compulsory process for obtaining witnesses in his favor, and to have the Assistance of Counsel for his defence."

The **Supreme Court** elaborated a four-part test to determine whether a defendant's right to a speedy trial has been abrogated. In *Barker v. Wingo* (1972) the majority held that the criteria include the length of delay, the reason for the delay, the time and manner in which the defendant has asserted his or her Sixth Amendment right, and the degree of prejudice to the defendant arising from the delay. In *Strunk v. United States* (1973) the court elucidated that the only remedy to a violation of the right to a speedy trial is a dismissal of the indictment or invalidation of a conviction, and the **Fifth Amendment** right not to face double jeopardy attaches.

Defendants in a trial have a right to confront their accusers, and the courts may compel witnesses to testify. **Article III**, Section 2, of the Constitution mandates that trials take place where the alleged crime was committed. The Sixth Amendment requires that juries be selected from the jurisdiction in which the trial is held (vicinage). In *Reynolds v. United States* (1878) the Supreme Court rejected the argument that religious obligation exempted individuals from criminal indictment; the case pivoted on a Mormon in Utah Territory charged with polygamy.

The most significant development in the 20th century was the expansive interpretation of the understanding of "assistance to counsel" elaborated by the Supreme Court under **Chief Justice Earl Warren** in the case of ***Gideon v. Wainwright*** (1963). The court had previously determined that defendants in capital cases unable to employ counsel, or otherwise incapable of self-representation, were entitled to such in *Powell v. Alabama* (1932). In *Johnson v. Zerbst* (1938) the majority ruled that poor defendants were entitled to counsel in *all* federal courts if they could not afford an attorney. In *Hamilton v. Alabama* (1961) the court **incorporated** the decision in *Powell* to apply to the states via the **Fourteenth Amendment**, holding that defendants in capital cases were entitled to counsel regardless of "special circumstances" such as "ignorance, feeble mindedness, illiteracy, or the like." In *Gideon*, however, the Warren Court asserted that defendants in *any* felony case were entitled to counsel (public defender) if they did not have the means to pay for one.

***SLAUGHTERHOUSE CASES* (1873)**

This **Supreme Court** decision involved an amalgam of cases litigated over a charter by the Louisiana legislature granting a private corporation an exclusive franchise for the butcher business in New Orleans. The putative rationale behind the legislative act, titled "An Act to Protect the

Health of the City of New Orleans," was to halt the frequent outbreak of cholera by relocating all butchering activities to the south of the city. The implications of the ruling relative to the **Fourteenth Amendment** were far-reaching with respect to **civil rights** and the failure of **incorporation** of the **Bill of Rights** during the era of **Reconstruction**.

More than 400 members of the Butchers' Benevolent Association sued to halt the state-mandated monopoly over their businesses. They did so on the basis of the Fourteenth Amendment guarantees of **due process**, privileges and immunities, and **equal protection**, which they alleged the state had contravened. In a 5–4 decision—with **Chief Justice Salmon P. Chase** dissenting—the majority on the court took a narrow view of citizenship rights incongruous with the intent of the Fourteenth Amendment according to critics.

As Associate Justice Samuel F. Miller elaborated in the **majority opinion**, "there is a citizenship of the United States, and a citizenship of a state, which are distinct from each other, and which depend upon different characteristics or circumstances in the individual." Miller asserted that the plaintiffs erred, as the Fourteenth Amendment "speaks only of privileges and immunities of citizens of the United States, and does not speak of those of citizens of the several states. . . . Was it the purpose of the fourteenth amendment, by the simple declaration that no State should make or enforce any law which shall abridge the privileges and immunities of citizens of the United States, to transfer the security and protection of all the civil rights which we have mentioned, from the States to the Federal government? And where is it declared that Congress Shall have the power to enforce that article, was it intended to bring within the power of Congress the entire domain of civil rights heretofore belonging exclusively to the States?" Miller opined that the effect "is to fetter and degrade the State governments by subjecting them to the control of Congress in the exercise of powers heretofore universally conceded to them of the most ordinary and fundamental character."

Miller's articulation of "dual citizenship" and the inapplicability of the Fourteenth Amendment guarantees to state actions laid the groundwork for a host of insidious local ordinances and state statutes that solidified segregation through **Jim Crow laws**, the abrogation of **voting rights** for blacks, and other forms of discrimination that were deemed constitutional under the guise of **states' rights**. *See also BARRON V. BALTIMORE* (1833); *GITLOW V. NEW YORK* (1925); *PLESSY V. FERGUSON* (1896); *U.S. V. CRUIKSHANK* (1876).

**SODOMY LAWS**

*See* GAY RIGHTS; *BOWERS V. HARDWICK* (1986); *LAWRENCE V. TEXAS* (2003).

**SOLICITOR GENERAL**

The number three position in the Department of Justice behind the attorney general and deputy attorney general, the solicitor general represents the U.S. government before the **Supreme Court** in the latter's **Article III** jurisdiction. The position was created in 1870. As of 2015 the Office of the Solicitor General had four deputies and 17 assistants who report to the solicitor general.

**STARE DECISIS**

From the Latin for "let the decision stand," the legal doctrine stare decisis is the principle of following precedents and standards established by cases already ruled upon by the courts. The practice follows two essential rules. The first is that rulings by a superior (higher) court are binding on lower courts. The second is that no court should contravene the precedents it sets, and should look to lower-court rulings for guidance when questions arise. In deciding the constitutionality of state or federal statutes, as well as in **judicial review** of the actions of the executive, the **Supreme Court** relies heavily on precedential cases for its interpretations. *See also MARBURY V. MADISON* (1803).

**STATES' RIGHTS**

The notion of states' rights refers to **federalism**, or the division of powers between the federal government and the states. In particular, states' rights advocates emphasize the **reserved powers** of the states in the **Tenth Amendment** and the (limited) **enumerated powers** accorded to Congress.

Controversies concerning which level of government is (or should be) predominant in the federal system have abounded since the early Republic. In 1819 the **Supreme Court** enunciated in ***McCulloch v. Maryland*** that the range of congressional power vis-à-vis the states extended beyond enumerated powers due to the "necessary and proper clause" in **Article I**, Section 8, of the Constitution. Nonetheless, detractors—including Vice President John C. Calhoun following passage of the Tariff of 1828 (the "Tariff of Abominations")—advocated a doctrine of *nullification* by which states had the right to invalidate a federal law. Notwithstanding a constitutional amendment, a federal law nullified by a state could not be operative. The Compromise Tariff of 1833, adopted during the presidency of Andrew Jackson, ended the nullification crisis alongside the Force Bill, which clarified presidential authority to enforce federal laws.

The issue of slavery, and the resulting Civil War begun in 1861, was as much about states' rights as the normative arguments against the institution of bondage. The Supreme Court decision in ***Dred Scott v. Sanford*** (1857) heralded civil conflict as slave states contended the ruling protected their property rights, while abolitionist states asserted the enforcement of the Fugitive Slave Act violated their rights. The question was scarcely settled during **Reconstruction**, despite the adoption of the **Thirteenth**, **Fourteenth**, and **Fifteenth Amendments**. In ***Texas v. White*** (1869) the Supreme Court ruled that secession was unconstitutional and all laws adopted by Confederate states were null. Regardless, during the era of Reconstruction the high court elucidated a position that the **Civil War Amendments** did *not* apply to the states and refused to **incorporate** the **Bill of Rights** to state actions. In the ***Slaughterhouse Cases*** (1873) the court asserted that the privileges and immunities clause of the Fourteenth Amendment did *not* convey citizenship rights at the state level. Further, in ***U.S. v. Cruikshank*** (1876) the court elaborated that neither **First** nor the **Second Amendment** protections applied to state government actions. Finally, in 1883 the court invalidated the Civil Rights Act of 1875, citing a lack of authority by Congress under the Fourteenth Amendment to bar racial discrimination. The aggregate result of these and other rulings was passage of **Jim Crow laws**, or local ordinances and state laws that preserved and expanded racial segregation, violated the **voting rights** of blacks, an even condoned lynchings (*U.S. v. Harris*, 1883). State policies mandating the segregation of the races were confirmed as constitutional in the case of ***Plessy v. Ferguson*** (1896).

States' rights remained closely aligned with proponents of racial segregation during the **civil rights** movement in the 1950s and 1960s after the Supreme Court invalidated the "separate but equal" doctrine in ***Brown v. Board of Education*** (1954) and Congress passed legislation banning discrimination in employment, housing, and voting during the presidency of Lyndon Johnson (1964–1969). Contemporary debates have shifted significantly away from race to issues of the federal–state balance of power, especially in terms of fiscal federalism, congressional regulation, and issues of governmental efficiency. States' rights advocates point to the decline in federal aid to states since the 1970s and the increase of congressional "mandates" with which they must comply without compensation (i.e., grants-in-aid). In the 1990s the Supreme Court limited congressional power relative to the commerce clause in ***U.S. v. Lopez*** (1995) and curbed Congress's enforcement power under the Fourteenth Amendment in ***City of Boerne v. Flores*** (1997). Many states' rights advocates champion an **original intent** argument relative to the Tenth Amendment and posit that states are "laboratories of democracy" wherein innovative policies can be designed and reject a federal, "one size fits all" approach. Critics of states' rights fear other motives, such as hostility toward minorities including homosexuals. Opponents to same-sex marriage in a majority of states, for example, passed legislation or state constitutional amendments barring the practice until the Supreme Court's ruling in ***Obergefell v. Hodges*** (2015) legalized it. *See also* GAY RIGHTS.

**STONE, HARLAN FISKE (1872–1946)**

A native of Chesterfield, New Hampshire, Stone graduated from Amherst College in 1894 and earned a law degree from Columbia University in 1898. He practiced law in the private sphere while teaching at Columbia University for more than two decades. In 1924 President Calvin Coolidge appointment him attorney general; a year later, Coolidge nominated him as an associate justice to the **Supreme Court**, a position in which he served for 16 years. In 1941 President Franklin Roosevelt nominated him as **chief justice**. Stone was regarded as a steadfast supporter of Roosevelt's New Deal. Among the most famous cases over which he presided as chief justice was the Nazi saboteur controversy in ***Ex Parte Quirin*** (1942). He died of a cerebral hemorrhage on 22 April 1946. He is interred at Rock Creek Park Cemetery in Washington, DC.

**STRICT CONSTRUCTIONISM**

*See* ORIGINAL INTENT.

**STRICT SCRUTINY**

This term refers to the most stringent standard of constitutional **judicial review** by the **Supreme Court**. Generally, the court applies strict scrutiny to cases involving "suspect classifications" such as race, or when a statute or action challenges a fundamental constitutional right (such as the protections afforded in the **Bill of Rights**) or challenges **due process** rights under the **Fourteenth Amendment**. Strict scrutiny differs from lesser standards, such as rationale basis or **intermediate scrutiny** typical for cases involving **gender**. Rather, the standards of strict scrutiny hold that for a law or action to be deemed constitutional, a law must be fashioned using the least restrictive means possible, there must be a "compelling government interest," and the law must be "narrowly tailored." The standard of strict scrutiny is frequently applied to cases involving **affirmative action** and **voting rights**.

***STROMBERG V. CALIFORNIA* (1931)**

This landmark **Supreme Court** case considered the **incorporation** of the **First Amendment** right to symbolic speech through the **Fourteenth Amendment**. At issue was a 1919 California law that barred the public display of red flags—frequently a symbol of communists or communist sympathizers. Yetta Stromberg, a Young Communist worker at a summer camp, was charged with, and convicted of a criminal act when a police raid uncovered a red flag and her leading of a daily ceremony in pledging allegiance to the "workers' flag."

In a 7–2 decision the Supreme Court invalidated the California law on the basis that it was too vague in its application to Stromberg's conviction. The central issue was the statute's provision that banned the red flag "as a sign, symbol or emblem of opposition to organized government." Most importantly, the court contended that symbolic or expressive speech under the First Amendment was applicable to the states under the Fourteenth Amendment. In his **majority opinion**, **Chief Justice Charles Evans Hughes** found that the simple display of a red flag did not conform to the "clear and present danger" test elaborated in ***Schenck v. United States*** (1919). As he concluded, Evans wrote that "The maintenance of the opportunity for free political discussion to the end that government may be responsive to the will of the people and that changes may be obtained by lawful means, an opportunity essential to the security of the Republic, is a fundamental principle of our constitutional system. A statute which, upon its face and as authoritatively construed, is so vague and indefinite as to permit the punishment of the fair use of this opportunity is repugnant to the guaranty of liberty contained in the Fourteenth Amendment."

**SUCCESSION (PRESIDENTIAL)**

The earliest legislation mandating the order of succession of power in case of the president's death dates to the presidency of **George Washington**. The Presidential Succession Act of 1792 assigned (in order) the vice president, the president pro tempore of the Senate, and finally the speaker of the House of Representatives. In 1886 Congress altered the order of succession by replacing the president pro tempore of the Senate and speaker of the House with cabinet officers.

The current order of succession follows the Presidential Succession Act of 1947, adopted during the presidency of Harry S. Truman. The act established the following order in the case of the president's death: the vice president, speaker of the House, president pro tempore of the Senate, and cabinet secretaries in order of the creation of their departments (e.g., State, Treasury, War [Defense], Interior, etc.).

**SUPREMACY CLAUSE**

*See* ARTICLE I (CONSTITUTION).

**SUPREME COURT**

The Supreme Court is the only court in the United States that is specifically mentioned in the Constitution. Congress created a framework for the federal district and appellate courts in the Judiciary Act of 1789. The number of justices on the court is set by Congress; currently there are nine. Presidents **appoint** members of the Supreme Court upon the **advice and consent** of the Senate (confirmation) by a majority vote, and the justices receive lifetime appointments. The Constitution does not specify qualifications for justices, but historically all have been trained in the law. Justices are subject to **impeachment** and removal from office per **Article I**, Section 4, of the Constitution (the only justice to have impeachment charges levied against him by the House of Representatives was Samuel Chase, who was acquitted in the Senate). The **chief justice** leads the court in terms of administration of the court's business and generally writes the **majority opinion** if in agreement with the majority. The chief justice also presides over impeachment proceedings against the president, as **Salmon P. Chase** did in the trial of Andrew Johnson and **William H. Rehnquist** did in the trial of William Clinton.

The Supreme Court is a court of *original jurisdiction*, where cases are first heard, and an *appellate court*. Its original jurisdiction stems from provisions in **Article III** of the Constitution. The high court deals with specific types of cases, including those involving foreign dignitaries, disputes between the states, and disputes between the federal government and the states. The solicitor general—the third highest position in the Department of Justice—represents the federal government before the Supreme Court.

As an appellate court, the Supreme Court reviews cases at its discretion and only once certain criteria have been met. The court typically agrees to hear less than one percent of cases brought before the justices. Petitioners must secure a **writ of certiorari** whereby four of the nine justices agree to hear the case. Cases must be "ripe," or have exhausted all other avenues of appeal in the federal court system or at the state level. Moreover, cases must be "real and adverse." An actual dispute must be at issue, as the Supreme Court does not provide advisory opinions or engage in hypothetical cases. Further, petitioners must have "standing" and be an actual party to the dispute. Finally, the Supreme Court also hears emergency appeals, including petitions for **habeas corpus**. These most often arise with respect to **death penalty** cases and requests for stays of execution, or emergency injunctions to halt lower-court decisions.

A quorum of six justices is required to decide a case. Justices may participate in a case by listening to audio recordings of the oral arguments and reading the transcripts. Statutorily, the term of the Supreme Court commences on the first Monday in October. The term generally continues until June or July and is divided between "sittings," when justices hear cases through oral arguments and deliver opinions, and recesses when they consider the business of the court and also write opinions. Oral arguments generally last 30 minutes, and there are no witnesses and no jury. Justices are free to query parties to the case.

Once a decision has been reached, justices are free to write **concurring opinions** with the majority or **dissenting opinions** in which they lay out their rationale for disagreement with the majority. Generally, the principle of **stare decisis** or precedent plays a pivotal role in the collective decision making of the court. Interest groups and other parties may also file **amicus curiae**, or "friend of the court," briefs in which they lay out an interpretation of a particular case and a legal rationale, but it remains unclear how influential such briefs are vis-à-vis the justices. While analysis of individual members' opinions may cast light on their legal and constitutional approach to any case, the proceedings of court deliberations are not open to the public.

In rare cases the court does not reach a majority opinion. In such cases a plurality of justices typically agrees on select issues of the case, but disagrees on others, and no single opinion receives a majority. In *Marks v. United States* (1977) the court elaborated how plurality opinions should be interpreted: "When a fragmented Court decides a case and no single rationale explaining the result enjoys the assent of five Justices, the holding of the Court may be viewed as that position taken by those Members who concurred in the judgments on the narrowest grounds." Examples of plurality opinions include the **civil rights** cases of ***Regents of the University of California v. Bakke*** (1978) and ***Schuette v. Coalition to Defend Affirmative Action*** (2014), the **voting rights** case of ***Bush v. Vera*** (1996), and the **abortion** case of ***Planned Parenthood v. Casey*** (1992). The absence of a controlling, majority opinion in such cases complicates interpretations by policy makers and lower courts in the implementation of the court's decision.

***SWANN V. CHARLOTTE-MECKLENBURG BOARD OF EDUCATION* (1971)**

This controversial **Supreme Court civil rights** decision addressed the question of busing children across school district lines to achieve racial integration. The case stemmed from the 1954 decision in ***Brown v. Board of Education***, and *Brown II* a year later, in which the Supreme Court ordered desegregation of public school systems around the nation "with all deliberate speed." The constitutional question centered on Charlotte, North Carolina's consolidation of school districts after the state formally ended segregation. Due to residential patterns and the design of the zoning plan, most African American children in urban areas continued to attend nearly all-black schools. Litigation ensued in lower courts, which mandated a busing plan aimed at promoting integration.

In a unanimous opinion authored by **Chief Justice Warren Burger**, the Supreme Court held that busing was constitutional. Burger contended that "The objective [in *Brown*] is to dismantle the dual school system. 'Racially neutral' assignment plans proposed by school authorities to a district court may be inadequate; such plans may fail to counteract the continuing effects of past school segregation resulting from discriminatory location of school sites or distortion of school size in order to achieve or maintain an artificial racial separation." He further argued that "the pairing and grouping of noncontiguous school zones is a permissible tool, and such action is to be considered in light of the objectives sought. . . . No rigid guidelines as to student transportation can be given for application to the infinite variety of problems presented in thousands of situations. . . . District courts must weigh the soundness of any transportation plan. . . . It hardly needs stating that the limits on time of travel will vary with many factors, but probably with none more than the age of the students. The reconciliation of competing values in a desegregation case is, of course, a difficult task with many sensitive facets, but fundamentally no more so than remedial measures courts of equity have traditionally employed."

The court's affirmation of busing as a tool to achieve integration led to protests and a public backlash as school systems around the country, and especially in the South, sought to achieve racial balance. Three years later, however, the court placed a significant restriction on the use of busing in ***Milliken v. Bradley*** (1974). In *Milliken* the court determined that busing could be used in school districts where there had been prior de jure (legally mandated) segregation, but not in cases of de facto segregation, including residential mobility patterns, in which past discriminatory policies were absent.

***SWEATT V. PAINTER* (1950)**

Like ***McLaurin v. Oklahoma State Regents*** (1950), this **Supreme Court** case involving segregation in higher education was a precursor to the landmark decision in ***Brown v. Board of Education*** (1954) that overturned the "separate but equal" doctrine enunciated in ***Plessy v. Ferguson*** (1896). This **civil rights** case considered the establishment of separate law school facilities provided for an African American man, Herman Sweatt, to study law after he was denied admission into the University of Texas Law School. At the time the Texas state constitution prohibited integrated educational facilities. Sweatt refused to enroll in the special Houston-based facility called the Thurgood Marshall School of Law at Texas Southern University. The separate facility had only five full-time faculty, a far less extensive legal library, many fewer students than the University of Texas Law School, and was not yet accredited.

In a unanimous decision authored by **Chief Justice Fred Vinson**, the Supreme Court held that the University of Texas Law School's denial of admission to Sweatt on the basis of race violated his **Fourteenth Amendment** rights to **equal protection** of the laws. In his majority opinion Vinson wrote, "petitioner may claim his full constitutional right: legal education equivalent to that offered by the State to students of other races. Such education is not available to him in a separate law school as offered by the State." Vinson elaborated that "we cannot find substantial equality in the educational opportunities offered white and Negro law students by the State. In terms of number of the faculty, variety of courses and opportunity for specialization, size of the student body, scope of the library, availability of law review and similar activities, the University of Texas Law School is superior. What is more important, the University of Texas Law School possesses to a far greater degree those qualities which are incapable of objective measurement but which make for greatness in a law school. Such qualities, to name but a few, include reputation of the faculty, experience of the administration, position and influence of the alumni, standing in the community, traditions and prestige. It is difficult to believe that one who had a free choice between these law schools would consider the question close." "The State," Vinson asserted, "must provide [legal education] for [petitioner] in conformity with the equal protection clause of the Fourteenth Amendment and provide it as soon as it does for applicants of any other group." The decision ordering Sweatt's admission to the University of Texas Law School was an influential precedent in the court's decision in *Brown* four years later.

**SYMBOLIC SPEECH**

This category of constitutionally protected speech falls under **First Amendment** rights. Symbolic speech may take the form of political speech, per se, as well as figurative actions including flag burning or emblematic signs, pictures, and words on clothing. *See also STROMBERG*

*V. CALIFORNIA* (1931); *TEXAS V. JOHNSON* (1989); *TINKER V. DES MOINES INDEPENDENT COMMUNITY SCHOOL DISTRICT* (1969).

# T

**TAFT, WILLIAM HOWARD (1857–1930)**

The 27th president was born in Cincinnati, Ohio. He graduated from Yale University in 1878 and Cincinnati Law School in 1880. In the early 1880s he served as a prosecutor for Hamilton County, Ohio, as well as collector of revenue. In 1887 he was appointed a judge for Cincinnati. In 1890 President Benjamin Harrison made him solicitor general of the United States, and two years later appointed him a judge of the Sixth Federal Circuit Court. In 1900 President William McKinley charged Taft with organizing a civil government in the Philippines following the Spanish–American War. In 1906 President Theodore Roosevelt briefly appointed him the First Provisional Governor of Cuba. From 1904 to 1908, Taft served as secretary of war to Roosevelt and was the latter's handpicked successor for the presidency in 1908.

Disagreements between Taft and Roosevelt split the Republican Party in 1912 and enabled Democrat Woodrow Wilson to carry the election with just less than 42 percent of the popular vote and 40 states. Taft placed third behind Roosevelt and carried just two states in the **Electoral College**.

Taft, who always aspired to be a **Supreme Court** judge, realized his dream in 1921, when President Warren Harding appointed him as **chief justice**. In 1929, the year before his passing, he successfully argued in favor of an independent building to be constructed for the Supreme Court. In 1926, his opinion for the majority in *Myers v. United States* found that the **Tenure of Office Act**, which had been used as a basis for President Andrew Johnson's impeachment, was unconstitutional.

Taft, who struggled with obesity issues and heart disease, retired from the Supreme Court in February 1930 in ill health. He died on 8 March 1930 and is buried at Arlington National Cemetery. As a former president, he is the only chief justice of the Supreme Court to have had a state funeral to date.

**TANEY, ROGER BROOKE (1777–1864)**

A native of Calvert County, Maryland, Taney graduated from Dickinson College in 1795. He read law in Annapolis and in 1799 was admitted to the Maryland bar and elected to the Maryland state legislature. Unsuccessful in his reelection bid, he pursued private law practice in Frederick, Maryland, until his election to the state senate in 1816. In 1827 he was appointed attorney general in Maryland. President Andrew Jackson appointed him attorney general of the United States in 1831. Two years later Jackson made Taney secretary of the treasury via a recess **appointment**. In 1834 Jackson formally nominated Taney to the post, but the Senate failed to confirm him. Similarly, a year later Jackson nominated him to the **Supreme Court** and the upper chamber again declined to confirm him. In both cases the anti-Jackson, Whig-controlled Senate rejected Jackson's close advisor because of his support of the president's opposition to the Bank of the United States.

In 1835 Jackson successfully nominated Taney as **chief justice** of the Supreme Court thanks to a slim Democratic majority in the Senate. Taney served 28 years in the position. His tenure remains controversial most particularly for the rulings over which he presided regarding slavery in ***Dred Scott v. Sanford*** (1857) and President Abraham Lincoln's suspension of the writ of **habeas corpus** in ***Ex Parte Merryman*** (1861).

Taney died on 13 October 1864 and is interred at St. Johns Cemetery in Frederick, Maryland. He was succeeded as chief justice by **Salmon P. Chase**.

**TENTH AMENDMENT**

Ratified on 15 December 1791, the Tenth Amendment is part of the **Bill of Rights** and enshrines the doctrine of **federalism** as the operational basis of the division of powers between levels of government in the republic. The Tenth Amendment reads: "The powers not delegated to the United States by the Constitution, nor prohibited by it to the States, are reserved to the States respectively, or to the people." The scope of **reserved powers** to the states, or to the people, is open to some interpretation. **States' rights** advocates embrace the Tenth Amendment to argue against federal preemption of state laws, the promulgation of federal regulations, and so forth. However, the framers of the Tenth Amendment did not include the word "express" in front of the phrase "powers not delegated to the United States Constitution," and thus the amendment does *not* conflict with the necessary and proper clause in **Article I**, which enables Congress to implement the laws it passes.

Only rarely has the **Supreme Court** adjudicated cases involving Tenth Amendment claims by the states to circumvent federal regulations. In *United States v. Darby Lumber* (1941) the high court determined that "The amendment states but a truism that all is retained which has not been surrendered. There is nothing in the history of its adoption to suggest that it was more than declaratory of the relationship between the national and state governments as it had been established by the Constitution before the amendment or that its purpose was other than to allay fears that the new national government might seek to exercise powers not granted, and that the states might not be able to exercise fully their reserved powers."

In a handful of cases in the last several decades, however, the Supreme Court has struck down attempts by the federal government to mandate that states implement federal laws and regulations. Among the most controversial was the Court's invalidation of the Brady Handgun Violation Act, passed in 1993, which compelled state and local law enforcement officials to conduct background checks on purchasers. In ***Printz v. United States*** (1997) the majority concluded that enforcement of federal laws lay with the president and that attempts to force state and local officials to implement them were unconstitutional.

**TENURE OF OFFICE ACT (1867)**

This statute was passed by the Republican congressional majorities during **Reconstruction**. Directed at President Andrew Johnson for his opposition to congressional policies toward the South, the act prohibited the president from removing any appointee without the **advice and consent** of the Senate.

In August 1867, in defiance of the law, President Johnson sought to remove Secretary of War Edwin M. Stanton while the Senate was out of session. When the Senate returned to decide on the matter, a majority voted to disapprove of the removal. As Johnson set out to appoint a new secretary of war, the House of Representatives drew up articles of **impeachment** against him. Stanton resigned in 1868 following Johnson's acquittal in the Senate.

Congress repealed the Tenure of Office Act in 1887. Further, in a 1929 **Supreme Court** ruling in *Myers v. United States*, presided over by **Chief Justice Charles Evans Hughes**, a similar law precluding the president from removing appointees was declared unconstitutional.

***TEXAS V. JOHNSON* (1989)**

This landmark **Supreme Court** case addressed the question of **symbolic speech** and **First Amendment** rights. The case pivoted on a Texas law that barred the desecration of a venerated object. Gregory Lee Johnson, a communist and opponent of the policies of President Ronald Reagan, protested at the Republican National Convention in Dallas in 1984, where he doused an American flag with kerosene and lit it on fire. He was arrested, convicted, and sentenced to one year in prison and fined $2,000 under the Texas law. He lost an appeal to a state circuit court but prevailed in the Texas Court of Criminal Appeals. The State of Texas then appealed the case to the Supreme Court.

In a 5–4 decision the high court invalidated the Texas law. Associate Justice William Brennan delivered the **majority opinion**. Brennan elaborated that "The First Amendment literally forbids the abridgment only of 'speech,' but we have long recognized that its protection does not end at the spoken or written word. While we have rejected 'the view that an apparently limitless variety of conduct can be labeled "speech" whenever the person engaging in the conduct intends thereby to express an idea,' ***United States v. O'Brien***, . . . we have acknowledged that conduct may be 'sufficiently imbued with elements of communication to fall within the scope of the First and **Fourteenth Amendments**.' . . . In deciding whether particular conduct possesses sufficient communicative elements to bring the First Amendment into play, we have asked whether '[a]n intent to convey a particularized message was present, and [whether] the likelihood was great that the message would be understood by those who viewed it.'" Brennan further noted that "we have recognized the expressive nature of students' wearing of black armbands to protest American military involvement in Vietnam, ***Tinker v. Des Moines Independent Community School Dist.***, . . . of a sit-in by blacks in a 'whites only' area to protest segregation . . . of the wearing of American military uniforms in a dramatic presentation criticizing American involvement in Vietnam . . . and of picketing about a wide variety of causes." The majority rejected Texas's argument that Johnson had breached the peace. Brennan posited that "a principal 'function of free speech under our system of government is to invite dispute. It may indeed best serve its high purpose when it induces a condition of unrest, creates dissatisfaction with conditions as they are, or even stirs people to anger.'" Brennan concluded: "Johnson was convicted for engaging in expressive conduct. The State's interest in preventing breaches of the peace does not support his conviction, because Johnson's conduct did not threaten to disturb the peace. Nor does the State's interest in preserving the flag as a symbol of nationhood and national unity justify his criminal conviction for engaging in political expression.

**Chief Justice William Rehnquist** authored the **dissenting opinion**. Rehnquist emphasized that "For more than 200 years, the American flag has occupied a unique position as the symbol of our Nation, a uniqueness that justifies a governmental prohibition against flag burning in the way respondent Johnson did here." Rehnquist continued: "The American flag, then, throughout more than 200 years of our history, has come to be the visible symbol embodying our Nation. It does not represent the views of any particular political party, and it does not represent any particular political philosophy. The flag is not simply another 'idea' or 'point of view' competing for recognition in the marketplace of ideas. Millions and millions of Americans regard it with an almost mystical reverence, regardless of what sort of social, political, or philosophical beliefs they may have. I cannot agree that the First Amendment invalidates the Act of Congress, and the laws of 48 of the 50 States, which make criminal the public burning of the flag."

A closer reading of both the majority and dissenting opinions is notable for the reference to the historical symbolism of the American flag in history, poetry, war, and the national anthem. Public opinion polls showed that 71 percent of Americans supported a constitutional amendment to prohibit flag burning after the court's ruling. Twenty-five years later, in 2006, support for such an amendment had fallen to 56 percent, the last time a proposed amendment failed in the Senate by a single vote. A congressional statute passed in 1989 that protected the American flag was invalidated by the Supreme Court in the case of ***U.S. v. Eichman*** in 1990. *See also STROMBERG V. CALIFORNIA* (1931).

***TEXAS V. WHITE* (1869)**

This **Reconstruction**-era **Supreme Court** case involved the sale of United States bonds owned by the State of Texas and sold by the Confederate state legislature during the Civil War after the state had seceded from the Union. The prima facie issue considered who owned the bonds. The larger question was the constitutionality of the secession of the 13 states of the Confederacy, per se. The case occurred while Texas was still under federal military control.

In a 5–3 decision for which **Chief Justice Salmon P. Chase** authored the **majority opinion**, the court held that the Constitution prohibited states from seceding from the Union. Chase wrote: "Considered therefore as transactions under the Constitution, the ordinance of secession, adopted by the convention and ratified by a majority of the citizens of Texas, and all the acts of her legislature intended to give effect to that ordinance, were absolutely null. They were utterly without operation in law. The obligations of the State, as a member of the Union, and of every citizen of the State, as a citizen of the United States, remained perfect and unimpaired. It certainly follows that the State did not cease to be a State, nor her citizens to be citizens of the Union." Chase further argued that "It is not necessary to attempt any exact definitions within which the acts of such a State government must be treated as valid or invalid. It may be said, perhaps with sufficient accuracy, that acts necessary to peace and good order among citizens, such for example, as acts sanctioning and protecting marriage and the domestic relations, governing the course of descents, regulating the conveyance and transfer of property, real and personal, and providing remedies for injuries to person and estate, and other similar acts, which would be valid if emanating from a lawful government must be regarded in general as valid when proceeding from an actual, though unlawful, government, and that acts in furtherance or support of rebellion against the United States, or intended to defeat the just rights of citizens, and other acts of like nature, must, in general, be regarded as invalid and void." The decision upheld the State of Texas's ownership of the bonds, which were either to be returned from the purchasers or the proceeds from their redemption paid to the state.

**THIRD AMENDMENT**

This constitutional amendment, adopted as part of the **Bill of Rights** on 15 December 1791, was a direct response to the British Quartering Acts during the Revolutionary War, during which time British soldiers were empowered to take up residence in private homes. The amendment states the following: "No Soldier shall, in time of peace be quartered in any house, without the consent of the Owner, nor in time of war, but in a manner to be prescribed by law." As of 2016, this amendment has not been subject to any **Supreme Court** litigation.

**THIRTEENTH AMENDMENT**

The first of three amendments adopted after the Civil War and during **Reconstruction**, the Thirteenth was ratified on 6 December 1865 and formally abolished slavery. The text reads: "Neither slavery nor involuntary servitude, except as a punishment for crime whereof the party shall have been duly convicted, shall exist within the United States, or any place subject to their jurisdiction." Section 2 states that "Congress shall have the power to enforce this article by appropriate legislation."

The Thirteenth Amendment codified Abraham Lincoln's Emancipation Proclamation of 1863 and overturned Article I, Section 2 (Clause 3), of the Constitution as adopted in 1787, which provided that slaves be counted as three-fifths of a person for the purposes of congressional representation (thereby enshrining slavery in the foundational document). Despite passage of the amendment, states adopted **black codes** and **Jim Crow laws** that defied its letter and spirit, leaving many freedmen in continued, de facto economic bondage. *See also* FIFTEENTH AMENDMENT; FOURTEENTH AMENDMENT; INCORPORATION DOCTRINE.

**THREE-FIFTHS COMPROMISE**

*See* ARTICLE I (CONSTITUTION); THIRTEENTH AMENDMENT.

***TINKER V. DES MOINES INDEPENDENT COMMUNITY SCHOOL DISTRICT* (1969)**

This **Supreme Court** case pivoted on **symbolic speech** and the **First Amendment** rights of school children. The Iowa case involved four siblings' plan to wear black armbands to school as a means of protesting the Vietnam War. The Des Moines school district adopted a policy that students who did not remove the armbands would be suspended immediately. The Tinker siblings purposely violated the policy, and two of the older children were suspended until the following year, when their protest was scheduled to end. The **American Civil Liberties Union** assisted the family in pursuing the case to the Supreme Court.

Drawing on the precedent in ***Stromberg v. California*** (1931), a 7–2 majority on the court found that school districts had to present constitutionally valid reasons for censoring students' speech—and the Des Moines school district had not done so. Associate Justice Abe Fortas wrote the **majority opinion** and was joined by **Chief Justice Earl Warren**. The majority held that "First Amendment rights, applied in light of the special characteristics of the school environment, are available to teachers and students. It can hardly be argued that either students or teachers shed their constitutional rights to freedom of speech or expression at the schoolhouse gate. . . . On the other hand, the Court has repeatedly emphasized the need for affirming the comprehensive authority of the States and of school officials, consistent with fundamental constitutional safeguards, to prescribe and control conduct in the schools." Fortas continued: "The school officials banned and sought to punish petitioners for a silent, passive expression of opinion, unaccompanied by any disorder or disturbance on the part of petitioners. There is here no evidence whatever of petitioners' interference, actual or nascent, with the schools' work or of collision with the rights of other students to be secure and to be let alone. Accordingly, this case does not concern speech or action that intrudes upon the work of the schools or the rights of other students. . . . In order for the State in the person of school officials to justify prohibition of a particular expression of opinion, it must be able to show that its action was caused by something more than a mere desire to avoid the discomfort and unpleasantness that always accompany an unpopular viewpoint." The majority also chastised the school district for singling out students with black armbands, when other students wore a host of other symbolic jewelry or clothing items. The fundamentals of the *Tinker* decision have since remained intact, although schools *have* been able to limit speech that is indecent, that promotes illegal drug use, or otherwise interferes with teaching. *See also TEXAS V. JOHNSON* (1989).

**TREASON**

*See* IMPEACHMENT.

**TREATIES**

*See* ADVICE AND CONSENT.

**TWELFTH AMENDMENT**

Ratified on 15 June 1804, the Twelfth Amendment altered the system for electing the president and vice president in the **Electoral College**. Essentially, the amendment "encouraged" the formation of a single presidential and vice presidential ticket insofar as electors cast a single ballot for the two offices, rather than two ballots for president under the original provision of **Article II**, Section 1.

Problems arose in the elections of 1796 and 1800 with the development of the First Party System. The second-highest vote getter in the presidential election became vice president. This pitted the president against his rival (i.e., **John Adams** and **Thomas Jefferson** in 1796, and Jefferson and Aaron Burr in 1800), precluding a harmonious working relationship. Moreover, the 1800 election underscored that under the original system, a tie for president was most likely if electors voted along straight party lines. The 1804 election, in which Jefferson was reelected, was the first under which the provisions of the Twelfth Amendment were implemented. The amendment did not alter the requirements for eligibility for the presidential office, nor did it change the process of choosing the president (House of Representatives) or the vice president (Senate) if there is no majority in the Electoral College.

**TWENTIETH AMENDMENT**

Ratified on 23 January 1933, this amendment to the Constitution changed the president's term of office to end at noon on 20 January, mandated that senators' and representatives' terms end on 3 January, and elucidated that if the president-elect dies, the vice president becomes president. Moreover, the Congress must meet at noon on 3 January unless another date is chosen. Finally, if there is a deadlock in the **Electoral College**, the Twentieth Amendment specifies that the incoming Congress—not the outgoing members—will choose the president (House) or vice president (Senate).

The amendment arose primarily to reduce the "lame duck" status of outgoing presidents, whose successors would assume office on 4 March and face a new Congress that would assemble on 23 January.

**TWENTY-FIFTH AMENDMENT**

Adopted on 10 February 1967, this amendment to the Constitution addresses the question of presidential disability. Specifically, the language of the amendment addressed ambiguities in **Article II**, Section 1, by elucidating that the vice president becomes president (not acting president) if the president dies in office. Section 2 delineates that in case of vacancy of the vice presidency, the president may nominate a candidate who requires a majority confirmation in both the House of Representatives and the Senate. Section 3 clarifies that the vice president becomes acting president when the president transmits to the president pro tempore of the Senate and the speaker of the House of Representatives that he is "unable to discharge the powers and duties of his office." Finally, in case of emergency, Section 4 enables that if the vice president and a "majority of either the principal officers of the executive departments or of such other body as Congress may by law provide" transmit to the president pro tempore of the Senate and speaker of the House that the president is unable to fulfill his duties, the vice president becomes acting president.

The issue of presidential succession had plagued the Republic since President William Henry Harrison died in office in 1841. His successor, Vice President John Tyler, contended he was "acting president"; his critics gave him the sobriquet "His Accidency." President Woodrow Wilson was incapacitated by a stroke that left him unable to discharge his duties at the end of his second term. And repeatedly the office of the vice presidency has laid vacant when an incumbent died, as there was no provision in Article II to allow for a replacement. The assassination of John F. Kennedy in November 1963 catalyzed Senator Birch Bayh (D-IN) and Representative Emmanuel Celler (D-NY) to propose an amendment that would remedy filling a vacancy in the presidency and vice presidency and determine presidential disability.

**TWENTY-FIRST AMENDMENT**

Ratified on 5 December 1933, this amendment nullified the **Eighteenth Amendment** prohibition on alcohol sales, manufacture, and transport. The amendment was largely the result of a grassroots movement for the repeal of prohibition and the rampant criminality that resulted from the inability to effectively enforce the Eighteenth Amendment.

**TWENTY-FOURTH AMENDMENT**

Adopted on 23 January 1964, this amendment to the Constitution addressed **voting rights** by abolishing the **poll tax**. Poll taxes, along with literacy tests, **grandfather clauses**, and all-white primaries, had disenfranchised blacks since **Reconstruction** despite **Fifteenth Amendment** guarantees. In 1937 the **Supreme Court** held poll taxes constitutional at the state level. Federal involvement in voting, particularly in the south, commenced during the presidency of John F. Kennedy. **Civil rights** groups and federal oversight led to some important progress, and by the time of the adoption of the Twenty-Fourth Amendment only five states—Alabama, Arkansas, Mississippi, Texas, and Virginia—still had poll taxes. In 1966 the high court ruled in *Harper v. Virginia State Board of Elections* that poll taxes at any level of government violated the **equal protection clause** of the **Fourteenth Amendment**. Federal courts had previously struck down Alabama and Texas poll taxes that continued to operate after adoption of the Twenty-Fourth Amendment.

**TWENTY-SECOND AMENDMENT**

Ratified on 27 February 1951, this amendment to the Constitution limits the president of the United States to two four-year terms in office. One catalyst for the amendment was Franklin D. Roosevelt's election to a third term in 1940, and a fourth term in 1944 (though he died 89 days into his fourth term). Proponents of the amendment, including prominent Republicans such as Thomas E. Dewey (Republican candidate for the presidency in 1944 and 1948), suggested that 16 years in office endangered liberty. Moreover, advocates of the amendment pointed to the precedents of the early Republic, including **George Washington**, **Thomas Jefferson**, and **James Madison**, all of whom stepped down after two terms. Finally, other presidents, including Ulysses S. Grant, Grover Cleveland, and Theodore Roosevelt, had been unsuccessful in running for the presidency thrice. Detractors of the amendment contend that presidents should be able to serve as long as voters wish to elect them. Several attempts at repealing the amendment since the presidency of Ronald Reagan, however, have failed to pass congressional muster.

**TWENTY-SEVENTH AMENDMENT**

Ratified on 7 May 1992, this most recent amendment to the Constitution precludes Congress from increasing or decreasing the legislature's salary until the next legislative session. The proposed amendment dated to September 1789 when Congress and the states took up the **Bill of Rights**. It languished for nearly two centuries until a student at the University of Texas became interested in the matter and embarked on a writing campaign. Seven states had ratified the amendment by the end of 1791, Ohio did so in 1873, and subsequently more than two dozen did so in the 1980s. Alabama, Missouri, and Michigan were the last states to do so in May 1992. Given the time that had passed since the amendment had been proposed, the House of Representatives and the Senate passed a concurrent resolution upholding the validity of state ratification the same month.

**TWENTY-SIXTH AMENDMENT**

Adopted on 1 July 1971, this amendment to the Constitution addressed **voting rights** by according the franchise to all Americans who are at least 18 years of age. A year earlier the **Supreme Court** enunciated in *Oregon v. Mitchell* (1970) that while Congress may establish the voting eligibility age for federal elections, states and localities did not have to follow suit. Passage of the amendment was in large measure due to the military draft imposed during the Vietnam War and the student movement in opposition to U.S. engagement in Southeast Asia in the 1960s. Young men were eligible for the draft at age 18 but could not vote until age 21. President Richard M. Nixon signed legislation in 1970 lowering the federal voting age to 18, but 17 states still retained the age of 21 as a threshold for voting well before the Vietnam conflict ended. *See also* FIFTEENTH AMENDMENT; NINETEENTH AMENDMENT.

**TWENTY-THIRD AMENDMENT**

Formally ratified by the states on 29 March 1961, this amendment to the Constitution made residents of the District of Columbia eligible to vote in presidential elections and accorded the federal city representation in the **Electoral College**. Prior to adoption of the amendment, presidential elections followed **Article II**, Section 1, of the Constitution, which elaborated that electors to the Electoral College came from the states on the basis of population. The text reads: "A number of electors of President and Vice President equal to the whole number of Senators and Representatives in Congress to which the District would be entitled if it were a State, but in no event more than the least populous State; they shall be in addition to those appointed by the States, but they shall be considered, for the purposes of the election of President and Vice President, to be electors appointed by a State; and they shall meet in the District and perform such duties as provided by the twelfth article of amendment."

Currently, the District of Columbia has as many Electoral College votes—three—as the least populous states in the country (Alaska, Delaware, Montana, North Dakota, South Dakota, Vermont, and Wyoming). The Twenty-Third Amendment did not address issues of "home rule" for the federal city (which is controlled by Congress) or congressional representation for residents. The District of Columbia Voting Rights Amendment, which would have rectified these questions, was passed by Congress in 1978 but failed to be ratified by the states seven years later.

**TWO TREATISES ON GOVERNMENT**

*See* LOCKE, JOHN (1632–1704).

# U

**UNREASONABLE SEARCH AND SEIZURE**

*See* FOURTH AMENDMENT; *MAPP V. OHIO* (1961); *U.S. V. LEON* (1984).

***U.S. V. CRUIKSHANK* (1876)**

This **Reconstruction**-era **Supreme Court** case addressed the applicability of the **Fourteenth Amendment** and the **incorporation** of the **Bill of Rights** to state actions following the Civil War. The case arose as a result of a disputed gubernatorial election in Louisiana in 1872. A federal judge ordered that the Republican members of the legislature be seated. White Democrats objected, and some attacked freed African Americans in Colfax, Louisiana sought to preclude Democrats from taking up parish offices. The white insurrectionaries were convicted under the Enforcement Act of 1870 for violations of the freedmen's **First Amendment** right of assembly and **Second Amendment** rights to keep and bear arms. The federal statute made it a crime to deprive individuals of their constitutional rights.

In a 5–4 decision, the Supreme Court took a narrow view of the Fourteenth Amendment and found that the Bill of Rights did *not* apply to the states. **Chief Justice Morrison Waite** wrote the majority opinion and drew upon the precedent in the ***Slaughterhouse Cases*** (1873). He contended that "We have in our political system a government of the United States and a government of each of the several States. Each one of these governments is distinct from the others, and each has citizens of its own who owe it allegiance and whose rights, within its jurisdiction, it must protect. The same person may be at the same time a citizen of the United States and a citizen of a State, but his rights of citizenship under one of these governments will be different from those he has under the other." Waite concluded that "The first amendment to the Constitution prohibits Congress from abridging 'the right of the people to assemble and to petition the government for a redress of grievances.' This, like the other amendments proposed and adopted at the same time, was not intended to limit the powers of the State governments in respect to their own citizens, but to operate upon the National Government alone," and that "The second amendment declares that it shall not be infringed, but this, as has been seen, means no more than that it shall not be infringed by Congress. This is one of the amendments that has no other effect than to restrict the powers of the national government, leaving the people to look for their protection against any violation by their fellow citizens of the rights it recognizes."

The convictions of the white Democrats under the federal statute were thus struck down. This case, like the *Slaughterhouse Cases*, undermined the fundamental rationale of the adoption of the Fourteenth Amendment. Blacks had recourse only to protections by the states, and many adopted insidious policies, "**black codes**," and **Jim Crow laws** that were aimed at disenfranchising, intimidating, and segregating African Americans in violation of their **civil rights**. *See also* VOTING RIGHTS.

***U.S. V. CURTISS-WRIGHT EXPORT CORP.*** **(1936)**

This landmark **Supreme Court** case involved the question of the federal government's ability to regulate foreign affairs, generally, and the president's powers in this regard more specifically. The case arose from a congressional resolution that authorized the president to place an embargo on trade with the countries of Bolivia and Paraguay during the Chaco War. Curtiss-Wright Export Corp. was indicted in federal court for violating the embargo by selling aircraft to Bolivia. The company contended that the embargo was an unconstitutional delegation of authority by Congress to the executive branch.

Associate Justice George Sutherland wrote the **majority opinion** in the case. Only Justice James Clark McReynolds **dissented**. Sutherland drew a sharp distinction between constitutionally **enumerated powers**, **implied powers**, and foreign and domestic policy. He asserted that "The broad statement that the federal government can exercise no powers except those specifically enumerated in the Constitution, and such implied powers as are necessary and proper to carry into effect the enumerated powers, is categorically true only in respect of our internal affairs. . . . It is important to bear in mind that we are here dealing not alone with an authority vested in the President by an exertion of legislative power, but with such an authority plus the very delicate, plenary and exclusive power of the President as the sole organ of the federal government in the field of international relations—a power which does not require as a basis for its exercise an act of Congress but which, of course, like every other governmental power, must be exercised in subordination to the applicable provisions of the Constitution. It is quite apparent that if, in the maintenance of our international relations, embarrassment—perhaps serious embarrassment—is to be avoided and success for our aims achieved, congressional legislation which is to be made effective through negotiation and inquiry within the international field must often accord to the President a degree of discretion and freedom from statutory restriction which would not be admissible were domestic affairs alone involved. Moreover, he, not Congress, has the better opportunity of knowing the conditions which prevail in foreign countries, and especially is this true in time of war. He has his confidential sources of information. He has his agents in the form of diplomatic, consular and other officials.

Secrecy in respect of information gathered by them may be highly necessary, and the premature disclosure of it productive of harmful results."

Sutherland's use of the adjective *plenary* with respect to presidential power in foreign affairs remains controversial. Some scholars contend that the ruling undergirded a growing imbalance between Congress and the president in terms of the war power and led to the "imperial presidency" of Lyndon Johnson and Richard Nixon in the 1960s and 1970s, whereby the executive became (putatively) less accountable. Congressional passage of the **War Powers Resolution**, over President Nixon's **veto** in 1973, was aimed at reigning in presidential adventurism as a result of the protracted war in Vietnam. Nonetheless, the broad language of the *Curtiss-Wright* decision continues to be cited as a justification for far-reaching implied and discretionary powers of the president in foreign affairs. *See also* WAR ON TERROR, WAR ON TERRORISM.

***U.S. V. EICHMAN* (1990)**

This **Supreme Court** case addressed the question of **symbolic speech** and a federal law banning desecration of the American flag following the decision in ***Texas v. Johnson*** (1989). Congress adopted the Flag Protection Act of 1989 in the wake of the high court's decision that a Texas state law barring flag burning was unconstitutional. The statute, which amended a 1968 bill, made it a crime punishable by no more than one year in jail to mutilate, deface, trample upon, or burn the American flag. The statute gave the Supreme Court the sole authority to hear appeals.

The case arose when protestors of the law—on the day it was adopted—burned the flag in Seattle, Washington, and on the steps of Capitol Hill and were subsequently arrested and charged with violating the federal law. In a 5–4 decision penned by Associate Justice William Brennan, the majority held that congressional intent to preserve the American flag as a symbol of national unity did not prevail over **First Amendment** rights to the freedom of expression.

Brennan contended that "Although Congress cast the Flag Protection Act in somewhat broader terms than the Texas statute at issue in *Johnson,* the Act still suffers from the same fundamental flaw: it suppresses expression out of concern for its likely communicative impact. . . . We decline the Government's invitation to reassess this conclusion in light of Congress' recent recognition of a purported 'national consensus' favoring a prohibition on flag-burning. Even assuming such a consensus exists, any suggestion that the Government's interest in suppressing speech becomes more weighty as popular opposition to that speech grows is foreign to the First Amendment. . . . If there is a bedrock principle underlying the First Amendment, it is that the Government may not prohibit the expression of an idea simply because society finds the idea itself offensive or disagreeable. Punishing desecration of the flag dilutes the very freedom that makes this emblem so revered, and worth revering."

***U.S. V. LEON* (1984)**

This **Supreme Court** case was significant insofar as the justices enunciated a "good faith" rule regarding **Fourth Amendment** search and seizures and the "exclusionary rule" elaborated in ***Mapp v. Ohio*** (1961). In *Mapp* the court elucidated that evidence obtained illegally by the police must be excluded from criminal trials. The question in *Leon* centered on a search warrant authorizing the police to surveil suspects on the basis of tips from informants. Although the search warrant was deemed invalid due to a lack of probable cause, the evidence obtained through the surveillance against the suspects, Patsy Stewart and Armando Sanchez, was upheld in court.

In a 6–3 decision, the majority on the court ruled that the evidence in question had been gathered in "good faith" and was admissible. The majority held that "The Fourth Amendment exclusionary rule should not be applied so as to bar the use in the prosecution's case in chief of evidence obtained by officers acting in reasonable reliance on a search warrant issued by a detached and neutral magistrate but ultimately found to be invalid." Author of the **majority opinion**, Associate Justice Byron Wright, asserted that "The deterrent purpose of the exclusionary rule necessarily assumes that the police have engaged in willful, or at the very least negligent, conduct which has deprived the defendant of some right. By refusing to admit evidence gained as a result of such conduct, the courts hope to instill in those particular investigating officers, or in their future counterparts, a greater degree of care toward the rights of an accused. Where the official action was pursued in complete good faith, however, the deterrence rationale loses much of its force. If the purpose of the exclusionary rule is to deter unlawful police conduct, then evidence obtained from a search should be suppressed only if it can be said that the law enforcement officer had knowledge, or may properly be charged with knowledge, that the search was unconstitutional under the Fourth Amendment."

Proponents of law enforcement hailed the decision, contending that the exclusionary rule had led to the suppression of evidence based on technical violations by the police. Critics of the decision, however, posited that the court set aside traditional notions of Fourth Amendment protections by shifting the burden to individuals to suppress evidence from search warrants deemed by the trial court to have been invalid. *See also* SIXTH AMENDMENT.

***U.S. V. LOPEZ* (1995)**

This pivotal **Supreme Court** case was the first to reconsider the extent of congressional power under the **commerce clause** in **Article I** of the Constitution since the New Deal of President Franklin Roosevelt in the 1930s. The case turned on the Gun Free School Zones Act of 1990. The statute, passed by Congress, forbade the possession or discharge of a firearm that "has moved in or that otherwise affects interstate or foreign commerce at a place that the person knows is a school zone." Supporters of the statute contended that gun violence broadly affected economic intercourse given the disruptions it may cause, including the creation of a learning environment in which students could not thrive and bolster future economic productivity in their employment. Critics charged that Congress was circumventing **Second Amendment** protections by invoking the commerce clause inappropriately and arrogating power to enact gun control legislation.

Alfonso Lopez, a student in San Antonio, Texas, was arrested at Edison High School for bringing a revolver and ammunition onto school grounds in violation of the statute. He was tried and convicted in federal court. The Fifth Circuit Court of Appeals, however, reversed the conviction.

In a 5–4 decision, the majority on the Supreme Court, led by **Chief Justice William Rehnquist**, invalidated the statute on grounds that Congress had exceeded its authority under the commerce clause. The majority held that "The Act exceeds Congress' Commerce Clause authority. First, although this Court has upheld a wide variety of congressional Acts regulating intrastate economic activity that substantially affected interstate commerce, the possession of a gun in a local school zone is in no sense an economic activity that might, through repetition elsewhere, have such a substantial effect on interstate commerce. . . . Second, [the statute] contains no jurisdictional element that would ensure, through case-by-case inquiry, that the firearms possession in question has the requisite nexus with interstate commerce."

In his **majority opinion**, Rehnquist declared that "The Government admits, under its 'costs of crime' reasoning, that Congress could regulate not only all violent crime, but all activities that might lead to violent crime, regardless of how tenuously they relate to interstate commerce. . . . Similarly, under the Government's 'national productivity' reasoning, Congress could regulate any activity that it found was related to the economic productivity of individual citizens: family law (including marriage, divorce, and child custody), for example. Under the theories that the Government presents . . . it is difficult to perceive any limitation on federal power, even in areas such as criminal law enforcement or education where States historically have been sovereign. Thus, if we were to accept the Government's arguments, we are hard pressed to posit any activity by an individual that Congress is without power to regulate."

***U.S. V. MILLER* (1939)**

*See* SECOND AMENDMENT.

***U.S. V. NIXON* (1974)**

This **Supreme Court** case occurred in the midst of the Watergate scandal during the presidency of Richard Nixon. At issue was the president's claim of **executive privilege** after federal judge John Sirica ordered the president to turn over tape recordings to the special prosecutor, Leon Jaworski, overseeing the investigation of the break-in at the Democratic

Party headquarters at the Watergate Hotel in Washington, DC. Jaworski had obtained a subpoena for secretly recorded tapes that Nixon had made during discussions with his advisory staff. Nixon complied partially. He turned over *transcripts* of the tapes, which were edited and replete with the phrase "expletive deleted." When Nixon refused to turn over the actual tapes, which Jaworski suspected might connect the president to figures in the Watergate scandal indicted on criminal charges, the special prosecutor appealed the decision to the Supreme Court.

In a unanimous decision (8–0, with **William Rehnquist** not taking part), the justices rejected claims of executive privilege and ordered the president to turn over all tapes. Nixon had claimed an "absolute, unqualified Presidential privilege of immunity from judicial process under all circumstances" and had contended that compliance with the subpoena violated the doctrine of the **separation of powers**. Writing the opinion for the court, **Chief Justice Warren Burger** asserted that "neither the doctrine of separation of powers nor the need for confidentiality of high-level communications, without more, can sustain an absolute, unqualified Presidential privilege of immunity from judicial process under all circumstances. The President's need for complete candor and objectivity from advisers calls for great deference from the courts. However, when the privilege depends solely on the broad, undifferentiated claim of public interest in the confidentiality of such conversations, a confrontation with other values arises. Absent a claim of need to protect military, diplomatic, or sensitive national security secrets, we find it difficult to accept the argument that even the very important interest in confidentiality of Presidential communications is significantly diminished by production of such material for *in camera* inspection with all the protection that a district court will be obliged to provide. The impediment that an absolute, unqualified privilege would place in the way of the primary constitutional duty of the Judicial Branch to do justice in criminal prosecutions would plainly conflict with the function of the courts under **Art. III**. In designing the structure of our Government and dividing and allocating the sovereign power among three co-equal branches, the Framers of the Constitution sought to provide a comprehensive system, but the separate powers were not intended to operate with absolute independence."

The decision brought about the endgame to Nixon's presidency. He resigned 16 days later on 9 August 1974, at which time Vice President Gerald R. Ford took the **oath of office** and became the 38th president of the United States.

### *U.S. V. O'BRIEN* (1968)

This **First Amendment Supreme Court** case addressed the question of **symbolic speech** during the Vietnam War. Protestors routinely burned draft cards to protest the United States' involvement in the conflict in Southeast Asia. Congress amended the Selective Service Act in 1965 to criminalize the knowing mutilation or destruction of draft cards. David

Paul O'Brien burned his draft card in Boston at an antiwar protest and was subsequently arrested and convicted. A federal appeals court upheld his conviction on the basis of nonpossession of a draft card. O'Brien contended that the law was an unconstitutional violation of expressive speech and that Congress had specifically targeted antiwar protesters in passing the legislation.

In an 8–1 decision, the Supreme Court refused to strike down the law. **Chief Justice Earl Warren** delivered the **majority opinion**. Citing the government's interest in tracking those registered for the draft and Congress's broad authority to raise an army, Warren asserted that "The governmental interest and the scope of the 1965 Amendment are limited to preventing harm to the smooth and efficient functioning of the Selective Service System. When O'Brien deliberately rendered unavailable his registration certificate, he willfully frustrated this governmental interest. For this noncommunicative impact of his conduct, and for nothing else, he was convicted. . . . [W]e find that, because of the Government's substantial interest in assuring the continuing availability of issued Selective Service certificates, because amended [statute] § 462(b) is an appropriately narrow means of protecting this interest and condemns only the independent noncommunicative impact of conduct within its reach, and because the noncommunicative impact of O'Brien's act of burning his registration certificate frustrated the Government's interest, a sufficient governmental interest has been shown to justify O'Brien's conviction."

***U.S. V. REESE* (1876)**

This **Reconstruction**-era **Supreme Court** case addressed the **Fifteenth Amendment** and **voting rights**. The case arose from litigation surrounding the Enforcement Act of 1870 passed by Congress. A Kentucky clerk had denied an African American man's request to register to vote, in violation of Section 3 of the law. In a 7–2 decision the court under **Chief Justice Morrison Waite** found that section of the law to be invalid since it did not explicitly repeat the language in the Fifteenth Amendment prohibiting male suffrage on the basis of race, color, or condition of previous servitude. The ruling was a watershed in state and local governments' adoption of **poll taxes**, **grandfather clauses**, literacy tests, and other mechanisms aimed at precluding African Americans from exercising the vote.

***U.S. V. VIRGINIA* (1996)**

This landmark **Supreme Court** case addressed the constitutionality of the Virginia Military Institute's (VMI) policy of excluding females from admission to the school. A state-supported institution, VMI was established in Lexington, Virginia, in 1836 and maintained a male-only admission policy. A district court's finding that the policy was constitutional was overturned by the Fourth District Court of Appeals. In response, Virginia created a program for women, the Virginia Women's Institute of

Leadership at Mary Baldwin College (a private institution), that the state contended was an equivalent program.

In a 7–1 decision the Supreme Court found the male-only admission policy was a violation of the **equal protection clause** of the **Fourteenth Amendment**. Associate Justice Ruth Bader Ginsburg authored the **majority opinion**. Ginsburg asserted that "classifications may not be used, as they once were . . . to create or perpetuate the legal, social, and economic inferiority of women" and that "we find no persuasive evidence in this record that VMI's male-only admission policy 'is in furtherance of a state policy of 'diversity.''" Ginsburg continued, arguing that the separate women's institution was not adequate: "the Commonwealth has shown no 'exceedingly persuasive justification' for withholding from women qualified for the experience premier training of the kind VMI affords."

The decision, which was taken under **intermediate scrutiny** for which **gender** classifications are considered suspect, was a significant victory for women's rights. In effect, the case evidenced some parallels with the **civil rights** case of ***Sweatt v. Painter*** (1950), in which the Supreme Court first struck down separate-but-allegedly-equal educational facilities for African Americans.

***U.S. V. WINDSOR* (2013)**

This **gay rights Supreme Court** case addressed the constitutionality of the **Defense of Marriage Act** (DOMA), which defined marriage as the union of one man and one woman. At issue were two women, Edith Windsor and Thea Spyer, who were married in Ontario, Canada. Windsor lived in New York. Upon Spyer's death, Windsor attempted to claim a spousal exemption on estate taxes. The Internal Revenue Service found that same-sex couples were ineligible for the exemption per DOMA. The state of New York, however, recognized Windsor's and Spyer's marriage.

By a 5–4 majority, the Supreme Court struck down the part of DOMA that defined marriage as the union of a man and a woman. Associate Justice Anthony Kennedy authored the **majority opinion**. The majority held that Section 3 of DOMA was a "deprivation of liberty" of the individual guaranteed by the **Fifth Amendment**. Citing New York's recognition of the same-sex marriage, Kennedy posited that "When the State used its historic and essential authority to define the marital relation in this way, its role and its power in making the decision enhanced the recognition, dignity, and protection of the class in their own community. DOMA, because of its reach and extent, departs from this history and tradition of reliance on state law to define marriage. Discriminations of an unusual character especially suggest careful consideration to determine whether they are obnoxious to the constitutional provision. . . . For same-sex couples who wished to be married, the State acted to give their lawful conduct a lawful status. This status is a far-reaching legal acknowledgment of the intimate relationship between two people, a relationship deemed by the State worthy of dignity in the community equal with all other marriages. It reflects both the community's considered perspective on the historical roots of the institution of marriage and its evolving understanding of the meaning of equality. . . . DOMA seeks to injure the very class New York seeks to protect. By doing so it violates basic **due process** and **equal protection** principles applicable to the Federal Government. . . . The avowed purpose and practical effect of the law here in question are to impose a disadvantage, a separate status, and so a stigma upon all who enter into same-sex marriages made lawful by the unquestioned authority of the States."

The controversial decision was considered a major victory for gay rights advocates and set an important precedent that paved the way for the legalization of same-sex marriage in all 50 states in ***Obergefell v. Hodges*** (2015). *See also HOLLINGSWORTH V. PERRY* (2013).

# V

## VETO (POWER)

**Article I**, Section 7, of the Constitution (**presentment clause**) provides the president with the power to approve or disapprove legislation passed by Congress. Article I, Section 7, states: "Every Bill which shall have passed the House of Representatives and the Senate, shall, before it become a Law, be presented to the President of the United States; If he approve he shall sign it, but if not he shall return it, with his Objections to that House in which it shall have originated, who shall enter the Objections at large on their Journal, and proceed to reconsider it." In returning legislation back to Congress, presidents pen "messages" in which they clarify, in greater or lesser detail, their objections to the bill. Since the beginning of the Republic, veto messages have been archived in the Public Papers of the Presidents.

The president does not have the final word on legislation, however. Congress can override the president's objections and pass the disputed bill with a supermajority of two-thirds of each chamber. Article I, Section 7, elucidates: "If after such Reconsideration two thirds of that House shall agree to pass the Bill, it shall be sent, together with the Objections, to the other House, by which it shall likewise be reconsidered, and if approved by two thirds of that House, it shall become a Law. But in all such Cases the Votes of both Houses shall be determined by Yeas and Nays, and the Names of the Persons voting for and against the Bill shall be entered on the Journal of each House respectively." Congressional overrides of presidential vetoes may be considered a sign of a weak executive. However, from 1789 to 2013, of the 1,497 vetoes presidents have cast, only 109 (7.3 percent) have been successfully overridden.

Scholars often cast the veto as a *negative* presidential power. However, the foundations of Article I, Section 7, may enable the president to *threaten* a veto of legislation in the bid to shape legislative outcomes. For example, in the modern era presidents may issue a veto threat to committee chairs in Congress via "statements of administration policy" whereby legislative aides to the president maintain they will recommend a veto if certain statutory provisions are omitted or retained. Presidents' success in altering legislation to their liking, particularly under conditions of divided government, remains a topic of significant scholarly interest and debate. *See also* *CITY OF NEW YORK V. CLINTON* (1998); POCKET VETO.

**VINSON, FREDERICK "FRED" MOORE (1890–1953)**

A native of Louisa, Kentucky, Vinson graduated from Centre College in 1909 and earned a law degree there in 1911. He became city attorney for Ashland, Kentucky, in 1911 and county attorney in 1921. He was elected to the U.S. House of Representatives in 1924 and was reelected in 1926. After a two-year hiatus, during which time he was in private law practice, he won election to the House again in 1926 and was reelected thrice. President Franklin Roosevelt appointed him to the District of Columbia Circuit Court of Appeals in 1938. During World War II, he served in numerous positions in the Roosevelt administration, including as director of the Office of War Mobilization and Conversion. In 1945 President Harry Truman appointed him secretary of the treasury. A year later Truman appointed him **chief justice** of the **Supreme Court**. He served for seven years until his death on 8 September 1953. He is interred at Pinehill Cemetery in Louisa, Kentucky.

**VIRGINIA PLAN**

Sponsored by Edmund Randolph, the Virginia Plan was offered as a model of legislative representation at the Constitutional Convention in Philadelphia in 1787. The plan called for a bicameral legislature for which both houses would be elected on the basis of population. By contrast, the **New Jersey Plan** advocated a unicameral legislature with equal state representation. The **Great Compromise**, or Connecticut Compromise, emerged as an alternative to reconcile differences between large and small states. The ultimate structure upon which the delegates to the Convention agreed included a House of Representatives elected proportionate to population, with slaves counted as three-fifths of a person, and a Senate with two members elected by each state legislature.

**VOTING RIGHTS**

The issue of voting rights has historically concerned (1) individual **civil rights** and discriminatory practices and (2) questions of representation and fairness in boundaries for legislative districts for Congress and at the state level.

The **Fifteenth Amendment**, adopted during **Reconstruction**, set out to ensure that African Americans could exercise the franchise effectively following the Civil War. The Supreme Court's narrow interpretation of citizenship rights in ***U.S. v. Reese*** (1876) effectively denied blacks the right to vote. Further, the **Fourteenth Amendment** guaranteed **due process** of law and **equal protection** of the laws. Regardless, the **Supreme Court** took a narrow view of these **Civil War Amendments** and undermined both their spirit and letter in the late 19th century. States erected a panoply of barriers to the African American vote, including **poll taxes**, **grandfather clauses**, and all-white primaries. In the ***Slaughterhouse Cases*** (1873) the high court asserted that the Fourteenth Amendment did not apply to state-level actions, paving the way for **Jim Crow laws** that disenfranchised blacks. In the *Civil Rights Cases* (1883), a consolidation of five cases, the high court struck down the 1875 Civil Rights Act, which set out to prohibit segregation, as unconstitutional.

It was not until the early 20th century that the court reversed course and began **incorporating** the protections in the **Bill of Rights** to the states regarding voting. In ***Guinn v. United States*** (1915) the justices struck down the use of grandfather clauses to determine voter eligibility. Further, the court asserted that all-white primaries violated the Fourteenth Amendment in *Nixon v. Herndon* (1927) and struck down the practice with regard to state actions to transfer authority to political parties in *Smith v. Allwright* (1944). In 1964 the **Twenty-Fourth Amendment** abolished the poll tax. The Voting Rights Act of 1965 was perhaps the most important subsequent factor that enabled parity in black and white voter registration and electoral participation within a decade.

Women similarly struggled in the 19th century in their bid to exercise the franchise. In ***Minor v. Happersett*** (1875) the Supreme Court found no intrinsic right in the Constitution regarding the women's vote. Only passage of the **Nineteenth Amendment** in 1920, after decades of lobbying by the suffragette movement, enshrined a prohibition on **gender discrimination**. In the 20th century young Americans earned the right to vote at age 18 with ratification of the **Twenty-Sixth Amendment** in 1971. The push to lower the voting age from 21 years in most states emanated from the student movement against the Vietnam War and the imposition of the military draft.

In the last half century the Supreme Court has struggled considerably with the issue of redistricting at the congressional and state levels. In ***Baker v. Carr*** (1962) the majority of justices set aside the notion that redistricting constituted a "political question" and established federal oversight of cases regarding congressional districts. In 1964 the decisions in ***Reynolds v. Sims*** and ***Wesberry v. Sanders*** addressed issues of unequal population apportionment of congressional districts and mandated "one person, one vote" to ensure that districts were drawn fairly so as not to advantage more or less populated districts over one another.

The most controversial cases of redistricting involve **gerrymandering**, which is an effort to draw legislative districts to benefit one political party or another. In the case of racial gerrymandering, the issue concerns attempts either to disenfranchise some segment of the population based on race or to *promote* the potential representation of a racial group by the drawing of boundaries (e.g., minority-majority districts in Congress). In ***Gomillion v. Lightfoot*** (1960) the court struck down efforts to redraw the boundaries of Tuskegee, Alabama, to dilute the black vote on Fifteenth Amendment grounds. The case of ***Shaw v. Reno*** (1993) addressed the drawing of congressional districts to favor election of minorities. The Supreme Court held that while states must take into account the mandates of the 1965 Voting Rights Act, drawing of districts along racial lines is subject to **strict scrutiny** under the **equal protection clause** of the Fourteenth Amendment. The high court reaffirmed this view in ***Miller v. Johnson*** (1995) when it struck down an oddly shaped Georgia congressional district with an African American majority. In ***Bush v. Vera*** (1996) the court reiterated that redistricting cases that appear to favor one racial group over another must be narrowly tailored in support of a compelling state interest. In ***Shelby County v. Holder*** (2013) the court invalidated a provision of the 1965 Voting Rights Act requiring states to gain "preclearance" from the Department of Justice before redrawing congressional districts. The majority contended that the formula to determine past discrimination by states was outdated.

# W

**WAITE, MORRISON REMICK (1816–1888)**
Born in Lyme, Connecticut, Waite graduated from Yale College in 1837. He relocated to Ohio where he read law and became an attorney in Maumee City. He practiced law in Toledo, Ohio, until 1874. He was elected to the Ohio legislature in 1850, serving a single term and unsuccessfully pursuing a seat in the U.S. House of Representatives in 1846 and 1862. In 1871 President Ulysses S. Grant appointed him to the commission to settle the United States' claims against Great Britain stemming from that country's support of the Confederacy during the Civil War. While serving as president of the Ohio Constitutional Convention in 1872, Waite was appointed **chief justice** of the **Supreme Court** by President Grant. He served for 14 years, during which time the court took a narrow view of the **Thirteenth**, **Fourteenth**, and **Fifteenth Amendments** passed after the Civil War. Prominent cases decided during Waite's tenure include the ***Slaughterhouse Cases*** (1873), ***Minor v. Happersett*** (1875), and ***U.S. v. Cruikshank*** (1875). Waite died on 23 March 1888 and is interred at Woodlawn Cemetery in Toledo, Ohio.

**WAR ON TERROR, WAR ON TERRORISM**
The United States' general mobilization of governmental, diplomatic, and military resources to combat terrorism during the presidency of George W. Bush occurred after the 11 September 2001 attacks on the World Trade Center in New York City and the Pentagon in Washington, DC. Terrorists hijacked commercial aircraft and used the fuel-laden aircraft as missiles to inflict maximum casualties and damage.

The constitutional issues raised by the War on Terror and the governmental response to combat terror threats have centered particularly on the growth of the national security state and **civil liberties**, the detention of enemy combatants captured in Afghanistan and Iraq at Guantanamo Bay, Cuba, and military tribunals the president and Congress attempted to establish to prosecute suspected terrorists. Passed in October 2001, the USA PATRIOT Act enabled federal agencies to gather intelligence more easily, detain immigrants indefinitely, and perform warrantless searches of electronic communications and financial records. Further, the *New York Times* exposed the National Security Agency's (NSA) warrantless wiretapping of foreign nationals, including those communicating with U.S. citizens, in violation of the **Foreign Intelligence Surveillance Act** (FISA). Subsequent legislation clarified compliance with FISA. Nonetheless, President Barack Obama's detractors posit that he has kept, expanded, or even gone beyond Bush's policies. Obama signed an extension of PATRIOT Act provisions in 2011 that continued wiretapping provisions and expanded government access to business and telephone records, which critics charge is a violation of **Fourth Amendment** protections regarding search and seizure. Obama also has come under criticism for his use of drones in Afghanistan and Iraq, which have contributed to civilian deaths and, in the case of Anwar al-Awlaki, the targeted killing by drones of an American-born suspected terrorist. Critics contend that the targeting of Americans abroad violates their constitutional rights to **due process** under the **Fifth Amendment**.

Another facet of the War on Terror that raises constitutional issues includes captured terrorists and their detainment at the U.S. military base at Guantanamo Bay, Cuba. President Bush claimed that those captured in Afghanistan were "enemy combatants" without Geneva Convention or constitutional protections. Some detainees claimed they had been tortured through techniques such as waterboarding or simulated drowning. Bush and Congress tried to set up military tribunals for the prosecution of captured terrorists, but the **Supreme Court** reaffirmed detainees' rights to **habeas corpus**, struck down Bush's unilateral attempt to create tribunals, and invalidated Congress's Military Commissions Act by contending that detainees had constitutional protections. The controlling cases are ***Rasul v. Bush*** (2004), ***Hamdi v. Rumsfeld*** (2004), ***Hamdan v. Rumsfeld*** (2006), and ***Boumediene v. Bush*** (2008).

As a candidate in 2008, Barack Obama promised to close the detainee facility in Guantanamo Bay, Cuba. He sought to try the detainees in U.S. civilian courts but faced a significant public backlash. Similarly, the transfer of detainees to U.S. prisons proved highly unpopular. As of 2015, the president has instead quietly transferred more than 100 detainees to other countries, and approximately 120 remain at Guantanamo Bay, down from a high-water mark of over 600.

**WAR POWER**

*See* ARTICLE I (CONSTITUTION).

**WAR POWERS RESOLUTION**

The purpose of this act of Congress was to compel the president to consult with Congress prior to and after introducing armed forces into hostilities. Passed over President Richard M. Nixon's **veto** in 1973, the statute mandates that the president inform the speaker of the House and the president pro tempore of the Senate within 48 hours when armed forces are committed to military action. The law specifies that within 60 days the president shall "terminate any use of United States Armed Forces . . . unless the Congress has declared war or has enacted specific authorization for such use of United States Armed Forces, has extended by law such sixty-day period, or is physically unable to meet as a result of an armed attack upon the United States. Such sixty-day period shall be extended for not more than an additional thirty days if the President determines and certifies to the Congress in writing that unavoidable military necessity respecting the safety of United States Armed Forces requires the continued use of such armed forces in the course of bringing about a prompt removal of such forces."

The law emerged as a result of legislators' frustration with presidents' deployment of troops in long-term conflicts for which Congress had not declared war, including the Korean War and, most significantly at the time of the law's adoption, the Vietnam War. Since passage of the law, presidents have submitted more than 130 reports on the use of military force to Congress, yet no president has acknowledged the constitutionality of the statute. The language used in presidential reports is paramount: presidents have informed Congress "consistent with" the War Powers Resolution instead of "in compliance with" the statute.

Presidents have viewed the statute as an interference with the Constitution's prescribed role for the executive as **commander-in-chief**. Moreover, the constitutionality of the law is questionable as an improper legislative veto under the **Supreme Court**'s ruling in ***INS v. Chadha*** (1983). Congress, however, maintains the sole constitutional responsibility for declaring war and raising and supporting the armed forces as provided in Article I, Section 8, of the Constitution. The authors of the law also reference the "necessary and proper clause" (or elastic clause) in Article I, Section 8, that provides Congress "the power to make all laws necessary and proper for carrying into execution, not only its own powers but also all other powers vested by the Constitution in the Government of the United States, or in any department or officer hereof."

Proponents of the War Powers Resolution maintain that the statute has reigned in presidential military adventurism. Detractors contend that the statute is unconstitutional, that consultation with Congress is unworkable given the need for "secrecy and despatch" (as **Alexander Hamilton** argued in **Federalist** no. 70) in military operations and foreign affairs, and that it should be repealed. Given the delicate balance in the division of war powers between the branches, neither has had an incentive to demand a definitive interpretation of the constitutionality of the statute by the Supreme Court.

**WARRANT**

*See* FOURTH AMENDMENT.

**WARRANTLESS WIRETAPS**

*See* WAR ON TERROR, WAR ON TERRORISM.

**WARREN, EARL (1891–1974)**

A native of Los Angeles, California, Warren earned undergraduate and law degrees from the University of California in 1912 and 1914, respectively. After practicing in the private sphere, he became deputy city attorney for Oakland, California, in 1919. In 1920 he served as deputy assistant district attorney for Alameda County. Five years later he was appointed district attorney for Alameda County and won election to the office in 1926. In 1942 he ran successfully for the governorship of California and was reelected twice. In 1948 he ran on the Republican ticket as the vice presidential running mate to Thomas Dewey. In 1952 he lost the Republican nomination for president to Dwight D. Eisenhower. In 1953 President Eisenhower nominated Warren as **chief justice** of the **Supreme Court** as a recess **appointment**. The Senate confirmed his appointment in 1954. In 1963 he chaired the so-called Warren Commission to investigate the assassination of President John F. Kennedy. He retired from the Supreme Court in June 1969 after 15 years as chief justice.

The Warren Court is widely regarded for its progressive decisions regarding the expansion of **civil liberties** and **civil rights**, with a particular focus on rights of the accused and desegregation. Prominent decisions included ***Brown v. Board of Education*** (1954), ***Gideon v. Wainwright*** (1963), ***Reynolds v. Sims*** (1964), ***Miranda v. Arizona*** (1966), and ***Loving v. Virginia*** (1967). President Eisenhower once opined that his appointment of Warren was one of two mistakes he made during his two terms, as he expected Warren to take a more reserved approach on the bench.

Warren died on 9 July 1974. He is buried at Arlington National Cemetery in Arlington, Virginia.

**WASHINGTON, GEORGE (1732–1799)**

The commander of the Continental Army during the Revolutionary War, presiding officer at the Constitutional Convention in 1787, and first American president was born in Westmoreland County, Virginia. Historians have ascertained little about his childhood. In 1750, at the age of 17, he became a surveyor of Culpeper County, Virginia. He fought in the French and Indian War, obtaining the rank of lieutenant colonel in 1754. He was elected to the Virginia colonial legislature (House of Burgesses) in 1759 and gradually became a proponent of the state's revolutionary movement against Great Britain.

A member of the first and second Continental Congresses, Washington was chosen to lead the Continental Army on 15 June 1775. He suffered a number of defeats, including the Battle of Brandywine, and stunning victories such as Saratoga, New York; endured significant casualties at Valley Forge, Pennsylvania; and watched from afar in New York as Cornwallis was defeated with French assistance at Yorktown. During the Revolutionary War, he often quarreled with Congress over funding for the troops, nearly lost his command, and was the subject of derision, as reflected in the Conway Cabal. He returned to his cherished Mount Vernon, Virginia, estate after the Revolution but was recalled to public service as the presiding officer of the Constitutional Convention in Philadelphia in 1787, which set out to rectify the dysfunctions of the **Articles of Confederation**. He was the first signatory to the new Constitution.

Although it may be argued that Founders of the Constitution, including its architect **James Madison**, never anticipated presidential candidates would routinely win a majority of the **Electoral College**—thereby throwing the decision to the House of Representatives—Washington was elected *unanimously* in the 1788 and 1792 elections. **John Adams** received the second-highest number of electoral votes and became vice president.

Washington's cabinet departments numbered three: state, treasury, and war (defense). He made his appointments not on the basis of partisanship, as formal political parties did not yet exist, but rather on nominees' support of the Constitution. He chose **Alexander Hamilton** as secretary of the treasury, **Thomas Jefferson** as secretary of state, Henry Knox as secretary of war, and Edmund Randolph as attorney general. The rift between Jefferson and Hamilton over the latter's economic policies would commence a rivalry between the **Federalists** and the emerging Democratic-Republicans that would solidify the First Party System by the 1800 election.

As the first chief executive of the United States, Washington's presidency was naturally precedent setting. He believed in strict separation of the branches. Events in Europe and domestically solidified the parameters of the **commander-in-chief** role and presidential primacy in foreign affairs. In May 1793 Washington issued the Neutrality Proclamation, declaring the United States impartial in the war between France and Britain despite a formal alliance that still existed between France and the United States. Further, with the Jay Treaty, ultimately approved by the Senate, the president successfully established peace with Britain, to the expense of supporters of France, including Jefferson. Finally, when residents of western Pennsylvania refused to pay an excise task on whiskey passed by Congress, Washington acted swiftly to enlist state militias to put down the insurrection. Of those convicted of treason, the president exercised his prerogative of the **pardon power**.

Washington also established an important precedent—unbroken until the presidency of Andrew Jackson—that the **veto power** was to be used on constitutional grounds. In 1792 he issued the first veto, rejecting an apportionment act. Washington contended that the bill provided for unequal representation in the House of Representatives. In 1797 he vetoed a military bill that terminated two cavalry companies and, objecting as commander-in-chief, returned the bill to Congress. The House swiftly repassed legislation without the objectionable provision.

Washington oversaw the establishment of the federal judiciary, made treaties with natives and Spain, and with Hamilton's early assistance set out to expand the national economy while freeing the inchoate nation from debt. He made the decision to leave office after two terms—another precedent that remained unbroken until the presidency of Franklin D. Roosevelt in 1940. His farewell address to the nation warned of the dangers of sectionalism, as well as the "baneful effects of the spirit of party" and cautioned the young nation to avoid "interweaving our destiny with that of any part of Europe" and "entangl[ing] our peace and prosperity in the toils of European ambition, rivalship, interest, humor or caprice."

The sage general's admonitions notwithstanding, John Adams's tumultuous presidency would buttress the development of party factions, and not only would the U.S. engage France in the Quasi-War but also less than a decade later America would square off militarily with Britain in the War of 1812. And Washington's warnings about sectionalism were lost on his successors, who oversaw significant territorial expansion but could not resolve the issue of slavery, leading to southern secession and the Civil War—fundamental challenges to the constitutional order of which Washington could scarcely conceive as he retired to Mount Vernon in 1797.

Washington died on 14 December 1799 after falling ill inspecting his plantation on horseback in cold weather. He is buried in a tomb at his Mount Vernon estate.

***WEBSTER V. REPRODUCTIVE HEALTH SERVICES* (1989)**

This pivotal **Supreme Court** decision addressed state-level attempts to curtail the use of public funds for **abortions**. The case arose from a Missouri statute that prohibited the abortion of fetuses deemed viable, precluded state facilities from performing abortions, and banned public funds from being used to counsel women to have abortions unless the mother's life was in danger. A federal district court and an appeals court both struck down the law on grounds that the statute was inconsistent with the right to abortion held in ***Roe v. Wade*** (1973).

The decision by the Supreme Court resulted in a somewhat complicated plurality opinion. **Chief Justice William Rehnquist** wrote the opinion, which was joined fully by only two other justices and with parts of which other justices concurred. In effect, the court ruled that although abortion was constitutional under the **due process clause** of the **Fourteenth Amendment**, the fetal viability was also constitutional insofar as there is a state interest in protecting the life of the unborn. In her **concurring opinion**, Associate Justice Sandra Day O'Connor asserted that she disagreed with the fetal viability provision of the state law and called for judicial restraint, but nonetheless upheld the Missouri law on the basis that it did not impose an "undue burden" on women. Associate Justice Antonin Scalia concurred but chastised his colleagues for failing to overturn *Roe* in toto.

The net effect of the ruling was to narrow abortion rights, which was welcomed by pro-life groups and signaled a setback for pro-choice groups that championed unrestricted access to abortions. *See also GONZALES V. CARHART* (2007); *PLANNED PARENTHOOD V. CASEY* (1992).

***WESBERRY V. SANDERS* (1964)**

This **Supreme Court voting rights** case centered on congressional districts in Georgia that did not have proportionate populations. As the syllabus of the case read, the petitioners were "qualified voters in Georgia's Fifth Congressional District, the population of which is two to three times greater than that of some other congressional districts in the State. Since there is only one Congressman for each district, appellants claimed debasement of their right to vote resulting from the 1931 Georgia apportionment statute and failure of the legislature to realign that State's congressional districts more nearly to equalize the population of each." The constitutional question focused on whether districts' population imbalance violated the **equal protection clause** of the **Fourteenth Amendment**.

In a 6–3 decision for which Associate Justice Hugo Black authored the **majority opinion**, the court held that Georgia's malapportionment discriminated against voters. By obliging one member of Congress to represent up to three times more voters in one district than another, the apportionment scheme ran afoul of the "one man, one vote" standard that the court enunciated more fully in ***Reynolds v. Sims*** (1964). As Black contended, the notion that "a vote is worth more in one district than in another would not only run counter to our fundamental ideas of democratic government, it would cast aside the principle of a House of Representatives elected 'by the People.'" As a result of the ruling, states around the country were required to draw congressional district boundaries roughly equal in population. As of 2015, a single congressional district has an approximate population of 700,000. Nonetheless, state legislatures' attempts to **gerrymander** congressional districts on the basis of partisanship, ethnicity, or race remain a litigious issue following the decennial census. *See also BAKER V. CARR* (1962).

**WHITE, EDWARD DOUGLASS (1845–1921)**

A native of Lafourche Parish, Louisiana, White's studies at Georgetown College (now University) were interrupted by the outbreak of the Civil War. He halted his studies to join the Confederate Army but was captured in 1863 and held until 1865 by Union forces. At the end of the conflict, White read law and studied at the University of Louisiana. In 1866 he established a law practice in New Orleans. He was elected to the Louisiana State Senate in 1874 and served on the Louisiana Supreme Court from 1878 to 1880. In 1891 he was elected to the U.S. Senate. President Grover Cleveland nominated him to the **Supreme Court** in February 1894. In 1910 President William Taft nominated him as **chief justice**, and he served in the position until 1921.

White voted with the majority in the 1896 case of ***Plessy v. Ferguson*** that validated "separate but equal" facilities for blacks and whites in a ratification of state segregation policies. However, while serving as chief justice, White authored the **majority opinion** in ***Guinn v. United States*** in which **grandfather clauses** and literacy tests aimed at precluding African Americans from voting were invalidated.

White died on 19 May 1921. He is buried in Oak Hill Cemetery in Washington, DC.

***WHITNEY V. CALIFORNIA* (1927)**

This **First Amendment Supreme Court** case pivoted on the conviction of a young woman, Anita Whitney, for violating a 1919 California Criminal Syndicalism Act, which prohibited advocating the violent overthrow of the government. The law, like others adopted around the country, arose during the First Red Scare following World War I. Whitney was convicted for her involvement in the Agricultural Workers' Industrial Union meetings across the Imperial Valley in California. She and others convicted under the statute were sentenced to more than 40 years in prison or deportation.

In a 9–0 decision, the majority on the Supreme Court upheld her and others' convictions, ruling the statute was constitutionally valid and did not violate either the **due process clause** or the **equal protection clause** of the Constitution. In his **majority opinion**, Associate Justice Edward T. Sanford drew upon the "the clear and present danger" principle articulated in ***Schenck v. United States*** (1919) but went further to argue that "utterances inimical to the public welfare, tending to incite crime, disturb the public peace, or endanger the foundations of organized government and threaten its overthrow" were subject to criminalization.

Justice Louis Brandeis's **concurring opinion** is nonetheless frequently cited as one of the most remarkable defenses of free speech in the court's history. Brandeis opined that "Whenever the fundamental rights of free speech and assembly are alleged to have been invaded, it must remain open to a defendant to present the issue whether there actually did exist at the time a clear danger; whether the danger, if any, was imminent; and whether the evil apprehended was one so substantial as to justify the stringent restriction interposed by the legislature." Citing the Republic's Revolutionary War leaders, Brandeis asserted that "They did not fear political change. They did not exalt order at the cost of liberty. To courageous, self-reliant men, with confidence in the power of free and fearless reasoning applied through the processes of popular government, no danger flowing from speech can be deemed clear and present unless the incidence of the evil apprehended is so imminent that it may befall before there is opportunity for full discussion. If there be time to expose through discussion the falsehood and fallacies, to avert the evil by the processes of education, the remedy to be applied is more speech, not enforced silence. Only an emergency can justify repression. Such must be the rule if authority is to be reconciled with freedom. Such, in my opinion, is the command of the Constitution. It is therefore always open to Americans to challenge a law abridging free speech and assembly by showing that there was no emergency justifying it."

The precedent in *Whitney* was effectively overturned in the landmark case of ***Brandenburg v. Ohio*** (1969).

**WILSON, JAMES (1742–1798)**

Born near St. Andrews, Scotland, Wilson came to pre-Revolutionary America in 1766. Having studied at the Universities of St. Andrews, Glasgow, and Edinburgh, Wilson did not receive a degree until he was awarded an honorary degree from the Academy and College of Philadelphia (now the University of Pennsylvania). He read law and in 1767 set up a private law practice in Reading, Pennsylvania. He was a founding trustee of Dickinson College.

Wilson played a major intellectual role in Revolutionary thought and in the Founding of the American Republic. In 1774 he authored a pamphlet titled "Considerations on the Nature and Extent of the Legislative Authority of the British Government." In this exposition he asserted that the colonies owed an allegiance to the king but that Parliament had no right to pass laws affecting the colonies because the latter had no representation. During the Revolutionary War, he rose to the rank of brigadier general of the Pennsylvania militia. He was a member of the Continental Congress and signer of the **Declaration of Independence**.

Considered one of the most erudite Founders at the Constitutional Convention in Philadelphia in 1787 alongside **James Madison**, Wilson served on the Committee of Detail. He is credited with proposing the Three-Fifths Compromise to solve the matter of representation in the House of Representatives between slave and nonslave states. His arguments in favor of a strong executive helped shape **Article II** of the Constitution and the contours of presidential power. Unlike many of his contemporaries who feared a strong executive, Wilson made the case that an energetic president was essential to cementing the nation's **republican** virtues. He played a crucial role in debates about ratification of the Constitution. Many historians argue that his "speech in the statehouse yard" in October 1787 was pivotal in shaping the contours of the ratification debate. It was reprinted throughout the states and was nearly as prominent as the **Federalist Papers** in support of the new governmental structure.

President **George Washington** nominated Wilson to the **Supreme Court** as an associate justice in September 1789. He took part in the first major precedential case on the high court in 1793 in *Chisholm v. Georgia,* which led to the adoption of the **Eleventh Amendment** and forbade citizens of one state from suing another state in a federal court. Wilson died on 21 August 1798. He is buried in Christ Episcopal Church and Churchyard in Philadelphia, Pennsylvania.

**WOMEN, WOMEN'S RIGHTS**

*See* GENDER, GENDER DISCRIMINATION.

**WRIT OF CERTIORARI**

In order for a case to proceed to the **Supreme Court**, a minimum of four of nine justices must agree to hear the matter. When at least four of nine justices assent to hear the case, certiorari is granted, which comprises a review of inferior courts' rulings. *See also* ARTICLE III (CONSTITUTION).

# Y

***YOUNGSTOWN SHEET AND TUBE V. SAWYER* (1952)**

This **Supreme Court** case centered on President Harry S. Truman's seizure of steel mills in the United States during the Korean War. The Truman administration's policies of holding down wage increases through a Wage Stabilization Board prompted the United Steelworkers of America to contemplate a widespread labor strike. Rather than pursue an injunction against a strike available under statutory authority (Taft-Hartley), the president instead claimed inherent powers to seize private property during a national emergency.

In a stunning rebuke to Truman, the high court, by a 7–2 decision, struck down the president's seizure of the mills. Writing for the majority, Justice Hugo Black cited the lack of any authority enumerated in **Article II** of the Constitution or by any statute passed by Congress conferring such power to the president. The administration's claim of an emergency was weak at best, given relative stockpiles of steel products available for the war effort in Korea. Following the court's decision, Truman ordered Secretary of Commerce Charles Sawyer to return the mills to their rightful owners, and the steelworkers subsequently embarked on a 50-day strike. The case is regarded as one of the most critical in the post–World War II era in limiting broad executive claims to implied constitutional powers. *See also* EXECUTIVE ORDER.

# Z

## *ZELMAN V. SIMMONS-HARRIS* (2002)

This **Supreme Court** case considered the constitutionality of **school vouchers** and whether such programs violated the establishment clause of the **First Amendment**. At issue was a pilot program in Cleveland, Ohio. Parents were provided tuition vouchers, based on financial need, redeemable at public *or* private schools. Advocates of the voucher program emphasized school choice as a means to circumvent the failures of the Cleveland public school system. Opponents pointed to the religious affiliation of the private schools in the program and contended it ran afoul of the separation of church and state.

By a 5–4 decision, the court held that the voucher program did not violate the establishment clause based on a review of the program's implementation and its objectives. **Chief Justice William Rehnquist** wrote the **majority opinion**. Rehnquist asserted that "We believe that the program challenged here is a program of true private choice consistent with *Mueller, Witters,* and *Zobrest* [precedential cases], and thus constitutional. As was true in those cases, the Ohio program is neutral in all respects toward religion. It is part of a general and multifaceted undertaking by the State of Ohio to provide educational opportunities to the children of a failed school district. It confers educational assistance directly to a broad class of individuals defined without reference to religion, i.e., any parent of a school-age child who resides in the Cleveland City School District. The program permits the participation of *all* schools within the district, religious or nonreligious. Adjacent public schools also may participate and have a financial incentive to do so. Program benefits are available to participating families on neutral terms, with no reference to religion. The only preference stated anywhere in the program is a preference for low-income families, who receive greater assistance and are given priority for admission at participating schools."

As of late 2015, 13 states and the District of Columbia have school voucher programs. Eligibility criteria for students vary widely, from socioeconomic status to disabilities to individual education plans.

## *ZORACH V. CLAUSON* (1952)

This **Supreme Court** case addressed the constitutionality of a New York statute that permitted children to leave public school for part of the day for religious instruction. The constitutional question pivoted on whether the policy was a violation of the establishment clause of the **First**

**Amendment**. By a 6–3 decision, the court found that the policy was constitutional since the religious instruction took place off of school grounds and there were no public funds expended. Associate Justice William O. Douglas penned the **majority opinion** and was joined by **Chief Justice Fred Vinson** and four other justices. As Douglas posited, "we do not see how New York by this type of 'released time' program has made a law respecting an establishment of religion within the meaning of the First Amendment. There is much talk of the separation of Church and State in the history of the Bill of Rights and in the decisions clustering around the First Amendment. *See* ***Everson v. Board of Education****,* 330 U. S. 1; *McCollum v. Board of Education, supra.* There cannot be the slightest doubt that the First Amendment reflects the philosophy that Church and State should be separated. And so far as interference with the 'free exercise' of religion and an 'establishment' of religion are concerned, the separation must be complete and unequivocal. The First Amendment within the scope of its coverage permits no exception; the prohibition is absolute. . . . The First Amendment, however, does not say that, in every and all respects there shall be a separation of Church and State. Rather, it studiously defines the manner, the specific ways, in which there shall be no concert or union or dependency one on the other. That is the common sense of the matter. . . . We would have to press the concept of separation of Church and State to these extremes to condemn the present law on constitutional grounds."

# Appendix A: The Declaration of Independence and Signatories

IN CONGRESS, July 4, 1776.

The unanimous Declaration of the thirteen united States of America,

When in the Course of human events, it becomes necessary for one people to dissolve the political bands which have connected them with another, and to assume among the powers of the earth, the separate and equal station to which the Laws of Nature and of Nature's God entitle them, a decent respect to the opinions of mankind requires that they should declare the causes which impel them to the separation.

We hold these truths to be self-evident, that all men are created equal, that they are endowed by their Creator with certain unalienable Rights, that among these are Life, Liberty and the pursuit of Happiness.—That to secure these rights, Governments are instituted among Men, deriving their just powers from the consent of the governed, —That whenever any Form of Government becomes destructive of these ends, it is the Right of the People to alter or to abolish it, and to institute new Government, laying its foundation on such principles and organizing its powers in such form, as to them shall seem most likely to effect their Safety and Happiness. Prudence, indeed, will dictate that Governments long established should not be changed for light and transient causes; and accordingly all experience hath shewn, that mankind are more disposed to suffer, while evils are sufferable, than to right themselves by abolishing the forms to which they are accustomed. But when a long train of abuses and usurpations, pursuing invariably the same Object evinces a design to reduce them under absolute Despotism, it is their right, it is their duty, to throw off such Government, and to provide new Guards for their future security.—Such has been the patient sufferance of these Colonies; and such is now the necessity which constrains them to alter their former Systems of Government. The history of the present King of Great Britain is a history of repeated injuries and usurpations, all having in direct object the establishment of an absolute Tyranny over these States. To prove this, let Facts be submitted to a candid world.

He has refused his Assent to Laws, the most wholesome and necessary for the public good.

He has forbidden his Governors to pass Laws of immediate and pressing importance, unless suspended in their operation till his Assent should be obtained; and when so suspended, he has utterly neglected to attend to them.

He has refused to pass other Laws for the accommodation of large districts of people, unless those people would relinquish the right of Representation in the Legislature, a right inestimable to them and formidable to tyrants only.

He has called together legislative bodies at places unusual, uncomfortable, and distant from the depository of their public Records, for the sole purpose of fatiguing them into compliance with his measures.

He has dissolved Representative Houses repeatedly, for opposing with manly firmness his invasions on the rights of the people.

He has refused for a long time, after such dissolutions, to cause others to be elected; whereby the Legislative powers, incapable of Annihilation, have returned to the People at large for their exercise; the State remaining in the mean time exposed to all the dangers of invasion from without, and convulsions within.

He has endeavoured to prevent the population of these States; for that purpose obstructing the Laws for Naturalization of Foreigners; refusing to pass others to encourage their migrations hither, and raising the conditions of new Appropriations of Lands.

He has obstructed the Administration of Justice, by refusing his Assent to Laws for establishing Judiciary powers.

He has made Judges dependent on his Will alone, for the tenure of their offices, and the amount and payment of their salaries.

He has erected a multitude of New Offices, and sent hither swarms of Officers to harrass our people, and eat out their substance.

He has kept among us, in times of peace, Standing Armies without the Consent of our legislatures.

He has affected to render the Military independent of and superior to the Civil power.

He has combined with others to subject us to a jurisdiction foreign to our constitution, and unacknowledged by our laws; giving his Assent to their Acts of pretended Legislation:

For Quartering large bodies of armed troops among us:

For protecting them, by a mock Trial, from punishment for any Murders which they should commit on the Inhabitants of these States:

For cutting off our Trade with all parts of the world:

For imposing Taxes on us without our Consent:

For depriving us in many cases, of the benefits of Trial by Jury:

For transporting us beyond Seas to be tried for pretended offences:

For abolishing the free System of English Laws in a neighbouring Province, establishing therein an Arbitrary government, and enlarging its

Boundaries so as to render it at once an example and fit instrument for introducing the same absolute rule into these Colonies:

For taking away our Charters, abolishing our most valuable Laws, and altering fundamentally the Forms of our Governments:

For suspending our own Legislatures, and declaring themselves invested with power to legislate for us in all cases whatsoever.

He has abdicated Government here, by declaring us out of his Protection and waging War against us.

He has plundered our seas, ravaged our Coasts, burnt our towns, and destroyed the lives of our people.

He is at this time transporting large Armies of foreign Mercenaries to compleat the works of death, desolation and tyranny, already begun with circumstances of Cruelty & perfidy scarcely paralleled in the most barbarous ages, and totally unworthy the Head of a civilized nation.

He has constrained our fellow Citizens taken Captive on the high Seas to bear Arms against their Country, to become the executioners of their friends and Brethren, or to fall themselves by their Hands.

He has excited domestic insurrections amongst us, and has endeavoured to bring on the inhabitants of our frontiers, the merciless Indian Savages, whose known rule of warfare, is an undistinguished destruction of all ages, sexes and conditions.

In every stage of these Oppressions We have Petitioned for Redress in the most humble terms: Our repeated Petitions have been answered only by repeated injury. A Prince whose character is thus marked by every act which may define a Tyrant, is unfit to be the ruler of a free people.

Nor have We been wanting in attentions to our Brittish brethren. We have warned them from time to time of attempts by their legislature to extend an unwarrantable jurisdiction over us. We have reminded them of the circumstances of our emigration and settlement here. We have appealed to their native justice and magnanimity, and we have conjured them by the ties of our common kindred to disavow these usurpations, which, would inevitably interrupt our connections and correspondence. They too have been deaf to the voice of justice and of consanguinity. We must, therefore, acquiesce in the necessity, which denounces our Separation, and hold them, as we hold the rest of mankind, Enemies in War, in Peace Friends.

We, therefore, the Representatives of the united States of America, in General Congress, Assembled, appealing to the Supreme Judge of the world for the rectitude of our intentions, do, in the Name, and by Authority of the good People of these Colonies, solemnly publish and declare, That these United Colonies are, and of Right ought to be Free and Independent States; that they are Absolved from all Allegiance to the British Crown, and that all political connection between them and the State of Great Britain, is and ought to be totally dissolved; and that as Free and Independent States, they have full Power to levy War, conclude Peace, contract Alliances, establish Commerce, and to do all other Acts and Things which Independent States may of right do. And for the support of this Declaration, with a firm reliance on the protection of divine Providence, we mutually pledge to each other our Lives, our Fortunes and our sacred Honor.

The 56 signatures on the Declaration appear in the positions indicated:

Column 1
Georgia

Button Gwinnett
Lyman Hall
George Walton

Column 2
North Carolina

William Hooper
Joseph Hewes
John Penn

South Carolina

Edward Rutledge
Thomas Heyward Jr.
Thomas Lynch Jr.
Arthur Middleton

Column 3
Massachusetts

John Hancock

Maryland

Samuel Chase
William Paca
Thomas Stone
Charles Carroll of Carrollton

Virginia

George Wythe
Richard Henry Lee
Thomas Jefferson
Benjamin Harrison
Thomas Nelson Jr.
Francis Lightfoot Lee
Carter Braxton

Column 4

Pennsylvania

Robert Morris
Benjamin Rush
Benjamin Franklin
John Morton
George Clymer
James Smith
George Taylor
James Wilson
George Ross

Delaware

Caesar Rodney
George Read
Thomas McKean

Column 5

New York

William Floyd
Philip Livingston
Francis Lewis
Lewis Morris

New Jersey

Richard Stockton
John Witherspoon
Francis Hopkinson
John Hart
Abraham Clark

Column 6

New Hampshire

Josiah Bartlett
William Whipple

Massachusetts

Samuel Adams
John Adams
Robert Treat Paine
Elbridge Gerry

Rhode Island

Stephen Hopkins
William Ellery

Connecticut

Roger Sherman
Samuel Huntington
William Williams
Oliver Wolcott

New Hampshire

Matthew Thornton

*Source:* National Archives and Records Administration, http://www.archives.gov/exhibits/charters/declaration_transcript.html.

# Appendix B: The Constitution of the United States

We the People of the United States, in Order to form a more perfect Union, establish Justice, insure domestic Tranquility, provide for the common defence, promote the general Welfare, and secure the Blessings of Liberty to ourselves and our Posterity, do ordain and establish this Constitution for the United States of America.

## ARTICLE. I.

*Section. 1.*

All legislative Powers herein granted shall be vested in a Congress of the United States, which shall consist of a Senate and House of Representatives.

*Section. 2.*

The House of Representatives shall be composed of Members chosen every second Year by the People of the several States, and the Electors in each State shall have the Qualifications requisite for Electors of the most numerous Branch of the State Legislature.

No Person shall be a Representative who shall not have attained to the Age of twenty five Years, and been seven Years a Citizen of the United States, and who shall not, when elected, be an Inhabitant of that State in which he shall be chosen.

Representatives and direct Taxes shall be apportioned among the several States which may be included within this Union, according to their respective Numbers, which shall be determined by adding to the whole Number of free Persons, including those bound to Service for a Term of Years, and excluding Indians not taxed, three fifths of all other Persons. The actual Enumeration shall be made within three Years after the first Meeting of the Congress of the United States, and within every subsequent Term of ten Years, in such Manner as they shall by Law direct. The Number of Representatives shall not exceed one for every thirty Thousand, but each State shall have at Least one Representative; and until such enumeration shall be made, the State of New Hampshire shall be entitled to chuse three, Massachusetts eight, Rhode-Island and Providence Plantations one, Connecticut five, New-York six, New Jersey four, Pennsylvania eight, Delaware one, Maryland six, Virginia ten, North Carolina five, South Carolina five, and Georgia three.

When vacancies happen in the Representation from any State, the Executive Authority thereof shall issue Writs of Election to fill such Vacancies.

The House of Representatives shall chuse their Speaker and other Officers; and shall have the sole Power of Impeachment.

*Section. 3.*

The Senate of the United States shall be composed of two Senators from each State, chosen by the Legislature thereof, for six Years; and each Senator shall have one Vote.

Immediately after they shall be assembled in Consequence of the first Election, they shall be divided as equally as may be into three Classes. The Seats of the Senators of the first Class shall be vacated at the Expiration of the second Year, of the second Class at the Expiration of the fourth Year, and of the third Class at the Expiration of the sixth Year, so that one third may be chosen every second Year; and if Vacancies happen by Resignation, or otherwise, during the Recess of the Legislature of any State, the Executive thereof may make temporary Appointments until the next Meeting of the Legislature, which shall then fill such Vacancies.

No Person shall be a Senator who shall not have attained to the Age of thirty Years, and been nine Years a Citizen of the United States, and who shall not, when elected, be an Inhabitant of that State for which he shall be chosen.

The Vice President of the United States shall be President of the Senate, but shall have no Vote, unless they be equally divided.

The Senate shall chuse their other Officers, and also a President pro tempore, in the Absence of the Vice President, or when he shall exercise the Office of President of the United States.

The Senate shall have the sole Power to try all Impeachments. When sitting for that Purpose, they shall be on Oath or Affirmation. When the President of the United States is tried, the Chief Justice shall preside: And no Person shall be convicted without the Concurrence of two thirds of the Members present.

Judgment in Cases of Impeachment shall not extend further than to removal from Office, and disqualification to hold and enjoy any Office of honor, Trust or Profit under the United States: but the Party convicted shall nevertheless be liable and subject to Indictment, Trial, Judgment and Punishment, according to Law.

*Section. 4.*

The Times, Places and Manner of holding Elections for Senators and Representatives, shall be prescribed in each State by the Legislature thereof; but the Congress may at any time by Law make or alter such Regulations, except as to the Places of chusing Senators.

The Congress shall assemble at least once in every Year, and such Meeting shall be on the first Monday in December, unless they shall by Law appoint a different Day.

*Section. 5.*

Each House shall be the Judge of the Elections, Returns and Qualifications of its own Members, and a Majority of each shall constitute a Quorum to do Business; but a smaller Number may adjourn from day to day, and may be authorized to compel the Attendance of absent Members, in such Manner, and under such Penalties as each House may provide.

Each House may determine the Rules of its Proceedings, punish its Members for disorderly Behaviour, and, with the Concurrence of two thirds, expel a Member.

Each House shall keep a Journal of its Proceedings, and from time to time publish the same, excepting such Parts as may in their Judgment require Secrecy; and the Yeas and Nays of the Members of either House on any question shall, at the Desire of one fifth of those Present, be entered on the Journal.

Neither House, during the Session of Congress, shall, without the Consent of the other, adjourn for more than three days, nor to any other Place than that in which the two Houses shall be sitting.

*Section. 6.*

The Senators and Representatives shall receive a Compensation for their Services, to be ascertained by Law, and paid out of the Treasury of the United States. They shall in all Cases, except Treason, Felony and Breach of the Peace, be privileged from Arrest during their Attendance at the Session of their respective Houses, and in going to and returning from the same; and for any Speech or Debate in either House, they shall not be questioned in any other Place.

No Senator or Representative shall, during the Time for which he was elected, be appointed to any civil Office under the Authority of the United States, which shall have been created, or the Emoluments whereof shall have been encreased during such time; and no Person holding any Office under the United States, shall be a Member of either House during his Continuance in Office.

*Section. 7.*

All Bills for raising Revenue shall originate in the House of Representatives; but the Senate may propose or concur with Amendments as on other Bills.

Every Bill which shall have passed the House of Representatives and the Senate, shall, before it become a Law, be presented to the President of the United States; If he approve he shall sign it, but if not he shall return it, with his Objections to that House in which it shall have originated, who shall enter the Objections at large on their Journal, and proceed to reconsider it. If after such Reconsideration two thirds of that House shall agree to pass the Bill, it shall be sent, together with the Objections, to the other House, by which it shall likewise be reconsidered, and if approved by two thirds of that House, it shall become a Law. But in all such Cases the Votes of both Houses shall be determined by yeas and Nays, and the Names of the Persons voting for and against the Bill shall be entered on the Journal of each House respectively. If any Bill shall not be returned by the President within ten Days (Sundays excepted) after it shall have been presented to him, the Same shall be a Law, in like Manner as if he had signed it, unless the Congress by their Adjournment prevent its Return, in which Case it shall not be a Law.

Every Order, Resolution, or Vote to which the Concurrence of the Senate and House of Representatives may be necessary (except on a question of Adjournment) shall be presented to the President of the United States; and before the Same shall take Effect, shall be approved by him, or being disapproved by him, shall be repassed by two thirds of the Senate and House of Representatives, according to the Rules and Limitations prescribed in the Case of a Bill.

*Section. 8.*

The Congress shall have Power To lay and collect Taxes, Duties, Imposts and Excises, to pay the Debts and provide for the common Defence and general Welfare of the United States; but all Duties, Imposts and Excises shall be uniform throughout the United States;

To borrow Money on the credit of the United States;

To regulate Commerce with foreign Nations, and among the several States, and with the Indian Tribes;

To establish an uniform Rule of Naturalization, and uniform Laws on the subject of Bankruptcies throughout the United States;

To coin Money, regulate the Value thereof, and of foreign Coin, and fix the Standard of Weights and Measures;

To provide for the Punishment of counterfeiting the Securities and current Coin of the United States;

To establish Post Offices and post Roads;

To promote the Progress of Science and useful Arts, by securing for limited Times to Authors and Inventors the exclusive Right to their respective Writings and Discoveries;

To constitute Tribunals inferior to the supreme Court;

To define and punish Piracies and Felonies committed on the high Seas, and Offences against the Law of Nations;

To declare War, grant Letters of Marque and Reprisal, and make Rules concerning Captures on Land and Water;

To raise and support Armies, but no Appropriation of Money to that Use shall be for a longer Term than two Years;

To provide and maintain a Navy;

To make Rules for the Government and Regulation of the land and naval Forces;

To provide for calling forth the Militia to execute the Laws of the Union, suppress Insurrections and repel Invasions;

To provide for organizing, arming, and disciplining, the Militia, and for governing such Part of them as may be employed in the Service of the United States, reserving to the States respectively, the Appointment of the Officers, and the Authority of training the Militia according to the discipline prescribed by Congress;

To exercise exclusive Legislation in all Cases whatsoever, over such District (not exceeding ten Miles square) as may, by Cession of particular States, and the Acceptance of Congress, become the Seat of the Government of the United States, and to exercise like Authority over all Places purchased by the Consent of the Legislature of the State in which the Same shall be, for the Erection of Forts, Magazines, Arsenals, dock-Yards, and other needful Buildings;—And

To make all Laws which shall be necessary and proper for carrying into Execution the foregoing Powers, and all other Powers vested by this Constitution in the Government of the United States, or in any Department or Officer thereof.

*Section. 9.*

The Migration or Importation of such Persons as any of the States now existing shall think proper to admit, shall not be prohibited by the Congress prior to the Year one thousand eight hundred and eight, but a Tax or duty may be imposed on such Importation, not exceeding ten dollars for each Person.

The Privilege of the Writ of Habeas Corpus shall not be suspended, unless when in Cases of Rebellion or Invasion the public Safety may require it.

No Bill of Attainder or ex post facto Law shall be passed.

No Capitation, or other direct, Tax shall be laid, unless in Proportion to the Census or enumeration herein before directed to be taken.

No Tax or Duty shall be laid on Articles exported from any State.

No Preference shall be given by any Regulation of Commerce or Revenue to the Ports of one State over those of another: nor shall Vessels bound to, or from, one State, be obliged to enter, clear, or pay Duties in another.

No Money shall be drawn from the Treasury, but in Consequence of Appropriations made by Law; and a regular Statement and Account of the Receipts and Expenditures of all public Money shall be published from time to time.

No Title of Nobility shall be granted by the United States: And no Person holding any Office of Profit or Trust under them, shall, without the Consent of the Congress, accept of any present, Emolument, Office, or Title, of any kind whatever, from any King, Prince, or foreign State.

*Section. 10.*

No State shall enter into any Treaty, Alliance, or Confederation; grant Letters of Marque and Reprisal; coin Money; emit Bills of Credit; make any Thing but gold and silver Coin a Tender in Payment of Debts; pass any Bill of Attainder, ex post facto Law, or Law impairing the Obligation of Contracts, or grant any Title of Nobility.

No State shall, without the Consent of the Congress, lay any Imposts or Duties on Imports or Exports, except what may be absolutely necessary for executing it's inspection Laws: and the net Produce of all Duties and Imposts, laid by any State on Imports or Exports, shall be for the Use of the Treasury of the United States; and all such Laws shall be subject to the Revision and Controul of the Congress.

No State shall, without the Consent of Congress, lay any Duty of Tonnage, keep Troops, or Ships of War in time of Peace, enter into any Agreement or Compact with another State, or with a foreign Power, or engage in War, unless actually invaded, or in such imminent Danger as will not admit of delay.

## ARTICLE. II.

*Section. 1.*

The executive Power shall be vested in a President of the United States of America. He shall hold his Office during the Term of four Years, and, together with the Vice President, chosen for the same Term, be elected, as follows

Each State shall appoint, in such Manner as the Legislature thereof may direct, a Number of Electors, equal to the whole Number of Senators and Representatives to which the State may be entitled in the Congress:

but no Senator or Representative, or Person holding an Office of Trust or Profit under the United States, shall be appointed an Elector.

The Electors shall meet in their respective States, and vote by Ballot for two Persons, of whom one at least shall not be an Inhabitant of the same State with themselves. And they shall make a List of all the Persons voted for, and of the Number of Votes for each; which List they shall sign and certify, and transmit sealed to the Seat of the Government of the United States, directed to the President of the Senate. The President of the Senate shall, in the Presence of the Senate and House of Representatives, open all the Certificates, and the Votes shall then be counted. The Person having the greatest Number of Votes shall be the President, if such Number be a Majority of the whole Number of Electors appointed; and if there be more than one who have such Majority, and have an equal Number of Votes, then the House of Representatives shall immediately chuse by Ballot one of them for President; and if no Person have a Majority, then from the five highest on the List the said House shall in like Manner chuse the President. But in chusing the President, the Votes shall be taken by States, the Representation from each State having one Vote; A quorum for this Purpose shall consist of a Member or Members from two thirds of the States, and a Majority of all the States shall be necessary to a Choice. In every Case, after the Choice of the President, the Person having the greatest Number of Votes of the Electors shall be the Vice President. But if there should remain two or more who have equal Votes, the Senate shall chuse from them by Ballot the Vice President.

The Congress may determine the Time of chusing the Electors, and the Day on which they shall give their Votes; which Day shall be the same throughout the United States.

No Person except a natural born Citizen, or a Citizen of the United States, at the time of the Adoption of this Constitution, shall be eligible to the Office of President; neither shall any Person be eligible to that Office who shall not have attained to the Age of thirty five Years, and been fourteen Years a Resident within the United States.

In Case of the Removal of the President from Office, or of his Death, Resignation, or Inability to discharge the Powers and Duties of the said Office, the Same shall devolve on the Vice President, and the Congress may by Law provide for the Case of Removal, Death, Resignation or Inability, both of the President and Vice President, declaring what Officer shall then act as President, and such Officer shall act accordingly, until the Disability be removed, or a President shall be elected.

The President shall, at stated Times, receive for his Services, a Compensation, which shall neither be encreased nor diminished during the Period for which he shall have been elected, and he shall not receive within that Period any other Emolument from the United States, or any of them.

Before he enter on the Execution of his Office, he shall take the following Oath or Affirmation:—"I do solemnly swear (or affirm) that I will faithfully execute the Office of President of the United States, and will to the best of my Ability, preserve, protect and defend the Constitution of the United States."

*Section. 2.*

The President shall be Commander in Chief of the Army and Navy of the United States, and of the Militia of the several States, when called into the actual Service of the United States; he may require the Opinion, in writing, of the principal Officer in each of the executive Departments, upon any Subject relating to the Duties of their respective Offices, and he shall have Power to grant Reprieves and Pardons for Offences against the United States, except in Cases of Impeachment.

He shall have Power, by and with the Advice and Consent of the Senate, to make Treaties, provided two thirds of the Senators present concur; and he shall nominate, and by and with the Advice and Consent of the Senate, shall appoint Ambassadors, other public Ministers and Consuls, Judges of the supreme Court, and all other Officers of the United States, whose Appointments are not herein otherwise provided for, and which shall be established by Law: but the Congress may by Law vest the Appointment of such inferior Officers, as they think proper, in the President alone, in the Courts of Law, or in the Heads of Departments.

The President shall have Power to fill up all Vacancies that may happen during the Recess of the Senate, by granting Commissions which shall expire at the End of their next Session.

*Section. 3.*

He shall from time to time give to the Congress Information of the State of the Union, and recommend to their Consideration such Measures as he shall judge necessary and expedient; he may, on extraordinary Occasions, convene both Houses, or either of them, and in Case of Disagreement between them, with Respect to the Time of Adjournment, he may adjourn them to such Time as he shall think proper; he shall receive Ambassadors and other public Ministers; he shall take Care that the Laws be faithfully executed, and shall Commission all the Officers of the United States.

*Section. 4.*

The President, Vice President and all civil Officers of the United States, shall be removed from Office on Impeachment for, and Conviction of, Treason, Bribery, or other high Crimes and Misdemeanors.

## ARTICLE III.

*Section. 1.*

The judicial Power of the United States, shall be vested in one supreme Court, and in such inferior Courts as the Congress may from time to time ordain and establish. The Judges, both of the supreme and inferior Courts, shall hold their Offices during good Behaviour, and shall, at stated Times, receive for their Services, a Compensation, which shall not be diminished during their Continuance in Office.

*Section. 2.*

The judicial Power shall extend to all Cases, in Law and Equity, arising under this Constitution, the Laws of the United States, and Treaties made, or which shall be made, under their Authority;—to all Cases affecting Ambassadors, other public Ministers and Consuls;—to all Cases of admiralty and maritime Jurisdiction;—to Controversies to which the United States shall be a Party;—to Controversies between two or more States;— between a State and Citizens of another State,—between Citizens of different States,—between Citizens of the same State claiming Lands under Grants of different States, and between a State, or the Citizens thereof, and foreign States, Citizens or Subjects.

In all Cases affecting Ambassadors, other public Ministers and Consuls, and those in which a State shall be Party, the supreme Court shall have original Jurisdiction. In all the other Cases before mentioned, the supreme Court shall have appellate Jurisdiction, both as to Law and Fact, with such Exceptions, and under such Regulations as the Congress shall make.

The Trial of all Crimes, except in Cases of Impeachment, shall be by Jury; and such Trial shall be held in the State where the said Crimes shall have been committed; but when not committed within any State, the Trial shall be at such Place or Places as the Congress may by Law have directed.

*Section. 3.*

Treason against the United States, shall consist only in levying War against them, or in adhering to their Enemies, giving them Aid and Comfort. No Person shall be convicted of Treason unless on the Testimony of two Witnesses to the same overt Act, or on Confession in open Court.

The Congress shall have Power to declare the Punishment of Treason, but no Attainder of Treason shall work Corruption of Blood, or Forfeiture except during the Life of the Person attainted.

## ARTICLE. IV.

*Section. 1.*

Full Faith and Credit shall be given in each State to the public Acts, Records, and judicial Proceedings of every other State. And the Congress may by general Laws prescribe the Manner in which such Acts, Records and Proceedings shall be proved, and the Effect thereof.

*Section. 2.*

The Citizens of each State shall be entitled to all Privileges and Immunities of Citizens in the several States.

A Person charged in any State with Treason, Felony, or other Crime, who shall flee from Justice, and be found in another State, shall on Demand of the executive Authority of the State from which he fled, be delivered up, to be removed to the State having Jurisdiction of the Crime.

No Person held to Service or Labour in one State, under the Laws thereof, escaping into another, shall, in Consequence of any Law or Regulation therein, be discharged from such Service or Labour, but shall be delivered up on Claim of the Party to whom such Service or Labour may be due.

*Section. 3.*

New States may be admitted by the Congress into this Union; but no new State shall be formed or erected within the Jurisdiction of any other State; nor any State be formed by the Junction of two or more States, or Parts of States, without the Consent of the Legislatures of the States concerned as well as of the Congress.

The Congress shall have Power to dispose of and make all needful Rules and Regulations respecting the Territory or other Property belonging to the United States; and nothing in this Constitution shall be so construed as to Prejudice any Claims of the United States, or of any particular State.

*Section. 4.*

The United States shall guarantee to every State in this Union a Republican Form of Government, and shall protect each of them against Invasion; and on Application of the Legislature, or of the Executive (when the Legislature cannot be convened), against domestic Violence.

## ARTICLE. V.

The Congress, whenever two thirds of both Houses shall deem it necessary, shall propose Amendments to this Constitution, or, on the Application of the Legislatures of two thirds of the several States, shall call a Convention for proposing Amendments, which, in either Case, shall be valid to all Intents and Purposes, as Part of this Constitution, when ratified by the Legislatures of three fourths of the several States, or by Conventions in three fourths thereof, as the one or the other Mode of Ratification may be proposed by the Congress; Provided that no Amendment which may be made prior to the Year One thousand eight hundred and eight shall in any Manner affect the first and fourth Clauses in the Ninth Section of the first Article; and that no State, without its Consent, shall be deprived of its equal Suffrage in the Senate.

## ARTICLE. VI.

All Debts contracted and Engagements entered into, before the Adoption of this Constitution, shall be as valid against the United States under this Constitution, as under the Confederation.

This Constitution, and the Laws of the United States which shall be made in Pursuance thereof; and all Treaties made, or which shall be made, under the Authority of the United States, shall be the supreme Law of the Land; and the Judges in every State shall be bound thereby, any Thing in the Constitution or Laws of any State to the Contrary notwithstanding.

The Senators and Representatives before mentioned, and the Members of the several State Legislatures, and all executive and judicial Officers, both of the United States and of the several States, shall be bound by Oath or Affirmation, to support this Constitution; but no religious Test shall ever be required as a Qualification to any Office or public Trust under the United States.

ARTICLE. VII.

The Ratification of the Conventions of nine States, shall be sufficient for the Establishment of this Constitution between the States so ratifying the Same.

The Word, "the," being interlined between the seventh and eighth Lines of the first Page, The Word "Thirty" being partly written on an Erazure in the fifteenth Line of the first Page, The Words "is tried" being interlined between the thirty second and thirty third Lines of the first Page and the Word "the" being interlined between the forty third and forty fourth Lines of the second Page.

Attest William Jackson Secretary

done in Convention by the Unanimous Consent of the States present the Seventeenth Day of September in the Year of our Lord one thousand seven hundred and Eighty seven and of the Independance of the United States of America the Twelfth In witness whereof We have hereunto subscribed our Names,

G. Washington
Presidt and deputy from Virginia

Delaware

Geo: Read
Gunning Bedford jun
John Dickinson
Richard Bassett
Jaco: Broom

Maryland

James McHenry
Dan of St Thos. Jenifer
Danl. Carroll

Virginia

John Blair
James Madison Jr.

North Carolina

Wm. Blount
Richd. Dobbs Spaight
Hu Williamson

South Carolina

J. Rutledge
Charles Cotesworth Pinckney
Charles Pinckney
Pierce Butler

Georgia

William Few
Abr Baldwin

New Hampshire

John Langdon
Nicholas Gilman

Massachusetts

Nathaniel Gorham
Rufus King

Connecticut

Wm. Saml. Johnson
Roger Sherman

New York

Alexander Hamilton

New Jersey

Wil: Livingston
David Brearley
Wm. Paterson
Jona: Dayton

Pensylvania

B Franklin
Thomas Mifflin
Robt. Morris
Geo. Clymer
Thos. FitzSimons
Jared Ingersoll
James Wilson
Gouv Morris

*Source:* National Archives and Records Administration, http://www.archives.gov/exhibits/charters/constitution_transcript.html.

AMENDMENT I (RATIFIED 15 DECEMBER 1791)

Congress shall make no law respecting an establishment of religion, or prohibiting the free exercise thereof; or abridging the freedom of speech, or of the press; or the right of the people peaceably to assemble, and to petition the Government for a redress of grievances.

AMENDMENT II (RATIFIED 15 DECEMBER 1791)

A well regulated Militia, being necessary to the security of a free State, the right of the people to keep and bear Arms, shall not be infringed.

AMENDMENT III (RATIFIED 15 DECEMBER 1791)

No Soldier shall, in time of peace be quartered in any house, without the consent of the Owner, nor in time of war, but in a manner to be prescribed by law.

AMENDMENT IV (RATIFIED 15 DECEMBER 1791)

The right of the people to be secure in their persons, houses, papers, and effects, against unreasonable searches and seizures, shall not be violated, and no Warrants shall issue, but upon probable cause, supported by Oath or affirmation, and particularly describing the place to be searched, and the persons or things to be seized.

AMENDMENT V (RATIFIED 15 DECEMBER 1791)

No person shall be held to answer for a capital, or otherwise infamous crime, unless on a presentment or indictment of a Grand Jury, except in cases arising in the land or naval forces, or in the Militia, when in actual service in time of War or public danger; nor shall any person be subject for the same offence to be twice put in jeopardy of life or limb; nor shall be compelled in any criminal case to be a witness against himself, nor be deprived of life, liberty, or property, without due process of law; nor shall private property be taken for public use, without just compensation.

AMENDMENT VI (RATIFIED 15 DECEMBER 1791)

In all criminal prosecutions, the accused shall enjoy the right to a speedy and public trial, by an impartial jury of the State and district wherein the crime shall have been committed, which district shall have been previously ascertained by law, and to be informed of the nature and cause of the accusation; to be confronted with the witnesses against him; to have compulsory process for obtaining witnesses in his favor, and to have the Assistance of Counsel for his defence.

## AMENDMENT VII (RATIFIED 15 DECEMBER 1791)

In Suits at common law, where the value in controversy shall exceed twenty dollars, the right of trial by jury shall be preserved, and no fact tried by a jury, shall be otherwise re-examined in any Court of the United States, than according to the rules of the common law.

## AMENDMENT VIII (RATIFIED 15 DECEMBER 1791)

Excessive bail shall not be required, nor excessive fines imposed, nor cruel and unusual punishments inflicted.

## AMENDMENT IX (RATIFIED 15 DECEMBER 1791)

The enumeration in the Constitution, of certain rights, shall not be construed to deny or disparage others retained by the people.

## AMENDMENT X (RATIFIED 15 DECEMBER 1791)

The powers not delegated to the United States by the Constitution, nor prohibited by it to the States, are reserved to the States respectively, or to the people.

## AMENDMENT XI (RATIFIED 7 FEBRUARY 1795)

The Judicial power of the United States shall not be construed to extend to any suit in law or equity, commenced or prosecuted against one on the United States by Citizens of another State, or by Citizens or Subjects of any Foreign State.

## AMENDMENT XII (RATIFIED 15 JUNE 1804)

The Electors shall meet in their respective states and vote by ballot for President and Vice-President, one of whom, at least, shall not be an inhabitant of the same state with themselves; they shall name in their ballots the person voted for as President, and in distinct ballots the person voted for as Vice-President, and they shall make distinct lists of all persons voted for as President, and of all persons voted for as Vice-President, and of the number of votes for each, which lists they shall sign and certify, and transmit sealed to the seat of the government of the United States, directed to the President of the Senate;—The President of the Senate shall, in the presence of the Senate and House of Representatives, open all the certificates and the votes shall then be counted;—The person having the greatest Number of votes for President, shall be the President, if such number be a majority of the whole number of Electors appointed; and if no person have such majority, then from the persons having the highest numbers not exceeding three on the list of those voted for as President, the House of Representatives shall choose immediately, by ballot, the President. But in choosing the President, the votes shall be taken by states, the representation from each state having one vote; a quorum for this purpose shall consist of a member or members from two-thirds of the states, and a majority of all the states shall be necessary to a choice. And if the House of Representatives shall not choose a President whenever the right of choice shall devolve upon them, before the fourth day of March next following, then the Vice-President shall act as President, as in the case of the death or other constitutional disability of the President—The person having the greatest number of votes as Vice-President, shall be the Vice-President, if such number be a majority of the whole number of Electors appointed, and if no person have a majority, then from the two highest numbers on the list, the Senate shall choose the Vice-President; a quorum for the purpose shall consist of two-thirds of the whole number of Senators, and a majority of the whole number shall be necessary to a choice. But no person constitutionally ineligible to the office of President shall be eligible to that of Vice-President of the United States.

## AMENDMENT XIII (RATIFIED 6 DECEMBER 1865)

**Section 1.** Neither slavery nor involuntary servitude, except as a punishment for crime whereof the party shall have been duly convicted, shall exist within the United States, or any place subject to their jurisdiction.

**Section 2.** Congress shall have power to enforce this article by appropriate legislation.

## AMENDMENT XIV (RATIFIED 9 JULY 1868)

**Section 1.** All persons born or naturalized in the United States and subject to the jurisdiction thereof, are citizens of the United States and of the State wherein they reside. No State shall make or enforce any law which shall abridge the privileges or immunities of citizens of the United States; nor shall any State deprive any person of life, liberty, or property, with- out due process of law; nor deny to any person within its jurisdiction the equal protection of the laws.

**Section 2.** Representatives shall be apportioned among the several States according to their respective umbers, counting the whole number of persons in each State, excluding Indians not taxed. But when the right to vote at any election for the choice of electors for President and Vice President of the United States, Representatives in Congress, the Executive and Judicial officers of a State, or the members of the Legislature thereof, is denied to any of the male inhabitants of such State, being twenty-one years of age, and citizens of the United States, or in any way abridged, except for participation in rebellion, or other crime, the basis of representation therein shall be reduced in the proportion which the number of such male citizens shall bear to the whole number of male citizens twenty-one years of age in such State.

**Section 3.** No person shall be a Senator or Representative in Congress, or elector of President and Vice President, or hold any office, civil or military, under the United States, or under any State, who, having previously taken an oath, as a member of Congress, or as an officer of the United States, or as a member of any State legislature, or as an executive or judicial officer of any State, to support the Constitution of the United States, shall have engaged in insurrection or rebellion against the same, or given aid or comfort to the enemies thereof. But Congress may by a vote of two-thirds of each House, remove such disability.

**Section 4.** The validity of the public debt of the United States, authorized by law, including debts incurred for payment of pensions and bounties for services in suppressing insurrection or rebellion, shall not be questioned. But neither the Unit- ed States nor any State shall assume or pay any debt or obligation incurred in aid of insurrection or rebellion against the United States, or any claim for the loss or emancipation of any slave; but all such debts, obligations and claims shall be held illegal and void.

**Section 5.** The Congress shall have power to enforce, by appropriate legislation, the provisions of this article.

## AMENDMENT XV (RATIFIED 3 FEBRUARY 1870)

**Section 1.** The right of citizens of the United States to vote shall not be denied or abridged by the United States or by any State on account of race, color, or previous condition of servitude.

**Section 2.**The Congress shall have power to enforce this article by appropriate legislation.

## AMENDMENT XVI (RATIFIED 3 FEBRUARY 1913)

The Congress shall have power to lay and collect taxes on incomes, from whatever source derived, without apportionment among the several States, and without regard to any census or enumeration.

## AMENDMENT XVII (RATIFIED 8 APRIL 1913)

The Senate of the United States shall be composed of two Senators from each State, elected by the people thereof, for six years; and each Senator shall have one vote. The electors in each State shall have the qualifications requisite for electors of the most numerous branch of the State legislatures.

When vacancies happen in the representation of any State in the Senate, the executive authority of such State shall issue writs of election to fill such vacancies: Provided, That the legislature of any State may empower the executive thereof to make temporary appointments until the people fill the vacancies by election as the legislature may direct.

This amendment shall not be so construed as to affect the election or term of any Senator chosen before it becomes valid as part of the Constitution.

## AMENDMENT XVIII (RATIFIED 16 JANUARY 1919)

**Section 1.** After one year from the ratification of this article the manufacture, sale, or transportation of intoxicating liquors within, the importation thereof into, or the exportation thereof from the United States and all territory subject to the jurisdiction thereof for beverage purposes is hereby prohibited.

**Section 2.** The Congress and the several States shall have concurrent power to enforce this article by appropriate legislation.

**Section 3.** This article shall be inoperative unless it shall have been ratified as an amendment to the Constitution by the legislatures of the several States, as provided in the Constitution, within seven years from the date of the submission hereof to the States by the Congress.

## AMENDMENT XIX (RATIFIED 18 AUGUST 1920)

The right of citizens of the United States to vote shall not be denied or abridged by the United States or by any State on account of sex.

Congress shall have power to enforce this article by appropriate legislation.

## AMENDMENT XX (RATIFIED 23 JANUARY 1933)

**Section 1.** The terms of the President and Vice President shall end at noon on the 20th day of January, and the terms of Senators and Representatives at noon on the 3d day of January, of the years in which such terms would have ended if this article had not been ratified; and the terms of their successors shall then begin.

**Section 2.** The Congress shall assemble at least once in every year, and such meeting shall begin at noon on the 3d day of January, unless they shall by law appoint a different day.

**Section 3.** If, at the time fixed for the beginning of the term of the President, the President elect shall have died, the Vice President elect shall become President. If a President shall not have been chosen before the time fixed for the beginning of his term, or if the President elect shall have failed to qualify, then the Vice President elect shall act as President until a President shall have qualified; and the Congress may by law provide for the case wherein neither a President elect nor a Vice President elect shall have qualified, declaring who shall then act as President, or the manner in which one who is to act shall be selected, and such person shall act accordingly until a President or Vice President shall have qualified.

**Section 4.** The Congress may by law provide for the case of the death of any of the persons from whom the House of Representatives may choose a President whenever the right of choice shall have devolved upon them, and for the case of the death of any of the persons from whom the Senate may choose a Vice President whenever the right of choice shall have devolved upon them.

**Section 5.** Sections 1 and 2 shall take effect on the 15th day of October following the ratification of this article.

**Section 6.** This article shall be inoperative unless it shall have been ratified as an amendment to the Constitution by the legislatures of three-fourths of the several States within seven years from the date of its submission.

## AMENDMENT XXI (RATIFIED 5 DECEMBER 1933)

**Section 1.** The eighteenth article of amendment to the Constitution of the United States is hereby repealed.

**Section 2.** The transportation or importation into any State, Territory, or possession of the United States for delivery or use therein of intoxicating liquors, in violation of the laws thereof, is hereby prohibited.

**Section 3.**This article shall be inoperative unless it shall have been ratified as an amendment to the Constitution by conventions in the several States, as provided in the Constitution, within seven years from the date of the submission hereof to the States by the Congress.

AMENDMENT XXII (RATIFIED 27 FEBRUARY 1951)

**Section 1.** No person shall be elected to the office of the President more than twice, and no person who has held the office of President, or acted as President, for more than two years of a term to which some other person was elected President shall be elected to the office of the President more than once. But this Article shall not apply to any person holding the office of President, when this Article was proposed by the Congress, and shall not prevent any person who may be holding the office of President, or acting as President, during the term within which this Article becomes operative from holding the office of President or acting as President during the remainder of such term.

**Section 2.** This article shall be inoperative unless it shall have been ratified as an amendment to the Constitution by the legislatures of three-fourths of the several States within seven years from the date of its submission to the States by the Congress.

AMENDMENT XXIII (RATIFIED 29 MARCH 1961)

**Section 1.** The District constituting the seat of Government of the United States shall appoint in such manner as the Congress may direct:

A number of electors of President and Vice President equal to the whole number of Senators and Representatives in Congress to which the District would be entitled if it were a State, but in no event more than the least populous State; they shall be in addition to those appointed by the States, but they shall be considered, for the purposes of the election of President and Vice President, to be electors appointed by a State; and they shall meet in the District and perform such duties as provided by the twelfth article of amendment.

**Section 2.** The Congress shall have power to enforce this article by appropriate legislation.

AMENDMENT XXIV (RATIFIED 23 JANUARY 1964)

**Section 1.** The right of citizens of the United States to vote in any primary or other election for President or Vice President, for electors for President or Vice President, or for Senator or Representative in Congress, shall not be denied or abridged by the United States or any State by reason of failure to pay any poll tax or other tax.

**Section 2.** The Congress shall have power to enforce this article by appropriate legislation.

AMENDMENT XXV (RATIFIED 10 FEBRUARY 1967)

**Section 1.** In case of the removal of the President from office or of his death or resignation, the Vice President shall become President.

**Section 2.** Whenever there is a vacancy in the office of the Vice President, the President shall nominate a Vice President who shall take office upon confirmation by a majority vote of both Houses of Congress.

**Section 3.** Whenever the President transmits to the President pro tempore of the Senate and the Speaker of the House of Representatives has written declaration that he is unable to discharge the powers and duties of his office, and until he transmits to them a written declaration to the contrary, such powers and duties shall be discharged by the Vice President as Acting President.

**Section 4.** Whenever the Vice President and a majority of either the principal officers of the executive departments or of such other body as Congress may by law provide, transmit to the President pro tempore of the Senate and the Speaker of the House of Representatives their written declaration that the President is unable to discharge the powers and duties of his office, the Vice President shall immediately assume the powers and duties of the office as Acting President.

Thereafter, when the President transmits to the President pro tempore of the Senate and the Speaker of the House of Representatives has written declaration that no inability exists, he shall resume the powers and duties of his office unless the Vice President and a majority of either the principal officers of the executive department or of such other body as Congress may by law provide, transmit within four days to the President pro tempore of the Senate and the Speaker of the House of Representatives their written declaration that the President is unable to discharge the powers and duties of his office. Thereupon Congress shall decide the issue, assembling within forty-eight hours for that purpose if not in session. If the Congress, within twenty-one days after receipt of the latter written declaration, or, if Congress is not in session, within twenty-one days after Congress is required to assemble, determines by two-thirds vote of both Houses that the President is unable to dis- charge the powers and duties of his office, the Vice President shall continue to discharge the same as Acting President; otherwise, the President shall resume the powers and duties of his office.

## AMENDMENT XXVI (RATIFIED 1 JULY 1971)

**Section 1.** The right of citizens of the United States, who are eighteen years of age or older, to vote shall not be denied or abridged by the United States or by any State on account of age.

**Section 2.** The Congress shall have power to enforce this article by appropriate legislation.

## AMENDMENT XXVII (RATIFIED 7 MAY 1992)

No law varying the compensation for the services of the Senators and Representatives shall take effect, until an election of Representatives shall have intervened.

# Appendix C: Federalist No. 1

*Source:* Federalist Papers included in the appendixes are from https://www.congress.gov/resources/display/content/The+Federalist+Papers.

For the *Independent Journal*

Author: Alexander Hamilton

To the People of the State of New York:

AFTER an unequivocal experience of the inefficiency of the subsisting federal government, you are called upon to deliberate on a new Constitution for the United States of America. The subject speaks its own importance; comprehending in its consequences nothing less than the existence of the UNION, the safety and welfare of the parts of which it is composed, the fate of an empire in many respects the most interesting in the world. It has been frequently remarked that it seems to have been reserved to the people of this country, by their conduct and example, to decide the important question, whether societies of men are really capable or not of establishing good government from reflection and choice, or whether they are forever destined to depend for their political constitutions on accident and force. If there be any truth in the remark, the crisis at which we are arrived may with propriety be regarded as the era in which that decision is to be made; and a wrong election of the part we shall act may, in this view, deserve to be considered as the general misfortune of mankind.

This idea will add the inducements of philanthropy to those of patriotism, to heighten the solicitude which all considerate and good men must feel for the event. Happy will it be if our choice should be directed by a judicious estimate of our true interests, unperplexed and unbiased by considerations not connected with the public good. But this is a thing more ardently to be wished than seriously to be expected. The plan offered to our deliberations affects too many particular interests, innovates upon too many local institutions, not to involve in its discussion a variety of objects foreign to its merits, and of views, passions and prejudices little favorable to the discovery of truth.

Among the most formidable of the obstacles which the new Constitution will have to encounter may readily be distinguished the obvious interest of a certain class of men in every State to resist all changes which may hazard a diminution of the power, emolument, and consequence of the offices they hold under the State establishments; and the perverted ambition of another class of men, who will either hope to aggrandize themselves by the confusions of their country, or will flatter themselves with fairer prospects of elevation from the subdivision of the empire into several partial confederacies than from its union under one government.

It is not, however, my design to dwell upon observations of this nature. I am well aware that it would be disingenuous to resolve indiscriminately the opposition of any set of men (merely because their situations might subject them to suspicion) into interested or ambitious views. Candor will oblige us to admit that even such men may be actuated by upright intentions; and it cannot be doubted that much of the opposition which has made its appearance, or may hereafter make its appearance, will spring from sources, blameless at least, if not respectable--the honest errors of minds led astray by preconceived jealousies and fears. So numerous indeed and so powerful are the causes which serve to give a false bias to the judgment, that we, upon many occasions, see wise and good men on the wrong as well as on the right side of questions of the first magnitude to society. This circumstance, if duly attended to, would furnish a lesson of moderation to those who are ever so much persuaded of their being in the right in any controversy. And a further reason for caution, in this respect, might be drawn from the reflection that we are not always sure that those who advocate the truth are influenced by purer principles than their antagonists. Ambition, avarice, personal animosity, party opposition, and many other motives not more laudable than these, are apt to operate as well upon those who support as those who oppose the right side of a question. Were there not even these inducements to moderation, nothing could be more ill-judged than that intolerant spirit which has, at all times, characterized political parties. For in politics, as in religion, it is equally absurd to aim at making proselytes by fire and sword. Heresies in either can rarely be cured by persecution.

And yet, however just these sentiments will be allowed to be, we have already sufficient indications that it will happen in this as in all former cases of great national discussion. A torrent of angry and malignant passions will be let loose. To judge from the conduct of the opposite parties, we shall be led to conclude that they will mutually hope to evince the justness of their opinions, and to increase the number of their converts by the loudness of their declamations and the bitterness of their invectives. An enlightened zeal for the energy and efficiency of government will be stigmatized as the offspring of a temper fond of despotic power and hostile to the principles of liberty. An over-scrupulous jealousy of danger to the rights of the people, which is more commonly the fault of the head than of the heart, will be represented as mere pretense and artifice, the stale bait for popularity at the expense of the public good. It will be forgotten, on the one hand, that jealousy is the usual concomitant of love, and that the noble enthusiasm of liberty is apt to be infected with a spirit of narrow and illiberal distrust. On the other hand, it will be equally forgotten that the vigor of government is essential to the security of liberty; that, in the contemplation of a sound and well-informed judgment, their interest can never be separated; and that a dangerous ambition more often lurks behind the specious mask of zeal for the rights of the people than under the forbidden appearance of zeal for the firmness and efficiency of government. History will teach us that the former has been found a much more certain road to the introduction of despotism than the latter, and that of those men who have overturned the liberties of republics, the greatest number have begun their career by paying an obsequious court to the people; commencing demagogues, and ending tyrants.

In the course of the preceding observations, I have had an eye, my fellow-citizens, to putting you upon your guard against all attempts, from whatever quarter, to influence your decision in a matter of the utmost moment to your welfare, by any impressions other than those which may result from the evidence of truth. You will, no doubt, at the same time, have collected from the general scope of them, that they proceed from a source not unfriendly to the new Constitution. Yes, my countrymen, I own to you that, after having given it an attentive consideration, I am clearly of opinion it is your interest to adopt it. I am convinced that this is the safest course for your liberty, your dignity, and your happiness. I affect not reserves which I do not feel. I will not amuse you with an appearance of deliberation when I have decided. I frankly acknowledge to you my convictions, and I will freely lay before you the reasons on which they are founded. The consciousness of good intentions disdains ambiguity. I shall not, however, multiply professions on this head. My motives must remain in the depository of my own breast. My arguments will be open to all, and may be judged of by all. They shall at least be offered in a spirit which will not disgrace the cause of truth.

I propose, in a series of papers, to discuss the following interesting particulars:

THE UTILITY OF THE UNION TO YOUR POLITICAL PROSPERITY THE INSUFFICIENCY OF THE PRESENT CONFEDERATION TO PRESERVE THAT UNION THE NECESSITY OF A GOVERNMENT AT LEAST EQUALLY ENERGETIC WITH THE ONE PROPOSED, TO THE ATTAINMENT OF THIS OBJECT THE CONFORMITY OF THE PROPOSED CONSTITUTION TO THE TRUE PRINCIPLES OF REPUBLICAN GOVERNMENT ITS ANALOGY TO YOUR OWN STATE CONSTITUTION and lastly, THE ADDITIONAL SECURITY WHICH ITS ADOPTION WILL AFFORD TO THE PRESERVATION OF THAT SPECIES OF GOVERNMENT, TO LIBERTY, AND TO PROPERTY.

In the progress of this discussion I shall endeavor to give a satisfactory answer to all the objections which shall have made their appearance, that may seem to have any claim to your attention.

It may perhaps be thought superfluous to offer arguments to prove the utility of the UNION, a point, no doubt, deeply engraved on the hearts of the great body of the people in every State, and one, which it may be imagined, has no adversaries. But the fact is, that we already hear it whispered in the private circles of those who oppose the new Constitution, that the thirteen States are of too great extent for any general system, and that we must of necessity resort to separate confederacies of distinct portions of the whole.[i]This doctrine will, in all probability, be gradually propagated, till it has votaries enough to countenance an open avowal of it. For nothing can be more evident, to those who are able to take an enlarged view of the subject, than the alternative of an adoption of the new Constitution or a dismemberment of the Union. It will therefore be of use to begin by examining the advantages of that Union, the certain evils, and the probable dangers, to which every State will be exposed from its dissolution. This shall accordingly constitute the subject of my next address.

PUBLIUS.

# Appendix D: Federalist No. 2: Concerning Dangers from Foreign Force and Influence

For the *Independent Journal*

Author: John Jay

To the People of the State of New York:

WHEN the people of America reflect that they are now called upon to decide a question, which, in its consequences, must prove one of the most important that ever engaged their attention, the propriety of their taking a very comprehensive, as well as a very serious, view of it, will be evident.

Nothing is more certain than the indispensable necessity of government, and it is equally undeniable, that whenever and however it is instituted, the people must cede to it some of their natural rights in order to vest it with requisite powers. It is well worthy of consideration therefore, whether it would conduce more to the interest of the people of America that they should, to all general purposes, be one nation, under one federal government, or that they should divide themselves into separate confederacies, and give to the head of each the same kind of powers which they are advised to place in one national government.

It has until lately been a received and uncontradicted opinion that the prosperity of the people of America depended on their continuing firmly united, and the wishes, prayers, and efforts of our best and wisest citizens have been constantly directed to that object. But politicians now appear, who insist that this opinion is erroneous, and that instead of looking for safety and happiness in union, we ought to seek it in a division of the States into distinct confederacies or sovereignties. However extraordinary this new doctrine may appear, it nevertheless has its advocates; and certain characters who were much opposed to it formerly, are at present of the number. Whatever may be the arguments or inducements which have wrought this change in the sentiments and declarations of these gentlemen, it certainly would not be wise in the people at large to adopt these new political tenets without being fully convinced that they are founded in truth and sound policy.

It has often given me pleasure to observe that independent America was not composed of detached and distant territories, but that one connected, fertile, widespreading country was the portion of our western sons of liberty. Providence has in a particular manner blessed it with a variety of soils and productions, and watered it with innumerable streams, for the delight and accommodation of its inhabitants. A succession of navigable waters forms a kind of chain round its borders, as if to bind it together; while the most noble rivers in the world, running at convenient distances, present them with highways for the easy communication of friendly aids, and the mutual transportation and exchange of their various commodities.

With equal pleasure I have as often taken notice that Providence has been pleased to give this one connected country to one united people--a people descended from the same ancestors, speaking the same language, professing the same religion, attached to the same principles of government, very similar in their manners and customs, and who, by their joint counsels, arms, and efforts, fighting side by side throughout a long and bloody war, have nobly established general liberty and independence.

This country and this people seem to have been made for each other, and it appears as if it was the design of Providence, that an inheritance so proper and convenient for a band of brethren, united to each other by the strongest ties, should never be split into a number of unsocial, jealous, and alien sovereignties.

Similar sentiments have hitherto prevailed among all orders and denominations of men among us. To all general purposes we have uniformly been one people each individual citizen everywhere enjoying the same national rights, privileges, and protection. As a nation we have made peace and war; as a nation we have vanquished our common enemies; as a nation we have formed alliances, and made treaties, and entered into various compacts and conventions with foreign states.

A strong sense of the value and blessings of union induced the people, at a very early period, to institute a federal government to preserve and perpetuate it. They formed it almost as soon as they had a political existence; nay, at a time when their habitations were in flames, when many of their citizens were bleeding, and when the progress of hostility and desolation left little room for those calm and mature inquiries and reflections which must ever precede the formation of a wise and wellbalanced government for a free people. It is not to be wondered at, that a government instituted in times so inauspicious, should on experiment be found greatly deficient and inadequate to the purpose it was intended to answer.

This intelligent people perceived and regretted these defects. Still continuing no less attached to union than enamored of liberty, they observed the danger which immediately threatened the former and more remotely the latter; and being pursuaded that ample security for both could only be found in a national government more wisely framed, they as with one voice, convened the late convention at Philadelphia, to take that important subject under consideration.

This convention composed of men who possessed the confidence of the people, and many of whom had become highly distinguished by their patriotism, virtue and wisdom, in times which tried the minds and hearts of men, undertook the arduous task. In the mild season of peace, with minds unoccupied by other subjects, they passed many months in cool, uninterrupted, and daily consultation; and finally, without having been awed by power, or influenced by any passions except love for their country, they presented and recommended to the people the plan produced by their joint and very unanimous councils.

Admit, for so is the fact, that this plan is only RECOMMENDED, not imposed, yet let it be remembered that it is neither recommended to BLIND approbation, nor to BLIND reprobation; but to that sedate and candid consideration which the magnitude and importance of the subject demand, and which it certainly ought to receive. But this (as was remarked in the foregoing number of this paper) is more to be wished than expected, that it may be so considered and examined. Experience on a former occasion teaches us not to be too sanguine in such hopes. It is not yet forgotten that well-grounded apprehensions of imminent danger induced the people of America to form the memorable Congress of 1774. That body recommended certain measures to their constituents, and the event proved their wisdom; yet it is fresh in our memories how soon the press began to teem with pamphlets and weekly papers against those very measures. Not only many of the officers of government, who obeyed the dictates of personal interest, but others, from a mistaken estimate of consequences, or the undue influence of former attachments, or whose ambition aimed at objects which did not correspond with the public good, were indefatigable in their efforts to pursuade the people to reject the advice of that patriotic Congress. Many, indeed, were deceived and deluded, but the great majority of the people reasoned and decided judiciously; and happy they are in reflecting that they did so.

They considered that the Congress was composed of many wise and experienced men. That, being convened from different parts of the country, they brought with them and communicated to each other a variety of useful information. That, in the course of the time they passed together in inquiring into and discussing the true interests of their country, they must have acquired very accurate knowledge on that head. That they were individually interested in the public liberty and prosperity, and therefore that it was not less their inclination than their duty to recommend only such measures as, after the most mature deliberation, they really thought prudent and advisable.

These and similar considerations then induced the people to rely greatly on the judgment and integrity of the Congress; and they took their advice, notwithstanding the various arts and endeavors used to deter them from it. But if the people at large had reason to confide in the men of that Congress, few of whom had been fully tried or generally known, still greater reason have they now to respect the judgment and advice of the convention, for it is well known that some of the most distinguished members of that Congress, who have been since tried and justly approved for patriotism and abilities, and who have grown old in acquiring political information, were also members of this convention, and carried into it their accumulated knowledge and experience.

It is worthy of remark that not only the first, but every succeeding Congress, as well as the late convention, have invariably joined with the people in thinking that the prosperity of America depended on its Union. To preserve and perpetuate it was the great object of the people in forming that convention, and it is also the great object of the plan which the convention has advised them to adopt. With what propriety, therefore, or for what good purposes, are attempts at this particular period made by some men to depreciate the importance of the Union? Or why is it suggested that three or four confederacies would be better than one? I am persuaded in my own mind that the people have always thought right on this subject, and that their universal and uniform attachment to the cause of the Union rests on great and weighty reasons, which I shall endeavor to develop and explain in some ensuing papers. They who promote the idea of substituting a number of distinct confederacies in the room of the plan of the convention, seem clearly to foresee that the rejection of it would put the continuance of the Union in the utmost jeopardy. That certainly would be the case, and I sincerely wish that it may be as clearly foreseen by every good citizen, that whenever the dissolution of the Union arrives, America will have reason to exclaim, in the words of the poet: "FAREWELL! A LONG FAREWELL TO ALL MY GREATNESS."

*PUBLIUS.*

# Appendix E: Federalist No. 9: The Union as a Safeguard Against Domestic Faction and Insurrection

For the *Independent Journal*

Author: Alexander Hamilton

To the People of the State of New York:

A FIRM Union will be of the utmost moment to the peace and liberty of the States, as a barrier against domestic faction and insurrection. It is impossible to read the history of the petty republics of Greece and Italy without feeling sensations of horror and disgust at the distractions with which they were continually agitated, and at the rapid succession of revolutions by which they were kept in a state of perpetual vibration between the extremes of tyranny and anarchy. If they exhibit occasional calms, these only serve as short-lived contrast to the furious storms that are to succeed. If now and then intervals of felicity open to view, we behold them with a mixture of regret, arising from the reflection that the pleasing scenes before us are soon to be overwhelmed by the tempestuous waves of sedition and party rage. If momentary rays of glory break forth from the gloom, while they dazzle us with a transient and fleeting brilliancy, they at the same time admonish us to lament that the vices of government should pervert the direction and tarnish the lustre of those bright talents and exalted endowments for which the favored soils that produced them have been so justly celebrated.

From the disorders that disfigure the annals of those republics the advocates of despotism have drawn arguments, not only against the forms of republican government, but against the very principles of civil liberty. They have decried all free government as inconsistent with the order of society, and have indulged themselves in malicious exultation over its friends and partisans. Happily for mankind, stupendous fabrics reared on the basis of liberty, which have flourished for ages, have, in a few glorious instances, refuted their gloomy sophisms. And, I trust, America will be the broad and solid foundation of other edifices, not less magnificent, which will be equally permanent monuments of their errors.

But it is not to be denied that the portraits they have sketched of republican government were too just copies of the originals from which they were taken. If it had been found impracticable to have devised models of a more perfect structure, the enlightened friends to liberty would have been obliged to abandon the cause of that species of government as indefensible. The science of politics, however, like most other sciences, has received great improvement. The efficacy of various principles is now well understood, which were either not known at all, or imperfectly known to the ancients. The regular distribution of power into distinct departments; the introduction of legislative balances and checks; the institution of courts composed of judges holding their offices during good behavior; the representation of the people in the legislature by deputies of their own election: these are wholly new discoveries, or have made their principal progress towards perfection in modern times. They are means, and powerful means, by which the excellences of republican government may be retained and its imperfections lessened or avoided. To this catalogue of circumstances that tend to the amelioration of popular systems of civil government, I shall venture, however novel it may appear to some, to add one more, on a principle which has been made the foundation of an objection to the new Constitution; I mean the ENLARGEMENT of the ORBIT within which such systems are to revolve, either in respect to the dimensions of a single State or to the consolidation of several smaller States into one great Confederacy. The latter is that which immediately concerns the object under consideration. It will, however, be of use to examine the principle in its application to a single State, which shall be attended to in another place.

The utility of a Confederacy, as well to suppress faction and to guard the internal tranquillity of States, as to increase their external force and security, is in reality not a new idea. It has been practiced upon in different countries and ages, and has received the sanction of the most approved writers on the subject of politics. The opponents of the plan proposed have, with great assiduity, cited and circulated the observations of Montesquieu on the necessity of a contracted territory for a republican government. But they seem not to have been apprised of the sentiments of that great man expressed in another part of his work, nor to have adverted to the consequences of the principle to which they subscribe with such ready acquiescence.

When Montesquieu recommends a small extent for republics, the standards he had in view were of dimensions far short of the limits of almost every one of these States. Neither Virginia, Massachusetts, Pennsylvania, New York, North Carolina, nor Georgia can by any means be compared with the models from which he reasoned and to which the terms of his description apply. If we therefore take his ideas on this point as the criterion of truth, we shall be driven to the alternative either of taking refuge at once in the arms of monarchy, or of splitting ourselves into an infinity of little, jealous, clashing, tumultuous commonwealths, the wretched nurseries of unceasing discord, and the miserable objects of universal pity or contempt. Some of the writers who have come forward on the other side of the question seem to have been aware of the dilemma; and have even been bold enough to hint at the division of the larger States as a desirable thing. Such an infatuated policy, such a desperate expedient, might, by the multiplication of petty offices, answer the views of men who possess not qualifications to extend their influence beyond the narrow circles of personal intrigue, but it could never promote the greatness or happiness of the people of America.

Referring the examination of the principle itself to another place, as has been already mentioned, it will be sufficient to remark here that, in the sense of the author who has been most emphatically quoted upon the occasion, it would only dictate a reduction of the SIZE of the more considerable MEMBERS of the Union, but would not militate against their being all comprehended in one confederate government. And this is the true question, in the discussion of which we are at present interested.

So far are the suggestions of Montesquieu from standing in opposition to a general Union of the States, that he explicitly treats of a CONFEDERATE REPUBLIC as the expedient for extending the sphere of popular government, and reconciling the advantages of monarchy with those of republicanism.

"It is very probable," (says he)[i] "that mankind would have been obliged at length to live constantly under the government of a single person, had they not contrived a kind of constitution that has all the internal advantages of a republican, together with the external force of a monarchical government. I mean a CONFEDERATE REPUBLIC.

"This form of government is a convention by which several smaller STATES agree to become members of a larger ONE, which they intend to form. It is a kind of assemblage of societies that constitute a new one, capable of increasing, by means of new associations, till they arrive to such a degree of power as to be able to provide for the security of the united body.

"A republic of this kind, able to withstand an external force, may support itself without any internal corruptions. The form of this society prevents all manner of inconveniences.

"If a single member should attempt to usurp the supreme authority, he could not be supposed to have an equal authority and credit in all the confederate states. Were he to have too great influence over one, this would alarm the rest. Were he to subdue a part, that which would still remain free might oppose him with forces independent of those which he had usurped and overpower him before he could be settled in his usurpation.

"Should a popular insurrection happen in one of the confederate states the others are able to quell it. Should abuses creep into one part, they are reformed by those that remain sound. The state may be destroyed on one side, and not on the other; the confederacy may be dissolved, and the confederates preserve their sovereignty.

"As this government is composed of small republics, it enjoys the internal happiness of each; and with respect to its external situation, it is possessed, by means of the association, of all the advantages of large monarchies."

I have thought it proper to quote at length these interesting passages, because they contain a luminous abridgment of the principal arguments in favor of the Union, and must effectually remove the false impressions which a misapplication of other parts of the work was calculated to make. They have, at the same time, an intimate connection with the more immediate design of this paper; which is, to illustrate the tendency of the Union to repress domestic faction and insurrection.

A distinction, more subtle than accurate, has been raised between a CONFEDERACY and a CONSOLIDATION of the States. The essential characteristic of the first is said to be, the restriction of its authority to the members in their collective capacities, without reaching to the individuals of whom they are composed. It is contended that the national council ought to have no concern with any object of internal administration. An exact equality of suffrage between the members has also been insisted upon as a leading feature of a confederate government. These positions are, in the main, arbitrary; they are supported neither by principle nor precedent. It has indeed happened, that governments of this kind have generally operated in the manner which the distinction taken notice of, supposes to be inherent in their nature; but there have been in most of them extensive exceptions to the practice, which serve to prove, as far as example will go, that there is no absolute rule on the subject. And it will be clearly shown in the course of this investigation that as far as the principle contended for has prevailed, it has been the cause of incurable disorder and imbecility in the government.

The definition of a CONFEDERATE REPUBLIC seems simply to be "an assemblage of societies," or an association of two or more states into one state. The extent, modifications, and objects of the federal authority are mere matters of discretion. So long as the separate organization of the members be not abolished; so long as it exists, by a constitutional necessity, for local purposes; though it should be in perfect subordination to the general authority of the union, it would still be, in fact and in theory, an association of states, or a confederacy. The proposed Constitution, so far from implying an abolition of the State governments, makes them constituent parts of the national sovereignty, by allowing them a direct representation in the Senate, and leaves in their possession certain exclusive and very important portions of sovereign power. This fully corresponds, in every rational import of the terms, with the idea of a federal government.

In the Lycian confederacy, which consisted of twenty-three CITIES or republics, the largest were entitled to THREE votes in the COMMON COUNCIL, those of the middle class to TWO, and the smallest to ONE. The COMMON COUNCIL had the appointment of all the judges and magistrates of the respective CITIES. This was certainly the most, delicate species of interference in their internal administration; for if there be any thing that seems exclusively appropriated to the local jurisdictions, it is the appointment of their own officers. Yet Montesquieu, speaking of this association, says: "Were I to give a model of an excellent Confederate Republic, it would be that of Lycia." Thus we perceive that the distinctions insisted upon were not within the contemplation of this enlightened civilian; and we shall be led to conclude, that they are the novel refinements of an erroneous theory.

*PUBLIUS.*

NOTE

1. "Spirit of Laws," vol. i., book ix., chap. i.

# Appendix F: Federalist No. 10: The Same Subject Continued: The Union as a Safeguard Against Domestic Faction and Insurrection

From the *New York Packet*
Friday, 23 November 1787
Author: James Madison
To the People of the State of New York:

AMONG the numerous advantages promised by a well-constructed Union, none deserves to be more accurately developed than its tendency to break and control the violence of faction. The friend of popular governments never finds himself so much alarmed for their character and fate, as when he contemplates their propensity to this dangerous vice. He will not fail, therefore, to set a due value on any plan which, without violating the principles to which he is attached, provides a proper cure for it. The instability, injustice, and confusion introduced into the public councils, have, in truth, been the mortal diseases under which popular governments have everywhere perished; as they continue to be the favorite and fruitful topics from which the adversaries to liberty derive their most specious declamations. The valuable improvements made by the American constitutions on the popular models, both ancient and modern, cannot certainly be too much admired; but it would be an unwarrantable partiality, to contend that they have as effectually obviated the danger on this side, as was wished and expected. Complaints are everywhere heard from our most considerate and virtuous citizens, equally the friends of public and private faith, and of public and personal liberty, that our governments are too unstable, that the public good is disregarded in the conflicts of rival parties, and that measures are too often decided, not according to the rules of justice and the rights of the minor party, but by the superior force of an interested and overbearing majority. However anxiously we may wish that these complaints had no foundation, the evidence, of known facts will not permit us to deny that they are in some degree true. It will be found, indeed, on a candid review of our situation, that some of the distresses under which we labor have been erroneously charged on the operation of our governments; but it will be found, at the same time, that other causes will not alone account for many of our heaviest misfortunes; and, particularly, for that prevailing and increasing distrust of public engagements, and alarm for private rights, which are echoed from one end of the continent to the other. These must be chiefly, if not wholly, effects of the unsteadiness and injustice with which a factious spirit has tainted our public administrations.

By a faction, I understand a number of citizens, whether amounting to a majority or a minority of the whole, who are united and actuated by some common impulse of passion, or of interest, adversed to the rights of other citizens, or to the permanent and aggregate interests of the community.

There are two methods of curing the mischiefs of faction: the one, by removing its causes; the other, by controlling its effects.

There are again two methods of removing the causes of faction: the one, by destroying the liberty which is essential to its existence; the other, by giving to every citizen the same opinions, the same passions, and the same interests.

It could never be more truly said than of the first remedy, that it was worse than the disease. Liberty is to faction what air is to fire, an aliment without which it instantly expires. But it could not be less folly to abolish liberty, which is essential to political life, because it nourishes faction, than it would be to wish the annihilation of air, which is essential to animal life, because it imparts to fire its destructive agency.

The second expedient is as impracticable as the first would be unwise. As long as the reason of man continues fallible, and he is at liberty to exercise it, different opinions will be formed. As long as the connection subsists between his reason and his self-love, his opinions and his passions will have a reciprocal influence on each other; and the former will be objects to which the latter will attach themselves. The diversity in the faculties of men, from which the rights of property originate, is not less an insuperable obstacle to a uniformity of interests. The protection of these faculties is the first object of government. From the protection of different and unequal faculties of acquiring property, the possession of different degrees and kinds of property immediately results; and from the influence of these on the sentiments and views of the respective proprietors, ensues a division of the society into different interests and parties.

The latent causes of faction are thus sown in the nature of man; and we see them everywhere brought into different degrees of activity, according to the different circumstances of civil society. A zeal for different opinions concerning religion, concerning government, and many other points, as well of speculation as of practice; an attachment to different leaders ambitiously contending for pre-eminence and power; or to persons of other descriptions whose fortunes have been interesting to the human passions, have, in turn, divided mankind into parties, inflamed them with mutual animosity, and rendered them much more disposed to vex and oppress each other than to co-operate for their common good. So strong is this propensity of mankind to fall into mutual animosities, that where no substantial occasion presents itself, the most frivolous and fanciful distinctions have been sufficient to kindle their unfriendly passions and excite their most violent conflicts. But the most common and durable source of factions has been the various and unequal distribution of property. Those who hold and those who are without property have ever formed distinct interests in society. Those who are creditors, and those who are debtors, fall under a like discrimination. A landed interest, a manufacturing interest, a mercantile interest, a moneyed interest, with many lesser interests, grow up of necessity in civilized nations, and divide them into different classes, actuated by different sentiments and views. The regulation of these various and interfering interests forms the principal task of modern legislation, and involves the spirit of party and faction in the necessary and ordinary operations of the government.

No man is allowed to be a judge in his own cause, because his interest would certainly bias his judgment, and, not improbably, corrupt his integrity. With equal, nay with greater reason, a body of men are unfit to be both judges and parties at the same time; yet what are many of the most important acts of legislation, but so many judicial determinations, not indeed concerning the rights of single persons, but concerning the rights of large bodies of citizens? And what are the different classes of legislators but advocates and parties to the causes which they determine? Is a law proposed concerning private debts? It is a question to which the creditors are parties on one side and the debtors on the other. Justice ought to hold the balance between them. Yet the parties are, and must be, themselves the judges; and the most numerous party, or, in other words, the most powerful faction must be expected to prevail. Shall domestic manufactures be encouraged, and in what degree, by restrictions on foreign manufactures? are questions which would be differently decided by the landed and the manufacturing classes, and probably by neither with a sole regard to justice and the public good. The apportionment of taxes on the various descriptions of property is an act which seems to require the most exact impartiality; yet there is, perhaps, no legislative act in which greater opportunity and temptation are given to a predominant party to trample on the rules of justice. Every shilling with which they overburden the inferior number, is a shilling saved to their own pockets.

It is in vain to say that enlightened statesmen will be able to adjust these clashing interests, and render them all subservient to the public good. Enlightened statesmen will not always be at the helm. Nor, in many cases, can such an adjustment be made at all without taking into view indirect and remote considerations, which will rarely prevail over the immediate interest which one party may find in disregarding the rights of another or the good of the whole.

The inference to which we are brought is, that the CAUSES of faction cannot be removed, and that relief is only to be sought in the means of controlling its EFFECTS.

If a faction consists of less than a majority, relief is supplied by the republican principle, which enables the majority to defeat its sinister views by regular vote. It may clog the administration, it may convulse the society; but it will be unable to execute and mask its violence under the forms of the Constitution. When a majority is included in a faction, the form of popular government, on the other hand, enables it to sacrifice to its ruling passion or interest both the public good and the rights of other citizens. To secure the public good and private rights against the danger of such a faction, and at the same time to preserve the spirit and the form of popular government, is then the great object to which our inquiries are directed. Let me add that it is the great desideratum by which this form of government can be rescued from the opprobrium under which it has so long labored, and be recommended to the esteem and adoption of mankind.

By what means is this object attainable? Evidently by one of two only. Either the existence of the same passion or interest in a majority at the same time must be prevented, or the majority, having such coexistent passion or interest, must be rendered, by their number and local situation, unable to concert and carry into effect schemes of oppression. If the impulse and the opportunity be suffered to coincide, we well know that neither moral nor religious motives can be relied on as an adequate control. They are not found to be such on the injustice and violence of individuals, and lose their efficacy in proportion to the number combined together, that is, in proportion as their efficacy becomes needful.

From this view of the subject it may be concluded that a pure democracy, by which I mean a society consisting of a small number of citizens, who assemble and administer the government in person, can admit of no cure for the mischiefs of faction. A common passion or interest will, in almost every case, be felt by a majority of the whole; a communication and concert result from the form of government itself; and there is nothing to check the inducements to sacrifice the weaker party or an obnoxious individual. Hence it is that such democracies have ever been spectacles of turbulence and contention; have ever been found incompatible with personal security or the rights of property; and have in general been as short in their lives as they have been violent in their deaths. Theoretic politicians, who have patronized this species of government, have erroneously supposed that by reducing mankind to a perfect equality in their political rights, they would, at the same time, be perfectly equalized and assimilated in their possessions, their opinions, and their passions.

A republic, by which I mean a government in which the scheme of representation takes place, opens a different prospect, and promises the cure for which we are seeking. Let us examine the points in which it varies from pure democracy, and we shall comprehend both the nature of the cure and the efficacy which it must derive from the Union.

The two great points of difference between a democracy and a republic are: first, the delegation of the government, in the latter, to a small number of citizens elected by the rest; secondly, the greater number of citizens, and greater sphere of country, over which the latter may be extended.

The effect of the first difference is, on the one hand, to refine and enlarge the public views, by passing them through the medium of a chosen body of citizens, whose wisdom may best discern the true interest of their country, and whose patriotism and love of justice will be least likely to sacrifice it to temporary or partial considerations. Under such a regulation, it may well happen that the public voice, pronounced by the representatives of the people, will be more consonant to the public good than if pronounced by the people themselves, convened for the purpose. On the other hand, the effect may be inverted. Men of factious tempers, of local prejudices, or of sinister designs, may, by intrigue, by corruption, or by other means, first obtain the suffrages, and then betray the interests, of the people. The question resulting is, whether small or extensive republics are more favorable to the election of proper guardians of the public weal; and it is clearly decided in favor of the latter by two obvious considerations:

In the first place, it is to be remarked that, however small the republic may be, the representatives must be raised to a certain number, in order to guard against the cabals of a few; and that, however large it may be, they must be limited to a certain number, in order to guard against the confusion of a multitude. Hence, the number of representatives in the two cases not being in proportion to that of the two constituents, and being proportionally greater in the small republic, it follows that, if the proportion of fit characters be not less in the large than in the small republic, the former will present a greater option, and consequently a greater probability of a fit choice.

In the next place, as each representative will be chosen by a greater number of citizens in the large than in the small republic, it will be more difficult for unworthy candidates to practice with success the vicious arts by which elections are too often carried; and the suffrages of the people being more free, will be more likely to centre in men who possess the most attractive merit and the most diffusive and established characters.

It must be confessed that in this, as in most other cases, there is a mean, on both sides of which inconveniences will be found to lie. By enlarging too much the number of electors, you render the representatives too little acquainted with all their local circumstances and lesser interests; as by reducing it too much, you render him unduly attached to these, and too little fit to comprehend and pursue great and national objects. The federal Constitution forms a happy combination in this respect; the great and aggregate interests being referred to the national, the local and particular to the State legislatures.

The other point of difference is, the greater number of citizens and extent of territory which may be brought within the compass of republican than of democratic government; and it is this circumstance principally which renders factious combinations less to be dreaded in the former than in the latter. The smaller the society, the fewer probably will be the distinct parties and interests composing it; the fewer the distinct parties and interests, the more frequently will a majority be found of the same party; and the smaller the number of individuals composing a majority, and the smaller the compass within which they are placed, the more easily will they concert and execute their plans of oppression. Extend the sphere, and you take in a greater variety of parties and interests; you make it less probable that a majority of the whole will have a common motive to invade the rights of other citizens; or if such a common motive exists, it will be more difficult for all who feel it to discover their own strength, and to act in unison with each other. Besides other impediments, it may be remarked that, where there is a consciousness of unjust or dishonorable purposes, communication is always checked by distrust in proportion to the number whose concurrence is necessary.

Hence, it clearly appears, that the same advantage which a republic has over a democracy, in controlling the effects of faction, is enjoyed by a large over a small republic,—is enjoyed by the Union over the States composing it. Does the advantage consist in the substitution of representatives whose enlightened views and virtuous sentiments render them superior to local prejudices and schemes of injustice? It will not be denied that the representation of the Union will be most likely to possess these requisite endowments. Does it consist in the greater security afforded by a greater variety of parties, against the event of any one party being able to outnumber and oppress the rest? In an equal degree does the increased variety of parties comprised within the Union, increase this security. Does it, in fine, consist in the greater obstacles opposed to the concert and accomplishment of the secret wishes of an unjust and interested majority? Here, again, the extent of the Union gives it the most palpable advantage.

The influence of factious leaders may kindle a flame within their particular States, but will be unable to spread a general conflagration through the other States. A religious sect may degenerate into a political faction in a part of the Confederacy; but the variety of sects dispersed over the entire face of it must secure the national councils against any danger from that source. A rage for paper money, for an abolition of debts, for an equal division of property, or for any other improper or wicked project, will be less apt to pervade the whole body of the Union than a particular member of it; in the same proportion as such a malady is more likely to taint a particular county or district, than an entire State.

In the extent and proper structure of the Union, therefore, we behold a republican remedy for the diseases most incident to republican government. And according to the degree of pleasure and pride we feel in being republicans, ought to be our zeal in cherishing the spirit and supporting the character of Federalists.

# Appendix G: Federalist No. 13: Advantage of the Union in Respect to Economy in Government

For the *Independent Journal*
Author: Alexander Hamilton
To the People of the State of New York:

As CONNECTED with the subject of revenue, we may with propriety consider that of economy. The money saved from one object may be usefully applied to another, and there will be so much the less to be drawn from the pockets of the people. If the States are united under one government, there will be but one national civil list to support; if they are divided into several confederacies, there will be as many different national civil lists to be provided for—and each of them, as to the principal departments, coextensive with that which would be necessary for a government of the whole. The entire separation of the States into thirteen unconnected sovereignties is a project too extravagant and too replete with danger to have many advocates. The ideas of men who speculate upon the dismemberment of the empire seem generally turned toward three confederacies—one consisting of the four Northern, another of the four Middle, and a third of the five Southern States. There is little probability that there would be a greater number. According to this distribution, each confederacy would comprise an extent of territory larger than that of the kingdom of Great Britain. No well-informed man will suppose that the affairs of such a confederacy can be properly regulated by a government less comprehensive in its organs or institutions than that which has been proposed by the convention. When the dimensions of a State attain to a certain magnitude, it requires the same energy of government and the same forms of administration which are requisite in one of much greater extent. This idea admits not of precise demonstration, because there is no rule by which we can measure the momentum of civil power necessary to the government of any given number of individuals; but when we consider that the island of Britain, nearly commensurate with each of the supposed confederacies, contains about eight millions of people, and when we reflect upon the degree of authority required to direct the passions of so large a society to the public good, we shall see no reason to doubt that the like portion of power would be sufficient to perform the same task in a society far more numerous. Civil power, properly organized and exerted, is capable of diffusing its force to a very great extent; and can, in a manner, reproduce itself in every part of a great empire by a judicious arrangement of subordinate institutions.

The supposition that each confederacy into which the States would be likely to be divided would require a government not less comprehensive than the one proposed, will be strengthened by another supposition, more probable than that which presents us with three confederacies as the alternative to a general Union. If we attend carefully to geographical and commercial considerations, in conjunction with the habits and prejudices of the different States, we shall be led to conclude that in case of disunion they will most naturally league themselves under two governments. The four Eastern States, from all the causes that form the links of national sympathy and connection, may with certainty be expected to unite. New York, situated as she is, would never be unwise enough to oppose a feeble and unsupported flank to the weight of that confederacy. There are other obvious reasons that would facilitate her accession to it. New Jersey is too small a State to think of being a frontier, in opposition to this still more powerful combination; nor do there appear to be any obstacles to her admission into it. Even Pennsylvania would have strong inducements to join the Northern league. An active foreign commerce, on the basis of her own navigation, is her true policy, and coincides with the opinions and dispositions of her citizens. The more Southern States, from various circumstances, may not think themselves much interested in the encouragement of navigation. They may prefer a system which would give unlimited scope to all nations to be the carriers as well as the purchasers of their commodities. Pennsylvania may not choose to confound her interests in a connection so adverse to her policy. As she must at all events be a frontier, she may deem it most consistent with her safety to have her exposed side turned towards the weaker power of the Southern, rather than towards the stronger power of the Northern, Confederacy. This would give her the fairest chance to avoid being the Flanders of America. Whatever may be the determination of Pennsylvania, if the Northern Confederacy includes New Jersey, there is no likelihood of more than one confederacy to the south of that State.

Nothing can be more evident than that the thirteen States will be able to support a national government better than one half, or one third, or any number less than the whole. This reflection must have great weight in obviating that objection to the proposed plan, which is founded on the principle of expense; an objection, however, which, when we come to take a nearer view of it, will appear in every light to stand on mistaken ground.

If, in addition to the consideration of a plurality of civil lists, we take into view the number of persons who must necessarily be employed to guard the inland communication between the different confederacies against illicit trade, and who in time will infallibly spring up out of the necessities of revenue; and if we also take into view the military establishments which it has been shown would unavoidably result from the jealousies and conflicts of the several nations into which the States would be divided, we shall clearly discover that a separation would be not less injurious to the economy, than to the tranquillity, commerce, revenue, and liberty of every part.

*PUBLIUS.*

# Appendix H: Federalist No. 15: The Insufficiency of the Present Confederation to Preserve the Union

For the *Independent Journal*
Author: Alexander Hamilton
To the People of the State of New York:

IN THE course of the preceding papers, I have endeavored, my fellow-citizens, to place before you, in a clear and convincing light, the importance of Union to your political safety and happiness. I have unfolded to you a complication of dangers to which you would be exposed, should you permit that sacred knot which binds the people of America together be severed or dissolved by ambition or by avarice, by jealousy or by misrepresentation. In the sequel of the inquiry through which I propose to accompany you, the truths intended to be inculcated will receive further confirmation from facts and arguments hitherto unnoticed. If the road over which you will still have to pass should in some places appear to you tedious or irksome, you will recollect that you are in quest of information on a subject the most momentous which can engage the attention of a free people, that the field through which you have to travel is in itself spacious, and that the difficulties of the journey have been unnecessarily increased by the mazes with which sophistry has beset the way. It will be my aim to remove the obstacles from your progress in as compendious a manner as it can be done, without sacrificing utility to despatch.

In pursuance of the plan which I have laid down for the discussion of the subject, the point next in order to be examined is the "insufficiency of the present Confederation to the preservation of the Union." It may perhaps be asked what need there is of reasoning or proof to illustrate a position which is not either controverted or doubted, to which the understandings and feelings of all classes of men assent, and which in substance is admitted by the opponents as well as by the friends of the new Constitution. It must in truth be acknowledged that, however these may differ in other respects, they in general appear to harmonize in this sentiment, at least, that there are material imperfections in our national system, and that something is necessary to be done to rescue us from impending anarchy. The facts that support this opinion are no longer objects of speculation. They have forced themselves upon the sensibility of the people at large, and have at length extorted from those, whose mistaken policy has had the principal share in precipitating the extremity at which we are arrived, a reluctant confession of the reality of those defects in the scheme of our federal government, which have been long pointed out and regretted by the intelligent friends of the Union.

We may indeed with propriety be said to have reached almost the last stage of national humiliation. There is scarcely anything that can wound the pride or degrade the character of an independent nation which we do not experience. Are there engagements to the performance of which we are held by every tie respectable among men? These are the subjects of constant and unblushing violation. Do we owe debts to foreigners and to our own citizens contracted in a time of imminent peril for the preservation of our political existence? These remain without any proper or satisfactory provision for their discharge. Have we valuable territories and important posts in the possession of a foreign power which, by express stipulations, ought long since to have been surrendered? These are still retained, to the prejudice of our interests, not less than of our rights. Are we in a condition to resent or to repel the aggression? We have neither troops, nor treasury, nor government.[i] Are we even in a condition to remonstrate with dignity? The just imputations on our own faith, in respect to the same treaty, ought first to be removed. Are we entitled by nature and compact to a free participation in the navigation of the Mississippi? Spain excludes us from it. Is public credit an indispensable resource in time of public danger? We seem to have abandoned its cause as desperate and irretrievable. Is commerce of importance to national wealth? Ours is at the lowest point of declension. Is respectability in the eyes of foreign powers a safeguard against foreign encroachments? The imbecility of our government even forbids them to treat with us. Our ambassadors abroad are the mere pageants of mimic sovereignty. Is a violent and unnatural decrease in the value of land a symptom of national distress? The price of improved land in most parts of the country is much lower than can be accounted for by the quantity of waste land at market, and can only be fully explained by that want of private and public confidence, which are so alarmingly prevalent among all ranks, and which have a direct tendency to depreciate property of every kind. Is private credit the friend and patron of industry? That most useful kind which relates to borrowing and lending is reduced within the narrowest limits, and this still more from an opinion of insecurity than from the scarcity of money. To shorten an enumeration of particulars which can afford neither pleasure nor instruction, it may in general be demanded, what indication is there of national disorder, poverty, and insignificance that could befall a community so peculiarly blessed with natural advantages as we are, which does not form a part of the dark catalogue of our public misfortunes?

This is the melancholy situation to which we have been brought by those very maxims and councils which would now deter us from adopting the proposed Constitution; and which, not content with having conducted us to the brink of a precipice, seem resolved to plunge us into the abyss that awaits us below. Here, my countrymen, impelled by every motive that ought to influence an enlightened people, let us make a firm stand for our safety, our tranquillity, our dignity, our reputation. Let us at last break the fatal charm which has too long seduced us from the paths of felicity and prosperity.

It is true, as has been before observed that facts, too stubborn to be resisted, have produced a species of general assent to the abstract proposition that there exist material defects in our national system; but the usefulness of the concession, on the part of the old adversaries of federal measures, is destroyed by a strenuous opposition to a remedy, upon the only principles that can give it a chance of success. While they admit that the government of the United States is destitute of energy, they contend against conferring upon it those powers which are requisite to supply that energy. They seem still to aim at things repugnant and irreconcilable; at an augmentation of federal authority, without a diminution of State authority; at sovereignty in the Union, and complete independence in the members. They still, in fine, seem to cherish with blind devotion the political monster of an imperium in imperio. This renders a full display of the principal defects of the Confederation necessary, in order to show that the evils we experience do not proceed from minute or partial imperfections, but from fundamental errors in the structure of the building, which cannot be amended otherwise than by an alteration in the first principles and main pillars of the fabric.

The great and radical vice in the construction of the existing Confederation is in the principle of LEGISLATION for STATES or GOVERNMENTS, in their CORPORATE or COLLECTIVE CAPACITIES, and as contradistinguished from the INDIVIDUALS of which they consist. Though this principle does not run through all the powers delegated to the Union, yet it pervades and governs those on which the efficacy of the rest depends. Except as to the rule of appointment, the United States has an indefinite discretion to make requisitions for men and money; but they have no authority to raise either, by regulations extending to the individual citizens of America. The consequence of this is, that though in theory their resolutions concerning those objects are laws, constitutionally binding on the members of the Union, yet in practice they are mere recommendations which the States observe or disregard at their option.

It is a singular instance of the capriciousness of the human mind, that after all the admonitions we have had from experience on this head, there should still be found men who object to the new Constitution, for deviating from a principle which has been found the bane of the old, and which is in itself evidently incompatible with the idea of GOVERNMENT; a principle, in short, which, if it is to be executed at all, must substitute the violent and sanguinary agency of the sword to the mild influence of the magistracy.

There is nothing absurd or impracticable in the idea of a league or alliance between independent nations for certain defined purposes precisely stated in a treaty regulating all the details of time, place, circumstance, and quantity; leaving nothing to future discretion; and depending for its execution on the good faith of the parties. Compacts of this kind exist among all civilized nations, subject to the usual vicissitudes of peace and war, of observance and non-observance, as the interests or passions of the contracting powers dictate. In the early part of the present century there was an epidemical rage in Europe for this species of compacts, from which the politicians of the times fondly hoped for benefits which were never realized. With a view to establishing the equilibrium of power and the peace of that part of the world, all the resources of negotiation were exhausted, and triple and quadruple alliances were formed; but they were scarcely formed before they were broken, giving an instructive but afflicting lesson to mankind, how little dependence is to be placed on treaties which have no other sanction than the obligations of good faith, and which oppose general considerations of peace and justice to the impulse of any immediate interest or passion.

If the particular States in this country are disposed to stand in a similar relation to each other, and to drop the project of a general DISCRETIONARY SUPERINTENDENCE, the scheme would indeed be pernicious, and would entail upon us all the mischiefs which have been enumerated under the first head; but it would have the merit of being, at least, consistent and practicable Abandoning all views towards a confederate government, this would bring us to a simple alliance offensive and defensive; and would place us in a situation to be alternate friends and enemies of each other, as our mutual jealousies and rivalships, nourished by the intrigues of foreign nations, should prescribe to us.

But if we are unwilling to be placed in this perilous situation; if we still will adhere to the design of a national government, or, which is the same thing, of a superintending power, under the direction of a common council, we must resolve to incorporate into our plan those ingredients which may be considered as forming the characteristic difference between a league and a government; we must extend the authority of the Union to the persons of the citizens, --the only proper objects of government.

Government implies the power of making laws. It is essential to the idea of a law, that it be attended with a sanction; or, in other words, a penalty or punishment for disobedience. If there be no penalty annexed to disobedience, the resolutions or commands which pretend to be laws will, in fact, amount to nothing more than advice or recommendation. This penalty, whatever it may be, can only be inflicted in two ways: by the agency of the courts and ministers of justice, or by military force; by the COERCION of the magistracy, or by the COERCION of arms. The first kind can evidently apply only to men; the last kind must of necessity, be employed against bodies politic, or communities, or States. It is evident that there is no process of a court by which the observance of the laws can, in the last resort, be enforced. Sentences may be denounced against them for violations of their duty; but these sentences can only be carried into execution by the sword. In an association where the general authority is confined to the collective bodies of the communities, that compose it, every breach of the laws must involve a state of war; and military execution must become the only instrument of civil obedience. Such a state of things can certainly not deserve the name of government, nor would any prudent man choose to commit his happiness to it.

There was a time when we were told that breaches, by the States, of the regulations of the federal authority were not to be expected; that a sense of common interest would preside over the conduct of the respective members, and would beget a full compliance with all the constitutional requisitions of the Union. This language, at the present day, would appear as wild as a great part of what we now hear from the same quarter will be thought, when we shall have received further lessons from that best oracle of wisdom, experience. It at all times betrayed an ignorance of the true springs by which human conduct is actuated, and belied the original inducements to the establishment of civil power. Why has government been instituted at all? Because the passions of men will not conform to the dictates of reason and justice, without constraint. Has it been found that bodies of men act with more rectitude or greater disinterestedness than individuals? The contrary of this has been inferred by all accurate observers of the conduct of mankind; and the inference is founded upon obvious reasons. Regard to reputation has a less active influence, when the infamy of a bad action is to be divided among a number than when it is to fall singly upon one. A spirit of faction, which is apt to mingle its poison in the deliberations of all bodies of men, will often hurry the persons of whom they are composed into improprieties and excesses, for which they would blush in a private capacity.

In addition to all this, there is, in the nature of sovereign power, an impatience of control, that disposes those who are invested with the exercise of it, to look with an evil eye upon all external attempts to restrain or direct its operations. From this spirit it happens, that in every political association which is formed upon the principle of uniting in a common interest a number of lesser sovereignties, there will be found a kind of eccentric tendency in the subordinate or inferior orbs, by the operation of which there will be a perpetual effort in each to fly off from the common centre. This tendency is not difficult to be accounted for. It has its origin in the love of power. Power controlled or abridged is almost always the rival and enemy of that power by which it is controlled or abridged. This simple proposition will teach us how little reason there is to expect, that the persons intrusted with the administration of the affairs of the particular members of a confederacy will at all times be ready, with perfect good-humor, and an unbiased regard to the public weal, to execute the resolutions or decrees of the general authority. The reverse of this results from the constitution of human nature.

If, therefore, the measures of the Confederacy cannot be executed without the intervention of the particular administrations, there will be little prospect of their being executed at all. The rulers of the respective members, whether they have a constitutional right to do it or not, will undertake to judge of the propriety of the measures themselves. They will consider the conformity of the thing proposed or required to their immediate interests or aims; the momentary conveniences or inconveniences that would attend its adoption. All this will be done; and in a spirit of interested and suspicious scrutiny, without that knowledge of national circumstances and reasons of state, which is essential to a right judgment, and with that strong predilection in favor of local objects, which can hardly fail to mislead the decision. The same process must be repeated in every member of which the body is constituted; and the execution of the plans, framed by the councils of the whole, will always fluctuate on the discretion of the ill-informed and prejudiced opinion of every part. Those who have been conversant in the proceedings of popular assemblies; who have seen how difficult it often is, where there is no exterior pressure of circumstances, to bring them to harmonious resolutions on important points, will readily conceive how impossible it must be to induce a number of such assemblies, deliberating at a distance from each other, at different times, and under different impressions, long to co-operate in the same views and pursuits.

In our case, the concurrence of thirteen distinct sovereign wills is requisite, under the Confederation, to the complete execution of every important measure that proceeds from the Union. It has happened as was to have been foreseen. The measures of the Union have not been executed; the delinquencies of the States have, step by step, matured themselves to an extreme, which has, at length, arrested all the wheels of the national government, and brought them to an awful stand. Congress at this time scarcely possess the means of keeping up the forms of administration, till the States can have time to agree upon a more substantial substitute for the present shadow of a federal government. Things did not come to this desperate extremity at once. The causes which have been specified produced at first only unequal and disproportionate degrees of compliance with the requisitions of the Union. The greater deficiencies of some States furnished the pretext of example and the temptation of interest to the complying, or to the least delinquent States. Why should we do more in proportion than those who are embarked with us in the same political voyage? Why should we consent to bear more than our proper share of the common burden? These were suggestions which human selfishness could not withstand, and which even speculative men, who looked forward to remote consequences, could not, without hesitation, combat. Each State, yielding to the persuasive voice of immediate interest or convenience, has successively withdrawn its support, till the frail and tottering edifice seems ready to fall upon our heads, and to crush us beneath its ruins.

*PUBLIUS.*

## NOTE

1. "I mean for the Union."

# Appendix I: Federalist No. 37: Concerning the Difficulties of the Convention in Devising a Proper Form of Government

From the *Daily Advertiser*
Friday, 11 January 1788
Author: James Madison
To the People of the State of New York:

IN REVIEWING the defects of the existing Confederation, and showing that they cannot be supplied by a government of less energy than that before the public, several of the most important principles of the latter fell of course under consideration. But as the ultimate object of these papers is to determine clearly and fully the merits of this Constitution, and the expediency of adopting it, our plan cannot be complete without taking a more critical and thorough survey of the work of the convention, without examining it on all its sides, comparing it in all its parts, and calculating its probable effects.

That this remaining task may be executed under impressions conducive to a just and fair result, some reflections must in this place be indulged, which candor previously suggests.

It is a misfortune, inseparable from human affairs, that public measures are rarely investigated with that spirit of moderation which is essential to a just estimate of their real tendency to advance or obstruct the public good; and that this spirit is more apt to be diminished than promoted, by those occasions which require an unusual exercise of it. To those who have been led by experience to attend to this consideration, it could not appear surprising, that the act of the convention, which recommends so many important changes and innovations, which may be viewed in so many lights and relations, and which touches the springs of so many passions and interests, should find or excite dispositions unfriendly, both on one side and on the other, to a fair discussion and accurate judgment of its merits. In some, it has been too evident from their own publications, that they have scanned the proposed Constitution, not only with a predisposition to censure, but with a predetermination to condemn; as the language held by others betrays an opposite predetermination or bias, which must render their opinions also of little moment in the question. In placing, however, these different characters on a level, with respect to the weight of their opinions, I wish not to insinuate that there may not be a material difference in the purity of their intentions. It is but just to remark in favor of the latter description, that as our situation is universally admitted to be peculiarly critical, and to require indispensably that something should be done for our relief, the predetermined patron of what has been actually done may have taken his bias from the weight of these considerations, as well as from considerations of a sinister nature. The predetermined adversary, on the other hand, can have been governed by no venial motive whatever. The intentions of the first may be upright, as they may on the contrary be culpable. The views of the last cannot be upright, and must be culpable. But the truth is, that these papers are not addressed to persons falling under either of these characters. They solicit the attention of those only, who add to a sincere zeal for the happiness of their country, a temper favorable to a just estimate of the means of promoting it.

Persons of this character will proceed to an examination of the plan submitted by the convention, not only without a disposition to find or to magnify faults; but will see the propriety of reflecting, that a faultless plan was not to be expected. Nor will they barely make allowances for the errors which may be chargeable on the fallibility to which the convention, as a body of men, were liable; but will keep in mind, that they themselves also are but men, and ought not to assume an infallibility in rejudging the fallible opinions of others.

With equal readiness will it be perceived, that besides these inducements to candor, many allowances ought to be made for the difficulties inherent in the very nature of the undertaking referred to the convention.

The novelty of the undertaking immediately strikes us. It has been shown in the course of these papers, that the existing Confederation is founded on principles which are fallacious; that we must consequently change this first foundation, and with it the superstructure resting upon it. It has been shown, that the other confederacies which could be consulted as precedents have been vitiated by the same erroneous principles, and can therefore furnish no other light than that of beacons, which give warning of the course to be shunned, without pointing out that which ought to be pursued. The most that the convention could do in such a situation, was to avoid the errors suggested by the past experience of other countries, as well as of our own; and to provide a convenient mode of rectifying their own errors, as future experiences may unfold them.

Among the difficulties encountered by the convention, a very important one must have lain in combining the requisite stability and energy in government, with the inviolable attention due to liberty and to the republican form. Without substantially accomplishing this part of their undertaking, they would have very imperfectly fulfilled the object of their appointment, or the expectation of the public; yet that it could not be easily accomplished, will be denied by no one who is unwilling to betray his ignorance of the subject. Energy in government is essential to that security against external and internal danger, and to that prompt and salutary execution of the laws which enter into the very definition of good government. Stability in government is essential to national character and to the advantages annexed to it, as well as to that repose and confidence in the minds of the people, which are among the chief blessings of civil society. An irregular and mutable legislation is not more an evil in itself than it is odious to the people; and it may be pronounced with assurance that the people of this country, enlightened as they are with regard to the nature, and interested, as the great body of them are, in the effects of good government, will never be satisfied till some remedy be applied to the vicissitudes and uncertainties which characterize the State administrations. On comparing, however, these valuable ingredients with the vital principles of liberty, we must perceive at once the difficulty of mingling them together in their due proportions. The genius of republican liberty seems to demand on one side, not only that all power should be derived from the people, but that those intrusted with it should be kept in independence on the people, by a short duration of their appointments; and that even during this short period the trust should be placed not in a few, but a number of hands. Stability, on the contrary, requires that the hands in which power is lodged should continue for a length of time the same. A frequent change of men will result from a frequent return of elections; and a frequent change of measures from a frequent change of men: whilst energy in government requires not only a certain duration of power, but the execution of it by a single hand.

How far the convention may have succeeded in this part of their work, will better appear on a more accurate view of it. From the cursory view here taken, it must clearly appear to have been an arduous part.

Not less arduous must have been the task of marking the proper line of partition between the authority of the general and that of the State governments. Every man will be sensible of this difficulty, in proportion as he has been accustomed to contemplate and discriminate objects extensive and complicated in their nature. The faculties of the mind itself have never yet been distinguished and defined, with satisfactory precision, by all the efforts of the most acute and metaphysical philosophers. Sense, perception, judgment, desire, volition, memory, imagination, are found to be separated by such delicate shades and minute gradations that their boundaries have eluded the most subtle investigations, and remain a pregnant source of ingenious disquisition and controversy. The boundaries between the great kingdom of nature, and, still more, between the various provinces, and lesser portions, into which they are subdivided, afford another illustration of the same important truth. The most sagacious and laborious naturalists have never yet succeeded in tracing with certainty the line which separates the district of vegetable life from the neighboring region of unorganized matter, or which marks the ermination of the former and the commencement of the animal empire. A still greater obscurity lies in the distinctive characters by which the objects in each of these great departments of nature have been arranged and assorted.

When we pass from the works of nature, in which all the delineations are perfectly accurate, and appear to be otherwise only from the imperfection of the eye which surveys them, to the institutions of man, in which the obscurity arises as well from the object itself as from the organ by which it is contemplated, we must perceive the necessity of moderating still further our expectations and hopes from the efforts of human sagacity. Experience has instructed us that no skill in the science of government has yet been able to discriminate and define, with sufficient certainty, its three great provinces the legislative, executive, and judiciary; or even the privileges and powers of the different legislative branches. Questions daily occur in the course of practice, which prove the obscurity which reins in these subjects, and which puzzle the greatest adepts in political science.

The experience of ages, with the continued and combined labors of the most enlightened legislatures and jurists, has been equally unsuccessful in delineating the several objects and limits of different codes of laws and different tribunals of justice. The precise extent of the common law, and the statute law, the maritime law, the ecclesiastical law, the law of corporations, and other local laws and customs, remains still to be clearly and finally established in Great Britain, where accuracy in such subjects has been more industriously pursued than in any other part of the world. The jurisdiction of her several courts, general and local, of law, of equity, of admiralty, etc., is not less a source of frequent and intricate discussions, sufficiently denoting the indeterminate limits by which they are respectively circumscribed. All new laws, though penned with the greatest technical skill, and passed on the fullest and most mature deliberation, are considered as more or less obscure and equivocal, until their meaning be liquidated and ascertained by a series of particular discussions and adjudications. Besides the obscurity arising from the complexity of objects, and the imperfection of the human faculties, the medium through which the conceptions of men are conveyed to each other adds a fresh embarrassment. The use of words is to express ideas. Perspicuity, therefore, requires not only that the ideas should be distinctly formed, but that they should be expressed by words distinctly and exclusively appropriate to them. But no language is so copious as to supply words and phrases for every complex idea, or so correct as not to include many equivocally denoting different ideas. Hence it must happen that however accurately objects may be discriminated in themselves, and however accurately the discrimination may be considered, the definition of them may be rendered inaccurate by the inaccuracy of the terms in which it is delivered. And this unavoidable inaccuracy must be greater or less, according to the complexity and novelty of the objects defined. When the Almighty himself condescends to address mankind in their own language, his meaning, luminous as it must be, is rendered dim and doubtful by the cloudy medium through which it is communicated.

Here, then, are three sources of vague and incorrect definitions: indistinctness of the object, imperfection of the organ of conception, inadequateness of the vehicle of ideas. Any one of these must produce a certain degree of obscurity. The convention, in delineating the boundary between the federal and State jurisdictions, must have experienced the full effect of them all.

To the difficulties already mentioned may be added the interfering pretensions of the larger and smaller States. We cannot err in supposing that the former would contend for a participation in the government, fully proportioned to their superior wealth and importance; and that the latter would not be less tenacious of the equality at present enjoyed by them. We may well suppose that neither side would entirely yield to the other, and consequently that the struggle could be terminated only by compromise. It is extremely probable, also, that after the ratio of representation had been adjusted, this very compromise must have produced a fresh struggle between the same parties, to give such a turn to the organization of the government, and to the distribution of its powers, as would increase the importance of the branches, in forming which they had respectively obtained the greatest share of influence. There are features in the Constitution which warrant each of these suppositions; and as far as either of them is well founded, it shows that the convention must have been compelled to sacrifice theoretical propriety to the force of extraneous considerations.

Nor could it have been the large and small States only, which would marshal themselves in opposition to each other on various points. Other combinations, resulting from a difference of local position and policy, must have created additional difficulties. As every State may be divided into different districts, and its citizens into different classes, which give birth to contending interests and local jealousies, so the different parts of the United States are distinguished from each other by a variety of circumstances, which produce a like effect on a larger scale. And although this variety of interests, for reasons sufficiently explained in a former paper, may have a salutary influence on the administration of the government when formed, yet every one must be sensible of the contrary influence, which must have been experienced in the task of forming it.

Would it be wonderful if, under the pressure of all these difficulties, the convention should have been forced into some deviations from that artificial structure and regular symmetry which an abstract view of the subject might lead an ingenious theorist to bestow on a Constitution planned in his closet or in his imagination? The real wonder is that so many difficulties should have been surmounted, and surmounted with a unanimity almost as unprecedented as it must have been unexpected. It is impossible for any man of candor to reflect on this circumstance without partaking of the astonishment. It is impossible for the man of pious reflection not to perceive in it a finger of that Almighty hand which has been so frequently and signally extended to our relief in the critical stages of the revolution.

We had occasion, in a former paper, to take notice of the repeated trials which have been unsuccessfully made in the United Netherlands for reforming the baneful and notorious vices of their constitution. The history of almost all the great councils and consultations held among mankind for reconciling their discordant opinions, assuaging their mutual jealousies, and adjusting their respective interests, is a history of factions, contentions, and disappointments, and may be classed among the most dark and degraded pictures which display the infirmities and depravities of the human character. If, in a few scattered instances, a brighter aspect is presented, they serve only as exceptions to admonish us of the general truth; and by their lustre to darken the gloom of the adverse prospect to which they are contrasted. In revolving the causes from which these exceptions result, and applying them to the particular instances before us, we are necessarily led to two important conclusions. The first is, that the convention must have enjoyed, in a very singular degree, an exemption from the pestilential influence of party animosities the disease most incident to deliberative bodies, and most apt to contaminate their proceedings. The second conclusion is that all the deputations composing the convention were satisfactorily accommodated by the final act, or were induced to accede to it by a deep conviction of the necessity of sacrificing private opinions and partial interests to the public good, and by a despair of seeing this necessity diminished by delays or by new experiments.

*PUBLIUS.*

# Appendix J: Federalist No. 46: The Influence of the State and Federal Governments Compared

From the *New York Packet*
Tuesday, 29 January 1788
Author: James Madison
To the People of the State of New York:

RESUMING the subject of the last paper, I proceed to inquire whether the federal government or the State governments will have the advantage with regard to the predilection and support of the people. Notwithstanding the different modes in which they are appointed, we must consider both of them as substantially dependent on the great body of the citizens of the United States.

I assume this position here as it respects the first, reserving the proofs for another place. The federal and State governments are in fact but different agents and trustees of the people, constituted with different powers, and designed for different purposes. The adversaries of the Constitution seem to have lost sight of the people altogether in their reasonings on this subject; and to have viewed these different establishments, not only as mutual rivals and enemies, but as uncontrolled by any common superior in their efforts to usurp the authorities of each other. These gentlemen must here be reminded of their error. They must be told that the ultimate authority, wherever the derivative may be found, resides in the people alone, and that it will not depend merely on the comparative ambition or address of the different governments, whether either, or which of them, will be able to enlarge its sphere of jurisdiction at the expense of the other. Truth, no less than decency, requires that the event in every case should be supposed to depend on the sentiments and sanction of their common constituents. Many considerations, besides those suggested on a former occasion, seem to place it beyond doubt that the first and most natural attachment of the people will be to the governments of their respective States.

Into the administration of these a greater number of individuals will expect to rise. From the gift of these a greater number of offices and emoluments will flow. By the superintending care of these, all the more domestic and personal interests of the people will be regulated and provided for. With the affairs of these, the people will be more familiarly and minutely conversant. And with the members of these, will a greater proportion of the people have the ties of personal acquaintance and friendship, and of family and party attachments; on the side of these, therefore, the popular bias may well be expected most strongly to incline. Experience speaks the same language in this case. The federal administration, though hitherto very defective in comparison with what may be hoped under a better system, had, during the war, and particularly whilst the independent fund of paper emissions was in credit, an activity and importance as great as it can well have in any future circumstances whatever.

It was engaged, too, in a course of measures which had for their object the protection of everything that was dear, and the acquisition of everything that could be desirable to the people at large. It was, nevertheless, invariably found, after the transient enthusiasm for the early Congresses was over, that the attention and attachment of the people were turned anew to their own particular governments; that the federal council was at no time the idol of popular favor; and that opposition to proposed enlargements of its powers and importance was the side usually taken by the men who wished to build their political consequence on the prepossessions of their fellow-citizens. If, therefore, as has been elsewhere remarked, the people should in future become more partial to the federal than to the State governments, the change can only result from such manifest and irresistible proofs of a better administration, as will overcome all their antecedent propensities. And in that case, the people ought not surely to be precluded from giving most of their confidence where they may discover it to be most due; but even in that case the State governments could have little to apprehend, because it is only within a certain sphere that the federal power can, in the nature of things, be advantageously administered. The remaining points on which I propose to compare the federal and State governments, are the disposition and the faculty they may respectively possess, to resist and frustrate the measures of each other. It has been already proved that the members of the federal will be more dependent on the members of the State governments, than the latter will be on the former. It has appeared also, that the prepossessions of the people, on whom both will depend, will be more on the side of the State governments, than of the federal government. So far as the disposition of each towards the other may be influenced by these causes, the State governments must clearly have the advantage.

But in a distinct and very important point of view, the advantage will lie on the same side. The prepossessions, which the members themselves will carry into the federal government, will generally be favorable to the States; whilst it will rarely happen, that the members of the State governments will carry into the public councils a bias in favor of the general government. A local spirit will infallibly prevail much more in the members of Congress, than a national spirit will prevail in the legislatures of the particular States. Every one knows that a great proportion of the errors committed by the State legislatures proceeds from the disposition of the members to sacrifice the comprehensive and permanent interest of the State, to the particular and separate views of the counties or districts in which they reside. And if they do not sufficiently enlarge their policy to embrace the collective welfare of their particular State, how can it be imagined that they will make the aggregate prosperity of the Union, and the dignity and respectability of its government, the objects of their affections and consultations? For the same reason that the members of the State legislatures will be unlikely to attach themselves sufficiently to national objects, the members of the federal legislature will be likely to attach themselves too much to local objects. The States will be to the latter what counties and towns are to the former. Measures will too often be decided according to their probable effect, not on the national prosperity and happiness, but on the prejudices, interests, and pursuits of the governments and people of the individual States. What is the spirit that has in general characterized the proceedings of Congress? A perusal of their journals, as well as the candid acknowledgments of such as have had a seat in that assembly, will inform us, that the members have but too frequently displayed the character, rather of partisans of their respective States, than of impartial guardians of a common interest; that where on one occasion improper sacrifices have been made of local considerations, to the aggrandizement of the federal government, the great interests of the nation have suffered on a hundred, from an undue attention to the local prejudices, interests, and views of the particular States. I mean not by these reflections to insinuate, that the new federal government will not embrace a more enlarged plan of policy than the existing government may have pursued; much less, that its views will be as confined as those of the State legislatures; but only that it will partake sufficiently of the spirit of both, to be disinclined to invade the rights of the individual States, or the preorgatives of their governments. The motives on the part of the State governments, to augment their prerogatives by defalcations from the federal government, will be overruled by no reciprocal predispositions in the members. Were it admitted, however, that the Federal government may feel an equal disposition with the State governments to extend its power beyond the due limits, the latter would still have the advantage in the means of defeating such encroachments. If an act of a particular State, though unfriendly to the national government, be generally popular in that State and should not too grossly violate the oaths of the State officers, it is executed immediately and, of course, by means on the spot and depending on the State alone. The opposition of the federal government, or the interposition of federal officers, would but inflame the zeal of all parties on the side of the State, and the evil could not be prevented or repaired, if at all, without the employment of means which must always be resorted to with reluctance and difficulty.

On the other hand, should an unwarrantable measure of the federal government be unpopular in particular States, which would seldom fail to be the case, or even a warrantable measure be so, which may sometimes be the case, the means of opposition to it are powerful and at hand. The disquietude of the people; their repugnance and, perhaps, refusal to co-operate with the officers of the Union; the frowns of the executive magistracy of the State; the embarrassments created by legislative devices, which would often be added on such occasions, would oppose, in any State, difficulties not to be despised; would form, in a large State, very serious impediments; and where the sentiments of several adjoining States happened to be in unison, would present obstructions which the federal government would hardly be willing to encounter. But ambitious encroachments of the federal government, on the authority of the State governments, would not excite the opposition of a single State, or of a few States only. They would be signals of general alarm. Every government would espouse the common cause. A correspondence would be opened. Plans of resistance would be concerted. One spirit would animate and conduct the whole. The same combinations, in short, would result from an apprehension of the federal, as was produced by the dread of a foreign, yoke; and unless the projected innovations should be voluntarily renounced, the same appeal to a trial of force would be made in the one case as was made in the other. But what degree of madness could ever drive the federal government to such an extremity. In the contest with Great Britain, one part of the empire was employed against the other.

The more numerous part invaded the rights of the less numerous part. The attempt was unjust and unwise; but it was not in speculation absolutely chimerical. But what would be the contest in the case we are supposing? Who would be the parties? A few representatives of the people would be opposed to the people themselves; or rather one set of representatives would be contending against thirteen sets of representatives, with the whole body of their common constituents on the side of the latter. The only refuge left for those who prophesy the downfall of the State governments is the visionary supposition that the federal government may previously accumulate a military force for the projects of ambition. The reasonings contained in these papers must have been employed to little purpose indeed, if it could be necessary now to disprove the reality of this danger. That the people and the States should, for a sufficient period of time, elect an uninterupted succession of men ready to betray both; that the traitors should, throughout this period, uniformly and systematically pursue some fixed plan for the extension of the military establishment; that the governments and the people of the States should silently and patiently behold the gathering storm, and continue to supply the materials, until it should be prepared to burst on their own heads, must appear to every one more like the incoherent dreams of a delirious jealousy, or the misjudged exaggerations of a counterfeit zeal, than like the sober apprehensions of genuine patriotism.

Extravagant as the supposition is, let it however be made. Let a regular army, fully equal to the resources of the country, be formed; and let it be entirely at the devotion of the federal government; still it would not be going too far to say, that the State governments, with the people on their side, would be able to repel the danger. The highest number to which, according to the best computation, a standing army can be carried in any country, does not exceed one hundredth part of the whole number of souls; or one twenty-fifth part of the number able to bear arms. This proportion would not yield, in the United States, an army of more than twenty-five or thirty thousand men. To these would be opposed a militia amounting to near half a million of citizens with arms in their hands, officered by men chosen from among themselves, fighting for their common liberties, and united and conducted by governments possessing their affections and confidence. It may well be doubted, whether a militia thus circumstanced could ever be conquered by such a proportion of regular troops. Those who are best acquainted with the last successful resistance of this country against the British arms, will be most inclined to deny the possibility of it. Besides the advantage of being armed, which the Americans possess over the people of almost every other nation, the existence of subordinate governments, to which the people are attached, and by which the militia officers are appointed, forms a barrier against the enterprises of ambition, more insurmountable than any which a simple government of any form can admit of. Notwithstanding the military establishments in the several kingdoms of Europe, which are carried as far as the public resources will bear, the governments are afraid to trust the people with arms. And it is not certain, that with this aid alone they would not be able to shake off their yokes. But were the people to possess the additional advantages of local governments chosen by themselves, who could collect the national will and direct the national force, and of officers appointed out of the militia, by these governments, and attached both to them and to the militia, it may be affirmed with the greatest assurance, that the throne of every tyranny in Europe would be speedily overturned in spite of the legions which surround it. Let us not insult the free and gallant citizens of America with the suspicion, that they would be less able to defend the rights of which they would be in actual possession, than the debased subjects of arbitrary power would be to rescue theirs from the hands of their oppressors. Let us rather no longer insult them with the supposition that they can ever reduce themselves to the necessity of making the experiment, by a blind and tame submission to the long train of insidious measures which must precede and produce it. The argument under the present head may be put into a very concise form, which appears altogether conclusive. Either the mode in which the federal government is to be constructed will render it sufficiently dependent on the people, or it will not. On the first supposition, it will be restrained by that dependence from forming schemes obnoxious to their constituents. On the other supposition, it will not possess the confidence of the people, and its schemes of usurpation will be easily defeated by the State governments, who will be supported by the people. On summing up the considerations stated in this and the last paper, they seem to amount to the most convincing evidence, that the powers proposed to be lodged in the federal government are as little formidable to those reserved to the individual States, as they are indispensably necessary to accomplish the purposes of the Union; and that all those alarms which have been sounded, of a meditated and consequential annihilation of the State governments, must, on the most favorable interpretation, be ascribed to the chimerical fears of the authors of them.

*PUBLIUS.*

# Appendix K: Federalist No. 51: The Structure of the Government Must Furnish the Proper Checks and Balances Between the Different Departments

From the *New York Packet*
Friday, 8 February 1788
Author: Alexander Hamilton or James Madison
To the People of the State of New York:

TO WHAT expedient, then, shall we finally resort, for maintaining in practice the necessary partition of power among the several departments, as laid down in the Constitution? The only answer that can be given is, that as all these exterior provisions are found to be inadequate, the defect must be supplied, by so contriving the interior structure of the government as that its several constituent parts may, by their mutual relations, be the means of keeping each other in their proper places. Without presuming to undertake a full development of this important idea, I will hazard a few general observations, which may perhaps place it in a clearer light, and enable us to form a more correct judgment of the principles and structure of the government planned by the convention.

In order to lay a due foundation for that separate and distinct exercise of the different powers of government, which to a certain extent is admitted on all hands to be essential to the preservation of liberty, it is evident that each department should have a will of its own; and consequently should be so constituted that the members of each should have as little agency as possible in the appointment of the members of the others. Were this principle rigorously adhered to, it would require that all the appointments for the supreme executive, legislative, and judiciary magistracies should be drawn from the same fountain of authority, the people, through channels having no communication whatever with one another. Perhaps such a plan of constructing the several departments would be less difficult in practice than it may in contemplation appear. Some difficulties, however, and some additional expense would attend the execution of it. Some deviations, therefore, from the principle must be admitted. In the constitution of the judiciary department in particular, it might be inexpedient to insist rigorously on the principle: first, because peculiar qualifications being essential in the members, the primary consideration ought to be to select that mode of choice which best secures these qualifications; secondly, because the permanent tenure by which the appointments are held in that department, must soon destroy all sense of dependence on the authority conferring them.

It is equally evident, that the members of each department should be as little dependent as possible on those of the others, for the emoluments annexed to their offices. Were the executive magistrate, or the judges, not independent of the legislature in this particular, their independence in every other would be merely nominal. But the great security against a gradual concentration of the several powers in the same department, consists in giving to those who administer each department the necessary constitutional means and personal motives to resist encroachments of the others. The provision for defense must in this, as in all other cases, be made commensurate to the danger of attack. Ambition must be made to counteract ambition. The interest of the man must be connected with the constitutional rights of the place. It may be a reflection on human nature, that such devices should be necessary to control the abuses of government. But what is government itself, but the greatest of all reflections on human nature? If men were angels, no government would be necessary. If angels were to govern men, neither external nor internal controls on government would be necessary. In framing a government which is to be administered by men over men, the great difficulty lies in this: you must first enable the government to control the governed; and in the next place oblige it to control itself.

A dependence on the people is, no doubt, the primary control on the government; but experience has taught mankind the necessity of auxiliary precautions. This policy of supplying, by opposite and rival interests, the defect of better motives, might be traced through the whole system of human affairs, private as well as public. We see it particularly displayed in all the subordinate distributions of power, where the constant aim is to divide and arrange the several offices in such a manner as that each may be a check on the other that the private interest of every individual may be a sentinel over the public rights. These inventions of prudence cannot be less requisite in the distribution of the supreme powers of the State. But it is not possible to give to each department an equal power of self-defense. In republican government, the legislative authority necessarily predominates. The remedy for this inconveniency is to divide the legislature into different branches; and to render them, by different modes of election and different principles of action, as little connected with each other as the nature of their common functions and their common dependence on the society will admit. It may even be necessary to guard against dangerous encroachments by still further precautions. As the weight of the legislative authority requires that it should be thus divided, the weakness of the executive may require, on the other hand, that it should be fortified.

An absolute negative on the legislature appears, at first view, to be the natural defense with which the executive magistrate should be armed. But perhaps it would be neither altogether safe nor alone sufficient. On ordinary occasions it might not be exerted with the requisite firmness, and on extraordinary occasions it might be perfidiously abused. May not this defect of an absolute negative be supplied by some qualified connection between this weaker department and the weaker branch of the stronger department, by which the latter may be led to support the constitutional rights of the former, without being too much detached from the rights of its own department? If the principles on which these observations are founded be just, as I persuade myself they are, and they be applied as a criterion to the several State constitutions, and to the federal Constitution it will be found that if the latter does not perfectly correspond with them, the former are infinitely less able to bear such a test.

There are, moreover, two considerations particularly applicable to the federal system of America, which place that system in a very interesting point of view. First. In a single republic, all the power surrendered by the people is submitted to the administration of a single government; and the usurpations are guarded against by a division of the government into distinct and separate departments. In the compound republic of America, the power surrendered by the people is first divided between two distinct governments, and then the portion allotted to each subdivided among distinct and separate departments. Hence a double security arises to the rights of the people. The different governments will control each other, at the same time that each will be controlled by itself. Second. It is of great importance in a republic not only to guard the society against the oppression of its rulers, but to guard one part of the society against the injustice of the other part. Different interests necessarily exist in different classes of citizens. If a majority be united by a common interest, the rights of the minority will be insecure.

There are but two methods of providing against this evil: the one by creating a will in the community independent of the majority that is, of the society itself; the other, by comprehending in the society so many separate descriptions of citizens as will render an unjust combination of a majority of the whole very improbable, if not impracticable. The first method prevails in all governments possessing an hereditary or self-appointed authority. This, at best, is but a precarious security; because a power independent of the society may as well espouse the unjust views of the major, as the rightful interests of the minor party, and may possibly be turned against both parties. The second method will be exemplified in the federal republic of the United States. Whilst all authority in it will be derived from and dependent on the society, the society itself will be broken into so many parts, interests, and classes of citizens, that the rights of individuals, or of the minority, will be in little danger from interested combinations of the majority.

In a free government the security for civil rights must be the same as that for religious rights. It consists in the one case in the multiplicity of interests, and in the other in the multiplicity of sects. The degree of security in both cases will depend on the number of interests and sects; and this may be presumed to depend on the extent of country and number of people comprehended under the same government. This view of the subject must particularly recommend a proper federal system to all the sincere and considerate friends of republican government, since it shows that in exact proportion as the territory of the Union may be formed into more circumscribed Confederacies, or States oppressive combinations of a majority will be facilitated: the best security, under the republican forms, for the rights of every class of citizens, will be diminished: and consequently the stability and independence of some member of the government, the only other security, must be proportionately increased. Justice is the end of government. It is the end of civil society. It ever has been and ever will be pursued until it be obtained, or until liberty be lost in the pursuit. In a society under the forms of which the stronger faction can readily unite and oppress the weaker, anarchy may as truly be said to reign as in a state of nature, where the weaker individual is not secured against the violence of the stronger; and as, in the latter state, even the stronger individuals are prompted, by the uncertainty of their condition, to submit to a government which may protect the weak as well as themselves; so, in the former state, will the more powerful factions or parties be gradnally induced, by a like motive, to wish for a government which will protect all parties, the weaker as well as the more powerful.

It can be little doubted that if the State of Rhode Island was separated from the Confederacy and left to itself, the insecurity of rights under the popular form of government within such narrow limits would be displayed by such reiterated oppressions of factious majorities that some power altogether independent of the people would soon be called for by the voice of the very factions whose misrule had proved the necessity of it. In the extended republic of the United States, and among the great variety of interests, parties, and sects which it embraces, a coalition of a majority of the whole society could seldom take place on any other principles than those of justice and the general good; whilst there being thus less danger to a minor from the will of a major party, there must be less pretext, also, to provide for the security of the former, by introducing into the government a will not dependent on the latter, or, in other words, a will independent of the society itself. It is no less certain than it is important, notwithstanding the contrary opinions which have been entertained, that the larger the society, provided it lie within a practical sphere, the more duly capable it will be of self-government. And happily for the REPUBLICAN CAUSE, the practicable sphere may be carried to a very great extent, by a judicious modification and mixture of the FEDERAL PRINCIPLE.

*PUBLIUS.*

# Appendix L: Federalist No. 52: The House of Representatives

From the *New York Packet*
Friday, 8 February 1788
Author: Alexander Hamilton or James Madison
To the People of the State of New York:

FROM the more general inquiries pursued in the four last papers, I pass on to a more particular examination of the several parts of the government. I shall begin with the House of Representatives. The first view to be taken of this part of the government relates to the qualifications of the electors and the elected. Those of the former are to be the same with those of the electors of the most numerous branch of the State legislatures. The definition of the right of suffrage is very justly regarded as a fundamental article of republican government. It was incumbent on the convention, therefore, to define and establish this right in the Constitution. To have left it open for the occasional regulation of the Congress, would have been improper for the reason just mentioned. To have submitted it to the legislative discretion of the States, would have been improper for the same reason; and for the additional reason that it would have rendered too dependent on the State governments that branch of the federal government which ought to be dependent on the people alone. To have reduced the different qualifications in the different States to one uniform rule, would probably have been as dissatisfactory to some of the States as it would have been difficult to the convention. The provision made by the convention appears, therefore, to be the best that lay within their option.

It must be satisfactory to every State, because it is conformable to the standard already established, or which may be established, by the State itself. It will be safe to the United States, because, being fixed by the State constitutions, it is not alterable by the State governments, and it cannot be feared that the people of the States will alter this part of their constitutions in such a manner as to abridge the rights secured to them by the federal Constitution. The qualifications of the elected, being less carefully and properly defined by the State constitutions, and being at the same time more susceptible of uniformity, have been very properly considered and regulated by the convention. A representative of the United States must be of the age of twenty-five years; must have been seven years a citizen of the United States; must, at the time of his election, be an inhabitant of the State he is to represent; and, during the time of his service, must be in no office under the United States. Under these reasonable limitations, the door of this part of the federal government is open to merit of every description, whether native or adoptive, whether young or old, and without regard to poverty or wealth, or to any particular profession of religious faith.

The term for which the representatives are to be elected falls under a second view which may be taken of this branch. In order to decide on the propriety of this article, two questions must be considered: first, whether biennial elections will, in this case, be safe; secondly, whether they be necessary or useful. First. As it is essential to liberty that the government in general should have a common interest with the people, so it is particularly essential that the branch of it under consideration should have an immediate dependence on, and an intimate sympathy with, the people. Frequent elections are unquestionably the only policy by which this dependence and sympathy can be effectually secured. But what particular degree of frequency may be absolutely necessary for the purpose, does not appear to be susceptible of any precise calculation, and must depend on a variety of circumstances with which it may be connected.

Let us consult experience, the guide that ought always to be followed whenever it can be found. The scheme of representation, as a substitute for a meeting of the citizens in person, being at most but very imperfectly known to ancient polity, it is in more modern times only that we are to expect instructive examples. And even here, in order to avoid a research too vague and diffusive, it will be proper to confine ourselves to the few examples which are best known, and which bear the greatest analogy to our particular case. The first to which this character ought to be applied, is the House of Commons in Great Britain. The history of this branch of the English Constitution, anterior to the date of Magna Charta, is too obscure to yield instruction. The very existence of it has been made a question among political antiquaries. The earliest records of subsequent date prove that parliaments were to SIT only every year; not that they were to be ELECTED every year. And even these annual sessions were left so much at the discretion of the monarch, that, under various pretexts, very long and dangerous intermissions were often contrived by royal ambition. To remedy this grievance, it was provided by a statute in the reign of Charles II. , that the intermissions should not be protracted beyond a period of three years. On the accession of William III. , when a revolution took place in the government, the subject was still more seriously resumed, and it was declared to be among the fundamental rights of the people that parliaments ought to be held FREQUENTLY. By another statute, which passed a few years later in the same reign, the term "frequently," which had alluded to the triennial period settled in the time of Charles II. , is reduced to a precise meaning, it being expressly enacted that a new parliament shall be called within three years after the termination of the former. The last change, from three to seven years, is well known to have been introduced pretty early in the present century, under on alarm for the Hanoverian succession.

From these facts it appears that the greatest frequency of elections which has been deemed necessary in that kingdom, for binding the representatives to their constituents, does not exceed a triennial return of them. And if we may argue from the degree of liberty retained even under septennial elections, and all the other vicious ingredients in the parliamentary constitution, we cannot doubt that a reduction of the period from seven to three years, with the other necessary reforms, would so far extend the influence of the people over their representatives as to satisfy us that biennial elections, under the federal system, cannot possibly be dangerous to the requisite dependence of the House of Representatives on their constituents. Elections in Ireland, till of late, were regulated entirely by the discretion of the crown, and were seldom repeated, except on the accession of a new prince, or some other contingent event. The parliament which commenced with George II. was continued throughout his whole reign, a period of about thirty-five years. The only dependence of the representatives on the people consisted in the right of the latter to supply occasional vacancies by the election of new members, and in the chance of some event which might produce a general new election.

The ability also of the Irish parliament to maintain the rights of their constituents, so far as the disposition might exist, was extremely shackled by the control of the crown over the subjects of their deliberation. Of late these shackles, if I mistake not, have been broken; and octennial parliaments have besides been established. What effect may be produced by this partial reform, must be left to further experience. The example of Ireland, from this view of it, can throw but little light on the subject. As far as we can draw any conclusion from it, it must be that if the people of that country have been able under all these disadvantages to retain any liberty whatever, the advantage of biennial elections would secure to them every degree of liberty, which might depend on a due connection between their representatives and themselves. Let us bring our inquiries nearer home. The example of these States, when British colonies, claims particular attention, at the same time that it is so well known as to require little to be said on it. The principle of representation, in one branch of the legislature at least, was established in all of them. But the periods of election were different. They varied from one to seven years. Have we any reason to infer, from the spirit and conduct of the representatives of the people, prior to the Revolution, that biennial elections would have been dangerous to the public liberties? The spirit which everywhere displayed itself at the commencement of the struggle, and which vanquished the obstacles to independence, is the best of proofs that a sufficient portion of liberty had been everywhere enjoyed to inspire both a sense of its worth and a zeal for its proper enlargement This remark holds good, as well with regard to the then colonies whose elections were least frequent, as to those whose elections were most frequent Virginia was the colony which stood first in resisting the parliamentary usurpations of Great Britain; it was the first also in espousing, by public act, the resolution of independence.

In Virginia, nevertheless, if I have not been misinformed, elections under the former government were septennial. This particular example is brought into view, not as a proof of any peculiar merit, for the priority in those instances was probably accidental; and still less of any advantage in SEPTENNIAL elections, for when compared with a greater frequency they are inadmissible; but merely as a proof, and I conceive it to be a very substantial proof, that the liberties of the people can be in no danger from BIENNIAL elections. The conclusion resulting from these examples will be not a little strengthened by recollecting three circumstances. The first is, that the federal legislature will possess a part only of that supreme legislative authority which is vested completely in the British Parliament; and which, with a few exceptions, was exercised by the colonial assemblies and the Irish legislature. It is a received and well-founded maxim, that where no other circumstances affect the case, the greater the power is, the shorter ought to be its duration; and, conversely, the smaller the power, the more safely may its duration be protracted. In the second place, it has, on another occasion, been shown that the federal legislature will not only be restrained by its dependence on its people, as other legislative bodies are, but that it will be, moreover, watched and controlled by the several collateral legislatures, which other legislative bodies are not. And in the third place, no comparison can be made between the means that will be possessed by the more permanent branches of the federal government for seducing, if they should be disposed to seduce, the House of Representatives from their duty to the people, and the means of influence over the popular branch possessed by the other branches of the government above cited. With less power, therefore, to abuse, the federal representatives can be less tempted on one side, and will be doubly watched on the other.

*PUBLIUS.*

# Appendix M: Federalist No. 62: The Senate

For the *Independent Journal*

Author: Alexander Hamilton or James Madison

To the People of the State of New York:

HAVING examined the constitution of the House of Representatives, and answered such of the objections against it as seemed to merit notice, I enter next on the examination of the Senate.

The heads into which this member of the government may be considered are: I. The qualification of senators; II. The appointment of them by the State legislatures; III. The equality of representation in the Senate; IV. The number of senators, and the term for which they are to be elected; V. The powers vested in the Senate.

I. The qualifications proposed for senators, as distinguished from those of representatives, consist in a more advanced age and a longer period of citizenship. A senator must be thirty years of age at least; as a representative must be twenty-five. And the former must have been a citizen nine years; as seven years are required for the latter. The propriety of these distinctions is explained by the nature of the senatorial trust, which, requiring greater extent of information and stability of character, requires at the same time that the senator should have reached a period of life most likely to supply these advantages; and which, participating immediately in transactions with foreign nations, ought to be exercised by none who are not thoroughly weaned from the prepossessions and habits incident to foreign birth and education. The term of nine years appears to be a prudent mediocrity between a total exclusion of adopted citizens, whose merits and talents may claim a share in the public confidence, and an indiscriminate and hasty admission of them, which might create a channel for foreign influence on the national councils.

II. It is equally unnecessary to dilate on the appointment of senators by the State legislatures. Among the various modes which might have been devised for constituting this branch of the government, that which has been proposed by the convention is probably the most congenial with the public opinion. It is recommended by the double advantage of favoring a select appointment, and of giving to the State governments such an agency in the formation of the federal government as must secure the authority of the former, and may form a convenient link between the two systems.

III. The equality of representation in the Senate is another point, which, being evidently the result of compromise between the opposite pretensions of the large and the small States, does not call for much discussion. If indeed it be right, that among a people thoroughly incorporated into one nation, every district ought to have a PROPORTIONAL share in the government, and that among independent and sovereign States, bound together by a simple league, the parties, however unequal in size, ought to have an EQUAL share in the common councils, it does not appear to be without some reason that in a compound republic, partaking both of the national and federal character, the government ought to be founded on a mixture of the principles of proportional and equal representation. But it is superfluous to try, by the standard of theory, a part of the Constitution which is allowed on all hands to be the result, not of theory, but "of a spirit of amity, and that mutual deference and concession which the peculiarity of our political situation rendered indispensable." A common government, with powers equal to its objects, is called for by the voice, and still more loudly by the political situation, of America. A government founded on principles more consonant to the wishes of the larger States, is not likely to be obtained from the smaller States. The only option, then, for the former, lies between the proposed government and a government still more objectionable. Under this alternative, the advice of prudence must be to embrace the lesser evil; and, instead of indulging a fruitless anticipation of the possible mischiefs which may ensue, to contemplate rather the advantageous consequences which may qualify the sacrifice.

In this spirit it may be remarked, that the equal vote allowed to each State is at once a constitutional recognition of the portion of sovereignty remaining in the individual States, and an instrument for preserving that residuary sovereignty. So far the equality ought to be no less acceptable to the large than to the small States; since they are not less solicitous to guard, by every possible expedient, against an improper consolidation of the States into one simple republic.

Another advantage accruing from this ingredient in the constitution of the Senate is, the additional impediment it must prove against improper acts of legislation. No law or resolution can now be passed without the concurrence, first, of a majority of the people, and then, of a majority of the States. It must be acknowledged that this complicated check on legislation may in some instances be injurious as well as beneficial; and that the peculiar defense which it involves in favor of the smaller States, would be more rational, if any interests common to them, and distinct from those of the other States, would otherwise be exposed to peculiar danger. But as the larger States will always be able, by their power over the supplies, to defeat unreasonable exertions of this prerogative of the lesser States, and as the faculty and excess of law-making seem to be the diseases to which our governments are most liable, it is not impossible that this part of the Constitution may be more convenient in practice than it appears to many in contemplation.

IV. The number of senators, and the duration of their appointment, come next to be considered. In order to form an accurate judgment on both of these points, it will be proper to inquire into the purposes which are to be answered by a senate; and in order to ascertain these, it will be necessary to review the inconveniences which a republic must suffer from the want of such an institution.

First. It is a misfortune incident to republican government, though in a less degree than to other governments, that those who administer it may forget their obligations to their constituents, and prove unfaithful to their important trust. In this point of view, a senate, as a second branch of the legislative assembly, distinct from, and dividing the power with, a first, must be in all cases a salutary check on the government. It doubles the security to the people, by requiring the concurrence of two distinct bodies in schemes of usurpation or perfidy, where the ambition or corruption of one would otherwise be sufficient. This is a precaution founded on such clear principles, and now so well understood in the United States, that it would be more than superfluous to enlarge on it. I will barely remark, that as the improbability of sinister combinations will be in proportion to the dissimilarity in the genius of the two bodies, it must be politic to distinguish them from each other by every circumstance which will consist with a due harmony in all proper measures, and with the genuine principles of republican government.

Secondly. The necessity of a senate is not less indicated by the propensity of all single and numerous assemblies to yield to the impulse of sudden and violent passions, and to be seduced by factious leaders into intemperate and pernicious resolutions. Examples on this subject might be cited without number; and from proceedings within the United States, as well as from the history of other nations. But a position that will not be contradicted, need not be proved. All that need be remarked is, that a body which is to correct this infirmity ought itself to be free from it, and consequently ought to be less numerous. It ought, moreover, to possess great firmness, and consequently ought to hold its authority by a tenure of considerable duration.

Thirdly. Another defect to be supplied by a senate lies in a want of due acquaintance with the objects and principles of legislation. It is not possible that an assembly of men called for the most part from pursuits of a private nature, continued in appointment for a short time, and led by no permanent motive to devote the intervals of public occupation to a study of the laws, the affairs, and the comprehensive interests of their country, should, if left wholly to themselves, escape a variety of important errors in the exercise of their legislative trust. It may be affirmed, on the best grounds, that no small share of the present embarrassments of America is to be charged on the blunders of our governments; and that these have proceeded from the heads rather than the hearts of most of the authors of them. What indeed are all the repealing, explaining, and amending laws, which fill and disgrace our voluminous codes, but so many monuments of deficient wisdom; so many impeachments exhibited by each succeeding against each preceding session; so many admonitions to the people, of the value of those aids which may be expected from a well-constituted senate?

A good government implies two things: first, fidelity to the object of government, which is the happiness of the people; secondly, a knowledge of the means by which that object can be best attained. Some governments are deficient in both these qualities; most governments are deficient in the first. I scruple not to assert, that in American governments too little attention has been paid to the last. The federal Constitution avoids this error; and what merits particular notice, it provides for the last in a mode which increases the security for the first.

Fourthly. The mutability in the public councils arising from a rapid succession of new members, however qualified they may be, points out, in the strongest manner, the necessity of some stable institution in the government. Every new election in the States is found to change one half of the representatives. From this change of men must proceed a change of opinions; and from a change of opinions, a change of measures. But a continual change even of good measures is inconsistent with every rule of prudence and every prospect of success. The remark is verified in private life, and becomes more just, as well as more important, in national transactions.

V. To trace the mischievous effects of a mutable government would fill a volume. I will hint a few only, each of which will be perceived to be a source of innumerable others.

In the first place, it forfeits the respect and confidence of other nations, and all the advantages connected with national character. An individual who is observed to be inconstant to his plans, or perhaps to carry on his affairs without any plan at all, is marked at once, by all prudent people, as a speedy victim to his own unsteadiness and folly. His more friendly neighbors may pity him, but all will decline to connect their fortunes with his; and not a few will seize the opportunity of making their fortunes out of his. One nation is to another what one individual is to another; with this melancholy distinction perhaps, that the former, with fewer of the benevolent emotions than the latter, are under fewer restraints also from taking undue advantage from the indiscretions of each other. Every nation, consequently, whose affairs betray a want of wisdom and stability, may calculate on every loss which can be sustained from the more systematic policy of their wiser neighbors. But the best instruction on this subject is unhappily conveyed to America by the example of her own situation. She finds that she is held in no respect by her friends; that she is the derision of her enemies; and that she is a prey to every nation which has an interest in speculating on her fluctuating councils and embarrassed affairs.

The internal effects of a mutable policy are still more calamitous. It poisons the blessing of liberty itself. It will be of little avail to the people, that the laws are made by men of their own choice, if the laws be so voluminous that they cannot be read, or so incoherent that they cannot be understood; if they be repealed or revised before they are promulgated, or undergo such incessant changes that no man, who knows what the law is to-day, can guess what it will be to-morrow. Law is defined to be a rule of action; but how can that be a rule, which is little known, and less fixed?

Another effect of public instability is the unreasonable advantage it gives to the sagacious, the enterprising, and the moneyed few over the industrious and uniformed mass of the people. Every new regulation concerning commerce or revenue, or in any way affecting the value of the different species of property, presents a new harvest to those who watch the change, and can trace its consequences; a harvest, reared not by themselves, but by the toils and cares of the great body of their fellow-citizens. This is a state of things in which it may be said with some truth that laws are made for the FEW, not for the MANY.

In another point of view, great injury results from an unstable government. The want of confidence in the public councils damps every useful undertaking, the success and profit of which may depend on a continuance of existing arrangements. What prudent merchant will hazard his fortunes in any new branch of commerce when he knows not but that his plans may be rendered unlawful before they can be executed? What farmer or manufacturer will lay himself out for the encouragement given to any particular cultivation or establishment, when he can have no assurance that his preparatory labors and advances will not render him a victim to an inconstant government? In a word, no great improvement or laudable enterprise can go forward which requires the auspices of a steady system of national policy.

But the most deplorable effect of all is that diminution of attachment and reverence which steals into the hearts of the people, towards a political system which betrays so many marks of infirmity, and disappoints so many of their flattering hopes. No government, any more than an individual, will long be respected without being truly respectable; nor be truly respectable, without possessing a certain portion of order and stability.

*PUBLIUS.*

# Appendix N: Federalist No. 67: The Executive Department

From the *New York Packet*
Tuesday, 11 March 1788
Author: Alexander Hamilton
To the People of the State of New York:

THE constitution of the executive department of the proposed government, claims next our attention.

There is hardly any part of the system which could have been attended with greater difficulty in the arrangement of it than this; and there is, perhaps, none which has been inveighed against with less candor or criticised with less judgment.

Here the writers against the Constitution seem to have taken pains to signalize their talent of misrepresentation. Calculating upon the aversion of the people to monarchy, they have endeavored to enlist all their jealousies and apprehensions in opposition to the intended President of the United States; not merely as the embryo, but as the full-grown progeny, of that detested parent. To establish the pretended affinity, they have not scrupled to draw resources even from the regions of fiction. The authorities of a magistrate, in few instances greater, in some instances less, than those of a governor of New York, have been magnified into more than royal prerogatives. He has been decorated with attributes superior in dignity and splendor to those of a king of Great Britain. He has been shown to us with the diadem sparkling on his brow and the imperial purple flowing in his train. He has been seated on a throne surrounded with minions and mistresses, giving audience to the envoys of foreign potentates, in all the supercilious pomp of majesty. The images of Asiatic despotism and voluptuousness have scarcely been wanting to crown the exaggerated scene. We have been taught to tremble at the terrific visages of murdering janizaries, and to blush at the unveiled mysteries of a future seraglio.

Attempts so extravagant as these to disfigure or, it might rather be said, to metamorphose the object, render it necessary to take an accurate view of its real nature and form: in order as well to ascertain its true aspect and genuine appearance, as to unmask the disingenuity and expose the fallacy of the counterfeit resemblances which have been so insidiously, as well as industriously, propagated.

In the execution of this task, there is no man who would not find it an arduous effort either to behold with moderation, or to treat with seriousness, the devices, not less weak than wicked, which have been contrived to pervert the public opinion in relation to the subject. They so far exceed the usual though unjustifiable licenses of party artifice, that even in a disposition the most candid and tolerant, they must force the sentiments which favor an indulgent construction of the conduct of political adversaries to give place to a voluntary and unreserved indignation. It is impossible not to bestow the imputation of deliberate imposture and deception upon the gross pretense of a similitude between a king of Great Britain and a magistrate of the character marked out for that of the President of the United States. It is still more impossible to withhold that imputation from the rash and barefaced expedients which have been employed to give success to the attempted imposition.

In one instance, which I cite as a sample of the general spirit, the temerity has proceeded so far as to ascribe to the President of the United States a power which by the instrument reported is EXPRESSLY allotted to the Executives of the individual States. I mean the power of filling casual vacancies in the Senate.

This bold experiment upon the discernment of his countrymen has been hazarded by a writer who (whatever may be his real merit) has had no inconsiderable share in the applauses of his party;[1] and who, upon this false and unfounded suggestion, has built a series of observations equally false and unfounded. Let him now be confronted with the evidence of the fact, and let him, if he be able, justify or extenuate the shameful outrage he has offered to the dictates of truth and to the rules of fair dealing.

The second clause of the second section of the second article empowers the President of the United States "to nominate, and by and with the advice and consent of the Senate, to appoint ambassadors, other public ministers and consuls, judges of the Supreme Court, and all other OFFICERS of United States whose appointments are NOT in the Constitution OTHERWISE PROVIDED FOR, and WHICH SHALL BE ESTABLISHED BY LAW." Immediately after this clause follows another in these words: "The President shall have power to fill up ?? VACANCIES that may happen DURING THE RECESS OF THE SENATE, by granting commissions which shall EXPIRE AT THE END OF THEIR NEXT SESSION." It is from this last provision that the pretended power of the President to fill vacancies in the Senate has been deduced. A slight attention to the connection of the clauses, and to the obvious meaning of the terms, will satisfy us that the deduction is not even colorable.

The first of these two clauses, it is clear, only provides a mode for appointing such officers, "whose appointments are NOT OTHERWISE PROVIDED FOR in the Constitution, and which SHALL BE ESTABLISHED BY LAW"; of course it cannot extend to the appointments of senators, whose appointments are OTHERWISE PROVIDED FOR in the

Constitution,[2] and who are ESTABLISHED BY THE CONSTITUTION, and will not require a future establishment by law. This position will hardly be contested.

The last of these two clauses, it is equally clear, cannot be understood to comprehend the power of filling vacancies in the Senate, for the following reasons: First. The relation in which that clause stands to the other, which declares the general mode of appointing officers of the United States, denotes it to be nothing more than a supplement to the other, for the purpose of establishing an auxiliary method of appointment, in cases to which the general method was inadequate. The ordinary power of appointment is confined to the President and Senate JOINTLY, and can therefore only be exercised during the session of the Senate; but as it would have been improper to oblige this body to be continually in session for the appointment of officers and as vacancies might happen IN THEIR RECESS, which it might be necessary for the public service to fill without delay, the succeeding clause is evidently intended to authorize the President, SINGLY, to make temporary appointments "during the recess of the Senate, by granting commissions which shall expire at the end of their next session."

Secondly. If this clause is to be considered as supplementary to the one which precedes, the VACANCIES of which it speaks must be construed to relate to the "officers" described in the preceding one; and this, we have seen, excludes from its description the members of the Senate. Thirdly. The time within which the power is to operate, "during the recess of the Senate," and the duration of the appointments, "to the end of the next session" of that body, conspire to elucidate the sense of the provision, which, if it had been intended to comprehend senators, would naturally have referred the temporary power of filling vacancies to the recess of the State legislatures, who are to make the permanent appointments, and not to the recess of the national Senate, who are to have no concern in those appointments; and would have extended the duration in office of the temporary senators to the next session of the legislature of the State, in whose representation the vacancies had happened, instead of making it to expire at the end of the ensuing session of the national Senate. The circumstances of the body authorized to make the permanent appointments would, of course, have governed the modification of a power which related to the temporary appointments; and as the national Senate is the body, whose situation is alone contemplated in the clause upon which the suggestion under examination has been founded, the vacancies to which it alludes can only be deemed to respect those officers in whose appointment that body has a concurrent agency with the President.

But lastly, the first and second clauses of the third section of the first article, not only obviate all possibility of doubt, but destroy the pretext of misconception. The former provides, that "the Senate of the United States shall be composed of two Senators from each State, chosen BY THE LEGISLATURE THEREOF for six years"; and the latter directs, that, "if vacancies in that body should happen by resignation or otherwise, DURING THE RECESS OF THE LEGISLATURE OF ANY STATE, the Executive THEREOF may make temporary appointments until the NEXT MEETING OF THE LEGISLATURE, which shall then fill such vacancies." Here is an express power given, in clear and unambiguous terms, to the State Executives, to fill casual vacancies in the Senate, by temporary appointments; which not only invalidates the supposition, that the clause before considered could have been intended to confer that power upon the President of the United States, but proves that this supposition, destitute as it is even of the merit of plausibility, must have originated in an intention to deceive the people, too palpable to be obscured by sophistry, too atrocious to be palliated by hypocrisy.

I have taken the pains to select this instance of misrepresentation, and to place it in a clear and strong light, as an unequivocal proof of the unwarrantable arts which are practiced to prevent a fair and impartial judgment of the real merits of the Constitution submitted to the consideration of the people. Nor have I scrupled, in so flagrant a case, to allow myself a severity of animadversion little congenial with the general spirit of these papers. I hesitate not to submit it to the decision of any candid and honest adversary of the proposed government, whether language can furnish epithets of too much asperity, for so shameless and so prostitute an attempt to impose on the citizens of America.

*PUBLIUS.*

## NOTES

1. See CATO, No. V.
2. Article I, section 3, clause I.

# Appendix O: Federalist No. 70: The Executive Department Further Considered

Author: Alexander Hamilton

To the People of the State of New York:

THERE is an idea, which is not without its advocates, that a vigorous Executive is inconsistent with the genius of republican government. The enlightened well-wishers to this species of government must at least hope that the supposition is destitute of foundation; since they can never admit its truth, without at the same time admitting the condemnation of their own principles. Energy in the Executive is a leading character in the definition of good government. It is essential to the protection of the community against foreign attacks; it is not less essential to the steady administration of the laws; to the protection of property against those irregular and high-handed combinations which sometimes interrupt the ordinary course of justice; to the security of liberty against the enterprises and assaults of ambition, of faction, and of anarchy. Every man the least conversant in Roman story, knows how often that republic was obliged to take refuge in the absolute power of a single man, under the formidable title of Dictator, as well against the intrigues of ambitious individuals who aspired to the tyranny, and the seditions of whole classes of the community whose conduct threatened the existence of all government, as against the invasions of external enemies who menaced the conquest and destruction of Rome.

There can be no need, however, to multiply arguments or examples on this head. A feeble Executive implies a feeble execution of the government. A feeble execution is but another phrase for a bad execution; and a government ill executed, whatever it may be in theory, must be, in practice, a bad government.

Taking it for granted, therefore, that all men of sense will agree in the necessity of an energetic Executive, it will only remain to inquire, what are the ingredients which constitute this energy? How far can they be combined with those other ingredients which constitute safety in the republican sense? And how far does this combination characterize the plan which has been reported by the convention?

The ingredients which constitute energy in the Executive are, first, unity; secondly, duration; thirdly, an adequate provision for its support; fourthly, competent powers.

The ingredients which constitute safety in the republican sense are, first, a due dependence on the people, secondly, a due responsibility.

Those politicians and statesmen who have been the most celebrated for the soundness of their principles and for the justice of their views, have declared in favor of a single Executive and a numerous legislature. They have with great propriety, considered energy as the most necessary qualification of the former, and have regarded this as most applicable to power in a single hand, while they have, with equal propriety, considered the latter as best adapted to deliberation and wisdom, and best calculated to conciliate the confidence of the people and to secure their privileges and interests.

That unity is conducive to energy will not be disputed. Decision, activity, secrecy, and despatch will generally characterize the proceedings of one man in a much more eminent degree than the proceedings of any greater number; and in proportion as the number is increased, these qualities will be diminished.

This unity may be destroyed in two ways: either by vesting the power in two or more magistrates of equal dignity and authority; or by vesting it ostensibly in one man, subject, in whole or in part, to the control and co-operation of others, in the capacity of counsellors to him. Of the first, the two Consuls of Rome may serve as an example; of the last, we shall find examples in the constitutions of several of the States. New York and New Jersey, if I recollect right, are the only States which have intrusted the executive authority wholly to single men.[1] Both these methods of destroying the unity of the Executive have their partisans; but the votaries of an executive council are the most numerous. They are both liable, if not to equal, to similar objections, and may in most lights be examined in conjunction.

The experience of other nations will afford little instruction on this head. As far, however, as it teaches any thing, it teaches us not to be enamoured of plurality in the Executive. We have seen that the Achaeans, on an experiment of two Praetors, were induced to abolish one. The Roman history records many instances of mischiefs to the republic from the dissensions between the Consuls, and between the military Tribunes, who were at times substituted for the Consuls. But it gives us no specimens of any peculiar advantages derived to the state from the circumstance of the plurality of those magistrates. That the dissensions between them were not more frequent or more fatal, is a matter of astonishment, until we advert to the singular position in which the republic was almost continually placed, and to the prudent policy pointed out by the circumstances of the state, and pursued by the Consuls, of making a division of the government between them. The patricians engaged in a perpetual struggle with the plebeians for the preservation of their ancient authorities and dignities; the Consuls, who were generally chosen out of the former body, were commonly united by the personal interest they had in the defense of the privileges of their order. In addition to this motive of union, after the arms of the republic had considerably expanded the bounds of its empire, it became an established custom with the Consuls to divide the administration between themselves by lot one of them remaining at Rome to govern the city and its environs, the other taking the command in the more distant provinces. This expedient must, no doubt, have had great influence in preventing those collisions and rivalships which might otherwise have embroiled the peace of the republic.

But quitting the dim light of historical research, attaching ourselves purely to the dictates of reason and good sense, we shall discover much greater cause to reject than to approve the idea of plurality in the Executive, under any modification whatever.

Wherever two or more persons are engaged in any common enterprise or pursuit, there is always danger of difference of opinion. If it be a public trust or office, in which they are clothed with equal dignity and authority, there is peculiar danger of personal emulation and even animosity. From either, and especially from all these causes, the most bitter dissensions are apt to spring. Whenever these happen, they lessen the respectability, weaken the authority, and distract the plans and operation of those whom they divide. If they should unfortunately assail the supreme executive magistracy of a country, consisting of a plurality of persons, they might impede or frustrate the most important measures of the government, in the most critical emergencies of the state. And what is still worse, they might split the community into the most violent and irreconcilable factions, adhering differently to the different individuals who composed the magistracy.

Men often oppose a thing, merely because they have had no agency in planning it, or because it may have been planned by those whom they dislike. But if they have been consulted, and have happened to disapprove, opposition then becomes, in their estimation, an indispensable duty of self-love. They seem to think themselves bound in honor, and by all the motives of personal infallibility, to defeat the success of what has been resolved upon contrary to their sentiments. Men of upright, benevolent tempers have too many opportunities of remarking, with horror, to what desperate lengths this disposition is sometimes carried, and how often the great interests of society are sacrificed to the vanity, to the conceit, and to the obstinacy of individuals, who have credit enough to make their passions and their caprices interesting to mankind. Perhaps the question now before the public may, in its consequences, afford melancholy proofs of the effects of this despicable frailty, or rather detestable vice, in the human character.

Upon the principles of a free government, inconveniences from the source just mentioned must necessarily be submitted to in the formation of the legislature; but it is unnecessary, and therefore unwise, to introduce them into the constitution of the Executive. It is here too that they may be most pernicious. In the legislature, promptitude of decision is oftener an evil than a benefit. The differences of opinion, and the jarrings of parties in that department of the government, though they may sometimes obstruct salutary plans, yet often promote deliberation and circumspection, and serve to check excesses in the majority. When a resolution too is once taken, the opposition must be at an end. That resolution is a law, and resistance to it punishable. But no favorable circumstances palliate or atone for the disadvantages of dissension in the executive department. Here, they are pure and unmixed. There is no point at which they cease to operate. They serve to embarrass and weaken the execution of the plan or measure to which they relate, from the first step to the final conclusion of it. They constantly counteract those qualities in the Executive which are the most necessary ingredients in its composition, vigor and expedition, and this without any counterbalancing good. In the conduct of war, in which the energy of the Executive is the bulwark of the national security, every thing would be to be apprehended from its plurality.

It must be confessed that these observations apply with principal weight to the first case supposed that is, to a plurality of magistrates of equal dignity and authority a scheme, the advocates for which are not likely to form a numerous sect; but they apply, though not with equal, yet with considerable weight to the project of a council, whose concurrence is made constitutionally necessary to the operations of the ostensible Executive. An artful cabal in that council would be able to distract and to enervate the whole system of administration. If no such cabal should exist, the mere diversity of views and opinions would alone be sufficient to tincture the exercise of the executive authority with a spirit of habitual feebleness and dilatoriness.

But one of the weightiest objections to a plurality in the Executive, and which lies as much against the last as the first plan, is, that it tends to conceal faults and destroy responsibility. Responsibility is of two kinds to censure and to punishment. The first is the more important of the two, especially in an elective office. Man, in public trust, will much oftener act in such a manner as to render him unworthy of being any longer trusted, than in such a manner as to make him obnoxious to legal punishment. But the multiplication of the Executive adds to the difficulty of detection in either case. It often becomes impossible, amidst mutual accusations, to determine on whom the blame or the punishment of a pernicious measure, or series of pernicious measures, ought really to fall. It is shifted from one to another with so much dexterity, and under such plausible appearances, that the public opinion is left in suspense about the real author.

The circumstances which may have led to any national miscarriage or misfortune are sometimes so complicated that, where there are a number of actors who may have had different degrees and kinds of agency, though we may clearly see upon the whole that there has been mismanagement, yet it may be impracticable to pronounce to whose account the evil which may have been incurred is truly chargeable. "I was overruled by my council. The council were so divided in their opinions that it was impossible to obtain any better resolution on the point." These and similar pretexts are constantly at hand, whether true or false. And who is there that will either take the trouble or incur the odium, of a strict scrutiny into the secret springs of the transaction? Should there be found a citizen zealous enough to undertake the unpromising task, if there happen to be collusion between the parties concerned, how easy it is to clothe the circumstances with so much ambiguity, as to render it uncertain what was the precise conduct of any of those parties?

In the single instance in which the governor of this State is coupled with a council that is, in the appointment to offices, we have seen the mischiefs of it in the view now under consideration. Scandalous appointments to important offices have been made. Some cases, indeed, have been so flagrant that ALL PARTIES have agreed in the impropriety of the thing. When inquiry has been made, the blame has been laid by the governor on the members of the council, who, on their part, have charged it upon his nomination; while the people remain altogether at a loss to determine, by whose influence their interests have been committed to hands so unqualified and so manifestly improper. In tenderness to individuals, I forbear to descend to particulars.

It is evident from these considerations, that the plurality of the Executive tends to deprive the people of the two greatest securities they can have for the faithful exercise of any delegated power, first, the restraints of public opinion, which lose their efficacy, as well on account of the division of the censure attendant on bad measures among a number, as on account of the uncertainty on whom it ought to fall; and, secondly, the opportunity of discovering with facility and clearness the misconduct of the persons they trust, in order either to their removal from office or to their actual punishment in cases which admit of it.

In England, the king is a perpetual magistrate; and it is a maxim which has obtained for the sake of the public peace, that he is unaccountable for his administration, and his person sacred. Nothing, therefore, can be wiser in that kingdom, than to annex to the king a constitutional council, who may be responsible to the nation for the advice they give. Without this, there would be no responsibility whatever in the executive department an idea inadmissible in a free government. But even there the king is not bound by the resolutions of his council, though they are answerable for the advice they give. He is the absolute master of his own conduct in the exercise of his office, and may observe or disregard the counsel given to him at his sole discretion.

But in a republic, where every magistrate ought to be personally responsible for his behavior in office the reason which in the British Constitution dictates the propriety of a council, not only ceases to apply, but turns against the institution. In the monarchy of Great Britain, it furnishes a substitute for the prohibited responsibility of the chief magistrate, which serves in some degree as a hostage to the national justice for his good behavior. In the American republic, it would serve to destroy, or would greatly diminish, the intended and necessary responsibility of the Chief Magistrate himself.

The idea of a council to the Executive, which has so generally obtained in the State constitutions, has been derived from that maxim of republican jealousy which considers power as safer in the hands of a number of men than of a single man. If the maxim should be admitted to be applicable to the case, I should contend that the advantage on that side would not counterbalance the numerous disadvantages on the opposite side. But I do not think the rule at all applicable to the executive power. I clearly concur in opinion, in this particular, with a writer whom the celebrated Junius pronounces to be "deep, solid, and ingenious," that "the executive power is more easily confined when it is ONE";[2] that it is far more safe there should be a single object for the jealousy and watchfulness of the people; and, in a word, that all multiplication of the Executive is rather dangerous than friendly to liberty.

A little consideration will satisfy us, that the species of security sought for in the multiplication of the Executive, is unattainable. Numbers must be so great as to render combination difficult, or they are rather a source of danger than of security. The united credit and influence of several individuals must be more formidable to liberty, than the credit and influence of either of them separately. When power, therefore, is placed in the hands of so small a number of men, as to admit of their interests and views being easily combined in a common enterprise, by an artful leader, it becomes more liable to abuse, and more dangerous when abused, than if it be lodged in the hands of one man; who, from the very circumstance of his being alone, will be more narrowly watched and more readily suspected, and who cannot unite so great a mass of influence as when he is associated with others. The Decemvirs of Rome, whose name denotes their number,[3] were more to be dreaded in their usurpation than any ONE of them would have been. No person would think of proposing an Executive much more numerous than that body; from six to a dozen have been suggested for the number of the council. The extreme of these numbers, is not too great for an easy combination; and from such a combination America would have more to fear, than from the ambition of any single individual. A council to a magistrate, who is himself responsible for what he does, are generally nothing better than a clog upon his good intentions, are often the instruments and accomplices of his bad and are almost always a cloak to his faults.

I forbear to dwell upon the subject of expense; though it be evident that if the council should be numerous enough to answer the principal end aimed at by the institution, the salaries of the members, who must be drawn from their homes to reside at the seat of government, would form an item in the catalogue of public expenditures too serious to be incurred for an object of equivocal utility. I will only add that, prior to the appearance of the Constitution, I rarely met with an intelligent man from any of the States, who did not admit, as the result of experience, that the UNITY of the executive of this State was one of the best of the distinguishing features of our constitution.

*PUBLIUS.*

## NOTES

1. New York has no council except for the single purpose of appointing to offices; New Jersey has a council whom the governor may consult. But I think, from the terms of the constitution, their resolutions do not bind him.
2. De Lolme.
3. Ten.

# Appendix P: Federalist No. 78: The Judiciary Department

From *McLean's Edition*, New York

Author: Alexander Hamilton

To the People of the State of New York:

WE PROCEED now to an examination of the judiciary department of the proposed government.

In unfolding the defects of the existing Confederation, the utility and necessity of a federal judicature have been clearly pointed out. It is the less necessary to recapitulate the considerations there urged, as the propriety of the institution in the abstract is not disputed; the only questions which have been raised being relative to the manner of constituting it, and to its extent. To these points, therefore, our observations shall be confined.

The manner of constituting it seems to embrace these several objects: 1st. The mode of appointing the judges. 2d. The tenure by which they are to hold their places. 3d. The partition of the judiciary authority between different courts, and their relations to each other.

First. As to the mode of appointing the judges; this is the same with that of appointing the officers of the Union in general, and has been so fully discussed in the two last numbers, that nothing can be said here which would not be useless repetition.

Second. As to the tenure by which the judges are to hold their places; this chiefly concerns their duration in office; the provisions for their support; the precautions for their responsibility.

According to the plan of the convention, all judges who may be appointed by the United States are to hold their offices DURING GOOD BEHAVIOR; which is conformable to the most approved of the State constitutions and among the rest, to that of this State. Its propriety having been drawn into question by the adversaries of that plan, is no light symptom of the rage for objection, which disorders their imaginations and judgments. The standard of good behavior for the continuance in office of the judicial magistracy, is certainly one of the most valuable of the modern improvements in the practice of government. In a monarchy it is an excellent barrier to the despotism of the prince; in a republic it is a no less excellent barrier to the encroachments and oppressions of the representative body. And it is the best expedient which can be devised in any government, to secure a steady, upright, and impartial administration of the laws.

Whoever attentively considers the different departments of power must perceive, that, in a government in which they are separated from each other, the judiciary, from the nature of its functions, will always be the least dangerous to the political rights of the Constitution; because it will be least in a capacity to annoy or injure them. The Executive not only dispenses the honors, but holds the sword of the community. The legislature not only commands the purse, but prescribes the rules by which the duties and rights of every citizen are to be regulated. The judiciary, on the contrary, has no influence over either the sword or the purse; no direction either of the strength or of the wealth of the society; and can take no active resolution whatever. It may truly be said to have neither FORCE nor WILL, but merely judgment; and must ultimately depend upon the aid of the executive arm even for the efficacy of its judgments.

This simple view of the matter suggests several important consequences. It proves incontestably, that the judiciary is beyond comparison the weakest of the three departments of power;[1] that it can never attack with success either of the other two; and that all possible care is requisite to enable it to defend itself against their attacks. It equally proves, that though individual oppression may now and then proceed from the courts of justice, the general liberty of the people can never be endangered from that quarter; I mean so long as the judiciary remains truly distinct from both the legislature and the Executive. For I agree, that "there is no liberty, if the power of judging be not separated from the legislative and executive powers."[2] And it proves, in the last place, that as liberty can have nothing to fear from the judiciary alone, but would have every thing to fear from its union with either of the other departments; that as all the effects of such a union must ensue from a dependence of the former on the latter, notwithstanding a nominal and apparent separation; that as, from the natural feebleness of the judiciary, it is in continual jeopardy of being overpowered, awed, or influenced by its co-ordinate branches; and that as nothing can contribute so much to its firmness and independence as permanency in office, this quality may therefore be justly regarded as an indispensable ingredient in its constitution, and, in a great measure, as the citadel of the public justice and the public security.

The complete independence of the courts of justice is peculiarly essential in a limited Constitution. By a limited Constitution, I understand one which contains certain specified exceptions to the legislative authority; such, for instance, as that it shall pass no bills of attainder, no ex-post-facto laws, and the like. Limitations of this kind can be preserved in practice no other way than through the medium of courts of justice, whose duty it must be to declare all acts contrary to the manifest tenor of the Constitution void. Without this, all the reservations of particular rights or privileges would amount to nothing.

Some perplexity respecting the rights of the courts to pronounce legislative acts void, because contrary to the Constitution, has arisen from an imagination that the doctrine would imply a superiority of the judiciary to the legislative power. It is urged that the authority which can declare the acts of another void, must necessarily be superior to the one whose acts may be declared void. As this doctrine is of great importance in all the American constitutions, a brief discussion of the ground on which it rests cannot be unacceptable.

There is no position which depends on clearer principles, than that every act of a delegated authority, contrary to the tenor of the commission under which it is exercised, is void. No legislative act, therefore, contrary to the Constitution, can be valid. To deny this, would be to affirm, that the deputy is greater than his principal; that the servant is above his master; that the representatives of the people are superior to the people themselves; that men acting by virtue of powers, may do not only what their powers do not authorize, but what they forbid.

If it be said that the legislative body are themselves the constitutional judges of their own powers, and that the construction they put upon them is conclusive upon the other departments, it may be answered, that this cannot be the natural presumption, where it is not to be collected from any particular provisions in the Constitution. It is not otherwise to be supposed, that the Constitution could intend to enable the representatives of the people to substitute their WILL to that of their constituents. It is far more rational to suppose, that the courts were designed to be an intermediate body between the people and the legislature, in order, among other things, to keep the latter within the limits assigned to their authority. The interpretation of the laws is the proper and peculiar province of the courts. A constitution is, in fact, and must be regarded by the judges, as a fundamental law. It therefore belongs to them to ascertain its meaning, as well as the meaning of any particular act proceeding from the legislative body. If there should happen to be an irreconcilable variance between the two, that which has the superior obligation and validity ought, of course, to be preferred; or, in other words, the Constitution ought to be preferred to the statute, the intention of the people to the intention of their agents.

Nor does this conclusion by any means suppose a superiority of the judicial to the legislative power. It only supposes that the power of the people is superior to both; and that where the will of the legislature, declared in its statutes, stands in opposition to that of the people, declared in the Constitution, the judges ought to be governed by the latter rather than the former. They ought to regulate their decisions by the fundamental laws, rather than by those which are not fundamental.

This exercise of judicial discretion, in determining between two contradictory laws, is exemplified in a familiar instance. It not uncommonly happens, that there are two statutes existing at one time, clashing in whole or in part with each other, and neither of them containing any repealing clause or expression. In such a case, it is the province of the courts to liquidate and fix their meaning and operation. So far as they can, by any fair construction, be reconciled to each other, reason and law conspire to dictate that this should be done; where this is impracticable, it becomes a matter of necessity to give effect to one, in exclusion of the other. The rule which has obtained in the courts for determining their relative validity is, that the last in order of time shall be preferred to the first. But this is a mere rule of construction, not derived from any positive law, but from the nature and reason of the thing. It is a rule not enjoined upon the courts by legislative provision, but adopted by themselves, as consonant to truth and propriety, for the direction of their conduct as interpreters of the law. They thought it reasonable, that between the interfering acts of an EQUAL authority, that which was the last indication of its will should have the preference.

But in regard to the interfering acts of a superior and subordinate authority, of an original and derivative power, the nature and reason of the thing indicate the converse of that rule as proper to be followed. They teach us that the prior act of a superior ought to be preferred to the subsequent act of an inferior and subordinate authority; and that accordingly, whenever a particular statute contravenes the Constitution, it will be the duty of the judicial tribunals to adhere to the latter and disregard the former.

It can be of no weight to say that the courts, on the pretense of a repugnancy, may substitute their own pleasure to the constitutional intentions of the legislature. This might as well happen in the case of two contradictory statutes; or it might as well happen in every adjudication upon any single statute. The courts must declare the sense of the law; and if they should be disposed to exercise WILL instead of JUDGMENT, the consequence would equally be the substitution of their pleasure to that of the legislative body. The observation, if it prove any thing, would prove that there ought to be no judges distinct from that body.

If, then, the courts of justice are to be considered as the bulwarks of a limited Constitution against legislative encroachments, this consideration will afford a strong argument for the permanent tenure of judicial offices, since nothing will contribute so much as this to that independent spirit in the judges which must be essential to the faithful performance of so arduous a duty.

This independence of the judges is equally requisite to guard the Constitution and the rights of individuals from the effects of those ill humors, which the arts of designing men, or the influence of particular conjunctures, sometimes disseminate among the people themselves, and which, though they speedily give place to better information, and more deliberate reflection, have a tendency, in the meantime, to occasion dangerous innovations in the government, and serious oppressions of the minor party in the community. Though I trust the friends of the proposed Constitution will never concur with its enemies,[3] in questioning that fundamental principle of republican government, which admits the right of the people to alter or abolish the established Constitution, whenever they find it inconsistent with their happiness, yet it is not to be inferred from this principle, that the representatives of the people, whenever a momentary inclination happens to lay hold of a majority of their constituents, incompatible with the provisions in the existing Constitution, would, on that account, be justifiable in a violation of those provisions; or that the courts would be under a greater obligation to connive at infractions in this shape, than when they had proceeded wholly from the cabals of the representative body. Until the people have, by some solemn and authoritative act, annulled or changed the established form, it is binding upon themselves collectively, as well as individually; and no presumption, or even knowledge, of their sentiments, can warrant their representatives in a departure from it, prior to such an act. But it is easy to see, that it would require an uncommon portion of fortitude in the judges to do their duty as faithful guardians of the Constitution, where legislative invasions of it had been instigated by the major voice of the community.

But it is not with a view to infractions of the Constitution only, that the independence of the judges may be an essential safeguard against the effects of occasional ill humors in the society. These sometimes extend no farther than to the injury of the private rights of particular classes of citizens, by unjust and partial laws. Here also the firmness of the judicial magistracy is of vast importance in mitigating the severity and confining the operation of such laws. It not only serves to moderate the immediate mischiefs of those which may have been passed, but it operates as a check upon the legislative body in passing them; who, perceiving that obstacles to the success of iniquitous intention are to be expected from the scruples of the courts, are in a manner compelled, by the very motives of the injustice they meditate, to qualify their attempts. This is a circumstance calculated to have more influence upon the character of our governments, than but few may be aware of. The benefits of the integrity and moderation of the judiciary have already been felt in more States than one; and though they may have displeased those whose sinister expectations they may have disappointed, they must have commanded the esteem and applause of all the virtuous and disinterested. Considerate men, of every description, ought to prize whatever will tend to beget or fortify that temper in the courts: as no man can be sure that he may not be to-morrow the victim of a spirit of injustice, by which he may be a gainer to-day. And every man must now feel, that the inevitable tendency of such a spirit is to sap the foundations of public and private confidence, and to introduce in its stead universal distrust and distress.

That inflexible and uniform adherence to the rights of the Constitution, and of individuals, which we perceive to be indispensable in the courts of justice, can certainly not be expected from judges who hold their offices by a temporary commission. Periodical appointments, however regulated, or by whomsoever made, would, in some way or other, be fatal to their necessary independence. If the power of making them was committed either to the Executive or legislature, there would be danger of an improper complaisance to the branch which possessed it; if to both, there would be an unwillingness to hazard the displeasure of either; if to the people, or to persons chosen by them for the special purpose, there would be too great a disposition to consult popularity, to justify a reliance that nothing would be consulted but the Constitution and the laws.

There is yet a further and a weightier reason for the permanency of the judicial offices, which is deducible from the nature of the qualifications they require. It has been frequently remarked, with great propriety, that a voluminous code of laws is one of the inconveniences necessarily connected with the advantages of a free government. To avoid an arbitrary discretion in the courts, it is indispensable that they should be bound down by strict rules and precedents, which serve to define and point out their duty in every particular case that comes before them; and it will readily be conceived from the variety of controversies which grow out of the folly and wickedness of mankind, that the records of those precedents must unavoidably swell to a very considerable bulk, and must demand long and laborious study to acquire a competent knowledge of them. Hence it is, that there can be but few men in the society who will have sufficient skill in the laws to qualify them for the stations of judges. And making the proper deductions for the ordinary depravity of human nature, the number must be still smaller of those who unite the requisite integrity with the requisite knowledge. These considerations apprise us, that the government can have no great option between fit character; and that a temporary duration in office, which would naturally discourage such characters from quitting a lucrative line of practice to accept a seat on the bench, would have a tendency to throw the administration of justice into hands less able, and less well qualified, to conduct it with utility and dignity. In the present circumstances of this country, and in those in which it is likely to be for a long time to come, the disadvantages on this score would be greater than they may at first sight appear; but it must be confessed, that they are far inferior to those which present themselves under the other aspects of the subject.

Upon the whole, there can be no room to doubt that the convention acted wisely in copying from the models of those constitutions which have established GOOD BEHAVIOR as the tenure of their judicial offices, in point of duration; and that so far from being blamable on this account, their plan would have been inexcusably defective, if it had wanted this important feature of good government. The experience of Great Britain affords an illustrious comment on the excellence of the institution.

*PUBLIUS.*

NOTES

1. The celebrated Montesquieu, speaking of them, says: "Of the three powers above mentioned, the judiciary is next to nothing." "Spirit of Laws." vol. i., page 186.

2. Idem, page 181.

3. Vide "Protest of the Minority of the Convention of Pennsylvania," Martin's Speech, etc.

# Appendix Q: Federalist No. 85: Concluding Remarks

From *McLean's Edition*, New York

Author: Alexander Hamilton

To the People of the State of New York:

ACCORDING to the formal division of the subject of these papers, announced in my first number, there would appear still to remain for discussion two points: "the analogy of the proposed government to your own State constitution," and "the additional security which its adoption will afford to republican government, to liberty, and to property." But these heads have been so fully anticipated and exhausted in the progress of the work, that it would now scarcely be possible to do any thing more than repeat, in a more dilated form, what has been heretofore said, which the advanced stage of the question, and the time already spent upon it, conspire to forbid.

It is remarkable, that the resemblance of the plan of the convention to the act which organizes the government of this State holds, not less with regard to many of the supposed defects, than to the real excellences of the former. Among the pretended defects are the re-eligibility of the Executive, the want of a council, the omission of a formal bill of rights, the omission of a provision respecting the liberty of the press. These and several others which have been noted in the course of our inquiries are as much chargeable on the existing constitution of this State, as on the one proposed for the Union; and a man must have slender pretensions to consistency, who can rail at the latter for imperfections which he finds no difficulty in excusing in the former. Nor indeed can there be a better proof of the insincerity and affectation of some of the zealous adversaries of the plan of the convention among us, who profess to be the devoted admirers of the government under which they live, than the fury with which they have attacked that plan, for matters in regard to which our own constitution is equally or perhaps more vulnerable.

The additional securities to republican government, to liberty and to property, to be derived from the adoption of the plan under consideration, consist chiefly in the restraints which the preservation of the Union will impose on local factions and insurrections, and on the ambition of powerful individuals in single States, who may acquire credit and influence enough, from leaders and favorites, to become the despots of the people; in the diminution of the opportunities to foreign intrigue, which the dissolution of the Confederacy would invite and facilitate; in the prevention of extensive military establishments, which could not fail to grow out of wars between the States in a disunited situation; in the express guaranty of a republican form of government to each; in the absolute and universal exclusion of titles of nobility; and in the precautions against the repetition of those practices on the part of the State governments which have undermined the foundations of property and credit, have planted mutual distrust in the breasts of all classes of citizens, and have occasioned an almost universal prostration of morals.

Thus have I, fellow-citizens, executed the task I had assigned to myself; with what success, your conduct must determine. I trust at least you will admit that I have not failed in the assurance I gave you respecting the spirit with which my endeavors should be conducted. I have addressed myself purely to your judgments, and have studiously avoided those asperities which are too apt to disgrace political disputants of all parties, and which have been not a little provoked by the language and conduct of the opponents of the Constitution. The charge of a conspiracy against the liberties of the people, which has been indiscriminately brought against the advocates of the plan, has something in it too wanton and too malignant, not to excite the indignation of every man who feels in his own bosom a refutation of the calumny. The perpetual changes which have been rung upon the wealthy, the well-born, and the great, have been such as to inspire the disgust of all sensible men. And the unwarrantable concealments and misrepresentations which have been in various ways practiced to keep the truth from the public eye, have been of a nature to demand the reprobation of all honest men. It is not impossible that these circumstances may have occasionally betrayed me into intemperances of expression which I did not intend; it is certain that I have frequently felt a struggle between sensibility and moderation; and if the former has in some instances prevailed, it must be my excuse that it has been neither often nor much.

Let us now pause and ask ourselves whether, in the course of these papers, the proposed Constitution has not been satisfactorily vindicated from the aspersions thrown upon it; and whether it has not been shown to be worthy of the public approbation, and necessary to the public safety and prosperity. Every man is bound to answer these questions to himself, according to the best of his conscience and understanding, and to act agreeably to the genuine and sober dictates of his judgment. This is a duty from which nothing can give him a dispensation. 'T is one that he is called upon, nay, constrained by all the obligations that form the bands of society, to discharge sincerely and honestly. No partial motive, no particular interest, no pride of opinion, no temporary passion or prejudice, will justify to himself, to his country, or to his posterity, an improper election of the part he is to act. Let him beware of an obstinate adherence to party;

let him reflect that the object upon which he is to decide is not a particular interest of the community, but the very existence of the nation; and let him remember that a majority of America has already given its sanction to the plan which he is to approve or reject.

I shall not dissemble that I feel an entire confidence in the arguments which recommend the proposed system to your adoption, and that I am unable to discern any real force in those by which it has been opposed. I am persuaded that it is the best which our political situation, habits, and opinions will admit, and superior to any the revolution has produced.

Concessions on the part of the friends of the plan, that it has not a claim to absolute perfection, have afforded matter of no small triumph to its enemies. "Why," say they, "should we adopt an imperfect thing? Why not amend it and make it perfect before it is irrevocably established?" This may be plausible enough, but it is only plausible. In the first place I remark, that the extent of these concessions has been greatly exaggerated. They have been stated as amounting to an admission that the plan is radically defective, and that without material alterations the rights and the interests of the community cannot be safely confided to it. This, as far as I have understood the meaning of those who make the concessions, is an entire perversion of their sense. No advocate of the measure can be found, who will not declare as his sentiment, that the system, though it may not be perfect in every part, is, upon the whole, a good one; is the best that the present views and circumstances of the country will permit; and is such an one as promises every species of security which a reasonable people can desire.

I answer in the next place, that I should esteem it the extreme of imprudence to prolong the precarious state of our national affairs, and to expose the Union to the jeopardy of successive experiments, in the chimerical pursuit of a perfect plan. I never expect to see a perfect work from imperfect man. The result of the deliberations of all collective bodies must necessarily be a compound, as well of the errors and prejudices, as of the good sense and wisdom, of the individuals of whom they are composed. The compacts which are to embrace thirteen distinct States in a common bond of amity and union, must as necessarily be a compromise of as many dissimilar interests and inclinations. How can perfection spring from such materials?

The reasons assigned in an excellent little pamphlet lately published in this city,[1] are unanswerable to show the utter improbability of assembling a new convention, under circumstances in any degree so favorable to a happy issue, as those in which the late convention met, deliberated, and concluded. I will not repeat the arguments there used, as I presume the production itself has had an extensive circulation. It is certainly well worthy the perusal of every friend to his country. There is, however, one point of light in which the subject of amendments still remains to be considered, and in which it has not yet been exhibited to public view. I cannot resolve to conclude without first taking a survey of it in this aspect.

It appears to me susceptible of absolute demonstration, that it will be far more easy to obtain subsequent than previous amendments to the Constitution. The moment an alteration is made in the present plan, it becomes, to the purpose of adoption, a new one, and must undergo a new decision of each State. To its complete establishment throughout the Union, it will therefore require the concurrence of thirteen States. If, on the contrary, the Constitution proposed should once be ratified by all the States as it stands, alterations in it may at any time be effected by nine[2] States. Here, then, the chances are as thirteen to nine in favor of subsequent amendment, rather than of the original adoption of an entire system.

This is not all. Every Constitution for the United States must inevitably consist of a great variety of particulars, in which thirteen independent States are to be accommodated in their interests or opinions of interest. We may of course expect to see, in any body of men charged with its original formation, very different combinations of the parts upon different points. Many of those who form a majority on one question, may become the minority on a second, and an association dissimilar to either may constitute the majority on a third. Hence the necessity of moulding and arranging all the particulars which are to compose the whole, in such a manner as to satisfy all the parties to the compact; and hence, also, an immense multiplication of difficulties and casualties in obtaining the collective assent to a final act. The degree of that multiplication must evidently be in a ratio to the number of particulars and the number of parties.

But every amendment to the Constitution, if once established, would be a single proposition, and might be brought forward singly. There would then be no necessity for management or compromise, in relation to any other point no giving nor taking. The will of the requisite number would at once bring the matter to a decisive issue. And consequently, whenever nine, or rather ten States, were united in the desire of a particular amendment, that amendment must infallibly take place. There can, therefore, be no comparison between the facility of affecting an amendment, and that of establishing in the first instance a complete Constitution.

In opposition to the probability of subsequent amendments, it has been urged that the persons delegated to the administration of the national government will always be disinclined to yield up any portion of the authority of which they were once possessed. For my own part I acknowledge a thorough conviction that any amendments which may, upon mature consideration, be thought useful, will be applicable to the organization of the government, not to the mass of its powers; and on this account alone, I think there is no weight in the observation just stated. I also think there is little weight in it on another account. The intrinsic difficulty of governing thirteen States at any rate, independent of calculations upon an ordinary degree of public spirit and integrity, will, in my opinion constantly impose on the national rulers the necessity of a spirit of accommodation to the reasonable expectations of their constituents. But there is yet a further consideration, which proves beyond the possibility of a doubt, that the observation is futile. It is this that the national rulers, whenever nine States concur, will have no option upon the subject. By the fifth article of the plan, the Congress will be obliged "on the application of the legislatures of two thirds of the States (which at present amount to nine), to call a convention for proposing amendments, which shall be valid, to all intents and purposes, as part of the Constitution, when ratified by the legislatures of three fourths of the States, or by conventions in three fourths thereof." The words of this article are peremptory. The Congress "shall call a convention." Nothing in this particular is left to the discretion of that body. And of consequence, all the declamation about the disinclination to a change vanishes in air. Nor however difficult it may be supposed to unite two thirds or three fourths of the State legislatures, in amendments which may affect local interests, can there be any room to apprehend any such difficulty in a union on points which are merely relative to the general liberty or security of the people. We may safely rely on the disposition of the State legislatures to erect barriers against the encroachments of the national authority.

If the foregoing argument is a fallacy, certain it is that I am myself deceived by it, for it is, in my conception, one of those rare instances in which a political truth can be brought to the test of a mathematical demonstration. Those who see the matter in the same light with me, however zealous they may be for amendments, must agree in the propriety of a previous adoption, as the most direct road to their own object.

The zeal for attempts to amend, prior to the establishment of the Constitution, must abate in every man who is ready to accede to the truth of the following observations of a writer equally solid and ingenious: "To balance a large state or society (says he), whether monarchical or republican, on general laws, is a work of so great difficulty, that no human genius, however comprehensive, is able, by the mere dint of reason and reflection, to effect it. The judgments of many must unite in the work; experience must guide their labor; time must bring it to perfection, and the feeling of inconveniences must correct the mistakes which they INEVITABLY fall into in their first trials and experiments."[3] These judicious reflections contain a lesson of moderation to all the sincere lovers of the Union, and ought to put them upon their guard against hazarding anarchy, civil war, a perpetual alienation of the States from each other, and perhaps the military despotism of a victorious demagoguery, in the pursuit of what they are not likely to obtain, but from time and experience. It may be in me a defect of political fortitude, but I acknowledge that I cannot entertain an equal tranquillity with those who affect to treat the dangers of a longer continuance in our present situation as imaginary. A nation, without a national government, is, in my view, an awful spectacle. The establishment of a Constitution, in time of profound peace, by the voluntary consent of a whole people, is a prodigy, to the completion of which I look forward with trembling anxiety. I can reconcile it to no rules of prudence to let go the hold we now have, in so arduous an enterprise, upon seven out of the thirteen States, and after having passed over so considerable a part of the ground, to recommence the course. I dread the more the consequences of new attempts, because I know that powerful individuals, in this and in other States, are enemies to a general national government in every possible shape.

*PUBLIUS.*

## NOTES

1. Entitled "An Address to the People of the State of New York."
2. It may rather be said TEN, for though two thirds may set on foot the measure, three fourths must ratify.
3. Hume's "Essays," vol. i., page 128: "The Rise of Arts and Sciences."

# Appendix R: Anti-Federalist No. 1: General Introduction: A Dangerous Plan of Benefit Only to the "Aristocratick Combination"

*Source:* Anti-Federalist Papers included in the appendixes are from http://www.thefederalistpapers.org/anti-federalist-papers

Author: John Dewitt

I am pleased to see a spirit of inquiry burst the band of constraint upon the subject of the NEW PLAN for consolidating the governments of the United States, as recommended by the late Convention. If it is suitable to the GENIUS and HABITS of the citizens of these states, it will bear the strictest scrutiny. The PEOPLE are the grand inquest who have a RIGHT to judge of its merits.

The hideous daemon of Aristocracy has hitherto had so much influence as to bar the channels of investigation, preclude the people from inquiry and extinguish every spark of liberal information of its qualities. At length the luminary of intelligence begins to beam its effulgent rays upon this important production; the deceptive mists cast before the eyes of the people by the delusive machinations of its INTERESTED advocates begins to dissipate, as darkness flies before the burning taper; and I dare venture to predict, that in spite of those mercenary dectaimers, the plan will have a candid and complete examination.

Those furious zealots who are for cramming it down the throats of the people, without allowing them either time or opportunity to scan or weigh it in the balance of their understandings, bear the same marks in their features as those who have been long wishing to erect an aristocracy in THIS COMMONWEALTH [of Massachusetts]. Their menacing cry is for a RIGID government, it matters little to them of what kind, provided it answers THAT description. As the plan now offered comes something near their wishes, and is the most consonant to their views of any they can hope for, they come boldly forward and DEMAND its adoption.

They brand with infamy every man who is not as determined and zealous in its favor as themselves. They cry aloud the whole must be swallowed or none at all, thinking thereby to preclude any amendment; they are afraid of having it abated of its present RIGID aspect. They have strived to overawe or seduce printers to stifle and obstruct a free discussion, and have endeavored to hasten it to a decision before the people can duty reflect upon its properties. In order to deceive them, they incessantly declare that none can discover any defect in the system but bankrupts who wish no government, and officers of the present government who fear to lose a part of their power. These zealous partisans may injure their own cause, and endanger the public tranquility by impeding a proper inquiry; the people may suspect the WHOLE to be a dangerous plan, from such COVERED and DESIGNING schemes to enforce it upon them.

Compulsive or treacherous measures to establish any government whatever, will always excite jealousy among a free people: better remain single and alone, than blindly adopt whatever a few individuals shall demand, be they ever so wise. I had rather be a free citizen of the small republic of Massachusetts, than an oppressed subject of the great American empire. Let all act understandingly or not at all. If we can confederate upon terms that wilt secure to us our liberties, it is an object highly desirable, because of its additional security to the whole. If the proposed plan proves such an one, I hope it will be adopted, but if it will endanger our liberties as it stands, let it be amended; in order to which it must and ought to be open to inspection and free inquiry.

The inundation of abuse that has been thrown out upon the heads of those who have had any doubts of its universal good qualities, have been so redundant, that it may not be improper to scan the characters of its most strenuous advocates. It will first be allowed that many undesigning citizens may wish its adoption from the best motives, but these are modest and silent, when compared to the greater number, who endeavor to suppress all attempts for investigation. These violent partisans are for having the people gulp down the gilded pill blindfolded, whole, and without any qualification whatever.

These consist generally, of the NOBLE order of C[incinnatu]s, holders of public securities, men of great wealth and expectations of public office, Bankers and Lawyers: these with their train of dependents form the Aristocratick combination. The Lawyers in particular, keep up an incessant declamation for its adoption; like greedy gudgeons they long to satiate their voracious stomachs with the golden bait. The numerous tribunals to be erected by the new plan of consolidated empire, will find employment for ten times their present numbers; these are the LOAVES AND FISHES for which they hunger. They will probably find it suited to THEIR HABITS, if not to the HABITS OF THE PEOPLE. There may be reasons for having but few of them in the State Convention, lest THEIR OWN INTEREST should be too strongly considered. The time draws near for the choice of Delegates. I hope my fellow-citizens will look well to the characters of their preference, and remember the Old Patriots of 75; they have never led them astray, nor need they fear to try them on this momentous occasion.

*A FEDERALIST*

# Appendix S: Anti-Federalist No. 3: New Constitution Creates a National Government; Will Not Abate Foreign Influence

There are but two modes by which men are connected in society, the one which operates on individuals, this always has been, and ought still to be called, national government; the other which binds States and governments together (not corporations, for there is no considerable nation on earth, despotic, monarchical, or republican, that does not contain many subordinate corporations with various constitutions) this last has heretofore been denominated a league or confederacy. The term federalists is therefore improperly applied to themselves, by the friends and supporters of the proposed constitution. This abuse of language does not help the cause; every degree of imposition serves only to irritate, but can never convince. They are national men, and their opponents, or at least a great majority of them, are federal, in the only true and strict sense of the word.

Whether any form of national government is preferable for the Americans, to a league or confederacy, is a previous question we must first make up our minds upon. . . .

That a national government will add to the dignity and increase the splendor of the United States abroad, can admit of no doubt: it is essentially requisite for both. That it will render government, and officers of government, more dignified at home is equally certain. That these objects are more suited to the manners, if not [the] genius and disposition of our people is, I fear, also true. That it is requisite in order to keep us at peace among ourselves, is doubtful. That it is necessary, to prevent foreigners from dividing us, or interfering in our government, I deny positively; and, after all, I have strong doubts whether all its advantages are not more specious than solid. We are vain, like other nations. We wish to make a noise in the world; and feel hurt that Europeans are not so attentive to America in peace, as they were to America in war. We are also, no doubt, desirous of cutting a figure in history. Should we not reflect, that quiet is happiness? That content and pomp are incompatible? I have either read or heard this truth, which the Americans should never forget: That the silence of historians is the surest record of the happiness of a people. The Swiss have been four hundred years the envy of mankind, and there is yet scarcely an history of their nation. What is history, but a disgusting and painful detail of the butcheries of conquerors, and the woeful calamities of the conquered? Many of us are proud, and are frequently disappointed that office confers neither respect or difference. No man of merit can ever be disgraced by office. A rogue in office may be feared in some governments—he will be respected in none. After all, what we call respect and difference only arise from contrast of situation, as most of our ideas come by comparison and relation. Where the people are free there can be no great contrast or distinction among honest citizens in or out of office. In proportion as the people lose their freedom, every gradation of distinction, between the Governors and governed obtains, until the former become masters, and the latter become slaves. In all governments virtue will command reverence. The divine Cato knew every Roman citizen by name, and never assumed any preeminence; yet Cato found, and his memory will find, respect and reverence in the bosoms of mankind, until this world returns into that nothing, from whence Omnipotence called it. That the people are not at present disposed for, and are actually incapable of, governments of simplicity and equal rights, I can no longer doubt. But whose fault is it? We make them bad, by bad governments, and then abuse and despise them for being so. Our people are capable of being made anything that human nature was or is capable of, if we would only have a little patience and give them good and wholesome institutions; but I see none such and very little prospect of such. Alas! I see nothing in my fellow-citizens, that will permit my still fostering the delusion, that they are now capable of sustaining the weight of SELF-GOVERNMENT: a burden to which Greek and Roman shoulders proved unequal. The honor of supporting the dignity of the human character, seems reserved to the hardy Helvetians alone. If the body of the people will not govern themselves, and govern themselves well too, the consequence is unavoidable—a FEW will, and must govern them. Then it is that government becomes truly a government by force only, where men relinquish part of their natural rights to secure the rest, instead of an union of will and force, to protect all their natural rights, which ought to be the foundation of every rightful social compact.

Whether national government will be productive of internal peace, is too uncertain to admit of decided opinion. I only hazard a conjecture when I say, that our state disputes, in a confederacy, would be disputes of levity and passion, which would subside before injury. The people being free, government having no right to them, but they to government, they would separate and divide as interest or inclination prompted—as they do at this day, and always have done, in Switzerland. In a national government, unless cautiously and fortunately administered, the disputes will be the deep-rooted differences of interest, where part of the empire must be injured by the operation of general law; and then should the sword of government be once drawn (which Heaven avert) I fear it will not be sheathed, until we have waded through that series of desolation, which France, Spain, and the other great kingdoms of the world have suffered, in order to bring so many separate States into uniformity, of government and law; in which event the legislative power can only be entrusted to one man (as it is with them) who can have no local attachments, partial interests, or private views to gratify.

That a national government will prevent the influence or danger of foreign intrigue, or secure us from invasion, is in my judgment directly the reverse of the truth. The only foreign, or at least evil foreign influence, must be obtained through corruption. Where the government is lodged in the body of the people, as in Switzerland, they can never be corrupted; for no prince, or people, can have resources enough to corrupt the majority of a nation; and if they could, the play is not worth the candle. The facility of corruption is increased in proportion as power tends by representation or delegation, to a concentration in the hands of a few. . . .

As to any nation attacking a number of confederated independent republics . . . it is not to be expected, more especially as the wealth of the empire is there universally diffused, and will not be collected into any one overgrown, luxurious and effeminate capital to become a lure to the enterprising ambitious. That extensive empire is a misfortune to be deprecated, will not now be disputed. The balance of power has long engaged the attention of all the European world, in order to avoid the horrid evils of a general government. The same government pervading a vast extent of territory, terrifies the minds of individuals into meanness and submission. All human authority, however organized, must have confined limits, or insolence and oppression will prove the offspring of its grandeur, and the difficulty or rather impossibility of escape prevents resistance. Gibbon relates that some Roman Knights who had offended government in Rome were taken up in Asia, in a very few days after. It was the extensive territory of the Roman republic that produced a Sylla, a Marius, a Caligula, a Nero, and an Elagabalus. In small independent States contiguous to each other, the people run away and leave despotism to reek its vengeance on itself; and thus it is that moderation becomes with them, the law of self-preservation. These and such reasons founded on the eternal and immutable nature of things have long caused and will continue to cause much difference of sentiment throughout our wide extensive territories. From our divided and dispersed situation, and from the natural moderation of the American character, it has hitherto proved a warfare of argument and reason.

# Appendix T: Anti-Federalist No. 9: A Consolidated Government Is a Tyranny

From *Independent Gazetteer*
17 October 1787

We the Aristocratic party of the United States, lamenting the many inconveniences to which the late confederation subjected the well-born, the better kind of people, bringing them down to the level of the rabble—and holding in utter detestation that frontispiece to every bill of rights, "that all men are born equal"—beg leave (for the purpose of drawing a line between such as we think were ordained to govern, and such as were made to bear the weight of government without having any share in its administration) to submit to our Friends in the first class for their inspection, the following defense of our monarchical, aristocratical democracy.

1st. As a majority of all societies consist of men who (though totally incapable of thinking or acting in governmental matters) are more readily led than driven, we have thought meet to indulge them in something like a democracy in the new constitution, which part we have designated by the popular name of the House of Representatives. But to guard against every possible danger from this lower house, we have subjected every bill they bring forward, to the double negative of our upper house and president. Nor have we allowed the populace the right to elect their representatives annually . . . lest this body should be too much under the influence and control of their constituents, and thereby prove the "weatherboard of our grand edifice, to show the shiftings of every fashionable gale,"—for we have not yet to learn that little else is wanting to aristocratize the most democratical representative than to make him somewhat independent of his political creators. We have taken away that rotation of appointment which has so long perplexed us—that grand engine of popular influence. Every man is eligible into our government from time to time for life. This will have a two-fold good effect. First, it prevents the representatives from mixing with the lower class, and imbibing their foolish sentiments, with which they would have come charged on re-election.

2d. They will from the perpetuality of office be under our eye, and in a short time will think and act like us, independently of popular whims and prejudices. For the assertion "that evil communications corrupt good manners," is not more true than its reverse. We have allowed this house the power to impeach, but we have tenaciously reserved the right to try. We hope gentlemen, you will see the policy of this clause—for what matters it who accuses, if the accused is tried by his friends. In fine, this plebian house will have little power, and that little be rightly shaped by our house of gentlemen, who will have a very extensive influence—from their being chosen out of the genteeler class . . . It is true, every third senatorial seat is to be vacated duennually, but two-thirds of this influential body will remain in office, and be ready to direct or (if necessary) bring over to the good old way, the young members, if the old ones should not be returned. And whereas many of our brethren, from a laudable desire to support their rank in life above the commonalty, have not only deranged their finances, but subjected their persons to indecent treatment (as being arrested for debt, etc.) we have framed a privilege clause, by which they may laugh at the fools who trusted them. But we have given out, that this clause was provided, only that the members might be able without interruption, to deliberate on the important business of their country.

We have frequently endeavored to effect in our respective states, the happy discrimination which pervades this system; but finding we could not bring the states into it individually, we have determined . . . and have taken pains to leave the legislature of each free and independent state, as they now call themselves, in such a situation that they will eventually be absorbed by our grand continental vortex, or dwindle into petty corporations, and have power over little else than yoaking hogs or determining the width of cart wheels. But (aware that an intention to annihilate state legislatures, would be objected to our favorite scheme) we have made their existence (as a board of electors) necessary to ours. This furnishes us and our advocates with a fine answer to any clamors that may be raised on this subject. We have so interwoven continental and state legislatures that they cannot exist separately; whereas we in truth only leave them the power of electing us, for what can a provincial legislature do when we possess the exclusive regulation of external and internal commerce, excise, duties, imposts, post-offices and roads; when we and we alone, have the power to wage war, make peace, coin money (if we can get bullion) if not, borrow money, organize the militia and call them forth to execute our decrees, and crush insurrections assisted by a noble body of veterans subject to our nod, which we have the power of raising and keeping even in the time of peace.

What have we to fear from state legislatures or even from states, when we are armed with such powers, with a president at our head? (A name we thought proper to adopt in conformity to the prejudices of a silly people who are so foolishly fond of a Republican government, that we were obliged to accommodate in names and forms to them, in order more effectually to secure the substance of our proposed plan; but we all know that Cromwell was a King, with the title of Protector). I repeat it, what have we to fear armed with such powers, with a president at our head who is captain-general of the army, navy and militia of the United States, who can make and unmake treaties, appoint and commission ambassadors and other ministers, who can grant or refuse reprieves or pardons, who can make judges of the supreme and other continental courts—in short, who will be the source, the fountain of honor, profit and power, whose influence like the rays of the sun, will diffuse itself far and wide, will exhale all democratical vapors and break the clouds of popular insurrection?

But again gentlemen, our judicial power is a strong work, a masked battery, few people see the guns we can and will ere long play off from it. For the judicial power embraces every question which can arise in law or equity, under this constitution and under the laws of "the United States" (which laws will be, you know, the supreme laws of the land). This power extends to all cases, affecting ambassadors or other public ministers, "and consuls; to all cases of admiralty and maritime jurisdiction; to controversies to which the United States shall be a party; to controversies between two or more States; between a State and citizens of another State; between citizens of different States; between citizens of the same State, claiming lands under grants of different States; and between a State or the citizens thereof, and foreign States, citizens or subjects."

Now, can a question arise in the colonial courts, which the ingenuity or sophistry of an able lawyer may not bring within one or other of the above cases? Certainly not. Then our court will have original or appellate jurisdiction in all cases—and if so, how fallen are state judicatures—and must not every provincial law yield to our supreme fiat? Our constitution answers yes. . . . And finally we shall entrench ourselves so as to laugh at the cabals of the commonalty. A few regiments will do at first; it must be spread abroad that they are absolutely necessary to defend the frontiers. Now a regiment and then a legion must be added quietly; by and by a frigate or two must be built, still taking care to intimate that they are essential to the support of our revenue laws and to prevent smuggling. We have said nothing about a bill of rights, for we viewed it as an eternal clog upon our designs, as a lock chain to the wheels of government—though, by the way, as we have not insisted on rotation in our offices, the simile of a wheel is ill. We have for some time considered the freedom of the press as a great evil—it spreads information, and begets a licentiousness in the people which needs the rein more than the spur; besides, a daring printer may expose the plans of government and lessen the consequence of our president and senate—for these and many other reasons we have said nothing with respect to the "right of the people to speak and publish their sentiments" or about their "palladiums of liberty" and such stuff. We do not much like that sturdy privilege of the people—the right to demand the writ of habeas corpus. We have therefore reserved the power of refusing it in cases of rebellion, and you know we are the judges of what is rebellion. . . . Our friends we find have been assiduous in representing our federal calamities, until at length the people at large—frightened by the gloomy picture on one side, and allured by the prophecies of some of our fanciful and visionary adherents on the other—are ready to accept and confirm our proposed government without the delay or forms of examination—which was the more to be wished, as they are wholly unfit to investigate the principles or pronounce on the merit of so exquisite a system.

Impressed with a conviction that this constitution is calculated to restrain the influence and power of the LOWER CLASS—to draw that discrimination we have so long sought after; to secure to our friends privileges and offices, which were not to be . . . [obtained] under the former government, because they were in common; to take the burden of legislation and attendance on public business off the commonalty, who will be much better able thereby to prosecute with effect their private business; to destroy that political thirteen headed monster, the state sovereignties; to check the licentiousness of the people by making it dangerous to speak or publish daring or tumultuary sentiments; to enforce obedience to laws by a strong executive, aided by military pensioners; and finally to promote the public and private interests of the better kind of people—we submit it to your judgment to take such measures for its adoption as you in your wisdom may think fit.

Signed by unanimous order of the lords spiritual and temporal.

*MONTEZUMA*

# Appendix U: Anti-Federalist No. 14: Extent of Territory under Consolidated Government Too Large to Preserve Liberty or Protect Property

From *New-York Journal*
25 October 1787
Author: George Clinton

. . . The recital, or premises on which the new form of government is erected, declares a consolidation or union of all the thirteen parts, or states, into one great whole, under the form of the United States, for all the various and important purposes therein set forth. But whoever seriously considers the immense extent of territory comprehended within the limits of the United States, together with the variety of its climates, productions, and commerce, the difference of extent, and number of inhabitants in all; the dissimilitude of interest, morals, and politics, in almost every one, will receive it as an intuitive truth, that a consolidated republican form of government therein, can never form a perfect union, establish justice, insure domestic tranquility, promote the general welfare, and secure the blessings of liberty to you and your posterity, for to these objects it must be directed. This unkindred legislature therefore, composed of interests opposite and dissimilar in their nature, will in its exercise, emphatically be like a house divided against itself.

The governments of Europe have taken their limits and form from adventitious circumstances, and nothing can be argued on the motive of agreement from them; but these adventitious political principles have nevertheless produced effects that have attracted the attention of philosophy, which have established axioms in the science of politics therefrom, as irrefragable as any in Euclid. It is natural, says Montesquieu, to a republic to have only a small territory, otherwise it cannot long subsist: in a large one, there are men of large fortunes, and consequently of less moderation; there are too great deposits to trust in the hands of a single subject, an ambitious person soon becomes sensible that he may be happy, great, and glorious by oppressing his fellow citizens, and that he might raise himself to grandeur, on the ruins of his country. In large republics, the public good is sacrificed to a thousand views, in a small one, the interest of the public is easily perceived, better understood, and more within the reach of every citizen; abuses have a less extent, and of course are less protected. He also shows you, that the duration of the republic of Sparta was owing to its having continued with the same extent of territory after all its wars; and that the ambition of Athens and Lacedemon to command and direct the union, lost them their liberties, and gave them a monarchy.

From this picture, what can you promise yourselves, on the score of consolidation of the United States into one government? Impracticability in the just exercise of it, your freedom insecure, even this form of government limited in its continuance, the employments of your country disposed of to the opulent, to whose contumely you will continually be an object. You must risk much, by indispensably placing trusts of the greatest magnitude, into the hands of individuals whose ambition for power, and aggrandizement, will oppress and grind you. Where, from the vast extent of your territory, and the complication of interests, the science of government will become intricate and perplexed, and too mysterious for you to understand and observe; and by which you are to be conducted into a monarchy, either limited or despotic; the latter, Mr. Locke remarks, is a government derived from neither nature nor compact.

Political liberty, the great Montesquieu again observes, consists in security, or at least in the opinion we have of security; and this security, therefore, or the opinion, is best obtained in moderate governments, where the mildness of the laws, and the equality of the manners, beget a confidence in the people, which produces this security, or the opinion. This moderation in governments depends in a great measure on their limits, connected with their political distribution.

The extent of many of the states of the Union, is at this time almost too great for the superintendence of a republican form of government, and must one day or other revolve into more vigorous ones, or by separation be reduced into smaller and more useful, as well as moderate ones. You have already observed the feeble efforts of Massachusetts against their insurgents; with what difficulty did they quell that insurrection; and is not the province of Maine at this moment on the eve of separation from her? The reason of these things is, that for the security of the property of the community—in which expressive term Mr. Locke makes life, liberty, and estate, to consist the wheels of a republic are necessarily slow in their operation. Hence, in large free republics, the evil sometimes is not only begun, but almost completed, before they are in a situation to turn the current into a contrary progression. The extremes are also too remote from the usual seat of government, and the laws, therefore, too feeble to afford protection to all its parts, and insure domestic tranquility without the aid of another principle. If, therefore, this state [New York], and that of North Carolina, had an army under their control, they never would have lost Vermont, and Frankland, nor the state of Massachusetts suffered an insurrection, or the dismemberment of her fairest district; but the exercise of a principle which would have prevented these things, if we may believe the experience of ages, would have ended in the destruction of their liberties.

Will this consolidated republic, if established, in its exercise beget such confidence and compliance, among the citizens of these states, as to do without the aid of a standing army? I deny that it will. The malcontents in each state, who will not be a few, nor the least important, will be exciting factions against it. The fear of a dismemberment of some of its parts, and the necessity to enforce the execution Of revenue laws (a fruitful source of oppression) on the extremes and in the other districts of the government, will incidentally and necessarily require a permanent force, to be kept on foot. Will not political security, and even the opinion of it, be extinguished? Can mildness and moderation exist in a government where the primary incident in its exercise must be force? Will not violence destroy confidence, and can equality subsist where the extent, policy, and practice of it will naturally lead to make odious distinctions among citizens?

The people who may compose this national legislature from the southern states, in which, from the mildness of the climate, the fertility of the soil, and the value of its productions, wealth is rapidly acquired, and where the same causes naturally lead to luxury, dissipation, and a passion for aristocratic distinction; where slavery is encouraged, and liberty of course less respected and protected; who know not what it is to acquire property by their own toil, nor to economize with the savings of indus—will these men, therefore, be as tenacious of the liberties and interests of the more northern states, where freedom, independence, industry, equality and frugality are natural to the climate and soil, as men who are your own citizens, legislating in your own state, under your inspection, and whose manners and fortunes bear a more equal resemblance to your own?

It may be suggested, in answer to this, that whoever is a citizen of one state is a citizen of each, and that therefore he will be as interested in the happiness and interest of all, as the one he is delegated from. But the argument is fallacious, and, whoever has attended to the history of mankind, and the principles which bind them together as parents, citizens, or men, will readily perceive it. These principles are, in their exercise, like a pebble cast on the calm surface of a river—the circles begin in the center, and are small, active and forcible, but as they depart from that point, they lose their force, and vanish into calmness.

The strongest principle of union resides within our domestic walls. The ties of the parent exceed that of any other. As we depart from home, the next general principle of union is amongst citizens of the same state, where acquaintance, habits, and fortunes, nourish affection, and attachment. Enlarge the circle still further, and, as citizens of different states, though we acknowledge the same national denomination, we lose in the ties of acquaintance, habits, and fortunes, and thus by degrees we lessen in our attachments, till, at length, we no more than acknowledge a sameness of species. Is it, therefore, from certainty like this, reasonable to believe, that inhabitants of Georgia, or New Hampshire, will have the same obligations towards you as your own, and preside over your lives, liberties, and property, with the same care and attachment? Intuitive reason answers in the negative. . . .

*CATO*

# Appendix V: Anti-Federalist No. 21: Why the Articles Failed

From *Independent Gazetteer*
5 October and 30 November 1787

That the present confederation is inadequate to the objects of the union, seems to be universally allowed. The only question is, what additional powers are wanting to give due energy to the federal government? We should, however, be careful, in forming our opinion on this subject, not to impute the temporary and extraordinary difficulties that have hitherto impeded the execution of the confederation, to defects in the system itself. For years past, the harpies of power have been industriously inculcating the idea that all our difficulties proceed from the impotency of Congress, and have at length succeeded to give to this sentiment almost universal currency and belief. The devastations, losses and burdens occasioned by the late war; the excessive importations of foreign merchandise and luxuries, which have drained the country of its specie and involved it in debt, are all overlooked, and the inadequacy of the powers of the present confederation is erroneously supposed to be the only cause of our difficulties. Hence persons of every description are revelling in the anticipation of the halcyon days consequent on the establishment of the new constitution. What gross deception and fatal delusion! Although very considerable benefit might be derived from strengthening the hands of Congress, so as to enable them to regulate commerce, and counteract the adverse restrictions of other nations, which would meet with the concurrence of all persons; yet this benefit is accompanied in the new constitution with the scourge of despotic power. . . .

Taxation is in every government a very delicate and difficult subject. Hence it has been the policy of all wise statesmen, as far as circumstances permitted, to lead the people by small beginnings and almost imperceptible degrees, into the habits of taxation. Where the contrary conduct has been pursued, it has ever failed of full success, not unfrequently proving the ruin of the projectors. The imposing of a burdensome tax at once on a people, without the usual gradations, is the severest test that any government can be put to; despotism itself has often proved unequal to the attempt. Under this conviction, let us take a review of our situation before and since the revolution.

From the first settlement of this country until the commencement of the late war, the taxes were so light and trivial as to be scarcely felt by the people. When we engaged in the expensive contest with Great Britain, the Congress, sensible of the difficulty of levying the monies necessary to its support, by direct taxation, had resource to an anticipation of the public resources, by emitting bills of credit, and thus postponed the necessity of taxation for several years. This means was pursued to a most ruinous length. But about the year 80 or 81, it was wholly exhausted, the bills of credit had suffered such a depreciation from the excessive quantities in circulation, that they ceased to be useful as a medium. The country at this period was very much impoverished and exhausted; commerce had been suspended for near six years; the husbandman, for want of a market, limited his crops to his own subsistence; the frequent calls of the militia and long continuance in actual service, the devastations of the enemy, the subsistence of our own armies, the evils of the depreciation of the paper money, which fell chiefly upon the patriotic and virtuous part of the community, had all concurred to produce great distress throughout America. In this situation of affairs, we still had the same powerful enemy to contend with, who had even more numerous and better appointed armies in the field than at any former time. Our allies were applied to in this exigency, but the pecuniary assistance that we could procure from them was soon exhausted. The only resource now remaining was to obtain by direct taxation, the moneys necessary for our defense. The history of mankind does not furnish a similar instance of an attempt to levy such enormous taxes at once, nor of a people so wholly unprepared and uninured to them—the lamp of sacred liberty must indeed have burned with unsullied lustre, every sordid principle of the mind must have been then extinct, when the people not only submitted to the grievous impositions, but cheerfully exerted themselves to comply with the calls of their country. Their abilities, however, were not equal to furnish the necessary sums—indeed, the requisition of the year 1782, amounted to the whole income of their farms and other property, including the means of their subsistence.

Perhaps the strained exertions of two years would not have sufficed to the discharge of this requisition. How then can we impute the difficulties of the people to a due compliance with the requisitions of Congress, to a defect in the confederation? Any government, however energetic, in similar circumstances, would have experienced the same fate. If we review the proceedings of the States, we shall find that they gave every sanction and authority to the requisitions of Congress that their laws could confer, that they attempted to collect the sums called for in the same manner as is proposed to be done in future by the general government, instead of the State legislatures. . . .

The wheels of the general government having been thus clogged, and the arrearages of taxes still accumulating, it may be asked what prospect is there of the government resuming its proper tone, unless more compulsory powers are granted? To this it may be answered, that the produce of imposts on commerce, which all agree to vest in Congress, together with the immense tracts of land at their disposal, will rapidly lessen and eventually discharge the present encumbrances. When this takes place, the mode by requisition will be found perfectly adequate to the extraordinary exigencies of the union. Congress have lately sold land to the amount of eight millions of dollars, which is a considerable portion of the whole debt.

It is to be lamented that the interested and designing have availed themselves so successfully of the present crisis, and under the specious pretence of having discovered a panacea for all the ills of the people, they are about establishing a system of government, that will prove more destructive to them than the wooden horse filled with soldiers did in ancient times to the city of Troy. This horse was introduced by their hostile enemy the Grecians, by a prostitution of the sacred rites of their religion; in like manner, my fellow citizens, are aspiring despots among yourselves prostituting the name of a Washington to cloak their designs upon your liberties.

I would ask how was the proposed Constitution to have showered down those treasures upon every class of citizens, as has been so industriously inculcated and so fondly believed by some? Would it have been by the addition of numerous and expensive establishments? By doubling our judiciaries, instituting federal courts in every county of every state? By a superb presidential court? By a large standing army? In short, by putting it in the power of the future government to levy money at pleasure, and placing this government so independent of the people as to enable the administration to gratify every corrupt passion of the mind, to riot on your spoils, without check or control?

A transfer to Congress of the power of imposing imposts on commerce, the unlimited regulation of trade, and to make treaties, I believe is all that is wanting to render America as prosperous as it is in the power of any form of government to render her; this properly understood would meet the views of all the honest and well meaning.

What gave birth to the late continental Convention? Was it not the situation of our commerce, which lay at the mercy of every foreign power, who, from motives of interest or enmity, could restrict and control it without risking a retaliation on the part of America, as Congress was impotent on this subject? Such indeed was the case with respect to Britain, whose hostile regulations gave such a stab to our navigation as to threaten its annihilation, it became the interest of even the American merchant to give a preference to foreign bottoms; hence the distress of our seamen, shipwrights, and every mechanic art dependent on navigation.

By these regulations too, we were limited in markets for our produce; our vessels were excluded from their West India islands; many of our staple commodities were denied entrance in Britain. Hence the husbandman were distressed by the demand for their crops being lessened and their prices reduced. This is the source to which may be traced every evil we experience, that can be relieved by a more energetic government. Recollect the language of complaint for years past; compare the recommendations of Congress, founded on such complaints, pointing out the remedy; examine the reasons assigned by the different states for appointing delegates to the late Convention; view the powers vested in that body—they all harmonize in the sentiment, that the due regulation of trade and navigation was the anxious wish of every class of citizens, was the great object of calling the Convention.

This object being provided for by the Constitution proposed by the general Convention, people overlooked and were not sensible of the needless sacrifice they were making for it. Allowing for a moment that it would be possible for trade to flourish under a despotic government, of what avail would be a prosperous state of commerce, when the produce of it would be at the absolute disposal of an arbitrary unchecked general government, who may levy at pleasure the most oppressive taxes; who may destroy every principle of freedom; who may even destroy the privilege of complaining. . . .

After so recent a triumph over British despots, after such torrents of blood and treasure have been spent, after involving ourselves in the distresses of an arduous war, and incurring such a debt, for the express purpose of asserting the rights of humanity, it is truly astonishing that a set of men among ourselves should have had the effrontery to attempt the destruction of our liberties. But in this enlightened age, to dupe the people by the arts they are practising, is still more extraordinary. . . .

*CENTINEL*

# Appendix W: Anti-Federalist No. 22: Articles of Confederation Simply Requires Amendments, Particularly for Commercial Power and Judicial Power; Constitution Goes Too Far

From *Boston Independent Chronicle*
6 and 20 December 1787
Author: Benjamin Austin

. . . Many people are sanguine for the Constitution, because they apprehend our commerce will be benefited. I would advise those persons to distinguish between the evils that arise from extraneous causes and our private imprudencies, and those that arise from our government. It does not appear that the embarrassments of our trade will be removed by the adoption of this Constitution. The powers of Europe do not lay any extraordinary duties on our oil, fish, or tobacco, because of our government; neither do they discourage our ship building on this account. I would ask what motive would induce Britain to repeal the duties on our oil, or France on our fish, if we should adopt the proposed Constitution? Those nations laid these duties to promote their own fishery, etc., and let us adopt what mode of government we please, they will pursue their own politics respecting our imports and exports, unless we can check them by some commercial regulations.

But it may be said, that such commercial regulations will take place after we have adopted the Constitution, and that the northern states would then become carriers for the southern. The great question then is, whether it is necessary in order to obtain these purposes, for every state to give up their whole power of legislation and taxation, and become an unwieldy republic, when it is probable the important object of our commerce could be effected by a uniform navigation act, giving Congress full power to regulate the whole commerce of the States? This power Congress have often said was sufficient to answer all their purposes. The circular letter from the Boston merchants and others, was urgent on this subject. Also the navigation act of this state [Massachusetts], was adopted upon similar principles, and . . . was declared by our Minister in England, to be the most effectual plan to promote our navigation, provided it had been adopted by the whole confederacy.

But it may be said, this regulation of commerce, without energy to enforce a compliance, is quite ideal. Coercion with some persons seems the principal object, but I believe we have more to expect from the affections of the people, than from an armed body of men. Provided a uniform commercial system was adopted, and each State felt its agreeable operations, we should have but little occasion to exercise force. But however, as power is thought necessary to raise an army, if required, to carry into effect any federal measure, I am willing to place it, where it is likely to be used with the utmost caution. This power I am willing to place among the confederated States, to be exercised when two thirds of them in their legislative capacities shall say the common good requires it. But to trust this power in the hands of a few men delegated for two, four and six years, is complimenting the ambition of human nature too highly, to risk the tranquility of these States on their absolute determination.

Certain characters now on the stage, we have reason to venerate, but though this country is now blessed with a Washington, Franklin, Hancock and Adams, yet posterity may have reason to rue the day when their political welfare depends on the decision of men who may fill the places of these worthies. . . .

The advocates for the Constitution, have always assumed an advantage by saying, that their opposers have never offered any plan as a substitute; the following outlines are therefore submitted, not as originating from an individual, but as copied from former resolutions of Congress, and united with some parts of the Constitution proposed by the respectable convention. This being the case, I presume it will not be invalidated by the cant term of antifederalism.

1st. That the Legislature of each state, empower Congress to frame a navigation act, to operate uniformly throughout the states; receiving to Congress all necessary powers to regulate our commerce with foreign nations, and among the several states, and with the Indian tribes. The revenue arising from the impost to be subject to their appropriations, "to enable them to fulfill their public engagements with foreign creditors."

2nd. That the Legislature of each state, instruct their delegates in Congress, to frame a treaty of AMITY for the purposes of discharging each state's proportion of the public debt, either foreign or domestic, and to enforce (if necessary) their immediate payment. Each state obligating themselves in the treaty of amity, to furnish (whenever required by Congress) a proportionate number of the Militia who are ever to be well organized and disciplined, for the purposes of repelling any invasion; suppressing any insurrection; or reducing any delinquent state within the confederacy, to a compliance with the federal treaty of commerce and amity. Such assistance to be furnished by the Supreme Executive of each state, on the application of Congress. The troops in cases of invasion to be under the command of the Supreme Executive of the state immediately in danger; but in cases of insurrection, and when employed against any delinquent state in the confederacy, the troops to be under the command of Congress.

3d. That such states as did not join the confederacy of commerce and amity, should be considered as aliens; and any goods brought from such state into any of the confederated states, together with their vessels, should be subject to heavy extra duties.

4th. The treaty of amity, agreed to by the several states, should expressly declare that no State (without the consent of Congress) should enter into any treaty, alliances, or confederacy; grant letters of marque and reprisal; make anything but gold and silver coin a tender in payment of debts; pass any bill of attainder or ex post facto law, or impair the obligations of contracts; engage in war, or declare peace.

5th. A Supreme Judicial Court to be constituted for the following federal purposes—to extend to all treaties made previous to, or which shall be made under the authority of the confederacy; all cases affecting Ambassadors, and other public Ministers and Consuls; controversies between two or more states; and between citizens of the same state claiming lands under grants of different states; to define and punish piracies, and felonies committed on the high seas, and offenses against the law of nations.

6th. That it be recommended to Congress, that the said navigation act, and treaty of amity, be sent to the Legislatures (or people) of the several states, for their assenting to, and ratifying the same.

7th. A regular statement and account of the receipts and expenditures, of all public monies, should be published from time to time.

The above plan it is humbly conceived—secures the internal government of the several states; promotes the commerce of the whole union; preserves a due degree of energy; lays restraints on aliens; secures the several states against invasions and insurrection by a MILITIA, rather than a STANDING ARMY; checks all ex post facto laws; cements the states by certain federal restrictions; confines the judiciary powers to national matters; and provides for the public information of receipts and expenditures. In a word, it places us in a complete federal state.

The resolves of Congress, 18th April, 1783, "recommends to the several States, to invest them with powers to levy for the use of the United States, certain duties upon goods, imported from any foreign port, island or plantation;" which measures is declared by them, "to be a system more free, from well founded exception, and is better calculated to receive the approbation of the several States, than any other, that the wisdom of Congress could devise; and if adopted, would enable them to fulfill their public engagements with their foreign creditors." . . .

Should we adopt this plan, no extraordinary expenses would arise, and Congress having but one object to attend, every commercial regulation would be uniformly adopted; the duties of impost and excise, would operate equally throughout the states; our ship building and carrying trade, would claim their immediate attention; and in consequence thereof, our agriculture, trade and manufactures would revive and flourish. No acts of legislation, independent of this great business, would disaffect one State against the other; but the whole, . . . in one Federal System of commerce, would serve to remove all local attachments, and establish our navigation upon a most extensive basis. The powers of Europe, would be alarmed at our Union, and would fear lest we should retaliate on them by laying restrictions on their trade. . . .

These states, by the blessing of Heaven, are now in a very tranquil state. This government, in particular, has produced an instance of ENERGY, in suppressing a late rebellion, which no absolute monarchy can boast. And notwithstanding the insinuations of a "small party," who are ever branding the PEOPLE with the most opprobrious epithets—representing them as aiming to level all distinctions; emit paper money; encourage the rebellion—yet the present General Court, the voice of that body, whom they have endeavored to stigmatize, have steadily pursued measures foreign from the suggestions of such revilers. And the public credit has been constantly appreciating since the present Administration.

Let us then be cautious how we disturb this general harmony. Every exertion is now making, by the people, to discharge their taxes. Industry and frugality prevail. Our commerce is every day increasing by the enterprise of our merchants. And above all, the PEOPLE of the several states are convinced of the necessity of adopting some Federal Commercial Plan. . . .

*CANDIDUS*

# Appendix X: Anti-Federalist No. 37: Factions and the Constitution

To have a just idea of the government before us, and to show that a consolidated one is the object in view, it is necessary not only to examine the plan, but also its history, and the politics of its particular friends.

The confederation was formed when great confidence was placed in the voluntary exertions of individuals, and of the respective states; and the framers of it, to guard against usurpation, so limited, and checked the powers, that, in many respects, they are inadequate to the exigencies of the union. We find, therefore, members of congress urging alterations in the federal system almost as soon as it was adopted. It was early proposed to vest congress with powers to levy an impost, to regulate trade, etc. , but such was known to be the caution of the states in parting with power, that the vestment even of these, was proposed to be under several checks and limitations.

During the war, the general confusion, and the introduction of paper money, infused in the minds of the people vague ideas respecting government and credit. We expected too much from the return of peace, and of course we have been disappointed. Our governments have been new and unsettled; and several legislatures, by making tender, suspension, and paper money laws, have given just cause of uneasiness to creditors. By these and other causes, several orders of men in the community have been prepared, by degrees, for a change of government. And this very abuse of power in the legislatures, which in some cases has been charged upon the democratic part of the community, has furnished aristocratical men with those very weapons, and those very means, with which, in great measure, they are rapidly effecting their favorite object. And should an oppressive government be the consequence of the proposed change, posterity may reproach not only a few overbearing, unprincipled men, but those parties in the states which have misused their powers.

The conduct of several legislatures, touching paper money, and tender laws, has prepared many honest men for changes in government, which otherwise they would not have thought of—when by the evils, on the one hand, and by the secret instigations of artful men, on the other, the minds of men were become sufficiently uneasy, a bold step was taken, which is usually followed by a revolution, or a civil war. A general convention for mere commercial purposes was moved for—the authors of this measure saw that the people's attention was turned solely to the amendment of the federal system; and that, had the idea of a total change been started, probably no state would have appointed members to the convention. The idea of destroying ultimately, the state government, and forming one consolidated system, could not have been admitted—a convention, therefore, merely for vesting in congress power to regulate trade was proposed.

This was pleasing to the commercial towns; and the landed people had little or no concern about it. In September, 1786, a few men from the middle states met at Annapolis, and hastily proposed a convention to be held in May, 1787, for the purpose, generally, of amending the confederation. This was done before the delegates of Massachusetts, and of the other states arrived—still not a word was said about destroying the old constitution, and making a new one. The states still unsuspecting, and not aware that they were passing the Rubicon, appointed members to the new convention, for the sole and express purpose of revising and amending the confederation—and, probably, not one man in ten thousand in the United States, till within these ten or twelve days, had an idea that the old ship was to be destroyed, and be put to the alternative of embarking in the new ship presented, or of being left in danger of sinking. The States, I believe, universally supposed the convention would report alterations in the confederation, which would pass an examination in congress, and after being agreed to there, would be confirmed by all the legislatures, or be rejected.

Virginia made a very respectable appointment, and placed at the head of it the first man in America. In this appointment there was a mixture of political characters; but Pennsylvania appointed principally those men who are esteemed aristocratical. Here the favorite moment for changing the government was evidently discerned by a few men, who seized it with address. Ten other states appointed, and tho' they chose men principally connected with commerce and the judicial department yet they appointed many good republican characters. Had they all attended we should now see, I am persuaded, a better system presented.

The nonattendance of eight or nine men, who were appointed members of the convention, I shall ever consider as a very unfortunate event to the United States. Had they attended, I am pretty clear that the result of the convention would not have had that strong tendency to aristocracy now discernible in every part of the plan. There would not have been so great an accumulation of powers, especially as to the internal police of this country in a few hands as the constitution reported proposes to vest in them—the young visionary men, and the consolidating aristocracy, would have been more restrained than they have been. Eleven states met in the convention, and after four months close attention presented the new constitution, to be adopted or rejected by the people. The uneasy and fickle part of the community may be prepared to receive any form of government; but I presume the enlightened and substantial part will give any constitution presented for their adoption a candid and thorough examination. . . .

We shall view the convention with proper respect—and, at the same time, that we reflect there were men of abilities and integrity in it, we must recollect how disproportionately the democratic and aristocratic parts of the community were represented. Perhaps the judicious friends and opposers of the new constitution will agree, that it is best to let it rely solely on its own merits, or be condemned for its own defects. . . .

This subject of consolidating the states is new. And because forty or fifty men have agreed in a system, to suppose the good sense of this country, an enlightened nation, must adopt it without examination, and though in a state of profound peace, without endeavoring to amend those parts they perceive are defective, dangerous to freedom, and destructive of the valuable principles of republican government—is truly humiliating. It is true there may be danger in delay; but there is danger in adopting the system in its present form.

And I see the danger in either case will arise principally from the conduct and views of two very unprincipled parties in the United States—two fires, between which the honest and substantial people have long found themselves situated. One party is composed of little insurgents, men in debt, who want no law, and who want a share of the property of others; these are called revellers, Shayites, etc. The other party is composed of a few, but more dangerous men, with their servile dependents; these avariciously grasp at all power and property; you may discover in all the actions of these men, an evident dislike to free and equal government, and they will go systematically to work to change, essentially, the forms of government in this country; these are called aristocrats, monarchists, etc. Between these two parties is the weight of the community; the men of middling property, men not in debt on the one hand, and men, on the other, content with republican governments, and not aiming at immense fortunes, offices, and power. In 1786, the little insurgents, the revellers, came forth, invaded the rights of others, and attempted to establish governments according to their wills. Their movements evidently gave encouragement to the other party, which, in 1787, has taken the political field, and with its fashionable dependents, and the tongue and the pen, is endeavoring to establish in a great haste, a politer kind of government. These two parties, which will probably be opposed or united as it may suit their interests and views, are really insignificant, compared with the solid, free, and independent part of the community. It is not my intention to suggest, that either of these parties, and the real friends of the proposed constitution, are the same men.

The fact is, these aristocrats support and hasten the adoption of the proposed constitution, merely because they think it is a stepping stone to their favorite object. I think I am well founded in this idea. I think the general politics of these men support it, as well as the common observation among them: That the proffered plan is the best that can be got at present, it will do for a few years, and lead to something better. The sensible and judicious part of the community will carefully weigh all these circumstances; they will view the late convention as a respectable body of men—America probably never will see an assembly of men, of a like number, more respectable. But the members of the convention met without knowing the sentiments of one man in ten thousand in these states respecting the new ground taken. Their doings are but the first attempts in the most important scene ever opened. Though each individual in the state conventions will not, probably, be so respectable as each individual in the federal convention, yet as the state conventions will probably consist of fifteen hundred or two thousand men of abilities, and versed in the science of government, collected from all parts of the community and from all orders of men, it must be acknowledged that the weight of respectability will be in them. In them will be collected the solid sense and the real political character of the country. Being revisers of the subject, they will possess peculiar advantages. To say that these conventions ought not to attempt, coolly and deliberately, the revision of the system, or that they cannot amend it, is very foolish or very assuming. . . .

*THE FEDERAL FARMER*

# Appendix Y: Anti-Federalist No. 47: "Balance" of Departments Not Achieved under New Constitution

From *Independent Gazetteer*
5 and 24 October 1787

I am fearful that the principles of government inculcated in Mr. [John] Adams' treatise ["Defence of the Constitutions of Government of the United States of America"], and enforced in the numerous essays and paragraphs in the newspapers, have misled some well designing members of the late Convention. But it will appear in the sequel, that the construction of the proposed plan of government is infinitely more extravagant.

I have been anxiously expecting that some enlightened patriot would, ere this, have taken up the pen to expose the futility, and counteract the baneful tendency of such principles. Mr. Adams' sine qua non of a good government is three balancing powers; whose repelling qualities are to produce an equilibrium of interests, and thereby promote the happiness of the whole community. He asserts that the administrators of every government, will ever be actuated by views of private interest and ambition, to the prejudice of the public good; that therefore the only effectual method to secure the rights of the people and promote their welfare, is to create an opposition of interests between the members of two distinct bodies, in the exercise of the powers of government, and balanced by those of a third. This hypothesis supposes human wisdom competent to the task of instituting three co-equal orders in government, and a corresponding weight in the community to enable them respectively to exercise their several parts, and whose views and interests should be so distinct as to prevent a coalition of any two of them for the destruction of the third. Mr. Adams, although he has traced the constitution of every form of government that ever existed, as far as history affords materials, has not been able to adduce a single instance of such a government. He indeed says that the British constitution is such in theory, but this is rather a confirmation that his principles are chimerical and not to be reduced to practice. If such an organization of power were practicable, how long would it continue? Not a day-for there is so great a disparity in the talents, wisdom and industry of mankind, that the scale would presently preponderate to one or the other body, and with every accession of power the means of further increase would be greatly extended. The state of society in England is much more favorable to such a scheme of government than that of America. There they have a powerful hereditary nobility, and real distinctions of rank and interests; but even there, for want of that perfect equality of power and distinction of interests in the three orders of government, they exist but in name. The only operative and efficient check upon the conduct of administration, is the sense of the people at large.

Suppose a government could be formed and supported on such principles, would it answer the great purposes of civil society? If the administrators of every government are actuated by views of private interest and ambition, how is the welfare and happiness of the community to be the result of such jarring adverse interests?

Therefore, as different orders in government will not produce the good of the whole, we must recur to other principles. I believe it will be found that the form of government, which holds those entrusted with power in the greatest responsibility to their constituents, the best calculated for freemen. A republican, or free government, can only exist where the body of the people are virtuous, and where property is pretty equally divided. In such a government the people are the sovereign and their sense or opinion is the criterion of every public measure. For when this ceases to be the case, the nature of the government is changed, and an aristocracy, monarchy or despotism will rise on its ruin. The highest responsibility is to be attained in a simple structure of government, for the great body of the people never steadily attend to the operations of government, and for want of due information are liable to be imposed on. If you complicate the plan by various orders, the people will be perplexed and divided in their sentiment about the source of abuses or misconduct; some will impute it to the senate, others to the house of representatives, and so on, that the interposition of the people may be rendered imperfect or perhaps wholly abortive. But if, imitating the constitution of Pennsylvania, you vest all the legislative power in one body of men (separating the executive and judicial) elected for a short period, and necessarily excluded by rotation from permanency, and guarded from precipitancy and surprise by delays imposed on its proceedings, you will create the most perfect responsibility. For then, whenever the people feel a grievance, they cannot mistake the authors, and will apply the remedy with certainty and effect, discarding them at the next election. This tie of responsibility will obviate all the dangers apprehended from a single legislature, and will the best secure the rights of the people.

Having premised this much, I shall now proceed to the examination of the proposed plan of government, and I trust, shall make it appear to the meanest capacity, that it has none of the essential requisites of a free government; that it is neither founded on those balancing restraining powers, recommended by Mr. Adams and attempted in the British constitution, or possessed of that responsibility to its constituents, which, in my opinion, is the only effectual security for the liberties and happiness of the people. But on the contrary, that it is a most daring attempt to establish a despotic aristocracy among freemen, that the world has ever witnessed. . . .

Thus we see, the house of representatives are on the part of the people to balance the senate, who I suppose will be composed of the better sort, the well born, etc. The number of the representatives (being only one for every 30,000 inhabitants) appears to be too few, either to communicate the requisite information of the wants, local circumstances and sentiments of so extensive an empire, or to prevent corruption and undue influence, in the exercise of such great powers; the term for which they are to be chosen, too long to preserve a due dependence and accountability to their constituents; and the mode and places of their election not sufficiently ascertained, for as Congress have the control over both, they may govern the choice, by ordering the representatives of a whole State, to be elected in one place, and that too may be the most inconvenient.

The senate, the great efficient body in this plan of government, is constituted on the most unequal principles. The smallest State in the Union has equal weight with the great States of Virginia, Massachusetts, or Pennsylvania. The senate, besides its legislative functions, has a very considerable share in the executive; none of the principal appointments to office can be made without its advice and consent. The terin and mode of its appointment will lead to permanency. The members are chosen for six years, the mode is under the control of Congress, and as there is no exclusion by rotation, they may be continued for life, which, from their extensive means of influence, would follow of course. The President, who would be a mere pageant of State, unless he coincides with the views of the senate, would either become the bead of the aristocratic junto in that body, or its minion; besides, their influence being the most predominant, could the best secure his re-election to office. And from his power of granting pardons, he might screen from punishment the most treasonable attempts on the liberties of the people, when instigated by the senate. . . .

Mr. [James] Wilson asserts that never was charge made with less reason, than that which predicts the institution of a baneful aristocracy in the federal Senate. In my first number, I stated that this body would be a very unequal representation of the several States, that the members being appointed for the long term of six years, and there being no exclusion by rotation, they might be continued for life, which would follow of course from their extensive means of influence, and that possessing a considerable share in the executive as well as the legislative, it would become a permanent aristocracy, and swallow up the other orders in the government.

That these fears are not imaginary, a knowledge of the history of other nations, where the powers of government have been injudiciously placed, will fully demonstrate. Mr. Wilson says, "the senate branches into two characters; the one legislative and the other executive. In its legislative character it can effect no purpose, without the co-operation of the house of representatives, and in its executive character it can accomplish no object without the concurrence of the president. Thus fettered, I do not know any act which the senate can of itself perform, and such dependence necessarily precludes every idea of influence and superiority." This I confess is very specious, but experience demonstrates that checks in government, unless accompanied with adequate power and independently placed, prove merely nominal, and will be inoperative. Is it probable, that the President of the United States, limited as he is in power, and dependent on the will of the senate, in appointments to office, will either have the firmness or inclination to exercise his prerogative of a conditional control upon the proceedings of that body, however injurious they may be to the public welfare? It will be his interest to coincide with the views of the senate, and thus become the head of the aristocratic junto. The king of England is a constituent part in the legislature, but although an hereditary monarch, in possession of the whole executive power, including the unrestrained appointment to offices, and an immense revenue, enjoys but in name the prerogative of a negative upon the parliament. Even the king of England, circumstanced as he is, has not dared to exercise it for near a century past. The check of the house of representatives upon the senate will likewise be rendered nugatory for want of due weight in the democratic branch, and from their constitution they may become so independent of the people as to be indifferent of its interests. Nay, as Congress would have the control over the mode and place of their election, by ordering the representatives of a whole state to be elected at one place, and that too the most inconvenient, the ruling powers may govern the choice, and thus the house of representatives may be composed of the creatures of the senate. Still the semblance of checks may remain, but without operation.

This mixture of the legislative and executive moreover highly tends to corruption. The chief improvement in government, in modern times, has been the complete separation of the great distinctions of power; placing the legislative in different hands from those which hold the executive; and again severing the judicial part from the ordinary administrative. "When the legislative and executive powers (says Montesquieu) are united in the same person or in the same body of magistrates, there can be no liberty."

*CENTINEL*

# Appendix Z: Anti-Federalist No. 67: Various Fears Concerning the Executive Department

From *The New-York Journal*
8 November 1787
Author: George Clinton

I shall begin with observations on the executive branch of this new system; and though it is not the first in order, as arranged therein, yet being the chief, is perhaps entitled by the rules of rank to the first consideration. The executive power as described in the 2d article, consists of a president and vice-president, who are to hold their offices during the term of four years; the same article has marked the manner and time of their election, and established the qualifications of the president; it also provides against the removal, death, or inability of the president and vice-president—regulates the salary of the president, delineates his duties and powers; and, lastly, declares the causes for which the president and vice-president shall be removed from office.

Notwithstanding the great learning and abilities of the gentlemen who composed the convention, it may be here remarked with deference, that the construction of the first paragraph of the first section of the second article is vague and inexplicit, and leaves the mind in doubt as to the election of a president and vice-president, after the expiration of the election for the first term of four years; in every other case, the election of these great officers is expressly provided for; but there is no explicit provision for their election which is to set this political machine in motion; no certain and express terms as in your state constitution, that statedly once in every four years, and as often as these offices shall become vacant, by expiration or otherwise, as is therein expressed, an election shall be held as follows, etc.; this inexplicitness perhaps may lead to an establishment for life.

It is remarked by Montesquieu, in treating of republics, that in all magistracies, the greatness of the power must be compensated by the brevity of the duration, and that a longer time than a year would be dangerous. It is, therefore, obvious to the least intelligent mind to account why great power in the hands of a magistrate, and that power connected with considerable duration, may be dangerous to the liberties of a republic. The deposit of vast trusts in the hands of a single magistrate enables him in their exercise to create a numerous train of dependents. This tempts his ambition, which in a republican magistrate is also remarked, to be pernicious, and the duration of his office for any considerable time favors his views, gives him the means and time to perfect and execute his designs; he therefore fancies that he may be great and glorious by oppressing his fellow citizens, and raising himself to permanent grandeur on the ruins of his country. And here it may be necessary to compare the vast and important powers of the president, together with his continuance in office, with the foregoing doctrine—his eminent magisterial situation will attach many adherents to him, and he will be surrounded by expectants and courtiers. His power of nomination and influence on all appointments; the strong posts in each state comprised within his superintendence, and garrisoned by troops under his direction; his control over the army, militia, and navy; the unrestrained power of granting pardons for treason, which may be used to screen from punishment those whom he had secretly instigated to commit the crime, and thereby prevent a discovery of his own guilt; his duration in office for four years—these, and various other principles evidently prove the truth of the position, that if the president is possessed of ambition, he has power and time sufficient to ruin his country.

Though the president, during the sitting of the legislature, is assisted by the senate, yet he is without a constitutional council in their recess. He will therefore be unsupported by proper information and advice, and will generally be directed by minions and favorites, or a council of state will grow out of the principal officers of the great departments, the most dangerous council in a free country. . . . The language and the manners of this court will be what distinguishes them from the rest of the community, not what assimilates them to it; and in being remarked for a behavior that shows they are not meanly born, and in adulation to people of fortune and power.

The establishment of a vice-president is as unnecessary as it is dangerous. This officer, for want of other employment, is made president of the senate, thereby blending the executive and legislative powers, besides always giving to some one state, from which he is to come, an unjust preeminence.

It is a maxim in republics that the representative of the people should be of their immediate choice; but by the manner in which the president is chosen, he arrives to this office at the fourth or fifth hand. Nor does the highest vote, in the way he is elected, determine the choice—for it is only necessary that he should be taken from the highest of five, who may have a plurality of votes. . . .

And wherein does this president, invested with his powers and prerogatives, essentially differ from the king of Great Britain (save as to name, the creation of nobility, and some immaterial incidents, the offspring of absurdity and locality)? The direct prerogatives of the president, as springing from his political character, are among the following: It is necessary, in order to distinguish him from the rest of the community, and enable him to keep, and maintain his court, that the compensation for his services, or in other words, his revenue, should be such as to enable him to appear with the splendor of a prince. He has the power of receiving ambassadors from, and a great influence on their appointments to foreign courts; as also to make treaties, leagues, and alliances with foreign states, assisted by the Senate, which when made becomes the supreme law of land. He is a constituent part of the legislative power, for every bill which shall pass the House of Representatives and Senate is to be presented to him for approbation. If he approves of it he is to sign it, if he disapproves he is to return it with objections, which in many cases will amount to a complete negative; and in this view he will have a great share in the power of making peace, coining money, etc., and all the various objects of legislation, expressed or implied in this Constitution. For though it may be asserted that the king of Great Britain has the express power of making peace or war, yet he never thinks it prudent to do so without the advice of his Parliament, from whom be is to derive his support—and therefore these powers, in both president and king, are substantially the same. He is the generalissimo of the nation, and of course has the command and control of the army, navy and militia; he is the general conservator of the peace of the union—he may pardon all offenses, except in cases of impeachment, and the principal fountain of all offices and employments. Will not the exercise of these powers therefore tend either to the establishment of a vile and arbitrary aristocracy or monarchy? The safety of the people in a republic depends on the share or proportion they have in the government; but experience ought to teach you, that when a man is at the head of an elective government invested with great powers, and interested in his re-election, in what circle appointments will be made; by which means an imperfect aristocracy bordering on monarchy may be established. You must, however, my countrymen, beware that the advocates of this new system do not deceive you by a fallacious resemblance between it and your own state government [New York] which you so much prize; and, if you examine, you will perceive that the chief magistrate of this state is your immediate choice, controlled and checked by a just and full representation of the people, divested of the prerogative of influencing war and peace, making treaties, receiving and sending embassies, and commanding standing armies and navies, which belong to the power of the confederation, and will be convinced that this government is no more like a true picture of your own than an Angel of Darkness resembles an Angel of Light.

*CATO*

# Appendix AA: Anti-Federalist No. 84: On the Lack of a Bill of Rights

Author: Robert Yates (likely)

When a building is to be erected which is intended to stand for ages, the foundation should be firmly laid. The Constitution proposed to your acceptance is designed, not for yourselves alone, but for generations yet unborn. The principles, therefore, upon which the social compact is founded, ought to have been clearly and precisely stated, and the most express and full declaration of rights to have been made. But on this subject there is almost an entire silence.

If we may collect the sentiments of the people of America, from their own most solemn declarations, they hold this truth as self-evident, that all men are by nature free. No one man, therefore, or any class of men, have a right, by the law of nature, or of God, to assume or exercise authority over their fellows. The origin of society, then, is to be sought, not in any natural right which one man has to exercise authority over another, but in the united consent of those who associate. The mutual wants of men at first dictated the propriety of forming societies: and when they were established, protection and defense pointed out the necessity of instituting government. In a state of nature every individual pursues his own interest; in this pursuit it frequently happened, that the possessions or enjoyments of one were sacrificed to the views and designs of another; thus the weak were a prey to the strong, the simple and unwary were subject to impositions from those who were more crafty and designing. In this state of things, every individual was insecure; common interest, therefore, directed that government should be established, in which the force of the whole community should be collected, and under such directions, as to protect and defend every one who composed it. The common good, therefore, is the end of civil government, and common consent, the foundation on which it is established. To effect this end, it was necessary that a certain portion of natural liberty should be surrendered, in order that what remained should be preserved. How great a proportion of natural freedom is necessary to be yielded by individuals, when they submit to government, I shall not inquire. So much, however, must be given, as will be sufficient to enable those to whom the administration of the government is committed, to establish laws for the promoting the happiness of the community, and to carry those laws into effect. But it is not necessary, for this purpose, that individuals should relinquish all their natural rights. Some are of such a nature that they cannot be surrendered. Of this kind are the rights of conscience, the right of enjoying and defending life, etc. Others are not necessary to be resigned in order to attain the end for which government is instituted; these therefore ought not to be given up. To surrender them, would counteract the very end of government, to wit, the common good. From these observations it appears, that in forming a government on its true principles, the foundation should be laid in the manner I before stated, by expressly reserving to the people such of their essential rights as are not necessary to be parted with. The same reasons which at first induced mankind to associate and institute government, will operate to influence them to observe this precaution. If they had been disposed to conform themselves to the rule of immutable righteousness, government would not have been requisite. It was because one part exercised fraud, oppression and violence, on the other, that men came together, and agreed that certain rules should be formed to regulate the conduct of all, and the power of the whole community lodged in the hands of rulers to enforce an obedience to them. But rulers have the same propensities as other men; they are as likely to use the power with which they are vested, for private purposes, and to the injury and oppression of those over whom they are placed, as individuals in a state of nature are to injure and oppress one another. It is therefore as proper that bounds should be set to their authority, as that government should have at first been instituted to restrain private injuries.

This principle, which seems so evidently founded in the reason and nature of things, is confirmed by universal experience. Those who have governed, have been found in all ages ever active to enlarge their powers and abridge the public liberty. This has induced the people in all countries, where any sense of freedom remained, to fix barriers against the encroachments of their rulers. The country from which we have derived our origin, is an eminent example of this. Their magna charta and bill of rights have long been the boast, as well as the security of that nation. I need say no more, I presume, to an American, than that this principle is a fundamental one, in all the Constitutions of our own States; there is not one of them but what is either founded on a declaration or bill of rights, or has certain express reservation of rights interwoven in the body of them. From this it appears, that at a time when the pulse of liberty beat high, and when an appeal was made to the people to form Constitutions for the government of themselves, it was their universal sense, that such declarations should make a part of their frames of government. It is, therefore, the more astonishing, that this grand security to the rights of the people is not to be found in this Constitution.

It has been said, in answer to this objection, that such declarations of rights, however requisite they might be in the Constitutions of the States, are not necessary in the general Constitution, because, "in the former case, every thing which is not reserved is given; but in the latter, the reverse of the proposition prevails, and every thing which is not given is reserved." It requires but little attention to discover, that this mode of reasoning is rather specious than solid. The powers, rights and authority, granted to the general government by this Constitution, are as complete, with respect to every object to which they extend, as that of any State government—it reaches to every thing which concerns human happiness—life, liberty, and property are under its control. There is the same reason, therefore, that the exercise of power, in this case, should be restrained within proper limits, as in that of the State governments. To set this matter in a clear light, permit me to instance some of the articles of the bills of rights of the individual States, and apply them to the case in question.

For the security of life, in criminal prosecutions, the bills of rights of most of the States have declared, that no man shall be held to answer for a crime until he is made fully acquainted with the charge brought against him; he shall not be compelled to accuse, or furnish evidence against himself—the witnesses against him shall be brought face to face, and he shall be fully heard by himself or counsel. That it is essential to the security of life and liberty, that trial of facts be in the vicinity where they happen. Are not provisions of this kind as necessary in the general government, as in that of a particular State? The powers vested in the new Congress extend in many cases to life; they are authorized to provide for the punishment of a variety of capital crimes, and no restraint is laid upon them in its exercise, save only, that "the trial of all crimes, except in cases of impeachment, shall be by jury; and such trial shall be in the State where the said crimes shall have been committed."

No man is secure of a trial in the county where he is charged to have committed a crime; he may be brought from Niagara to New York, or carried from Kentucky to Richmond for trial for an offense supposed to be committed. What security is there, that a man shall be furnished with a full and plain description of the charges against him? That he shall be allowed to produce all proof he can in his favor? That he shall see the witnesses against him face to face, or that he shall be fully heard in his own defense by himself or counsel?

For the security of liberty it has been declared, "that excessive bail should not be required, nor excessive fines imposed, nor cruel or unusual punishments inflicted. That all warrants, without oath or affirmation, to search suspected places, or seize any person, his papers or property, are grievous and oppressive."

These provisions are as necessary under the general government as under that of the individual States; for the power of the former is as complete to the purpose of requiring bail, imposing fines, inflicting punishments, granting search warrants, and seizing persons, papers, or property, in certain cases, as the other.

For the purpose of securing the property of the citizens, it is declared by all the States, "that in all controversies at law, respecting property, the ancient mode of trial by jury is one of the best securities of the rights of the people, and ought to remain sacred and inviolable."

Does not the same necessity exist of reserving this right under their national compact, as in that of the States? Yet nothing is said respecting it. In the bills of rights of the States it is declared, that a well regulated militia is the proper and natural defense of a free government; that as standing armies in time of peace are dangerous, they are not to be kept up, and that the military should be kept under strict subordination to, and controlled by, the civil power.

The same security is as necessary in this Constitution, and much more so; for the general government will have the sole power to raise and to pay armies, and are under no control in the exercise of it; yet nothing of this is to be found in this new system.

I might proceed to instance a number of other rights, which were as necessary to be reserved, such as, that elections should be free, that the liberty of the press should be held sacred; but the instances adduced are sufficient to prove that this argument is without foundation. Besides, it is evident that the reason here assigned was not the true one, why the framers of this Constitution omitted a bill of rights; if it had been, they would not have made certain reservations, while they totally omitted others of more importance.

We find they have, in the ninth section of the first article declared, that the writ of habeas corpus shall not be suspended, unless in cases of rebellion, that no bill of attainder, or ex post facto law, shall be passed, that no title of nobility shall be granted by the United States, etc. If every thing which is not given is reserved, what propriety is there in these exceptions? Does this Constitution any where grant the power of suspending the habeas corpus, to make ex post facto laws, pass bills of attainder, or grant titles of nobility? It certainly does not in express terms. The only answer that can be given is, that these are implied in the general powers granted. With equal truth it may be said, that all the powers which the bills of rights guard against the abuse of, are contained or implied in the general ones granted by this Constitution.

So far is it from being true, that a bill of rights is less necessary in the general Constitution than in those of the States, the contrary is evidently the fact. This system, if it is possible for the people of America to accede to it, will be an original compact; and being the last wilt, in the nature of things, vacate every former agreement inconsistent with it. For it being a plan of government received and ratified by the whole people, all other forms which are in existence at the time of its adoption, must yield to it. This is expressed in positive and unequivocal terms in the sixth article:

"That this Constitution, and the laws of the United States which shall be made in pursuance thereof, and all treaties made, or which shall be made, under the authority of the United States, shall be the supreme law of the land; and the judges in every State shall be bound thereby, any thing in the Constitution, or laws of any State, to the contrary notwithstanding."

"The senators and representatives before-mentioned, and the members of the several State legislatures, and all executive and judicial officers, both of the United States, and of the several States, shall be bound, by oath or affirmation, to support this Constitution."

It is therefore not only necessarily implied thereby, but positively expressed, that the different State Constitutions are repealed and entirely done away, so far as they are inconsistent with this, with the laws which shall be made in pursuance thereof, or with treaties made, or which shall be made, under the authority of the United States. Of what avail will the Constitutions of the respective States be to preserve the rights of its citizens? Should they be pled, the answer would be, the Constitution of the United States, and the laws made in pursuance thereof, is the supreme law, and all legislatures and judicial officers, whether of the General or State governments, are bound by oath to support it. No privilege, reserved by the bills of rights, or secured by the State governments, can limit the power granted by this, or restrain any laws made in pursuance of it. It stands, therefore, on its own bottom, and must receive a construction by itself, without any reference to any other. And hence it was of the highest importance, that the most precise and express declarations and reservations of rights should have been made.

This will appear the more necessary, when it is considered, that not only the Constitution and laws made in pursuance thereof, but alt treaties made, under the authority of the United States, are the supreme law of the land, and supersede the Constitutions of all the States. The power to make treaties, is vested in the president, by and with the advice and consent of two-thirds of the senate. I do not find any limitation or restriction to the exercise of this power. The most important article in any Constitution may therefore be repealed, even without a legislative act. Ought not a government, vested with such extensive and indefinite authority, to have been restricted by a declaration of rights? It certainly ought.

So clear a point is this, that I cannot help suspecting that persons who attempt to persuade people that such reservations were less necessary under this Constitution than under those of the States, are wilfully endeavoring to deceive, and to lead you into an absolute state of vassalage.

*BRUTUS*

# Appendix BB: Anti-Federalist No. 85: Concluding Remarks: Evils under Confederation Exaggerated; Constitution Must Be Drastically Revised Before Adoption

Author: Melancthon Smith

. . . It is agreed, the plan is defective—that some of the powers granted are dangerous—others not well defined—and amendments are necessary—why then not amend it? Why not remove the cause of danger, and, if possible, even the apprehension of it? The instrument is yet in the hands of the people; it is not signed, sealed, and delivered, and they have power to give it any form they please.

But it is contended, adopt it first, and then amend it. I ask, why not amend, and then adopt it? Most certainly the latter mode of proceeding is more consistent with our ideas of prudence in the ordinary concerns of life If men were about entering into a contract respecting their private concerns it would be highly absurd in them to sign and seal an instrument containing stipulations which are contrary to their interests and wishes, under the expectation, that the parties, after its execution, would agree to make alteration agreeable to their desire. They would insist upon the exceptionable clause being altered before they would ratify the contract. And is a compact for the government of ourselves and our posterity of less moment than contract between individuals? Certainly not. But to this reasoning, which at first vie would appear to admit of no reply, a variety of objections are made, and number of reasons urged for adopting the system, and afterwards proposing amendments. Such as have come under my observation, I shall state, an remark upon.

It is insisted, that the present situation of our country is such, as not t admit of a delay in forming a new government, or of time sufficient to deliberate and agree upon the amendments which are proper, without involving ourselves in a state of anarchy and confusion.

On this head, all the powers of rhetoric, and arts of description, ar employed to paint the condition of this country, in the most hideous an frightful colors. We are told, that agriculture is without encouragement trade is languishing; private faith and credit are disregarded, and public credit is prostrate; that the laws and magistrates are condemned and set at naught; that a spirit of licentiousness is rampant, and ready to break over every bound set to it by the government; that private embarrassments and distresses invade the house of every man of middling property, and insecurity threatens every man in affluent circumstances: in short, that we are in a state of the most grievous calamity at home, and that we are contemptible abroad, the scorn of foreign nations, and the ridicule of the world. From this high wrought picture, one would suppose that we were in a condition the most deplorable of any people upon earth. But suffer me, my countrymen, to call your attention to a serious and sober estimate of the situation in which you are placed, while I trace the embarrassments under which you labor, to their true sources, What is your condition? Does not every man sit under his own vine and under his own fig-tree, having none to make him afraid? Does not every one follow his calling without impediments and receive the reward of his well-earned industry? The farmer cultivates his land, and reaps the fruit which the bounty of heaven bestows on his honest toil. The mechanic is exercised in his art, and receives the reward of his labor. The merchant drives his commerce, and none can deprive him of the gain he honestly acquires; all classes and callings of men amongst us are protected in their various pursuits, and secured by the laws in the possession and enjoyment of the property obtained in those pursuits. The laws are as well executed as they ever were, in this or any other country. Neither the hand of private violence, nor the more to be dreaded hand of legal oppression, are reached out to distress us.

It is true, many individuals labor under embarrassments, but these are to be imputed to the unavoidable circumstances of things, rather than to any defect in our governments. We have just emerged from a long and expensive war. During its existence few people were in a situation to increase their fortunes, but many to diminish them. Debts contracted before the war were left unpaid while it existed, and these were left a burden too heavy to be home at the commencement of peace. Add to these, that when the war was over, too many of us, instead of reassuming our old habits of frugality, and industry, by which alone every country must be placed in a prosperous condition, took up the profuse use of foreign commodities. The country was deluged with articles imported from abroad, and the cash of the country has been sent to pay for them, and still left us laboring under the weight of a huge debt to persons abroad. These are the true sources to which we are to trace all the private difficulties of individuals. But will a new government relieve you from these? . . . Your present condition is such as is common to take place after the conclusion of a war. Those who can remember our situation after the termination of the war preceding the last, will recollect that our condition was similar to the present, but time and industry soon recovered us from it. Money was scarce, the produce of the country much lower than it has been since the peace, and many individuals were extremely embarrassed with debts; and this happened although we did not experience the ravages, desolations, and loss of property, that were suffered during the late war.

With regard to our public and national concerns, what is there in our condition that threatens us with any immediate danger? We are at peace with all the world; no nation menaces us with war; nor are we called upon by any cause of sufficient importance to attack any nation. The state governments answer the purposes of preserving the peace, and providing for present exigencies. Our condition as a nation is in no respect worse than it has been for several years past. Our public debt has been lessened in various ways, and the western territory, which has been relied upon as a productive fund to discharge the national debt has at length been brought to market, and a considerable part actually applied to its reduction. I mention these things to show, that there is nothing special, in our present situation, as it respects our national affairs, that should induce us to accept the proffered system, without taking sufficient time to consider and amend it. I do not mean by this, to insinuate, that our government does not stand in need of reform. It is admitted by all parties, that alterations are necessary in our federal constitution, but the circumstances of our case do by no means oblige us to precipitate this business, or require that we should adopt a system materially defective. We may safely take time to deliberate and amend, without in the meantime hazarding a condition, in any considerable degree, worse than the present.

But it is said that if we postpone the ratification of this system until the necessary amendments are first incorporated, the consequence will be a civil war among the states. . . . The idea of [New York] being attacked by the other states, will appear visionary and chimerical, if we consider that tho' several of them have adopted the new constitution, yet the opposition to it has been numerous and formidable. The eastern states from whom we are told we have most to fear, should a civil war be blown up, would have full employ to keep in awe those who are opposed to it in their own governments. Massachusetts, after a long and dubious contest in their convention, has adopted it by an inconsiderable majority, and in the very act has marked it with a stigma in its present form. No man of candor, judging from their public proceedings, will undertake to say on which side the majority of the people are. Connecticut, it is true, have acceded to it, by a large majority of their convention; but it is a fact well known, that a large proportion of the yeomanry of the country are against it. And it is equally true, that a considerable part of those who voted for it in the convention, wish to see it altered. In both these states the body of the common people, who always do the fighting of a country, would be more likely to fight against than for it. Can it then be presumed, that a country divided among themselves, upon a question where even the advocates for it, admit the system they contend for needs amendments, would make war upon a sister state? . . . The idea is preposterous. . . .

The reasonings made use of to persuade us, that no alterations can be agreed upon previous to the adoption of the system, are as curious as they are futile. It is alleged, that there was great diversity of sentiments in forming the proposed constitution; that it was the effect of mutual concessions and a spirit of accommodation, and from hence it is inferred, that further changes cannot be hoped for. I should suppose that the contrary inference was the fair one. If the convention, who framed this plan, were possessed of such a spirit of moderation and condescension, as to be induced to yield to each other certain points, and to accommodate themselves to each other's opinions, and even prejudices, there is reason to expect, that this same spirit will continue and prevail in a future convention, and produce an union of sentiments on the points objected to. There is more reason to hope for this, because the subject has received a full discussion, and the minds of the people much better known than they were when the convention sat. Previous to the meeting of the convention, the subject of a new form of government had been little thought of, and scarcely written upon at all. It is true, it was the general opinion, that some alterations were requisite in the federal system. This subject had been contemplated by almost every thinking man in the union. It had been the subject of many well-written essays, and it was the anxious wish of every true friend to America. But it was Dever in the contemplation of one in a thousand of those who had reflected on the matter, to have an entire change in the nature of our federal government—to alter it from a confederation of states, to that of one entire government, which will swallow up that of the individual states. I will venture to say, that the idea of a government similar to the one proposed, never entered the minds of the legislatures who appointed the convention, and of but very few of the members who composed it, until they had assembled and heard it proposed in that body: much less had the people any conception of such a plan until after it was promulgated, While it was agitated, the debates of the convention were kept an impenetrable secret, and no opportunity was given for well informed men to offer their sentiments upon the subject. The system was therefore never publicly discussed, nor indeed could be, because it was not known to the people until after it was proposed. Since then, it has been the object of universal attention—it has been thought of by every reflecting man—been discussed in a public and private manner, in conversation and in print; its defects have been pointed out, and every objection to it stated; able advocates have written in its favor, and able opponents have written against it.

And what is the result? It cannot be denied but that the general opinion is, that it contains material errors, and requires important amendments. This then being the general sentiment, both of the friends and foes of the system, can it be doubted, that another convention would concur in such amendments as would quiet the fears of the opposers, and effect a great degree of union on the subject?—An event most devoutly to be wished. But it is further said, that there can be no prospect of procuring alterations before it is acceded to, because those who oppose it do not agree among themselves with respect to the amendments that are necessary. To this I reply, that this may be urged against attempting alterations after it is received, with as much force as before; and therefore, if it concludes anything, it is that we must receive any system of government proposed to us, because those who object to it do not entirely concur in their objections. But the assertion is not true to any considerable extent. There is a remarkable uniformity in the objections made to the constitution, on the most important points. It is also worthy of notice, that very few of the matters found fault with in it, are of a local nature, or such as affect any particular state; on the contrary, they are such as concern the principles of general liberty, in which the people of New Hampshire, New York and Georgia are equally interested. . . .

It has been objected too that the new system . . . is calculated to and will effect such a consolidation of the States, as to supplant and overturn the state governments. . . .

It has been said that the representation in the general legislature is too small to secure liberty, or to answer the intention of representation. In this there is an union of sentiments in the opposers.

The constitution has been opposed, because it gives to the legislature an unlimited power of taxation both with respect to direct and indirect taxes, a right to lay and collect taxes, duties, imposts and excises of every kind and description, and to any amount. In this there has been as general a concurrence of opinion as in the former.

The opposers to the constitution have said that it is dangerous, because the judicial power may extend to many cases which ought to be reserved to the decision of the State courts, and because the right of trial by jury is not secured in the judicial courts of the general government, in civil cases. All the opposers are agreed in this objection.

The power of the general legislature to alter and regulate the time, place and manner of holding elections, has been stated as an argument against the adoption of the system. The opposers to the constitution universally agree in this objection. . . .

The mixture of legislative, judicial, and executive powers in the Senate; the little degree of responsibility under which the great officers of government will be held; and the liberty granted by the system to establish and maintain a standing army without any limitation or restriction, are also objected to the constitution; and in these there is a great degree of unanimity of sentiment in the opposers. . . .

You have heard that both sides on this great question, agree, that there are in it great defects; yet the one side tell you, choose such men as will adopt it, and then amend it—while the other say, amend previous to its adoption. I have stated to you my reasons for the latter, and I think they are unanswerable.

Consider, you the common people, the yeomanry of the country, for to such I principally address myself, you are to be the principal losers, if the constitution should prove oppressive. When a tyranny is established, there are always masters as well as slaves; the great and well-born are generally the former, and the middling class the latter. Attempts have been made, and will be repeated, to alarm you with the fear of consequences; but reflect there are consequences on both sides, and none can be apprehended more dreadful, than entailing on ourselves and posterity a government which will raise a few to the height of human greatness and wealth, while it will depress the many to the extreme of poverty and wretchedness. Consequences are under the control of that all-wise and all-powerful being, whose providence conducts the affairs of all men. Our part is to act right, and we may then have confidence that the consequences will be favorable. The path in which you should walk is plain and open before you; be united as one man, and direct your choice to such men as have been uniform in their opposition to the proposed system in its present form, or without proper alterations. In men of this description you have reason to place confidence, while on the other hand, you have just cause to distrust those who urge the adoption of a bad constitution, under the delusive expectation of making amendments after it is acceded to. Your jealousy of such characters should be the more excited, when you consider that the advocates for the constitution have shifted their ground. When men are uniform in their opinions, it affords evidence that they are sincere. When they are shifting, it gives reason to believe, they do not change from conviction. It must be recollected, that when this plan was first announced to the public, its supporters cried it up as the most perfect production of human wisdom, It was represented either as having no defects, or if it had, they were so trifling and inconsiderable, that they served only, as the shades in a fine picture, to set off the piece to the greater advantage. One gentleman in Philadelphia went so far in the ardor of his enthusiasm in its favor, as to pronounce, that the men who formed it were as really under the guidance of Divine Revelation, as was Moses, the Jewish lawgiver. Their language is now changed; the question has been discussed; the objections to the plan ably stated, and they are admitted to be unanswerable. The same men who held it almost perfect, now admit it is very imperfect; that it is necessary it should be amended. The only question between us, is simply this: shall we accede to a bad constitution, under the uncertain prospect of getting it amended, after we have received it, or shall we amend it before we adopt it? Common sense will point out which is the most rational, which is the most secure line of conduct. May heaven inspire you with wisdom, union, moderation and firmness, and give you hearts to make a proper estimate of your invaluable privileges, and preserve them to you, to be transmitted to your posterity unimpaired, and may they be maintained in this our country, while Sun and Moon endure.

*A PLEBEIAN*

# Appendix CC: Chief Justices of the Supreme Court, 1789–2016

| Name | Years of Service | Home State |
|---|---|---|
| John Jay | 1789–1795 | New York |
| John Rutledge | 1795 | South Carolina |
| Oliver Ellsworth | 1796–1800 | Connecticut |
| John Marshall | 1801–1835 | Virginia |
| Roger B. Taney | 1836–1864 | Maryland |
| Salmon P. Chase | 1864–1873 | New Hampshire/Ohio |
| Morrison R. Waite | 1874–1888 | Connecticut/Ohio |
| Melville W. Fuller | 1888–1910 | Maine/Illinois |
| Edward D. White | 1910–1921 | Louisiana |
| William H. Taft | 1921–1930 | Ohio/Connecticut |
| Charles E. Hughes | 1930–1941 | New York |
| Harlan F. Stone | 1941–1946 | New Hampshire/ New York |
| Frederick M. Vinson | 1946–1953 | Kentucky |
| Earl Warren | 1953–1969 | California |
| Warren Burger | 1969–1986 | Minnesota/Virginia |
| William Rehnquist | 1986–2005 | Wisconsin/Arizona |
| John G. Roberts Jr. | 2005– | New York/District of Columbia |

# Bibliography

CONTENTS

## I. INTRODUCTION

Few subjects have generated as much scholarly and critical attention as the United States Constitution, from its intellectual foundations to contemporary Supreme Court interpretations. The bibliography that follows includes books, scholarly articles, biographies, and edited volumes in the realms of history, law, and political science that address the themes covered in the dictionary. The bibliographic entries are arranged alphabetically by topic, are arrayed for a general audience, and should be considered a launching point for students and scholars wishing to undertake further research on particular subject.

The bibliographic entries, with few exceptions, do *not* include the extensive literature published in law reviews. Readers with an interest in legal interpretations and debates should consider consulting the many prominent legal journals that focus sharply on constitutional issues and past and pending Supreme Court decisions. Such law reviews include the *William & Mary Bill of Rights Journal, Journal of Supreme Court History, Supreme Court Review, Duke Journal of Constitutional Law and Public Policy,* and the more than 100 university law reviews in the United States published generally on a quarterly basis.

One excellent means to commence research on the foundation of the American Republic is with primary documents on the Constitutional Convention and its aftermath available from the Library of Congress website (http://www.loc.gov/rr/program/bib/ourdocs/). Extensive biographical accounts of the major founders—including the authors of the Federalist Papers (Alexander Hamilton, John Jay, and James Madison) and Thomas Jefferson, author of the Declaration of Independence—are included in the bibliography. The bibliography also contains a fairly broad entry for the Anti-Federalists and their arguments against the ratification of the Constitution that is essential in grasping the groundwork for the Bill of Rights.

Topics related to the Bill of Rights and the subsequent 17 amendments to the Constitution are organized by the number of the amendment. Thus readers wishing to consult material on freedom of speech, conscience, press, assembly, and petition should consult the bibliographic entry for the First Amendment; material on the right to bear arms is in the entry for the Second Amendment; material on the death penalty is located in the entry for the Eighth Amendment; and so forth. Readers should consult the references (and cross-references) by subject and amendment number in the dictionary entries.

Finally, the bibliography also comprises biographies for Supreme Court chief justices, the major decisions during their tenure, and the issues with which their "courts" (the associate justices whom they oversaw) dealt. Readers are invited to consult Artemus Ward, Christopher Brough, and Robert Arnold, *The Historical Dictionary of the Supreme Court* (Lanham, MD: Rowman & Littlefield, 2015) for a more detailed treatment of other justices, as well as features and processes that define the dynamics of the high court. Readers may also wish to consult Melvin I. Urofsky, *Biographical Encyclopedia of the Supreme Court: The Lives and Legal Philosophies of the Justices* (Washington, DC: CQ Press, 2006); Leon Friedman and Fred L. Israel, *The Justices of the United States Supreme Court: Their Lives and Major Opinions* (New York: Chelsea House, 1997); and Timothy L. Hall, *Supreme Court Justices: A Bibliographical Dictionary* (New York: Facts on File, 2001).

## II. ABORTION, *ROE V. WADE* (1973), AND THE CONSTITUTION

Garrow, David J. *Liberty and Sexuality: The Right to Privacy and the Making of Roe v. Wade*. New York: Macmillan, 1994.

Graber, Mark A. *Rethinking Abortion: Equal Choice, the Constitution, and Reproductive Politics*. Princeton, NJ: Princeton University Press, 1996.

Horan, Dennis J., et al. *Abortion and the Constitution: Reversing Roe v. Wade through the Courts*. Washington, DC: Georgetown University Press, 1987.

Hull, N. E. H., and Peter Charles Hoffer. *Roe V. Wade: The Abortion Rights Controversy in American History*. Lawrence: University Press of Kansas, 2010.

Krason, Stephen M. *Abortion: Politics, Morality, and the Constitution*. Lanham, MD: University Press of America, 1984.

McBride, Dorothy E. *Abortion in the United States: A Reference Handbook*. Santa Barbara, CA: ABC-CLIO, 2008.

Tribe, Laurence H. *Abortion: The Clash of Absolutes*. New York: W. W. Norton, 1990.

## III. ADAMS, JOHN

Adams, Charles Francis, ed. *The Works of John Adams, Second President of the United States*. 10 vols. Boston: Little, Brown and Company, 1850–1856.

Brown, Ralph A. *The Presidency of John Adams*. Lawrence: University Press of Kansas, 1975.

Diggins, John P. *John Adams*. New York: Times Books, 2003.

Ellis, Joseph J. *First Family: Abigail and John*. New York: Alfred A. Knopf, 2010.

———. *Passionate Sage: The Character and Legacy of John Adams*. New York: W. W. Norton, 1993.

Ferling, John E. *Adams vs. Jefferson: The Tumultuous Election of 1800*. New York: Oxford University Press, 2004.
———, comp. *John Adams: A Bibliography*. Westport, CT: Greenwood Press, 1994.
———. *John Adams: A Life*. Knoxville: University of Tennessee Press, 1992.
Grant, James. *John Adams: Party of One*. New York: Farrar, Straus and Giroux, 2005.
Haraszti, Zoltan. *John Adams and the Prophets of Progress*. Cambridge, MA: Harvard University Press, 1952.
McCullough, David G. *John Adams*. New York: Simon & Schuster, 2001.
Shaw, Peter. *The Character of John Adams*. Chapel Hill: University of North Carolina Press, 1976.

## IV. AFFIRMATIVE ACTION

Anderson, Terry H. *The Pursuit of Fairness: A History of Affirmative Action*. New York: Oxford University Press, 2004.
Belz, Herman. *Equality Transformed: A Quarter-Century of Affirmative Action*. Vol. 15. New Brunswick, NJ: Transaction, 1991.
Bergmann, Barbara R. *In Defense of Affirmative Action*. New York: Basic Books, 1997.
Carter, Stephen L. *Reflections of an Affirmative Action Baby*. New York: Basic Books, 1991.
Chin, Gabriel J. *Affirmative Action and the Constitution*. New York: Garland, 1998.
Eastland, Terry. *Ending Affirmative Action: The Case for Colorblind Justice*. New York: Basic Books, 1997.
Jones, James E., Jr. "The Origins of Affirmative Action." *UC Davis Law Review* 21 (1987): 383–419.
Rosenfeld, Michel. *Affirmative Action and Justice: A Philosophical and Constitutional Inquiry*. New Haven, CT: Yale University Press, 1993.
———. "Decoding Richmond: Affirmative Action and the Elusive Meaning of Constitutional Equality." *Michigan Law Review* 87 (1989): 1729–94.
Schnapper, Eric. "Affirmative Action and the Legislative History of the Fourteenth Amendment." *Virginia Law Review* 71 (1985): 753–98.
Schuck, Peter H. "Affirmative Action: Past, Present, and Future." *Yale Law & Policy Review* 20 (2002): 1–96.

## V. AMENDMENTS

Anastaplo, George. *The Amendments to the Constitution: A Commentary*. Baltimore: Johns Hopkins University Press, 1995.
Grimes, Alan Pendleton. *Democracy and the Amendments to the Constitution*. Lexington, MA: Lexington Books, 1978.
Grossman, Mark. *Constitutional Amendments: An Encyclopedia of the People, Procedures, Politics, Primary Documents and Campaigns for the 27 Amendments to the Constitution of the United States*. Armenia, NY: Grey House, 2012.
Levinson, Sanford, ed. *Responding to Imperfection: The Theory and Practice of Constitutional Amendment*. Princeton, NJ: Princeton University Press, 1995.
Vile, John R. *A Companion to the United States Constitution and Its Amendments*. Santa Barbara, CA: Praeger, 2000.

## VI. ANTI-FEDERALISTS

Ketcham, Ralph, ed. *The Anti-Federalist Papers and the Constitutional Convention Debates*. New York: New American Library, 1986.

Main, Jackson Turner. *The Anti-Federalists: Critics of the Constitution, 1781–1788*. Chapel Hill: University of North Carolina Press, 1961.

Storing, Herbert J. *What the Antifederalists Were For*. Chicago: University of Chicago Press, 1981.

## VII. APPOINTMENTS (SUPREME COURT)

Abraham, Henry J. *Justices and Presidents: A Political History of Appointments to the Supreme Court*. New York: Oxford University Press, 1992.

———. *Justices, Presidents, and Senators: A History of the U.S. Supreme Court Appointments from Washington to Clinton*. Lanham, MD: Rowman & Littlefield, 1999.

Bronner, Ethan. *How the Bork Nomination Shook America*. New York: W. W. Norton, 1989.

Danelski, David J. *A Supreme Court Justice Is Appointed*. New York: Random House, 1964.

Eisgruber, Christopher L. *The Next Justice: Repairing the Supreme Court Appointments Process*. Princeton, NJ: Princeton University Press, 2007.

Maltese, John Anthony. *The Selling of Supreme Court Nominees*. Baltimore: Johns Hopkins University Press, 1995.

Owens, Lori Jean. *Original Intent and the Struggle for the Supreme Court: The Politics of Judicial Appointments*. Lewiston, NY: Edwin Mellen Press, 2005.

Perry, Barbara A. *A Representative Court? The Impact of Race, Religion, and Gender on Appointments*. New York: Greenwood Press, 1991.

Segal, Jeffrey A., Richard J. Timpone, and Robert M. Howard. "Buyer Beware? Presidential Success through Supreme Court Appointments." *Political Research Quarterly* 53 (2000): 557–73.

Vieira, Norman, and Leonard Gross. *Supreme Court Appointments: Judge Bork and the Politicization of Senate Confirmations*. Carbondale: Southern Illinois University Press, 1998.

Watson, George, and John A. Stookey. *Shaping America: The Politics of Supreme Court Appointments*. New York: HarperCollins, 1995.

## VIII. BILL OF RIGHTS

Amar, Akhil Reed. *The Bill of Rights: Creation and Reconstruction*. New Haven, CT: Yale University Press, 1998.

Brant, Irving. *The Bill of Rights: Its Origin and Meaning*. Indianapolis: Bobbs-Merrill, 1965.

Conley, Patrick T., and John P. Kaminski, eds. *The Bill of Rights and the States: The Colonial and Revolutionary Origins of American Liberties*. Lanham, MD: Rowman & Littlefield, 1992.

Davey, Joseph Dillon. *The Bill of Rights Today: Constitutional Limits on the Powers of Government*. Lanham, MD: University Press of America, 2008.

Hand, Learned. *The Bill of Rights*. Cambridge, MA: Harvard University Press, 1958.

Hickok, Eugene W., Jr. *The Bill of Rights: Original Meaning and Current Understanding*. Charlottesville: University Press of Virginia, 1991.

Lacey, Michael J., and Knud Haakonssen, eds. *A Culture of Rights: The Bill of Rights in Philosophy, Politics, and Law, 1791 and 1991*. New York: Cambridge University Press, 1991.

Rutland, Robert Allen. *The Birth of the Bill of Rights, 1776–1791*. Boston: Northeastern University Press, 1991.

Schwartz, Bernard. *The Great Rights of Mankind: A History of the American Bill of Rights*. New York: Oxford University Press, 1977.

Wiltshire, Susan Ford. *Greece, Rome, and the Bill of Rights*. Norman: University of Oklahoma Press, 1992.

## IX. *BROWN V. BOARD OF EDUCATION* (1954) AND SCHOOL DESEGREGATION

Bell, Derrick. *Silent Covenants: Brown v. Board of Education and the Unfulfilled Hopes for Racial Reform*. New York: Oxford University Press, 2004.
Friedman, Leon. *Brown v. Board: The Landmark Oral Argument before the Supreme Court*. New York: New Press, 2004.
Kluger, Richard. *Simple Justice: The History of Brown v. Board of Education and Black America's Struggle for Equality*. New York: Alfred A. Knopf, 1975.
Lau, Peter F. *From the Grassroots to the Supreme Court: Brown v. Board of Education and American Democracy*. Durham, NC: Duke University Press, 2004.
Ogletree, Charles J. *All Deliberate Speed: Reflections on the First Half Century of Brown v. Board of Education*. New York: W. W. Norton, 2004.
Patterson, James T., and William W. Freehling. *Brown v. Board of Education: A Civil Rights Milestone and Its Troubled Legacy*. New York: Oxford University Press, 2001.
Rountree, Clarke, ed. *Brown v. Board of Education at Fifty: A Rhetorical Perspective*. Lanham, MD: Lexington Books, 2004.
Wilkinson, J. Harvie, III. *From Brown to Bakke: The Supreme Court and School Integration*. New York: Oxford University Press, 1979.

## X. BURGER, WARREN EARL

Blasi, Vincent, ed. *The Burger Court: The Counter-Revolution That Wasn't*. New Haven, CT: Yale University Press, 1983.
Friedman, Leon, and Fred I. Israel, eds. *The Justices of the United States Supreme Court, Their Lives, and Major Opinions*. Vol. 4, *The Burger Court, 1969–1978*. New York: Chelsea House, 1997.
Lamb, Charles M., and Stephen C. Halpern, eds. *The Burger Court: Political and Judicial Profiles*. Champaign-Urbana: University of Illinois Press, 1991.
Maltz, Earl M. *The Chief Justiceship of Warren Burger, 1969–1986*. Columbia: University of South Carolina Press, 2000.
Maveety, Nancy. *Representation Rights and the Burger Years*. Ann Arbor: University of Michigan Press, 1991.
Schwartz, Herman. *The Burger Years: Rights and Wrongs in the Supreme Court, 1969–1986*. New York: Viking, 1987.
Yarbrough, Tinsley E. *The Burger Court: Justices, Rulings, and Legacy*. Santa Barbara, CA: ABC-CLIO, 2000.

## XI. CHASE, SALMON PORTLAND

Blue, Frederick J. *Salmon P. Chase: A Life in Politics*. Kent, OH: Kent State University Press, 1987.
Donald, David Herbert. *Inside Lincoln's Cabinet: The Civil War Diaries of Salmon P. Chase*. New York: Longmans & Green, 1954.
Myman, Harold Melvin. *The Reconstruction Justice of Salmon P. Chase: In Re Turner and Texas v. White*. Lawrence: University Press of Kansas, 1997.
Niven, John. *Salmon P. Chase: A Biography*. New York: Oxford University Press, 1995.
———. *The Salmon P. Chase Papers*. Kent, OH: Kent State University Press, 1998.

## XII. CIVIL WAR AND RECONSTRUCTION

Belz, Herman. *Emancipation and Equal Rights: Politics and Constitutionalism in the Civil War Era*. New York: W. W. Norton, 1978.
Benedict, Michael Les. *A Compromise of Principle: Congressional Republicans and Reconstruction, 1863–1869*. New York: W. W. Norton, 1974.
Kutler, Stanley I. *Judicial Power and Reconstruction Politics*. Chicago: University of Chicago Press, 1968.
Maltz, Earl M. *Civil Rights, the Constitution, and Congress, 1863–1869*. Lawrence: University Press of Kansas, 1990.
Richards, David R. *Conscience and the Constitution: History, Theory, and Law of the Reconstruction*. Princeton, NJ: Princeton University Press, 1993.

## XIII. CONGRESS, THE CONSTITUTION, AND THE SUPREME COURT

Berger, Raoul. *Congress v. the Supreme Court*. Cambridge, MA: Harvard University Press, 1969.
Fisher, Louis. *The Supreme Court and Congress: Rival Interpretations*. Washington, DC: CQ Press, 2009.
Glidden, William. *The Supreme Court versus Congress: Disrupting the Balance of Power, 1789–2014*. Santa Barbara, CA: Praeger, 2015.
Harris, Robert Jennings. *The Quest for Equality: The Constitution, Congress, and the Supreme Court*. Baton Rouge: Louisiana State University Press, 1960.
Koh, Harold H. *The National Security Constitution: Sharing Power after the Iran-Contra Affair*. New Haven, CT: Yale University Press, 1990.
Murphy, Walter F. *Congress and the Court: A Case Study in the American Political Process*. Chicago: University of Chicago Press, 1962.
Pritchett, C. Herman. *Congress versus the Supreme Court, 1957–1960*. Minneapolis: University of Minnesota Press, 1961.
Rogers, James R., Roy B. Flemming, and Jon R. Bond. *Institutional Games and the U.S. Supreme Court*. Charlottesville: University of Virginia Press, 2006.
Schmidhauser, John R., and Larry L. Berg. *The Supreme Court and the Congress: Conflict and Interaction, 1945–1968*. New York: Free Press, 1972.
Vile, M. J. C. *Constitutionalism and the Separation of Powers*. Indianapolis: Liberty Fund, 2014.

## XIV. CONSTITUTIONAL CONVENTION (1787)

Alexander, John K. *The Selling of the Constitutional Convention: A History of News Coverage*. Madison, WI: Madison House, 1990.
Bowen, Catherine Drinker. *Miracle at Philadelphia: The Story of the Constitutional Convention, May to September 1787*. Boston: Little, Brown & Company, 1986.
Farrand, Max. *The Framing of the Constitution of the United States*. New Haven, CT: Yale University Press, 1913.
Haesly, Richard. *The Constitutional Convention*. San Diego, CA: Greenhaven Press, 2002.
Madison, James, Edward J. Larson, and Michael Winship. *The Constitutional Convention: A Narrative History from the Notes of James Madison*. New York: Modern Library, 2005.
Morton, Joseph C. *Shapers of the Great Debate at the Constitutional Convention of 1787: A Biographical Dictionary*. Westport, CT: Greenwood Press, 2006.
Rossiter, Clinton. *1787: The Grand Convention*. New York: Macmillan, 1966.

Stewart, David O. *The Summer of 1787: The Men Who Invented the Constitution*. New York: Simon & Schuster, 2007.
Vile, John R. *The Constitutional Convention of 1787: A Comprehensive Encyclopedia of America's Founding*. San Diego, CA: ABC-CLIO, 2005.

## XV. CONSTITUTIONAL DEVELOPMENT, INTERPRETATION, AND THE SUPREME COURT

Bickel, Alexander M. *The Supreme Court and the Idea of Progress*. New Haven, CT: Yale University Press, 1978.
Corwin, Edward S. *The Constitution and What It Means Today*. Princeton, NJ: Princeton University Press, 1947.
———. *The Twilight of the Supreme Court: A History of Our Constitutional Theory*. Hamden, CT: Archon Books, 1970.
Currie, David P. *The Constitution in the Supreme Court: The First Hundred Years, 1789–1888*. Chicago: University of Chicago Press, 1985.
———. *The Constitution in the Supreme Court: The Second Century, 1888–1986*. Chicago: University of Chicago Press, 1990.
David, S. Rufus. *The Federal Principle: A Journey through Time in Quest of Meaning*. Berkeley: University of California Press, 1978.
Hall, Kermit L., et al., eds. *The Oxford Companion to the Supreme Court of the United States*. New York: Oxford University Press, 1992.
Hyman, Harold M., and William M. Wiecek. *Equal Justice under Law: Constitutional Development, 1835–1875*. New York: Harper & Row, 1982.
Jackson, Robert H. *The Supreme Court in the American System of Government*. Cambridge, MA: Harvard University Press, 1955.
Konefsky, Samuel J. *The Legacy of Holmes and Brandeis: A Study in the Influence of Ideas*. New York: Macmillan, 1956.
Miller, Arthur S. *Politics, Democracy, and the Supreme Court: Essays on the Frontier of Constitutional Theory*. Westport, CT: Greenwood Press, 1985.
Murphy, Paul L. *The Constitution in Crisis Times, 1918–1969*. New York: Harper & Row, 1972.
Perry, Michael J. *The Constitution in the Courts: Law or Politics?* New York: Oxford University Press, 1994.
Powell, Thomas Reed. *Vagaries and Varieties in Constitutional Interpretation*. New York: Columbia University Press, 1966.
Rostow, Eugene V. *The Sovereign Prerogative: The Supreme Court and the Quest for Law*. New Haven, CT: Yale University Press, 1962.
Schwartz, Bernard. *A Basic History of the U.S. Supreme Court*. New York: Robert E. Krieger, 1979.
Shnayerson, Robert. *The Illustrated History of the Supreme Court of the United States*. New York: Harry N. Abrams, 1986.
Sullivan, Winnifred Fallers. *Paying the Words Extra: Religious Discourse in the Supreme Court of the United States*. Cambridge, MA: Harvard University Press, 1994.
Wiecek, William A. *Liberty under Law: The Supreme Court in American Life*. Baltimore: Johns Hopkins University Press, 1988.
Wolfe, Christopher. *The Rise of Modern Judicial Review: From Constitutional Interpretation to Judge-Made Law*. Lanham, MD: Rowman & Littlefield, 1994.

## XVI. CONSTITUTIONAL FOUNDATIONS: IDEOLOGICAL AND INTELLECTUAL ORIGINS

Adler, Mortimer J. *We Hold These Truths: Understanding the Ideas and Ideals of the Constitution*. New York: Macmillan, 1987.
Anastaplo, George. *The Constitution of 1787: A Commentary*. Baltimore: Johns Hopkins University Press, 1989.
Bailyn, Bernard. *The Ideological Origins of the American Revolution*. Cambridge, MA: Belknap Press, 1992.
Beard, Charles A. *An Economic Interpretation of the Constitution of the United States*. New York: Macmillan, 1913.
Beeman, Richard, et al., eds. *Beyond Confederation: Origins of the Constitution and American National Identity*. Chapel Hill: University of North Carolina Press, 1987.
Kelly, Alfred H., et al. *The American Constitution: Its Origins and Development*. New York: W. W. Norton, 1991.
Lerner, Ralph. *The Thinking Revolutionary: Principle and Practice in the New Republic*. Ithaca, NY: Cornell University Press, 1987.
Levy, Leonard W. *Original Intent and the Framers' Constitution*. New York: Macmillan, 1988.
McDonald, Forrest. *Novus Ordo Seclorum: The Intellectual Origins of the Constitution*. Lawrence: University Press of Kansas.
McGinnis, John O., and Michael B. Rappaport. *Originalism and the Good Constitution*. Cambridge, MA: Harvard University Press, 2013.
Morgan, Edmund S. *The Birth of the Republic, 1763–1789*. Chicago: University of Chicago Press, 1992.
Morris, Richard B. *The Forging of the Union, 1781–89*. New York: Harper & Row, 1987.
———. *Witnesses at the Creation: Hamilton, Madison, Jay, and the Constitution*. New York: Holt, Rinehart and Winston, 1985.
Thomas, George. *The Madisonian Constitution*. Baltimore: Johns Hopkins University Press, 2008.
Wood, Gordon S. *The Creation of the American Republic, 1776–1787*. Chapel Hill: University of North Carolina Press, 1969.

## XVII. CRITICAL VIEWS OF THE CONSTITUTION

Barber, Sotirios A. *On What the Constitution Means*. Baltimore: Johns Hopkins University Press, 1984.
Bernstein, Richard B., and Jerome Agel. *Amending America: If We Love the Constitution So Much, Why Do We Keep Trying to Change It?* New York: Times Books, 1993.
Bickel, Alexander M. *The Least Dangerous Branch: The Supreme Court at the Bar of Politics*. New Haven, CT: Yale University Press, 1986.
Bloom, Allan, ed. *Confronting the Constitution: The Challenge to Locke, Montesquieu, Jefferson, and the Federalists*. Washington, DC: AEI Press, 1990.
Bork, Robert H. *The Tempting of America: The Political Seduction of the Law*. New York: Free Press, 1990.
Burt, Robert A. *The Constitution in Conflict*. Cambridge, MA: Belknap Press, 1992.
Fisher, Louis. *Defending Congress and the Constitution*. Lawrence: University Press of Kansas, 2011.
Glendon, Mary Ann. *Rights Talk: The Impoverishment of Political Discourse*. New York: Free Press, 1991.
Kairys, David. *With Liberty and Justice for Some: A Critique of the Conservative Supreme Court*. New York: Free Press, 1993.
Lobel, Jules, ed. *A Less Than Perfect Union: Alternative Perspectives on the U.S. Constitution*. New York: Monthly Review Press, 1988.

Lusky, Louis. *By What Right? A Commentary on the Supreme Court's Power to Revise the Constitution*. Charlottesville, VA: Michie, 1975.
Manley, John F., and Kenneth M. Dolbeare, eds. *The Case against the Constitution: From the Antifederalists to the Present*. West Armonk, NY: M.E. Sharpe, 1987.
Marshall, Burke, ed. *Workable Government? The Constitution after 200 Years*. New York: W. W. Norton, 1987.
Ollman, Bertell, and Jonathan Birnbaum. *The United States Constitution: 200 Years of Anti-Federalist, Abolitionist, Feminist, Muckraking, Progressive, and Especially Socialist Criticism*. New York: New York University Press, 1990.
Posner, Richard A. *Not a Suicide Pact: The Constitution in a Time of National Emergency*. New York: Oxford University Press, 2006.
Romero, Victor C. *Alienated: Immigrant Rights, the Constitution, and Equality in America*. New York: New York University Press, 2005.
Rossiter, Clinton L. *Constitutional Dictatorship: Crisis Government in Modern Democracies*. Princeton, NJ: Princeton University Press, 1948.
Sunstein, Cass R. *The Partial Constitution*. Cambridge, MA: Harvard University Press, 1993.
Wilson, Woodrow. *Constitutional Government in the United States*. New York: Columbia University Press, 1908.

## XVIII. DECLARATION OF INDEPENDENCE

Armitage, David. *The Declaration of Independence: A Global History*. Cambridge, MA: Harvard University Press, 2007.
Boyd, Julian P. *The Declaration of Independence: The Evolution of the Text*. Charlottesville, VA: International Center for Jefferson Studies at Monticello in association with the Library of Congress, 1999.
Dupont, Christian Y., and Peter S. Onuf, eds. *Declaring Independence: The Origin and Influence of America's Founding Document*. Charlottesville: University of Virginia Library, 2008.
Ferris, Robert G., ed. *Signers of the Declaration: Historic Places Commemorating the Signing of the Declaration of Independence*. Washington, DC: United States Department of the Interior, National Park Service, 1975.
Friedenwald, Herbert. *The Declaration of Independence: An Interpretation and an Analysis*. New York: Macmillan, 1904.
Gerber, Scott Douglas, ed. *The Declaration of Independence: Origins and Impact*. Washington, DC: CQ Press, 2002.
Maier, Pauline. *American Scripture: Making the Declaration of Independence*. New York: Alfred A. Knopf, 1997.
Shain, Barry Alan, ed. *The Declaration of Independence in Historical Context: American State Papers, Petitions, Proclamations, and Letters of the Delegates to the First National Congress*. New Haven, CT: Yale University Press, 2014.

## XIX. EIGHTEENTH AMENDMENT

Blumenthal, Karen, and Jay Colvin. *Bootleg: Murder, Moonshine, and the Lawless Years of Prohibition*. New York: Roaring Brook Press, 2011.
Goff, Brian, and Gary Anderson. "The Political Economy of Prohibition in the United States, 1919–1933." *Social Science Quarterly* 75 (1994): 270–83.
Greenberg, Martin Alan. *Prohibition Enforcement: Charting a New Mission*. Springfield, IL: Charles Thomas, 1999.
Hamm, Richard F. *Shaping the Eighteenth Amendment: Temperance Reform, Legal Culture, and the Polity, 1880–1920*. Chapel Hill: University of North Carolina Press, 1995.

Nicholson, Dorothy, and Richard Perrin Graves. *Selective Bibliography on the Operation of the Eighteenth Amendment*. Berkeley: University of California, Bureau of Public Administration, 1931.

Shaw, Elton Raymond, and Wayne Bidwell Wheeler. *Prohibition: Going or Coming? The Eighteenth Amendment and the Volstead Act*. Berwyn, IL: Shaw, 1924.

Timberlake, James H. *Prohibition and the Progressive Movement, 1900–1920*. Vol. 162. New York: Atheneum, 1970.

## XX. EIGHTH AMENDMENT

Bedau, Hugo Adam. *The Death Penalty in America: Current Controversies*. New York: Oxford University Press, 1997.

Berns, Walter. *For Capital Punishment: Crime and the Morality of the Death Penalty*. New York: Basic Books, 1979.

Bessler, John D. *Cruel and Unusual: The American Death Penalty and the Founders' Eighth Amendment*. Boston: Northeastern University Press, 2012.

Black, Charles L., Jr. *Capital Punishment: The Inevitability of Caprice and Mistake*. New York: W. W. Norton, 1981.

Mandery, Evan J. *A Wild Justice: The Death and Resurrection of Capital Punishment in America*. New York: W. W. Norton, 2013.

Mello, Michael. *Against the Death Penalty: The Relentless Dissents of Justices Brennan and Marshall*. Boston: Northeastern University Press, 1996.

Meltsner, Michael. *Cruel and Unusual: The Supreme Court and Capital Punishment*. New York: Random House, 1973.

Parrish, Michael E. *The Supreme Court and Capital Punishment: Judging Death*. Washington, DC: CQ Press, 2010.

Virginia Commission on Constitutional Government. *Nor Cruel and Unusual Punishment Inflicted: A Few Observations on the Meaning of the Eighth Amendment*. Richmond, VA: Virginia Commission on Constitutional Government, 1965.

Vollum, Scott. *The Death Penalty: Constitutional Issues, Commentaries, and Case Briefs*. New York: Routledge, 2015.

## XXI. ELECTION LAW, CAMPAIGN FINANCE, AND THE CONSTITUTION

Anzalone, Christopher A. *Supreme Court Cases on Political Representation, 1787–2001*. Armonk, NY: M.E. Sharpe, 2002.

Hasen, Richard L. *The Supreme Court and Election Law: Judging Equality from Baker v. Carr to Bush v. Gore*. New York: New York University Press, 2003.

Mason, Thomas O., and Sophie A. James. *Campaign Finance and the Citizens United Supreme Court Case*. New York: Nova Science, 2011.

Pinaire, Brian K. *The Constitution of Electoral Speech Law: The Supreme Court and Freedom of Expression in Campaigns and Elections*. Stanford, CA: Stanford Law Books, 2008.

Posner, Richard A. *Breaking the Deadlock: The 2000 Election, the Constitution, and the Courts*. Princeton, NJ: Princeton University Press, 2001.

Post, Robert. *Citizens Divided: Campaign Finance Reform and the Constitution*. Cambridge, MA: Harvard University Press, 2014.

Ryden, David K. *The U.S. Supreme Court and the Electoral Process*. Washington, DC: Georgetown University Press, 2000.

Urofsky, Melvin I. *Money and Free Speech: Campaign Finance Reform and the Courts*. Lawrence: University Press of Kansas, 2005.

Zelden, Charles L. *The Supreme Court and Elections: Into the Political Thicket*. Washington, DC: CQ Press, 2010.

## XXII. ELLSWORTH, OLIVER


Casto, William R. *The Supreme Court in the Early Republic: The Justiceships of John Jay and Oliver Ellsworth*. Columbia: University of South Carolina Press, 1995.

Harrington, Matthew P. *Jay and Ellsworth, the First Courts: Justices, Rulings, and Legacy*. Santa Barbara, CA: ABC-CLIO, 2008.

Toth, Michael C. *Founding Federalist: The Life of Oliver Ellsworth*. Wilmington, DE: ISI Books, 2011.


## XXIII. FEDERALISM


Baier, Gerald. *Courts and Federalism: Judicial Doctrine in the United States, Australia, and Canada*. Vancouver: University of British Columbia Press, 2006.

Banks, Christopher P., and John C. Blakeman. *The U.S. Supreme Court and New Federalism: From the Rehnquist to the Roberts Court*. Lanham, MD: Rowman & Littlefield, 2012.

Beer, Samuel H. *To Make a Nation: The Rediscovery of American Federalism*. New York: Belknap Press, 1993.

Conlan, Timothy J. *New Federalism: Intergovernmental Reform from Nixon to Reagan*. Washington, DC: Brookings Institution, 1988.

Derthick, Martha. *Keeping the Compound Republic: Essays on American Federalism*. Washington, DC: Brookings Institution, 2001.

Doernberg, Donald L. *Sovereign Immunity and/or the Rule of Law: The New Federalism*. Durham, NC: Carolina Academic Press, 2004.

Drake, Frederick D., and Lynn R. Nelson. *States' Rights and American Federalism: A Documentary History*. Westport, NY: Greenwood Press, 1999.

Ferejohn, John A., and Barry R. Weingast, eds. *The New Federalism: Can the States Be Trusted?* Stanford, CA: Hoover Institution Press, 1997.

Gerston, Larry N. *American Federalism: A Concise Introduction*. Armonk, NY: M.E. Sharpe, 2007.

Kettl, Donald F. *The Regulation of American Federalism: With a New Epilogue*. Baltimore: Johns Hopkins University Press, 1987.

Lively, Donald E. *The Constitution, Race, and Renewed Relevance of Original Intent: Reclaiming the Lost Opportunity of Federalism*. Amherst, NY: Cambria Press, 2008.

Sprague, John D. *Voting Patterns of the United States Supreme Court: Cases in Federalism, 1889–1959*. Indianapolis: Bobbs-Merrill, 1968.

Zimmerman, Joseph Francis. *Contemporary American Federalism: The Growth of National Power*. Albany, NY: State University of New York Press, 2008.


## XXIV. FEDERALISTS AND THE FEDERALIST PAPERS


Adair, Douglass. "The Authorship of the Disputed Federalist Papers." *William & Mary Quarterly* 1 (April 1944): 97–122.

———. "The Authorship of the Disputed Federalist Papers: Part II." *William & Mary Quarterly* 1 (July 1944): 235–64.

Cooke, Jacob E., ed. *The Federalist*. Middletown, CT: Wesleyan University Press, 1961.

Dietze, Gottfried. *The Federalist: A Classic on Federalism and Free Government*. Baltimore: Johns Hopkins University Press, 1999.

Duvall, Edward D. *The Federalist Companion: A Guide to Understanding the Federalist Papers*. Gilbert, AZ: Fremont Valley Books, 2011.

Morris, Richard B. *Witnesses at the Creation: Hamilton, Madison, Jay, and the Constitution*. New York: Holt, Rinehart and Winston, 1985.

Rossiter, Clinton, ed. *The Federalist Papers: Alexander Hamilton, James Madison, John Jay*. New York: Mentor, 1989.
Taylor, Quentin P., ed. *The Essential Federalist: A New Reading of the Federalist Papers*. Madison, WI: Madison House, 1998.
White, Morton. *Philosophy, the Federalist, and the Constitution*. New York: Oxford University Press, 1987.

## XXV. FIFTEENTH AMENDMENT

Avins, Alfred, ed. *The Reconstruction Amendments' Debates: The Legislative History and Contemporary Debates in Congress on the 13th, 14th, and 15th Amendments*. Richmond: Virginia Commission on Constitutional Government, 1967.
Darling, Marsha J. Tyson, ed. *Race, Voting, Redistricting, and the Constitution: Sources and Explorations on the Fifteenth Amendment*. New York: Routledge, 2001.
Gillette, William. *The Right to Vote: Politics and the Passage of the Fifteenth Amendment*. Baltimore: Johns Hopkins University Press, 1969.
Hay, Jeff, ed. *Amendment XV: Race and the Right to Vote*. Farmington Hills, MI: Greenhaven Press, 2009.
Maltz, Earl M. *Civil Rights, the Constitution, and Congress, 1863–1869*. Lawrence: University Press of Kansas, 1990.
Mathews, John Mabry. *Legislative and Judicial History of the Fifteenth Amendment*. Baltimore: Johns Hopkins University Press, 1909.

## XXVI. FIFTH AMENDMENT

Allen, Ronald J., Richard B. Kuhns, and William J. Stuntz. *Constitutional Criminal Procedure: An Examination of the Fourth, Fifth, and Sixty Amendments, and Related Areas*. Boston: Little, Brown, 1995.
Dershowitz, Alan M. *Is There a Right to Remain Silent? Coercive Interrogation and the Fifth Amendment after 9/11*. New York: Oxford University Press, 2008.
Epstein, Richard A. *Takings: Private Property and the Power of Eminent Domain*. Cambridge, MA: Harvard University Press, 1985.
Garcia, Alfredo. *The Fifth Amendment: A Comprehensive Approach*. Westport, CT: Greenwood Press, 2002.
Leo, Richard A., and George C. Thomas. *The Miranda Debate: Law, Justice, and Policing*. Boston: Northeastern University Press, 1998.
Levy, Leonard W. *Origins of the Fifth Amendment: The Right against Self-Incrimination*. New York: Oxford University Press, 1968.
Rudstein, David S. *Double Jeopardy: A Reference Guide to the United States Constitution*. Westport, CT: Praeger, 2004.
Salky, Steven M. *The Privilege of Silence: Fifth Amendment Protections against Self-Incrimination*. Chicago: American Bar Association, Criminal Justice Section, 2009.
Sigler, Jay A. *Double Jeopardy: The Development of a Legal and Social Policy*. Ithaca, NY: Cornell University Press, 1969.
Stuart, Gary L. *Miranda: The Story of America's Right to Remain Silent*. Tucson: University of Arizona Press, 2004.
Thomas, George C., III *Double Jeopardy: The History, the Law*. New York: New York University Press, 1998.
Wrightsman, Lawrence S., and Mary L. Pitman. *The Miranda Ruling: Its Past, Present, and Future*. New York: Oxford University Press, 2010.

## XXVII. FIRST AMENDMENT


Bollinger, Lee C. *The Tolerant Society: Freedom of Speech and Extremist Speech in America.* New York: Oxford University Press, 1986.

Brownstein, Alan. *The Establishment of Religion Clause: The First Amendment, Its Constitutional History and the Contemporary Debate.* Amherst, NY: Prometheus Books, 2007.

Emerson, Thomas I. *The System of Freedom of Expression.* New York: Random House, 1970.

Fish, Stanley. *There's No Such Thing as Free Speech and It's a Good Thing, Too.* New York: Oxford University Press, 1994.

Friendly, Fred W. *Minnesota Rag: The Dramatic Story of the Landmark Supreme Court Case That Gave New Meaning to Freedom of the Press.*

Greenawalt, Kent. *Fighting Words: Individuals, Communities, and Liberties of Speech.* Princeton, NJ: Princeton University Press, 1995.

Haynes, Charles C., Sam Chaltain, and Susan M. Glisson. *First Freedoms: A Documentary History of First Amendment Rights in America.* New York: Oxford University Press, 2006.

Howe, Mark Dewolfe. *The Garden and the Wilderness: Religion and Government in American Constitutional History.* Chicago: University of Chicago Press, 1965.

Inazu, John D. *Liberty's Refuge: The Forgotten Freedom of Assembly.* New Haven, CT: Yale University Press, 2012.

Kalven, Jr., Harry. *A Worthy Tradition: Freedom of Speech in America.* New York: Harper & Row, 1988.

Levy, Leonard W. *Emergence of a Free Press.* New York: Oxford University Press, 1985.

———. *The Establishment Clause: Religion and the First Amendment.* Chapel Hill: University of North Carolina Press, 1994.

Lewis, Anthony. *Make No Law: The Sullivan Case and the First Amendment.* New York: Random House, 1991.

Mountjoy, Shane. *Engel V. Vitale: School Prayer and the Establishment Clause.* New York: Chelsea House, 2007.

O'Brien, David M., and Ronald K. L. Collins. *Congress Shall Make No Law: The First Amendment, Unprotected Expression, and the Supreme Court.* Lanham, MD: Rowman & Littlefield, 2010.

Redish, Martin H. *Freedom of Expression: A Critical Analysis.* Charlottesville, VA: Michie, 1984.

Schauer, Frederick. *Free Speech: A Philosophical Enquiry.* New York: Cambridge University Press, 1982.

Shiffrin, Steven H. *The First Amendment, Democracy, and Romance.* Cambridge, MA: Harvard University Press, 1990.

Smith, Steven D. *Foreordained Failure: The Quest for a Constitutional Principle of Religious Freedom.* New York: Oxford University Press, 1995.

Smolla, Rodney A. *Jerry Falwell v. Larry Flynt: The First Amendment on Trial.* New York: St. Martin's Press, 1988.

Waltman, Jerrold L. *Congress, the Supreme Court, and Religious Liberty: The Case of City of Boerne v. Flores.* New York: Palgrave Macmillan, 2013.


## XXVIII. FOURTEENTH AMENDMENT


Avins, Alfred, ed. *The Reconstruction Amendments' Debates: The Legislative History and Contemporary Debates in Congress on the 13th, 14th, and 15th Amendments.* Richmond: Virginia Commission on Constitutional Government, 1967.

Berger, Raoul. *The Fourteenth Amendment and the Bill of Rights.* Norman: University of Oklahoma Press, 1989.

———. *Government by Judiciary: The Transformation of the Fourteenth Amendment*. Indianapolis: Liberty Fund, 1997.
Bond, James E. *No Easy Walk to Freedom: Reconstruction and the Ratification of the Fourteenth Amendment*. Westport, CT: Praeger, 1997.
Curtis, Michael Kent. *No State Shall Abridge: The Fourteenth Amendment and the Bill of Rights*. Durham, NC: Duke University Press, 1986.
Epps, Garrett. *Democracy Reborn: The Fourteenth Amendment and the Fight for Equal Rights in Post–Civil War America*. New York: H. Holt, 2006.
Flack, Horace Edgar. *The Adoption of the Fourteenth Amendment*. Buffalo, NY: W. S. Hein, 2003.
Hay, Jeff, ed. *Amendment XIV: Citizenship for All*. Farmington Hills, MI: Greenhaven Press, 2009.
James, Joseph B. *The Ratification of the Fourteenth Amendment*. Macon, GA: Mercer University Press, 1984.
Labbé, Ronald M. *The Slaughterhouse Cases: Regulation, Reconstruction, and the Fourteenth Amendment*. Lawrence: University Press of Kansas, 2003.
Meyer, Howard N. *The Amendment That Refused to Die: Equality and Justice Deferred; The History of the Fourteenth Amendment*. Lanham, MD: Madison Books, 2000.
Mykkeltvedt, Roald Y. *The Nationalization of the Bill of Rights: Fourteenth Amendment Due Process and the Procedural Rights*. Port Washington, NY: Associated Faculty Press, 1983.
Nelson, William E. *The Fourteenth Amendment: From Political Principle to Judicial Doctrine*. Cambridge, MA: Harvard University Press, 1988.
Perry, Michael J. *We the People: The Fourteenth Amendment and the Supreme Court*. New York: Oxford University Press, 1999.

## XXIX. FOURTH AMENDMENT

Clancy, Thomas K. *The Fourth Amendment: Its History and Interpretation*. Durham, NC: Carolina Academic Press, 2008.
Cuddihy, William John. *The Fourth Amendment: Origins and Original Meaning, 602–1791*. New York: Oxford University Press, 2009.
Greenhalgh, William W. *The Fourth Amendment Handbook: A Chronological Survey of Supreme Court Decisions*. Chicago: Criminal Justice Section, American Bar Association, 2003.
LaFave, Wayne R. *Search and Seizure: A Treatise on the Fourth Amendment*. Vol. 4. St. Paul, MN: West Group, 2004.
Landynski, Jacob W. *Search and Seizure and the Supreme Court: A Study in Constitutional Interpretation*. Vol. 4. Baltimore: Johns Hopkins University Press, 1966.
Lind, Nancy S., and Erik Rankin, eds. *Privacy in the Digital Age: 21st-Century Challenges to the Fourth Amendment*. Santa Barbara, CA: Praeger, 2015.
Maclin, Tracey. *The Supreme Court and the Fourth Amendment's Exclusionary Rule*. New York: Oxford University Press, 2013.
McInnis, Thomas N. *The Evolution of the Fourth Amendment*. Lanham, MD: Lexington Books, 2009.
Newman, Bruce A. *Against that "Powerful Engine of Despotism": The Fourth Amendment and General Warrants at the Founding and Today*. Lanham, MD: University Press of America, 2007.
Schulhofer, Stephen J. *More Essential Than Ever: The Fourth Amendment in the Twenty-First Century*. New York: Oxford University Press, 2012.
Slobogin, Christopher. *Privacy at Risk: The New Government Surveillance and the Fourth Amendment*. Chicago: University of Chicago Press, 2008.
Taslitz, Andrew E. *Reconstructing the Fourth Amendment: A History of Search and Seizure, 1789–1868*. New York: New York University Press, 2006.

Vile, John R. *Encyclopedia of the Fourth Amendment*. Thousand Oaks, CA: CQ Press, 2013.

Wilson, Bradford P. *Enforcing the Fourth Amendment: A Jurisprudential History*. New York: Garland, 1986.

## XXX. FULLER, MELVILLE WESTON

Ely, James W. *The Chief Justice of Melville W. Fuller, 1888–1910*. Columbia: University of South Carolina Press, 1995.

———. *The Fuller Court: Justices, Rulings, and Legacy*. Santa Barbara, CA: ABC-CLIO, 2003.

Furer, Howard B., ed. *The Fuller Court, 1888–1910*. New York: Associated Faculty Press, 1986.

King, Willard L. *Melville Weston Fuller: Chief Justice of the United States, 1888–1910*. New York: Macmillan, 1950.

## XXXI. HAMILTON, ALEXANDER

Ambrose, Douglas, and Robert W. T. Martin, eds. *The Many Faces of Alexander Hamilton: The Life and Legacy of America's Most Elusive Founding Father*. New York: New York University Press, 2006.

Brookhiser, Richard. *Alexander Hamilton, American*. New York: Free Press, 1999.

Cantor, Milton. *Hamilton*. Englewood Cliffs, NJ: Prentice-Hall, 1971.

Chernow, Ron. *Alexander Hamilton*. New York: Penguin, 2004.

Cooke, Jacob Ernest. *Alexander Hamilton*. New York: Scribner's, 1982.

Fleming, Thomas J. *Duel: Alexander Hamilton, Aaron Burr, and the Future of America*. New York: Basic Books, 1999.

Flexner, James Thomas. *The Young Hamilton: A Biography*. New York: Fordham University Press, 1997.

Freeman, Joanne B., ed. *Alexander Hamilton: Writings*. New York: Library of America, 2001.

Frisch, Morton J., ed. *Selected Writings and Speeches of Alexander Hamilton*. Washington, DC: American Enterprise Institute for Public Policy Research, 1985.

Gaylord, Irving C., comp. *The Burr-Hamilton Duel, with Correspondence Preceding Same, etc.* New York: Hamilton Bank, 1889.

Goebel, Julius, Jr., ed. *The Law Practice of Alexander Hamilton: Documents and Commentary*. 5 vols. New York: Columbia University Press, 1964–1981.

Harper, John Lamberton. *American Machiavelli: Alexander Hamilton and the Origins of U.S. Foreign Policy*. New York: Cambridge University Press, 2004.

Hecht, Marie B. *Odd Destiny: The Life of Alexander Hamilton*. New York: Macmillan, 1982.

Kline, Mary-Jo, ed. *Alexander Hamilton: A Biography in His Own Words*. New York: Harper & Row, 1973.

Knott, Stephen F. *Hamilton and the Persistence of Myth*. Lawrence: University Press of Kansas, 2005.

Lodge, Henry Cabot, ed. *The Works of Alexander Hamilton*. 12 vols. New York: G. P. Putnam's Sons, 1904.

McDonald, Forrest. *Alexander Hamilton: A Biography*. New York: W. W. Norton, 1979.

Miller, John Chester. *Alexander Hamilton: Portrait in Paradox*. New York: Harper, 1959.

Mitchell, Broadus. *Alexander Hamilton*. 2 vols. New York: Macmillan, 1957–1962.

———. *Alexander Hamilton: A Concise Biography*. New York: Oxford University Press, 1976.

———. *Alexander Hamilton: The Revolutionary Years*. New York: Crowell, 1970.

Randall, Willard Sterne. *Alexander Hamilton: A Life*. New York: HarperCollins, 2003.

Schachner, Nathan. *Alexander Hamilton*. New York: D. Appleton-Century, 1946.
Syrett, Harold C., and Jacob E. Cooke, eds. *The Papers of Alexander Hamilton*. 27 vols. New York: Columbia University Press, 1961–1987.
Vernier, Richard B., ed. *The Revolutionary Writings of Alexander Hamilton*. Indianapolis: Liberty Fund, 2008.

## XXXII. HUGHES, CHARLES EVANS

Hendel, Samuel. *Charles Evans Hughes and the Supreme Court*. New York: King's Crown Press, 1951.
Hughes, Charles Evans. *The Supreme Court of the United States: Its Foundation, Methods, and Achievements; An Interpretation*. New York: Columbia University Press, 1928.
Pusey, Merlo J. *Charles Evans Hughes*. New York: Macmillan, 1951.
Ross, William G. *The Chief Justiceship of Charles Evans Hughes, 1930–1941*. Columbia: University of South Carolina Press, 2007.
Simon, James F. *FDR and Chief Justice Hughes: The President, the Supreme Court, and the Epic Battle over the New Deal*. New York: Simon & Schuster, 2012.

## XXXIII. JAY, JOHN

Jay, William. *The Life of John Jay: With Selections from His Correspondence and Miscellaneous Papers*. 2 vols. New York, 1833.
Johnson, Herbert A. *John Jay, 1745–1829*. Albany: N.Y. State American Revolution Bicentennial Commission, 1970.
———. *John Jay, Colonial Lawyer*. New York: Garland, 1989.
Johnston, Henry P. Johnston, ed. *The Correspondence and Public Papers of John Jay, 1763–1826*. 4 vols. New York: G. P. Putnam's Sons, 1890–1893.
Monaghan, Frank. *John Jay: Defender of Liberty*. New York: Bobbs-Merrill, 1935.
Morris, Richard B. *John Jay: The Making of a Revolutionary, 1745–1780*. New York: Harper & Row, 1975.
———. *John Jay: The Winning of the Peace, 1780–1784*. New York: Harper & Row, 1980.
———. *Seven Who Shaped Our Destiny*. New York: Harper & Row, 1973.
Pellew, George. *John Jay*. Boston: Houghton Mifflin, 1890.

## XXXIV. JEFFERSON, THOMAS

Appleby, Joyce. *Thomas Jefferson*. New York: Times Books, 2003.
Boyd, Julian P., et al., eds. *The Papers of Thomas Jefferson*. Princeton, NJ: Princeton University Press, 1950.
Bernstein, Richard B. *Thomas Jefferson*. New York: Oxford University Press, 2003.
Burstein, Andrew. *The Inner Jefferson: Portrait of a Grieving Optimist*. Charlottesville: University Press of Virginia, 1995.
Cappon, Lester J., ed. *The Adams-Jefferson Letters: The Complete Correspondence between Thomas Jefferson and Abigail and John Adams*. 1959. Reprint, Chapel Hill: University of North Carolina Press, 1988.
Cunningham, Noble E. *In Pursuit of Reason: The Life of Thomas Jefferson*. Baton Rouge: Louisiana State University Press, 1987.
Ellis, Joseph J. *American Sphinx: The Character of Thomas Jefferson*. New York: Alfred A. Knopf, 1997.
Ford, Paul Leicester, ed. *The Works of Thomas Jefferson*. 12 vols. New York: Knickerbocker Press, 1904.

Kimball, Fiske, ed. *Thomas Jefferson: Architect; Original Designs in the Collection of Thomas Jefferson Coolidge, Junior, with an Essay and Notes by Fiske Kimball*. Cambridge, MA: Riverside Press, 1916.
Lipscomb, Andrew A., and Albert Ellery Bergh, eds. *The Writings of Thomas Jefferson*. 20 vols. Washington, DC: Thomas Jefferson Memorial Association, 1905.
Malone, Dumas. *Jefferson and His Time*. 6 vols. Boston: Little, Brown, 1948–1981.
Meacham, Jon. *Thomas Jefferson: The Art of Power*. New York: Random House, 2012.
Peterson, Merrill D. *Thomas Jefferson and the New Nation: A Biography*. New York: Oxford University Press, 1970.
———. *Thomas Jefferson: A Reference Biography*. New York: Charles Scribner's Sons, 1986.
———, ed. *Thomas Jefferson: Writings*. New York: Library of America, 1984.
Smith, James Morton, ed. *The Republic of Letters: The Correspondence between Thomas Jefferson and James Madison, 1776–1826*. 3 vols. New York: W. W. Norton, 1995.
Shuffelton, Frank. *Thomas Jefferson, 1981–1990: An Annotated Bibliography*. New York: Garland, 1992.
———. *Thomas Jefferson: A Comprehensive, Annotated Bibliography of Writings about Him (1826–1980)*. New York: Garland, 1983.

## XXXV. JUDICIAL REVIEW AND *MARBURY V. MADISON*

Clinton, Robert Lowry. *Marbury v. Madison and Judicial Review*. Lawrence: University Press of Kansas, 1989.
Dewey, Donald Odell. *Marshall versus Jefferson: The Political Background of Marbury v. Madison*. New York: Alfred A. Knopf, 1970.
Ely, John Hart. *Democracy and Distrust: A Theory of Judicial Review*. Cambridge, MA: Harvard University Press, 1980.
Goldstone, Lawrence. *The Activist: John Marshall, Marbury v. Madison, and the Myth of Judicial Review*. New York: Walker, 2008.
Graber, Mark A., and Michael Perhac. *Marbury v. Madison: Documents and Commentary*. Washington, DC: CQ Press, 2002.
Kahn, Paul W. *The Reign of Law: Marbury v. Madison and the Construction of America*. New Haven, CT: Yale University Press, 1997.
Nelson, William Edward. *Marbury v. Madison: The Origins and Legacy of Judicial Review*. Lawrence: University Press of Kansas, 2000.
Tushnet, Mark V. *Arguing Marbury v. Madison*. Stanford, CA: Stanford Law and Politics, 2005.

## XXXVI. MADISON, JAMES

Banning, Lance. *The Sacred Fire of Liberty: James Madison and the Founding of the Federal Republic*. Ithaca, NY: Cornell University Press, 1995.
Brant, Irving. *James Madison*. 6 vols. Indianapolis: Bobbs-Merrill, 1941–1961.
Broadwater, Jeff. *James Madison: A Son of Virginia and a Founder of the Nation*. Chapel Hill: University of North Carolina Press, 2012.
Gutzman, Kevin Raeder. *James Madison and the Making of America*. New York: St. Martin's Press, 2012.
Hunt, Gaillard, ed. *The Writings of James Madison*. 9 vols. New York: G. P. Putnam's Sons, 1900–1910.
Hutchinson, William T., et al., eds. *The Papers of James Madison: Congressional Series*. 17 vols. Chicago: University of Chicago Press; Charlottesville: University of Virginia Press, 1962–1991.
Ketcham, Ralph. *James Madison: A Biography*. New York: Macmillan, 1971.

Koch, Adrienne. *Jefferson and Madison: The Great Collaboration*. 1950. Reprint, Lanham, MD: University Press of America, 1986.
Labunski, Richard E. *James Madison and the Struggle for the Bill of Rights*. New York: Oxford University Press, 2006.
Leibiger, Stuart. *Founding Friendship: George Washington, James Madison, and the Creation of the American Republic*. Charlottesville: University Press of Virginia, 1999.
McCoy, Drew R. *The Last of the Fathers: James Madison and the Republican Legacy*. Cambridge: Cambridge University Press, 1989.
Meyers, Marvin, ed. *The Mind of the Founder: Sources of the Political Thought of James Madison*. Rev. ed. Hanover, NH: University Press of New England, 1981.
Rakove, Jack N. *James Madison and the Creation of the American Republic*. 3rd ed. New York: Pearson Longman, 2007.
Rosen, Gary. *American Compact: James Madison and the Problem of Founding*. Lawrence: University Press of Kansas, 1999.
Rutland, Robert Allen. *James Madison and the Search for Nationhood*. With Conover Hunt Jones and Kym S. Rice, guest curators. Washington, DC: Library of Congress, 1981.
———. *James Madison: The Founding Father*. Columbia: University of Missouri Press, 1997.
———. *The Presidency of James Madison*. Lawrence: University Press of Kansas, 1990.
Rutland, Robert A., et al., eds. *The Papers of James Madison: Presidential Series*. Charlottesville: University Press of Virginia, 1984–.
Sheldon, Garrett Ward. *The Political Philosophy of James Madison*. Baltimore: Johns Hopkins University Press, 2001.
Stagg, J. C. A. *Mr. Madison's War: Politics, Diplomacy, and Warfare in the Early American Republic, 1783–1830*. Princeton, NJ: Princeton University Press, 1983.
Wills, Garry. *James Madison*. New York: Times Books, 2002.

## XXXVII. MARSHALL, JOHN

Baker, Leonard. *John Marshall: A Life in Law*. New York: Collier Macmillan, 1974.
Beveridge, Albert J. *The Life of John Marshall*. New York: Houghton Mifflin, 1916–1919.
Feinberg, Barbara Silberdick. *John Marshall: The Great Chief Justice*. Springfield, NJ: Enslow, 1995.
Hobson, Charles F. *The Great Chief Justice: John Marshall and the Rule of Law*. Lawrence: University Press of Kansas, 1996.
Johnson, Herbert Alan. *The Chief Justiceship of John Marshall, 1801–1835*. Columbia: University of South Carolina Press, 1997.
Jones, W. Melville. *Chief Justice John Marshall: A Reappraisal*. Ithaca, NY: Cornell University Press, 1956.
Loth, David. *Chief Justice John Marshall and the Growth of the Republic*. New York: W. W. Norton, 1949.
Newmyer, R. Kent. *John Marshall and the Heroic Age of the Supreme Court*. Baton Rouge: Louisiana State University Press, 2001.
Robarge, David Scott. *A Chief Justice's Progress: John Marshall from Revolutionary Virginia to the Supreme Court*. Westport, CT: Greenwood Press, 2000.
Rudko, Frances Howell. *John Marshall and International Law: Statesman and Chief Justice*. New York: Greenwood Press, 1991.
Sites, Francis N. *John Marshall, Defender of the Constitution*. Boston: Little, Brown, 1981.
Smith, Jean Edward. *John Marshall: Definer of a Nation*. New York: Holt, 1996.
Surrency, Erwin C. *The Marshall Reader: The Life and Contributions of Chief Justice John Marshall*. New York: Oceana, 1955.
Swindler, William Finley. *The Constitution and Chief Justice Marshall*. New York: Dodd, Mead, 1978.
Unger, Harlow G. *John Marshall: The Chief Justice Who Saved the Nation*. Boston: Da Capo Press, 2014.

Zellar, Ronald C. *A Brave Man Stands Firm: The Historic Battles between Chief Justice John Marshall and President Thomas Jefferson*. New York: Algora, 2011.

## XXXVIII. NINETEENTH AMENDMENT

Buechler, Steven M. *Women's Movements in the United States: Woman Suffrage, Equal Rights, and Beyond*. New Brunswick, NJ: Rutgers University Press, 1990.
Clift, Eleanor. *Founding Sisters and the Nineteenth Amendment*. Hoboken, NJ: Wiley & Sons, 2003.
Fredericks, Carrie. *Amendment XIX: Granting Women the Right to Vote*. Detroit: Greenhaven Press, 2009.
Keyssar, Alexander. *The Right to Vote: The Contested History of Democracy in the United States*. New York: Basic Books, 2000.

## XXXIX. PRESIDENCY AND THE SUPREME COURT

Baker, Leonard. *Back to Back: The Duel between F.D.R. and the Supreme Court*. New York: Macmillan, 1967.
Burland, Philip B. *Watergate and the Constitution*. Chicago: University of Chicago Press, 1978.
Burns, James MacGregor. *Packing the Court: The Rise of Judicial Power and the Coming Crisis of the Supreme Court*. New York: Penguin, 2009.
Craig, Barbara Hinkson. *Chadha: The Story of an Epic Constitutional Struggle*. New York: Oxford University Press, 1988.
Ellis, Richard. *Judging Executive Power: Sixteen Supreme Court Cases That Have Shaped the American Presidency*. Lanham, MD: Rowman & Littlefield, 2009.
Feldman, Noah. *Scorpions: The Battles and Triumphs of FDR's Great Supreme Court Justices*. New York: Twelve, 2010.
Fisher, Louis. *Constitutional Conflicts between Congress and the President*. Lawrence: University of Kansas Press, 1991.
Friedman, Leon. *United States v. Nixon: The President before the Supreme Court*. New York: Chelsea House, 1974.
Henkin, Louis. *Constitutionalism, Democracy, and Foreign Affairs*. New York: Columbia University Press, 1990.
Leuchtenburg, William E. *The Supreme Court Reborn: The Constitutional Revolution in the Age of Roosevelt*. New York: Oxford University Press, 1995.
Marcus, Maeva. *Truman and the Steel Seizure Case: The Limits of Presidential Power*. New York: Columbia University Press, 1977.
Novkov, Julie. *The Supreme Court and the Presidency: Struggles for Supremacy*. Thousand Oaks, CA: CQ Press, 2013.
Pritchett, C. Herman. *The Roosevelt Court: A Study in Judicial Politics and Values, 1937–1947*. New York: Macmillan, 1948.
Rossiter, Clinton, and Richard P. Longaker. *The Supreme Court and the Commander in Chief*. Ithaca, NY: Cornell University Press, 1976.
Scigliano, Robert. *The Supreme Court and the Presidency*. New York: Free Press, 1971.
Toobin, Jeffrey. *The Oath: The Obama White House and the Supreme Court*. New York: Doubleday, 2012.
Westin, Alan F. *The Anatomy of a Constitutional Law Case: Youngstown Sheet and Tube Co. v. Sawyer; the Steel Seizure Decision*. New York: Columbia University Press, 1996.
Whittington, Keith E. *Political Foundations of Judicial Supremacy: The Presidency, the Supreme Court, and Constitutional Leadership in U.S. History*. Princeton, NJ: Princeton University Press, 2007.
Witt, Elder. *A Different Justice: Reagan and the Supreme Court*. Washington, DC: Congressional Quarterly, 1986.

Yates, Jeff. *Popular Justice: Presidential Prestige and Executive Success in the Supreme Court*. Albany: State University of New York Press, 2002.

## XL. RACE AND THE CONSTITUTION

Anastaplo, George. *Reflections on Slavery and the Constitution*. Lanham, MD: Lexington Books, 2012.
Bracey, Christopher Alan, Paul Finkelman, and David Thomas Konig. *The Dred Scott Case: Historical and Contemporary Perspectives on Race and Law*. Athens: Ohio University Press, 2010.
Darling, Marsha J. Tyson. *Race, Voting, Redistricting, and the Constitution: Sources and Explorations on the Fifteenth Amendment*. New York: Routledge, 2001.
Davis, Abraham L., and Barbara Luck Graham. *The Supreme Court, Race, and Civil Rights*. Thousand Oaks, CA: Sage, 1995.
Finkelman, Paul. *Race and the Constitution: From the Philadelphia Convention to the Age of Segregation*. Washington, DC: American Historical Association, 2010.
———. *Slavery and the Founders: Race and Liberty in the Age of Jefferson*. Armonk, NY: M.E. Shape, 1996.
Franklin, John Hope. *From Slavery to Freedom: A History of Negro Americans*. New York: McGraw-Hill, 1994.
Franklin, John Hope, and Genna Rae McNeil, eds. *African Americans and the Living Constitution*. Washington, DC: Smithsonian Institution Press, 1995.
Goldwin, Robert A., and Art Kaufman. *Slavery and Its Consequences: The Constitution, Equality, and Race*. Washington, DC: AEI Press, 1988.
Higginbotham, F. Michael. *Race Law: Cases, Commentary, and Questions*. Durham, NC: Carolina Academic Press, 2010.
Kull, Andrew. *The Color-Blind Constitution*. Cambridge, MA: Harvard University Press, 1998.
Lively, Donald E. *The Constitution and Race*. New York: Praeger, 1992.
Napolitano, Andrew P. *Dred Scott's Revenge: A Legal History of Race and Freedom in America*. Nashville: Thomas Nelson, 2009.
Spann, Girardeau A. *Race against the Court: The Supreme Court and Minorities in Contemporary America*. New York: New York University Press, 1993.
Woodward, C. Vann. *The Strange Career of Jim Crow*. New York: Oxford University Press, 1974.

## XLI. REHNQUIST, WILLIAM HUBBS

Belsky, Martin H. *The Rehnquist Court: A Retrospective*. New York: Oxford University Press, 2002.
Boles, Donald E. *Mr. Justice Rehnquist: Judicial Activist*. Ames: Iowa State University Press, 1987.
Bradley, Craig M. *The Rehnquist Legacy*. New York: Cambridge University Press, 2006.
Cameron, Scott. *William H. Rehnquist: Chief Justice of the Supreme Court*. New York: Ferguson, 2005.
Davis, Derek. *Original Intent: Chief Justice Rehnquist and the Course of American Church/State Relations*. New York: Prometheus Books, 1991.
Davis, Sue. *Justice Rehnquist and the Constitution*. Princeton, NJ: Princeton University Press, 1989.
Gottlieb, Stephen E. *Morality Imposed: The Rehnquist Court and Liberty in America*. New York: New York University Press, 2000.
Hensley, Thomas R., et al. *The Rehnquist Court: Justices, Rulings, and Legacy*. Santa Barbara, CA: ABC-CLIO, 2006.

Irons, Peter H. *Brennan vs. Rehnquist: The Battle for the Constitution*. New York: Alfred A. Knopf, 1994.
Jenkins, John A. *The Partisan: The Life of William Rehnquist*. New York: PublicAffairs, 2012.
Marshall, Thomas R. *Public Opinion and the Rehnquist Court*. Albany: State University of New York Press, 2008.
Rehnquist, William H. *All the Laws but One: Civil Liberties in Wartime*. New York: Alfred A. Knopf, 1998.
———. *Grand Inquests: The Historic Impeachments of Justice Samuel Chase and Andrew Johnson*. New York: William Morrow, 1992.
Savage, David G. *Turning Right: The Making of the Rehnquist Supreme Court*. New York: Wiley & Sons, 1992.
Schwartz, Herman. *The Rehnquist Court: Judicial Activist on the Right*. New York: Hill and Wang, 2003.
Tushnet, Mark. *A Court Divided: The Rehnquist Court and the Future of Constitutional Law*. New York: W. W. Norton, 2005.
Yarbrough, Tinsley E. *The Rehnquist Court and the Constitution*. New York: Oxford University Press, 2000.

## XLII. ROBERTS, JOHN GLOVER

Coyle, Marcia. *The Roberts Court: The Struggle for the Constitution*. New York: Simon & Schuster, 2013.
Meinhold, Stephen Scott. *Battle Supreme: The Confirmation of Chief Justice Roberts and the Future of the Supreme Court*. Belmont, CA: Thomson/Wadsworth, 2006.
Tribe, Laurence H., and Joshua Matz. *Uncertain Justice: The Roberts Court and the Constitution*. New York: Holt, 2014.
Tushnet, Mark V. *In the Balance: Law and Politics on the Roberts Court*. New York: W. W. Norton, 2013.

## XLIII. RUTLEDGE, JOHN WILEY

Ferren, John M. *Salt of the Earth, Conscience of the Court: The Story of Justice Wiley Rutledge*. Chapel Hill: University of North Carolina Press, 2004.
Gerber, Scott Douglas. *Seriatim: The Supreme Court before John Marshall*. New York: New York University Press, 1998.
Haw, James. *John and Edward Rutledge of South Carolina*. Athens: University of Georgia Press, 1997.

## XLIV. SECOND AMENDMENT

Bogus, Carl T., ed. *The Second Amendment in Law and History: Historians and Constitutional Scholars on the Right to Bear Arms*. New York: New Press, 2000.
Cornell, Saul. *A Well-Regulated Militia: The Founding Fathers and the Origins of Gun Control in America*. Oxford: Oxford University Press, 2006.
Cress, Lawrence Delbert. *Citizens in Arms: The Army and the Militia in American Society to the War of 1812*. Chapel Hill: University of North Carolina Press, 1982.
Halbrook, Stephen P. *A Right to Bear Arms: State and Federal Bills of Rights and Constitutional Guarantees*. New York: Greenwood Press, 1989.
Malcolm, Joyce Lee. *To Keep and Bear Arms: The Origins of an Anglo-American Right*. Cambridge, MA: Harvard University Press, 1994.

McClurg, Andrew J., David B. Kopel, and Brannon P. Denning, eds. *Gun Control and Gun Rights: A Reader and Guide*. New York: New York University Press, 2002.
Spitzer, Robert J. *The Politics of Gun Control*. Washington, DC: CQ Press, 2008.
Tushnet, Mark V. *Out of Range: Why the Constitution Can't End the Battle over Guns*. New York: Oxford University Press, 2007.
Uviller, H. Richard, and William G. Merkel. *The Militia and the Right to Bear Arms; or, How the Second Amendment Fell Silent*. Durham, NC: Duke University Press, 2002.
Williams, David C. *The Mythic Meanings of the Second Amendment: Taming Political Violence in a Constitutional Republic*. New Haven, CT: Yale University Press, 2003.

## XLV. SEVENTEENTH AMENDMENT

Bernhard, William, and Brian R. Sala. "The Remaking of an American Senate: The 17th Amendment and Ideological Responsiveness." *Journal of Politics* 68 (2006): 345–57.
Buenker, John D. "The Urban Political Machine and the Seventeenth Amendment." *Journal of American History* 56 (1969): 305–22.
Crook, Sara Brandes, and John R. Hibbing. "A Not-So-Distant Mirror: The 17th Amendment and Congressional Change." *American Political Science Review* 91 (1997): 845–53.
Hoebeke, Christopher Hyde. *The Road to Mass Democracy: Original Intent and the Seventeenth Amendment*. New Brunswick, NJ: Transaction, 2014.
King, Ronald F., and Susan Ellis. "Partisan Advantage and Constitutional Change: The Case of the Seventeenth Amendment." *Studies in American Political Development* 10 (1996): 69–102.
Riker, William H. "The Senate and American Federalism." *American Political Science Review* 49 (1955): 452–69.
Rossum, Ralph. *Federalism, the Supreme Court, and the Seventeenth Amendment: The Irony of Constitutional Democracy*. Lanham, MD: Lexington Books, 2001.
Schiller, Wendy J., and Charles Stewart III. *Electing the Senate: Indirect Democracy before the Seventeenth Amendment*. Princeton, NJ: Princeton University Press, 2014.

## XLVI. SIXTH AMENDMENT

Garcia, Alfredo. *The Sixth Amendment in Modern American Jurisprudence: A Critical Perspective*. New York: Greenwood Press, 1992.
Heller, Francis Howard. *The Sixth Amendment to the Constitution of the United States: A Study in Constitutional Development*. Lawrence: University of Kansas Press, 1951.
Houppert, Karen. *Chasing Gideon: The Elusive Quest for Poor People's Justice*. New York: Free Press, 2013.
Lewis, Anthony. *Gideon's Trumpet*. New York: Random House, 1964.
Marcus, Paul, et al. *The Rights of the Accused under the Sixth Amendment: Trials, Presentation of Evidence, and Confrontation*. Chicago: American Bar Association, Criminal Justice Section, 2012.

## XLVII. STONE, HARLAN FISKE

Konefsky, Samuel Joseph. *Chief Justice Stone and the Supreme Court*. New York: Hafner, 1971.
Mason, Alpheus T. *Harlan Fiske Stone: Pillar of the Law*. New York: Viking Press, 1956.
Renstrom, Peter G. *The Stone Court: Justices, Rulings, and Legacy*. Santa Barbara, CA: ABC-CLIO, 2001.

Stone, Harlan Fiske. *Law and Its Administration*. New York: Columbia University Press, 1915.
Urofsky, Melvin I. *Division and Discord: The Supreme Court under Stone and Vinson, 1941–1953*. Columbia: University of South Carolina Press, 1997.

## XLVIII. TAFT, WILLIAM HOWARD

Anderson, Judith Icke. *William Howard Taft, an Intimate History*. New York: W. W. Norton, 1981.
Lurie, Jonathan. *William Howard Taft: The Travails of a Progressive Conservative*. New York: Cambridge University Press, 2012.
Mason, Alpheus T. *William Howard Taft: Chief Justice*. New York: Simon & Schuster, 1964.
Pringle, Henry F. *The Life and Times of William Howard Taft: A Biography*. 2 vols. 1939. Reprint, Norwalk, CT: Easton Press, 1986.
Renstrom, Peter G. *The Taft Court: Justices, Rulings, and Legacy*. Santa Barbara, CA: ABC-CLIO, 2003.
Taft, William H. *Ethics in Service*. New Haven, CT: Yale University Press, 1915.
———. *Liberty under Law: An Interpretation of the Principles of Our Constitutional Government*. New Haven, CT: Yale University Press, 1922.
———. *Our Chief Magistrate and His Powers*. New York: Columbia University Press, 1916.
———. *Popular Government: Its Essence, Its Permanence and Its Perils*. New Haven, CT: Yale University Press, 1913.

## XLIX. TANEY, ROGER BROOKE

Fehrenbacher, Don E. *The Dred Scott Case: Its Significance In American Law and Politics*. New York: Oxford University Press, 1978.
Freedman, Suzanne. *Roger Taney: The Dred Scott Legacy*. Springfield, NJ: Enslow Publishers, 1995.
Huebner, Timothy S. *The Taney Court: Justices, Rulings, and Legacy*. Santa Barbara, CA: ABC-CLIO, 2003.
Lewis, H. H. Walker. *Without Fear or Favor: A Biography of Chief Justice Roger Brooke Taney*. Boston: Houghton Mifflin, 1965.
Newmyer, R. Kent. *The Supreme Court under Marshall and Taney*. New York: Crowell, 1968.
Simon, James F. *Lincoln and Chief Justice Taney: Slavery, Secession, and the President's War Powers*. New York: Simon & Schuster, 2006.
Steiner, Bernard C. *Life of Roger Brooke Taney, Chief Justice of the United States Supreme Court*. Westport, CT: Greenwood Press, 1970.
Swisher, Carl Brent. *Roger B. Taney*. New York: Macmillan, 1935.
Tyler, Samuel, and Roger Brooke Taney. *Memoir of Roger Brooke Taney, LL.D.: Chief Justice of the Supreme Court of the United States*. Baltimore: J. Murphy & Co., 1872.

## L. TENTH AMENDMENT

Devine, Donald John. *Restoring the Tenth Amendment: The New American Federalist Agenda*. Fort Lauderdale, FL: VYTIS, 1996.
Killenbeck, Mark R., ed. *The Tenth Amendment and State Sovereignty: Constitutional History and Contemporary Issues*. Lanham, MD: Rowman & Littlefield, 2002.

McAffee, Thomas B., Jay S. Bybee, and A. Christopher Bryant. *Powers Reserved for the People and the States: A History of the Ninth and Tenth Amendments*. Westport, CT: Praeger, 2006.

## LI. THIRTEENTH AMENDMENT

Holzer, Harold, and Sara Vaughn Gabbard. *Lincoln and Freedom: Slavery, Emancipation, and the Thirteenth Amendment*. Carbondale: Southern Illinois University Press, 2007.
Richards, Leonard L. *Who Freed the Slaves? The Fight over the Thirteenth Amendment*. Chicago: University of Chicago Press, 2015.
Samito, Christian G. *Lincoln and the Thirteenth Amendment*. Carbondale: Southern Illinois University Press, 2015.
Tsesis, Alexander. *The Promises of Liberty: The History and Contemporary Relevance of the Thirteenth Amendment*. New York: Columbia University Press, 2010.
Vorenberg, Michael. *Final Freedom: The Civil War, the Abolition of Slavery, and the Thirteenth Amendment*. New York: Cambridge University Press, 2001.

## LII. TWENTY-FIFTH AMENDMENT

Abrams, Herbert L. "Can the Twenty-Fifth Amendment Deal with a Disabled President? Preventing Future White House Cover-Ups." *Presidential Studies Quarterly* 29 (1999): 115–33.
Feerick, John D. *The Twenty-Fifth Amendment: Its Complete History and Earliest Applications*. New York: Fordham University Press, 1976.
Gilbert, Robert E. "The Contemporary Presidency: The Twenty-Fifth Amendment: Recommendations and Deliberations of the Working Group on Presidential Disability." *Presidential Studies Quarterly* 33 (2003): 877–88.
———, ed. *Managing Crisis: Presidential Disability and the Twenty-Fifth Amendment*. New York: Fordham University Press, 2000.
Kassop, Nancy. "When Law and Politics Collide: Presidents and the Use of the Twenty-Fifth Amendment." *Presidential Studies Quarterly* 35 (2005): 147–65.
Toole, James F., and Robert J. Joynt. *Presidential Disability: Papers, Discussions, and Recommendations on the Twenty-Fifth Amendment and Issues of Inability and Disability among Presidents of the United States*. Rochester, NY: University of Rochester Press, 2001.

## LIII. TWENTY-FIRST AMENDMENT

Brown, Everett S. "The Ratification of the Twenty-First Amendment." *American Political Science Review* 29 (1935): 1005–17.
Engelmann, Larry. *Intemperance, the Lost War against Liquor*. New York: Free Press, 1979.
Kyvig, David E., and Honorée Fanonne Jeffers. *Repealing National Prohibition*. Kent, OH: Kent State University Press, 2000.
Munger, Michael, and Thomas Schaller. "The Prohibition-Repeal Amendments: A Natural Experiment in Interest Group Influence." *Public Choice* 90 (1997): 139–63.
Root, Grace McClure Dixon Cogswell. *Women and Repeal: The Story of the Women's Organization for National Prohibition Reform*. New York: Harper & Brothers, 1934.
Schrad, Mark Lawrence. "Constitutional Blemishes: American Alcohol Prohibition and Repeal as Policy Punctuation." *Policy Studies Journal* 35 (2007): 437–63.
Sinclair, Andrew. *Prohibition, the Era of Excess: With an Introduction by Richard Hofstadter*. Boston: Little, Brown, 1962.

## LIV. TWENTY-FOURTH AMENDMENT

Lawson, Steven F. *Black Ballots: Voting Rights in the South, 1944–1969*. New York: Columbia University Press, 1976.
Ogden, Frederic D. *The Poll Tax in the South*. Birmingham: University of Alabama Press, 1958.
Ackerman, Bruce, and Jennifer Nou. "Canonizing the Civil Rights Revolution: The People and the Poll Tax." *Northwestern University Law Review* 103 (2009): 63–148.

## LV. TWENTY-SECOND AMENDMENT

Crockett, David A. "'An Excess of Refinement': Lame Duck Presidents in Constitutional and Historical Context." *Presidential Studies Quarterly* 38 (2008): 707–21.
Davis, Paul B. "The Results and Implications of the Enactment of the Twenty-Second Amendment." *Presidential Studies Quarterly* 9 (1979): 289–303.
Korzi, Michael J. *Presidential Term Limits in American History: Power, Principles, and Politics*. College Station: Texas A&M University Press, 2011.
Willis, Paul G., and George L. Willis. "The Politics of the Twenty-Second Amendment." *Western Political Quarterly* 5 (1952): 469–82.

## LVI. TWENTY-SEVENTH AMENDMENT

Paulsen, Michael Stokes. "A General Theory of Article V: The Constitutional Lessons of the Twenty-Seventh Amendment." *Yale Law Journal* 103 (1993): 677–789.

## LVII. TWENTY-SIXTH AMENDMENT

Bernstein, Richard B. "The Sleeper Wakes: The History and Legacy of the Twenty-Seventh Amendment." *Fordham Law Review* 61 (1992): 497–557.

## LVIII. TWENTY-THIRD AMENDMENT

Crockett, David A. "Dodging the Bullet: Election Mechanics and the Problem of the Twenty-Third Amendment." *PS: Political Science and Politics* 36 (2003): 423–26.

## LIX. VINSON, FREDERICK MOORE

Belknap, Michal R. *The Vinson Court: Justices, Rulings, and Legacy*. Santa Barbara, CA: ABC-CLIO, 2004.
Pritchett, C. Herman. *Civil Liberties and the Vinson Court*. Chicago: University of Chicago Press, 1969.
St. Clair, James E., and Linda C. Gugin. *Chief Justice Fred M. Vinson of Kentucky: A Political Biography*. Lexington: University Press of Kentucky, 2002.
Urofsky, Melvin I. *Division and Discord: The Supreme Court under Stone and Vinson, 1941–1953*. Columbia: University of South Carolina Press, 1997.

## LX. VOTING RIGHTS

Bybee, Keith J. *Mistaken Identity: The Supreme Court and the Politics of Minority Representation*. Princeton, NJ: Princeton University Press, 1998.

Elliott, Ward E. Y. *The Rise of Guardian Democracy: The Supreme Court's Role in Voting Rights Disputes, 1845–1969*. Cambridge, MA: Harvard University Press, 1974.

Peacock, Anthony A. *Deconstructing the Republic: Voting Rights, the Supreme Court, and the Founders' Republicanism Reconsidered*. Washington, DC: AEI Press, 2008.

Rush, Mark E. *Voting Rights and Redistricting in the United States*. Westport, CT: Greenwood Press, 1998.

Thernstrom, Abigail M. *Whose Votes Count? Affirmative Action and Minority Voting Rights*. Cambridge, MA: Harvard University Press, 1987.

## LXI. WAITE, MORRISON REMICK

Kens, Paul. *The Supreme Court under Morrison R. Waite, 1874–1888*. Columbia: University of South Carolina Press, 2010.

Magrath, C. Peter, ed. *Morrison R. Waite: The Triumph of Character*. New York: Macmillan, 1963.

Stephenson, D. Grier. *The Waite Court: Justices, Rulings, and Legacy*. Santa Barbara, CA: ABC-CLIO, 2003.

Trimble, Bruce R. *Chief Justice Waite: Defender of the Public Interest*. Princeton, NJ: Princeton University Press, 1938.

## LXII. WARREN, EARL

Belknap, Michal R. *The Supreme Court under Earl Warren, 1953–1969*. Columbia: University of South Carolina Press, 2005.

Burland, Philip B. *Politics, the Constitution and the Warren Court*. Chicago: University of Chicago Press, 1970.

Compston, Christine L. *Earl Warren: Justice For All*. New York: Oxford University Press, 2001.

Goldberg, Arthur J. *Equal Justice: The Warren Era of the Supreme Court*. Chicago: Northwestern University Press, 1971.

Katcher, Leo. *Earl Warren: A Political Biography*. New York: McGraw-Hill, 1967.

Newton, Jim. *Earl Warren and the Nation He Made*. New York: Riverhead Books, 2006.

Pollack, Jack Harrison. *Earl Warren: The Judge Who Changed America*. Englewood Cliffs, NJ: Prentice Hall, 1979.

Schwartz, Bernard. *Super Chief: Earl Warren and His Supreme Court—a Judicial Biography*. New York: New York University Press, 1983.

Tushnet, Mark, ed. *The Warren Court in Historical and Political Perspective*. Charlottesville: University Press of Virginia, 1993.

Warren, Earl. *The Memoirs of Earl Warren*. New York: Doubleday, 1977.

Warren, Earl, and Henry M. Christman. *The Public Papers of Chief Justice Earl Warren*. New York: Simon & Schuster, 1959.

White, G. Edward. *Earl Warren: A Public Life*. New York: Oxford University Press, 1982.

## LXIII. WASHINGTON, GEORGE

Abbot, W. W., et al., eds. *The Papers of George Washington*. Charlottesville: University Press of Virginia.

Achenbach, Joel. *The Grand Idea: George Washington's Potomac and the Race to the West.* New York: Simon & Schuster, 2004.
Alden, John R. *George Washington: A Biography*. Baton Rouge: Louisiana State University Press, 1984.
Chernow, Ron. *Washington: A Life*. New York: Penguin, 2010.
Cunliffe, Marcus. *George Washington, Man and Monument.* Boston: Little, Brown, 1958.
Dalzell, Robert F., Jr., and Lee Brown Dalzell. *George Washington's Mount Vernon: At Home in Revolutionary America.* New York: Oxford University Press, 1998.
Ellis, Joseph J. *His Excellency: George Washington.* New York: Alfred A. Knopf, 2004.
Fischer, David Hackett. *Washington's Crossing.* New York: Oxford University Press, 2004.
Fitzpatrick, John C., ed. *The Writings of George Washington from the Original Manuscript Sources, 1745–1799.* 39 vols. Washington, DC: U.S. Government Printing Office, 1931–1944.
Flexner, James Thomas. *George Washington.* 4 vols. Boston: Little, Brown, 1965–1972.
———. *Washington: The Indispensable Man.* Boston: Little, Brown. 1974.
Freeman, Douglas Southall. *George Washington: A Biography.* 7 vols. New York: Scribner's, 1948–1957.
———. *Washington.* New York: Scribner's, 1968.
Gilbert, Felix. *To the Farewell Address: Ideas of Early American Foreign Policy.* Princeton, NJ: Princeton University Press, 1961.
Henriques, Peter R. *Realistic Visionary: A Portrait of George Washington.* Charlottesville: University of Virginia Press, 2006.
Higginbotham, Don. *George Washington and the American Military Tradition.* Athens: University of Georgia Press, 1985.
Leibiger, Stuart Eric. *Founding Friendship: George Washington, James Madison, and the Creation of the American Republic.* Charlottesville: University Press of Virginia, 1999.
Longmore, Paul K. *The Invention of George Washington.* Berkeley: University of California Press, 1988.
McDonald, Forrest. *The Presidency of George Washington.* Lawrence: University Press of Kansas, 1974.
Morgan, Edmund S. *The Genius of George Washington.* New York: W. W. Norton, 1980.
Randall, Willard Sterne. *George Washington: A Life.* New York: Henry Holt & Co., 1997.
Rhodehame, John H., ed. *George Washington: Writings.* New York: Library of America, 1997.
Smith, Richard Norton. *Patriarch: George Washington and the New American Nation.* Boston: Houghton Mifflin, 1993.
Twohig, Dorothy, ed. *George Washington's Diaries: An Abridgment*. Charlottesville: University Press of Virginia, 1999.
Wiencek, Henry. *An Imperfect God: George Washington, His Slaves, and the Creation of America.* New York: Farrar, Straus and Giroux, 2003.

## LXIV. WHITE, EDWARD DOUGLASS

Highsaw, Robert B. *Edward Douglass White: Defender of the Conservative Faith*. Baton Rouge: Louisiana State University Press, 1981.
Klinkhammer, Marie. *Edward Douglass White, Chief Justice of the United States.* Washington, DC: Catholic University of America Press, 1943.
Pratt, Walter F. *The Supreme Court under Edward Douglass White, 1910–1921.* Columbia: University of South Carolina Press, 1999.

## LXV. WOMEN AND THE CONSTITUTION

Baker, Jean H. *Women and the U.S. Constitution, 1776–1920*. Washington, DC: American Historical Association, 2009.
Berry, Mary Frances. *Why ERA Failed: Politics, Women's Rights, and the Amending Process of the Constitution*. Bloomington: Indiana University Press, 1986.
Cushman, Clare, and Talbot D'Alemberte. *Supreme Court Decisions and Women's Rights: Milestones to Equality*. Washington, DC: CQ Press, 2001.
Hall, Kermit L. *Women, the Law, and the Constitution: Major Historical Interpretations*. New York: Garland, 1987.
Lynn, Naomi B. *Women, Politics, and the Constitution*. New York: Haworth Press, 1990.
McKenney, Janice E. *Women of the Constitution: Wives of the Signers*. Lanham, MD: Scarecrow Press, 2013.
Richards, David A. *Women, Gays, and the Constitution: The Grounds for Feminism and Gay Rights in Culture and Law*. Chicago: University of Chicago Press, 1998.
Schwarzenbach, Sibyl, and Patricia Smith. *Women and the United States Constitution: History, Interpretation, and Practice*. New York: Columbia University Press, 2003.
Sullivan, Kathleen S. *Constitutional Context: Women and Rights Discourse in Nineteenth-Century America*. Baltimore: Johns Hopkins University Press, 2007.
Wolgast, Elizabeth H. *Equality and the Rights of Women*. Ithaca, NY: Cornell University Press, 1980.

# About the Author

**Richard S. Conley** was born in 1967 in Southern California. He attended the University of California, Irvine, from 1985 to 1989 and majored in political science. He earned a master's degree from McGill University in Montreal, Quebec, Canada, in 1993 and completed his doctorate in political science at the University of Maryland, College Park, in 1998. His dissertation, which focused on presidential–congressional relations in the post–World War II era during periods of divided government, won the Department of Government and Politics' Dillon Award.

Dr. Conley has taught at the University of Florida since 1998. He is an associate professor who teaches courses on American politics and is a specialist on the U.S. presidency and executive–legislative relations. He also has an interest in comparative politics and teaches courses in Canadian, French, and Irish politics. He has led numerous study-abroad programs in France, Ireland, and recently China.

Dr. Conley is author of *The Presidency, Congress, and Divided Government: A Post-War Assessment* (2002), *Historical Dictionary of the Reagan–Bush Era* (2007), *Historical Dictionary of the George W. Bush Era* (2010), *Historical Dictionary of the Clinton Era* (2012), and *Historical Dictionary of the U.S. Presidency* (2016). He is editor of *Reassessing the Reagan Presidency* (2003) and *Transforming the American Polity: The Presidency of George W. Bush and the War on Terrorism* (2005). His scholarly articles on American and comparative politics have appeared in *American Politics Research, American Review of Canadian Studies, Canadian Parliamentary Affairs, Comparative Political Studies, Congress and the Presidency, French Politics, Irish Political Studies, Political Research Quarterly, Politics and Policy, Political Studies, Presidential Studies Quarterly,* and *White House Studies*. He has authored more than a dozen book chapters on presidential politics in the United States. He is currently working on several books, including one on presidential–congressional relations, one on Canadian prime ministers, and a longer-term project tentatively titled *Deteriorating Foundations: American National Institutions and the Politics of the Post-Constitutional Republic.*

Dr. Conley resides in Havana, Florida, in the Panhandle of the Sunshine State.

www.ingramcontent.com/pod-product-compliance
Ingram Content Group UK Ltd.
Pitfield, Milton Keynes, MK11 3LW, UK
UKHW041129071026
15587UKWH00009B/297

9 781442 271883